"Dr. Samuel Mitcham's newest book, *The Encyclopedia of Confederate Generals*, offers the most complete survey yet of its subject matter and includes Dr. Mitcham's assessment of each general's effectiveness. Sometimes I would debate that assessment, but then, such a debate is where all the fun is!"

—**MAJOR GENERAL (RET.) JOHN SCALES,** author of *The Battles and Campaigns of Confederate General Nathan Bedford Forrest*

"Dr. Mitcham is an extraordinary researcher and has given us a priceless and wonderfully illuminating Civil War research tool with brief but fascinating biographies of the 426 Confederate generals."

—**LIEUTENANT COLONEL (RET.) LEONARD M. (MIKE) SCRUGGS,** author of *The Un-Civil War: Shattering the Historical Myths*

"Dr. Mitcham's book is an excellent reading adventure into the military leaders of the South."

—**PAUL GRAMLING, JR.**, past Commander-In-Chief, Sons of Confederate Veterans

THE ENCYCLOPEDIA OF CONFEDERATE GENERALS

The ENCYCLOPEDIA *of*

CONFEDERATE GENERALS

The Definitive Guide *to the* 426 Leaders *of the* South's War Effort

Samuel W. Mitcham, Jr.

REGNERY
HISTORY
Washington, D.C.

Regnery History™ is a trademark of Salem Communications Holding Cor-
poration
Regnery® is a registered trademark and its colophon is a trademark of Salem
Communications Holding Corporation

Cataloging-in-Publication data on file with the Library of Congress

ISBN: 978-1-68451-244-7
eISBN: 978-1-68451-279-9
Library of Congress Control Number: 2021946354

Published in the United States by
Regnery History, an Imprint of
Regnery Publishing
A Division of Salem Media Group
Washington, D.C.
www.RegneryHistory.com

Manufactured in the United States of America

10 9 8 7 6 5 4 3 2 1

Books are available in quantity for promotional or premium use. For information on discounts and terms, please visit our website: www.Regnery.com.

Contents

INTRODUCTION

In recent years, monuments to American heroes—everyone from Thomas Jefferson to Abraham Lincoln, from Christopher Columbus to Jesus Christ to Ulysses S. Grant—have been defaced, destroyed, or displaced, sometimes by ignorant thugs, sometimes by ignorant or cowardly authorities. Confederate monuments were some of the first to go, because they were allegedly "racist"—a term that has expanded almost infinitely to incorporate ever more Americans of the past. The argument goes that the Confederacy was racist because it fought to perpetuate the evil institution of slavery. That argument has *some* truth in it in individual cases, but it is overly simplistic and overlooks a more complex reality. For many Confederate generals, the cause of the Confederacy and of "states rights" was about more than slavery; it was about tariffs; it was about the rightful limits of Federal power; it was about the right of states to withdraw from a Union they thought no longer served their interests. A great many Confederate generals simply believed that their primary loyalty was to their state—a widespread belief in 1861, even among Northern officers. When their states withdrew from the Union, many officers followed and fought in defense of their homes. Some regarded Federal troops as invaders; some fought out of a sense of duty; some fought for glory; others fought out of ambition. Their motivations were manifold, and, where possible, the motivations of individual Confederate generals are touched upon in this work. More than that, the purpose of this book is to make the reader feel as if he has come to know, even if only glancingly, every Confederate general: who he was, what he did, and how well he did his job.

There are three dates of importance concerning Confederate generals. They are as follows: (1) date of nomination, (2) date of rank, and (3) date of confirmation by the Confederate Senate. Generally speaking, the date of nomination is the most important. That is the day Confederate President Jefferson Davis appointed (nominated) them for promotion in rank.

Their date of rank might have been that same day they were nominated. It might also have been an earlier day or (in rare cases) a later day.
It was important in determining seniority. A major general with a date
of rank of September 1, 1862, for example, outranked a major general
with a date of rank of November 1, 1862, even if the latter had been
nominated earlier. This would be especially important if jealousy entered
the picture, which it often did. Wade Hampton, for example, threatened
to resign his commission when Stephen Dill Lee was promoted to the
same rank as he but with an earlier date of rank. (Lee had been a junior
officer under Hampton's command when the war began.) Faced with the
threat of losing Hampton, who was a great cavalry general, President
Davis adjusted Lee's promotion to give him the same date of rank as
Hampton, an arrangement which seems to have been satisfactory to all
concerned. Unfortunately for the South, such happy resolutions were
rare (see the essay on Joseph E. Johnston).

Some authors have mistaken date of rank for date of promotion. For
example, Jones M. Withers was nominated (promoted) to major general
on August 16, 1862. His date of rank, however, was April 6, 1862, the
day he distinguished himself while commanding a division in the Battle
of Shiloh. He was not, however, a major general on April 7, 1862. He
commanded his division in the Siege of Corinth and the retreat to
Tupelo as a brigadier general. He did not actually become a major general
until August 16.

Dates of appointment (nomination) and dates of rank were often the
same day. In this book, if the reader sees a date of promotion without a
date of rank given, it is safe to assume that the dates were the same.

Dates of confirmation are, generally speaking, less important. By
law, all nominations for ranks of brigadier general and higher had to be
confirmed by the Confederate Senate; however, by a law passed on September 1, 1861, President Davis was authorized to make recess appointments, which he often did. The confirmation process was most
important when the Senate rejected a promotion. This did not happen
often, but it wasn't exactly rare, either. Early in the war, the Senate tended

to act quickly on Davis's nominations. The date of confirmation came later as the war progressed.

Sometimes, a brigadier general's nomination was rejected by the Senate. These officers reverted to their lower rank, which was usually colonel. Sometimes, such officers were renominated. Joseph R. "Joe" Davis is a good example. The president nominated Joe Davis, his nephew, for brigadier general on September 15, 1862, but his nomination was rejected by the Senate on October 3, and he reverted to the rank of colonel. Apparently, his uncle, President Davis, made a political deal with Senator Ben Hill of Georgia. This was never proven, but Joe's nomination was reconsidered and confirmed on October 8.

Some generals were never confirmed. Colonel Thomas R. R. Cobb, for example, was promoted (nominated) to brigadier general on November 1, 1862. He commanded his brigade as a brigadier general until he was killed in action at the Battle of Fredericksburg on December 13. Such officers will be treated at their higher rank in his book. In my opinion, Cobb and officers like him were brigadier generals.

On May 31, 1864, the Confederate Congress passed an act establishing the rank of "temporary brigadier general" or "brigadier general (temporary rank)." This rank was normally given to colonels who were acting as brigade commanders (often when the brigade commander was wounded). John D. Barry is one example. He was the commander of the 18th North Carolina Infantry Regiment when Brigadier General James H. Lane, his commanding officer, was wounded at Cold Harbor. As senior regimental commander, Barry replaced him on June 2, 1864, as a brigadier general (temporary rank). He reverted to the rank of colonel when Lane returned on August 29. Barry ended the war as a colonel. Was Barry a Confederate general? My answer is yes—for a few weeks he was. His story is therefore told in this book.

Thirty-five temporary brigadier generals were eventually appointed. Only three, David Weisiger, William MacRae, and Bradley Johnson, were later promoted to permanent rank. This, however, is a matter of little consequence. A temporary general, after all, was still a general.

All books on Civil War generals will forever be measured against Ezra J. Warner's classics, *Generals in Gray: Lives of the Confederate Commanders* and

Generals in Blue: Lives of the Union Commanders. The former was first published in 1959 and covered 425 Confederate generals. I list 426. Warner chose not to include Raphael Semmes, the famous sea raider, as a Confederate general, but President Davis appointed Semmes brigadier general on April 5, 1865. He commanded a brigade for three weeks and was paroled as both a rear admiral and a brigadier general. As short as his tenure was, he was still a brigadier general—and there were others with shorter tenures than his—so I've included him.

A note about the term "chief of staff": In the Confederate Army, the man who functioned as the chief of staff was most likely the assistant adjutant general, though in some large field armies, the title "chief of staff" was held by a general officer. Nathan Bedford Forrest, for example, commanded a cavalry corps but had no chief of staff. Functionally speaking, Major Charles Anderson, his assistant adjutant general, was his chief of staff—but he never officially held the title.

Two other aspects of Confederate generals must be addressed. First, there were state generals and militia generals who never held Confederate rank at the general level. Sometimes, these men were called "General," which they were, but they were not *Confederate* generals. This sometimes confuses people. There were also "Trans-Mississippi Generals"—men "assigned to duty" as generals by Edmund Kirby Smith, the commander of the Trans-Mississippi Department, in 1864 and 1865. Their appointments were of dubious legality because they were never nominated by the president or confirmed by the Senate. They were Arthur P. Bagby, Xavier B. Debray, Wilburn H. King, Robert P. Maclay, Horace Randal, Benjamin Franklin Gordon, Sidney D. Jackson, Levin M. Lewis, and Alexander W. Terrell. The biographies of these men—worthy though they were—will not be covered in this book.

The second aspect is the insignia of a general. U.S. generals were (and are) distinguished by the number of stars on their shoulder boards. A brigadier general wears one star and is often called a one-star general. A major general has two stars, a lieutenant general three stars, and a general (often called a "full general") wears four. When we had "Generals of the Army" during World War II, they wore five stars. The Confederacy did not do it that way. All generals, regardless of grade, wore an insignia of three gold stars, enclosed by a wreath. The middle star was larger than the other two. A brigadier general was distinguished from other generals by the arrangement of the buttons on his coat. A brigadier general wore

buttons in two rows, in groups of two buttons each. Other generals had two rows in groups of three. Full ("four-star") generals wore a sleeve insignia. Robert E. Lee was an exception to the rule. He chose to wear the rank insignia of a colonel, which had three stars of the same size and no wreath. As with Lee, many liberties were taken with the uniform as the war wore on. A Confederate colonel, for example, was unlikely to discard a warm coat (if he had one) just because he was promoted to brigadier general. He would probably just change his collar insignia to reflect his new rank.

John C. Brown in the uniform of a major general

Colonels wore a collar insignia of three stars, lieutenant colonels wore two, and majors wore a single star. They all had a single line of buttons. Captains wore a collar insignia of three stripes, first lieutenants two stripes, and second lieutenants a single stripe.

A note on brevet rank: A "brevet" was normally an honorary promotion, given for bravery in the field or upon retirement. It had no impact on a man's pay. In the antebellum Regular Army, however, it was sometimes used as a rank just below second lieutenant. It was, for practical purposes, equivalent to the rank of "third lieutenant." Typically, this circumstance applied only to recent West Point graduates.

A note on the names of battles: In those days, the North and the South could not even agree on the names of some of the battles. They still can't. Southerners generally called them after the nearest place. Northerners often called them after the nearest body of water. On September 17, 1862, for example, the North fought the Battle of Antietam, while the South fought the Battle of Sharpsburg—even though it was the same battle. I tend to use the Southern names. I am, after all, a Southern officer and a Southern historian, as well as a member of the Sons of Confederate Veterans, writing from a Southern perspective about Southern generals fighting primarily in the South.

Finally, a word about footnotes. Essentially there aren't any—just a handful of informational notes. Some readers will wish there were. So do I. When I started this book, I wanted to tell the story of each man in great detail. But by the time I was ready to approach a publisher, the manuscript was approaching 500,000 words in length, and I was in 3- or 4-volume territory. The average book is 60,000 to 70,000 words long. Four-volume sets generally lose money, and publishing is a business, after all, so I was limited to 250,000 words—the maximum for a single volume. This required a lot of cutting. The choice came between cutting information, cutting the photographs, cutting footnotes, or scrapping the project altogether, so I cut the notes. There is a rather extensive bibliography at the end of the book for those who are interested.

James Cantey in a brigadier general's uniform

Thanks go to everyone who assisted me in researching and writing this book, including James Ronald Kennedy and Walter Donald Kennedy, who allowed me to use parts of their extensive libraries. Thanks also go to the various people who worked so hard to get this book to press, including Alex Novak, Harry Crocker III, Tad Wojcik, and Joshua Monnington. Also to my long-suffering wife, Donna Mitcham, who took time away from her own freelance work as a writer and editor to proofread this book. She is also an extremely good sport, as I have taken her across most of America's Civil War battlefields. Thanks also go to a myriad of librarians, park rangers, museum curators, and scholars (especially at the Abbeville Institute and the Stephen Dill Lee Institute), who are too numerous to mention individually. The same goes for the members of the Sons of Confederate Veterans, the Military Order of the Stars and Bars, and the United Daughters of the Confederacy, who always share their abundant knowledge with anyone who shows an interest.

—Dr. Samuel W. Mitcham, Jr.

A

ADAMS – ASHBY

DANIEL WEISIGER "DAN" ADAMS was born in Frankfort, Kentucky, on May 1, 1821, but grew up in Mississippi. He became a prominent attorney and served in the Mississippi State Senate (1852–56). In 1843, a newspaper editor attacked him, and Adams shot him in the head with a derringer. Adams was indicted and tried for murder but was acquitted.

Adams moved to New Orleans in the 1850s, and on March 13, 1861, he became lieutenant colonel of the 1st Louisiana Infantry Regiment. Promoted to colonel on October 30, he led the 1st Louisiana at Shiloh on April 6, 1862, when his brigade commander, General Gladden, was killed. Adams assumed command of the brigade and led it against the Hornet's Nest, where a rifle ball blinded him in his left eye.

Adams was promoted to brigadier general on May 23, 1862, and returned to duty on August 13. He led his brigade at Perryville and the Second Battle of Murfreesboro (Stone River), where, on December 31, he was wounded by a shell fragment in the left arm.* He served in the Vicksburg relief campaign and at Chickamauga, where he was wounded and taken prisoner. In October, the Yankees returned Adams to Confederate lines at the special request of Braxton Bragg, who liked him.

After he recovered, General Adams served as a cavalry brigade leader and commander of the districts of North Alabama, Central Alabama, and Alabama. He fought in the Battle of Selma, supervised the evacuation of Montgomery on April 11, and fought in the Battle of Columbus, Georgia, the last major action east of the Mississippi River, on April 16. He surrendered on May 9, 1865, in Meridian, Mississippi.

Despite a total lack of military training or experience, Dan Adams proved to be a capable and effective brigade commander. This was true of a great many generals on both sides during the War for Southern Independence. Adams was also noted for being cheerful, even when in pain.

---

* Appendix I shows the dates of the major battles, campaigns, and events of the war.

A

Adams went to England after the war but soon returned to the United States and became a law partner with Harry T. Hays, another former Confederate general, in New Orleans.

On June 13, 1872, General Adams was working in his office when he simply put his head down on his desk and died of a massive stroke. He was fifty-one years old. He is buried next to his brother, William W. Adams, also a Confederate general, in the family plot in Greenwood Cemetery, Jackson, Mississippi. His grave is unmarked, although there is a cenotaph (a tombstone without a body beneath it) erected in his honor in the Confederate section of the cemetery.

JOHN ADAMS, whose parents were Irish immigrants, was born in Nashville, Tennessee, on July 1, 1825. Through hard work, he gained admission to West Point, from which he graduated in 1846. He was commissioned a brevet second lieutenant of cavalry on July 1. Sent to Mexico, he fought in the Battle of Santa Cruz de Rosales and earned a brevet to first lieutenant for gallantry.

Postwar, Adams served principally on the Western frontier and fought Indians. He was a captain when Tennessee seceded. He resigned his commission and was appointed captain in the Confederate Regular Army. He was placed in command of the post of Memphis, where his commander, General Leonidas Polk, was not satisfied with him and complained about his "bad habits" and lack of ability. On Polk's recommendation, Adams was transferred to command of the 1st Kentucky Cavalry Regiment in April 1862. He was promoted to colonel the following month. He served on the Western Front, where his performance was mixed. On June 4, the Yankees surprised Adams at Sweeten's Cove, Tennessee, and routed his regiment. He lost at least fifty-two men and several wagons. Two Northerners were killed and seven were wounded.

From August 1862 to May 1863, Adams labored in rear-area posts in Mississippi. He had not, however, lost the confidence of General

Joseph E. Johnston, who recommended Adams be promoted to brigadier general. He was appointed to this rank on January 9, 1863, but the Senate rejected his nomination, and he reverted to the rank of colonel.

Johnston gave Adams command of Lloyd Tilghman's brigade after that officer was killed on May 16. Adams was appointed brigadier general for the second time on May 23, 1863. This time he was confirmed.

Adams took part in the defense of eastern Mississippi. In 1864, Adams's brigade distinguished itself during the Atlanta campaign and was part of John Bell Hood's invasion of Tennessee in the winter of 1864, during which it captured several hundred Union prisoners. On November 30, 1864, during the Battle of Franklin, Adams was severely wounded in the right arm near the shoulder but refused to leave the field. He led his men in the final, desperate assault on the Union's prepared positions. They were slaughtered. As he leaped over the Union breastworks, his horse was killed, and General Adams was shot nine times. The Yankees captured him, pulled his dead horse off him, gave him water, and fashioned a cotton pillow for him. Adams thanked them for their courtesy. When the bluecoats expressed sorrow for his impending demise, Adams replied: "It is the fate of a soldier to die for his country." He passed away a few moments later. He was thirty-nine years old.

As a commander, John Adams clearly grew as the war progressed, and he was a fine brigade commander by 1864. He is buried in the Maplewood Cemetery, Pulaski, Tennessee.

WILLIAM WIRT ADAMS, the older brother of General Daniel W. Adams, was born in Frankfort, Kentucky, on March 22, 1819. His family moved to Mississippi in 1825. Adams graduated from Bardstown College in Kentucky in 1839 and promptly enlisted in the Army of the Republic of Texas as a private. He fought Indians in northeastern Texas and became a lieutenant and regimental adjutant. Later, he returned to Mississippi, became a successful planter, a banker, and a businessman, and owned an impressive plantation house, a sugar plantation in Iberville Parish, Louisiana, a $90,000 home in New Orleans (worth $2,025,000 in 2020 dollars), and many slaves. He was elected to the Mississippi House of Representatives in 1857 and reelected in 1860. He was a secessionist.

In February 1861, Jefferson Davis offered to name Adams postmaster general, but he opted for field duty instead. He organized the 1st Mississippi Cavalry Regiment, which he outfitted at his own expense. He fought at Shiloh, the siege of Corinth, the retreat to Tupelo, and the Battle of Iuka. Adams also led a number of successful raids into west Tennessee in the summer of 1862.

During the Vicksburg campaign, Adams's regiment formed virtually all the cavalry in the Army of Mississippi, a mission which exceeded their capabilities by a wide margin. Adams escaped being trapped in Vicksburg and harassed Sherman's forces as they advanced into central and eastern Mississippi.

Wirt Adams was promoted to brigadier general on September 25, 1863, and commanded a small cavalry brigade. He was an effective raider, and he and his men harassed Union forces from west Tennessee to Baton Rouge, much to the annoyance of Grant and Sherman. In early 1865, he was transferred to Alabama. On April 5, 1865, he smashed a Union brigade near Eutaw—one of the last victories ever won by the Confederate Army. General Adams surrendered on May 4 near Ramsey Station, Alabama, and was paroled at Gainesville on May 12.

After the war, Adams resumed business operations in Mississippi and became postmaster of Jackson in 1885. He grew to be the target of several scathing and sarcastic editorial attacks from newspaperman John H. Martin. On May 1, 1888, Adams ran into Martin on the street. After a short verbal altercation, the editor drew his revolver. Adams also pulled his pistol and both men started shooting. One of the bullets struck Adams in the heart, killing him instantly. Martin was also killed.

General Adams is buried in the Greenwood Cemetery in Jackson.

EDWARD PORTER ALEXANDER (commonly known as E. Porter Alexander and called "Porter") was born into a wealthy family in

Washington, Georgia, on May 26, 1835. Porter graduated from West Point in 1857 and was commissioned in the engineers. He taught practical military engineering and fencing at West Point before being transferred to Utah. He later did another tour of duty at West Point, followed by a stint in Washington, D.C., where he worked with the Army's foremost signals experts.

Alexander opposed secession but joined the Confederate Army as a captain of engineers when Georgia left the Union. General Beauregard named him chief engineer and signal officer of the Confederate Army of the Potomac on June 3. He was promoted to major on July 1.

Porter Alexander distinguished himself in the Battle of First Manassas (Bull Run) as the first man in history to use signal flags in combat to transmit messages over great distances and materially contributed to the Confederate victory. He served as chief of ordnance and chief signals officer on the staffs of Beauregard, Joseph E. Johnston, and Robert E. Lee. He transferred to the artillery (which offered greater scope for advancement) in November 1862 and was promoted to colonel on March 3, 1863.

Alexander became perhaps the most famous artillery officer in the Civil War. He set up the artillery defense of Marye's Heights in the Battle of Fredericksburg in December 1862, where the Union attackers were slaughtered. His most famous battle was Gettysburg, where on July 3, he conducted a massive two-hour, 140-gun bombardment on Cemetery Ridge. Unfortunately, many of the guns fired over the Union positions, smashing the Federal rear but leaving the Federal infantry intact. The result was the decisive defeat of Pickett's Charge. As chief of artillery of Longstreet's corps, he fought in Tennessee and returned to Virginia in early 1864. General Lee arranged for him to be promoted to brigadier general on February 26. He took part in the Overland Campaign and the Siege of Petersburg, where his tactical use of mortars was quite effective. He was severely wounded by a ricocheted Union bullet on June 30,

1864. He returned to duty that fall and was present at Appomattox. No other officer in the Civil War had as many varied assignments as Alexander, and none excelled more frequently than did he.

After the war, General Alexander taught mathematics at the University of South Carolina, served as executive superintendent or president of three railroads, and fixed the boundary between Nicaragua and Costa Rica, to the satisfaction of both countries. He returned to the United States in 1899. He published the highly acclaimed *Military Memoirs of a Confederate* in 1907. He also wrote a handful of books on railroad operations, as well as articles in *Battles and Leaders of the Civil War* and the *Southern Historical Society Papers*.

General E. Porter Alexander had a severe stroke in January 1910. He lapsed into a coma on April 27 and died in Savannah on April 28, 1910, at age seventy-four. He is buried in Magnolia Cemetery, Augusta, Georgia.

HENRY WATKINS ALLEN was, as Pulitzer Prize–winning historian Dr. Douglas Southall Freeman wrote, the one administrator who might have made a difference in the outcome of the war, had the Confederacy recognized his genius earlier. He was born on April 29, 1820, in Farmville, Virginia. His family moved to Missouri in 1833. Henry Allen was educated at local schools and attended Marion College in Philadelphia, Missouri, for two years. He left home at age seventeen and moved to Mississippi, where he studied law. When he returned for a visit ten years later, he was the richest person in the state.

Henry Allen was a small, physically unattractive man noted for his genius and his energy. An apparent spirit of adventure prompted him to join the Army of the Republic of Texas in 1842, where he rose from private to captain in six months before he returned to Mississippi, where he practiced law and politics, and also acquired a plantation in Tensas Parish, Louisiana, raising several cotton crops.

The tobacco-chewing Allen wed a beautiful woman, but she died after they had been married only seven years. He also had a fierce temper, which he did not always keep under control. In the 1850s, this led to a duel in which he was seriously wounded. It has been speculated that this is why he had no children.

Allen served in the Mississippi House of Representatives from 1845 to 1847 and later in the Louisiana legislature. He was the founding president of the Louisiana Historical Society. In 1852, he acquired a large sugarcane plantation in West Baton Rouge Parish, Louisiana, owned 125 slaves, and built his own railroad. He also journeyed throughout the South, studied law at Harvard, traveled extensively in Europe, and wrote a book about his adventures. In 1860, he enlisted in the Delta Rifle Company as a private.

Henry Allen took part in the seizure of the Federal arsenal in Baton Rouge in January 1861. In the spring of 1861, he joined the 4th Louisiana Infantry Regiment, was elected its lieutenant colonel, and was promoted to colonel on March 1, 1862. He fought at Shiloh, where a Yankee shot him in the cheek and knocked out several teeth. He nevertheless commanded an ad hoc brigade in the (First) Siege of Vicksburg and in the Battle of Baton Rouge on August 5, 1862. Here, a cannon blast at close range shattered both his legs. He was unable to walk without crutches for the rest of his life.

Allen returned to duty as a military judge. Despite his handicap, President Davis promoted him to brigadier general on August 19, 1863, and ordered him to Shreveport to organize paroled prisoners of war.

Meanwhile, Allen's friends placed his name on the gubernatorial ballot. He was so highly thought of that no one opposed him. He assumed office on January 1, 1864.

Governor Allen never allowed his wounds to sap his energy. For the details of his incredibly successful administration, see Samuel W. Mitcham, Jr., *Richard Taylor and the Red River Campaign*. After the war, he escaped to Mexico City, where he established an English-language newspaper.

Governor Allen died of a stomach disorder in Mexico City on April 22, 1866, at age forty-five. The people of Louisiana still loved him,

however, and his remains are now buried on the Old Capitol grounds in Baton Rouge. He is the only person in Louisiana history to ever be so honored.

WILLIAM WIRT ALLEN (who was called "Wirt" or "W. W.") was born in New York City on September 11, 1835. His father was a successful land speculator and entrepreneur with business interests in the South. He moved to South Carolina in 1818 and settled in Montgomery, Alabama, when W. W. was a child. The future general received his education there and at the College of New Jersey (later named Princeton), where he studied law. Wirt graduated in 1854 but preferred plantation life to a legal career. He married and eventually became the father of eleven children.

Allen was a tall, stout man who, by 1861, had developed the cordial, gracious manner of a Southern gentleman farmer. Although not a secessionist, he joined the Montgomery Mounted Rifles as a first lieutenant as soon as the war began. His company was incorporated into the 1st Alabama Cavalry Regiment, and Allen was elected its major on March 18, 1862. He first saw action at Shiloh, after which he became the colonel and regimental commander. He took part in the Kentucky Campaign of 1862 and was slightly wounded in the left arm in the Battle of Perryville. Advanced to brigade command, he distinguished himself in the Stones River Campaign, destroying a wagon train and capturing hundreds of prisoners. Early on the morning of January 1, 1863, he fought a sharp engagement north of Overall Creek, where he was shot and wounded so badly that it took him over a year to recover, and he never fully regained the use of his right hand. Back on field duty in April 1864, he took command of an Alabama cavalry brigade in northern Alabama and was promoted to brigadier general on March 1 to date from February 26.

Allen led his brigade in the Atlanta Campaign and in August became a division commander. He opposed Sherman's March to the Sea and his subsequent advance through the Carolinas. He was slightly wounded at Waynesboro, Georgia, on November 28. Jefferson Davis appointed him major general (temporary rank) on March 4, 1865. He surrendered in North Carolina and was paroled as a brigadier. During the war, he was seriously wounded three times and had ten horses shot out from under him. "As a soldier, he was cool and fearless in danger and tireless in the performance of duty," General Joe Wheeler recalled. He was probably the best commander in Wheeler's cavalry corps.

Postwar, Wirt Allen returned to Alabama and resumed farming. He was also involved in the railroad business, served several years as the state's adjutant general in the early 1870s, and became a U.S. marshal in Alabama. Allen also helped form the Confederate Survivors Association. W. W. Allen moved to Sheffield, Alabama, in 1893 and died there of heart disease on November 21, 1894, at age fifty-nine. He is buried in Elmwood Cemetery, Birmingham.

GEORGE BURGWYN ANDERSON was born on April 12, 1831, near Hillsboro in Orange County, North Carolina, the son of a planter. He enrolled in Caldwell Academy and then the University of North Carolina at Chapel Hill, graduating with highest honors. Admitted to West Point, he graduated in the class of 1852. Commissioned a brevet second lieutenant of cavalry, he was at various times stationed at Carlisle Barracks, Pennsylvania; Fort Chadbourne, Texas; and Fort Riley, Kansas, as well as in California and in the Utah War against the Mormons in 1858. He was at Fort Kearney, Nebraska, when he resigned his commission on April 25, 1861. He returned to North Carolina, where the governor named him colonel of the 4th North Carolina Infantry on July 16. Daniel Harvey Hill, Jr., later described him as "a magnificent specimen of manhood, full six feet, erect, broad-shouldered, round-limbed, with a deep, musical voice, and a smile wonderfully gentle and winning." He was known for his uncommonly friendly and positive personality.

Sent north, Anderson commanded the garrison at Manassas for six months. Hurriedly transferred to the peninsula in late March 1862, he performed well in the Battle of Williamsburg, where he grabbed the regimental colors and led a desperate charge witnessed by Jefferson Davis.

General D. H. Hill praised Anderson highly for his conduct at Seven Pines and on June 6 wrote directly to Secretary of War Judah Benjamin and asked that Anderson be promoted to brigadier general and assigned to his (Hill's) command. Anderson was promoted three days later.

Anderson fought in the Seven Days Battles, where he exhibited a talent for detecting weak points in the enemy's defenses. He was wounded in the hand during the Battle of Malvern Hill. During his convalescence, he temporarily commanded a brigade in the Richmond defenses in G. W. Smith's division.

General Anderson resumed command of his brigade that fall and led it in the Maryland Campaign, including the Battle of South Mountain, where he fought in the Fox Gap sector. Here, he lost a third of his command.

George Anderson had a reputation for being a furious fighter. During the Battle of Sharpsburg, he helped defend the Sunken Road, which was also known as the "Bloody Lane," where he was struck in the foot and right ankle by a minié ball. Although painful, his wound was not thought to be serious. Unfortunately, infection set in, and he was sent to Raleigh, North Carolina, where his foot was amputated. He did not rally from the surgery and died on October 16, 1862. He is buried in Historic Oakwood Cemetery in Raleigh. He was thirty-one years old.

General John Brown Gordon called him a "superb" man. D. H. Hill, Jr., called him "a man of spotless purity of life, integrity[,] and honor, as well as dauntless courage."

GEORGE THOMAS "TIGE" OR "TIGER" ANDERSON was born in Covington, Georgia, on February 3, 1824. He attended Emory College (Georgia) but dropped out and, on May 27, 1847, joined the Independent

Company of Georgia Mounted Rifles as a second lieutenant. He fought in the Mexican War, where he helped conquer New Mexico, Arizona, and California for the United States. Anderson secured a Regular Army commission as a captain in the 1st U.S. Cavalry in 1855 and served in Kansas, but he resigned on June 11, 1858. He remained in Kansas until Georgia seceded.

Anderson was a man of considerable means by the time the war began. He was elected colonel of the 11th Georgia Infantry and was sent to Virginia, where the unit became part of the Army of the Shenandoah. It was ordered to Manassas but arrived too late to participate in the First Battle of Bull Run.

"Tige" Anderson fought in the Siege of Yorktown, the Peninsula Campaign, the Seven Days Battles, Second Manassas, South Mountain, Sharpsburg, Fredericksburg, Suffolk, and Gettysburg, among other battles. He quickly gained a reputation as a good regimental and brigade commander and one of the Army's toughest warriors. During the Seven Days, he commanded a brigade, which he led most of the rest of the war. He was promoted to brigadier general on November 1, 1862.

Anderson was with Longstreet at Gettysburg and fought in the Wheatfield on July 2. His brigade performed "splendidly," but nearly half of its 1,497 men were killed, wounded, or captured. Of the 10 men on his staff (including couriers), 7 were killed or wounded. Among the casualties was Anderson himself, who was seriously wounded when a minié ball struck his right thigh between the femoral artery and the bone. He was sent to Charleston to recuperate. "Tiger" Anderson returned to duty on October 5 and served in Longstreet's East Tennessee Campaign. He was with William Mahone when he attacked and rolled up the Union left wing on May 6, 1864, during the Battle of the Wilderness. Anderson and his brigade fought at Spotsylvania, Cold Harbor, and the Siege of Petersburg. It surrendered at Appomattox with Charles Field's Division.

After the war, General Anderson became a freight agent and then went into law enforcement. He was chief of police of Atlanta (1877–81) before he moved to Anniston, Alabama, where he was both chief of police

A

and county tax collector. He died of chronic kidney and bladder inflammation in Anniston on April 4, 1901, at age seventy-seven and is buried there in Edgemont Cemetery.

JAMES PATTON ANDERSON was born in Franklin County, Tennessee, on February 16, 1822. He was called by his middle name. His family moved to Kentucky when he was nine and to Mississippi in 1838. James attended medical school but dropped out. He nevertheless began practicing medicine in 1842 but soon switched professions to law. He was admitted to the bar in 1843 and set up a practice at Hernando, Mississippi. When the Mexican War began in 1846, he joined the elite Mississippi Rifle Regiment, where he rose to the rank of lieutenant colonel.

Patton Anderson served in the Mississippi House of Representatives (1850–51) but was defeated in his bid for reelection. He returned to the practice of law with some success, and after a brief adventure as a gold prospector, he was appointed U.S. marshal for Washington Territory, a post he occupied for several years, and represented the territory in Congress (1855–57). Concerned that the Union was about to collapse, Anderson moved to Florida after his term expired, managed a plantation, and was a delegate to the Florida Secession Convention and then a member of the Provisional Confederate Congress. He became colonel of the 1st Florida Infantry Regiment on March 26, 1861, and resigned from Congress. Sent to Pensacola, he took part in the unsuccessful attack on the Union camp on Santa Rosa Island. He became a brigade commander on October 12, was promoted to brigadier general on February 10, 1862, and assumed command of a brigade on the Western Front.

General Anderson was a firm disciplinarian and was quick to execute deserters but was friendly and popular with his men. He distinguished himself at Shiloh and led his brigade through the battles of Farmington, Corinth, the Kentucky Campaign, Second Murfreesboro (where he captured three Union batteries on the first day), the Tullahoma Campaign, and Chickamauga. He was a temporary division commander at Chickamauga and Chattanooga, replacing a wounded General Thomas C. Hindman. Anderson's was the first division to break at Missionary Ridge on November 25. He was not held personally responsible for this defeat, however, and was promoted to major general on February 1, 1864.

Anderson was named commander of the District of Florida. Despite limited resources, he was able to contain the enemy in the Jacksonville area. Ordered back to Georgia, he assumed command of his old division on July 28. He fought in the Atlanta Campaign until August 31 when, during the Battle of Jonesboro, a minié ball broke his jaw. He was on a liquid diet for months.

Ignoring his doctors, he returned to duty on April 1, 1865. He was given command of Taliaferro's old division, which had only 890 men. He surrendered with the rest of the Army of Tennessee on April 26.

Patton Anderson lived in Memphis, Tennessee, after the war. He found it difficult to work because of the lingering effects of his wound. He died of pneumonia and in poverty on September 20, 1872, at the age of fifty. General Anderson is buried in Elmwood Cemetery, Memphis. He was eulogized as "the soul of honor and integrity."

JOSEPH REID ANDERSON was born on February 16, 1813, at "Walnut Hill" near Fincastle in Botetourt County, Virginia, the grandson of Scotch-Irish immigrants. He attended West Point and graduated fourth in the class of 1836 as an artillery second lieutenant. Later that year he transferred to the Corps of Engineers and was sent to Fort Pulaski, Georgia—an undesirable assignment. Seeking better prospects, he resigned from the army effective September 30, 1837, and became a civil engineer, working for the Commonwealth of Virginia. Eventually, he became assistant state engineer and chief engineer of the Valley Turnpike Company.

Anderson joined the Tredegar Iron Works company in Richmond in 1841. He leased the firm in 1843 and purchased it outright in 1848. He made it the largest ironworks south of the Mason-Dixon Line, producing steam locomotives, boilers, munitions, naval hardware, cables, and cannons. Anderson was the leading industrialist in the South by 1860. He was elected to the Virginia legislature in 1852 and was reelected several times.

After Lincoln was elected president in November 1860, Anderson supported secession and served in a local defense unit. He joined the Confederate Army as a major of artillery on August 27, 1861, and was promoted to brigadier general on September 3. Initially assigned to command Rebel forces in and around Wilmington, North Carolina, he was transferred to the Virginia front in the spring of 1862 and was given command of a brigade near Fredericksburg. Anderson's brigade joined A. P. Hill's famous "Light Division" in May and fought at Seven Pines and in the Seven Days Battles. On June 30, 1862, during the Battle of Frayser's Farm (also called Glendale and White Oak Swamp), Anderson was struck in the head by a Union bullet. Fortunately for him, the round was spent, but it still concussed him, and it took him several weeks to recover.

At the request of senior Confederate officials, he resigned from the Army on July 19, 1862. He was too valuable as the director of Tredegar. During the war, he manufactured 1,099 cannons for the Southern armies, as well as munitions, shells, machinery for the manufacture of small arms, machinery for Confederate warships, tools, and other equipment. He supplied the Southern armies until April 2–3, 1865, when General Lee evacuated Richmond.

Anderson regained control of Tredegar from the Federal government in 1867 and directed it until his death on September 7, 1892. He was elected to the Virginia House of Delegates in 1873, defeated in 1875, reelected in 1877, and served until 1879. He also served on the Richmond City Council. His elegant home on Franklin Street was the center of Richmond society.

Joseph Anderson died of cerebral atrophy while on vacation at the Isles of Shoals, New Hampshire. His body was returned to Richmond, where his funeral was attended by thirty thousand people. He is buried in Hollywood Cemetery, Richmond.

RICHARD HERON "DICK" ANDERSON was born at Borough House Plantation (also known as Hill Crest) near Statesburg, Sumter County, South Carolina, on October 7, 1821. He was a descendant of the famous William Wallace of Scotland.

Anderson attended West Point and graduated in 1842 as a second lieutenant of dragoons. He spent the next eighteen years on the frontier. He fought in the Mexican War (1846–48) and in the Utah War (1857–58). A captain in 1861, he resigned when South Carolina seceded and returned home, where he was named colonel of the 1st South Carolina Regulars.

Colonel Anderson took part in the bombardment of Fort Sumter and was left in charge of Charleston when General G. T. Beauregard left for Virginia on May 27. Anderson was promoted to brigadier general on July 19 and was transferred to the Army of Pensacola as a brigade commander. He fought in the Battle of Santa Rosa Island during the night of October 8–9, when the Confederates tried unsuccessfully to capture Fort Pickens. Anderson was severely wounded when a Union musket ball struck his left elbow. After he recuperated, he was transferred to the Army of the Potomac (later the Army of Northern Virginia) and assumed command of D. R. Jones's old brigade.

Anderson fought in the Peninsula Campaign and at Seven Pines gained the sobriquet "Fighting Dick." He took part in the Seven Days Battles, was promoted to major general on July 14, and took over General Benjamin Huger's division. He fought at the battles of Second Manassas, the Maryland Campaign, and Sharpsburg, where he was wounded in the thigh but refused to leave the field until he collapsed from loss of blood. He also led his division at Fredericksburg and Chancellorsville.

General Moxley Sorrel called him "lovable" but also noted, "He was indolent. His capacity and intelligence excellent, but it was hard to get him to use them." On the other hand, he had a knack for inspiring confidence in his men by his very presence. One soldier remembered: "When General Anderson was near, everyone felt better and braver."

Anderson has been rightly criticized for mismanaging his division at Gettysburg. On July 2, one of his brigades under Ambrose R. Wright penetrated Cemetery Ridge, which was not yet heavily defended, but Anderson failed to reinforce Wright, and fresh Union regiments threw him back. Meanwhile, one of Anderson's brigades was not engaged at all.

On May 6, 1864, after General Longstreet was critically wounded at the Battle of the Wilderness, Robert E. Lee named Anderson as Longstreet's temporary successor. He was promoted to lieutenant general (temporary rank) on May 31.

Fighting Dick did well in the battles of the Overland Campaign, including Spotsylvania Court House, North Anna, and Cold Harbor. After Longstreet returned from his convalescence, General Lee created a new IV Corps, which Anderson directed during the Siege of Petersburg. By this time, however, Anderson had become a defeatist, and his performance was lackluster.

During the retreat to Appomattox, Anderson's corps was overrun at Sayler's Creek on April 6, 1865. Anderson fled on horseback, earning him Lee's censure. General Lee relieved him of his command on April 8. Now a supernumerary, General Anderson headed for home on April 8, one day before Lee surrendered. Somehow, he escaped Grant's tightening encirclement. There is no record of his parole.

The rest of Richard Anderson's life was an unsuccessful struggle against poverty. His financial situation became so bad that, at one point, he joined a railroad construction gang as a day laborer. In Beaufort, South Carolina, on June 26, 1879, General Anderson suffered an attack of apoplexy (a cerebral hemorrhage or stroke) and was dead within an hour. He was fifty-seven years old. They buried Fighting Dick in the churchyard cemetery of St. Helena's Episcopal Church in Beaufort the next day.

ROBERT HOUSTON "BOB" ANDERSON was born on October 1, 1835, in Savannah, Georgia, the son of a local businessman. He was educated in local schools and at West Point, from which he graduated in 1857 as a second lieutenant of infantry. He was stationed at Fort Walla Walla in Washington Territory before he "went south" in March 1861 shortly after Georgia seceded. He joined the Confederate Army as a lieutenant of artillery.

Anderson was promoted to major in September 1861 and was assistant adjutant general (and de facto chief of staff) to Major General W. H. T. Walker at Pensacola. When Walker was transferred to Virginia, Anderson went with him. Walker resigned in October, and Anderson returned to Georgia in April 1862 to organize the 1st Georgia Sharpshooters Battalion at Fort McAllister on the Ogeechee River, just downriver from Savannah. Anderson became colonel of the 5th Georgia Cavalry Regiment on January 20, 1863, but he was still in the area in February when the Yankee gunboats attacked Fort McAllister. Anderson assumed command of the fort, repulsed the gunboats, and saved Savannah.

The 5th Georgia Cavalry defended South Carolina and parts of Georgia against Union incursions. It fought in several local battles and was generally successful. Colonel Anderson and the 5th Georgia Cavalry were sent to Florida in February 1864 but arrived too late to fight in the Battle of Olustee. They remained in Florida, where they performed scouting missions and coastal picket duty until the Atlanta Campaign began.

Anderson and his men joined General Joseph "Fighting Joe" Wheeler's cavalry corps in the Atlanta Campaign. In mid-June, Anderson was given command of W. W. Allen's cavalry brigade. He was wounded in late June but was promoted to brigadier general (temporary rank) on July 26, 1864. Four days later, he was wounded again in the Battle of Brown's Mill near Newman, Georgia, but did not miss much duty.

Anderson opposed Sherman's March to the Sea in late 1864 and was wounded in the Battle of Griswoldville on November 22 and near

Fayetteville, North Carolina, in March 1865. He surrendered with the rest of Johnston's Army of Tennessee on April 26, 1865, and was paroled at Hillsboro on May 3.

Robert H. Anderson returned home to Savannah, where he served as police chief from 1867 to 1888. His police force was considered one of the best in the nation. Chief Anderson preached reconciliation and hired both Union and Confederate veterans. He died of pneumonia in Savannah on February 8, 1888, and is buried in Bonaventure Cemetery. He was fifty-two years old.

SAMUEL READ ANDERSON was born on February 17, 1804, in Bedford County, Virginia, but was raised in Tennessee. By 1845, Anderson was a successful business-man and a leading citizen of Nashville, Tennessee. He served as lieutenant colonel of the 1st Tennessee Volunteer Infantry Regiment during the Mexican War. It fought in the American victories at Fort de la Teneria and Monterrey in northern Mexico before being transferred to Winfield Scott's army for the drive on Mexico City.** The 1st Tennessee fought in the Battle of Cerro Gordo and the subsequent pursuit; however, the twelve-month enlistments of the Tennesseans expired, and most of them opted not to reenlist.

Colonel Anderson worked for the Bank of Tennessee until 1853, when he became postmaster of Nashville. In 1861, Governor Isham G. Harris commissioned him major general of the Provisional Army of Tennessee. When this army was transferred to Confederate service, Anderson became a brigadier general on July 9.

Anderson became a brigade commander on August 5 and directed three Tennessee regiments (three thousand men) under Robert E. Lee in the unsuccessful Cheat Mountain campaign of 1861. His performance was credible but hardly brilliant. He spent the harsh winter of 1861–62

** Appendix II shows the chronology of the major battles of the Mexican War.

A ⬦

in the mountains of western Virginia and took part in Stonewall Jackson's operations around Hancock, Bath, and Romney, which undermined his health. That spring, he and his brigade fought in the Peninsula Campaign and in the successful attempt to check the Union advance at West Point, Virginia, (also known as Eltham's Landing) on May 7. Here he earned the praise of the overall Confederate commander, General W. H. C. Whiting, who was not an easy man to please. Three days later, on May 10, 1862, Anderson resigned for reasons of health and returned to Tennessee. He was a good commander but perhaps too old for field duty.

Samuel Anderson returned to the colors late in the conflict. Jefferson Davis reappointed him brigadier general on November 7, 1864, and named him chief of the Bureau of Conscription for Tennessee. Because most of the state was in Union hands, he was headquartered in Selma, Alabama. After the war, Anderson was paroled and returned to Nashville, where he became a successful businessman. He died there of "general disability" on January 2, 1883, at age seventy-eight, and is buried in the Old City Cemetery, Nashville.

JAMES JAY ARCHER was born at Stafford, near Havre de Grace, Maryland, on December 19, 1817, to wealthy parents. He graduated from the College of New Jersey (now Princeton), where he received the nickname "Sally" because of his frail health and small physique. He also attended Bacon College in Georgetown, Kentucky, and the University of Maryland, where he studied law. He was admitted to the bar and had a successful practice until 1846, when he volunteered for service in the Mexican War. Archer was commissioned captain in the Regiment of *Voltigeurs* (skirmishers) and won a brevet to major for bravery as a company commander in the Battle of Chapultepec.

After the war, Archer returned to Maryland and resumed his law practice but joined the Regular Army as a captain in 1855 and was sent to the Pacific Northwest. He was stationed at Fort Walla Walla, Washington, when the Civil War began.

Archer resigned his commission on May 14 and joined the Confederate Army. In September, President Davis created the 5th Texas Infantry Regiment from ten independent Texas companies then in Richmond and named Archer as commander. He fought in the Peninsula campaign and at Seven Pines.

He was not popular with his Texans, who considered him a martinet. Certainly he was a stern commander. He was nevertheless promoted to brigadier general on June 3, 1862, and given a brigade of Tennesseans after its commander, Robert H. Hatton, was killed in action at Seven Pines. Archer was more popular with the Tennesseans, who nicknamed him "the little gamecock" because of his small stature and his fierceness in battle. He fought in the Seven Days Battles, at Cedar Mountain, and at the Second Bull Run, where his horse was shot out from under him.

Archer directed his men from an ambulance during the Maryland campaign and took part in the capture of Harpers Ferry. He was too sick to lead it to Sharpsburg. Despite his fragile health, Archer led his troops at Fredericksburg, where he earned the praise of Stonewall Jackson. General Archer also distinguished himself at Chancellorsville, where on May 3 he led a charge against Hazel Grove, which was one of the key positions on the entire battlefield. He overran the position and captured one hundred bluecoats and four guns in the process. He briefly commanded the Light Division after Generals A. P. Hill, Henry Heth, and Dorsey Pender were all wounded.

Archer's worst battle was undoubtedly Gettysburg, where he did not handle his command with his customary skill. He was caught flat-footed by a Union counterattack and was captured at Willoughby Run. He was the first Confederate general from the Army of Northern Virginia taken prisoner.

Archer was sent to Johnson's Island prison camp on Lake Erie, where his health deteriorated due to the bitter cold, a lack of blankets, and an inadequate diet. After nearly a year, he was exchanged and returned to Petersburg, where he assumed command of his old brigade. He fought in the siege there and in the Battle of Peebles's Farm (September 30 to October 2, 1864) but collapsed altogether after the Union offensive was checked. He was taken to Richmond, where he died of pneumonia on October 24, 1864. James J. Archer is buried in Hollywood Cemetery, Richmond. He never married.

LEWIS ADDISON ARMISTEAD (pronounced UM-stead) was born in New Bern, North Carolina, on February 18, 1817, into a distinguished military family. Armistead's friends called him "Lo," after "Lothario," an unscrupulous seducer of women in the novel *Don Quixote*.

Armistead attended West Point but was forced to resign after breaking a plate over the head of Cadet Jubal Early in the mess hall. His father, General Armistead, had influence, however, and gained a commission for Lo in 1839. He served in Arkansas, the Indian Territory, and Mexico, where he fought at Contreras and Churubusco, for which he was brevetted captain, and at Chapultepec, where he was wounded. He was brevetted major for his actions at Chapultepec and at Molino del Rey.

He married Robert E. Lee's cousin in 1844, but she died in 1850. In 1853, Armistead married his second cousin. She perished in a cholera epidemic that swept Fort Riley, Kansas, in 1855. Armistead was heartbroken over her death and never fully got over it. He never remarried.

During the next three years, Captain Armistead served in various posts in the Kansas and Nebraska territories and in Utah. He also fought the Mohave Indians in California.

When the Civil War began, Armistead joined the Confederate Army as a major. He was promoted to colonel and commander of the 57th Virginia Infantry Regiment in September. He initially fought in western Virginia but joined Joseph E. Johnston's (later Lee's) staff in the latter part of 1861 as provost marshal of the army. General Lee commended him for his efficiency in this job.

Armistead was promoted to brigadier general on April 1, 1862, and was given command of a brigade that same month. He led it in several

major battles, including Sharpsburg, where he was wounded in the foot. He also fought at Fredericksburg and Suffolk.

Despite being a strict disciplinarian, Armistead was popular with his men. One of them called him a "gallant, kind and urbane old veteran." They would follow him anywhere, as they proved at Cemetery Ridge.

Armistead's brigade was part of George Pickett's division and took part in Pickett's Charge. With about two hundred men, Armistead reached the stone wall at "the Angle," which was the objective of the assault. Just after he crossed the wall, the enemy shot him three times, in the chest, arm, and left leg. He was captured almost immediately by a Union counterattack.

The Union surgeons did not believe Armistead's wounds were mortal, but he died in a Union field hospital (the Spangler farm) on July 5. He was forty-six years old. Lewis Addison Armistead was buried in Old St. Paul's Episcopal Cemetery, Baltimore, Maryland.

FRANK CRAWFORD ARMSTRONG was born on the Choctaw Agency in the Indian Territory (now Scullyville, Oklahoma) on November 22, 1835. Educated locally, Frank accompanied his stepfather, General Persifor F. Smith, on an expedition into New Mexico Territory, where he fought Indians. After that he attended the College of Holy Cross in Worcester, Massachusetts. Following graduation, thanks to the influence of his stepfather, he was commissioned directly into the Regular Army as a second lieutenant in the 2nd Dragoon Regiment in 1855. He fought in the Utah War against the Mormons.

In 1861, Armstrong was promoted to captain, Regular Army, and led a company of Union cavalry at Manassas. He resigned his commission on August 10 and joined the Confederacy. He was the only officer to become a general who had fought on both sides in the Civil War.

Armstrong joined the staff of General Ben McCulloch and later James M. McIntosh, both of whom were killed at Pea Ridge. Subsequently, he was assistant adjutant general of a brigade and then a division in Earl Van Dorn's Army of the West. Armstrong was elected colonel of the 3rd Louisiana Infantry Regiment on May 14, 1862, where his men found he strictly followed every military regulation, but he was always "affable, kind, and courteous" when dealing with his men. He led the 3rd Louisiana in the battles of Iuka and Second Corinth, where he distinguished himself by keeping the army's escape route open. He was placed in command of Major General Sterling Price's cavalry on July 7. Van Dorn "promoted" him to brigadier general the same day, but President Davis cancelled the promotion.

On December 30, Joseph E. Johnston, the commander of the Department of the West, requested that Davis promote Armstrong. Properly approached, Davis appointed him brigadier general on January 23, 1863, to rank from January 20.

Working under General Nathan Bedford Forrest, Armstrong fought at Thompson's Station (near Spring Hill, Tennessee) on March 4–5, at Brentwood on March 25, and at Franklin on April 10. He was captured near Franklin on June 4 but quickly escaped. He fought in the Tullahoma campaign and the Battle of Chickamauga, where he led a two-brigade division. Armstrong commanded a small division during Longstreet's unsuccessful Knoxville Campaign of late 1863.

He led a cavalry division in eastern Mississippi, the Atlanta Campaign, and John Bell Hood's disastrous Tennessee campaign, where he fought at Franklin, the Third Battle of Murfreesboro, and in the retreat from Nashville as part the rear guard. He fought at Selma, Alabama, in 1865 and was paroled in Columbus, Mississippi, on May 15.

After the war, Armstrong worked for the Overland Mail service in Texas and served as U.S. Indian Inspector. He was assistant commissioner for Indian Affairs from 1893 to 1895.

Frank C. Armstrong died of myocarditis in Bar Harbor, Maine, on September 8, 1909, and is buried in Rock Creek Cemetery, Washington, D.C. He was seventy-three years old.

TURNER ASHBY, JR., the "Black Knight of the Confederacy," was born on Rose Bank Plantation in Fauquier County, Virginia, on October 23, 1828. He loved the outdoors, became a superb equestrian, and won several riding tournaments, including one in which he dressed up as an American Indian and used neither saddle nor bridle.

Ashby was educated by private tutors and at Major Ambler's academy. As an adult, he ran a mill on his father's property and farmed the plantation. He also organized a militia cavalry company called the Mountain Rangers, which guarded John Brown before his execution. Although Ashby opposed secession, he left the Union when Virginia did. His Mountain Rangers became Company A, 7th Virginia Cavalry. He was stationed at Harpers Ferry, under the command of Colonel Thomas J. Jackson.

Early in the war, Ashby conducted raids against the Baltimore and Ohio (B & O) Railroad and the Chesapeake and Ohio Canal. In a skirmish on June 26, 1861, his brother Richard ("Dick") Ashby was wounded. As he lay helpless on the ground, a Union cavalryman ran him through. It took him eight days to die. "Turner became another man after Dick's death," Dr. Thomas A. Ashby recalled. His controlling motivation for the rest of his life was revenge. He remained a bold cavalier, noted for his physical endurance, but he also fought with a fierce hatred and became a hardened killer. He downed several Yankees in one-on-one combat, even after he suffered two wounds. He was promoted to lieutenant colonel on June 15, 1861, and to colonel on March 12, 1862.

Colonel Ashby's force was large and operated by its own rules. Not even Stonewall Jackson could impose discipline on Ashby and his men, and he did not press his luck. Ashby was popular with his followers, and Jackson feared mass desertion if Ashby resigned. Jackson opposed Ashby's promotion to brigadier general, but it was granted nevertheless on May 23, 1862.

Ashby's performance as Jackson's cavalry commander was mixed. His raids and screening operations were contributing factors to several of Jackson's victories, but his reconnaissance reports were frequently wrong. Acting on one of them, Jackson suffered his only defeat at Kernstown on March 22, 1862. Ashby also failed to cut off U.S. General Nathaniel Banks's retreat after Jackson's victory at Winchester—even though his wagon trains were completely exposed—because Ashby's men were too busy looting.

Turner Ashby relished combat and took unnecessary risks. On June 6, 1862, near Harrisonburg, Virginia, he led a charge on foot, and a Northern soldier shot him through the heart. He was thirty-three years old.

Turner Ashby never married. He was initially buried in the University of Virginia Cemetery but in 1866 was reinterred in the Stonewall Cemetery in Winchester, next to the body of his brother, Richard.

B

BAKER – BUTLER

B·

ALPHEUS BAKER was born at "Clover Hill" in the Abbeville District of South Carolina on May 28, 1828, where he became a schoolteacher at age fifteen. He moved to Eufaula, Alabama, in 1848, was admitted to the bar in 1849, and practiced law until the war began. He was a delegate to the state secession convention in 1861. After Alabama left the Union, he enlisted in the Eufaula Rifles as a private. He was elected captain and company commander later that year. The Rifles became Company B, 1st Alabama, which was briefly stationed at Pensacola before being transferred to Fort Pillow, Tennessee, in November 1861. When the enlistments of the 1st Alabama expired in early 1862, Baker became colonel of the 4th Confederate Infantry Regiment, which included companies from Alabama, Tennessee, Kentucky, and Mississippi. It fought in the Battle of Island Number 10, which ended with the capture of the Rebel garrison, including Colonel Baker. After he was exchanged in September, Baker was elected colonel of the newly formed 54th Alabama Infantry Regiment in October 1862. He led the 54th in the various campaigns aimed at capturing Vicksburg, including the Battle of Fort Pemberton on the Yazoo. During the last Vicksburg campaign, Colonel Baker was seriously wounded in the foot early in the Battle of Champion Hill on May 16, 1863. His regiment evaded capture.

After he recovered, Alpheus Baker assumed command of an Alabama brigade and was promoted to brigadier general on March 7, 1864, to date from March 5. He led his men in the Atlanta Campaign, where his horse was shot out from under him at Resaca. He was wounded again at the Battle of Ezra Church. During the Atlanta Campaign, his division commander, Henry Clayton, officially praised Baker several times, but his corps commander, Stephen Dill Lee, criticized him for "indecision and vacillation" and showing a lack of energy, which was probably too harsh. Baker's brigade was sent to the Mobile sector shortly after. It rejoined the Army of Tennessee for the closing campaign in the

Carolinas. During the Battle of Bentonville, Baker's diminished command (320 muskets) took more than 200 Northern prisoners.

After the war, Baker returned to his law practice. He moved to Louisville, Kentucky, in 1878. Alpheus Baker died of pyelitis on October 2, 1891, at age sixty-three. In accordance with his last wishes, he was buried in the Confederate section of Cave Hill Cemetery in Louisville.

Alpheus Baker was a popular man, considered a gentleman and a devout Christian and known for his eloquence and humor.

LAURENCE SIMMONS BAKER was born at Cole's Hill Plantation in Gates County, North Carolina, on May 15, 1830. He was educated at the Norfolk Academy and at West Point, where he graduated at the very bottom of the class of 1851. He spent the next nine years on the Western frontier with the Mounted Rifles Regiment. In May 1861, after North Carolina seceded, he joined the 1st North Carolina Cavalry as its lieutenant colonel, even though he personally opposed secession. He became regimental commander and was promoted to colonel on March 11, 1862.

On June 9, 1863, during the Battle of Brandy Station, Baker directed Wade Hampton's brigade and routed the 10th New York Cavalry. Robert E. Lee, who witnessed the contest, wrote to General Cooper: "Hampton's brigade . . . was very skillfully handled by Colonel Baker." That very day Lee recommended Baker be promoted to brigadier general.

Laurence Baker fought at Gettysburg on July 3. After Hampton was seriously wounded, Baker replaced him as brigade commander and was wounded himself but handled the brigade exceptionally well during the retreat from Pennsylvania. He was promoted to brigadier general on July 30, to rank from July 23. On July 31, while contesting a Union attempt to cross the Rappahannock River, General Baker was severely wounded in the right arm. He was incapacitated for months, and his shattered arm bothered him for the rest of his life.

B·

Baker assumed command of the 2nd North Carolina Military District on June 8, 1864, where he helped defend railroads and supply lines and was wounded in a skirmish on September 22. He briefly commanded a brigade in the defense of Savannah, Georgia, in December 1864. He then returned to the Old North State to command the North Carolina Junior Reserves, which was mainly an administrative post.

General Baker commanded a brigade in the Battle of Bentonville. In April 1865, instead of surrendering, Laurence Baker disbanded his command. He was paroled at Raleigh, North Carolina, on May 8.

After the war, Baker lived in New Bern, North Carolina. He later moved to the Norfolk, Virginia, area and became a farmer. Apparently unsuccessful in agriculture, he returned to North Carolina, where he labored in the insurance business until 1877. Finally, he became a station agent for the Seaboard and Roanoke Railroad in Suffolk, Virginia, where he worked for twenty-nine years. He was active in the United Confederate Veterans (now the Sons of Confederate Veterans) and was a member of St. Paul's Episcopal Church.

General Baker died in Suffolk on April 10, 1907, at the age of seventy-six. He was buried in the Cedar Hill Cemetery in Suffolk.

WILLIAM EDWIN BALDWIN was born in Stateburg, South Carolina, on July 28, 1827. His family moved to Mississippi when William was a child. He grew up and became a book and stationery store owner in Columbus, Mississippi, and served twelve years as a lieutenant in the local militia company, the "Columbus Riflemen." He was elected captain of the company after Mississippi seceded. Sent to Pensacola, he was elected colonel of the 14th Mississippi Infantry on June 5, 1861.

Baldwin led the 14th in East Tennessee and Kentucky before being sent to Fort Donelson in February 1862, where he was soon involved in heavy fighting. General Gideon J. Pillow praised Baldwin for his "gallant conduct and bearing" during the battle. Baldwin was captured when the fort surrendered and was incarcerated at Fort Warren, Boston Harbor, Massachusetts, until August 15, when he was exchanged. Baldwin was promoted to brigadier general on October 3, 1862, with a date of rank of September 19, and was sent to East Tennessee, where he received another brigade command.

Transferred to Mississippi, Baldwin resisted the various Union attempts to capture Vicksburg and fought in the battles of Coffeeville, Port Gibson, and Champion Hill, among others. He was finally caught up in the Siege of Vicksburg in May 1863, where he held a sector on the northern face of the fortress. He helped repulse two major Union attacks and was severely wounded on May 22 but returned to duty on June 13.

Vicksburg surrendered on July 4, 1863, and William Baldwin was again a prisoner of war. He was exchanged on October 13 and was sent to Georgia with what was left of his brigade. In November, he assumed command of a new brigade in John H. Forney's division. He and his men were hurriedly transferred to the Chattanooga sector, where they fought in the Battle of Missionary Ridge. On January 15, 1864, following the retreat to Dalton, Georgia, they were ordered back to Mobile.

On February 19, 1864, General Baldwin fell from his horse while riding near the Dog River Factory. He suffered a broken neck and died that evening. Some said he and his men had had too much whiskey, but the immediate cause of his fall was a broken stirrup. Baldwin was thirty-six years old. Initially buried in Magnolia Cemetery in Mobile, he was later reinterred in Friendship Cemetery in his hometown of Columbus, Mississippi. He was the only Confederate general to die during the war of a non-battle-related accident.

WILLIAM BARKSDALE was born in Smyrna, Tennessee, on August 21, 1821. William attended local schools and the University of Nashville. He moved to Mississippi, where he practiced law and became editor of the Columbus

B ·

Democrat. Barksdale rose from private to captain during the Mexican War, although he arrived too late to be involved in any fighting.

Barksdale ran for Congress in 1852, was elected, and served from March 4, 1853 to 1861. While there, he gained a reputation as a fierce "Fire-Eater" when it came to defending Southern rights, although he did not embrace secession until Lincoln was elected president in November 1860. After Mississippi seceded, William Barksdale resigned from Congress and became adjutant general and later quartermaster general of the state. On May 14, 1861, he was appointed colonel and commander of the 13th Mississippi Infantry Regiment. An excellent regimental commander and a ferocious warrior, he fought in the battles of First Manassas, Ball's Bluff, the Peninsula Campaign, and the Seven Days. Barksdale assumed command of the Mississippi Brigade after General Richard Griffith was mortally wounded at Savage Station.

Barksdale was promoted to brigadier general on August 12, 1862. In September, his attack on Maryland Heights sealed the fate of the Union garrison at Harpers Ferry, which was the largest mass surrender of U.S. troops during the war. At Sharpsburg, he held the West Woods against a Union division and saved Lee's left flank. On December 11, 1862, he brilliantly defended the Fredericksburg waterfront against Union forces trying to cross the Rappahannock. He held the city for sixteen hours. When he finally retreated, Barksdale and his men were cheered by the entire army. They remained in the Fredericksburg sector in 1863 and fought in the Battle of Chancellorsville.

William Barksdale was a large, portly man who relished combat. Gettysburg was his last battle. On July 2, he attacked a Union battery. "It was the grandest charge that was ever made by mortal man," one U.S. colonel recalled. He overran the Union infantry and took the guns but was not able to hold them. Meanwhile, Barksdale was wounded in his left knee, a cannonball struck his left foot, and two bullets plunged into his chest. In all, he was reportedly shot or struck by shrapnel nine times. "I am killed!" he told his aide. "Tell my wife and children that I died fighting at my post." His men were forced to leave him, and he was captured. He died in a Union field hospital the next day.

General Barksdale is buried in an unmarked grave in the Barksdale family plot of Greenwood Cemetery in Jackson, Mississippi. He has a marker in the Confederate section, although his body is not there.

RUFUS BARRINGER was born on December 2, 1821, in Cabarrus County, North Carolina. He graduated from Sugar Creek Academy and the University of North Carolina class of 1842. He was later admitted to the bar and practiced law in Concord, North Carolina. A strong supporter of the temperance movement, he served in the State General Assembly from 1848 to 1850 as a Whig. He was a Constitutional Union Party presidential elector in 1860.

Barringer opposed secession and even thought African Americans should be allowed to vote, but when North Carolina left the Union, he went with his state. He raised a company of one hundred cavalryman, the "Cabarrus Rangers," which became Company F of the 1st North Carolina Cavalry Regiment. Barringer became their captain on May 16, 1861. The 1st North Carolina Cavalry rode with Jeb Stuart in the Peninsula Campaign, the Seven Days Battles, Second Manassas, the Maryland Campaign, and the Battle of Brandy Station, where Barringer was severely wounded on June 9, 1863. A minié ball struck his right cheek and passed into his mouth, ejecting several teeth and damaging his upper jaw. It took him months to recover, and he was on medical leave until September. He was, meanwhile, promoted to major in August and to lieutenant colonel and commander of the 4th North Carolina Cavalry on October 17, 1863.

Rufus Barringer fought in seventy-six engagements during the war, was wounded three times, and was cited for gallantry on several occasions. He had two horses shot out from under him during the war and was wounded again at Bristoe Station on October 14, 1863, but this time only slightly. Promoted to brigadier general on May 30, 1864, Barringer assumed command of the cavalry brigade previously led by

B·

James B. Gordon on June 4. He led it until April 3, 1865, when his command was destroyed and he was captured in the Battle of Namozine Church during the retreat to Appomattox. He was paroled at Fort Delaware on July 24, 1865.

General Barringer returned to North Carolina and established a law practice at Charlotte. He urged North Carolinians to accept Reconstruction and played a significant role in railroad development in the state. He served as a delegate to the North Carolina Constitutional Convention in 1875 and, as a Republican, waged an unsuccessful campaign for lieutenant governor in 1880. He retired in 1884 and wrote a short history of the 1st North Carolina Cavalry, as well as a history of North Carolina railroads.

Rufus Barringer died of stomach cancer in Charlotte on February 3, 1895, at age seventy-three. He is buried in the Elmwood Cemetery in Charlotte.

JOHN DECATUR BARRY was born on June 21, 1839, in Wilmington, North Carolina, the son of a prosperous planter. He graduated with honors from the University of North Carolina in 1859 and went into the banking business. He enlisted as a private in the Wilmington Rifle Guards at Coosawhatchie, South Carolina before the start of the war. It became Company I of the 18th North Carolina Infantry Regiment, and Barry was elected captain in April 1862. Captain Barry fought in the Peninsula Campaign and in the Seven Days Battles, and he was slightly wounded at Gaines' Mill on June 27 and Frayser's Farm on June 30. Later, he fought at Second Manassas, Sharpsburg, and Fredericksburg. He was promoted to major on November 11, 1862.

On May 2, 1863, during the Battle of Chancellorsville, Stonewall Jackson chose to personally scout Union positions. As he and his party returned in the darkness, they ran into the skirmish line of the 18th North Carolina, which was commanded by Major Barry. He mistook them for Union cavalry, which was known to be operating in the area, and ordered his men to fire. Three bullets hit Stonewall Jackson. He was taken to the rear where it was thought for a time he would recover, but pneumonia set in, and he died on May 10.

Barry never forgave himself for giving the order to fire. His superiors, however, did not hold him responsible for Jackson's death.

The commander of the 18th North Carolina was killed at Chancellorsville, and his second-in-command was severely wounded. Barry succeeded them as regimental commander and was promoted to colonel on May 27, to rank from May 3. Despite being only twenty-three years old, he had risen from private to colonel in only thirteen months.

Barry led his regiment in Pickett's Charge at Gettysburg on July 3, 1863, and in the Overland Campaign of 1864, where he particularly distinguished himself in the Battle of the Wilderness. On June 2, 1864, his brigade commander, James Lane, was seriously wounded during the Battle of Cold Harbor. John Barry replaced him and was appointed brigadier general (temporary rank) on August 8, to rank from August 3. Meanwhile, on July 27, Colonel Barry was shot in the hand by a Union sharpshooter. Taken to a field hospital, the doctors amputated the second and third fingers on his right hand.

Barry's appointment to brigadier general was cancelled on or about September 18, after General Lane returned to duty. But John D. Barry was a Confederate general for a brief time.

Colonel Barry fought in the Siege of Petersburg and was wounded again on August 15 and also in September. He served in the trenches until February 1865, when he was given command of a district in North Carolina. He was here when the war ended. He was paroled in Raleigh on May 12.

After the surrender, John Barry became the editor of the Wilmington *Dispatch*, but he suffered from depression and passed away on March 24, 1867. His family said he "died of a broken heart" because he held himself responsible for killing Stonewall Jackson. He was buried in Oakdale Cemetery, Wilmington. He was twenty-seven years old.

SETH MAXWELL BARTON was born on September 8, 1829, in Fredericksburg, Virginia, the son of a prosperous attorney. Admitted to West Point at age fifteen, he graduated in 1849, before his twentieth birthday. He was commissioned a brevet second lieutenant in the infantry and spent most of his U.S. Army career on the Western frontier, participating in several campaigns against the Comanches. A captain by 1857, he resigned his commission on June 11, 1861, after he learned that Virginia had seceded. He was elected lieutenant colonel of the 3rd Arkansas Infantry Regiment on July 8 and traveled with it to western Virginia (now West Virginia), where he was an engineer officer for Henry Rootes Jackson, Robert E. Lee, and W. W. Loring. He was Stonewall Jackson's chief engineer in the Valley Campaign of 1862.

Seth Barton was promoted to brigadier general on March 14, 1862, to rank from March 11. He was transferred to East Tennessee that summer, where he commanded a brigade in the Cumberland Gap Campaign. Sent west, he took part in the various battles for Vicksburg, including Sherman's defeat at Chickasaw Bluffs, where he distinguished himself by holding the left-center of the Rebel line against five Union attacks in heavy fighting. Part of his brigade performed well in the Battle of Champion Hill, although not every regiment did so. The brigade gave a better account of itself in the Siege of Vicksburg. After the surrender of the city, Barton was one of the first officers for which the Confederacy arranged an exchange. That fall, after the Gettysburg campaign, he was given command of what was left of the late Lewis Armistead's brigade of Pickett's division.

In February 1864, Barton commanded a lead column as part of a campaign led by Pickett to retake New Bern, North Carolina, from the occupying Union forces. The operation was not successful, and Pickett filed a formal complaint against Barton for lack of cooperation. Barton was censured and transferred to Robert Ransom's command at Drewry's Bluff, Virginia, near Richmond. After the successful Battle of Drewry's

· B

Bluff, General Ransom leveled charges of lack of cooperation against Barton and relieved him of his command. Barton demanded a hearing, but it was not granted.

Perhaps because Barton's former regimental commanders made repeated applications for his reinstatement, Barton was given command of a brigade for the defense of Richmond in the fall of 1864. He was with Richard S. Ewell and Custis Lee in the Battle of Sayler's Creek (April 6, 1865), where he was captured, along with eight other Rebel generals. Barton was sent to Fort Warren, Massachusetts, in Boston Harbor. He was released on July 24, 1865.

Seth Barton always enjoyed chemistry. Before the war, it was a hobby. After Appomattox, he pursued it full time and eventually gained a reputation as one of the foremost chemists in the United States.

General Barton died suddenly while visiting one of his children in Washington, D.C., on April 11, 1900, at age seventy. His cause of death was listed as senility and mitral insufficiency of the heart. He is buried in Fredericksburg City Cemetery, Fredericksburg, Virginia.

WILLIAM BRIMAGE BATE was born on October 7, 1826, in Bledsoe's Lick (now Castalian Springs), Sumner County, in north-central Tennessee, the son of a small farmer. His father died when he was fifteen, so he left home to find work and became a clerk on a steamboat. During the Mexican War, he joined the 3rd Tennessee Volunteer Infantry as a lieutenant and saw action at the end of the conflict. Bate then returned to the family farm, established a Democratic newspaper, the Gallatin *Tenth Legion*, and was elected to the Tennessee legislature in 1849. He graduated from Cumberland Law School in 1852, set up a practice in Gallatin, and was elected district attorney in 1854. He was a strong supporter of states' rights, a staunch secessionist, and a presidential elector for John C. Breckinridge in 1860.

In April 1861, he joined the local volunteer company and was promptly elected captain. He was elected colonel of the 2nd Tennessee

B ·

Infantry on April 27, 1861. His regiment was quickly sent to Virginia but saw little action. It returned to Tennessee in February 1862 and fought at Shiloh, where his brother and three other relatives were killed. William Bate's horse was shot out from under him (the first of several), and he was seriously wounded in both legs when a minié ball passed completely through his second horse. Incapacitated for months, he walked with a limp for the rest of his life and had to ambulate on crutches for the rest of the war.

Bate was promoted to brigadier general on September 26, to rank from October 3. He was assigned to rear-area duties but soon demanded to be returned to the front. Braxton Bragg (with whom he was friendly) accommodated him and gave him James Rains's old brigade on March 12, 1863.

Bate fought in the Tullahoma Campaign and was wounded again in the Battle of Hoover's Gap, Tennessee, on June 24, 1863, where he held off the bluecoats for thirty-six hours and kept them from cutting Bragg's line of retreat, thus preventing a Confederate disaster. He fought at Chickamauga, after which he took command of Breckinridge's old division. He fought in the Siege of Chattanooga and the Battle of Missionary Ridge.

William Bate was promoted to major general on February 23, 1864, and participated in the Atlanta Campaign. On August 10, he was shot in the knee and was *hors de combat* for some weeks. He returned and fought in the Heartland Campaign. The morale of Bate's division was finally shattered at Franklin, and most of it was routed at the Third Battle of Murfreesboro and during the second day of the Battle of Nashville, where three of his brigadiers were captured.

William Bate led the remnants of his division in the Carolinas Campaign, including the Battle of Bentonville. He surrendered near Greensboro, North Carolina, on April 26, 1865, and was paroled on May 1.

General Bate returned to Tennessee, settled in Nashville, and opened up a law practice. Always known as a cordial man, he became a very effective speaker. He was elected governor in 1882 as the "low-tax" candidate and was reelected in 1884. He was in office from

January 15, 1883, to January 17, 1887. The legislature elected Bate U.S. senator in 1887, reelecting him three times. He caught pneumonia and, on March 9, 1905, just five days into his fourth term, his heart failed. He was buried in Mount Olivet Cemetery, Nashville. He was seventy-eight years old.

CULLEN ANDREWS BATTLE was born in Powelton, Georgia, on June 1, 1829, the son of a physician. In 1836, his family moved to the Irwinton, Alabama, area (near Eufaula) and became quite prosperous. Cullen received a good private education, attended the University of Alabama, from which he graduated in 1850, and became a lawyer.

Battle opened a law practice in Tuskegee in 1852. After John Brown raided Harpers Ferry, Battle raised and equipped the Tuskegee Light Infantry, a militia company, and became its captain. In 1861, it was incorporated into the 3rd Alabama Infantry Regiment, of which Cullen Battle was elected major. The regiment was sent to Virginia, mustered into Confederate service, and stationed at Norfolk, where it remained until the city was evacuated on May 9, 1862. Cullen Battle, promoted to lieutenant colonel, fought in the Peninsula Campaign and at Seven Pines, where the regiment's commander was killed and Battle was severely wounded. He did not return to duty until July 23. As part of Robert E. Rodes's brigade, the 3rd Alabama took part in the Maryland Campaign, including the battles of South Mountain and Sharpsburg. Battle (now a colonel) was slightly wounded in both actions.

Battle and his men fought at Fredericksburg, where the colonel was severely injured when his horse fell and landed on him. On April 29, 1863, as Rodes's division moved to confront the Yankees at the Battle of Chancellorsville, Battle's horse reared and fell into a ditch, and he was again severely injured. He accompanied his regiment to the battlefield in an ambulance but was not able to mount his horse and stay mounted.

B ·

Absolutely frustrated, Colonel Battle resigned his commission on the spot, but General Rodes refused to accept it and sent him to the rear.

Cullen Battle was back in action at Gettysburg, where he served with Edward O'Neal's brigade. On July 1, the brigade became terribly disorganized. Battle took matters into his own hands and attached himself and his regiment to General Stephen D. Ramseur's brigade. General Lee relieved O'Neal of his command and replaced him with Battle, who was promoted to brigadier general on August 25, to rank from August 20. He commanded the brigade through the Mine Run Campaign and the Bristoe Campaign, as well as the battles of the Wilderness, Spotsylvania Court House, the North Anna, Cold Harbor, Monocacy, Fort Stevens, Third Winchester, and Fisher's Hill. At Cedar Creek his brigade captured a six-gun battery and took "many prisoners," but he was badly wounded—shot in the left knee—and was forced to sit out the end of the war. He spent two years on crutches. He was paroled at Montgomery, Alabama, on May 16, 1865.

After the surrender, Cullen Battle reopened his law practice in Tuskegee. He was elected to Congress in 1868, but the Radical Republicans denied him his seat. He went back to Alabama and worked as a farmer and then as an editor. In 1888, he moved to New Bern, North Carolina, to be near his son. By 1890, he was the editor of the New Bern *Journal* and was

elected mayor, although he never sought the office. He also wrote a history of the 3rd Alabama. Cullen Andrews Battle died in Greensboro, North Carolina, on April 8, 1905, and is buried in Blandford Cemetery, Petersburg, Virginia. He was seventy-five years old.

RICHARD LEE TURBERVILLE BEALE was born on May 22, 1819, at "Hickory Hill," Westmoreland County, Virginia. Educated in local private academies, he attended Dickinson College in Carlisle, Pennsylvania, and studied law at the University of Virginia, from which he graduated in 1837. He set up a practice in Hague, Virginia.

Beale was elected to Congress as a Democrat in 1846 and served from March 4, 1847, to March 3, 1849, but was not a candidate for reelection. He was a delegate to the state constitutional convention in 1851 and became a Virginia state senator in 1858. When Virginia seceded, he joined "Lee's Light Horse," a cavalry company, as a lieutenant in April 1861. It soon became part of "Lee's Legion." Beale was rapidly promoted to captain and major. The battalion's commander, Fitzhugh Lee, repeatedly commended him for his excellent judgment. After the legion was expanded into the 9th Virginia Cavalry Regiment, Beale became its lieutenant colonel in April 1862. When Lee was promoted to brigadier general in July, Beale replaced him as commander of the 9th. He was promoted to colonel on September 15, 1862. Meanwhile, Beale served with Robert E. Lee in western Virginia in 1861 and with Stonewall Jackson in the Shenandoah Valley and fought in all the campaigns of the Army of Northern Virginia.

In December 1862, Colonel Beale led a bold romp through Rappahannock County and captured the entire Federal garrison at Leeds without losing a man. In April and May 1863, he played a major role in smashing Stoneman's raid into Virginia. At Brandy Station on June 9, 1863, after W. H. F. "Rooney" Lee was wounded, he assumed temporary command of Lee's brigade and led a brilliant charge that defeated the bluecoat cavalry. He was wounded in a skirmish near Middleburg on June 12, when a piece of shrapnel lodged in his right arm, but he was able to return to duty the next day.

After the Gettysburg campaign, Beale was wounded in a skirmish near Culpeper Court House on September 13, 1863, when a minié ball struck his right leg. He spent three months on convalescent leave but was again made a brigade commander when he returned to duty in January 1864.

For all his brilliance as a cavalry commander, Richard Beale was not an easy subordinate to command. His prickly personality probably explains why he was not promoted to brigadier general until January 7, 1865, to rank from January 6.

Early on the morning of April 9, 1865, Beale led a charge and captured two Federal guns near Appomattox Court House. The Yankees

B ·

counterattacked, however, and General Beale was wounded and captured. Sent to the Union rear, he was paroled at Ashland, Virginia, on April 27.

After the South surrendered, General Beale returned to Hague and his law practice. When his fellow Democrat, Congressman Beverly B. Douglas, died in office, Beale ran to succeed him and won. He successfully stood for reelection, serving from January 23, 1879, to March 3, 1881. Not a candidate for reelection, he again returned to his law practice and wrote a history of the 9th Virginia Cavalry. He died in Hague on April 18, 1893, at the age of seventy-three and is buried in Hickory Hill Cemetery, Hague.

WILLIAM NELSON RECTOR BEALL was born on March 20, 1825, in Bardstown, Kentucky. His family moved to Little Rock in 1840. Young Beall entered West Point in 1844 and graduated in 1848. Commissioned a brevet second lieutenant of infantry, he served in Texas and the Indian Territory. A captain in 1855, he transferred to the cavalry and served in the Kansas and Nebraska territories.

Beall resigned his commission on August 20, 1861. He was one of the last U.S. officers to resign and "go south." The Confederacy quickly appointed him a captain of cavalry. He held a number of staff appointments under Albert Sidney Johnston and Earl Van Dorn and was assistant adjutant general of the Trans-Mississippi Department. Beall fought at Pea Ridge and followed Van Dorn across the Mississippi after Shiloh. He was promoted to colonel in March 1862 and to brigadier general on April 12, 1862, to rank from April 11. He commanded cavalry forces in the Siege of Corinth and then was named cavalry commander of the Second District of the Department of Southern Mississippi and Eastern Louisiana. On August 29, he assumed command of the fortress of Port Hudson, where he worked on improving the fortifications. He was superseded as commandant of the fortress by Franklin Gardner in December but remained in the garrison as commander of a brigade. He performed well during the Siege of Port Hudson and held his line against strong Union attacks.

Port Hudson surrendered on July 9, 1863. Beall was sent to Johnson's Island, Ohio, which is located in Lake Erie. He was then named chief receiving agent, which allowed him to sell Confederate cotton to the North or Europe in exchange for clothing, blankets, and other items, which were then supplied to Confederate prisoners. He headquartered in New York City for the rest of the war.

William Beall was paroled and released on August 21, 1865, and he moved to St. Louis, Missouri, where he became a merchant and commission agent. He later moved to Tennessee and died in McMinnville on July 25, 1883, at age fifty-eight. He was buried in Mount Olivet Cemetery, Nashville, Tennessee.

PIERRE GUSTAVE TOUTANT BEAUREGARD, who went by "G. T.," was born in "Contreras," a sugarcane plantation about twenty miles southeast of New Orleans, on May 28, 1818. He did not begin learning English until he was twelve years old; nevertheless, he entered West Point in 1834 at age sixteen and graduated in 1838 as a second lieutenant of engineers.

Beauregard distinguished himself as a military engineer, especially in the Mexican War. He served on the staff of Winfield Scott, the general-in-chief, and conducted several dangerous reconnaissance missions. He was wounded twice and earned two brevets.

Beauregard was a small man who stood five feet, seven inches tall and weighed about 150 pounds. He spoke with a French accent, was courteous to all, was charismatic and flashy, and could be quite charming, especially to the ladies. His main character flaws were jealousy and vanity, which would eventually hamstring his career.

Brevet Major Beauregard spent the years 1848 to 1860 on engineering projects in the South. He resigned his commission when Louisiana

B·

seceded. President Davis appointed Beauregard brigadier general in the Provisional Confederate Army on March 1 and placed him in charge of the Charleston, South Carolina, defenses. The "Little Creole" thus became the first Confederate general. Eventually, he was ordered to fire on Fort Sumter, which surrendered on April 13.

Charged with defending northern Virginia, G. T. Beauregard routed the Union Army of the Potomac at the Battle of First Manassas on July 21, 1861. In subsequent weeks, however, his petulant behavior alienated President Jefferson Davis, who demoted him to second-in-command of Albert Sidney Johnston's Army of Central Kentucky (later Mississippi).

After Johnston was killed at Shiloh on April 6, 1862, Beauregard pushed Union General U. S. Grant back to his last line of defense but then declined to attack, ceding the initiative to the Yankees. Buell's Army of the Ohio joined Grant that night, and the Rebels were defeated the next day.

After Shiloh, Beauregard conducted a brilliant retreat to Corinth, which he abandoned on May 29. He then retreated to Tupelo, forty miles to the south. President Davis relieved him of his command on June 17 for taking unauthorized medical leave. Braxton Bragg replaced him.

Beauregard was unemployed until August 29, when Davis reluctantly named him commander of the Charleston sector. He defended the city brilliantly, with innovative use of submarines, fieldworks, and naval mines, which were called "torpedoes" in those days.

On April 18, 1864, Beauregard was given the task of defending Petersburg, Virginia, the key to Richmond. In May, with eighteen thousand troops, he defeated U.S. General Butler's Army of the James (thirty-nine thousand men) and brilliantly forced them into the Bermuda Hundred, a peninsula between the James and Appomattox Rivers. Butler's men remained bottled up there for virtually the rest of the war.

That summer, General Grant stole a march on Robert E. Lee and crossed the James River with 16,000 men. The only troops available to defend Petersburg were 5,400 men under Beauregard, who defeated the Federals in the Second Battle of Petersburg (June 15) and saved the city. This was arguably Beauregard's best performance of the war.

On October 2, President Davis named Beauregard commander of the Department of the West. His subsequent attempts to check Sherman's March to the Sea were ineffective, and he failed to halt the Union advance into South Carolina. Davis—on the recommendation of General Lee—replaced Beauregard with Johnston on February 22. Beauregard was Johnston's second-in-command until they surrendered to Sherman on April 26, 1865.

Some of G. T. Beauregard's campaigns were magnificent, but others were mediocre at best, and none justified his jealous and touchy temperament.

After the war, he was a railroad executive and a supervisor of the highly corrupt Louisiana Lottery. He also wrote numerous articles and *The Military Operations of General Beauregard in the War Between the States* (credited to Alfred Roman). Beauregard also served as adjutant general of Louisiana from 1879 to 1888, when he was elected commissioner of public works for New Orleans.

G. T. Beauregard died of heart disease in New Orleans on February 20, 1893, at the age of seventy-four. He is buried in the Army of Tennessee section of Metairie Cemetery in Orleans Parish.

BARNARD ELLIOTT BEE, JR., was born on February 8, 1824, in Charleston, South Carolina, to a prominent family. His older brother was Hamilton P. Bee, another future Confederate general, as was his brother-in-law, Clement H. "Rock" Stevens. The Bee family moved to the Republic of Texas in 1836, but young Barnard remained behind and attended the Pendleton Academy. He gained admission to West Point in 1841 and graduated in 1845. At the academy, he was known as a quiet and generally friendly young man, but he acquired many demerits for chewing tobacco on duty and the occasional fistfight. Commissioned in the infantry, he was stationed in Texas and fought in the Mexican War. He was brevetted for gallantry at Cerro Gordo (where he

B·

was wounded) and a second time for his part in storming Chapultepec on September 13, 1847.

Following the war, he was posted to Pascagoula, Mississippi, and then to the frontier, at Fort Fillmore in New Mexico Territory (1849–55) and at Fort Snelling, Minnesota Territory. He took part in the Utah War, where he received a brevet to lieutenant colonel. In 1860, he was at Fort Laramie, Wyoming, and briefly served as commander of the post.

Barnard Bee did not favor secession and even considered moving to far west Texas to take up cattle ranching on some of his brother's vast acreage. When South Carolina seceded, however, he resigned his commission and returned to Charleston, where he was elected lieutenant colonel of the 1st South Carolina Regulars on June 1. On June 17, 1861, he was appointed brigadier general and named commander of the 3rd Brigade in Joseph E. Johnston's Army of the Shenandoah. Sent to the Manassas sector, he conducted a stubborn defense against the initial Northern onslaughts. His brigade was finally pushed back in some disarray. General Bee rallied his men behind the 1st Virginia Brigade on Henry House Hill, yelling: "Look! There stands Jackson like a stone wall! Let us determine to die here, and we will conquer! Rally behind the Virginians!" They did.

Just as the tide of battle turned in favor of the Confederacy, a Union shell fragment struck him in the stomach. In considerable pain, he was taken to a small cabin four miles from the battlefield, where he had set up headquarters. He died there the following morning, July 22, 1861. General Beauregard called his loss "irreparable." Barnard E. Bee is buried beside his father in St. Paul's Episcopal Church Cemetery in Pendleton, South Carolina. He was thirty-seven years old.

HAMILTON PRIOLEAU BEE was the older brother of Confederate General Barnard E. Bee, Jr. He was born on July 22, 1822, in Charleston, South Carolina, but his father moved to Texas in 1836. Hamilton and most of the family followed in 1837. In 1839, Bee received a deed for 320 acres of land in Harrison County. He served on a council with the Comanches (1843), which resulted in a peace treaty the following year. In 1845, Bee lived in Washington, D.C., where he was an agent of the Texas Treasury Department. He became the first secretary of the Texas State Senate the following year.

When the Mexican War broke out, Bee enlisted as a private and rose to lieutenant, fighting in the Battles of Monterrey and Buena Vista. He moved to Laredo after the war and was elected to the Texas legislature, serving from 1849 to 1859. He was speaker of the house from 1855 to 1857.

When the war broke out, Bee was elected brigadier general of the Texas militia and was appointed brigadier general in the Confederate Army on March 5, 1862, with a date of rank of March 4. Hamilton Bee admitted that he was not much of a military man and applied for duty in southern Texas, so the Confederacy benefited from his considerable administrative ability and his fluency in Spanish. He used his position there to export cotton to Europe and import munitions, thus circumventing the Union blockade, but he saw little or no action against hostile forces.

General Bee had little experience commanding troops in combat when he was ordered to Louisiana in March 1864 to take part in the Red River Campaign. He nevertheless performed exceptionally well in the decisive Rebel victory at the Battle of Mansfield and with great gallantry at the Battle of Pleasant Hill, where he had two horses shot out from under him and was slightly wounded in the face.

When Thomas Green was killed in action on April 12, Hamilton Bee succeeded him as commander of the cavalry corps of Richard Taylor's Army of Western Louisiana. Commanding a corps proved too much for him, and he allowed the defeated Union Army to escape at Monett's Ferry on April 22 by ordering a premature retreat. After an investigation, Taylor relieved him of his command. General Walker, commander of the Greyhound Division, agreed with Taylor, remarking, "I would regard it as a public calamity to know of his being assigned to an important command."

General Bee returned to Texas, where General Edmund Kirby Smith gave him command of a cavalry division under General Gabriel

Wharton. Later, he directed an infantry brigade under General Samuel Maxey in the vicinity of Liverpool, Texas. Neither unit was involved in much more than patrolling along the upper Red River. General Bee was paroled at Columbus, Texas, on June 26, 1865.

After the surrender, Bee moved his family to Saltillo, Mexico, where they lived until 1876. Then, with Reconstruction over, he returned to San Antonio, where he practiced law and was a member of the Episcopal Church. He served a term as Texas Commissioner of Insurance.

Hamilton Bee died of heart disease in San Antonio on October 3, 1897, at the age of seventy-five. His funeral procession was more than a mile long.

TYREE HARRIS BELL was born in Covington, Kentucky, on September 5 or September 6, 1815, but grew up on his father's plantation in Gallatin, Sumner County, Tennessee. He acquired his own plantation in nearby Dyer County, Tennessee, and became a planter.

When the war began, Bell raised a company, the Newbern Blues, which became part of the 12th Tennessee Infantry Regiment in the Confederate Army. Bell was elected captain on June 4, 1861, and lieutenant colonel of the regiment the next day. He fought with his regiment at the Battle of Belmont, Missouri, where Grant suffered his first defeat. At Shiloh, Bell had two horses shot out from under him. His leg was injured when one of the animals landed on it. He also suffered a serious bullet wound. He was elected colonel and permanent commander of the 12th Tennessee in May 1862 while he was recovering. His regiment was consolidated with the 22nd Tennessee, with Bell retaining command. He led the 12th/22nd Tennessee in Edmund Kirby Smith's invasion of Kentucky, including the Battle of Richmond. Later, he fought in the Second Battle of Corinth, Mississippi.

After Corinth, the 12th/22nd was consolidated with the 47th Tennessee, and Bell was the odd man out. As a supernumerary without a command, he did a tour of garrison duty at Shelbyville, Tennessee. In the spring of 1863, he was assigned to Nathan Bedford Forrest's cavalry as a recruiting officer in western Tennessee (behind Union lines), where he was instrumental in raising several companies and battalions. As a result of his success, Forrest made him a brigade commander on January 25, 1864, and recommended he be promoted to brigadier general as early as March 1864. General Leonidas Polk concurred.

Tyree Bell was a lot like Nathan Bedford Forrest—tough, profane, and incredibly brave. He commanded a brigade under "the Wizard of the Saddle" for the rest of the war, except when he was recovering from wounds. He fought in the West Tennessee Raid of 1864, the Battle of Fort Pillow, the Battle of Brice's Crossroads, and the actions around Tupelo and Oxford. He was wounded in the chest and face by an exploding shell at Pulaski, Tennessee, on September 27, 1864. He was back in action in the Battle of Johnsonville (November 4–5), where Forrest destroyed a huge Union supply base.

Colonel Bell was seriously wounded in December 1864. Shortly after he returned to duty, he was finally promoted to brigadier general on March 2, 1865, to rank from February 28. He fought in the Battle of Selma, where Forrest's cavalry was, at last, decisively defeated. Along with the rest of Forrest's command, General Bell surrendered at Gainesville, Alabama, on May 9, 1865, and was paroled the next day.

Bell returned to a devastated Tennessee and resumed his agricultural activities, but with modest success. In 1875, he moved to Fresno, California, where he became a successful farmer and orange producer. He was active in civic affairs and in the United Confederate Veterans. In 1902, he visited his old hometown, Gallatin, Tennessee, and attended a U.C.V. reunion. He died suddenly in New Orleans of a blood clot in his brain on August 30, 1902. He was eighty-six years old. General Tyree Bell is buried in Bethel Cemetery in Sanger, California.

HENRY LEWIS "ROCK" BENNING was born on April 2, 1814, on a plantation in Columbia County, East Georgia. He graduated from Franklin College in Georgia in August 1834 with highest honors,

studied law, and was admitted to the bar in 1835 at age twenty-one. He moved to Columbus, in western Georgia, on the Alabama line, and became politically involved. Known for his intelligence and abundant energy, he became an advocate of states' rights and slavery. He was also a fine lawyer. He was appointed solicitor-general for the Chattahoochee Circuit in 1837 after the incumbent died. The following year, the state legislature elected him to a four-year term.

Henry Benning ran for Congress in 1850 but was defeated. He was elected associate justice of the Georgia Supreme Court in 1853 and established a reputation as a fine jurist. He was also a tall, large man of commanding physical presence, known for his generosity.

Judge Benning was a member of the Georgia Secession Convention in 1861 and eloquently urged the state to leave the Union. After Georgia seceded, he returned to Columbus and raised his own regiment, the 17th Georgia Infantry, and became its colonel on August 29, 1861. He was looked upon with suspicion in the higher echelons of the Confederate Army, which seemed to doubt his military ability and wondered about his courage. He did not see a major action until Malvern Hill on July 1, 1862, where his regiment was lightly engaged. In the Second Battle of Manassas, he performed well. At Sharpsburg, his regiment was part of Robert Toombs's brigade, which guarded Burnside's Bridge on Lee's far right flank. Benning replaced Toombs after he was wounded and held his position despite repeated attacks from significantly stronger enemy forces. After that, all doubts about his courage and ability were gone, and his men nicknamed him "Rock" because of his steadfastness. General Toombs, meanwhile, resigned his commission on October 27, and Benning succeeded him and was promoted to brigadier general on January 23, 1863, with a date of rank of January 17.

Benning's brigade fought at Fredericksburg and Suffolk. On July 2, Benning led a fierce assault on Devil's Den at Gettysburg and captured the position but suffered heavy losses. He excelled again at Chickamauga,

·B

where he had three horses shot out from under him. He later took part in the unsuccessful Siege of Knoxville. Benning and his men returned to Virginia in early 1864.

On May 5, 1864, during the Battle of the Wilderness, General Benning was severely wounded in the left shoulder and missed the rest of the Overland Campaign. He returned to duty on November 22, 1864. His men held their lines in the Petersburg trenches until the Army of Northern Virginia was finally defeated on April 2, 1865. A distraught Henry Benning surrendered the remnants of his command at Appomattox on April 9.

After the war, "Old Rock" returned to Columbus and resumed his law practice. On his way to court in 1875, he suffered a stroke. General Benning died on July 10, 1875, in Columbus and was buried there in the Linwood Cemetery. He was sixty-one years old. Fort Benning, Georgia, the home of the U.S. Army's Infantry School, is named after him.

SAMUEL BENTON was born on October 18, 1820, probably in Williamson County, Tennessee. His uncle was Senator Thomas Hart Benton of Missouri, a leading advocate of westward expansion and Manifest Destiny. Samuel worked briefly as a schoolteacher before moving to Holly Springs, Mississippi, as a young adult. He studied law, was admitted to the bar, and became a prominent attorney. Starting in 1853, he was also the editor of the Mississippi *Times* newspaper. An advocate of states' rights, he was elected to the legislature in 1852 and was a member of the secession convention in 1861. He voted to leave the Union.

In early 1861, Benton was elected captain in the 9th Mississippi Infantry, a regiment of twelve-month volunteers, which was organized in Holly Springs. It was sent initially to Mobile and then to Pensacola. When the 9th's enlistments expired, Benton was named colonel of the 34th Mississippi Infantry Regiment.

B ·

Also known as the 37th Mississippi, it first saw action in the Battle of Shiloh. He and his men performed well.

The 34th was with Bragg during the 1862 Kentucky Campaign and fought in the Battle of Perryville. It suffered heavy losses, including all three of its field-grade officers. It took Benton a year to recover from his wounds, but he was back in action at the Battle of Lookout Mountain (November 24, 1863), where the enemy overran part of his regiment and captured two hundred men.

When the Atlanta Campaign of 1864 began, Benton commanded an ad hoc brigade of three regiments during the Battle of Dug Gap (May 8), which was won by the Confederates. He reverted to the command of the 34th Mississippi regiment of Edward C. Walthall's brigade on May 11 and led it at Resaca. In early June, Walthall was promoted to division commander, and Benton succeeded him as commander of the brigade.

On July 22, during the Battle of Atlanta, Colonel Benton was severely wounded in the right foot. At almost the same time, a shell fragment hit him in the chest. Carried to the rear, doctors amputated his leg. He died in the field hospital at Griffin, Georgia, on July 28. He was forty-three years old. His promotion to brigadier general, to date from July 26, arrived two days after his death.

He was initially buried in Griffin but was reinterred in Holly Springs' Hill Crest Cemetery after the war. Benton County, Mississippi, which was created in 1870, is named after him.

ALBERT GALLATIN BLANCHARD was born in Charlestown, Massachusetts, on September 6, 1810. Selected for West Point, he graduated in 1829 at age nineteen and was commissioned a brevet second lieutenant of infantry.

Blanchard was sent to the Western frontier. Working mainly out of Fort Jesup, Louisiana, he engaged in routine duties and in improving the navigation of the Sabine River. He resigned his commission on October 1, 1840, and moved to his wife's hometown of New Orleans, where he worked in the mercantile business and as director of the city's public schools from 1843 to 1845. Blanchard joined the 2nd Louisiana Infantry Regiment as a captain and company commander when the Mexican War began and distinguished himself at Monterrey and in the Siege of Veracruz. He briefly served as a major in the U.S. 12th Infantry. Discharged in 1848, he returned to New Orleans and worked as a public-school teacher, surveyor, and a railroad executive. When the Civil War began, Blanchard was commissioned colonel of the 1st Louisiana Infantry Regiment on April 28, 1861.

Blanchard and his regiment were sent to Norfolk, Virginia. He was promoted to brigadier general on September 21, 1861, and given command of a brigade posted at Portsmouth, Virginia.

Compared to his excellent performance in Mexico, Blanchard's Civil War record is unimpressive. His brigade was in reserve at the Battle of Seven Pines. After his old classmate General Robert E. Lee succeeded Joseph E. Johnston as commander of the Army of Northern Virginia, Blanchard was replaced as brigade commander by Ambrose R. Wright, ostensibly on account of his advanced age, even though he was younger than Lee. Most of the rest of his postings involved training camps and conscription duty. In June 1862, Secretary of War George W. Randolph sent him to the Trans-Mississippi Department. General Richard Taylor, the commander of the Army of Western Louisiana, gave Blanchard command of northeast Louisiana, with headquarters in Monroe. The Yankees launched a series of raids into Blanchard's area of operations in late 1862, and he utterly failed to respond. He performed so poorly that President Jefferson Davis ordered General Taylor to investigate his actions (or lack thereof). Taylor judged Blanchard to be utterly incompetent. On February 11, 1863, the secretary of war relieved him of his position. Blanchard was unemployed for months. Apparently no one in authority in the Trans-Mississippi Department wanted Blanchard or knew what to do with him. Eventually transferred to the East, he was ordered to sit on the court of inquiry for Seth M. Barton on May 27, 1864, but this court never met.

B ·

Blanchard helped defend Augusta, Georgia, during Sherman's March to the Sea in late 1864. During the Carolina Campaign of 1865, he commanded the South Carolina Reserve Brigade in Lafayette McLaws's division and fought in the battles of Averasborough and Bentonville.

After the surrender, General Blanchard returned to New Orleans and became assistant city surveyor, a job which he held for the rest of his life. Henry G. Blanchard died of "cerebral softening" and neurasthenia in New Orleans on June 21, 1891, at age eighty. He is buried in St. Louis Cemetery Number 2 in New Orleans.

WILLIAM ROBERTSON BOGGS first saw the light of day on March 18, 1829, in Augusta, Georgia. He was the son of a successful merchant. William was educated at the Augusta Academy, entered West Point in 1849, and graduated in 1853. He was commissioned a brevet second lieutenant in the Topographical Bureau but transferred to the Ordnance Branch in 1854.

Lieutenant Boggs resigned his commission on February 1, 1861, shortly after Georgia seceded, and was immediately appointed a captain of engineers in the Confederate Army. Initially he was assigned to Charleston, South Carolina, but in early March he was transferred to his home state, where Governor Joseph E. Brown of Georgia named him state purchasing agent. Boggs was soon transferred to Florida as chief engineer and ordnance officer of the Army of Pensacola. He took part in the Battle of Santa Rosa Island, and on December 21, 1861, Boggs became chief engineer for the state of Georgia with the rank of colonel. He remained in Georgia as chief engineer and artillery officer of the militia, where he improved the defenses of Savannah and other places. When U.S. General Buell threatened Chattanooga in the summer of 1862, Boggs was attached to the staff of Henry Heth (commanding the Confederate forces in Chattanooga) as chief engineer until the emergency passed. He became Edmund Kirby Smith's chief of staff on July 14 during the Kentucky Campaign of 1862 and played a role in the victory at Richmond.

William R. Boggs was promoted to brigadier general on November 4. He accompanied Kirby Smith to Louisiana in March 1863, when he was appointed commander of the Trans-Mississippi Department. Boggs was Kirby Smith's chief of staff.

Boggs was a brilliant engineer. In 1864, when U.S. Admiral David Dixon Porter's huge inland fleet steamed up the Red River with an eye toward taking Shreveport, Boggs delayed his progress and ultimately foiled his plans altogether. Unable to defeat the fleet, he removed the river. The innovative genius blew up the levee and the Hotchkiss Dam, diverting at least half and perhaps as much as three-quarters of the water from the Red River into the Bayou Pierre drainage basin via Tones Bayou. It rained often, but the river continued to drop. It was dangerously low when an astonished and frustrated Porter (who did not know what Boggs had done) finally retreated. Shreveport was saved and Porter lost several vessels, including the *Eastport*, the largest ironclad in his fleet. It had struck a mine and was refloated, but then it ran aground. Porter could not free it and had to blow it up.

The headquarters of the Trans-Mississippi Department was infested with politics. As a result of a palace intrigue, General Boggs was replaced as chief of staff by a Kirby Smith favorite in early 1865. He was unemployed when the Trans-Mississippi Department surrendered.

Boggs returned to Georgia but soon moved to St. Louis, where he worked as a civil engineer and architect. In 1875, he became a professor of mechanics at Virginia Tech in Blacksburg. He was dismissed because of academic politics in 1881.

General William Robertson Boggs retired to Winston-Salem, North Carolina, where he wrote his *Military Reminiscences*, which is a valuable historical account of the Confederate Trans-Mississippi Department. He died on September 15, 1911, at age eighty-two in Winston-Salem, North Carolina. He is buried in Salem Cemetery, Winston-Salem.

MILLEDGE LUKE BONHAM (pronounced BONE-um) was a Christmas baby, being born near Redbank (later Saluda), South Carolina, on December 25, 1813. Milledge attended private schools in the Edgefield District and at Abbeville and graduated with honors from South Carolina College in Columbia in 1834. He fought in the Second Seminole War in 1836 as a captain and adjutant of the South Carolina (Militia) Brigade and was promoted to major. Meanwhile, his older brother, James Butler Bonham, was killed in the Alamo.

Milledge fought in the Mexican War as lieutenant colonel and later (from August 1847) as colonel and commander of the 12th U.S. Infantry Regiment, where he performed well. He was injured at Contreras on August 19, 1847, when he accidentally shot himself in the hand with his own pistol. The bullet went through the palm of his right hand and came out the wrist, tearing the tendons to his little and ring fingers.

Colonel Bonham returned to South Carolina in 1848. He was solicitor for the southern circuit of South Carolina from 1848 to 1857, when he succeeded his late cousin Preston S. Brooks as a U.S. congressman. He held this office from March 4, 1857, until South Carolina seceded on December 20, 1860. Bonham resigned the next day and was appointed commander-in-chief of the Army of the Republic of South Carolina. He cooperated well with G. T. Beauregard, who led the Confederate forces in South Carolina.

On April 23, 1861, Milledge Bonham was appointed brigadier general in the Confederate States Army. Although a strong disciplinarian, he was popular with his men. One described him as "one of the finest looking officers in the entire army" and added that his "tall, graceful figure, commanding appearance, noble bearing, and soldier mien, all excited the admiration and confidence of his troops." A brigade commander, he fought in the First Battle of Bull Run (Manassas), where he held Mitchell's Ford against half-hearted Union probes. He briefly commanded a division in January 1862.

General Bonham resigned his commission on January 27, 1862, to take his seat in the Confederate Congress. Here he supported states' rights and opposed the suspension of habeas corpus. On December 17, 1862, the South Carolina General Assembly elected Bonham governor. He enforced the Confederate draft and demanded that cotton fields be converted to grow food crops to feed the Rebel armies. He served from December 18, 1862, to December 18, 1864.

President Davis reappointed Bonham brigadier general on February 16, 1865, with a date of rank of February 9, and he served as a brigade commander in General Matthew Butler's cavalry division of General Wade Hampton's cavalry corps in the Carolina Campaign. He surrendered with the army on April 26.

After the war, Bonham resumed his law practice and planting. He served in the pre-Reconstruction South Carolina legislature (1865–67) and owned an insurance business in Edgefield and Atlanta from 1865 to 1878. He supported Wade Hampton's efforts to restore home rule in South Carolina. As a reward, he was appointed state railroad commissioner in 1878 and served until he died in White Sulphur Springs, West Virginia, on August 27, 1890. He was seventy-six years old. Milledge Luke Bonham is buried in Elmwood Memorial Gardens, Columbia, South Carolina.

JOHN STEVENS BOWEN was born on October 30, 1830, at Bowen's Creek, Georgia. He attended the University of Georgia, was admitted to West Point in 1848, and graduated in 1853. He was suspended for a year for violating the honor code by covering up for a classmate. Bowen was commissioned a brevet second lieutenant in the Mounted Rifle Regiment.

He was posted to the army cavalry school in Carlisle, Pennsylvania; then to St. Louis, where he met and married his wife; and then to West Texas, where he fought Comanches and Mescalero Apaches. He resigned his commission in 1856 and returned to St.

B ·

Louis, where he became a successful architect and lived in the affluent suburb of Carondelet.

Bowen became a lieutenant colonel of militia in 1859 and organized and commanded a battalion on the Kansas frontier, where he guarded against abolitionist raids. Missouri was a border state of divided loyalties, but Bowen's militia was made of firm secessionists. Federal forces moved quickly and, in a surprise attack, captured Bowen on May 10, 1861, at Camp Jackson near St. Louis. After his release, on a prisoner exchange, he raised a regiment of more than 1,100 men. A colonel as of June 11, his regiment, the 1st Missouri Infantry, became known for its proficiency in drill and combat.

A strict disciplinarian, John S. Bowen was respected by his men for his undeniable military competence, but he was not loved. Many of them considered him a bit of a martinet. He was given command of a brigade and was promoted to brigadier general on March 14, 1862. He distinguished himself at Shiloh, where two horses were shot out from under him. Late on the afternoon of April 6, a shell exploded near him, killing his horse and throwing many fragments into his right shoulder, neck, and side. He was not expected to recover, but he did. Bowen later fought in the defense of northern Mississippi.

General Pemberton, the commander of the Army of Mississippi, called Bowen "one of the best soldiers in the Confederate Army." He promoted him to divisional commander over the heads of several officers who were senior to him. Pemberton ordered him to fortify and hold Grand Gulf, the most likely place the Yankees would attack if they got south of Vicksburg. They did so on April 29, 1863, and Bowen smashed the Union flotilla. Grant landed further south and met Bowen again near Port Gibson on May 1, where the Missouri architect faced an entire U.S. corps with only two brigades. (Two more brigades reinforced him during the battle.) At the end of the day, he retreated in good order and escaped with his entire command. Grant was highly complimentary of his opponent, who used to buy firewood from Grant at Carondelet. By now, the men of the Army of Mississippi were calling Bowen "the Stonewall of the West."

Bowen also fought at Champion Hill on May 16, 1863. While his men fought extremely well, superior numbers told, and Grant finally pushed Pemberton, Bowen, and their men off the field. The next day, part of Bowen's depleted division was routed at Big Black River and forced back into the fortress of Vicksburg. Although he would not know it for a month, Bowen was promoted to major general on May 25, 1863.

After a siege of forty-seven days, the city surrendered on July 4, 1863. By now, John Bowen was terribly sick with dysentery. Grant and two of Bowen's West Point classmates offered him medical care from the best U.S. Army surgeons, but Bowen was too proud to accept. This cost him his life.

Bowen was placed in an ambulance to return him to the Confederate lines. He never reached them. John S. Bowen died at Walton Farm, about six miles west of Raymond, on the morning of July 13, 1863. He was thirty-two years old. His loss was a terrible blow to the Confederacy. He was first buried in the Waltons' garden. In 1877, he was reburied in Vicksburg's Cedar Hill Cemetery.

BRAXTON BRAGG was born on March 22, 1817, in Warrenton, North Carolina. His brother, Thomas Bragg, who was later attorney general of the Confederacy, paid for Braxton to attend the Warrenton Male Academy, which was one of the best schools in North Carolina. Braxton was admitted to West Point at age sixteen. He was not a popular cadet. He was tall, awkward, opinionated, sarcastic, gruff, without humor, physically unattractive, and possessed of a jealous temperament. He graduated in 1837 and was commissioned in the artillery.

Bragg served in the Second Seminole War but was often ill. He suffered from poor health most of his life. His ailments included dyspepsia, rheumatism, and diarrhea, but perhaps the most serious problem was frequent migraine headaches. These contributed to his constant irritability. He quarreled with almost everyone.

B ·

Bragg was a battery commander in the Mexican War, where he performed brilliantly and earned three brevets. At Buena Vista, he fought in support of Colonel Jefferson Davis's 1st Mississippi Rifle Regiment and may have saved Taylor's army.

Captain Bragg resigned his commission in 1855 and bought a 1,600-acre sugarcane plantation north of Thibodaux, Louisiana. He managed the plantation well, and at one time had 105 slaves. He opposed secession, but when Louisiana left the Union on January 26, 1861, Bragg went with her. He briefly commanded the Army of the Republic of Louisiana and was then commissioned as a brigadier general in the Confederate Army on March 7. President Davis posted him to Pensacola, Florida. He was promoted to major general on September 12 and commanded the Army of Pensacola. As a field commander, Bragg was a dismal failure, but he was an excellent training officer. The regiments coming out of Pensacola were some of the best in the Confederate Army.

Bragg commanded a corps in the Battle of Shiloh, where he delivered several uncoordinated, piecemeal assaults. In spite of his rather poor performance, President Davis promoted Bragg to full general on April 12. When Davis sacked General Beauregard for taking an unauthorized leave, he named Braxton Bragg commander of the Army of Mississippi (later Tennessee) on June 17, 1862.

It was one of the worst mistakes Davis made during the war.

Bragg's record of command was characterized by a strange combination of boldness, indecisiveness, and anxiety. He was clearly promoted above his head. Largely because of his petulant, vacillating, and grouchy personality, he failed to receive friendly cooperation from his generals.

He brilliantly outflanked the Yankees in the summer and fall of 1862 but lost his nerve at critical points, fighting an inconclusive engagement at Perryville in Kentucky on October 8 and then withdrawing into Tennessee. In late 1862, he fought a bloody but indecisive battle at Murfreesboro (Stones River) that not only failed to defeat the Federal forces but also lost Bragg the confidence of some of his subordinate generals, who did not trust his leadership.

The Federals maneuvered General Bragg out of Tennessee, but once he was reinforced by Longstreet's corps from Virginia, he won a great victory in Georgia at Chickamauga on September 20. Once again, however, Bragg failed to follow up on his initial success. His ill-managed siege of Chattanooga was broken by General Grant, who proceeded to rout the Confederate Army of Tennessee in the Battle of Missionary Ridge. Braxton Bragg submitted his resignation on November 29. On December 2, General William J. Hardee was named his temporary replacement. General Joseph E. Johnston arrived and assumed command on December 16.

In early 1864, Bragg became the principal military advisor to President Davis, "charged with the conduct of military operations of the Confederate States." In a sense, he was kicked upstairs. Here, he accomplished few positive results. Placed in command of Confederate forces in North Carolina in the fall of 1864, he mishandled the situation badly, and the South lost Fort Fisher and its last port. After Richmond fell, Bragg joined Davis's party in its flight to the south, but Bragg was captured in Monticello, Georgia, on May 9, and paroled the same day. President Davis was captured on May 10.

Braxton Bragg is remembered today as the worst of the South's senior generals. His plantation had been confiscated by the Federals in late 1862. Deprived of his living as a planter, his postwar career was a succession of appointments that were short-lived because of his irritable temper. On September 27, 1876, he was walking down the sidewalk in Galveston, Texas, when he suddenly collapsed and died about fifteen minutes later, apparently due to a brain seizure. He was fifty-nine years old. Braxton Bragg is buried in Magnolia Cemetery, Mobile, Alabama.

LAWRENCE O'BRYAN BRANCH was born in Enfield, North Carolina, on November 20, 1820. His parents died when he was a child, and his uncle, Governor John Branch of North Carolina, took him in as a

B·

ward. Governor Branch became secretary of the navy under President Andrew Jackson and brought young Lawrence Branch with him to Washington. Later, Lawrence Branch attended the Bingham Military School in North Carolina, the University of North Carolina at Chapel Hill, and the College of New Jersey (later Princeton), from which he graduated in 1838 first in his class. He briefly studied law and edited a newspaper in Nashville, Tennessee, before practicing law in Tallahassee, Florida.

Branch fought in the Seminole War in 1842. He eventually returned to North Carolina, where he continued to practice law, served as president of the Raleigh and Gaston Railroad, and was an elector for Franklin Pierce in 1852. Branch was three times elected to Congress as a Democrat, serving from March 4, 1855, to March 3, 1861. He was not a candidate for reelection in 1860.

After Lincoln was elected, Branch advocated immediate secession. He enlisted in the Raleigh Rifles as a private in May 1861. He became North Carolina state quartermaster general on May 20 and did a good job under the circumstances, but he resigned because he preferred field service. He was elected colonel of the 33rd North Carolina Infantry Regiment in September. He was promoted to brigadier general on March 14, 1862. Branch led his brigade (four thousand men) in the battle of New Bern, North Carolina, where he was defeated by General Ambrose Burnside, who had eleven thousand men. Still, Branch was credited with fighting well against heavy odds and conducting a successful retreat.

Sent to Virginia, General Branch was ordered to hold Hanover Court House. On May 27, he was attacked by U.S. General Fitz John Porter, who had about twelve thousand men. Outnumbered three to one, Branch was defeated again. He lost 73 killed, 192 wounded, and about 700 captured. Porter lost 62 killed, 223 wounded, and 10 missing. Robert E. Lee nevertheless sent Branch a dispatch expressing his approval of the manner in which the North Carolinian had discharged his duty.

Branch's brigade was part of the Light Division in the Seven Days Battles, where he fought well. He took part in the Second Manassas Campaign, as well as in the capture of Harpers Ferry. He picked up

B

soldiering quickly, and by the fall of 1862, he was considered a fine general.

On September 17, 1862, Branch force-marched his brigade from Harpers Ferry to Sharpsburg, arriving on the field at 2:30 p.m., just in time to check a Union advance. A. P. Hill recorded how Branch and Maxcy Gregg "sternly held their ground . . . pouring in destructive volleys" so that "the tide of the enemy surged back, and breaking in confusion, passed out of sight." Minutes later, as Branch stood talking with Generals Hill, Maxcy Gregg, William Dorsey Pender, and James J. Archer, a Federal sniper noted the clump of Confederate officers and fired into it. His bullet struck Branch in his right cheek and exited through his left ear, killing him instantly. He was forty-one years old.

General Branch is buried in Old City Cemetery in Raleigh.

WILLIAM LINDSAY BRANDON was born in Adams County, near Washington, Mississippi, though in what year is a matter of dispute. Most likely it was 1802. The son of an Irish immigrant, William was educated at Washington College in Virginia and the College of New Jersey (Princeton). He then returned to Mississippi and built a plantation, Arcole, out of the wilderness.

In addition to planting, Brandon was interested in politics, medicine, horses, hunting, and military affairs. He was so good at medicine that professional doctors consulted him. More than six feet tall, affable, and well-educated, Brandon was a popular man in his community, which elected him to the legislature. When the Mexican War broke out, he ran for the post of commander of the 1st Mississippi Rifle Regiment but lost to Jefferson Davis.

By 1860, he was worth $78,000 ($2,280,398 in 2020 money), and his property included 63 slaves and 16 slave quarters. When the Civil War began, he raised a company and became its captain. It became part of the 1st (Brandon's) Mississippi Infantry Battalion, and Brandon was promoted to major (June 11) and to lieutenant colonel (July 17). His battalion was

B ·

absorbed by the 21st Mississippi in October 1861, with Benjamin G. Humphreys as colonel and Brandon as its lieutenant colonel. It was stationed in northeast Virginia during the fall and winter of 1861–62 but was sent to the Virginia Peninsula in the spring. Despite his relatively advanced age (he was approximately sixty), Brandon fought in the Peninsula Campaign and was acting commander of the regiment during the Seven Days Battles.

On July 1, 1862, during the Battle of Malvern Hill, he was severely wounded when a musket ball went through his right ankle joint. The colonel was taken to a field hospital, where doctors amputated his leg. They doubted he would live, but he recuperated rapidly and rejoined his regiment.

During the Battle of Gettysburg, General William Barksdale, the brigade commander, was killed on July 2, and Benjamin Humphreys succeeded him as brigade commander, so Brandon again became regimental commander. He was promoted to colonel on August 12.

William Brandon resigned his commission on October 28, after the Chickamauga Campaign, feeling that age and disability were rendering him incapable of operating effectively in the field.

Instead of accepting his resignation, President Davis promoted him to brigadier general on June 18, 1864, and appointed him commander of the Mississippi Reserve Corps, which consisted of all men under the age of eighteen and above the age of forty-five. That fall, he was placed in charge of the Confederate Conscription Bureau for Mississippi, headquartered in Enterprise. He did a superb job and enrolled three thousand men within his first ninety days—a remarkable accomplishment in the third year of the war. He remained at his post until the surrender. He was paroled at Meridian on May 10, 1865.

After the war, General Brandon returned to Arcole and worked tirelessly to redeem his fortune until his death, which occurred on October 8, 1890. He was likely either eighty-seven or eighty-eight years old. William Lindsay Brandon was buried on his plantation.

WILLIAM FELIX BRANTLEY was born in Greene County, Alabama, on March 12, 1830, but moved to Mississippi with his family when

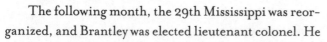

he was still a child. He studied law in Carroll County, Mississippi, and was a practicing attorney in Greensboro, Mississippi, by 1852.

By 1860, Brantley had moved to Choctaw County. A secessionist, he represented the county in the Mississippi Secession Convention and joined the state militia as a captain of the Wigfall Rifles. On May 21, 1861, the Rifles became Company D, 15th Mississippi Infantry, with Brandon as its captain. He fought in the battles of Mill Springs and Shiloh, where he was wounded on April 6, 1862.

The following month, the 29th Mississippi was reorganized, and Brantley was elected lieutenant colonel. He participated in the Kentucky Campaign and became colonel of his regiment on December 13. He fought at Murfreesboro (Stones River), where he was again slightly wounded, this time in the shoulder, by an exploding shell on December 31. He was back in command the next day.

Colonel Brandon fought in the Tullahoma Campaign, the Battle of Chickamauga, and the Siege of Chattanooga. He was officially cited for his conduct in the Battle of Lookout Mountain for his "skill, activity, zeal[,] and courage." He was again cited for his bravery in the Battle of Resaca, where he repulsed three separate Federal assaults on May 14, despite the fact that they were supported by twenty-four pieces of artillery. He then led a counterattack that routed the enemy.

The 29th Mississippi was under fire almost every day during the Atlanta Campaign. During the Battle of Atlanta, Brantley assumed command of the brigade after Samuel Benton was mortally wounded. He was promoted to brigadier general on July 26, 1864, and led the brigade for the rest of the war. He fought at Franklin and Nashville, where he smashed an attack by the African American brigades of U.S. General James B. Steedman. His surviving troops took part in the retreat to Tupelo, Mississippi, where Brantley furloughed his men and had them reassemble in Meridian on February 14, 1865. By now, it was obvious to many that the war was lost, and only 152 men returned. They traveled to

B.

Southfield, North Carolina, and fought in the Carolina Campaign. Brantley surrendered with the Army of Tennessee on April 26, 1865. He was paroled in Greensboro on May 1.

General Brantley returned home and resumed his law practice. His family was involved in a feud that had gone on since at least 1859. On November 10, 1870, on his way home from Winona, Mississippi, he was in his buggy when someone with a double-barreled shotgun fired a blast into his chest. He was forty years old. His assassin was never found.

William Felix Brantley was buried in New Greensboro Cemetery near Grady, Mississippi. Curiously, his tombstone lists his age at death as thirty-nine years, eight months, and twenty-four days.

JOHN BRATTON was born in Winnsboro, South Carolina, on March 7, 1831. He attended a local academy and South Carolina College in Columbia, from which he graduated in 1850, and then the South Carolina Medical College in Charleston. He practiced medicine in Winnsboro from 1853 to 1861. He also became a successful planter, and by 1860 he owned about seventy-five slaves on his plantation, which was known as Farmington.

Bratton entered Confederate service as a second lieutenant in Company C, 6th South Carolina Infantry Regiment on June 25, 1861. He was promoted to captain on July 1. Sent to Virginia, the regiment arrived too late to see action in the Battle of First Manassas. Remaining in Virginia, his company reenlisted for the duration of the war—the first one to do so. This attracted to Bratton the favorable notice of his superiors. He was promoted to lieutenant colonel on April 12, 1862, and he became colonel and regimental commander on May 1, 1862. Bratton fought at Dranesville and in the Peninsula Campaign, where he was wounded in the Battle of Williamsburg on May 5. He was wounded again and captured during the second day of the Battle of Seven Pines.

Exchanged at the end of August, Bratton rejoined the 6th South Carolina and fought at Fredericksburg and in Longstreet's Siege of

Suffolk, where he was a temporary brigade commander. His regiment was stationed in Richmond, guarding the capital during the Gettysburg Campaign, but it accompanied Longstreet's corps to Tennessee and took part in the sieges of Chattanooga and Knoxville. (It arrived too late to fight at Chickamauga.) He succeeded General Micah Jenkins, who was killed in action during the Battle of the Wilderness on May 6, 1864. He was promoted to brigadier general on June 1, to rank from May 6.

Bratton was such a good and steady commander that his men nicknamed him "Old Reliable." He fought in the Overland Campaign, including the battles of the Wilderness, Spotsylvania Court House, and Cold Harbor, and in the Siege of Petersburg. He was wounded in the shoulder on Darbytown Road (October 7, 1864) but was back in command in November. Along with the rest of the Army of Northern Virginia, he surrendered at Appomattox Court House on April 9, 1865. His brigade of 1,500 men was the largest in the army that day.

After the war, General Bratton engaged in livestock and cotton production. A political ally of Wade Hampton, he helped oust the corrupt carpetbagger regime in South Carolina. He served in the legislature in 1865 and 1866. After home rule was restored, the legislature elected Bratton comptroller general of the state in 1881. When Congressman John H. Evans died in 1884, John Bratton was elected to replace him, serving from December 8, 1884, to March 3, 1885. He was not a candidate for reelection.

John Bratton died in the town of his birth on January 12, 1898. He was sixty-six years old. He is buried in St. John's Episcopal Church Cemetery, Winnsboro.

JOHN CABELL BRECKINRIDGE was born near Lexington, Kentucky, on January 16, 1821 at his family estate, called Thorn Hill. He attended Centre College in Danville, Kentucky, and graduated in 1838. He did postgraduate studies at the College of New Jersey (Princeton) for a year, read law for a year, and attended Transylvania University in Lexington, where he received a bachelor of laws degree in 1841. He was a major in the 3rd Kentucky Infantry during the Mexican War but did not see combat.

From 1849 to 1861, Breckinridge was an active Kentucky politician. He was a state legislator (1849–50), congressman (1851–55), vice president of the United States under President James Buchanan (1857–61), unsuccessful presidential candidate (1860), and U.S. senator (1861). Breckinridge opposed secession, though he considered it legal; argued that slaveowners should voluntarily emancipate their slaves, but not be coerced by the government into doing so; and opposed in principle any usurpation of states' rights by the Federal government.

Kentucky's attempt at neutrality in the War Between the States failed, and Breckinridge "went south" on October 2, 1861. He was commissioned as a brigadier general in the Confederate Army on November 2 and assumed command of the 1st Kentucky Brigade on November 16.

Breckinridge was greeted as a hero in Richmond, Virginia. Louise Wigfall, the daughter of the influential Confederate States Senator Louis Wigfall of Texas, called him "[b]rilliant as he was and debonair, the highest type of Kentucky gentleman." He always made friends easily.

He fought in the Battle of Shiloh, where he commanded a three-brigade corps and was slightly wounded. He picked up soldiering quickly and his performance at Shiloh was judged to be good. The former vice president seemed to have an aptitude for commanding men in battle, and his eye for terrain was first-rate. He was promoted to major general on April 16, with a date of rank of April 14.

Breckinridge fought in many battles during the war, including the Siege of Corinth, the defense of Vicksburg, Baton Rouge, Second Murfreesboro, the Second Battle of Jackson (Mississippi), Chickamauga, the Siege of Chattanooga, Cold Harbor, Jubal Early's Maryland Campaign, and Saltville. After his failure at Chattanooga, Braxton Bragg needed a scapegoat, so he charged Breckinridge with drunkenness at Stones River (retroactively) and Chattanooga and relieved him of his command. While it was true that Breckinridge drank (and heavily), he held his liquor well, and Jefferson Davis and the War Department did not believe Bragg's charges. They replaced Bragg with Joseph E. Johnston and assigned the unemployed Breckinridge to command the Trans-Allegheny Department.

Breckinridge fought his most famous battle on May 15, 1864, when, with 4,800 men (including 261 Virginia Military Institute cadets), he crushed 6,500 Federals under General Franz Sigel at New Market.

On February 6, 1865, President Davis appointed Breckinridge secretary of war. He made the department more efficient and fired Lucius B. Northrop, the Confederate commissary general. He effectively disbanded the remnants of the Confederate government at Washington, Georgia, on May 4, 1865, and made his way to Cuba in an open boat. He remained in exile, in Europe and Canada, until 1869.

After the war, Breckinridge remained aloof from politics. He ran a railroad, was president of an insurance company, and resumed his law practice. His health slowly deteriorated and on May 17, 1875, at age fifty-four, he died. He was buried in the Lexington Cemetery.

Some sources cite cirrhosis of the liver as the cause of Breckinridge's death. Dr. Jack D. Welsh, M.D., who wrote a landmark study on the medical records of Confederate generals, doubts that. Breckinridge likely passed away as the result of a pulmonary hemorrhage.

THEODORE WASHINGTON BREVARD, JR., was born in Tuskegee, Alabama, on August 26, 1835. His family moved to Florida in 1847. He studied law at the University of Virginia; was admitted to the Florida bar; practiced law in Tallahassee; served with a company of Florida mounted volunteers, and fought the Seminoles in the Everglades in 1857, rising to the rank of captain. He was a member of the Florida House of Representatives from 1858 to 1859.

By 1861, Brevard was adjutant general of the state militia, but he resigned that position so he could do active field service. Newly commissioned as a captain, Brevard raised a company of infantry in Tallahassee that became Company D of the 2nd Florida Infantry

After the war, Theodore W. Brevard, Jr., resumed his law practice in Tallahassee and was highly successful. He died on June 20, 1882, at age forty-six. He is buried in St. John's Episcopal Church Cemetery in Tallahassee, Florida.

JOHN CALVIN BROWN was born on January 6, 1827, in Giles County, Tennessee. He graduated from Jackson College in Columbia in 1846, at age nineteen, was admitted to the bar in 1848, and practiced law in Pulaski, where he developed into a highly successful attorney.

He opposed secession and was a presidential elector for centrist candidate John Bell in the 1860 election but stayed loyal to Tennessee when it seceded. He enlisted as a private on May 1 but was elected colonel of the 3rd Tennessee Infantry Regiment on May 16, 1861. His regiment was sent to Fort Donelson, and on February 13, Brown became a temporary brigade commander. He was wounded during the battle (probably on the fifteenth) and was captured when the fort surrendered on February 16. He spent six months in prison at Fort Warren, Massachusetts, in Boston Harbor.

Colonel Brown was exchanged on August 15, 1862, and was promptly given another brigade. He was promoted to brigadier general on September 15, to rank from August 30. He served in the Heartland Campaign of 1862 and was shot through the right thigh in the Battle of Perryville.

Brown spent three months in various hospitals and was still on crutches when he returned to duty. As part of General Carter L. Stevenson's division, he rushed to Vicksburg in December 1862 and fought at Chickasaw Bluffs (also known as Chickasaw Bayou), Raymond, and the First Battle of Jackson. In September 1863, Brown fought at Chickamauga, where he shattered a Union division before he was hit by a spent grapeshot. He took part in the Siege of Chattanooga and in the unsuccessful defense of Missionary Ridge.

B·

General Brown's personal presence, Judge John S. Wilkes recalled, was "majestic and commanding," but he also noted that Brown "was not an orator." A born leader, he was a friendly, honest man who never spoke harshly. As a disciplinarian, he was strict but just. He was fearless, a gentleman to the core, and his officers and men loved him.

Brown distinguished himself in the retreat to Atlanta and subsequent battles around the city and was slightly wounded at Ezra Church on July 28. He assumed temporary command of a division on July 7 and was promoted to major general (temporary rank) on August 4, 1864. He commanded another division during the first stage of General John Bell Hood's Tennessee Campaign but was severely wounded in the Battle of Franklin on November 30. He did not recover until the following spring.

General Brown rejoined the Army of Tennessee in North Carolina on April 2, 1865. He surrendered with Joseph E. Johnston and the rest of the army at Bennett Place, Durham, North Carolina, on April 26.

After the war, Brown returned to Pulaski, where he resumed his law practice. He worked to restore home rule in Tennessee, was an early member of the Ku Klux Klan, and was elected to the legislature as a Democrat in 1867. He was president of the 1870 Constitutional Convention. The following year, he was elected the nineteenth governor of Tennessee. He was reelected in 1872 and served from October 10, 1871, to January 18, 1875.

After his second term as governor expired, Brown ran for the U.S. Senate but lost on the fifty-fourth ballot. General Brown then withdrew from public life. He became interested in railroads and industry and in 1889 became president of the Tennessee Coal, Iron, and Railroad Company, which was then the largest industrial concern in the South. He was also Grand Master of Masons in Tennessee.

General John Calvin Brown died in Red Boiling Springs, Macon County, Tennessee, on August 17, 1889, at age sixty-two. He is buried in Old Maplewood Cemetery, Pulaski, Giles County, Tennessee.

WILLIAM MONTAGUE BROWNE, JR., was born on July 7, 1823, in County Mayo, Ireland. The son of a member of parliament, he was

educated at Rugby and at Trinity College, Ireland, and
was considered polished, cultured, and sophisticated.
He served with the British Army during the Crimean
War and joined the British diplomatic service. He moved
to New York City in 1851 and was political editor for the
New York *Journal of Commerce*. Browne turned up in Washington, D.C., in 1857, as editor in chief of the Washington *Constitution*, a pro–Democratic Party newspaper. Here
he acquired the nickname "Constitution Browne."

By 1860, Browne was a well-known proponent of
secession. He moved to Athens, Georgia, shortly before
the war began, because it was the home of his good friends
and prominent political leaders, Howell Cobb (former
Speaker of the House, Georgia governor, and secretary of the treasury)
and Robert Toombs (former congressman and U.S. senator). When
Toombs became the Confederacy's first secretary of state, he appointed
Browne assistant secretary of state. Browne appears to have handled most
of the ministry's day-to-day business. He continued in his position after
Robert M. T. Hunter assumed the portfolio on July 25, 1861.

Browne moved to Richmond in 1861 and served as interim secretary
of state from February 17 to March 18, 1862. He resigned from the State
Department on April 9, after Judah Benjamin assumed the portfolio.

Browne excelled at making good friends quickly. Jefferson Davis,
another personal friend, appointed him a colonel of cavalry on April 19.
Browne served as aide-de-camp to the president from March 1862 to
April 5, 1864, when Davis named him director of conscription in Georgia, where Governor Joseph E. Brown was impeding the Southern war
effort. Browne handled the governor as well as anyone could have.

In late 1864, while keeping his conscription office, William Browne
formed a small seven hundred–man brigade of third- and fourth-class
reserve infantry against William T. Sherman in the defense of Savannah.
Browne had a talent for organization, which the president recognized.
Davis took this opportunity to promote his friend to brigadier general
(temporary rank) on December 13, 1864, to rank from November 11, but

B •

the Senate rejected Browne's nomination on February 18, 1865, and he reverted to the rank of colonel. He surrendered on May 8, 1865, but was paroled as a brigadier general.

Browne returned to Athens after the war, studied law, and was admitted to the bar in February 1866. He became editor of the Macon *Star* newspaper and the *Southern Banner* (an agricultural journal) in 1868 and filled the same role for the journal *Southern Farm and Home* from 1869 to 1873. He also wrote a biography of Confederate Vice President Alexander H. Stephens. Browne lived in relative poverty for much of the postwar era. In 1874, Browne was named professor of law, history, and political science at the University of Georgia, a post which he held for the rest of his life.

William Montague Browne died of pneumonia on April 28, 1883, at age fifty-nine. He is buried in Oconee Hill Cemetery in Athens.

GOODE BRYAN was born in Hancock County, Georgia, on August 31, 1811. He entered the U.S. Military Academy (West Point) in 1829 and graduated in 1834. Bryan was set back a year because of academic deficiencies. He served in the garrison at the Augusta Arsenal but resigned after ten months and became a civil engineer on the Athens and Augusta Railroad. In 1839, he moved to Tallapoosa County, Alabama, where he studied law, became a planter (thanks to his wealthy parents), and briefly served in the Alabama House of Representatives (1843).

When the Mexican War began, Bryan helped raise the 1st Alabama Volunteer Infantry. He became its major on June 27, 1846, and went to Mexico but did not fight in any battles. The regiment was disbanded in May 1847, and Bryan became a volunteer assistant quartermaster. He served until Mexico City fell. He then returned to Georgia.

In 1853, Goode Bryan moved to Richmond County, Georgia. A wealthy planter, he owned eighty-six slaves in 1859 and was worth

$110,500 ($3,464,494 in 2020 dollars) when the war started. He was a member of the Georgia Secession Convention of 1861 and voted in favor of leaving the Union. He joined the Confederate Army as a captain in the 16th Georgia Infantry but was promoted to lieutenant colonel on July 19, 1861. He became colonel of the regiment on February 15, 1862.

Bryan's regiment served in the Peninsula Campaign, the Seven Days Battles, Second Manassas, the Maryland Campaign, Fredericksburg, Chancellorsville, and Gettysburg with considerable success. On July 2, Colonel Bryan and his men were prepared to launch an attack against a weak point in the U.S. line near Little Round Top but were recalled by General James Longstreet. Bryan remained bitter about this until the last day of his life, asserting that he could have won the battle had Longstreet not stopped him.

Brigadier General Paul Jones Semmes was mortally wounded on July 2, and Bryan was selected to replace him as brigade commander. He was promoted to brigadier general on August 31, 1863, with a date of rank of August 29. He went with Longstreet's corps to Georgia but arrived too late to fight in the Battle of Chickamauga. He served in the Knoxville Campaign and led his men in the decisive and unsuccessful attack on Fort Sanders on November 29. He returned to Lee's Army of Northern Virginia that spring and fought in the Overland Campaign and the first part of the Siege of Petersburg. He resigned due to chronic illness (including dysentery and kidney problems) on September 20, 1864, and returned to Augusta. Bryan was paroled at Albany, Georgia, on May 19, 1865. He apparently went through the entire war without being wounded.

Although he never fully regained his health and spent much of his remaining years in semiretirement, Bryan helped establish the Confederate Survivors Association in 1878. He held minor posts in the city government for most of the postwar period.

Brigadier General Goode Bryan died in Augusta of "paralysis" on August 16, 1885, just two weeks before his seventy-fourth birthday. He is buried in Magnolia Cemetery, Augusta, Georgia.

SIMON BOLIVAR BUCKNER, SR., was born on his family's estate, Glen Lily, near Munfordville, Kentucky, on April 1, 1823. He was called "Bolivar." He enrolled at West Point in 1840 at age seventeen and graduated in 1844. During the Mexican War, he fought at Veracruz, San Antonio, and Churubusco, where he was slightly wounded and was brevetted first lieutenant. He was brevetted captain for his gallantry in the Battle of Molino del Rey. He also fought at Chapultepec and in the storming of the Belén Gate near Mexico City. He was given the honor of lowering the U.S. flag for the last time when the occupation of the Mexican capital ended.

After the war, Buckner did tours of duty in several locations, including the Western frontier. He developed a reputation for fairness in dealing with the Indians, and Chief Yellow Bear of the Oglala Sioux refused to deal with any white man except Buckner.

Buckner resigned from the army on March 26, 1855, to work for his father-in-law, who had extensive real estate holdings in Chicago and Kentucky. Buckner established a home in Louisville. He was a states' rights man but opposed secession. His family did not own slaves but felt that the issue of slavery was a matter to be decided by the separate states, not the Federal government. When the Civil War began, Kentucky Governor Beriah Magoffin appointed Buckner state adjutant general, and he organized sixty-one companies to defend the state's neutrality.

As Rebel and Union forces contested for the state, Buckner was forced to choose sides. He "went south." On September 14, 1861, he was commissioned a brigadier general in the Confederate Army and given command of a division in the Army of Central Kentucky.

The Battle of Fort Donelson in Tennessee was Buckner's first major action in the Civil War, and it proved to be his worst. He grossly overestimated the enemy's strength and urged General John Floyd to surrender. Floyd agreed but escaped by steamboat, leaving Buckner "holding the bag." Buckner surrendered twelve thousand men on the morning of February 16. He was imprisoned at Fort Warren in Boston Harbor. Held in solitary confinement, he spent five months writing poetry. He was exchanged on August 15 and was promoted to major general the next day. He was ordered to Chattanooga to join Braxton Bragg's Army of Tennessee immediately as a division commander. Shortly thereafter, he took part in Bragg's failed invasion of Kentucky.

From December 1862 through April 27, 1863, Buckner commanded the District of the Gulf, headquartered at Mobile. He then commanded the Department and Army of East Tennessee. In that role, he abandoned Knoxville, reinforced Bragg in Georgia, and commanded a corps in the Battle of Chickamauga, where he was part of Longstreet's breakthrough of the Union line. After this victory, he reported himself "sick" and took medical leave until Braxton Bragg (whom he despised) resigned his command.

After briefly commanding John Bell Hood's division, Buckner was transferred to the Trans-Mississippi Department on April 28, 1864. He assumed command of the Army (and Department) of Western Louisiana on August 4, a post which he held until April 19, 1865. At Edmund Kirby Smith's request, he was promoted to lieutenant general on September 20, 1864. On his own initiative, Buckner surrendered the Trans-Mississippi Department in New Orleans on May 26, 1865. It was one of history's ironies that Buckner was the first man to surrender a Confederate army: he was also the last.

After the war, Buckner filed a number of lawsuits and recovered most of his seized property, and he continued to make good business deals. (He had a talent for making money.) He served as governor of Kentucky from August 30, 1887, to September 1, 1891. At one point, Buckner loaned the state enough money from his personal funds to keep it solvent until more tax revenue could be collected.

Buckner ran for the U.S. Senate in 1895 but was defeated. He ran for vice president on a third-party ticket in 1896 but was easily defeated. He then retired to Glen Lily, where he continued to dabble in politics.

Simon Bolivar Buckner, Sr., the last surviving Confederate lieutenant general, died of uremic poisoning (acute kidney failure) on January 8, 1914, at his Glen Lily Plantation near Munfordville. He was ninety years old. He is buried at Frankfort Cemetery, Frankfort, Kentucky.

B ·

ABRAHAM "ABE" BUFORD was born in Woodford County, Kentucky, on January 18, 1820. He was home-schooled until he entered Centre College, a Presbyterian school in Danville, Kentucky. He left Centre to attend West Point in 1837. He graduated in 1841 and was commissioned a brevet second lieutenant in the cavalry. Lieutenant Buford served on the frontier from 1842 through 1846 in the Kansas Territory and the Indian Territory. He fought in Mexico and was brevetted captain for bravery at Buena Vista. He resigned from the army on October 12, 1854, and returned home to raise horses, establishing a successful thoroughbred horse farm near Versailles in Woodford County. He named it Bosque Bonita ("Beautiful Woods").

When the Civil War began, Buford tried to stay neutral. In the autumn of 1862, however, he joined the struggle and raised an impressive number of horsemen for the South. He was sent to Port Hudson, where he commanded an infantry brigade. In May 1863, Buford fought in the Battle of Champion Hill but escaped being trapped in Vicksburg. He participated in Joseph E. Johnston's abortive defense of Jackson and Leonidas Polk's unsuccessful defense of Meridian.

In early 1864, Buford and his brigade were designated cavalry and were attached to Nathan Bedford Forrest's corps. It was a perfect match. Buford and Forrest got along famously, and Buford and his men played key roles in several of Forrest's many victories. Buford hardly looked the part of a *beau cavalier*. He was more than six feet tall and weighed more than three hundred pounds. Normally a jovial, genial man, he could swear with the best of them when aroused. He also loved his Kentucky Bourbon—and dancing. Strangely, William Newton Mercer Otey of Forrest's staff recalled Buford as the most graceful dancer he ever saw.

While covering Hood's retreat from Nashville, Buford was wounded in the right leg at Richland Creek on December 17, 1864. On December 24, he was seriously wounded in another skirmish at Richland Creek. He did not return to duty until February 1865.

Buford participated in the Selma Campaign and surrendered with Forrest's cavalry corps on May 9. He returned to his Kentucky horse farm after the war and developed a national reputation for his outstanding animals. Lieutenant Colonel George Armstrong Custer was one of his customers. Many of the horses killed in the Battle of Little Bighorn were from Bosque Bonita.

Buford served a term in the Kentucky legislature after the war. But tragedy overtook him in the 1870s. In 1872, his only son died at the age of twenty-three. In 1879, his wife died, and he defended his brother from a murder charge (the brother was eventually found not guilty by reason of insanity). Buford also suffered a series of financial reverses that finally forced him into bankruptcy, and he lost his horse farm. Suffering from depression, Abe Buford went to visit his nephew in Danville, Indiana. Here, the sixty-four-year-old former general shot himself in the head on June 9, 1884. Abe Buford was buried in Lexington Cemetery, Lexington, Kentucky.

ROBERT BULLOCK was born in Greenville, North Carolina, on December 8, 1828. He attended public schools, moved to Florida, and settled at Fort King, near present-day Ocala, where he taught school. He was elected clerk of the circuit court for Marion County in 1849.

In 1855, Bullock organized a company of mounted volunteers and fought in the Third Seminole War. Captain Bullock proved to be a good and efficient officer. After a year and a half on active duty, he returned to Ocala, studied law, was admitted to the bar, and became clerk of the county court. Bullock joined the Confederate Army as a captain in 1861 and was elected lieutenant colonel of the 7th Florida Infantry in April 1862. He fought

B ·

in all of the major operations of the Army of Tennessee. He became commander of the 7th Florida on June 3, 1863, and was promoted to colonel. Bullock's regiment was heavily engaged in the Battle of Chickamauga. It was in a trench line at the base of Missionary Ridge when Grant unleashed his massive offensive of November 25. The bluecoats overran the position and Colonel Bullock was taken prisoner. Sent to Johnson's Island in Lake Erie, he was exchanged in March 1864 and rejoined his unit.

After General Jesse J. Finley was wounded in the Battle of Resaca, Bullock took command of his brigade, which was involved in some of the heaviest fighting in the Atlanta campaign. Bullock himself was wounded, but not seriously, at Utoy Creek near Atlanta on August 6. He was promoted to brigadier general (temporary rank) on December 13, 1864, with a date of rank of November 29.

General Bullock fought at Franklin, where he was wounded, and in the Third Battle of Murfreesboro, where he was wounded again and his brigade (part of General William Bate's division) was routed. General Bullock was sent to Mississippi to recover and was not able to return to active duty before the war ended. He was a good and solid commander.

After the war, General Bullock was elected probate court judge in Marion County (1866–68). After Reconstruction, he was elected to the Florida House of Representatives and was again clerk of the circuit court of Marion County. He served as a U.S. congressman from March 4, 1889, to March 3, 1893, but was not a candidate for reelection in 1892.

Robert Bullock retired from public life in 1893 and moved to the Lake Weir area, where he developed huge orange and lemon groves. They were destroyed, however, during the freeze of 1895. Bullock then returned to Ocala, where he was successively a state district judge, mayor, and postmaster.

General Bullock died in Ocala on July 27, 1905, at age seventy-six, fourteen months after his wife of more than fifty years had died. He took her sudden death so badly that his friends said he simply died of a broken heart. His official cause of death was chronic gastroduodenitis. He was buried in Evergreen Cemetery, Ocala, Florida.

MATTHEW CALBRAITH BUTLER was born at Eagle's Crag, his father's estate, on March 8, 1836, to a prominent Greenville, South Carolina, family. After his parents died, Calbraith (as he was called) was raised by his uncle. He was educated at the Edgefield Academy and at South Carolina College and became a lawyer in 1857. He was elected to the South Carolina House of Representatives as a secessionist in 1860.

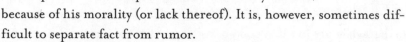

Butler married the daughter of Governor Francis Wilkinson Pickens, but their married life left much to be desired. Calbraith was not faithful; in fact, on one occasion, General Lee reportedly considered denying him a promotion, despite a stellar military record, because of his morality (or lack thereof). It is, however, sometimes difficult to separate fact from rumor.

Butler joined Hampton's Legion and was promoted to major to date from July 21, 1861, the day he fought in the First Battle of Bull Run. Although he had no military training whatsoever, he showed a definite aptitude for military leadership and excelled at every level from captain to major general. He was also noted for his fearlessness. He fought in the Peninsula Campaign, Seven Pines, and Seven Days.

The Legion's cavalry was consolidated with the 4th South Carolina Cavalry Battalion to form the 2nd South Carolina Cavalry Regiment, and Calbraith Butler was elected its commander on August 22, 1862. He led his men in all of the major operations of J. E. B. Stuart's cavalry until June 9, 1863. During the Battle of Brandy Station, Butler's regiment held off an entire Union division for much of the day, but Butler was hit by Union artillery shrapnel and lost his leg below the knee. Butler refused to let this injury end his military career or keep him out of the field. He was promoted to brigadier general on September 2, 1863, to rank from September 1, and returned to duty that same month, commanding a newly formed brigade of mounted infantry that became part of Hampton's division.

B ·

After General Stuart was mortally wounded on May 11, Butler was given command of a division. He played a major role in crushing Philip Sheridan's cavalry at Trevilian Station. He was promoted to major general on December 3, 1864, to rank from September 19.

Butler's division was sent south in early 1865, with orders to impede Sherman's advance through the Carolinas. He again did as well as could be expected, and his propensity for sharing their hardships made Butler very popular among his men. General Butler was with Joseph Johnston's Army of Tennessee when it surrendered at Bennett Place, Durham, North Carolina, on April 26. He was paroled at Greensboro on May 1.

Calbraith Butler lost all his material possessions during the war. "I was twenty-nine years old, with one leg gone, a wife and three children to support, with seventy slaves emancipated, a debt of $15,000, and in my pocket, $1.75," he recalled. He resumed his law practice, was elected to the legislature in 1866, and worked for a return to home rule in South Carolina.

The Democrats won the elections of 1876, and, in 1877, the legislature elected Calbraith Butler U.S. senator. He was reelected twice and served until 1895. He lost his 1894 reelection bid to Benjamin "Pitchfork Ben" Tillman.

Butler practiced law in Washington, D.C., from 1895 to 1898, when he was appointed U.S. Major General of Volunteers in the Spanish-American War; he did not see combat.

In 1904, Butler relocated to Mexico, where he served as vice president of a mining company, after which he lived in semiretirement. He died in Washington, D.C., on April 14, 1909, at age seventy-three. He is buried in Edgefield Village Cemetery.

C

CABELL – CUMMING

WILLIAM LEWIS "TIGE" CABELL was born in Danville, Virginia, on New Year's Day, 1827, the son of a major general. He gained admission to West Point in 1846 and graduated with the class of 1850. Commissioned a brevet second lieutenant of infantry, he served on the Western frontier, where he skirmished with Indians (and was wounded by a hostile's arrow) and fought Mormons in Utah.

Cabell resigned from the U.S. Army in 1861 and accepted a major's commission in the quartermaster department of the Confederate Army. On April 21, President Davis ordered him to Richmond to organize the quartermaster, commissary, and ordnance branches of the War Department. He fought in the First Battle of Bull Run as a member of Beauregard's staff. Later, he became Joseph E. Johnston's chief quartermaster. During the winter of 1861–62, Beauregard, Johnston, and Cabell reportedly designed what became known as the Confederate Battle Flag.

William Cabell was known for his efficiency, energy, and technical expertise. In January 1862, he was sent to Little Rock to remedy the tangled supply and logistical situation in the Trans-Mississippi Department, but there was insufficient time to do that before the poorly supplied Confederate Army of the West was defeated at the Battle of Pea Ridge in March 1862. After this defeat, Cabell transported Earl Van Dorn's entire field army across the Mississippi River to the east bank within a week, which demonstrated a high degree of logistical skill. In June, Van Dorn gave him command of a mixed Texas/Arkansas brigade, which he led in more than twenty engagements, including the battles of Iuka and Second Corinth. During the retreat from Corinth, Cabell made a stand at Davis Bridge, which saved Van Dorn's army. He was promoted to brigadier general on January 30, 1863, to rank from January 20.

In February, he was transferred back to Arkansas and attempted to regain control of northwest Arkansas but was checked in the Battle of Fayetteville (April 1863). His efforts to capture Fort Gibson in the

·C

Indian Territory also failed. General Cabell formed, organized, and led the 1st Arkansas Cavalry Brigade against the Union's Camden Expedition in April 1864 and in other operations. He proved a fine brigade commander, amassing an outstanding record, and played a role in the Confederate victories at Poison Spring and Marks' Mill, fought in many actions across Arkansas and Missouri, and was part of Sterling Price's Missouri Raid. He was captured on October 25, 1864, in the Battle of Mine Creek in Kansas. He was a prisoner at Johnson's Island, Ohio, and Fort Warren, Massachusetts, for the rest of the war. He was released on July 24, 1865.

After the war, William Cabell worked as a civil engineer and lawyer. In 1872, he moved to Dallas, where he served three terms as mayor (1874–76, 1877–79, and 1883–85). He was also vice president of a railroad until 1885, when he was appointed U.S. marshal for the Northern District of Texas.

General Cabell was elected national commander in chief of the United Confederate Veterans in 1908. He helped secure Texas state pensions for Confederate veterans and was instrumental in establishing the Home for Confederate Veterans in Austin. He also converted to Catholicism late in his life.

In poor health for some time, he died quietly at his home in Dallas (probably of heart failure) on February 22, 1911, at age eighty-four. He was buried in Greenwood Cemetery in Dallas. Fifty thousand people lined the streets for the parade held in his honor, and twenty-five thousand attended his funeral.

ALEXANDER WILLIAM CAMPBELL was born on June 4, 1828, in Nashville, Tennessee. He graduated from West Tennessee College (now Union University in Jackson) and Lebanon Law School and settled in Jackson, Tennessee, where he set up a law office.

Campbell enlisted in the Provisional Army of Tennessee as a private but was appointed major and assistant inspector on General Benjamin Cheatham's staff on May 9, 1861. He became colonel of the 33rd Tennessee Infantry Regiment on October 16. It was stationed at Columbus, Kentucky, which was evacuated on March 2, 1862. The 33rd was poorly armed, with many of its men carrying only shotguns, but saw heavy combat at Shiloh. Alexander Campbell was among the seriously wounded.

It took Campbell months to recover. When he did return, he discovered that he had not been reelected colonel. He joined Leonidas Polk's corps as a supernumerary officer. The general put him in charge of the ordnance train during the retreat from Kentucky in October 1862.

On December 28, just before the Second Battle of Murfreesboro, Polk appointed him an assistant adjutant general and inspector general. Later he was transferred to the Tennessee Conscription Bureau under Gideon Pillow.

Tennessee Governor Isham G. Harris sent Campbell on a mission behind enemy lines to recruit new volunteers in western Tennessee. He was captured at Lexington, Tennessee, on July 29, 1863, along with twenty-seven men, and was not exchanged until December 1864. He was appointed acting inspector general for Nathan Bedford Forrest. On March 1, he was given command of a brigade in William Hicks "Red" Jackson's cavalry division of Forrest's cavalry corps and was promoted to brigadier general on March 2, 1865, to rank from March 1. He (and Jackson) missed the Battle of Selma and surrendered at Gainesville on May 9. He was paroled on May 11.

Campbell was viewed by everyone as a gentleman of refinement, and was well-liked by Forrest's veterans, but why he was promoted over veteran brigade commanders like Clark Barteau and Robert "Black Bob" McCulloch when he had not commanded a troop for almost three years is a mystery.

After the war, Campbell returned to Jackson, resumed his law practice, and became a banker. He ran for governor in 1880 but lost. He developed cancer, which started in his tongue two years before his death. He passed away in Jackson on June 13, 1893, at age sixty-five. General Campbell is buried in Riverside Cemetery, Jackson, Tennessee.

JAMES CANTEY was born on December 30, 1818, in Camden, South Carolina, the son of a planter. He graduated from South Carolina College, studied law, was admitted to the bar in 1840, and set up a practice in Camden. In 1846, he was elected to the South Carolina House of Representatives and served two terms. He joined the Palmetto Regiment and fought in the Mexican War, where he was seriously wounded. He was a captain when the Mexican capital fell.

After Mexico, Cantey moved to Fort Mitchell, Alabama, which is eight miles south of Phenix City, to operate a plantation owned by his father. When the Civil War began, he organized Cantey's Rifles, which became part of the 15th Alabama Infantry. Cantey was elected commander on July 27, 1861, and led the regiment in Stonewall Jackson's Valley Campaign of 1862, where he particularly distinguished himself at the First Battle of Winchester on May 25. During the Battle of Cross Keys, he was cut off from the Rebel main force but slashed his way through Union lines, restored the front, outflanked the Yankees, and drove them back.

Cantey and his regiment fought under Stonewall Jackson in the Seven Days Battles, then he was posted to detached duty at Pollard, Alabama, in the Department of the Gulf. His poorly equipped command was short at least 1,600 arms, which probably explains why it remained in a secondary theater of operations as long as it did. James Cantey, meanwhile, was promoted to brigadier general on January 8, 1863, and remained in Mobile until April 1864, when he and his men were transferred to the Army of Tennessee.

General Cantey was often absent due to illness during the last three years of the war. When present, he functioned well. He fought in the Atlanta Campaign, where he led up to four thousand men. He briefly led a division in May and June 1864 but was replaced by General Edward Walthall. On September 13, General John Bell Hood wrote General Samuel Cooper and asked that Cantey be replaced because he was "sick and not likely to return." Charles Shelley commanded the brigade for most of the rest of the war, although Cantey apparently returned occasionally. The Army of Tennessee surrendered at Bennett Place, Durham, North Carolina, on April 26, 1865, and Cantey capitulated with his brigade.

After the war, General Cantey resided on his plantation. He died at Fort Mitchell, Russell County, Alabama, on June 30, 1874, and is buried in Crowell Family Cemetery, Fort Mitchell. He was fifty-five years old.

ELLISON CAPERS was born at Bull Head, his father's plantation in St. Thomas Parish, South Carolina, about twenty miles north of Charleston, on October 14, 1837. His father was a bishop in the Methodist Episcopal Church. Ellison was educated at local schools and at the South Carolina Military Academy (now The Citadel), whose founding president was his older brother, Francis W. Capers. After he graduated at the head of his class in 1857, he became an assistant professor of mathematics at the academy.

Capers joined the 1st South Carolina Rifle Regiment, a militia unit, in the fall of 1860 and was elected its major. He was present during the Battle of Fort Sumter. He entered Confederate service as a major of the 24th South Carolina Infantry during the winter of 1861–62. The regiment remained in South Carolina until May 6, 1863, when Capers (a lieutenant colonel as of April 1, 1862) and his men were sent to Mississippi and fought in the First Battle of Jackson. Capers was wounded when a rifle ball entered his leg about six inches below the knee. He lost a great deal of blood and had to leave the field, but he eventually recovered.

Capers's regiment fought in the Second Battle of Jackson in July and in the Battle of Chickamauga, where he was wounded on September 20. He recovered quickly and took part in the Siege of Chattanooga, including the disastrous defeat at Missionary Ridge. Meanwhile, Capers succeeded Isaac Stevens as commander of the 24th South Carolina Infantry and was promoted to colonel on January 20, 1864. He led his regiment

·C

in the Atlanta Campaign and John Bell Hood's disastrous Tennessee Campaign, where he fought in the Battle of Franklin. General States Rights Gist was killed, and Colonel Capers was severely wounded in the foot. After he recovered, Capers assumed command of Gist's former brigade, which he led in the Carolinas campaign. He became a brigadier general on March 2, 1865, to rank from March 1. He was, however, captured during the Battle of Bentonville that same month.

After the war, General Capers returned home. In December 1865, he was elected secretary of state for South Carolina. He was ordained as an Episcopal priest in 1866 and was consecrated as a bishop in 1893. Meanwhile, he wrote the South Carolina volume of *Confederate Military History*. He was also chaplain of the United Confederate Veterans for many years.

By his speeches, sermons, writings, and personal contacts, Dr. Capers made great contributions to reuniting the nation. In 1904, he was inaugurated chancellor of the University of the South in Sewanee, Tennessee, a position he held until his death. He had a stroke in 1907 and succumbed to its effects on April 22, 1908, at age seventy. He is buried in Trinity Episcopal Cathedral Cemetery.

WILLIAM HENRY CARROLL was born in Nashville, Tennessee, probably in 1810. He was the son of William Carroll, a six-term governor of Tennessee.

Young William operated a plantation in Panola County, Mississippi, but returned to Tennessee in 1848. He became postmaster of Memphis and a wealthy planter.

Governor Isham Harris appointed Carroll brigadier general in the Army of the State of Tennessee on May 9, 1861. He took command of the Memphis sector, where he suppressed pro-Union gangs and reestablished civil stability.

Eastern Tennessee was strongly pro-Union in sentiment, and in September 1861, General Leonidas Polk sent Carroll to Knoxville to secure the area for the South and recruit troops. He quickly formed three regiments and was promoted to brigadier general in the Confederate Army on October 26. On December 11, General Carroll declared martial law in Knoxville and the surrounding area, which allowed him to arrest anti–Confederate leaders before restoring civil government.

By late 1861, Carroll commanded four thousand men, but only three hundred of them were armed. He fought in the Battle of Mill Springs, where U.S. General George Thomas defeated Confederate General George B. Crittenden and secured eastern Kentucky for the Union.

Many Civil War generals had a problem with alcohol, and Carroll was one of them. There were rumors that both Crittenden and Carroll were drunk at Mill Springs. When Albert Sidney Johnston began to assemble his army around Corinth for the offensive against Grant's concentration at Pittsburg Landing, Carroll's brigade was stationed at Iuka. General William Hardee went there to investigate reports of incompetence and drunkenness by both Crittenden and Carroll. He found both men intoxicated and arrested them.

A court of inquiry was held on August 3, and it suspended Carroll from duty. Braxton Bragg declared that he was "unfit for command" and "not a safe man to be trusted with any command." Afterward, under pressure from Bragg, Carroll resigned his commission on February 1, 1863. He and his family then moved to Montreal, Canada, stayed at the luxurious St. Lawrence Hall Hotel, and associated with members of the Confederate Secret Service and John Wilkes Booth. Carroll attempted to reenter the Confederacy via blockade runner but was captured off the coast of North Carolina. Imprisoned for a time in Fort Monroe, he was released at the end of the war and quickly returned to Montreal.

General Carroll was suspected of being involved in the conspiracy to assassinate Abraham Lincoln, but what role, if any, he played in the plot was never established. William Carroll died of unknown causes in Montreal on May 3, 1868. He is buried in Elmwood Cemetery, Memphis, Tennessee. He was fifty-seven or fifty-eight years old.

JOHN CARPENTER CARTER was born on December 19, 1837 in Waynesboro, Georgia. He attended the University of Virginia from 1854 to 1856 and studied law under Judge Adam Carruthers at Cumberland University in Lebanon, Tennessee. He ended up marrying the judge's daughter and becoming an instructor at the school. He established a law practice in Memphis in 1860 and was there when the war began.

Carter joined the Tennessee Militia as a private on January 13, 1861. He became a first lieutenant in the 22nd Tennessee (in Confederate service) on August 18 but transferred to the 38th Tennessee Infantry Regiment. He was promoted to captain on October 7. He fought at Shiloh, where he was highly praised for his courage. When the regiment was reorganized on April 25, Carter was elected colonel.

He had a talent for leadership. Colonel James D. Porter recalled that John Carter had a "wonderful gentleness of manner, coupled with a dauntless courage." Another officer said of him: "His habits are unsurpassed in the army for sobriety and morality."

John C. Carter fought in the Battle of Perryville (where he was wounded), the retreat to middle Tennessee, and the Second Battle of Murfreesboro, where he was wounded again. He also fought at Chickamauga and in the Knoxville and Atlanta campaigns.

Colonel Carter's tactical skills, courage, and presence of mind impressed his superiors, and he was promoted to brigadier general (temporary rank) on July 8, 1864, to rank from July 7, and served as an acting commander of Benjamin F. Cheatham's division in the Battle of Jonesboro.

When the Army of Tennessee was reorganized after the fall of Atlanta, Carter's brigade was broken up, and Carter was given command of Brigadier General George Earl Maney's old brigade. At Franklin, on November 30, on General John Bell Hood's orders, Carter charged the field fortifications at the center of the Union line. He was seriously wounded. Taken to the Harrison House, Carter succumbed on December 10, 1864. In nine days, he would have been twenty-seven years old. He is buried at Rose Hill Cemetery in Columbia, Tennessee.

JAMES RONALD CHALMERS was born in Halifax County, Virginia, on January 11, 1831, but his family moved to Jackson, Tennessee, and then to Holly Springs, Mississippi, when he was just a child. His father was a prominent cotton planter, lawyer, and U.S. senator.

Chalmers attended South Carolina College, from which he graduated in 1851. He settled in Holly Springs, read law, and was admitted to the bar in 1853. In 1858, Chalmers was elected district attorney and was a delegate to the Mississippi Secession Convention in 1861. He firmly supported states' rights and secession.

Chalmers joined the Confederate Army as a captain almost as soon as the nation was formed. He was elected colonel of the 9th Mississippi Infantry Regiment on March 27, 1861. Initially posted to Pensacola, he took part in the unsuccessful attack on Santa Rosa Island during the night of October 8–9. Though the attack failed, his performance in the field impressed Braxton Bragg, who praised him throughout the war. Chalmers was promoted to brigadier general on Feburary 10, 1862, to rank from February 13. He fought at Shiloh, where he led several attacks and advanced farther against the Yankee line than any Confederate unit. He fought in the Siege of Corinth, the retreat to Tupelo, and the defense of northern Mississippi. He later joined Bragg in Kentucky.

On New Year's Eve, Chalmers was wounded by an exploding shell in the Second Battle of Murfreesboro and was carried from the battlefield with a concussion.

On March 9, 1863, General Chalmers was given command of the two northern tiers of counties in Mississippi. Although he had only a skeleton force, he skirmished with Union cavalry and prevented them from penetrating farther south while simultaneously organizing a new cavalry brigade and briefly commanding a division in Stephen Dill Lee's cavalry corps. In January 1864, he became a division commander in Nathan Bedford Forrest's cavalry corps.

Chalmers was a short man who was affectionately called "Little 'un" by his men, who liked and admired him. He was also a great orator and a fierce warrior. He played a major role in many of Forrest's victories in 1864, including battles in western Kentucky, western Tennessee, and northern Mississippi. Chalmers further distinguished himself in General John Bell Hood's Tennessee Campaign, where he helped cover the army's retreat and personally killed a Northerner in hand-to-hand combat.

On February 13, 1865, General Forrest placed Chalmers in charge of all Confederate cavalry and partisans in northern Mississippi and western Tennessee. He surrendered at Gainesville, Alabama, and was paroled on May 10, 1865.

James Chalmers returned home and became a leader in the home rule movement and the "Red Shirts" paramilitary force in Mississippi. In 1875, he was elected to the Mississippi State Senate and was reelected the following year. He was elected to Congress in 1876, serving from 1877 to 1881. He also served parts of two contested terms. He was defeated in his attempt at reelection in 1884.

Following his failed reelection bid, James R. Chalmers quit politics and moved to Memphis, where he set up a successful legal practice. He died in Memphis on April 9, 1898, and was buried in historic Elmwood Cemetery. He was sixty-seven years old.

JOHN RANDOLPH CHAMBLISS, JR., was born on January 23, 1833, in Hicksford, Greensville County, Virginia. His father was a lawyer, a wealthy planter, and a member of the Confederate Congress.

Chambliss graduated from West Point in 1853. He was commissioned a brevet second lieutenant in the mounted rifles and was sent to Carlisle Barracks,

Pennsylvania, but resigned his commission in 1854 and returned home, where he became a planter.

Chambliss served as an officer in the Virginia state militia and was a military aide to Virginia governors Henry A. Wise and John Letcher. Chambliss was colonel of the 41st Virginia Infantry Regiment in May 1861 and became commander of the 13th Virginia Cavalry on July 13. He joined the Army of Northern Virginia for the Maryland Campaign in 1862, where he was placed in command of an ad hoc mixed brigade of cavalry and infantry forces on the Rappahannock River. During the Sharpsburg Campaign, Chambliss turned back Union probes and performed so well that he received a commendation from Robert E. Lee. He later participated in the Fredericksburg Campaign.

On June 9, 1863, he fought at Brandy Station. Confederate Brigadier General Rooney Lee was wounded in the engagement, and his successor in command, Colonel Solomon Williams, was killed soon after. Chambliss assumed command of the brigade and led it during the Gettysburg Campaign. On June 17, during the battles of Aldie and Middleburg, he overran the 1st Rhode Island Cavalry and took 160 prisoners. On June 30, he routed U.S. General Hugh Judson Kilpatrick's brigade at Hanover, chased it through the town, and captured its ambulances, several wagons, and a number of prisoners. Subsequently, on July 3, he fought in the cavalry action at Gettysburg, in what is now called East Cavalry Field. The battle was fierce but inconclusive. Chambliss's brigade covered the retreat of Lee's army into Virginia.

Chambliss continued to command Rooney Lee's brigade during the Bristoe Campaign of October and November 1863. He was promoted to brigadier general on January 9, 1864, to rank from December 19, 1863.

General Chambliss was widely regarded as one of the best cavalry commanders in an army known for its outstanding cavalry commanders. He fought in the Overland Campaign between the Rapidan and the James rivers. On August 16, 1864, while leading his men in a battle on Charles City Road, north of the James, John R. Chambliss, Jr., was killed by a Union volley during the Second Battle of Deep Bottom. An old friend and West Point classmate, Union General David M.

Gregg, saw to it that Chambliss's body was recovered and sent home. He was buried in the Chambliss family cemetery in Emporia, Virginia. He was thirty-one years old.

BENJAMIN FRANKLIN CHEATHAM was born on  Westover Plantation in Nashville, Tennessee, on October 20, 1820. His family was of Tennessee aristocracy, and Westover, at one time, covered three thousand acres.

Young Benjamin became a planter and served with the 1st Tennessee Volunteer Infantry Regiment in Mexico as a captain. After fighting in the Battle of Monterrey, he was named colonel of the 3rd Tennessee Infantry, which he led in the capture of Mexico City.

Physically, Cheatham was noted for his extraordinary strength. He was five feet eight and about two hundred pounds, with light brown hair, a thick moustache, and slightly rounded shoulders. He was known for his imperturbable good humor and his colorful language, and he enjoyed his whiskey and women. He was popular with his men because he talked with them, looked out for them, and was a good administrator. Politically, he was a pro-secessionist Democrat.

Benjamin Cheatham joined the Provisional Army of Tennessee as a major general on May 9, 1861. He became a brigadier general in the Confederate Army on July 9 and fought in the Battle of Belmont, Missouri. He was promoted to major general on March 11, 1862, to rank from March 10, and was given command of a division, which he led at Shiloh. He was slightly wounded, probably on the second day, and had three horses shot out from under him. He fought at Perryville and the Second Battle of Murfreesboro, which was his worst battle. He performed sluggishly and launched uncoordinated, piecemeal attacks. Observers later recalled that he was drinking heavily during the engagement.

Cheatham redeemed his reputation in subsequent battles, leading his division in the Battle of Chickamauga and the Siege of Chattanooga, where he briefly commanded a corps. In 1864, Cheatham fought in the Atlanta Campaign and inflicted heavy casualties on Sherman's legions during the Battle of Kennesaw Mountain. During the Battle of Ezra Church (July 28), Lieutenant General Alexander Stewart was wounded, and Cheatham assumed command of his corps, even though he was also wounded. After the fall of Atlanta, he took command of William Hardee's old corps.

Following the Battle of Spring Hill on November 29, the Yankees escaped because Cheatham did not cut the Columbia-Nashville Turnpike and block their retreat; it was the last chance for the Confederate Army in the West to inflict a serious defeat on the Northerners. General John Bell Hood accused Generals Cheatham and Patrick Cleburne of dereliction of duty for failing to attack. Cheatham argued that no such attack was ordered. The controversy continues to this day, but the weight of evidence supports Cheatham. Cheatham then commanded a division in the Carolinas Campaign and capitulated at the Bennett Place on April 26, 1865.

Following the surrender, Cheatham returned to his farm. He ran for Congress in 1872 but was defeated. He was appointed warden of a Tennessee state prison, a position he held for four years. Finally, in 1885, he was appointed postmaster of Nashville, a job he held until his death from heart disease in Nashville on September 4, 1886, at age sixty-five.

His funeral was said to be the largest ever held in the Tennessee capital city. He was buried in the historic Mount Olivet Cemetery in Nashville.

JAMES CHESNUT, JR., was born on January 18, 1815, on Mulberry Plantation near Camden, South Carolina. At one time, his father owned 448 slaves. Chesnut enrolled at the College of New Jersey (Princeton) in 1832 and graduated with highest honors in 1835. He returned home, read law, and was admitted to the bar in 1837. He set up a practice in Camden.

In 1840, Chesnut married Mary Boykin Miller (1823–86), the daughter of a former governor who became the most famous diarist of the Civil War. Theirs was not always a happy marriage. She was highly opinionated and emotional and viewed her husband as too cool and reserved. Most of the time, however, their relationship was warm and supportive. They had no children.

Chesnut was a fine orator. He served in the state house of representatives from 1840 to 1845 and from 1850 to 1851, and in the state senate from 1854 to 1858. The South Carolina legislature elected him to the U.S. Senate in 1858. After Lincoln was elected president, Chesnut resigned his seat on November 10—the first Southern senator to do so. He was elected to the Provisional Congress of the Confederate States of America in January 1861 and helped draft the Confederate Constitution. He supported the Davis administration.

After serving as an aide to General G. T. Beauregard during the Battle of First Manassas, Chesnut served as commander of the South Carolina Militia with the rank of major general. In the fall of 1862, Jefferson Davis (a personal friend from their time together in the U.S. Senate) asked him to return to Richmond to serve as his military advisor with the rank of colonel in the Confederate cavalry. While Chesnut was an immense help to the president from late 1862 to April 23, 1864, his contemporaries viewed him as amiable and capable, but not brilliant.

In the spring of 1864, Colonel Chesnut asked for field duty. Davis promoted him to brigadier general on April 23, 1864, and gave him command of the reserve forces of South Carolina, which he directed until the end of the war. After the fall of Atlanta, he assumed command of a brigade of reserves (about 1,600 men). He surrendered on or about May 10, 1865, although there is no record of his parole.

After the war, General Chesnut reopened his law office, and he and his wife lived at the Chesnut Cottage in Columbia, South Carolina. He devoted his energies to his law practice and to ending the corrupt carpetbagger rule in South Carolina, although he never again sought public office for himself.

James Chesnut, Jr., died at his home, Sarsfield, in Camden, South Carolina, on February 1, 1885, at age seventy. He was buried in Knights Hill Cemetery in Camden.

ROBERT HALL "BOB" CHILTON was born on February 25, 1815, in Loudoun County, Virginia. His family was locally prominent, and he was able to secure an appointment to West Point in 1833, graduating in 1837. Chilton was commissioned a brevet second lieutenant in the dragoons and sent to the Western frontier, where he fought in skirmishes against the Osage Indians. He served in Kansas, western Texas, and in the Choctaw Nation area of the Indian Territory. He fought in the Mexican War and was brevetted for gallantry at Buena Vista. After the Mexican War, he returned to frontier duty. In 1854, he became a staff officer, serving variously in Washington, D.C., New York City, Detroit, and San Antonio. When he learned that Virginia had seceded, he resigned his commission and returned to the Old Dominion, where he was appointed a lieutenant colonel in the Regular Army of the Confederacy. He served as adjutant to Robert E. Lee, an old personal friend. He was promoted to colonel on October 12. In June 1862, when Lee became commander of the Army of Northern Virginia, he became Lee's chief of staff.

Lee's generals did not think much of Robert Chilton's competence. He clashed repeatedly with members of Congress and with senior commanders, and even Lee chided him for interfering too much in other officers' duties. Nevertheless, Lee firmly supported Chilton's nomination for promotion to brigadier general on October 20, 1862, but the nomination was rejected by the Senate on April 11, 1863. He reverted to the rank of colonel and was not renominated for brigadier general until December 22, 1863, with a date of rank of December 21; this time he was confirmed on February 16, 1864.

On April 1, 1864, Chilton was transferred, at his own request, to a staff position as inspector general of the Army of Northern Virginia in Richmond. He resigned his commission as a brigadier general and accepted a demotion to lieutenant colonel. He was promoted to colonel (February 20, 1865).

In May 1864, the Union Army of the James raided the critical Richmond and Petersburg Railroad. In this emergency situation, General Chilton assumed command of an infantry brigade and some cavalry. He launched an attack on May 10, routed the Federals (who outnumbered him), and secured the railroad. For this, he was praised, but there was no thought of giving him a permanent field command. He surrendered with Johnston's army on April 26, 1865, and was paroled at Greensboro on May 1.

After the war, Chilton moved to Columbus, Georgia, where he became president of a manufacturing company. He died of "apoplexy" (a stroke) on February 18, 1879, in Columbus, Georgia. He was sixty-three years old. Robert H. Chilton was buried in Hollywood Cemetery, Richmond, Virginia.

THOMAS JAMES CHURCHILL was born on March 10, 1824, on his father's farm near Louisville, Kentucky. He attended public schools and graduated from St. Mary's College in Bardstown, Kentucky, in 1844, at the age of twenty. He studied law at Transylvania University in Lexington.

When the Mexican War began, Churchill enlisted in the 1st Kentucky Mounted Rifles, rising to the rank of first lieutenant. While on a scouting mission in January 1847, he was captured by an enemy cavalry patrol and sent to Mexico City, where he remained a prisoner of war until near the end of the conflict, when he was exchanged and rejoined his regiment. Thomas Churchill became a planter and was appointed postmaster of Little Rock by President Buchanan in 1857.

Churchill raised the 1st Arkansas Mounted Rifles and was elected colonel on June 9, 1861. He distinguished himself in the Battle of Wilson's Creek, where he had two horses shot from under him. He also fought in the Battle of Pea Ridge. Meanwhile, he was promoted to brigadier general on March 5, 1862, to rank from March 4, and ordered

Regiment. In July 1861, the regiment was sent Virginia. Brevard was promoted to major on August 14. In September, the 2nd Florida fought in the Siege of Yorktown and the Battle of Williamsburg. After these engagements the regiment was reorganized and held new elections for officers. Brevard was not reelected. He returned to Florida and raised Brevard's Partisan Rangers, a cavalry battalion that was later redesignated the 2nd Florida Partisan Ranger Battalion with Brevard as its major. It fought in numerous small skirmishes around Jacksonville in 1863, and Brevard performed well. He was promoted to lieutenant colonel on August 12, 1863, to rank from June 24.

The Partisan Rangers mostly operated independently in South Florida and along the Floridian coast, patrolling, repelling Yankee probes, rounding up deserters, guarding outposts, and protecting cattle herds, which were a major source of food for the main Confederate armies.

In May 1864, while the Army of Northern Virginia was engaged in the Overland Campaign, Brevard's men were ordered to Richmond. He fought in the last stages of the Battle of Cold Harbor. On June 8, with Ulysses Grant temporarily checked, the Florida units underwent a reorganization, and Theodore Brevard was appointed colonel of the newly formed 11th Florida Infantry Regiment. He fought in the Siege of Petersburg. Meanwhile, Brevard's division commander, General William Mahone, was dissatisfied with General Joseph Finegan, whom he considered lax. He told President Davis that Brevard was the only one who could lead the Florida Brigade effectively. Accordingly, Finegan was transferred back to Florida, and President Davis promoted Theodore Brevard to brigadier general on March 28, to rank from March 22. He was never confirmed by the Senate, which did not meet after March 22. He did not even learn of his appointment until after the war. For this reason, David Lang, the senior regimental commander, replaced Finegan as brigade commander. Theodore Brevard commanded what was left of his regiment until he was captured in the Battle of Sayler's Creek on April 6, 1865. He was sent to the Old Capitol Prison in Washington, D.C., and then to the Johnson's Island prison camp, where he was paroled on July 25.

east. In May, he commanded 2,332 men in the Siege of Corinth. He took part in the retreat to Tupelo and commanded a small division in Edmund Kirby Smith's victory in the Battle of Richmond, Kentucky. In that battle, Churchill launched a surprise flanking attack that was a decisive factor. On December 10, he was sent to command the garrison at Arkansas Post (4,900 men), which fell to U.S. General John Alexander McClernand and his 33,000 men on January 11, 1863.

Churchill spent three months in prison at Camp Chase, Ohio, where he was treated badly. He was exchanged in April 1863. In July, he was given command of a brigade in Patrick Cleburne's division, but he was relieved on December 10 and sent back to the Trans-Mississippi Department, where he was named commander of a Texas cavalry brigade. On March 24, 1864, he was given command of an Arkansas infantry division.

During the Red River Campaign, General Churchill fought in the Battle of Pleasant Hill on April 9, 1864, where his performance was poor. General Richard Taylor later commented, rightly, that General Churchill was a conspicuous gentleman but "unlucky at war." After Pleasant Hill, Churchill led his division in the Battle of Jenkins' Ferry, Arkansas, on April 30, 1864.

Churchill's command remained relatively inactive for the rest of the war. He was finally promoted to major general on March 18, 1865, to rank from March 17. He surrendered a few weeks later and was paroled at Shreveport on June 7.

After the war, Churchill returned to his farm near Little Rock. He remained politically active and was elected state treasurer, serving from 1875 to 1881. In the election of 1880, he was elected governor, serving from January 13, 1881, to January 13, 1883.

Churchill's administration was crippled by the discovery of financial discrepancies during his tenure as state treasurer. The former general eventually paid $23,973 to the state, although he insisted this was not an admission of guilt. As a result of the scandal, Churchill left politics and retired to his farm.

Churchill was a member of the United Confederate Veterans organization and in 1904 became major general of the Arkansas Division. General Thomas J. Churchill died in Little Rock on May 14, 1905, at age eighty-one, after a long illness. At his request, he was buried in his Confederate uniform in Mount Holly Cemetery, Little Rock, with full military honors.

JAMES HOLT CLANTON was born on January 8, 1827, in Columbia County, Georgia. His family moved to Macon County, Alabama, in 1835. He enrolled at the University of Alabama at Tuscaloosa but cut his education short because of the outbreak of the Mexican War. He joined the Palmetto Regiment as a private and was with it in the battles for Mexico City.

After the war, Clanton returned to Alabama, studied law in Tuskegee, and was admitted to the bar in 1850. He settled in Montgomery, established his practice, was elected to the legislature, and was an elector for the John Bell–Edward Everett ticket in 1860. He opposed secession but joined the Confederate Army after Alabama left the Union.

Clanton was initially posted to the Pensacola sector and was promoted to captain of cavalry on November 12. He returned to Alabama, organized the 1st Alabama Cavalry, and was elected colonel on December 3. He distinguished himself in the Battle of Shiloh. Clanton also fought at Farmington (where he commanded a brigade), in the Siege of Corinth, and the retreat to Tupelo. He became an aide to Alabama Governor John G. Shorter later that year. In early 1863, he established a headquarters at Montgomery, raised three regiments of infantry and one of cavalry, and on May 1, 1863, was ordered to take his command to Pollard, Alabama.

James Clanton was promoted to brigadier general on November 18, 1863, to rank from November 16. He and his men were transferred to

Leonidas Polk's command and operated in eastern Mississippi and northern Alabama.

General Clanton's brigade was not considered reliable; General Polk himself found Clanton "very efficient and enterprising," but Joseph E. Johnston considered him incompetent. He refused to allow Clanton's brigade to join his army in April 1864. It remained in northern Alabama and skirmished with Union cavalry several times in the summer and fall of 1864. That winter, he defeated a Union cavalry force that had hoped to attack Mobile from Pensacola.

On March 25, 1865, during the Battle of Bluff Springs, Florida, Clanton was badly wounded and was captured, along with 118 of his men. The rest of his small brigade scattered. He was paroled at Mobile on May 25, 1865, and returned home.

General Clanton resumed his law practice and was active in the effort to restore home rule to the South. He was allegedly the head of the Ku Klux Klan in Alabama. On September 27, 1871, in Knoxville, Tennessee, the intoxicated son of a pro-Unionist judge fired both barrels of a double-barreled shotgun into Clanton's chest, killing him. James Clanton was forty-four years old. A rigged trial followed, in which the assassin was acquitted within five minutes. Alabama newspapers denounced the trial as a farce.

The general was buried in Oakwood Cemetery, Montgomery, Alabama. His tombstone reads: "James Holt Clanton 1827–1871, Brigadier General, C.S.A. Leader of Democratic and Conservative Party of Alabama, Bulwark of His People Against Radical Reconstruction. Knight Without Fear and Without Reproach."

CHARLES CLARK was born on May 24, 1811, in Lebanon, Ohio, near Cincinnati. Of old Puritan stock, his ancestors came over on the *Mayflower*. He graduated from Augusta College, Kentucky, before moving to Mississippi, where he taught school in Natchez and Yazoo County. He became a lawyer and was twice elected to the

Mississippi House of Representatives as a Whig, serving from 1838 to 1839 and from 1842 to 1843. During the Mexican War, Clark organized an infantry company which became part of the 2nd Mississippi. Clark was elected colonel of the regiment in October 1847 and led it in Mexico, although he did not see combat.

After he returned home, Colonel Clark moved to Bolivar County and worked as a planter and an attorney. Meanwhile, he acquired five thousand acres near Beulah, Mississippi, and built a mansion called Doro on the property.

Colonel Clark was a delegate to the Mississippi Constitutional Convention in 1851 and served as a state representative from 1856 to 1861. He ran for Congress as a Democrat in 1857 but was defeated. Initially opposed to secession, by 1861 he had decided that it was in Mississippi's best interest to leave the Union.

Clark was appointed brigadier general in the Mississippi militia in January 1861 and in April was promoted to major general (state rank). He was appointed a brigadier general in the Confederate Army on May 22, 1861. Clark was stationed in Kentucky and fought at Shiloh, where he commanded a division and was severely wounded in the right shoulder on April 6, 1862. On August 5, he led a division in the Battle of Baton Rouge. He attacked with "great vigor," according to General John C. Breckinridge, until a bullet struck his right thigh. He was so badly injured that General Earl Van Dorn reported that he was mortally wounded. He was left on the battlefield at his own request and was taken prisoner.

General Clark's wound crippled him for life, and he could not walk without crutches. He was exchanged in February 1863 but resigned his commission on October 31, 1863, because he was no longer fit to lead troops in the field. Meanwhile, Clark ran for governor and won easily. He was inaugurated on November 16, 1863. Although he was a fine governor, he could do little to influence the course of the war.

Governor Clark was arrested on May 22, 1865, and was sent to Fort Pulaski, Georgia. His imprisonment was brief. After his release, he returned to Doro and Bolivar County, where he resumed his legal practice. He partially recouped his wealth and in 1871 purchased Routhland, an antebellum mansion in Natchez, which is still extant.

In 1876, with Reconstruction over, Clark became a judge and served on the bench until his death. He died of pneumonia on December 18, 1877, in Bolivar County, Mississippi, at age sixty-six. He was buried in Clark Cemetery, Beulah, Bolivar County, Mississippi.

JOHN BULLOCK CLARK, JR., was born on January 14, 1831, in Fayette, Missouri, the son of a prominent attorney and political figure who became a Confederate senator. Clark attended Fayette Academy and the University of Missouri before heading for California. He then attended law school at Harvard and graduated in 1854. He was admitted to the bar in 1855 and practiced until the outbreak of the Civil War.

Clark joined the Confederate Army as a lieutenant in the 6th Missouri Infantry (state troops) in 1861 and was soon promoted to captain and company commander. He fought in several battles, including Carthage, Wilson's Creek (where he was slightly wounded), and Springfield. Promoted to major in July, he assumed command of the 1st Missouri Infantry when its colonel was wounded.

He commanded the 3rd Missouri State Guard Division (six small regiments) at Pea Ridge in March 1862 and was officially commended by General Thomas Hindman. On June 28, John B. Clark, Jr., became the colonel and commander of the 6th State Guard Regiment. He was mustered into Confederate service as colonel and commander of the 9th Missouri Infantry on November 16, 1862.

In early 1863, Clark's command was assigned to defend lower Arkansas. In June 1863, it was harassing Union shipping on the Mississippi River. It took part in the unsuccessful defense of Little Rock in September 1863, after which it was stationed at Arkadelphia.

Clark was promoted to brigadier general on March 12, 1864, to date from March 6, and continued to serve in Arkansas and Missouri for the rest of the war. He was slightly wounded in the arm during the Battle of Jenkins' Ferry on April 30, 1864, "while leading his brigade with his accustomed skill and daring," according to his division commander. He assumed command of General John S. Marmaduke's division after Marmaduke was captured during the Battle of Mine Creek on October 25, 1864, and led it for the rest of the war. He was paroled at Shreveport on June 7, 1865.

Despite a lack of military training and background, General Clark was a fine brigade and division commander.

After the war, Clark returned to Fayette and resumed his law practice. He was elected to Congress and served from 1873 to 1883. Defeated in his 1882 reelection attempt, he remained in Washington and was the clerk of the U.S. House of Representatives from 1883 to 1889, when he retired from politics.

General Clark practiced law in the nation's capital until his death. He suffered paralysis during the last year of his life. He died in Washington, D.C., on September 7, 1903. He was seventy-two years old. John B. Clark, Jr., is buried in Rock Creek Cemetery, Washington, D.C.

HENRY DELAMAR CLAYTON, SR., was born on March 7, 1827, in Pulaski County, Georgia. His family moved to Lee County, Alabama, in the 1830s. He graduated from Emory and Henry College in Virginia, moved to Eufaula, Alabama, and read law. He was admitted to the bar in 1849 and opened a law office in Clayton, Alabama. He was elected to the Alabama legislature twice, serving from 1857 to 1861. He also joined the state militia as a private and in August 1860 was elected colonel of the 3rd Alabama Infantry Regiment, a militia unit.

When the 1st Alabama Infantry Regiment was mustered into Confederate service in Pensacola on March 28, 1861, Clayton was its first colonel. The regiment helped capture Fort Barrancas and performed well in the unsuccessful attempt to take Fort Pickens on October 8–9.

Clayton resigned his commission in January 1862, returning to Alabama. He raised a new regiment, the 39th Alabama, and became its first colonel (May 15). He took part in Braxton Bragg's Kentucky Campaign of 1862, and he fought in the Second Battle of Murfreesboro, where he was severely wounded in the right shoulder on the first day. It took Clayton three months to recover. On April 23, 1863, on the recommendation of General Bragg, Clayton was promoted to brigadier general with a date of rank of April 22.

Clayton participated in the Tullahoma Campaign and fought at Chickamauga, where, on the second day of the battle, his brigade overran a Wisconsin regiment and took 646 prisoners, but he was severely wounded by grapeshot in the process. He did not recover until spring.

General Clayton took part in the Atlanta Campaign, fighting in several battles. Now considered an experienced and effective leader, Henry Clayton was given command of General Alexander P. Stewart's old division. He was promoted to major general (temporary rank) on July 8, 1864, to date from July 7.

Clayton had three horses shot out from under him at Ezra Church on July 28. His troops were part of John Bell Hood's Tennessee Campaign and captured Florence, Alabama, on October 30, securing the Tennessee River crossings for the army. He arrived too late to participate in the disastrous attacks at Franklin. He fought in the Battle of Nashville and distinguished himself yet again in the retreat from Tennessee, forming part of the rear guard and saving much of the army's wagons and artillery. Clayton fought in the Carolinas Campaign, including the Battle of Bentonville. He surrendered at Durham Station on April 26, 1865, and was paroled at Greensboro on May 1.

General Clayton returned home and was elected circuit judge, but Federal officials removed him from office in 1868 because of his high Confederate rank. He returned to his plantation and his law office at Eufaula, where he opposed the violence of the Ku Klux Klan. In 1874, with Reconstruction ending, he was reelected circuit court judge and reelected again in 1880. In 1886, trustees of the University of Alabama elected him president and professor of international law. Henry D.

Clayton, Sr., died in Tuscaloosa on October 3, 1889, at age sixty-two. He was buried in Fairview Cemetery in Eufaula, Alabama.

PATRICK RONAYNE CLEBURNE (pronounced KLAY-burn) was born on March 17, 1828, at Bride Park Cottage near Desertmore, County Cork, Ireland. He attended a Church of Ireland boarding school nearby at Ballincollig.

After his father's death, Patrick was forced to drop out of school for financial reasons. Ronayne, as his family called him, became a druggist's apprentice. At age seventeen, he enlisted in the British Army and was stationed in Ireland during the Potato Famine violence. Shy and reserved by nature, and very serious most of the time, Cleburne proved to be a useful if inconspicuous soldier and was promoted to corporal. He purchased his discharge from the army in September 1849 and sailed for America three days later.

Cleburne was eager to assimilate. He ended up managing a drugstore in Helena, Arkansas, studied law in his spare time, and was admitted to the bar in 1856. He was a good attorney and became quite prosperous.

Pat Cleburne joined the "Yell Rifles," a militia company formed by local plantation owners, who promptly elected him captain. (The company was named after former Arkansas governor and Mexican War hero Archibald Yell.) On May 14, 1861, he was elected commander of the 1st (later 15th) Arkansas Infantry Regiment. Cleburne's men found him a tough but fair disciplinarian.

Good at drill, he was given command of a brigade on October 28 and was promoted to brigadier general on March 5, 1862, to rank from March 4. He led his command in ferocious fighting at Shiloh. Later that year, General Cleburne played a major role in the Battle of Richmond, Kentucky, where a Union ball ripped through his left cheek, took away some teeth, and exited through his open mouth. He was back in action at Perryville, where an artillery shell exploded near him, killing his horse and wounding him in the leg.

He was promoted to major general on December 20, 1862, with a date of rank of December 13. Pat Cleburne immediately became the best divisional commander in the Army of Tennessee and possibly the entire Confederate Army. President Jefferson Davis, who had promoted Cleburne reluctantly (because of his foreign birth), later dubbed him "the Stonewall of the West" and never had occasion to regret promoting the Irishman. General Cleburne distinguished himself in every campaign in which he participated, including the Second Battle of Murfreesboro, the Tullahoma Campaign, the Battle of Chickamauga, and the Siege of Chattanooga, where he smashed several of Sherman's formations.

On January 2, 1864, Cleburne proposed freeing any slaves who would fight for the South. His proposal was strategically brilliant, but his fellow generals vetoed it, and Joseph E. Johnston suppressed the idea.

General Cleburne continued to excel as a combat commander during the Atlanta Campaign. He directed William J. Hardee's corps in the Battle of Jonesboro, where he did not do as well as he did commanding a division. He was back leading his old command during the Tennessee Campaign in late 1864.

On November 30, during the Battle of Franklin, Cleburne had two horses shot out from under him and led the charge on foot. He was fifty yards from the U.S. line when a single Union bullet went through his heart. He died immediately. He was thirty-six years old. His fiancé learned of his death from a newspaper vendor.

Cleburne's body was taken by wagon to Columbia, Tennessee, and interred in the paupers' section. He was soon moved, however, to the small cemetery at Ash Hill, Lucius Polk's plantation. After the war, his remains were moved yet again to the Confederate section of Maple Hill Cemetery, Helena, Arkansas, where they still lie.

THOMAS LANIER CLINGMAN was born in Huntsville in Surry (now Yadkin) County, North Carolina, on July 27, 1812. His maternal great-grandfather was a Cherokee chief. He entered the University of

North Carolina as a sophomore in 1829, graduated at the top of his class in 1832, and became a lawyer.

In 1835, Clingman was elected to the North Carolina House of Representatives as a Whig but was defeated for reelection in 1836. He moved to the mountainous region of North Carolina soon after and settled near Asheville in Buncombe County. He set up a law practice and remained there his entire life.

In 1840, Clingman was elected to the state senate. In 1842, he was elected to Congress and was continually reelected, serving from 1843 to 1858, with one two-year break (he lost the election of 1844). He served in the U.S. Senate from 1858 to 1861.

He was present in Charleston, South Carolina, when Fort Sumter was bombarded on April 12–13, 1861. Clingman was expelled from the Senate on July 11, 1861. He was the last Southerner to leave Congress. On August 13, 1861, he was elected colonel of the 25th North Carolina Infantry Regiment, opting for field duty despite having no military training or experience. Clingman and his regiment were stationed in Kinston as part of the Army of Pamlico, and he became commander of the District of Pamlico and Cape Fear. He was promoted to brigadier general on September 17, 1862, to rank from May 17. Clingman served in North and South Carolina in 1861, 1862, and 1863, mostly defending Goldsboro.

Thomas Clingman's career as a brigadier was not distinguished. His brigade was not a particularly good one and was criticized by Generals D. H. Hill and W. H. Chase Whiting. When possible, Clingman's superior officers preferred to use the brigade where it would not see much action.

Ordered to Virginia in the winter of 1863–64, he took part in the battles of Drewry's Bluff and Cold Harbor (where a projectile grazed his head), the Siege of Petersburg, and in engagements in defense of the Petersburg and Weldon Railroad. On August 19, 1864, during the Battle of Globe Tavern, he was seriously wounded in the leg and did not return to duty until near the end of the war. By then his brigade had returned to North Carolina. He fought in the Battle of Bentonville.

Although he was undoubtedly a fearless man, Thomas Clingman was a poor brigade commander, regarded as arrogant, conceited, and unteachable.

After the war, Clingman devoted himself to the practice of law, the economic development of western North Carolina, and exploring and measuring the peaks of the Allegheny Mountain range. Clingmans Dome, one of the highest peaks in the eastern United States, is named for him. He also traveled extensively on the lecture circuit.

Thomas L. Clingman died November 3, 1897, in Morganton, North Carolina, after a lengthy illness. He was eighty-five years old. He is buried in Riverside Cemetery, Asheville, North Carolina. General Clingman never married, but he did have one son, Thomas Jefferson Eatman (1856–1938), who became a Baptist preacher.

HOWELL COBB, SR., was born on September 7, 1815, at the Cherry Hill Plantation in Jefferson County, Georgia, but his family moved to Athens when he was a child. One of his younger brothers was future Confederate general Thomas R. R. Cobb. Howell attended Franklin College, graduated in 1834, was admitted to the bar in 1836, and became solicitor general for the Western Judicial Circuit of Georgia.

He ran for Congress in 1842 and was elected, serving from 1843 to 1851. In 1849, the U.S. House of Representatives selected Cobb as its Speaker. He left the House to become governor of Georgia (1851 to 1853). He returned to the House in 1855. He was known for being cheerful and gregarious, as well as a gifted humorist and storyteller who loved fine food and wine, which showed in his girth. He also loved to hear himself talk. Beneath his image as a jolly, fat man lay a shrewd, intelligent, cunning, and ambitious politician who wanted to be president of the United States. He was a middle-of-the-road

Democrat, firmly opposed to secession and nullification and favoring a compromise on the high tariffs favored by the North and the low tariffs favored by the South.

In 1857, Cobb became James Buchanan's secretary of the treasury. He became a secessionist only after Abraham Lincoln was elected president, because he regarded Lincoln as a purely sectional candidate. Cobb resigned his cabinet post on December 10, 1860.

In early February 1861, Cobb presided over the Confederate Constitutional Convention in Montgomery, Alabama, and for a time it appeared that he might be chosen president of the Confederate States of America, but the delegates opted for Jefferson Davis instead.

Cobb disdained politics during the war. He was commissioned colonel of the 16th Georgia Infantry Regiment when it was formed on July 15, 1861. It was sent to the Virginia Peninsula, where Cobb was promoted to brigadier general on February 12, 1862. He participated in the Peninsula Campaign, where on April 16 he rallied the Southern troops in the Battle of Lee's Mill (Dam Number 1). Cobb took this as proof that "political generals" could be just as effective as professional soldiers.

He fought in the Seven Days Battles and in the invasion of Maryland, where his brigade was routed at Crampton's Gap on September 14. Cobb was severely criticized by Lafayette McLaws and others for his dismal performance. He missed the Battle of Sharpsburg because of a foot infection.

After Crampton's Gap, Cobb must have sensed that any hopes he had for advancement in Robert E. Lee's army were finished. He was also worried about his family back in Georgia, so he asked for a transfer. General Lee offered no objections, and Cobb was named commander of the District of Middle Florida on November 11, 1862. He was named commander of the Georgia Militia and promoted to major general on September 19, 1863, to rank from September 9, 1862. His title was changed to commander of the Georgia Reserves in December 1863.

Cobb's duties were mainly administrative until the Atlanta Campaign of 1864 and William T. Sherman's March to the Sea, when he commanded the Georgia Reserve Corps. During his drive to Savannah,

Sherman maliciously burned Cobb's plantation and seized his property, instructing his subordinates to "spare nothing."

General Cobb directed Rebel forces in the Battle of Columbus, which was the last major action of the war east of the Mississippi. He surrendered his troops and the city of Macon, Georgia, on April 20, 1865. He was arrested by Federal officers, but President Andrew Johnson learned about it and paroled him before he reached prison.

Financially, Howell Cobb, Sr., was ruined by the war. He returned to Athens and resumed his law practice. On October 9, 1868, he died in the lobby of the Fifth Avenue Hotel while on a visit to New York City. His body was returned to Athens, Georgia, where he was buried in Oconee Hill Cemetery.

THOMAS READE ROOTES "TOM" COBB was born on April 10, 1823, at Cherry Hill, his father's plantation in Jefferson County, Georgia. He weighed twenty-one and a half pounds at birth. His older brother was Howell Cobb. Tom lived in Athens most of his life. He graduated from Franklin College at the top of his class in 1841 and was admitted to the bar in 1842.

Like his brother, Tom was a moderate Democrat who opposed both Northern radicals and Southern Fire-Eaters. Unlike his brother, he did not want to hold public office. He devoted himself to furthering his legal career and was quite successful. By 1860, he was worth $120,000 ($3,763,084 in 2020 money) and owned twenty-three slaves.

Thomas Cobb was a prominent legal and Constitutional scholar who fervently defended the institution of slavery. Like his brother, he opposed secession until Abraham Lincoln was elected president; then he changed his position.

Cobb was also a deeply religious man and a leader in the Presbyterian Church in his hometown. In addition to being a fine orator, Thomas Cobb was also a superb preacher.

Temperamentally, Cobb was impulsive and sometimes volatile—even paranoid. During the war, he frequently clashed with both superiors and subordinates. He was not popular with his men. He was brilliant and brave but difficult.

In early 1861, Cobb served on the committee which drafted the Confederate Constitution, the original manuscript of which is believed to have been written in Cobb's hand. He was elected to the Confederate House of Representatives and was instrumental in establishing the Confederate judiciary. Though lacking military experience, he resigned from Congress in August to recruit his own command, Cobb's Legion. Cobb was commissioned a colonel on August 28, and the legion was sent to the Virginia Peninsula, where it saw action at Yorktown, Lee's Mill, the Seven Days Battles, and the Maryland Campaign, including the Battle of South Mountain (Crampton's Gap). Cobb was not present at Sharpsburg. He performed well but was frustrated with his superiors, thinking that President Jefferson Davis, General Robert E. Lee, and others were discriminating against him.

In October 1862, Tom Cobb assumed command of the brigade formerly led by his brother, Howell Cobb, and, on the recommendation of Robert E. Lee, was promoted to brigadier general on November 1, 1862.

During the Battle of Fredericksburg (December 13, 1862), Cobb's "Irish Brigade" was charged with defending a critical position, the now famous stone wall and Sunken Road, near the top of Marye's Heights. They smashed six Union attacks and inflicted disproportionately high rates of casualties on the enemy. General Cobb "was everywhere," one survivor recalled, "perfectly himself, cool and collected." In the thick of the fight, his leg was shredded by shrapnel. In great pain, he was carried to the rear, but surgeons were unable to stop the bleeding, and he died in a house on the battlefield a little after 2:00 p.m. He was thirty-nine years old.

Cobb's body was transported back to Athens, and he was buried in Oconee Hill Cemetery, where his brother Howell now also lies, along with his parents and other members of his family.

PHILIP ST. GEORGE COCKE was born on April 17, 1809, at Bremo Bluff, a family home in Fluvanna County, Virginia. Philip St. George Cocke attended the University of Virginia but dropped out after he won an appointment to West Point, from which he graduated in 1832. Commissioned in the artillery, he was based in Charleston, South Carolina, during the Nullification Crisis of 1832–33. He resigned his commission in April 1834 to get married and manage several large plantations in Virginia and Mississippi. By 1840, he owned 237 slaves on three plantations. By 1850, he owned 187 slaves in Lowndes County, Mississippi, alone. He built Belmead, an impressive two-story, Gothic Revival–style mansion in Powhatan County, central Virginia, in the late 1830s.

Philip Cocke achieved fame as an agricultural expert and wrote a book on plantation management, as well as numerous articles, and became a nationally recognized authority on agriculture. After John Brown's attack on Harpers Ferry in 1859, he organized the Powhatan Troop, a militia company designed to protect the county from a similar raid or a slave revolt in the future.

On April 21, 1861, Governor John Letcher appointed Cocke brigadier general of commonwealth forces and placed him in command of all troops along the Potomac River. He headquartered in Alexandria and later at Culpeper.

Acting under orders from General Robert E. Lee, Cocke organized a new defensive line at Manassas, with another concentration at Winchester in the Shenandoah Valley, with the two positions connected by the Manassas Gap Railroad. This was the genesis of the South's Bull Run strategy. When the Provisional Army of Virginia was absorbed by the Confederate Army, Cocke was demoted to colonel. General Lee smoothed over Cocke's hurt feelings, and Cocke became commander of the 19th Virginia Infantry Regiment. He was soon promoted to commander of the 5th Brigade in General G. T. Beauregard's army.

·C

Colonel Cocke performed well at Blackburn's Ford on July 18 and in the Battle of First Manassas, on July 21, joining the fight on the Confederate left at about 2:00 p.m. He was promoted to brigadier general on October 21.

Cocke was stationed on the front but saw no major action for six months. He also could not get along with General Beauregard and felt put-upon and slighted. The nervous strain led to exhaustion, despondency, and depression, and his health deteriorated. That winter, he returned to Belmead and declared that he was unfit for duty. On December 26, 1861, he sent his family off to a social affair, went outside, and shot himself in the head. He was fifty-two years old. General Cocke was buried on the grounds of his plantation but in 1904 was reinterred in Hollywood Cemetery, Richmond, Virginia.

Noted author and Civil War historian William C. Davis wrote that, to the Confederacy, "Cooke's loss was undoubtedly a great one." I agree. He certainly showed talent and ability during his brief period in command.

FRANCIS MARION COCKRELL was born on October 1, 1834, in Warrensburg, Johnson County, Missouri. He attended local schools and Chapel Hill College, from which he graduated in 1853. He read law and was admitted to the bar in 1855.

Cockrell maintained a law office at Warrensburg until the Civil War began. He joined the Missouri State Guard as a private but was promoted to captain almost immediately and fought at Carthage, Wilson's Creek, and Pea Ridge. His company was incorporated into the 2nd Missouri Regiment of the Confederate Army on January 15, 1862. The regiment was reorganized in May 1862, and Cockrell was elected lieutenant colonel. Six weeks later, Cockrell moved up in rank and position.

Sent to Mississippi, Cockrell fought in the Battle of Iuka and the Second Battle of Corinth, where he was wounded by a shell fragment. Though the battles were Confederate defeats, Cockrell's troops did well.

He then took part in the successful defense of Grand Gulf. When John S. Bowen was promoted to divisional commander in April 1863, Cockrell was given command of the 1st Missouri Brigade and led it at Port Gibson, where he again distinguished himself. He was one of the best brigade commanders in either army. His big moment came in the Battle of Champion Hill on May 16, when he launched a counterattack against Grant's victorious legions. He checked the Northern advance, threw the Yankees off the hill, brought Grant under fire, and almost won the battle for the South. Had he been reinforced, as General John C. Pemberton had planned, this charge might have influenced the outcome of the war.

Cockrell fought at Big Black River and the Siege of Vicksburg, where he was in heavy combat by May 22. At one point, Cockrell was wounded in the hand by an exploding shell; later, he was tossed high into the air when a Union mine exploded. Captured when Vicksburg fell, Colonel Cockrell was quickly exchanged. He was reorganizing his brigade when he was promoted to brigadier general on July 23, 1863, to rank from July 18, and was named commander of all Missouri troops east of the Mississippi. Stationed in eastern Mississippi until May 1864, he fought in several battles in the Atlanta Campaign, including the Battle of Kennesaw Mountain, where he was wounded in both hands by shell fragments.

Cockrell resumed command of his brigade on August 8. He took part in the remainder of the Atlanta Campaign and in John Bell Hood's invasion of Tennessee, where he was shot four times during the Battle of Franklin: twice in the right arm, once through the left leg, and once in the right ankle. He hobbled off the battlefield and could not resume command until early February 1865.

Cockrell and his brigade were sent to the Mobile sector, where he commanded a division. He was captured, along with 1,300 men, when Fort Blakely fell on April 9, 1865. He was paroled the following month.

After the war, General Cockrell returned to Missouri and resumed his law practice. The state legislature elected him to the U.S. Senate in 1874, and he served continuously for thirty years. He declined to run for reelection in 1904, but President Theodore Roosevelt appointed him to the Interstate Commerce Commission in 1905. He held this office until 1911, when he was appointed to negotiate the boundary between Texas and the New Mexico Territory. He died in Washington, D.C., on December 13, 1915, at the age of eighty-one. He was buried in Sunset Hill Cemetery, Warrensburg.

ALFRED HOLT COLQUITT was born on April 20, 1824, in Monroe, Georgia. His father was a lawyer who later became a U.S. congressman and senator. Young Alfred attended the College of New Jersey (Princeton), graduated in 1844, and was admitted to the bar in 1845.

Colquitt was a serious, pious man noted for his maturity and sobriety. During the Mexican War, he joined the U.S. Army, served as a paymaster, and reached the rank of major. After the war, he returned to his law practice. In 1852, at age twenty-eight, he was elected to the U.S. House of Representatives, serving from 1853 to 1855, and was elected to the state legislature in 1859. A strong states' rights advocate, he was a Breckinridge elector in 1860. After the election, Colquitt was actively involved in the secession movement and was a delegate to the Georgia Secession Convention. He was commissioned as a captain in the Confederate Army before Fort Sumter and was elected colonel of the 6th Georgia Infantry Regiment on May 27, 1861.

Sent to Virginia, Colonel Colquitt led his regiment in the Peninsula Campaign and fought at Seven Pines. He became a brigade commander on June 16. He took part in the Seven Days Battles and was at Turner's Gap on September 14, where his brigade stood almost alone against a huge Union onslaught. Eventually compelled to retreat, he did so in good order and was praised by Robert E. Lee for his leadership. He was promoted to brigadier general on September 15, 1862, with a date of rank of September 1, and fought on September 17 at Sharpsburg, where he held the line in the cornfield. By the time the

Union forces were checked, all of Colquitt's field-grade officers were casualties, and his old regiment, the 6th Georgia, had lost 90 percent of its men, but it still held its positions.

He fought at Fredericksburg, December 11–15, 1862, and was part of Stonewall Jackson's famous flanking attack of May 2, 1863, during the Battle of Chancellorsville, where his performance was again deemed magnificent. By now, however, his brigade was so reduced by casualties that General Lee decided to send it to a secondary and relatively inactive sector in North and South Carolina.

In February 1864, 5,500 Federals launched a drive on Tallahassee, Florida. G. T. Beauregard sent Colquitt to hurriedly reinforce the local Confederate commander, General Joseph Finegan. Colquitt arrived in time, and the Federals were thoroughly thrashed in the Battle of Olustee (Ocean Pond). Colquitt was dubbed "the hero of Olustee."

General Colquitt returned to Virginia in the summer of 1864 and fought in the Siege of Petersburg. In January 1865, he and his brigade were transferred back to North Carolina, where they were unable to prevent the overwhelming Union forces from capturing Fort Fisher. He surrendered in North Carolina at the end of the war and was paroled at Greensboro on May 1, 1865.

Alfred H. Colquitt was one of the best brigade commanders on either side during the War for Southern Independence.

Colquitt returned home and worked to end Reconstruction. He was elected governor in 1876, serving from 1877 to 1882. He did not stand for reelection.

The Georgia legislature elected Colquitt to the U.S. Senate in 1883, and he served until his death from cardiac arrest on March 26, 1894, in Washington, D.C. He was sixty-nine years old. General Colquitt was buried in Rose Hill Cemetery, Macon, Georgia.

RALEIGH EDWARD "OLD POLLY" COLSTON
was born in Paris, France, on October 31, 1825, and was the adopted son of Maria Teresa Gnudi, the Duchess of

Valmy, and Dr. Raleigh Travers Colston of Virginia. Young Raleigh was educated in Paris and then at the Virginia Military Institute. He graduated in July 1846.

Following graduation, Colston became an assistant professor of French (he earned the nickname "Old Polly" as a pun of the French word *parler*, "to talk") at VMI and served as the school's treasurer. He became a full professor in 1854—the first graduate of VMI to reach this rank at his alma mater.

After Virginia left the Union, Governor John Letcher appointed Colston a colonel, and he was sent to Norfolk as commander of the 26th (later 16th) Virginia Infantry on or about May 16. He directed it until December 23, when he was appointed a brigadier general in the Confederate Army, to rank from December 24.

Colston fought in the Peninsula Campaign, where he contracted "peninsula fever," jaundice, and malaria and was placed on medical leave. He returned to duty on December 20, 1862, and was assigned to command a brigade of Virginia troops in the Petersburg defenses and in the Blackwater area of southeastern Virginia.

Isaac Trimble fell ill that spring, and Stonewall Jackson—an old friend of Colston's from VMI—named him acting division commander on April 4, 1863, even though several of Jackson's officers (who were passed over for this promotion) wondered aloud if Colston could handle the job.

They were right. Colston moved far too slowly during the Battle of Chancellorsville and generally performed unsatisfactorily. Colston lost control of his command on May 3, and Robert Rodes had to intervene to avoid a possible disaster. Robert E. Lee relieved Colston of command and separated him from the Army of Northern Virginia with unusual speed.

Colston returned to VMI and made at least five applications for another field command. At last, on October 20, 1863, he was given a brigade at Savannah, but again, his work was considered inadequate, and he was sacked on April 16, 1864.

In early June, he was given command of the Petersburg garrison, which consisted mainly of invalids, old men, and young boys. He faced

C

a surprise Union attack on June 9 and succeeded brilliantly, turning back the veteran Northern troops with a ragtag band of third- and fourth-class troops. He was, nevertheless, posted to Lynchburg, Virginia, another backwater assignment, on July 6, and remained there until the end of the war.

Colston was more admired as a human being than as a soldier. He was a congenial person and was described as "a gentleman . . . slow to believe evil about his fellow man."

The rest of his life was a struggle against sickness and poverty. In 1873, he accepted a commission in the army of the Khedive of Egypt but was badly injured in a fall from a camel and became very ill with rheumatism, paralysis, and other maladies. He returned to the United States crippled and virtually penniless in 1878.

He finally secured employment as a clerk and translator at the War Department in Washington, D.C., in 1882, but he was ill almost constantly, was paralyzed from the waist down, and could not work regularly. The United Confederate Veterans eventually took charge of him, and his friends supported him financially.

General Colston died in the R. E. Lee Camp Soldiers' Home in Richmond on July 29, 1896, at age seventy. He was buried in Hollywood Cemetery, Richmond.

JAMES CONNER was born on September 1, 1829, in Charleston, South Carolina. His father was the president of the Bank of Charleston and president of the South Carolina Railroad Company. Conner received a good education and graduated from South Carolina College in 1849. He read law, was admitted to the bar, and practiced in Charleston. He was appointed a U.S. district attorney in 1857 and served until South Carolina seceded.

Like most South Carolinians, James Conner was a secessionist. He was offered an appointment as district attorney but opted for field service instead. Initially a

· C

captain in the Montgomery Guards, a militia unit, he was present during the bombardment of Fort Sumter. He was a captain in Hampton's Legion during the Battle of First Manassas. When all the field-grade officers were killed or wounded, Conner took temporary command of the legion and led the attack that captured Captain James B. Ricketts's artillery battery. This led to Conner's promotion to major, effective July 21, 1861, and a lifelong friendship with Wade Hampton. He continued with the legion through the Battle of Seven Pines, after which he was promoted to colonel on June 13, and was given command of the 22nd North Carolina Infantry Regiment. Conner was a disciplinarian and never earned the affection of his men, but they respected his courage and ability. At the Battle of Gaines' Mill on June 27, 1862, a rifle ball shattered Conner's leg. He could not return to duty for months.

Colonel Conner rejoined his regiment in 1863 and fought at Gettysburg. He gave up his command on August 13 for staff duty and became a member of the military court of General Richard S. Ewell's II Corps.

During the Overland Campaign of 1864, the Army of Northern Virginia lost so many senior officers that it was necessary for James Conner to return to the field. He was promoted to brigadier general on May 30, 1864, to rank from June 1. General Robert E. Lee gave him temporary command of General Samuel McGowan's brigade, and later he was acting commander of General James H. Lane's brigade. Finally, he commanded General Joseph Kershaw's old brigade in the Shenandoah Valley Campaign from August 29. He fought in the Siege of Petersburg and in the Shenandoah. On October 13, he took part in a skirmish at Cedar Creek, where a shell exploded ten feet in front of him. Physicians had to amputate his "unlucky leg" close to the hip.

Although no longer fit for field service, he joined the Army of Tennessee on February 25, 1865. Apparently, he surrendered with Joseph E. Johnston on April 26, although there is no record of his parole.

James Connor was a good commander but not a lucky one; he likely would have risen higher had he not spent much of the war recovering from wounds.

After the war, General Conner returned to his law practice. In 1876, he was elected attorney general of South Carolina. As such, he was able to obtain judicial confirmation of Wade Hampton's election as governor in 1877, after the results had been contested. He was a model of calm and self-control during an emotionally trying time.

James Conner died of bronchitis on June 26, 1883, in Richmond, Virginia, at the age of fifty-three. He is buried in Magnolia Cemetery, Charleston, South Carolina.

PHILIP COOK was born on July 31, 1817, in Twiggs County, Georgia. His father built Fort Hawkins, which is now Macon, Georgia. Young Philip was educated in private schools before he joined the U.S. Army and took part in the Seminole War in Florida in 1836. After his discharge, he attended Oglethorpe University near Milledgeville, Georgia, and later at the University of Virginia's law school. Admitted to the bar, he practiced law in Oglethorpe, where he remained until 1861.

When the Civil War began, Cook was a private in the Macon County Volunteers, which was mustered into Confederate service as part of the 4th Georgia Infantry Regiment. He was promoted to sergeant in May and to lieutenant and regimental adjutant on October 2, 1861. Initially sent to Portsmouth, Virginia, he took part in the Peninsula Campaign and Seven Days Battles and was wounded by a shell fragment at Malvern Hill on July 1, 1862. The regiment was reorganized, and Cook was elected lieutenant colonel. He fought at Second Manassas and was promoted to commander of the 4th Georgia after the Maryland Campaign. He was promoted to colonel on November 1, 1862.

Colonel Cook led his regiment at Fredericksburg and Chancellorsville, where he was wounded in the left leg by a minié ball and officially cited for gallantry. He returned to the field in the autumn of 1863, but, having been elected to the Georgia House of Representatives, he secured leave in 1864 to attend a legislative session.

·C

Philip Cook fought in the Overland Campaign of May and June 1864, including Cold Harbor, where General George P. Doles was killed on June 2. Cook took charge of the brigade and did well. He also took part in the Siege of Petersburg and was promoted to brigadier general on August 8, 1864, with a date of rank of August 5.

Wounded again during the siege, he rejoined his brigade in the Shenandoah Valley, where he fought in the Battle of Cedar Creek. By now, the brigade was down to four hundred men. Cook's brigade was recalled to the trenches and, on March 25, 1865, took part in the failed Battle of Fort Stedman. Wounded in the right elbow during the attack, General Cook was still hospitalized when General Lee evacuated Richmond and Petersburg. The Federals captured him on April 3.

After the war, Cook returned to Oglethorpe. He moved to Americus, Georgia, in 1870, where he established a law practice and was elected to the U.S. House of Representatives, serving from 1873 to 1883. He was the state capitol commissioner (1883–89) when the Georgia state capitol was built. He was elected secretary of state for Georgia by the state senate in 1890. Cook held this post until his death from pneumonia in Atlanta, at a daughter's home, on May 21, 1894. He was buried in Rose Hill Cemetery, Macon, Georgia. He was seventy-six years old.

JOHN ROGERS COOKE was born on June 9, 1833, at Jefferson Barracks, St. Louis, Missouri, where his father, Captain Philip St. George Cooke, was stationed. John Cooke was educated at Harvard as a civil engineer and was commissioned directly into the U.S. Army as a second lieutenant of infantry on June 30, 1856. He served in Texas, New Mexico, and Arizona.

The Civil War divided his family. His father became a Union general, while his sister Flora married Confederate cavalry leader J. E. B. Stuart. John became a first lieutenant in the Confederate Army and an aide to General Theophilus Holmes. After the Battle of First Manassas, Cooke raised a company of light artillery and served along the Potomac River. In February 1862, General Holmes was appointed commander of the Department of North Carolina, and Cooke was promoted to major and named chief of artillery for that department. On April 16, 1862, he was elected colonel of the 27th North Carolina Infantry Regiment.

Colonel Cooke was a popular commander with the 27th North Carolina. He was dutiful and disciplined, respected and admired, capable and kindhearted. The 27th went to Virginia in the spring of 1862 and served in the Peninsula Campaign, the Seven Days Battles, and the Maryland Campaign. Cooke and his regiment were heavily engaged at Sharpsburg, where he directed an ad hoc brigade-sized battle group. He held the center of General Robert E. Lee's line against fierce Union attacks for two and a half hours *after* he had completely run out of ammunition. The 27th North Carolina lost 203 of its 325 men in the process. Cooke himself was wounded—he was wounded seven times during the war—but he never left the battlefield. He was promoted to brigadier general on November 1, 1862.

During the Battle of Fredericksburg, John Cooke was badly wounded when a bullet fractured his skull just above his left eye. Fortunately for him, it was a glancing blow. He returned to duty in April 1863, rejoined his brigade, and, on May 22, 1863, fought in the victorious Battle of Gum Swamp near Kinston, North Carolina. Cooke's brigade returned to Lee's army near the end of the Battle of Chancellorsville. Posted to Richmond and later Fredericksburg, Cooke's brigade suffered heavy losses in the Battle of Bristoe Station on October 14, 1863. During the battle, Cooke's shinbone was shattered. He did not return to duty until April 1864. By now, General Lee was praising Cooke as his best brigadier commanding his best brigade.

Cooke's men played a major role in the Overland Campaign and took part in the Siege of Petersburg, including the fighting west of Hatcher's Run on the extreme right of the Rebel line. When General Grant finally scored his decisive breakthrough on April 2, Cooke found himself commanding four small brigades cut off from Lee's army. Cooke's brigades reached Lee's army during the retreat to Appomattox. On April 9, he surrendered 560 men.

After the war, Cooke went into the mercantile business in Richmond, Virginia. He also served as director of the Chamber of Commerce and president of the board of directors of the state penitentiary and was one of the founders of the Robert E. Lee Camp Confederate Soldiers' Home in Richmond. He was also active in the United Confederate Veterans and in the Southern Historical Society. Several years after the war, he and his divided family were reconciled.

General Cooke died of pneumonia in Richmond on April 10, 1891, at the age of fifty-seven. He is buried in Hollywood Cemetery, Richmond.

DOUGLAS HANCOCK COOPER was born on November 1, 1815, in Amite County, Mississippi Territory. He attended the University of Virginia from 1832 to 1834, but he disliked studying, dropped out, and returned to Mississippi, where he engaged in agriculture. He also entered local politics and was elected to the state legislature as a Whig.

Cooper raised a company of infantry and served in the Mexican War as part of Colonel Jefferson Davis's elite 1st Mississippi Rifle Regiment, which distinguished itself at de La Terenia, Monterrey, and Buena Vista. Captain Cooper was cited for his courage and gallantry. He also became a close friend of the future president.

In 1853, Secretary of War Jefferson Davis used his influence with President Franklin Pierce to have Cooper appointed Federal agent to the Choctaw tribe and later to the Chickasaws. Unlike many agents, Cooper was fair, honest, and open with the Indians. He worked so well with the Indians that the Chickasaws officially adopted him as a member of their nation. He also formed a Choctaw and Chickasaw militia, which operated against Comanche marauders. When the Civil War began, Confederate Secretary of War LeRoy P. Walker authorized Cooper to protect the tribes from "Northern aggression." Cooper raised a regiment, the 1st Choctaw and Chickasaw Mounted Rifles, and served as its colonel. He was officially appointed in November 1861.

Reinforced with white regiments and Stand Watie's Cherokees, Cooper fought pro-Union Creeks and Seminoles under Chief Opothleyahola, who had 9,000 people in his band (of which about 2,000 were warriors) against Cooper's 1,380 men. Cooper smashed the Union forces in the battles of Chusto-Talasah and Chustenahlah. Opothleyahola's band was forced to flee to Kansas in the dead of winter. This retreat became known as "the Trail of Blood on Ice." Cooper's men attacked them all the way to Fort Row, Kansas, in hit-and-run raids.

Cooper was named commander of the District of the Indian Territory on January 20, 1862. He led Confederate troops at Pea Ridge, where he was less successful. His Indians panicked when they were exposed to cannon fire for the first time, and they did not perform well.

After he returned to what later became Oklahoma, a complicated and tangled command situation evolved, and unity of command was not established until 1865. Cooper hurt his own case because of his excessive fondness for alcohol and drunken binges. He was nevertheless promoted to brigadier general on June 23, to rank from May 2, 1863.

Cooper won several victories but was finally defeated on July 17, 1863, at Elk Creek, near Honey Springs. The war in the Indian Territory was still not settled, however, until after Robert E. Lee surrendered. Cooper then ordered the surrender of all troops in the Indian Territory in June 1865—the last Confederate ground troops to lay down their arms.

General Cooper continued to live in the Indian Territory for the rest of his life and ardently supported the Choctaws and Chickasaws in every way he could. He was especially eager to pursue their land claims against the Federal government. He died April 29, 1879, in Bryan County, Indian Territory, and was buried in an unmarked grave in Fort Washita, Oklahoma.

SAMUEL COOPER was born in New Hackensack, Dutchess County, New York, on the Hudson River, on June 12, 1798. He entered West Point in May 1813 at the age of fourteen and graduated two years later. He was commissioned in the light artillery upon graduation and began a steady rise to the top. Cooper was well-connected by marriage, kinship, and friendship, and he embarked upon a career as a desk soldier.

Early in his career, Lieutenant Cooper served in a variety of artillery units. After that, except for a tour of duty in Florida (1841–42) during the Second Seminole War, Samuel Cooper spent his U.S. Army career in Washington, D.C. He only fought in one battle, at Pila-Kil-Kaha, Florida, on April 19, 1842. He was appointed judge advocate and then chief clerk of the War Department, a post he held for years. He was promoted to colonel in 1852.

Samuel Cooper was a born staff officer, and he did his job efficiently, agreeably, and well. He purchased Cameron, a family estate and farm near Alexandria, Virginia. In 1850, he owned six slaves.

In 1852, he was named adjutant general of the army. He was helped by the fact that he looked like a distinguished old soldier: tall, slim, and of stately demeanor. He also made it a point to attend every social function in Washington and had brandy and cigars with all of the right people.

By now, despite his Northern roots, he was thoroughly Southern in his feelings and sympathies. Seeing Virginia's secession on the horizon, he resigned his commission on March 7, 1861, and left Washington, D.C., for Montgomery, Alabama, where he met with President Davis and offered his services to the Confederacy. Davis named him adjutant and inspector general of the Confederate Army on March 16. He was appointed full general on August 31, 1861, the day the rank was established. His date of rank was March 16, 1861. Cooper was thus the senior officer in the Confederate Army and would be until February 1865, when Lee was named general-in-chief.

Cooper's high rank suggests that he would have a major impact on the War Between the States, but nothing could be further from the truth. Jefferson Davis was a micromanager and was, in effect, his own secretary of war and chief of staff. Cooper was little more than an administrator and a military bureaucrat with no real power except as an occasional consultant to the president. The decentralized nature of the Confederacy, which had enshrined states' rights, further limited his effectiveness, as did the fact that many generals treated him as an unimportant bureaucrat. It didn't help matters that most of the time he didn't even wear a uniform.

General Cooper's jobs included preparing and issuing all orders from the War Department, maintaining army records, and inspecting forts, other installations, units, and personnel. He served a fifty-two-year military career without ever having a command—which was a good thing, because he was indecisive. He was more than willing to follow the directions of President Davis.

Samuel Cooper fled Richmond with Jefferson Davis and stayed with him until April 26, 1865. General Cooper was too ill to travel farther and bid the president an affectionate farewell. Cooper surrendered and was paroled in Charlotte on May 3.

General Cooper made a valuable contribution to history by ensuring the safety of the Confederate government's records and their transfer to the Federal government.

General Cooper returned home to find that Cameron had been confiscated by the Yankee government and converted into a Union fort. His son-in-law, U.S. General Frank Wheaton, persuaded Washington philanthropist W. W. Corcoran to buy the farm and return it to the

Coopers. He was able to move into what was the overseer's house and become a small farmer.

Like most postwar Southerners, he spent the rest of his life in poverty. General Samuel Cooper died at home on December 3, 1876. He was seventy-eight years old. He was buried in Christ Church Episcopal Cemetery, Alexandria.

MONTGOMERY DENT CORSE was born on March 14, 1816, in Alexandria, Virginia. He was well educated at Major Bradley Lowe's military school at Colross and Benjamin Hallowell's school in Alexandria. He went into business before becoming a captain and company commander in the 1st Virginia Regiment during the Mexican War, where he did not see any combat.

In 1849, Corse sailed for California to take part in the Gold Rush. In 1856, he returned to Alexandria and went into the banking business with two of his brothers.

In 1860, he organized the Old Dominion Rifles, a militia company, serving as its captain. On April 10, 1861, he was appointed major in the 6th Virginia Infantry Battalion. He was stationed in Alexandria until May, when it was evacuated. He became colonel of the 17th Virginia Infantry Regiment on June 10. He led it successfully at Blackburn's Ford, the Battle of First Manassas, and in the Peninsula Campaign of 1862. He was acting commander of James L. Kemper's brigade during the Battle of Second Manassas (August 29–30, 1862), and was wounded in the thigh. He rejoined his regiment in Maryland and was slightly wounded on September 14, near Boonsboro. Three days later, he was severely wounded at the Battle of Sharpsburg and lay behind enemy lines before he was finally rescued. When General Robert E. Lee reorganized the Army of Northern Virginia that fall, he gave him command of George Pickett's old brigade. Corse was promoted to brigadier general on November 1, 1862.

Corse's brigade fought at Fredericksburg and was with James Longstreet in the expedition to southeastern Virginia in the spring of 1863. During Lee's second invasion of the North, Corse's unit was detached to guard Hanover Junction, north of Richmond. It was thus spared participating in Pickett's disastrous charge at Gettysburg.

Corse took part in Pickett's unsuccessful attempt to capture New Bern, North Carolina. In May 1864, his brigade successfully defended Drewry's Bluff against the bluecoats, and Corse was slightly wounded again. The brigade rejoined the Army of Northern Virginia in late May and fought at Cold Harbor and in the Siege of Petersburg, during which General Corse was wounded yet again. Corse remained one of the better Confederate brigadiers. Following the Battle of Dinwiddie Court House and the Five Forks debacle, he and his men joined the retreat toward Appomattox and maintained their unit integrity (unlike most of the

Rebel formations) but were captured in the Battle of Sayler's Creek on April 6, 1865. He was released on July 24, 1865.

After the war, he returned to Alexandria, and he and his brothers resumed their banking business. In April 1870, he was in the Virginia State Capitol when part of it collapsed. He was seriously injured and partially blind for some years after. Surgeries restored him to partial sight, but he could no longer read or write. Montgomery D. Corse died at his home in Alexandria on February 11, 1895, after a brief illness. He was seventy-eight years old. He is buried in St. Paul's Presbyterian Cemetery, Alexandria.

GEORGE BLAKE COSBY was born in Louisville, Kentucky, on January 19, 1830. His brother, Frank C. Cosby, became a rear admiral in the U.S. Navy. George was educated in private schools before receiving an appointment to West Point in 1848. He graduated in the class of 1852 and was commissioned a brevet second lieutenant of cavalry. Assigned to the U.S. Mounted Regiment, Cosby served on the Texas frontier. He was wounded fighting Comanche Indians at Lake Trinidad, Texas, on May 9, 1854. He suffered from this injury for the rest of his life.

Two days after he was promoted to captain on May 8, 1861, Cosby, then an instructor at West Point, resigned his commission. A firm believer in the principal of state sovereignty, he joined the Confederacy. On May 16, he was appointed a captain in the Confederate Army. He was promoted to major the following month.

George Cosby's Civil War career was not distinguished. He held staff officer positions until he was captured at Fort Donelson on February 16, 1862. He was imprisoned at Camp Chase, Ohio.

After he was exchanged on August 15, Cosby was promoted to colonel of cavalry on August 27 and was briefly chief of staff of the Army of Mississippi under his friend, Earl Van Dorn, who was his commander

· C

in the old Army. This was followed by a tour as chief of staff of the District of the Gulf, under General Simon Bolivar Buckner. Upon the recommendations of Buckner, Van Dorn, and Joseph E. Johnston, he was promoted to brigadier general on January 23, 1863, with a date of rank of January 20, and given command of a cavalry brigade in Mississippi. In February 1863, Cosby and his men were transferred to the Army of Tennessee. They served in Earl Van Dorn's cavalry corps during the Battle of Thompson's Station on March 5 and under Joseph E. Johnston's command in operations around Jackson, Mississippi, during the Vicksburg Campaign.

The Federals evacuated Jackson on July 23. Cosby pursued them beyond Clinton and then guarded the Big Black River crossings. In mid-October, U.S. Major General James E. McPherson struck toward Canton, Mississippi, but was turned back by Confederate resistance. McPherson officially lamented that the cavalries of Cosby, William Wirt Adams, and John W. Whitfield were "far superior to" the Union's. Even so, Cosby lost the respect of his officers and men, who did not trust his judgment. General Stephen Dill Lee relieved him of his command in late 1863. Cosby was unemployed for some weeks before he was sent to the Department of Southwest Virginia and East Tennessee in February 1864, where he took part in several minor operations. He disbanded his command after General Robert E. Lee surrendered and returned to Kentucky, where Cosby was paroled in May.

General Cosby suffered from his wound in the Indian Wars most of his life. He suffered an attack of paralysis around 1899 and spent the rest of his life as a semi-invalid. Alone, depressed, and in pain, he killed himself on June 29, 1909, at the age of seventy-nine, in Oakland, California, by opening up a gas valve. His body was cremated, and his ashes were buried in Sacramento City Cemetery.

WILLIAM RUFFIN COX was born on March 11, 1832, in Scotland Neck, Halifax County, North Carolina, the youngest of seven children. His father was a prosperous entrepreneur and planter. William graduated from Franklin College in 1850. He then studied law at Lebanon Law School, was admitted to the bar, and set up a practice in Nashville, Tennessee, for five years.

In 1857, he returned to the Old North State and began to develop Penelo, the family's plantation in Edgecombe County. He settled in Raleigh and opened a law practice while continuing to develop Penelo.

William R. Cox was a strong advocate of states' rights and became an ardent secessionist. Seeing that the nation was heading for a breakup, he began studying military tactics and created, funded, and organized his own artillery company. On May 8, 1861, Governor John W. Ellis appointed him major of the 2nd North Carolina Infantry Regiment, a militia unit. He became a major in Confederate service on June 19.

Cox led from the front, where the fighting was the hottest, inspiring the troops with his courage, and was wounded eleven times in action. It was amazing that he survived. The 2nd North Carolina had more than 1,300 men when the war started. At Appomattox, only 54 surrendered.

William Cox was severely wounded in the Battle of Malvern Hill on July 1, 1862, and could not return to his unit until the Maryland Campaign in September. He was promoted to lieutenant colonel on September 17, 1862, and to colonel and regimental commander on March 20, 1863. He distinguished himself at Chancellorsville (April 30 to May 6, 1863), where his regiment lost three hundred of its four hundred available men, and Cox was wounded five times but refused to leave the field until late in the evening of May 3. He could not return to active field duty for months.

Cox again distinguished himself in the Battle of the Wilderness and at Spotsylvania, where Robert E. Lee personally commended him for his bravery during the fighting on May 12, 1864. Lee arranged for Cox to be promoted to brigadier general over the heads of other colonels on June 2, 1864. His date of rank was May 31.

That summer, Cox's brigade was sent to the Shenandoah Valley, took part in Jubal Early's raid on Washington, D.C., in July (and reportedly caught a glimpse of the Capitol), and then fought in Early's Valley Campaign of 1864. He fought at Third Winchester, Fisher's Hill, and Cedar

Creek. Cox and his men returned to the Petersburg trenches for the final months of the war.

General Cox had a reputation for fighting fiercely and keeping his men together, no matter their casualty rate. He led the last charge of the Army of Northern Virginia on April 9, 1865. He surrendered the remnants of his command at Appomattox that same day.

After the war, General Cox returned to Raleigh and resumed his law practice. He became president of the Chatham Railroad and spent six years as solicitor for the City of Raleigh. During the days of Reconstruction, he devoted himself to helping overthrow the corrupt Republican regime and restoring home rule. He served in Congress from 1881 to 1887.

After his reelection defeat in 1886, Cox was elected secretary of the U.S. Senate, a post that he resigned in 1900, when he retired, returned to Penelo, and became a highly successful planter. A grand master of the North Carolina Masons, he was a prominent Episcopalian and served as a trustee of the University of the South.

General William Ruffin Cox died in Richmond, Virginia, on December 26, 1919, at age eighty-seven. He is buried in Oakwood Cemetery, Raleigh.

GEORGE BIBB CRITTENDEN was born on March 20, 1812, in Russellville, Kentucky, into a politically prominent family. One of his brothers, Thomas (1819–1893), became a Union brigadier. George Crittenden graduated from West Point in 1832 and was commissioned a brevet second lieutenant in the infantry. He fought in the Black Hawk War (1832) but resigned his commission the following year. He enrolled at Transylvania University, studied law, and was admitted to the bar, but after a short legal career, he moved west. He joined the Army of the Republic of Texas as a second lieutenant in 1842 and took part in the ill-fated Mier Expedition of 1842–43 against the Mexican Army. He was captured and spent a year in Mexican prisons.

After his release, Crittenden returned to Kentucky and practiced law, but again only briefly, until the Mexican War began in 1846. He rejoined the U.S. Army, was commissioned as a captain in the Mounted Rifles Regiment, and earned a brevet to major for his gallantry in the battles of Contreras and Churubusco. He received a permanent promotion to major in the Regular Army on March 15, 1848. He was cashiered (dishonorably discharged) from the Army on August 19, 1848, apparently due to drunkenness, but was restored to his former rank the following March, thanks to his politically influential friends. He was promoted to lieutenant colonel in 1856 and was in New Mexico when the Civil War began.

George Crittenden was appointed a colonel in the Confederate Army, and President Jefferson Davis promoted him to brigadier general on August 13, 1861, with a date of rank of August 15. He was briefly a brigade commander in G. T. Beauregard's Army of the Potomac. Despite having done nothing of importance, he was advanced to major general on November 9, 1861, and was given command of the District of East Tennessee. On January 19, 1862, he and Confederate Brigadier General Felix K. Zollicoffer were routed by Union General George H. Thomas at Mill Springs, Kentucky. It was the South's first major battlefield defeat of the war; General Zollicoffer was killed, and Crittenden was forced to abandon eastern Kentucky. The Confederate forces had been poorly led, and Crittenden's lackluster performance and alleged drunkenness were the subject of intense public criticism.

General Crittenden was transferred to the Army of Central Kentucky as a division commander. On March 31, a week before the Battle of Shiloh, his corps commander, General William J. Hardee, arrived at Iuka, inspected Crittenden's command, and found the general drunk on duty and his division "in a most wretched state of discipline and instruction." Hardee relieved Generals Crittenden and William Henry Carroll of their commands and arrested them on April 1. This effectively destroyed Crittenden's military career.

Crittenden was restored to command on April 18, only to have General Braxton Bragg order a court of inquiry into Crittenden's conduct.

Rather than face charges, General Crittenden (who was obviously guilty) resigned his commission on October 23, 1862.

Crittenden, however, was not quite done. He accepted a demotion to colonel and served in western Virginia under General John S. Williams. But he held no further commands or positions of importance.

George B. Crittenden returned to Kentucky after the war and became the state librarian in 1867, a position he held until 1874, when he retired. He died in Frankfort on November 27, 1880, at the age of sixty-eight. He is buried in Frankfort Cemetery.

ALFRED CUMMING was born on January 30, 1829, in Augusta, Georgia, where his father was a cotton mogul. The future Confederate general graduated from West Point in 1849. Assigned to the infantry, he spent most of his U.S. military career in the West, including two years as an aide to Brigadier General David E. Twiggs (later a Confederate general). Among other duties, he served along the Mexican border and in the Mormon Expedition to Utah (1857–59). He was promoted to captain on July 20, 1856.

Cumming resigned his commission on January 19, 1861, in order to accept the post of commander of the Augusta Volunteer Battalion as a lieutenant colonel. He was appointed a major in the Confederate Army and assigned to the 1st Georgia Infantry Regiment in May 1861. On June 17, he became lieutenant colonel of the 10th Georgia Infantry Regiment and was promoted to be its colonel on September 25.

The 10th Georgia was sent to Virginia in the fall of 1861, and Colonel Cumming led the 10th in the Peninsula Campaign. He was in reserve at the Battle of Seven Pines but was heavily engaged during the Seven Days Battles, including Malvern Hill, where he was hit by a shell fragment. His men carried their stunned commander off the field, but he was not absent for long. On September 14, Cumming, acting as temporary commander of Cadmus M. Wilcox's brigade, promptly checked a

Union advance towards Harpers Ferry. Three days later, on September 17, he was wounded in the Battle of Sharpsburg. He was *hors de combat* through October.

Alfred Cumming was promoted to brigadier general on October 29, 1862, and when he recovered, he was transferred to command an Alabama brigade in Mobile. In May 1863, he assumed command of a brigade in Mississippi and fought in the Battle of Champion's Hill, where part of his unit behaved badly and most of his brigade was pushed off the field. During the Siege of Vicksburg, General Cumming's brigade performed very well, cutting down Yankees by the score during Grant's ill-advised attacks of May 19 and May 22. Nevertheless, Cumming surrendered along with the rest of the garrison on July 4, 1863, and was paroled.

Cumming reformed a brigade at Decatur, Georgia, and distinguished himself at the Battle of Missionary Ridge on November 25, 1863. Cumming also participated in several battles during the Atlanta campaign. On August 31, 1864, during the Battle of Jonesboro, Cumming was seriously wounded in the hip joint and both hands. He did not recover until after the Confederacy perished.

After the war, Alfred Cumming became a farmer near Rome, Georgia, before returning to Augusta, where he held a number of minor government positions. In 1888, he was part of the American military commission to Korea.

Brigadier General Alfred Cumming died in Rome, Georgia, on December 5, 1910. He was eighty-one years old. He is buried in Summerville Cemetery in Augusta, Georgia.

D

DANIEL – DUNOVANT

JUNIUS DANIEL was born on June 27, 1828, in Halifax, North Carolina. He attended local schools in Halifax and then a private academy in Raleigh, North Carolina. He received a presidential appointment to West Point from James K. Polk in 1846 and graduated in 1851. Daniel's graduation was delayed a year because of an accident he suffered during artillery practice. He was commissioned a brevet second lieutenant in the infantry.

Daniel transferred to the 3rd U.S. Dragoons in 1852 and was posted to Fort Fillmore in Albuquerque, New Mexico Territory, where he fought Apaches. Meanwhile, his father moved to Shreveport, Louisiana. Junius Daniel resigned his commission in 1858 to join the elder Daniel and become a planter.

Junius Daniel moved back to North Carolina in late 1860 and on June 3, 1861, was chosen to be colonel of the 4th (later 14th) North Carolina Infantry Regiment, a one-year unit forming at Garysburg. When the 14th North Carolina's period of enlistment expired, he was offered command of four other regiments. He selected the 45th North Carolina Infantry Regiment on April 14, 1862.

Colonel Daniel was posted to Goldsboro, where he organized three different brigades, the last of which he took to Petersburg, Virginia, where he joined the Army of Northern Virginia. He participated in the Peninsula Campaign and the Seven Days Battles and was wounded near Malvern Hill on June 30 when a Union artillery shell exploded near where he was riding. Robert E. Lee thought Daniel had commanded well, promoted him to brigadier general on September 15, 1862, with a date of rank of September 1, and gave him command of a brigade. Daniel remained in the Richmond area until December, when he was ordered to North Carolina with George Pickett's division.

During the Pennsylvania Campaign in 1863, he fought at Gettysburg and was officially praised for his "coolness and intrepid conduct." After the battle, Daniel's men retreated to the Rappahannock with the Army of Northern Virginia. Daniel took medical leave on July 21 and did not return to duty until September. He and his men fought in the battles of the Wilderness and Spotsylvania Court House. On May 12, 1864, Daniel led a counterattack and was shot down by a minié ball. He was carried to a nearby field hospital, where he wrote a loving message to his wife. He died the next day; he was thirty-five years old. General Lee had already recommended him for promotion to major general, but the mortally wounded Daniel never knew it.

His body was returned to North Carolina and buried in the Colonial Churchyard, Halifax.

HENRY BREVARD DAVIDSON was born on January 28, 1831, in Shelbyville, Tennessee. He was educated in local schools and on June 2, 1846, at age fifteen, joined the 1st Tennessee Volunteer Infantry as a private. Davidson was commended for his gallantry in the Battle of Monterrey and was promoted to sergeant. He was discharged on May 23, 1847. Because of his sterling war record in Mexico, he received an appointment to West Point in 1848 and graduated in 1853. He was commissioned in the cavalry.

Lieutenant Davidson fought Apaches and skirmished with hostile Indians in Oregon in 1856. He was promoted to captain in 1861 but almost immediately resigned his commission to "go south." He accepted a captain's commission in the Confederate Army and was promoted to major in April 1861. He initially served in the adjutant general's branch and then on the staff of the inspector general.

In December 1861, Henry Davidson was on John Floyd's staff as assistant adjutant general (AAG) of the Army of the Kanawha. The following month, he joined the staff of Albert Sidney Johnston as AAG of the Army of Central Kentucky. Briefly he was Simon Buckner's chief of artillery but was not present when Fort Donelson surrendered. He became an AAG and de facto chief of staff to Brigadier General William W. Mackall in March 1862 and was included in the surrender of Island

D·

Number 10 on April 7, 1862. While a prisoner of war, he was promoted to colonel in June 1862. He was exchanged on August 27 and named commandant of Staunton, Virginia, in the Shenandoah Valley, where he remained for almost a year. On August 18, 1863, he was promoted to brigadier general and led a brigade under Nathan Bedford Forrest during the Chickamauga Campaign. From October 1863, he was commander of a cavalry brigade under Joseph "Fighting Joe" Wheeler, screening the front of the Army of Tennessee against U.S. General William Sherman. In the spring of 1864, Davidson and Wheeler had a falling out, and Davidson was relieved of his command and arrested for insubordination. On May 8, 1864, General Joseph E. Johnston came to his rescue, releasing Davidson from arrest and placing him in command of Rome, Georgia, with orders to organize the troops there and hold the place against the rapidly advancing Yankees. In this emergency situation, Davidson did a fine job. On May 17, 1864, he distinguished himself in a battle near Rome, Georgia, in which he drove off a sizable force of enemy cavalry.

After Atlanta fell, General Davidson was ordered back to Virginia, where he assumed command of a brigade of cavalry on September 27 and fought in the Shenandoah Valley. He took part in the Battle of Waynesboro, Virginia, on March 2, 1865, when the Confederate Army under General Jubal Early was effectively destroyed. Davidson escaped this debacle and was with General Johnston in North Carolina when he surrendered on April 26. He was paroled at Greensboro on May 1, 1865.

After the war, Henry Davidson moved to New Orleans and was a deputy sheriff of Orleans Parish in 1866 and 1867. Unable to make a decent living in the devastated South, Davidson moved to California in 1868. He had a number of different jobs, including deputy secretary of state for California. General Davidson died on March 4, 1899, in Livermore, Alameda County, California. He was sixty-eight years old. He is buried in Mountain View Cemetery, Oakland.

JOSEPH ROBERT "JOE" DAVIS, the nephew of President Jefferson Davis, was born in Woodville, Mississippi, on January 12, 1825. He was educated in Nashville, Tennessee, and at Miami University (of Ohio). He was admitted to the bar and set up a practice in Madison County, north of Jackson, Mississippi. He was elected to the state senate in 1860.

When the Confederacy was formed, Joseph Davis became a captain of a Madison County militia company. On April 12, 1861, he was named lieutenant colonel of the 10th Mississippi Infantry Regiment and was sent to Pensacola. He was transferred to his uncle's staff as a colonel of cavalry on August 31. He lived with President Davis and his family at the Confederate White House, accompanied the president on various trips throughout the South, and wrote reports on the military situation. Jefferson Davis called him "discreet, gentlemanly and sound of judgment." Among his peers and friends, he was known as an amiable, unpretentious man who was not above an occasional practical joke. Mary Chesnut criticized him in her diary, however, for cursing—saying "Damn Yankees" in front of children.

President Davis promoted his nephew to brigadier general on September 15, 1862, and assigned him command of an infantry brigade. The Confederate Senate initially rejected his nomination but approved it on October 8. General Davis's date of rank was September 15, 1862.

Davis' Brigade was sent to southwestern Virginia in the winter of 1862–63 and joined the main army for General Robert E. Lee's second invasion of the North. It first saw heavy action at Gettysburg on July 1, 1863, and the inexperienced brigade blundered into an ambush in the railroad cut, took heavy losses, and retreated in disorder. Two days later, the survivors were part of Pickett's Charge. During the three-day battle, all of Davis's regimental commanders were killed or wounded. Joseph Davis himself was wounded on July 3.

After the battle, he came down with typhoid fever and took sick leave in Richmond but did not attempt to contact the president. Apparently he was afraid that he had lost his uncle's confidence. Joseph Davis missed the Battle of the Wilderness but was present at Spotsylvania, where his performance was much better than it had been at Gettysburg. He fought in the rest of the Overland Campaign, in the Battle of Cold Harbor, and in the Siege of Petersburg. He surrendered at Appomattox on April 9, 1865.

Overall, Joseph R. Davis must be rated as a mediocre commander. He achieved his rank through nepotism, as the South had literally dozens of colonels better qualified to lead a brigade. His performance at Gettysburg was terrible, although he improved markedly as the war progressed.

After the war, Davis returned to Mississippi and eventually settled in Biloxi, where he spent the rest of his life practicing law. He died there on September 15, 1896. He was seventy-one years old. He is buried in the old French section of Biloxi City Cemetery.

WILLIAM GEORGE MACKEY DAVIS was born on May 9, 1812, in Portsmouth, Virginia. He basically ran away from home at age seventeen by taking a job on a ship. He disembarked at Savannah, Georgia, and eventually took up residence in Apalachicola, Florida, where he became a highly successful attorney and cotton speculator. He was a kindhearted man and made many friends. He was elected county judge of Franklin County in 1844 as a Whig. He moved to Tallahassee in 1848. He owned slaves of the domestic variety but had serious moral reservations about the institution, so he freed them in the 1850s. He was a delegate to the Florida Secession Convention and sought to delay the separation, but when the final vote came on January 10, 1861, he voted to leave the Union.

In April 1861, the wealthy Davis gave $50,000 ($1,461,794 in 2020 money) to the state to raise Florida's first infantry regiment (the 1st Florida) and eventually secured Secretary of War Judah P. Benjamin's permission to raise a cavalry battalion. He was promoted to lieutenant colonel on November 4, 1861, and on January 1, 1862, he became

colonel of the 1st Florida Cavalry Regiment. On March 25, 1862, it was ordered to Chattanooga and then to East Tennessee. It engaged in scouting, patrolling, and routine garrison duties.

Colonel Davis commanded a brigade during the Kentucky Campaign, although it was not present in the Battle of Perryville or Richmond. On November 4, 1862, William G. H. Davis was promoted to brigadier general and was named commander of the Department of East Tennessee. His command included three Florida regiments. He was a strict disciplinarian and enforced a meticulous dress code.

General Davis's health began to deteriorate in the fall of 1862, and he was frequently absent. He resigned his commission on May 6, 1863. Unable to serve in the field, he moved to Richmond and operated a fleet of blockade runners from Wilmington, North Carolina, until the city fell in 1865.

After the war, he moved to Washington, D.C., where he became a member of a law firm settling cotton claims with England. He moved to the United Kingdom for a time. He eventually returned to Virginia and purchased a plantation near Norfolk.

General Davis died at the home of a son in Alexandria, Virginia, on March 11, 1898. He was age eighty-five. According to an obituary notice, he "was a typical Southern gentleman of the old school; chivalrous and true, abounding with a kindly courtesy and a sweetness of disposition which endeared him to all." He was firm in his convictions and decisive in manner but noted for his generosity and kindness. As a military commander, he governed the strongly pro-Union region of East Tennessee but handled the citizens well, with a combination of firmness and discretion.

JAMES "JIM" DEARING was born on April 25, 1840, at Otterburne, near Altavista in Campbell County, Virginia, in the south-central part of the state. When his father died in 1843, Dearing was adopted by his uncle, who saw to it that he received the best possible education.

D.

In 1858, he was admitted to West Point, where he was called a "reckless, handsome boy." He stood six feet, two inches tall, was lean and muscular, and developed a reputation for strength and endurance. He was an advocate of secession and received demerits for his outspoken political views, but he was also known as a friendly young man and joined the Whist (card-playing) Club and two unofficial tobacco clubs. (Dearing loved smoking a pipe.) In addition, he was known for his banjo playing, singing, and his fluency in French.

Dearing resigned from the military academy on April 22, 1861, and was appointed lieutenant of artillery in the Virginia Militia. When the Washington Artillery of New Orleans arrived in Lynchburg, Virginia, he joined it as both a second lieutenant and a drill instructor.

Dearing fought in the Battle of First Manassas, where his battery supported Jubal Early's brigade. He was promoted to first lieutenant in early 1862 and to captain in April and was appointed commander of a battery, which was eventually renamed Dearing's battery. His unit was attached to George Pickett's brigade and fought in the Peninsula Campaign, the Battle of Seven Pines, the Seven Days Battles, and the Battle of Second Manassas.

Dearing commanded a battalion of three batteries during the Battle of Fredericksburg, where he again supported George Pickett's division. Eventually, his command was redesignated as the 38th Virginia Light Artillery Battalion. Dearing was promoted to major in early 1863 and took part in James Longstreet's operations against Suffolk in the spring of that year.

On July 2, during the Battle of Gettysburg, he received the first of two reprimands from Robert E. Lee for exposing himself needlessly to enemy fire. Despite this, Lee thought highly of Dearing and even referred to him as "Jim," which was unusually informal for him. Dearing's men also loved him, even though he was a firm disciplinarian. On July 3, his battalion supported Pickett's Charge and suffered heavy losses to Union counterbattery fire.

After Gettysburg, Dearing received permission to form a cavalry regiment. He was promoted to lieutenant colonel on January 13, 1864, and to colonel (temporary rank) the same day. His regiment was designated the 8th Confederate Cavalry.

On April 19, 1864, General Robert Hoke captured Plymouth, North Carolina, and Colonel Dearing played a critical role in the victory. A grateful Hoke wrote directly to Braxton Bragg (then military advisor to President Jefferson Davis) and asked that Dearing be promoted to brigadier general. Bragg secured the promotion for Dearing on April 29. His command served as a fire brigade for General G. T. Beauregard that spring and summer. He played a major role in saving Petersburg in June 1864 and in the battles on the Weldon Railroad. In early 1865, he took command of the Laurel Cavalry brigade.

On April 6, 1865, Dearing engaged in personal combat with Union Generals Theodore Read and Francis Washburn. He shot General Read, who died instantly. He also shot Washburn through the mouth while Read's orderly put a bullet through both of Dearing's lungs.

General Dearing was carried to Lynchburg, Virginia, where he died on April 22, 1865, the same day as General Washburn. He was the last Confederate general to die of wounds during the war. He was buried on his twenty-fifth birthday in Avoca Family Cemetery. In 1902, his widow had him disinterred and reburied in Spring Hill Cemetery, Lynchburg, where he now lies.

ZACHARIAH CANTEY DEAS was born on October 25, 1819, in Camden, South Carolina. He was the cousin of James Chesnut, Jr., another future Rebel general. Deas was educated in Columbia, South Carolina, at Caudebec in Calvados, France, and in Mobile, Alabama, where his family moved in 1835. He served in the Mexican War, returned home, and became a cotton broker. He was a prominent Episcopalian and a member of the Democratic Party. By 1860, he was quite wealthy.

Deas joined the Confederate Army after Alabama seceded and served on the staff of General Joseph E. Johnston during the Battle of First Manassas. He returned home and organized the 22nd Alabama Infantry Regiment and equipped it at his own expense. The cost was $28,000 in gold ($818,604 in 2020 money). Deas was reimbursed by the government a year later in Confederate bonds—which meant he lost heavily on the deal, but he never uttered a word of complaint. He armed his men with eight hundred ultramodern Enfield Rifles, which he purchased with gold. Deas was naturally chosen as colonel (October 25, 1861) and remained in Mobile until February 26, 1862. He led his men in the Battle of Shiloh, where he became an acting brigade commander after General Adley H. Gladden was mortally wounded, and his successor, Colonel Daniel Adams, was seriously wounded about 2:00 p.m. on April 6. Deas had two horses shot out from under him and was wounded several times, but he remained at the front. He was badly wounded on April 7 and was finally forced to leave the field because of loss of blood.

Colonel Deas returned to duty in August 1862 and took part in the Kentucky Campaign. He was promoted to brigadier general on December 20, 1862, to date from December 13, and commanded Franklin Gardner's old brigade at the Second Battle of Murfreesboro. At Chickamauga, he routed Philip Sheridan's division in fierce fighting. Deas's brigade captured seventeen Union guns but suffered more than 50 percent casualties. Deas later fought in the Siege of Chattanooga, at Missionary Ridge, in the Atlanta Campaign, and in the Nashville Campaign, where he was slightly wounded in the Battle of Franklin.

Deas assumed command of General Edward Johnson's division after Johnson was captured at Nashville on December 16 and led it during the retreat to Alabama and in the Carolinas Campaign until March 1865, when he fell ill. He was not present at the surrender in North Carolina at Bennett Place on April 26, 1865. He was paroled at Meridian, Mississippi, on May 12, 1865.

After the war, General Deas moved to New York City, established himself as a stockbroker, became highly prominent in the city's financial circles, and owned a seat on the New York Stock Exchange. His three-story summer cottage, Sea View Villa, was lavishly appointed with chandeliers, stained glass windows, and intricate woodwork and was located on Easton's Beach, Newport, Rhode Island. Sea View Villa is still extant.

General Deas suffered from chronic Bright's disease in his last years. He died of apoplexy in New York City on March 6, 1882, at age sixty-two. He is buried in Woodlawn Cemetery, Bronx, New York.

JULIUS ADOLPHUS DE LAGNEL was born in Newark, New Jersey, on July 24, 1827. Some sources list his middle name as Adolph. He was the descendent of Huguenots (French Protestants) who had fled France to escape religious persecution and fled Haiti during the slave revolt in 1791. His father was a West Point graduate who died in New York in 1840 as a captain with almost twenty years of service.

In 1847, at age twenty, Julius de Lagnel was commissioned directly into the 2nd U.S. Artillery Regiment (his father's old outfit) as a second lieutenant. He took part in General Winfield Scott's drive on Mexico City. Promoted to first lieutenant in 1849, he remained on active duty until May 17, 1861, when he followed his adopted state (Virginia) out of the Union. He was commissioned a captain of artillery on June 12 and was assigned to the Lee Artillery as a drill instructor. Later that month, de Lagnel was named chief of artillery to Brigadier General Robert S. Garnett in western Virginia (later West Virginia). After the Confederates were routed at the Battle of Philippi, Garnett ordered de Lagnel to reorganize the Rebel forces and hold the area around Rich Mountain. On July 11, de Lagnel (who had five companies of infantry and a single gun) was ordered to defend Buckhannon Pass. At 11:00 a.m., he was attacked by a massively superior Union force. His horse was shot out from under him, most of his men were overwhelmed, and the captain served the sole artillery piece by himself, firing three or four rounds until he was shot in the side. Confederate cartographer Jed Hotchkiss recalled that de Lagnel fought with "indominable [*sic*] courage." With the battle obviously lost, de Lagnel ordered his surviving infantry to save themselves if they could. He hid in a thicket, under cover of a rainstorm, and wandered in the woods for seventy-two hours with nothing to eat except berries. He eventually disguised himself as a herder but was identified as a soldier by his boots and was captured near Laurel Hill, Virginia.

De Lagnel was exchanged in December. By early 1862, he was commanding a naval battery on Mulberry Island near the Virginia Peninsula. On March 16, John Bankhead Magruder wrote Robert E. Lee and recommended de Lagnel be promoted to major so he could command all the batteries on the peninsula. Instead, he was appointed brigadier general on April 8, 1862 (to rank from April 15), but he declined the appointment on July 31. He was promoted to major in the 20th Virginia Artillery Battalion of the Army of Northern Virginia in June.

Julius de Lagnel served in the Seven Days Battles and was promoted to lieutenant colonel of ordnance in July 1862. He was named second in command to Brigadier General Josiah Gorgas in the Confederate Ordnance Bureau from August 1862 and was occasionally inspector of arsenals. He commanded the Fayetteville, North Carolina, arsenal from September 1862 to November 1863 and the Columbus, Georgia, arsenal from May to September 1864. He was paroled at Greensboro, North Carolina, on May 1, 1865.

After the war, he moved to Washington, D.C., and was engaged in the Pacific shipping business. He died on June 3, 1912, at the age of eighty-four, and is buried in St. Paul's Cemetery, Alexandria, Virginia.

JAMES DESHLER was born in Tuscumbia, Alabama, on February 18, 1833. His father, David, had come to Alabama from Pennsylvania in 1825 to help construct the Tuscumbia Railway, the state's first railroad. He remained in Alabama and became a wealthy merchant. James entered West Point in 1850. Fellow cadet E. Porter Alexander remembered him as "a first class man" and a "fine looking fellow with very attractive manners & qualities." Deshler graduated with the class of 1854 and was commissioned in the artillery.

Lieutenant Deshler served in the Nebraska Territory, where he saw his first combat against the Lakota Sioux. He took part in the Utah War (the Mormon War) in 1857 and 1858 and was at Fort Wise, Colorado Territory, in May 1861, when he resigned his commission and "went south."

James Deshler was appointed as a captain of artillery and sent to western Virginia as an adjutant to General Henry Jackson. He was mustered into Confederate service in July. Deshler fought in the Battle of Cheat Mountain (September 12–15, 1861) and at Allegheny Mountain (December 13). He was wounded in both thighs but refused to leave the trenches until nightfall. Promoted to colonel of artillery in early 1862, he was sent to North Carolina on April 20, where he was chief of artillery on the staff of General Theophilus H. Holmes. He fought in the Seven Days Battles and went with Holmes when he was transferred to the Trans-Mississippi Department. Deshler was dispatched to Austin, Arkansas (near Little Rock), where he assumed command of a brigade of Texas infantry in October. It was part of the garrison of Arkansas Post (Fort Hindman) when it surrendered on January 11, 1863.

When they were exchanged in June 1863, Deshler and his brigade joined the Army of Tennessee, which was then concentrated around Tullahoma, Tennessee, as part of Patrick Cleburne's division. Deshler was promoted to brigadier general on July 28, 1863.

James Deshler was very popular with his men and greatly improved the quality of the unit. He was killed in action on September 20, 1863, during the Battle of Chickamauga. While inspecting the cartridge boxes of his men, a shell struck him in the chest, tore him apart, and literally ripped his heart out. When General Robert E. Lee heard of his death, he exclaimed, "There was no braver soldier in the Confederate Army than Deshler." He was thirty years old.

James Deshler was buried on the battlefield. After the war, his father had his body removed and reinterred in Oakwood Cemetery, Tuscumbia, Alabama.

GEORGE GIBBS DIBRELL was born on April 12, 1822, in Sparta, Tennessee, where his father was a farmer. He attended East Tennessee College (now the University of Tennessee) in Knoxville and clerked in a branch office of the Bank of Tennessee. At age twenty-six, he was elected clerk of the court for White County in 1848 and held this office until 1860. Simultaneously, he became a successful merchant. He opposed secession until Lincoln's call for volunteers to invade the South. In 1861, he was elected to the Tennessee state legislature but left after the opening session to join the 25th Tennessee Infantry Regiment as a private. On August 10, 1861, he was elected to be its lieutenant colonel.

Dibrell fought in the disastrous Battle of Mill Springs and at Farmington, Mississippi, during the Siege of Corinth. When the Army of Tennessee reorganized on May 10, 1862, following the fall of Corinth, he lost his position. Undeterred, he went to Richmond and gained authorization to form his own regiment. He organized the 13th (later 8th) Tennessee Cavalry, which was initially a twelve-company partisan unit. It joined Nathan Bedford Forrest's cavalry brigade in the fall of 1862 and became a regular Confederate formation. Dibrell armed his command from captured Union weapons. Promoted to colonel in September 1862, he served Forrest well in the West Tennessee Raid of December 1862 and in subsequent operations. He was elevated to the command of Forrest's old brigade on July 1, 1863, although he was not promoted to brigadier general until January 24, 1865. His date of rank was July 26, 1864.

Colonel Dibrell continued to operate with the "Wizard of the Saddle" in the Tullahoma Campaign and at Chickamauga. He was transferred to Joseph Wheeler's cavalry during the winter of 1863–64 and was wounded on the Clinch River during the Knoxville Campaign, probably on December 21, 1863. He fought in the Atlanta Campaign, gaining special prominence when he routed the Union cavalry at Rocky Face Ridge. He opposed William Sherman's March to the Sea and, during

·D

one skirmish, had his horse shot out from under him. Promoted to divisional commander, Wheeler praised him as a "most excellent officer," adding, "You can hardly find a better or more reliable man." Dibbell also fought at Averasborough (March 16) and Bentonville (March 19–21) in the Carolinas campaign.

After the war, he returned to Tennessee and resumed his business career, becoming a highly successful planter and industrial entrepreneur. At one time he owned more than fifteen thousand acres in White County as well as the large Bon Air Coal & Coke Company and several coal mines. He also helped develop the Southwestern Railroad, connecting Sparta with Nashville and Chattanooga.

Meanwhile, Dibrell was elected to Congress in 1874 and was reelected four times, serving from 1875 to 1885. He ran for governor in 1886 but failed to get the Democratic nomination.

General George G. Dibrell died in the town of his birth on May 9, 1888, at age sixty-six. He is buried in Old Sparta Cemetery.

THOMAS PLEASANT DOCKERY was born on December 18, 1833, in Montgomery County, North Carolina. His father eventually moved to Tennessee and then to Columbia County, Arkansas, where he built a large plantation, was instrumental in establishing the first railroad in Arkansas, and was president of the Mississippi, Ouachita & Red River Railroad. Thomas inherited his father's energy and also became a man of property.

On June 17, 1861, Tom Dockery was commissioned captain of a Columbia County volunteer militia company. It was soon redesignated Company B, 5th Arkansas State Troops Infantry, and in June, Dockery was elected colonel of the new regiment, which was part of Nicholas B. Pearce's division of the Arkansas State Troops. As such, it fought in the Battle of Wilson's Creek, Missouri, on August 10, 1861—an overwhelming Confederate victory. After the battle, however, Pearce's

D·

division voted to disband rather than be transferred to Confederate service, where it might have been assigned to serve east of the Mississippi. Thomas Dockery took some of his troops and reorganized them as the 19th Arkansas Infantry Regiment, of which he was elected colonel.

The 19th Arkansas crossed the Mississippi and fought in the Second Battle of Corinth. Dockery briefly became commander of a subdistrict in Arkansas before being given command of the 2nd Brigade of General John Bowen's division, which he led in the Battles of Grand Gulf and Port Gibson in the last Vicksburg Campaign. He had a reputation for being a gallant and particularly aggressive commander. One of his men recalled: "It was one of Colonel Dockery's hobbies to volunteer to take some battery or storm some difficult stronghold." He launched a brilliant bayonet charge at Champion Hill that routed part of Grant's right flank, brought the Union commander personally under fire, and caused him some bad moments. Dockery fought in the center of the Confederate line during the Siege of Vicksburg. He replaced General Martin Green, who was killed by a Union sharpshooter on June 25, as brigade commander. Dockery was paroled after the city fell on July 4, 1863, and was soon exchanged. An officer with a reputation for competence and aggression, he was nominated for brigadier general on August 10, 1863.

General Dockery was sent back to Washington, Arkansas, and assumed command of a brigade that consisted mainly of Vicksburg parolees. He fought with considerable success against the Union's Camden Expedition in 1864.

Dockery's first nomination for brigadier general failed to win Senate confirmation, and he reverted to the rank of colonel. He was reappointed on June 1, 1864, and this time was confirmed. In November 1864, Dockery became commander of the Reserve Forces of the State of Arkansas. At the end of the war, he signed the document surrendering all remaining Confederate forces in the state. He was paroled at Washington, the Confederate capital of Arkansas, on June 20, 1865.

Thomas Dockery lost all his property during the war. He tried, with some initial success, to rebuild his fortunes with railroad construction, but he eventually had to abandon the project and moved to New York

City, hoping to renew his fortunes there. His business interests began well, but finally failed, and he died in poverty in Manhattan, New York, on February 27, 1898, at the age of sixty-four. His two daughters arranged to have his body buried in City Cemetery, Natchez, Mississippi, where they lived.

GEORGE PIERCE DOLES was born at Milledgeville, Georgia, on May 14, 1830, the son of a tailor. He was educated in the local schools and was a successful merchant and businessman before the war and was captain of the Baldwin Blues, a militia company. When Georgia mobilized, he became commander of Company H, 4th Georgia Infantry.

Despite a limited education and a modest, polite personality, George Doles proved to be a natural military leader. He was elevated to colonel of the 4th Georgia on May 9, 1861, and was stationed at Hampton Roads, Virginia, for about eleven months. Doles led his regiment in the Peninsula Campaign of 1862 and the Seven Days Battles. He was wounded by a shell burst during the Battle of Malvern Hill but was back in command later that month.

Doles's regiment was part of Roswell S. Ripley's brigade during the Maryland Campaign and fought at South Mountain and Sharpsburg. When General Ripley was wounded, Doles assumed command of the brigade and led an attack on the southern end of the Miller cornfield. After the campaign, Ripley was transferred south, and Doles assumed permanent command of the brigade. He was promoted to brigadier general on November 1.

General Doles performed well in the Battle of Fredericksburg, after which his divisional commander, D. H. Hill, praised him as a veteran who would "do well whenever called upon to meet the infernal Yankees." He did equally well at Chancellorsville, where he commanded the spearhead of Robert Rodes's division during Stonewall Jackson's famous flanking attack. On July 1, 1863, during the first day of the Battle of

D·

Gettysburg, his brigade (1,300 men) attacked the U.S. XI Corps near Rock Creek, north of the town, and pushed the enemy back for a mile. Doles himself was fortunate to survive this battle. His horse was shot down within fifty yards of the Federal line, but he emerged unhurt.

By this point, Doles was considered one of the best brigade commanders in the Army of Northern Virginia. His men were lightly engaged during the last two days at Gettysburg and in the Bristoe and Mine Run campaigns. They were heavily engaged in the Overland Campaign, including the Battle of the Wilderness. In the Battle of Spotsylvania Court House, the brigade defended in the Mule Shoe salient on May 12, 1864, when it was attacked by overwhelming forces and was largely overrun. It lost about 650 men, of whom 350 were captured. Doles himself was trapped behind Union lines but managed to escape by lying on the ground and playing dead until a counterattack rescued him. He rallied the remnants of his brigade and led another counterattack. Eventually, the Rebels recaptured the lost entrenchments.

On June 2, 1864, during the Battle of Cold Harbor, he was supervising the construction of the Confederate line at Bethesda Church when he was struck in the chest by a bullet from a Union sharpshooter. He died instantly. He was thirty-four years old.

General Doles was buried in Memory Hill Cemetery, Milledgeville.

DANIEL SMITH DONELSON was born on June 23, 1801, in Sumner County, Tennessee. His father died when Daniel was about five, and he moved to The Hermitage, the home of his aunt, Rachel Donelson Jackson, whose husband was future President Andrew Jackson. They adopted Daniel and his two brothers.

"Ol' Hickory" saw to it that Donelson received a good education. He attended a boarding school in Nashville, enrolled in West Point in 1821, and graduated in 1825. He was commissioned a second lieutenant in the artillery but resigned his commission about seven months later to return to Sumner County and work as a planter. He joined the Tennessee Militia and rose to the rank of brigadier general.

Donelson spent two years in Florida and returned to Tennessee. He became a member of the Tennessee legislature from 1841 to 1843 and from 1855 to 1861 and was speaker of the house from 1859 to 1861.

Daniel Donelson was appointed adjutant general of the state when Tennessee seceded. In May 1861, he approved the locations of Forts Henry and Donelson, the latter of which was named after himself. The location of Fort Henry was terrible, subject to floods, and it was easily captured by General U. S. Grant and Flag Officer Andrew Hull Foote on February 6, 1862, giving the Union control of the Tennessee River.

Daniel Donelson became a brigadier general in the Confederate Army on July 9, 1861. He led a brigade in William Wing Loring's division during the Western Virginia Campaign of 1861 and briefly commanded the 5th Subdistrict of South Carolina (March–April 1862) and a brigade in General Braxton Bragg's Kentucky Campaign. He fought successfully at Perryville and saw action at the Second Battle of Murfreesboro (Stones River), where he was part of the charge that smashed the Union right wing. His brigade also lost 691 men (102 of them killed), but it captured 1,000 prisoners and 11 guns in heavy fighting. He was praised by General Leonidas Polk for his leadership.

Daniel Donelson was named commander of the Department of East Tennessee on January 17, 1863, and promoted to major general on March 5, 1863, to date from January 17, 1863. His tenure, however, was brief. He died of chronic diarrhea at the Montvale Springs resort near Knoxville on April 17, 1863. He was sixty-one years old. "His comrades in the army, and those who served under his orders, will long remember his deeds and virtues," General Bragg wrote. But his abilities as a military engineer—as demonstrated by his choice of the location of Fort Henry—left much to be desired.

General Donelson was buried in Hendersonville Presbyterian Church Cemetery in Sumner County, Tennessee.

THOMAS FENWICK DRAYTON was born in South Carolina on August 24, 1808, probably in Charleston. He spent his early years in Drayton Hall, a magnificent plantation. He was sent to school in England. Upon his return to the New World, he gained admission into the U.S. Military Academy at West Point; he graduated in 1828. Drayton was commissioned a brevet second lieutenant of infantry and fought in the Black Hawk War (1831–32).

Thomas Drayton resigned his commission on August 15, 1836, to become resident engineer of the Louisville, Charleston & Cincinnati Railroad. Later, he moved back to Drayton Hall and became a planter. In 1860, he was president of the Charleston & Savannah Railroad, a position he left to become a brigadier general of the Confederate Army on September 25, 1861. On July 15, 1862, he and General Nathan George "Shanks" Evans were ordered to Virginia to join General Robert E. Lee with their brigades. Writing in late 1862, Lee commented that Drayton was "a source of delay and embarrassment from the time the army left Richmond." Generals James Longstreet, D. R. Jones, and Lafayette McLaws also criticized Drayton. He fought in the Battle of Second Manassas, the Battle of South Mountain (defending Turner's Gap) and at Sharpsburg, where his brigade was routed. He was relieved of his command and relegated to backwater assignments, which included sitting on the court of inquiry to investigate Mansfield Lovell's defense of New Orleans.

Still, Lee hoped that "some duty may be found" for Drayton that "he may be able to perform." On August 26, 1863, Drayton was ordered to report to General Theophilus H. Holmes, commanding the District of Arkansas in the Trans-Mississippi Department. There, General Sterling Price gave Drayton command of an infantry brigade and later his own old division, before General Edmund Kirby Smith reassigned Drayton to the Eastern Subdistrict of Texas on March 3, 1864. He sat out the rest of the war more or less unemployed.

Following the surrender, General Drayton found his property was confiscated. His attempt to manage a plantation in Dooly County, Georgia, failed. He moved to Charlotte, North Carolina, in 1871, where he set up a real estate and insurance agency. He was regarded as cheerful, hardworking, and uncomplaining no matter the circumstances. He was a member of the vestry of St. Peter's Episcopal Church of Charlotte and was considered "a most zealous and devout Christian." Clearly, he was a better man than he was a general.

In 1890, General Drayton suffered a stroke that left him partially paralyzed. He died at his daughter's home in Florence, South Carolina, on February 18, 1891, at age eighty-two. He was buried in Elmwood Cemetery, Charlotte, North Carolina.

DUDLEY MCIVER DUBOSE was born on October 28, 1834, in Shelby County, Tennessee, near the city of Memphis. His ancestors were French Huguenots. His father was a planter.

Dudley DuBose attended the University of Mississippi at Oxford. Then he returned to Tennessee and enrolled in the Lebanon Law School, from which he graduated in 1856. He was admitted to the bar in 1857, set up a law practice in Memphis, and in 1858 married Sarah Ann "Sallie" Toombs, a distant cousin. She was the only surviving child of U.S. Senator Robert Toombs of Georgia.

By 1860, DuBose moved his family to Augusta, Georgia, where he founded another law office. When the war began, he became a lieutenant in the 15th Georgia Infantry, and his father-in-law became his brigade commander. He was an aide to Toombs (1861–62) and was promoted to captain and assistant adjutant general on January 29, 1862. DuBose fought in the Seven Days Battles, the Battle of Second Manassas, and the battles of Sharpsburg and Fredericksburg. In January 1863, he was promoted to colonel and assumed command of the 15th Georgia.

D·

After taking part in the Siege of Suffolk, Colonel DuBose led his regiment at Gettysburg on July 2 and 3, mostly in the Devil's Den and Little Round Top sectors. He was wounded but not seriously.

In the fall of 1863, DuBose was with General Longstreet in his famous attack during the Battle of Chickamauga. Colonel DuBose was wounded, but he returned to duty to take part in the Siege of Knoxville. After Longstreet's corps returned to the Army of Northern Virginia, DuBose fought in the Battle of the Wilderness. He temporarily commanded Henry Benning's brigade at Spotsylvania and Cold Harbor and was promoted to brigadier general (temporary rank) on November 30, 1864, to date from November 16, taking command of William T. Wofford's brigade (Wofford had been wounded and reassigned) in General Joseph B. Kershaw's division.

Dudley DuBose led his brigade in the Siege of Petersburg and in the retreat to Appomattox, although he never made it there. He was captured at Sayler's Creek on April 6, 1865. Taken to Fort Warren in Boston Harbor, he was paroled and released on July 24.

General DuBose's veterans remembered him as a highly competent and demanding regimental and brigade commander. They respected him.

After the war, DuBose moved to his spouse's hometown of Washington, Georgia, in Wilkes County, fifty-five miles from Augusta. His wife died in 1866, and his mother-in-law moved in to run the household and take care of her grandchildren. DuBose, meanwhile, became deeply involved in the effort to restore home rule to Georgia during the Reconstruction era. Backed by Robert Toombs, General DuBose was elected to Congress in 1870, serving until March 3, 1873.

Following his Congressional term, Dudley DuBose returned to his law practice, where he was a partner with his father-in-law. In 1883, he suffered a stroke and died in Washington on March 2. He was forty-eight years old. General DuBose is buried in Resthaven Cemetery, Washington, Georgia, beside his wife. Robert Toombs and other members of the Toombs and DuBose families are interred nearby.

BASIL WILSON DUKE was born on May 28, 1838, in Scott County, near Georgetown, Kentucky, the only child of a career naval officer. Relatively tall (five feet ten) and very thin (130 pounds), he was educated at Georgetown College and Centre College in Kentucky (1853–55) before studying law at Transylvania University in Lexington, Kentucky, from which he graduated in 1858. That same year, he moved to Missouri. He was an ardent secessionist.

In April 1861, Basil Duke returned to Lexington to marry Henrietta Hunt Morgan, the sister of Confederate General John Hunt Morgan. Her sister, Catherine "Kitty" Morgan, married A. P. Hill.

In October 1861, Duke enlisted in Morgan's Lexington Rifles as a private and was quickly elected second lieutenant. He was promoted to first lieutenant in November 1861. The Rifles expanded and became the 2nd Kentucky Cavalry Regiment, and Duke was their training officer—a field in which he excelled. He was seriously wounded at Shiloh. After he recovered, he was promoted to lieutenant colonel in August 1862 and then to colonel on December 7.

As a leader, Duke had a way of issuing orders with gentleness, which made him popular among the troops. He was also cool and calm in a crisis and enjoyed combat.

Morgan's Cavalry was primarily a raiding force and was often called "Morgan's Raiders" instead of "Morgan's Cavalry." It captured twelve thousand prisoners in 1862 alone. On December 29, Duke was seriously wounded by a shell fragment while crossing a stream. He could not rejoin the Raiders until March 1863, when he became commander of the 2nd Kentucky Cavalry Regiment. A brigade commander by April 1863, he took part in Morgan's Ohio Raid and was captured in the Battle of Buffington Island on July 19, 1863.

Basil Duke was a prisoner of war until August 3, 1864, when he was exchanged. After Morgan was killed on September 4, Duke took charge of what was left of Morgan's command. He was promoted to brigadier

D·

general on September 19, to date from September 15. He skirmished with Union forces in East Tennessee and southwest Virginia until early 1865, when President Jefferson Davis ordered him to Richmond. He was with the president as the city fell and Davis had to flee from the Federals. Duke took part in the last Confederate war council in Abbeville, South Carolina, on May 2, 1865. General Duke surrendered to the bluecoats at Augusta, Georgia, on May 10.

After the war, Duke settled in Louisville and set up a law practice. He was a strong, public advocate of reconciliation after the war. He was a delegate to the Democratic National Convention in 1868 and was elected to the Kentucky House of Representatives in 1869. He was also a prolific writer on the subject of Southern and Confederate history. He was the editor of the *Southern Bivouac* (1885–87), wrote *History of Morgan's Cavalry* (1867), *History of the Bank of Kentucky, 1792–1895* (1895), and *Reminiscences of General Basil W. Duke* (1911), as well as dozens of articles. President Theodore Roosevelt appointed Duke commissioner of the Shiloh National Military Park in 1904. He was active in the United Confederate Veterans.

One of the last living Confederate generals, he was plagued by ill health in his last years. He died at the age of seventy-eight on September 16, 1916, in Manhattan, New York, where he had gone for surgeries that had resulted in two amputations. He is buried in Lexington Cemetery, Lexington, Kentucky. His grave is directly in front of General Morgan's.

JOHNSON KELLY DUNCAN was born on March 19, 1827, in York County, Pennsylvania, and was raised and educated in rural Pennsylvania. He was appointed to the U.S. Military Academy in 1845 and graduated in 1849. Commissioned a brevet second lieutenant in the artillery, he was sent to Florida, where he saw combat against the Seminoles.

From 1850–53 he was stationed in Maine at Fort Sullivan and Fort Preble and then took part in the Northern Pacific railroad exploration expedition to the northwest. He resigned from the army in 1855 and moved to New Orleans, where he worked as a civil engineer, surveyor, and architect. He became superintendent of government construction in New Orleans, worked with G. T. Beauregard on completing the New Orleans Branch Mint, and later became chief engineer of the board of public works for the state of Louisiana.

By the time the Civil War began, Duncan considered himself a Louisianian. President Jefferson Davis appointed him a colonel and he supervised the evacuation of Ship Island in the fall of 1861. Afterward, he was placed in charge of the coastal artillery defenses of New Orleans.

Duncan was one of the finest artillery officers available, but in defending New Orleans, he and his district commander, Major General Mansfield Lovell, had an impossible task. New Orleans was one of the least defensible cities in North America. Duncan's responsibility included Fort Jackson and Fort St. Philip, on the western and eastern banks of the lower Mississippi River, respectively. General Lovell was much pleased with Duncan's improvements to the forts. He wrote to President Davis and urged that Duncan be promoted to brigadier general, declaring, "He is worth a dozen of [men like Brigadier General Daniel] Ruggles." The president acted upon his recommendation, and Duncan was promoted to brigadier general on January 9, 1862, to date from January 7.

But Duncan could not do enough to prepare the city for defense. No one could have. He fought well but was forced to surrender Forts Jackson and St. Philip on April 28.

The citizens of New Orleans did not hold Duncan responsible for this disaster; rather, they blamed General Lovell and the Confederate Navy. When Duncan was brought into the city, a crowd formed and cheered him as a hero.

After he was exchanged on August 15, 1862, Johnson Duncan briefly commanded a brigade (August 21–October 12) and a reserve division (October 12–November 10) before he was appointed chief of staff to Braxton Bragg and the Army of Tennessee on November 20. He never assumed this post, however, because he came down with typhoid fever on November 15 and died December 18, 1862, in Knoxville, Tennessee. He was thirty-five years old.

General Duncan was an ardent Christian. He was buried in McGavock Confederate Cemetery on the Carnton Plantation in Franklin, Tennessee. His only child, a daughter, was born five months after her father's death.

JOHN DUNOVANT was born on March 5, 1825, in Chester, South Carolina, the son of a medical doctor. Little is known of John's early life and education. He joined the Palmetto Regiment as a private when the Mexican War broke out, and he rose to the rank of sergeant. He was severely wounded in the Battle of Chapultepec on the road to Mexico City. Discharged in late 1847, he was commissioned directly into the Regular Army as a captain in 1855, when the War Department was organizing a new regiment, the 10th Infantry, at Carlisle Barracks, Pennsylvania. An ardent secessionist, he resigned his commission on December 29, nine days after South Carolina seceded.

Dunovant was a major of militia during the operations against Fort Sumter. On July 22, he became colonel and commander of the 1st South Carolina Regulars and was stationed on Sullivan's Island and at Fort Moultrie. He remained there for some time. He was bored with garrison duty, drank a lot, and clashed with his superiors.

After the Battle of Secessionville on June 16, 1862, Colonel Dunovant was arrested, court-martialed, and cashiered for drunkenness on November 8, 1862. President Jefferson Davis endorsed the verdict and summarily dismissed Dunovant from the service. Governor Francis W. Pickens gave Dunovant a second chance when he appointed him colonel of the 5th South Carolina Cavalry on July 28, 1863. Dunovant spent the next ten months engaged in the Siege of Charleston.

On April 25, 1864, as Grant and his legions geared up for their offensive against Robert E. Lee's Army of Northern Virginia, Dunovant and his command were ordered to the Old Dominion.

Here, John Dunovant restored his reputation, as the performance of the 5th South Carolina Cavalry exceeded all expectations. It played a major role in the Confederate victory in the Second Battle of Drewry's Bluff on May 16, 1864, and in the subsequent battles against Philip Sheridan's cavalry, most of which the South won. Dunovant was wounded by a pistol ball in the left hand on May 28 but was back on duty and performed well in the Battles of Cold Harbor, Trevilian Station, and the early stages of the Siege of Petersburg.

It was obvious that John Dunovant did much better on the battlefield than in tedious garrison duty. He had so redeemed himself in the eyes of Jefferson Davis that the president, on the recommendation of Wade Hampton and with the concurrence of Robert E. Lee, promoted him to brigadier general (temporary rank) on August 22 and gave him command of Matthew C. Butler's old brigade of Wade Hampton's cavalry division.

General Dunovant was a fine regimental commander but was not so good at the brigade level. He made several tactical mistakes in the fall of 1864, and his reconnaissance reports were sometimes faulty. On the Vaughan Road south of the James River on October 1, 1864, he led a desperate (and possibly rash) cavalry charge, during which he was shot in the chest and died almost instantly.

General John Dunovant's body was buried in the Dunovant Family Burying Ground, three miles southeast of Chester.

E

EARLY – EWELL

JUBAL ANDERSON "JUBE" EARLY was born in Franklin County, Virginia, in the foothills of the Blue Ridge Mountains, on November 3, 1816, the son of a wealthy tobacco planter. Young "Jube" received a good education from local private schools. He was admitted to West Point in 1833 and graduated in the class of 1837.

He was commissioned in the artillery and fought the Seminoles. In 1838, Jubal Early resigned his commission and returned to Rocky Mount in Franklin County to study law. He was admitted to the bar in 1840, but as he admitted later, he was an indifferent businessman, so his practice was never very lucrative. Early was also fractious and ornery and loved liquor and chewing tobacco. He was, as Gilbert Moxley Sorrel recalled, "of a snarling, rasping disposition," which helped his business not at all.

Early won election to the Virginia House of Delegates as a Whig, serving in the 1841–42 term. He was the youngest member of the legislature at that time. He was defeated for reelection. From 1843 to 1852, Early was the commonwealth attorney (prosecuting attorney) for Franklin County. He became a major of volunteers in the Virginia Regiment during the Mexican War but arrived in northern Mexico too late to engage in combat. He did, however, start developing the painful chronic arthritis that left him with a permanent stoop and plagued him until his death.

Early was a member of the Virginia Secession Convention. He opposed leaving the Union, but when Virginia seceded, he went with it. On June 19, 1861, he was appointed colonel of the 24th Virginia Infantry Regiment. On July 21, 1861, his brilliant charge against the Union's right flank at the Battle of First Manassas routed the Union forces, and he was promoted to brigadier general that same day.

In most of the major battles the Army of Northern Virginia fought from the Seven Days (June–July 1862) to Cold Harbor (May–June 1864), Early distinguished himself as a brigade or division commander. He was twice wounded in the Battle of Williamsburg. He was promoted to major general on January 23, 1863. His date of rank was January 17.

Early was anything but popular with his men because of his profanity, sarcasm, and biting tongue, but he was an excellent tactical commander at the brigade and divisional levels. On the first day of the Battle of Gettysburg (July 1, 1863), he helped smash General John F. Reynolds's I Corps but then apparently lost his nerve, objecting to General Robert E. Lee's suggestion that General Richard S. Ewell (the new commander of II Corps) attack Cemetery Hill that evening. The attack did not happen, and Lee's army lost a major opportunity to take the high ground and turn the Union flank. Union reinforcements arrived that night, and the Confederate efforts to turn the U.S. right on July 2 and 3 were unsuccessful.

Early fought well in the Overland Campaign and replaced Ewell as commander of II Corps on May 29, 1864. He was promoted to lieutenant general (temporary rank) on May 31, 1864, and led the corps with considerable success at Cold Harbor.

"Old Jube" was sent to the Shenandoah Valley in June 1864, promptly clearing it of Federal forces and even threatening Washington, D.C. He was, however, outnumbered more than two to one and was eventually defeated in the Third Battle of Winchester. Early was also defeated at Fisher's Hill, despite having a good defensive position, and then again at Cedar Creek where, after a highly successful surprise attack, he became hesitant and indecisive. He allowed the Yankees time to rally and rout his forces.

After Cedar Creek, Lee recalled II Corps to Richmond, leaving Old Jube with only one brigade of infantry and Lunsford Lomax's cavalry. Philip Sheridan overwhelmed Early's ragtag band at Waynesboro on March 2, 1865, effectively clearing the Shenandoah of Confederate forces except for partisans and irregulars. General Lee relieved Early of his command on March 29. After Lee surrendered, Early escaped to Mexico and then Canada. He did not return to the United States until 1869. The former anti-secessionist was now an Unreconstructed Rebel and remained so until his death.

In 1866, he published *A Memoir of the Last Year of the War for Independence, in the Confederate States of America*. In 1873, he became a founder and president of the Southern Historical Society and was a frequent contributor to the *Southern Historical Society Papers*, where he attempted to destroy the military reputation of James Longstreet and glorify the Lost Cause. Along with General G. T. Beauregard, he supervised the drawings of the (corrupt) Louisiana lottery.

On February 16, 1894, he fell down the granite stairs at the Lynchburg post office and never recovered from his injuries. He died quietly at home on March 2. He was seventy-seven years old. General Early is buried in Spring Hill Cemetery, Lynchburg. His *Autobiographical Sketch and Narrative of the War Between the States* was published posthumously in 1912.

Early's performance as a general was uneven. He certainly proved to be a better brigade and division commander than he was a corps or army commander, although he had flashes of brilliance at those levels. His hesitations at Cemetery Hill and Cedar Creek, however, were devastating to the Confederacy.

JOHN ECHOLS was born on March 20, 1823, in Lynchburg, Virginia. He attended the Virginia Military Institute in Lexington but dropped out to attend Washington College, which was also in Lexington. He studied law at Harvard, was admitted to the bar, and opened up a practice in Monroe County, Virginia.

John Echols was a big man, standing six feet four and weighing 260 pounds (the average man of his day stood about five feet eight and weighed about 143 pounds). He was very congenial and was said to have rarely made an enemy and never lost a friend.

He was a member of the Virginia House of Delegates (1852–53) and the Virginia Secession Convention. He voted against secession but changed his mind after Lincoln called for seventy-five thousand volunteers to suppress the "rebellion."

During the organization of Confederate forces, Echols was appointed commander of the 27th Virginia Regiment on May 30, 1861. It was part of the Stonewall Brigade in the Battle of First Manassas. He was promoted to colonel on October 14, 1861. He fought in the First Battle of Kernstown on March 23, 1862, where he was severely wounded when a Union musket ball went through his arm near the shoulder and shattered the bone. While he was recovering, Echols was promoted to brigadier general on April 18, with a date of rank of April 16.

General Echols was given command of a brigade operating in western Virginia in September 1862 and took part in General William Loring's occupation of the Kanawha Valley. Echols fell ill, however, and took a medical leave of absence on November 10, 1862. He did not return to duty until April 1863. He was given command of a brigade in the Trans-Allegheny Department and led the Confederate forces in the Battle of Droop Mountain (November 6, 1863). He was outnumbered four to one (five thousand men to twelve hundred men). Echols performed capably but could not avoid defeat. He was more successful in the Battle of New Market (May 15, 1864) where, as part of John C. Breckinridge's command, he helped rout the Union Army of the Shenandoah under Franz Sigel.

Robert E. Lee recalled Echols's brigade to the Richmond sector after New Market. Echols took part in the Battle of Cold Harbor and commanded a division in the early stages of the Siege of Petersburg. He was named commander of the District of Southwestern Virginia and played a part in the First Battle of Saltville (October 2). From January until March 29, 1865, he led a division in Jubal Early's Army of the Valley before replacing him as commander of the Department of Western Virginia.

After Richmond fell, Echols accompanied President Davis as far as Augusta, Georgia. He was paroled on May 1 and pardoned on November 4, 1865. He returned home after the conflict to find that the new state of West Virginia had enacted a law which would not allow former Confederates to practice law within its borders. Echols moved to Staunton, established a law office there, and became a prominent businessman. He was also a leader in the United Confederate Veterans. He was elected to the Virginia legislature once more, serving from 1878 to 1881. Echols rebuilt his wealth and became president of the National Valley Bank in Staunton. He lived in Kentucky most of the last ten years of his life, managing a railroad.

General John Echols passed away from Bright's disease at his son's residence, Oakdene, in Staunton, Virginia, on May 24, 1896, at seventy-three. He is buried in the Thornrose Cemetery, Staunton.

MATTHEW DUNCAN ECTOR was born in Putnam County, Georgia, on February 28, 1822, but was raised in Meriwether County. He was educated at Centre College, Danville, Kentucky, and studied law in Greenville, Georgia. Admitted to the bar in 1844, he served a term in the Georgia legislature (1845–47) and in a Georgia regiment in Mexico before becoming a farmer. He moved to Texas in 1851, opened a law office in Henderson, and was elected to the Texas legislature in 1855. When the Civil War began, Ector enlisted as a private in the 3rd Texas Cavalry. Shortly after, he was promoted to lieutenant. He fought at Wilson's Creek, Missouri, Chustenahlah in the Cherokee Nation, Indian Territory, and Pea Ridge, Arkansas, as well as in the Siege of Corinth, Mississippi. In April and May 1862, he served as adjutant to Brigadier General Joseph L. Hogg. After Hogg's death in May, he was elected colonel of the 14th Texas Cavalry (Dismounted) and led this regiment successfully in the Battle of Richmond, Kentucky. He was promoted to brigadier general on September 15, to rank from August 23. He was given a brigade on October 23, and fought in the Second Battle of Murfreesboro, after which General William Hardee commended him. He and his men were then transferred to Mississippi in May 1863, where they formed part of the Army of Relief during the Vicksburg Campaign.

Ector fought at Chickamauga, where he received three slight wounds. His brigade was sent to Mississippi on September 22, 1863, but was recalled to Georgia in May 1864 and was heavily engaged in the struggle for Atlanta. His active military career ended in the Battle of New Hope Church on July 27, 1864, where he was badly wounded and had his left leg amputated at the knee.

Ector was well regarded, but the war ended before he was sufficiently recovered to assume a new command. He was paroled at Meridian, Mississippi, on May 10, 1865, and was pardoned on August 8, 1866.

After the war, General Ector returned to Henderson, Texas, where he resumed his law practice. He was elected a district judge but was removed from office by the corrupt carpetbagger regime in 1867 on the grounds that he was a "Southern obstructionist." The next year, he moved to Marshall, Texas, where he formed a law partnership. After home rule was restored, he was appointed judge of the 7th District and was elected to the court of appeals in 1875. His colleagues elected him presiding judge of the court of appeals in 1876. He held this position until he died of kidney disease in Tyler, Texas, on October 29, 1879. He was fifty-seven years old. General Matthew D. Ector is buried in Greenwood Cemetery, Marshall, Texas. Ector County, Texas, is named after him.

STEPHEN ELLIOTT, JR., was born on October 26, 1830, in Beaufort, South Carolina, the son of a large plantation owner. Elliot attended Harvard and graduated from South Carolina College in 1850. He then became a planter on Parris Island and a locally famous yachtsman and fisherman. He was elected to the legislature in 1859 and became captain of the Beaufort Volunteer Artillery.

He took part in the bombardment of Fort Sumter. His company became part of the 11th South Carolina Infantry Regiment on June 12, but it remained an artillery unit. Captain Elliott became famous in South Carolina both as a gunner and as a raider. Among other things, he captured a 1,200-ton Union sailing ship, sank the U.S.S. *George Washington*, and twice routed Union forces in the battles on the Pocotaligo River. He was promoted to major of artillery on April 10, 1863, to rank from November 15, 1862.

Elliott was in command of the Confederate forces at Fort Sumter when the Yankees made a major attempt to capture it on September 8–9, 1863. Elliott's men took 125 prisoners and captured five boats. There were no Confederate casualties.

The Yankees blasted Fort Sumter with nineteen thousand shells from September 5 to December 11. Elliott, though wounded twice, maintained his command amid the ruins of the famous fort. At G. T. Beauregard's request, he was promoted to lieutenant colonel on November 21, 1863, to rank from September 9.

On April 25, 1864, Elliott was promoted to colonel, with a date of rank of April 20. Sent to Virginia, he briefly commanded the Holcombe Legion, but he was promoted to brigadier general on May 25, 1864, to rank from May 24, and was given command of Nathan G. Evans's former brigade.

Elliott and his men were in combat in the Petersburg trenches within a week of his assumption of command. On July 30, 1864, Union engineers detonated four tons of explosives underneath his command, decimating two of his regiments and beginning the Battle of the Crater. The general was asleep when the bomb exploded and woke up to chaos. Fortunately, he had already developed a contingency plan for dealing with such an event and quickly launched a counterattack. This rapid reaction materially contributed to the eventual Southern victory. Elliott, however, was not there to see it. He was badly wounded by Union bullets in the upper left lung and left arm during the counterattack and was carried to the rear.

It took General Elliott months to recover. He returned to duty on January 2, 1865. He was given command of a brigade of South Carolinians and Georgians engaged in the defense of James Island and Charleston. They were largely inexperienced but nevertheless defeated several Union probes. They fought in the Battle of Bentonville, where General Elliott was hit in the arm and caught a piece of shrapnel in his leg. He was sent home to recover and was still there when Confederate General Joseph E. Johnston surrendered.

For all his daring, Stephen Elliott was a quiet man—Mary Chesnut described him as "modest"—and he did not live long after the war. His plantation was seized on the pretext that he had failed to pay taxes. He moved to Charleston, earned a living as a fisherman, and lived in a fishing hut. He was reelected to the South Carolina legislature but passed away before he could take office. He died from the effects of his wounds on February 21, 1866, in Aiken, South Carolina, at the age of thirty-five. He is buried in St. Helena's Episcopal Churchyard in the town of his birth.

ARNOLD ELZEY was born **ARNOLD ELZEY JONES, JR.,** on December 18, 1816, at Elmwood, a plantation along the Manokin River in Somerset County, Maryland. Young Arnold attended West Point and graduated in 1837. He then dropped the last name "Jones," adopted the name of his paternal grandmother, and became Arnold Elzey.

An artillery officer, he fought in the Second Seminole War in Florida. He served with both Zachary Taylor's and Winfield Scott's armies in the Mexican War, fighting at Fort Brown and from Veracruz to Mexico City. He was brevetted captain after Churubusco and was promoted to captain (full rank) in 1849. He also fought in the Third Seminole War (1849–50) and was commandant of the Augusta Arsenal in 1861.

Elzey resigned his commission on April 25 and was appointed major of artillery but was then named colonel of the newly formed 1st Maryland Infantry Regiment on June 17. His regiment was part of Edmund Kirby Smith's brigade, which was hurriedly transported by rail to Manassas in time for the battle on July 21. About five minutes into the fighting, Kirby Smith was seriously wounded. As senior colonel of the brigade, Elzey assumed command. He helped stabilize the

Rebel line, launched a successful charge, and played a conspicuous role in the Southern victory. General G. T. Beauregard called Elzey "the Blücher of the Day," referring to the hero of Waterloo. President Jefferson Davis was so pleased with his performance that he promoted him to brigadier general on the spot.

Elzey and his brigade took part in Stonewall Jackson's Valley Campaign of 1862. He was shot in the leg at Cross Keys and had a horse shot out from under him, but his injuries were not serious. His performance in the Shenandoah Valley was brilliant. General Richard Ewell officially gave Elzey credit for selecting the strong Rebel defensive position at Cross Keys that contributed to the Confederate victory. He continued with Jackson until the Battle of Gaines' Mill (June 27), when a minié ball struck the right side of his face just above the mouth and passed through his head and out behind his left ear. So bad was his wound that he was never again able to exercise active field command for any extended period of time.

He had only partially recovered on December 4, 1862, when he was promoted to major general and appointed commander of the Department of Richmond.

Elzey badly wanted to return to field duty in 1863 and 1864 and finally finagled a transfer to General John C. Breckinridge's command in the Shenandoah. His "division," however, was very small—only a thousand men. On September 8, he was appointed chief of artillery of the Army of Tennessee but did not take part in the Franklin-Nashville Campaign for health reasons. He was officially relieved as artillery commander on February 17, 1865. He was in Richmond when the city fell but managed to escape to the south. He was paroled in Washington, Georgia, on May 9, 1865.

Bradley T. Johnson called Elzey an "intrepid soldier and modest unassuming gentleman." Had he not been disabled at Gaines' Mill, he would have risen to the highest ranks of the Confederate Army.

After the surrender, Arnold Elzey returned to Maryland and worked a small farm near Jessup's Cut. General Elzey died on February 21, 1871, in the Church Home and Infirmary in Baltimore at age fifty-four. He is buried in Green Mount Cemetery.

CLEMENT ANSELM EVANS was born in Stewart County, near Lumpkin, Georgia, on February 25, 1833. He read law locally and in Augusta, Georgia, was admitted to the bar in January 1852 at age eighteen, setting up a practice at Lumpkin. He was elected county judge at the age of twenty-one.

Evans was elected to the Georgia Senate in 1859 as a member of the Know Nothing Party. After Lincoln was elected president, he helped form an infantry company in Stewart County. It became part of the 2nd Georgia Infantry Regiment, and Evans became a first lieutenant on January 26, 1861. He was promoted to major of the 31st Georgia Infantry effective November 18 and to colonel on May 13, 1862.

Clement Evans took part in nearly every major battle the Army of Northern Virginia fought from Seven Pines until Appomattox. He was wounded five times, most severely in the Battle of Monocacy on July 9, 1864, as General Jubal Early pushed on Washington. He was struck by two balls. One went through his left arm and the other lodged in his left side. He did not return to field duty until mid-September.

Evans served primarily under John B. Gordon. When Gordon moved up to divisional command, he succeeded him as brigadier commander on May 8, 1864, and was promoted to brigadier general on May 20, with a date of rank of May 19. When Gordon advanced to the command of the II Corps on December 9, 1864, Evans assumed command of his old division. It returned to the Richmond-Petersburg sector that same month and ended the war at Appomattox.

In December 1862, while overlooking the carnage at Fredericksburg, Evans felt that God was calling upon him to preach the lessons of brotherly love and Christian forbearance. He promised God that he would join the clergy after the war—and he did. Ordained in 1866, he

E ·

pastored several Georgia Methodist churches. He must have been an excellent preacher, because some of his sermons attracted more than one thousand people.

Clement Evans retired from the ministry in 1892. He then edited the twelve-volume *Confederate Military History*, which was first published in 1899. He was the author of the military history of Georgia, the sixth volume of the set. He also coedited the four-volume *Cyclopedia of Georgia*.

Clement Evans was active in the United Confederate Veterans, commanded its Georgia Division for years, and was commander in chief of the United Confederate Veterans from 1909 to 1911. He was also the trustee of three colleges and president of an educational loan fund association, which allowed more than one hundred young men to gain a college education.

General Evans died of interstitial nephritis and arteriosclerosis on July 2, 1911, in Atlanta, Georgia, at the age of seventy-eight. The legislature was in session but adjourned for the day so its members could attend his funeral. Three years later, it created Evans County in southeast Georgia and named it in his honor. He is buried in Oakland Cemetery, Atlanta, only a few feet from his old chieftain, General Gordon.

NATHAN GEORGE "SHANKS" EVANS was born on February 3, 1824, in Marion County, South Carolina. He attended Randolph-Macon College before gaining admission to West Point in 1844. His peers nicknamed him "Shanks" because he had skinny legs. He graduated in 1848, was commissioned in the cavalry, served on the Western frontier, and became a renowned Indian fighter. In the Battle of Wichita Village (October 1, 1858), he killed two Comanche chieftains in hand-to-hand combat. He also developed a serious drinking problem, which hamstrung his career.

Evans resigned his commission on February 27, 1861, and joined the army of his native state. Shortly after, he entered the Confederate Army as a major and was promoted to colonel in July. He briefly served as commander of the 4th South Carolina Infantry Regiment and led the 7th Brigade of G. T. Beauregard's Army of the Potomac at the Battle of First Manassas. There, Colonel Evans realized that the Union Army was attempting a turning movement against Beauregard's left flank and, on his own initiative, blocked it and probably saved the Confederate Army. He fought with fierce courage and seemed to be everywhere that day. Though Southern newspapers hailed him as a hero, his superiors did not hold him in high esteem, because of his alcoholism, crudeness, and arrogance. It is significant that he was not promoted to brigadier general until October 21, 1861, after he won a significant victory at Ball's Bluff on the Potomac.

After this victory, Evans was transferred to the command of "the Tramp Brigade" in Charleston, South Carolina, at the request of Governor Francis Pickens. Here, his leadership commanding the Confederate forces during the Battle of Secessionville was praiseworthy. Sent back to Virginia in early July, he fought in the Battle of Second Manassas under General James Longstreet. During the Maryland invasion, he directed an ad hoc division, consisting of his own brigade and that of John Bell Hood.

Evans's brigade suffered heavy losses at South Mountain and numbered fewer than three hundred men at Sharpsburg (Antietam). His division was dissolved after Sharpsburg, and he reverted to a brigade commander. In early November 1862, Evans's brigade was sent to eastern North Carolina, where it checked Union raids.

On December 14, during the Battle of Kinston, he performed poorly and was defeated. Afterward, he was court-martialed for intemperance but was acquitted. His drinking worsened after that, and his commander, W. H. C. Whiting, found Evans's brigade to be in a deplorable condition.

In 1863, Evans briefly served in the Army of Relief and the Army of Tennessee. He returned to Charleston that fall but quarreled with his superiors, and General Roswell S. Ripley (who was himself addicted to the bottle) had him arrested in September 1863 and tried for insubordination and intoxication on duty, and he was court-martialed again. Once more, though, he was acquitted.

On April 16, 1864, Evans was seriously injured in a carriage accident in Charleston. His brigade left for Virginia without him. General Evans never fully recovered from his injuries and never received another command.

After the war, General Evans became the principal of a high school in Cokesbury, South Carolina, after which he directed a Methodist Academy in Midway, Alabama. He died there on November 23, 1868, at age forty-four. He is buried in Tabernacle Cemetery, Cokesbury, South Carolina.

RICHARD STODDERT "OLD BALDY" OR "DICK" EWELL (pronounced YOU-ll) was born on February 8, 1817, in Georgetown in the District of Columbia. He was raised on the family farm, Stony Lonesome, in Prince William County, Virginia.

Dick Ewell grew up in relative poverty. Ewell's mother secured for him an appointment to West Point in 1836. He graduated in 1840 and was assigned to the 1st U.S. Dragoons. He served in the Indian Territory, on the Santa Fe and Oregon Trails, and with General Winfield Scott in Mexico, where he was brevetted captain for his courage at Contreras and Churubusco. Fully promoted to captain in 1849, he fought against Indians in the West and was wounded in a skirmish with the Apaches in 1859.

Richard Ewell was an eccentric. He was an odd-looking man: bald, with bulging eyes, he reminded many people of a bird. His voice was shrill, and in conversation his remarks were sometimes completely random. He was also noted for his hot temper and searing profanity. Religiously, he was an agnostic at best until he was converted to Christianity following his wound at the Battle of Second Manassas. "No man had a better heart nor a worse manner of showing it," General John B. Gordon recalled. He was considered likable despite his foul mouth. He was a strict disciplinarian and paid close attention to detail. He was also a bit of a hypochondriac and subsisted on frumenty, a dish of hulled wheat boiled in milk and sweetened with sugar. He was very brave.

Politically, Captain Ewell opposed secession, but after Virginia seceded, he resigned his commission on May 7, 1861, and was commissioned colonel of cavalry in the Provisional Army of Virginia on May 9. He entered Confederate service as a lieutenant colonel. He was shot in the shoulder during a skirmish near Fairfax Court House on June 1—the first field-grade officer in the Confederate Army to be wounded in action.

On June 17 1861, Richard S. Ewell was promoted to brigadier general. He commanded a brigade during the Battle of First Manassas. He was promoted to major general on January 24, 1862. That spring, Ewell (now a division commander) was sent to the Shenandoah Valley, where he labored under Stonewall Jackson.

Dick Ewell was an excellent division commander. He excelled in Stonewall Jackson's Valley Campaign and distinguished himself in the Seven Days Battles and in the Second Manassas Campaign, in which his performance was again superb. One could argue that he was the best infantry division commander in the Civil War. On August 28, during the early phase of the Battle of Second Manassas, he was seriously wounded and lost a leg.

In May 1863, Robert E. Lee reorganized his army into three infantry corps. He selected Richard S. Ewell to command the II Corps (Jackson's old command), and Ewell was promoted to lieutenant general on May 23, 1863. This appointment was a mistake. Leading a corps was too much for him. No doubt his amputation had much to do with it. At Gettysburg, his hesitation and failure to attack Cemetery Hill during the afternoon of July 1 cost the South the battle.

He performed well as a corps commander in the Battle of the Wilderness but poorly in the Battle of Spotsylvania. When his men retreated, Ewell became hysterical, causing Lee to snap, "General Ewell, you must restrain yourself! How can you expect to control these men when you have lost control of yourself? If you cannot repress your excitement, you had better retire!" Lee had to personally take command of the sector.

On May 27, 1864, Ewell was ill with diarrhea and turned command of the II Corps over to General Jubal Early. General Lee never allowed him to return to corps command; rather, he made Ewell the commander of the District of Richmond.

Richmond fell on April 3, 1865. Ewell's men were mostly clerks, older-age troops, and other noncombatants. They could not keep up with Lee's veterans during the retreat and were cut off and destroyed in the Battle of Sayler's Creek on April 6. Richard Ewell was captured and imprisoned until August 19.

Ewell retired to his wife's property near Spring Hill, Tennessee, where he became a "gentleman farmer." He died of pneumonia on January 25, 1872, in Spring Hill, Tennessee. He was fifty-four years old. He is buried in Old City Cemetery, Nashville, Tennessee.

F

FAGAN – FRY

F·

JAMES FLEMING FAGAN was born on March 1, 1828, in Clark County, Kentucky. The family moved to Little Rock, Arkansas, in 1838. He joined the 1st Arkansas Mounted Infantry as a private, served in the Mexican War, and rose to the rank of lieutenant.

In 1850, Fagan inherited his stepfather's farm in southern Arkansas. He served a term in the Arkansas House of Representatives as a Whig (1852–53) and in the Senate (1860–62). At the start of the Civil War, Fagan raised a company of infantry and became its captain. His troops were brought into the 1st Arkansas Infantry, formed on May 6, 1861, and he was elected colonel. The regiment was sent to Virginia and fought in the Battle of First Manassas on July 21, arriving late in the day. It was on garrison duty at Fredericksburg until February 1862, when it was transferred to the Army of Mississippi. It saw heavy combat at Shiloh, where it suffered 45 percent casualties.

Colonel Fagan and his men took part in the Battle of Farmington, and he led a brigade in the Siege of Corinth. He was, however, disliked by General Braxton Bragg, who suspended him from command. He was transferred west of the Mississippi River, where he assumed command of the 6th Arkansas Cavalry Regiment. He was promoted to brigadier general on September 26, 1862, with a date of rank of September 12, and led his brigade in the battles of Cane Hill and Prairie Grove.

On July 4, 1863, Fagan fought in the Battle of Helena, Arkansas, on the Mississippi River. Confederate Generals Theophilus Holmes, Sterling Price, and Fagan then retreated back to Little Rock, which fell on September 10. The Confederates continued their retreat into southwest Arkansas, where Fagan was given command of a cavalry division.

In 1864, Fagan distinguished himself in the Rebel victory at Marks' Mill (April 25), where he (the senior officer present) attacked the front of a Union column of 1,440 men and 250 supply wagons while Jo Shelby struck the rear. The Union column was wiped out; Fagan took more than a thousand prisoners, all of the wagons were captured or destroyed, and the Federals were forced to abandon their Camden (Arkansas) Expedition, which was intended to take Arkansas out of the war.

Fagan was promoted to major general on June 11, to rank from April 25, 1864, and took part in Sterling Price's disastrous Missouri Raid that fall. His division performed poorly in the Battle of Fort Davidson at Pilot Knob, Missouri. Fagan's command and that of General John S. Marmaduke were overwhelmed at Mine Creek by the Union Army of the Border on October 25. Fagan led the remnants of his formations back to Arkansas and assumed command of the 1st Cavalry Division of the cavalry corps of the Trans-Mississippi Department on December 3, 1864. He became commander of the District of Arkansas on March 31, 1865, a post he held until May 26, 1865, when the Trans-Mississippi Department surrendered. He was paroled at Washington, Arkansas, on June 20, 1865.

After the war, he returned to his farm. President U. S. Grant appointed James F. Fagan a U.S. marshal in 1875, and he served until 1877. Later that year, he became receiver for the land office in Little Rock, an office he held until 1890.

General Fagan died on September 1, 1893, at the age of sixty-five, in Little Rock, Arkansas. He is buried in Mount Holly Cemetery, Little Rock.

WINFIELD SCOTT "OLD SWET" FEATHER-STON was born on August 8, 1820, in Murfreesboro, Tennessee. He left school in 1836 and, at age seventeen, joined the local militia to fight the Creek Indians. After the war, he moved to Houston, Mississippi, where he studied law and was admitted to the bar in 1840. A strong supporter of states' rights, he was elected to Congress as a Democrat in 1846 and served from 1847 to 1851. He was defeated for reelection in 1850 by the Whig candidate.

When Mississippi seceded, Featherston organized the Mississippi Guards militia company and was elected

F .

its captain. He joined the Confederate Army on May 21, 1861, and raised the 17th Mississippi Infantry Regiment. He was elected its colonel on June 4, 1861. The regiment departed for Virginia a week later. He fought at the Battle of First Manassas and was officially praised for his gallantry at Ball's Bluff near Leesburg on October 21, 1861, where he captured two guns and more than five hundred prisoners. He was promoted to brigadier general on March 5, 1862, to rank from March 4, and was named commander of a brigade of General James Longstreet's division on April 6.

Featherston led his brigade in the first five days of the Seven Days Battles. On the sixth day, June 30, he was shot in the shoulder and severely wounded at Frayser's Farm. He recovered in time to fight in the Battle of Second Manassas, after which he was criticized by Generals James Longstreet and Cadmus Wilcox for disobeying orders. Featherston was not present during the Maryland campaign and played a minor role in the Battle of Fredericksburg. When General Robert E. Lee reorganized his army, Featherston was sacked on January 19, 1863. He asked to be transferred to the Army of Mississippi, and Featherston was given a brigade in the division of W. W. Loring (another Lee reject) during the campaigns for Vicksburg. At Champion Hill, Featherston's brigade escaped only with its foot soldiers, losing all of its guns, ambulances, supplies, and wagons while inflicting virtually no damage on the enemy.

Featherston later served in the Meridian Campaign, the Atlanta Campaign, and the Tennessee Campaign of 1864, including the battles of Franklin and Nashville. Featherston showed great courage at Franklin and in the retreat from Nashville. He commanded the remains of General Loring's division in the Carolinas, but there seems to have been no thought of promoting him to major general, even with temporary rank.

Winfield S. Featherston stood six feet two and looked like a soldier, but overall his performance during the war was mediocre. He surrendered with the Army of Tennessee on April 26, 1865, and was paroled at Greensboro, North Carolina, on May 1.

Featherston returned to his family in Holly Springs, Mississippi, resumed his law practice, and ran for the U.S. Senate in late 1865, but was unsuccessful. He played a major role in overthrowing the corrupt carpetbagger regime of Governor Adelbert Ames. He was elected to the state legislature and served from 1876 to 1878 and from 1880 to 1882. He became judge of the Second Judicial Circuit of Mississippi in 1882.

General Winfield Scott Featherston died at home of paralysis on May 28, 1891. He was seventy years old. He is buried in Hill Crest (Hillcrest) Cemetery, Holly Springs, Mississippi.

·F

SAMUEL WRAGG FERGUSON was born on November 3, 1834, in Charleston, South Carolina, the son of a planter. He was educated in private schools, was admitted to West Point in 1852, and graduated with the class of 1857 as a brevet second lieutenant. Assigned to the 1st Dragoons, Ferguson took part in the Utah War against the Mormons. He was promoted to second lieutenant on June 14, 1858, and was stationed in Walla Walla, Washington. After learning of Lincoln's election and South Carolina's secession, Ferguson resigned his commission. Returning to his home state, he first joined the militia and then became a lieutenant of cavalry in the Confederate Army and an aide to General G. T.  Beauregard. He was the first man to raise the Confederate flag over Fort Sumter in April 1861. He fought in the Battle of First Manassas, where his horse was killed by an artillery shell.

On February 24, 1862, he was named lieutenant colonel of the 28th Mississippi Cavalry Regiment and fought at Shiloh, where he briefly commanded a brigade. Later, he fought in the Battle of Farmington, the Siege of Corinth, the retreat to Tupelo, and at Vicksburg. He defended northern Mississippi from Union incursions, saw a great deal of action, and was highly praised by his commander, Major General Dabney H. Maury. He was promoted to colonel of cavalry (temporary rank) on May

F ·

7 and to brigadier general on July 28, 1863. His date of rank was July 23, the same day he assumed command of a brigade in James R. Chalmers's division. In early 1864, he opposed Sherman's Meridian Expedition. Ferguson was slightly wounded in a skirmish with Sherman's cavalry east of the Pearl River on February 24.

Ferguson's brigade was sent to the Army of Tennessee in North Georgia in early May 1864, where it performed well. It even won a victory against U.S. Colonel John T. Wilder's famous Lightning Brigade, which was armed with repeating rifles.

In late November 1864, Ferguson's former mentor, General Beauregard, recommended him for promotion to major general. This move was blocked by General Joseph Wheeler, who denounced Ferguson as insubordinate and inefficient, criticized his brigade for its high desertion rate and poor condition, and suggested that Ferguson was incompetent.

Still commanding a brigade, Ferguson opposed Sherman's march through the Carolinas, and, after Richmond fell, became part of Jefferson Davis's escort. He was paroled at Forsyth, Georgia, on May 9, 1865.

After the war, Ferguson moved to Greenville, Mississippi, read law, and was admitted to the bar. He was appointed to the Mississippi Levee Board in 1876. President Chester Alan Arthur appointed him to the Mississippi River Commission in 1885. He eventually became the Levee Board's treasurer. When it was revealed that the board's books were short $39,000, Ferguson was charged with malfeasance. He fled the country, spending several years in Ecuador, South America. Impoverished, he eventually returned to Mississippi. When he applied for a Confederate pension in 1916, he moaned that he had nothing: "I met with reverses some years ago. I lost all through the treachery of supposed friends in business."

General Ferguson died in State Hospital in Jackson, Mississippi, on February 3, 1917, at age eighty-two. He was the last of Mississippi's Confederate generals to pass away. His final resting place is Greenwood Cemetery, Jackson, Mississippi.

CHARLES WILLIAM FIELD was born on April 6, 1828, in Airy Mount, near Versailles, in Woodford County, Kentucky. President James K. Polk appointed Field to West Point as an "at large" cadet in 1845. He graduated with the class of 1849. Commissioned a brevet second lieutenant of cavalry, he spent six years on the Western frontier, fighting Indians in Texas, New Mexico, and the Great Plains. He was a cavalry instructor at West Point when Virginia seceded.

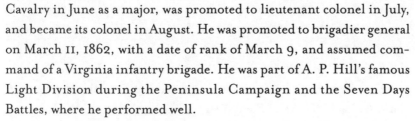

Captain Field resigned his commission on May 30, 1861, and left for Richmond, Virginia, where he was ordered to organize a school for cavalry instruction in Ashland, Virginia. He was assigned to the 6th Virginia Cavalry in June as a major, was promoted to lieutenant colonel in July, and became its colonel in August. He was promoted to brigadier general on March 11, 1862, with a date of rank of March 9, and assumed command of a Virginia infantry brigade. He was part of A. P. Hill's famous Light Division during the Peninsula Campaign and the Seven Days Battles, where he performed well.

General Field was large, jolly, and affable—well liked by his men and respected by his officers, because he was a highly competent and reliable commander at every level: regiment, brigade, and division.

Field was severely wounded in the leg on August 29 during the Battle of Second Manassas. The doctors managed to save the limb, but Field had a long recovery. He was still on crutches in May 1863 when he returned to limited active duty as chief of the Bureau of Conscription in the War Department on May 25, 1863.

On February 6, 1864, Charles Field was promoted to major general (to date from February 12) and, on the order of James Longstreet, assumed command of Simon B. Buckner's old division, which was very small. President Jefferson Davis, however, intended for him to be permanent commander of John Bell Hood's old division, the largest in the I Corps. Longstreet (who preferred Micah Jenkins) opposed this appointment so forcefully that he was reprimanded by Jefferson Davis.

The president was right: Field was a fine division leader, if not a particularly charismatic one. He fought in the Wilderness and briefly commanded the I Corps after Longstreet was wounded. He fought throughout the Overland Campaign, including at the Battle of Spotsylvania, despite being wounded twice. (Neither wound was serious.) He took part in the Battle of Cold Harbor, the Siege of Petersburg, and the retreat to Appomattox. On April 9, 1865, he still had five thousand men—the largest intact division in Robert E. Lee's army at the time of the surrender.

After the war, Field worked as a civil engineer and managed business interests in Georgia, Maryland, and the District of Columbia. In 1875, he went to Egypt, where he served Isma'il Pasha, the Khedive of Egypt, as a colonel of engineers, training Egyptian officers and directing the construction of several projects. He returned to the United States and was appointed the doorkeeper of the U.S. House of Representatives from 1878 to 1881.

From 1881 to 1888 he was a civil engineer; then he became superintendent of the Hot Springs Reservation (later named the Hot Springs National Park). General Field died on April 9, 1892, in Washington, D.C. He was sixty-four years old. He was buried in Loudon Park Cemetery, Baltimore.

JOSEPH FINEGAN (sometimes spelled Finnegan) was born in Clones (Cloonis), County Monaghan, Ireland, on November 17, 1814. He immigrated to New York in 1833 and to the Territory of Florida in 1834 but never lost his Irish brogue. He became a planter, the owner of a sawmill in Jacksonville, opened a law practice at Fernandina, and was a partner in the Florida Railroad.

The *Florida Times-Union* called him "hearty, unaffected, jovial, clear-headed, and keen-witted." No doubt he was a talented entrepreneur. By 1860, Finegan had built a forty-room mansion in Fernandina. He was elected to the Florida Secession Convention and voted to leave the Union.

He was soon named a lieutenant colonel in the Confederate Army and became commander of the 1st Florida Infantry Battalion on January 14, 1862. On April 5, Finegan was commissioned a brigadier general. Headquartered in Tallahassee, he was responsible for guarding middle and eastern Florida, worked well with Governor John Milton (who had initially opposed his appointment), rounded up Florida beef for the main Confederate armies to the north, skirmished with Union forces on the coast and prevented them from moving inland, and even recaptured Jacksonville in March 1863, although he held it only briefly.

On February 20, 1864, General Finegan fought at the Battle of Olustee, the largest battle fought in Florida during the Civil War, helping to defeat the Union forces and repulse their attempt to capture Tallahassee. For his part in the triumph, Finegan was voted the thanks of the Confederate Congress.

In May 1864, Finegan was given command of a Florida brigade and sent to the Army of Northern Virginia. He distinguished himself at Cold Harbor on June 3. He fought in the Siege of Petersburg and became acting commander of General William Mahone's division in early 1865. He led the division at Hatcher's Run and helped stop the Union advance. He continued to serve in the trenches until March 20, 1865, when he was sent back to Florida.

Joseph Finegan proved to be a useful and effective general throughout the war. He lost virtually everything he owned during the conflict but was able to sue and regain his mansion, which had been confiscated by the Freedmen's Bureau. He served as state senator for Nassau County from 1865–66, become a cotton broker in Savannah, Georgia, and eventually built a large orange grove in Orange County, Florida. After a brief illness, Joseph Finegan passed away on October 29, 1885, in Rutledge, Florida. He was seventy years old. He is buried in Old City Cemetery, Jacksonville, Florida.

F ·

JESSE JOHNSON FINLEY was born on November 18, 1812, in Wilson County, Tennessee, near Lebanon, where he was educated. Jesse read law but suspended his studies in 1836 to fight in the Second Seminole War, in which he was a captain and company commander. He returned home in 1838, finished his education, and was admitted to the bar in 1840.

Finley was a likable man, and it seemed easy for him to acquire political office. He moved to Mississippi County, Arkansas, in 1840 and was a member of the Arkansas state senate in 1841. He resigned his seat in 1842 and moved to Memphis and was mayor of the city in 1845. Next, he moved to Marianna, Florida, in November 1846, and was elected to the Florida state senate in 1850. He was judge of the Western Judicial Circuit of Florida (1853 to 1861). Under the Confederacy, he was a judge in the District of Florida, but in March 1862, he left the bench and enlisted in the Southern Army as a private.

Finley was soon elected captain of the Jackson County Volunteers, which became Companies D and E of the 6th Florida Infantry Regiment. On April 14, 1862, he was elected colonel of the 6th. He was sent to East Tennessee, where the regiment was involved in several skirmishes in the mountains and participated in the 1862 invasion of Kentucky, including the Battle of Richmond.

Finley and his men took part in the Tullahoma Campaign and the Battle of Chickamauga, where Colonel Finley distinguished himself. He captured more than five hundred prisoners on the second day of the battle.

On November 18, 1863, Finley was promoted to brigadier general to date from November 16 and assumed command of all Florida troops in the Army of Tennessee. His new brigade was caught up in the rout of Confederate forces at the Battle of Missionary Ridge, but it rallied and did well covering the retreat of the army. General Braxton Bragg wrote him a letter of commendation.

Finley was involved in heavy combat during the Atlanta Campaign, where he was badly wounded during the second day of the Battle of Resaca. He was seriously wounded again on August 31, 1864, when, in the Battle of Jonesboro, his horse was killed by shell fragments. Finley refused to be evacuated until all of his other wounded were cared for. His recuperation took months, and he was unable to return to his brigade, because a Union army stood between him and the brigade. Instead, he made his way to Columbus, Georgia, where he reported to Major General Howell Cobb. He was paroled to Quincy, Florida, on May 23.

After the war, Jesse Finley returned to Florida and the practice of law. He was elected to Congress three times and was defeated in 1882. The results of three of these four elections were contested, with Finley declared the winner twice and the loser once. He served in Congress from April 19, 1876, to March 3, 1877; February 20 to March 3, 1879; and March 4, 1881, to June 1, 1882. He was appointed to a U.S. Senate vacancy but was denied his seat due to a technicality.

General Jesse J. Finley died at his son's residence in Lake City, Florida, on November 12, 1904. Had he lived another six days, he would have been ninety-two years old. He is buried in Evergreen Cemetery, Lake City, Florida.

JOHN BUCHANAN FLOYD was born on June 1, 1806, at Smithfield in Montgomery County, Virginia (near Blacksburg), the son of John Floyd, governor of Virginia from 1830 to 1834. Young Floyd was homeschooled by his intellectual mother and studied law at South Carolina College, where he graduated in 1829.

Young Floyd and one of his brothers moved to Helena, Arkansas, to take advantage of the cotton boom but were ruined by the financial panic of 1837. John relocated to Abingdon in 1839 and set up a law practice.

Floyd proved to be a bad businessman (and bad with finances in general) but was a jovial and likable fellow who was described as muscular, athletic, and gregarious.

He was elected to the Virginia General Assembly in 1847 and was reelected in 1848. His colleagues elected him governor of Virginia in 1848. He ran on an internal improvement platform, and he served from January 1, 1849, to January 16, 1852.

As soon as his term as governor was over, Floyd was reelected to the Virginia House of Delegates. He was also a presidential elector for a personal friend, James Buchanan, in 1856. As a result, he was named secretary of war for the United States and took office on March 6, 1857.

Floyd's tenure as secretary was marked by incompetence and corruption. He was implicated in the Indian trust bonds scandal, which involved $870,000 in misappropriated bonds, and Floyd was eventually indicted for fraud, conspiracy, and malfeasance but managed to get the indictments quashed.

Secretary Floyd opposed secession until Abraham Lincoln was elected president. He strongly objected to President Buchanan's refusal to relinquish Fort Sumter to the now independent state of South Carolina and resigned on December 29, 1860. He was so broke that he had to borrow money to leave the capital.

After Virginia seceded, he was appointed major general in the Provisional Army of Virginia on April 27, 1861. John Floyd was appointed brigadier general in the Confederate Army on May 23. He was named commander of the Army of Kanawha, which contained 3,500 men. Operating in western Virginia (now West Virginia), he could not and would not cooperate with Henry A. Wise, another former governor and a hated political rival. The third general in the sector, W. W. Loring, would not cooperate with anybody. President Jefferson Davis sent Robert E. Lee to coordinate the three, but he was unsuccessful.

In July 1861, U.S. forces pushed the Confederates out of the Kanawha Valley. An investigator wrote to Davis urging that both former governors be removed because they hated each other worse than the enemy. Davis sacked Wise and on December 26 transferred Floyd to the Army of Central Kentucky. General Albert Sidney Johnston sent Floyd and his Virginia regiments to Fort Donelson in early 1862.

Floyd mishandled the Battle of Fort Donelson badly and, on the advice of General Simon Buckner, surrendered the fort (which he need not have done). He did not, however, surrender himself. Fearing trial before a Unionist court, he escaped in the middle of the night via steamboat, taking his 1,500 Virginia troops with him and leaving the rest of the garrison to its fate. General Grant captured 12,400 men. Floyd also mishandled the evacuation of Nashville, which fell on February 25.

Jefferson Davis relieved General Floyd of duty on March 11, 1862. Floyd used his political influence to be appointed a Virginia state major general (May 17, 1862), but his health soon failed him. Stress and despair no doubt contributed to his death, which occurred at his foster daughter's home in Abingdon on August 26, 1863. He was fifty-seven years old. He is buried in Sinking Spring Cemetery, Abingdon.

JOHN HORACE FORNEY was born August 12, 1829, in Lincolnton, North Carolina. He was the younger brother of William Henry Forney, who was also a future Confederate general. Forney's cousins included future Southern Generals Robert D. Johnston, Stephen D. Ramseur, and Robert F. Hoke.

The Forney family moved from North Carolina to Benton County (now Calhoun County), Alabama, in 1835. John was described as "a man of superb physique, a tall, majestic figure as handsome as any Vandyke or Velasquez picture." He was educated by private tutors and was admitted to West Point in 1848. He graduated in 1852 and was commissioned in the infantry. He fought Indians in New Mexico, the Dakota Territory, and Minnesota.

Forney resigned his commission on January 23, 1861, and was appointed colonel of artillery and commander of the 1st Alabama Artillery Regiment (state militia) and sent to Pensacola. He then became an infantry captain in the Confederate Army and was elected colonel of the 10th Alabama Infantry Regiment on June 4, 1861. Sent to Virginia, he led the regiment in the Battle of First Manassas. He fought in the Battle of Dranesville on December 20, 1861, where he led a charge through what J. E. B. Stuart described as "a shower of bullets." One of those bullets struck him in the arm, and the wound bothered John Forney for the rest of his life.

Forney was promoted to brigadier general on March 14, 1862, with a date of rank of March 10, and was sent to Mobile, where he commanded more than ten thousand men. He was promoted to major general on October 27, 1862. He commanded a division during the Siege of Vicksburg and defended two critical miles in the center of the Vicksburg perimeter. He played a major role in smashing Grant's assaults on the city on May 19 and 22, 1863, and held his lines until the garrison surrendered on July 4, despite repeated Union attacks and mining operations.

Forney was released on parole at Enterprise, Mississippi, on July 13. He was exchanged on October 13 and ordered to assume command of a division in the Department of Mississippi and East Louisiana. He held this command until May 1864. After a period of unemployment, he succeeded John G. Walker as commander of the famous Texas Greyhound Division on September 3, 1864. He was not popular with the Texans because he was a strict disciplinarian. He was commander of the Department of Texas, New Mexico, and Arizona from March 27 to May 12, 1865. General Forney was paroled at Galveston on June 20.

Forney returned to Alabama and farmed in Calhoun and Marengo counties. He later accepted a position as a civil engineer with the Selma, Rome, and Dalton Railroad. After that, he moved to Anniston, Alabama, to work for the city. Finally, he designed the waterworks for Jacksonville, Alabama, and the road from Jacksonville to White Plains, Alabama.

John H. Forney died in Jacksonville, Alabama, on September 13, 1902, at the age of seventy-three. He was buried in Jacksonville City Cemetery with full military honors.

WILLIAM HENRY FORNEY, the older brother of Confederate Major General John H. Forney, was born on November 9, 1823, in Lincolnton,

North Carolina, the third of nine children. He moved to Jacksonville, Alabama, with his family in 1835. Educated by private tutors, he attended the University of Alabama, where he received his bachelor's degree in 1844. He returned to Jacksonville and studied law in an older brother's law office.

Forney fought in the Mexican War with Winfield Scott's army. After Mexico, he returned to Jacksonville and continued his legal studies. He was admitted to the Alabama bar in 1848, opened up a law practice in Jacksonville, earned a master's degree from the University of Alabama in 1853, and was a trustee for the university from 1851 to 1860. He was elected to the Alabama legislature in 1859.

After Alabama seceded, Forney joined the Pope Walker Guards as its captain. It became Company G of the 10th Alabama. The regiment arrived in Virginia after the Battle of First Manassas, but William Forney fought in the Battle of Dranesville, where he was wounded in the shinbone—the first of thirteen wounds he suffered during the war. It took him two months to recover. He was promoted to major on January 28, 1862, and to lieutenant colonel on May 3.

William Forney took part in the Peninsula Campaign and was wounded at Williamsburg, where he was shot in the right shoulder. The bullet broke a bone. He was carried to William and Mary College, which was converted into a military hospital. He was captured when the Union army overran the place on May 6 but was paroled on July 29 and exchanged on August 31, 1862. He returned to his regiment to find that he was now its commander. His colonel had been killed at Gaines' Mill.

Forney led the 10th Alabama at Fredericksburg, Chancellorsville, and Salem Church. On July 2, 1863, during the Battle of Gettysburg, he directed his regiment in a counterattack near Plum Run and fought along the Emmitsburg Road, where he was wounded in the arm and chest. Forney continued to lead his men forward until he was shot in the right arm and left heel. He lost one-third of his heel bone, which left him maimed for life. His wounds were too severe for him to be moved, and he was captured on July 5.

William Forney was a prisoner of war until August 3, 1864, when he was exchanged. Despite being on crutches, he was named acting commander of John C. C. Sanders's brigade after that officer was killed in action on August 21. Later, he was given command of General Cadmus Wilcox's old Alabama brigade. He was promoted to brigadier general on February 22, 1865, with a date of rank of February 15. Meanwhile, he served in the Siege of Petersburg (including in the Bermuda Hundred trenches) and in the retreat to Appomattox. He surrendered with Robert E. Lee's army on April 9 and was paroled three days later.

After the war, Forney returned to his law practice. He was elected to the Alabama state senate in 1865 and 1866 but was ousted by the Radical Republicans when Congressional Reconstruction began in March 1867. A champion of home rule, General Forney was elected to the U.S. House of Representatives in 1876 and served from 1877 to 1893. He did not run for reelection in 1892. His death occurred in Jacksonville, Alabama, on January 16, 1894. He was seventy years of age. He is buried in Jacksonville City Cemetery.

NATHAN BEDFORD FORREST (called "Bedford") and his twin sister Frances "Fanny" Forrest were born near the hamlet of Chapel Hill, Tennessee, on July 13, 1821. He grew up in poverty.

Forrest's story is a prototypical American story. A first-grade dropout with no money, influence, or family connections, he became a highly successful businessman, worth $1,500,000 dollars ($43,853,810 in 2020 money). By 1860, he was a planter, land speculator, slave trader, and (after he saved a man from being lynched) was twice elected to the Memphis, Tennessee, City Council. He was an exemplary public servant.

Bedford Forrest was an outstanding physical specimen, and he had a fierce temper. Although he hated war,

Forrest got a thrill out of fighting. During his legendary career, he personally killed thirty Yankees in one-on-one combat, as well as two Confederates, a gunfighter and a wifebeater. He was severely wounded four times during the war and suffered many minor wounds. In battle, he could almost always be found in the front line.

Forrest married a demure Christian woman and was completely devoted to her; indeed, he treated all women as if they were queens. He did not believe in sex outside of marriage and once cashiered one of his best friends for having sexual relations with an unmarried female, stating that he would not have in his army anyone who would "do that" to a woman, nor would he tolerate any man telling dirty jokes in front of a woman.

Forrest was a strong Unionist until the John Brown attack on Harpers Ferry and Abraham Lincoln's call for seventy-five thousand men to suppress the "rebellion" in the cotton states. He joined the Confederate Army as a private on June 14, 1861, and rose to lieutenant general.

His victories are too numerous to discuss here. The people of what was then considered the "Old Southwest" looked upon him as a protector; he became a psychological threat to the Union troops, whose begrudging respect for him sometimes crossed the line into outright admiration; and the Union generals hated and feared him. Robert E. Lee (who never met him) called him the best general the Civil War produced, and Ulysses Grant, G. T. Beauregard, and Joe Johnston, among others, heaped praise on Forrest, as did William Tecumseh Sherman, who called him "the greatest cavalryman America ever produced."

Forrest was under enemy fire in battles and skirmishes 180 different times during the war. He was not decisively defeated until the Battle of Selma (April 2, 1865), when he fought General James H. Wilson's cavalry (13,000 men), who were armed with Spencer repeating rifles. Forrest had around 3,200 men, a third of whom were local defense troops.

Forrest was promoted to brigadier general on July 21, 1862, major general on December 4, 1863, and lieutenant general on March 2, 1865, to rank from February 28.

General Forrest surrendered at Gainesville, Alabama, on May 9, 1865. His last years were a struggle against poverty. Like most wealthy men of the defeated South, he lost everything during the war. He was Grand Wizard of the Ku Klux Klan from April 1866 to January 1869, when he ordered the organization to disband because it was turning into something of which he did not approve.

Forrest lost his plantation in Mississippi when he declared bankruptcy in 1868. He became president and major investor in a railroad but lost everything again during the Financial Panic of 1873.

Forrest's racial views evolved dramatically after the war. He addressed an early civil rights organization, was denounced by a Freedman's Bureau officer as being "too liberal" to the African Americans he employed, provoked the outrage of several editors by kissing a young black lady on the cheek after she presented him with a bouquet of flowers, was denounced by the (Confederate) Cavalry Survivors Association of Augusta for his positive attitude toward African Americans, hired them in responsible positions in his railroad (as foremen, conductors, architects, and engineers), and defended the right of African Americans to vote. He also made major contributions to an African American Baptist Church on Beall Street in Memphis.

General Forrest finally accepted Jesus Christ as his Savior and was baptized in 1875. He died from the effects of diabetes on October 29, 1877, in Memphis, Tennessee. Twenty thousand people lined the street for two miles with their hats off, respectfully mourning him as his hearse slowly passed by. These included more than three thousand African American mourners. One source places this number at six thousand.

Forrest was initially buried in Elmwood Cemetery, Memphis. In 1904, he and his wife were reinterred in Forrest Park (now the Health Sciences Park) in Memphis. Their graves were later desecrated. In September 2021, they were reburied on the grounds of the Headquarters of the Sons of Confederate Veterans at Elm Springs, Tennessee, where they are treated with respect.

JOHN WESLEY FRAZER (sometimes spelled "Frasier") was born on January 6, 1827, in Hardin County, Tennessee. By 1844, he was living in Mississippi. He attended West Point, graduated in 1849, and was commissioned a brevet second lieutenant in the infantry. His service was mostly in California, the Great Plains, and Washington Territory, where he fought in the Yakima (Indian) War.

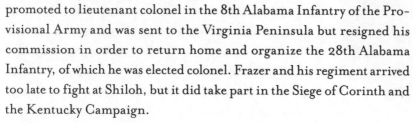

Captain Frazer resigned his commission on March 15, 1861. He was commissioned a captain of infantry in the Confederate Army and ordered to Louisiana on May 11 to supervise army recruiting in Baton Rouge. On June 17, as the Confederate Army rapidly expanded, he was promoted to lieutenant colonel in the 8th Alabama Infantry of the Provisional Army and was sent to the Virginia Peninsula but resigned his commission in order to return home and organize the 28th Alabama Infantry, of which he was elected colonel. Frazer and his regiment arrived too late to fight at Shiloh, but it did take part in the Siege of Corinth and the Kentucky Campaign.

Frazer resigned from the army in late 1862, then rejoined the army and was promoted to brigadier general on May 19, 1863, and was given command of a brigade of the Army of East Tennessee. General Simon B. Buckner ordered him to defend the Cumberland Gap at all costs. On September 7, he was loosely surrounded by U.S. General Ambrose Burnside, who demanded his surrender. Thinking he was badly outnumbered (which he was not), Frazer capitulated on September 9. Neither side suffered any casualties. Frazer surrendered 1,700 men and 12 guns.

Frazer's surrender was strongly criticized, and on February 16, 1864, his promotion to brigadier general was unanimously rejected. No attempt was made by the Confederate government to obtain his release, and he remained a prisoner of war at Fort Warren in Boston Harbor until July 24, 1865, when he was paroled.

General Frazer moved to Arkansas after the war, where he operated a plantation for several years. Later, he settled in New York City. He married Catherine Metcalf Tiffany (1831–1892) and became a successful businessman. He died on March 31, 1906, in New York City, at the age of seventy-nine. He is buried in Clifton Springs Village Cemetery, Clifton Springs, New York.

SAMUEL GIBBS FRENCH was born in Mullica Hill, Gloucester County, New Jersey, on November 22, 1818. He was educated mainly at a private academy in Burlington, New Jersey. He graduated from West Point in 1843 and was commissioned a brevet second lieutenant in the artillery. After three years of garrison duty, French fought in the Mexican War, including at the battles of Palo Alto, Resaca de la Palma, Monterrey, and Buena Vista, where he was severely wounded in the thigh by a musket ball and was carried to the hospital in the same wagon as Colonel Jefferson Davis. French was confined to a cot for forty days days and was eventually sent back to New Orleans. French transferred to the Quartermaster Department on January 12, 1848, and spent most of his time in Washington, D.C., and Fort Smith, Arkansas. He married the daughter of a prominent Natchez banker in 1853 and resigned his commission in 1856. The Frenches acquired a plantation along Deer Creek near Greenville, Mississippi, but tragically his wife died the following year.

After Mississippi seceded, French cast his lot with the South. Governor John J. Pettus appointed him colonel and chief of ordnance for the state forces on February 12, 1861. That April, he joined the Confederate Army as a major of artillery. He was appointed brigadier general by his old friend, President Davis, on October 23, 1861.

French commanded a brigade in the Aquia District of the Department of Northern Virginia from November 7, 1861 to March 1862. He was named commander of the Department of North Carolina and Southern Virginia on July 17, 1862, commanding a division. French was promoted to major general on October 22, 1862, to rank from August 31.

In 1863, he took part in James Longstreet's unsuccessful Siege of Suffolk. In May, he was given command of a division under Joseph E. Johnston in the unsuccessful attempt to break the Union Siege of Vicksburg. He remained in Mississippi as a division commander until the spring of 1864.

French's small division (he only had 2,500 men) fought in the Atlanta Campaign. After the city fell, the division was part of the Tennessee Campaign, where it suffered heavy casualties.

General French was a thoroughgoing professional. As Colonel Charles E. Hooker recalled, "Wherever French was engaged he and his men never failed to give a good account of themselves."

French contracted an eye infection that left him temporarily blind. He went on sick leave on December 15, 1864, and did not return to active duty until February 1865. He took part in the defense of Mobile, which fell on April 12. He was paroled at Mobile at the end of the war.

French worked to rebuild his Mississippi plantation until 1876, when he relocated to Georgia. He moved to Florida in 1881 and developed an orange grove. He also wrote *Two Wars: An Autobiography of General Samuel G. French*, a well-written memoir that is critical of several of his fellow Confederate generals, including James Longstreet, William J. Hardee, John Bell Hood, and Leonidas Polk.

General French died in Pensacola, Florida, on April 20, 1910, at the age of ninety-one. Senility was listed as the cause of death. He is buried in St. John's Cemetery, Pensacola.

DANIEL MARSH FROST was born on August 9, 1823, in Duanesburg, Schenectady County, New York. Well-connected, Daniel Frost received an appointment to West Point, from which he graduated in 1844. Frost was commissioned in the infantry but transferred to the Mounted Rifle Regiment in 1846. He was on garrison duty in various stations until the Mexican War began. He fought from the Siege of Veracruz to the fall of Mexico City and received a brevet for gallantry in the Battle of Cerro Gordo. After the war, he was stationed in the Oregon Territory and Jefferson Barracks in St. Louis, where he married a local lady in 1851.

Following a tour of duty in Europe, Frost was assigned to a regiment on the Texas frontier. Here he fought an Indian raiding party, was seriously wounded, and nearly lost an eye in 1852.

Mrs. Frost was not happy with life on the frontier, so Daniel resigned his commission in 1853. They returned to St. Louis, where he became a partner in a lumber planing mill and later established a fur trading company that operated from Kansas to the West Coast. He embraced Southern culture, cultivated a Southern drawl, and became a fervent advocate of states' rights and slavery. He was appointed a brigadier general in the state militia in 1858. His area of responsibility included St. Louis.

Daniel Frost concentrated pro-secessionist militia and paramilitary forces (635 men) at Camp Jackson, outside St. Louis. They planned to seize the St. Louis Arsenal, but U.S. Captain Nathaniel Lyon acted first and, with 700 men, surrounded Frost's camp on May 10 and forced him to surrender without firing a shot.

He was paroled on May 11 and returned home. He was exchanged on November 1, 1861. On March 5, 1862, he was commissioned a brigadier general in the Confederate Army (with a date of rank of March 3) and led the 7th and 9th Divisions of the Missouri State Guard (which together had the strength of a small brigade) at the Battle of Pea Ridge on March 7–8, 1862, a Confederate defeat in which Frost did not distinguish himself.

Frost was then sent to Memphis, where he became chief of artillery for General Sterling Price and took part in the Siege of Corinth and the retreat to Tupelo. On October 11, 1862, he was sent back to the Trans-Mississippi Department. He was given command of a division in Thomas Hindman's I Corps, Army of the Trans-Mississippi, which he led in the Battle of Prairie Grove.

In August 1863, Frost's family was forced to leave St. Louis and flee to Canada. When he heard the news, Daniel Frost left the army without bothering to inform the War Department and went to Canada. As a deserter, he was dropped from army rolls on December 9, 1863. He was the only Confederate general ever removed from the rolls in this manner.

Frost returned to Missouri after the war and became a farmer. He wrote a memoir that did not mention the Civil War period.

General Frost died at his estate, Hazelwood, on October 29, 1900, at the age of seventy-seven. He is buried in Calvary Cemetery and Mausoleum, St. Louis.

BIRKETT DAVENPORT FRY was born in Kanawha County, Virginia (present-day West Virginia), on June 24, 1822. He attended Washington College in Pennsylvania (1838–39) before entering the Virginia Military Institute in Lexington as a third classman (sophomore). He was accepted into the U.S. Military Academy at West Point in 1842 but was discharged in 1843 due to deficiencies in mathematics. He returned home and became a lawyer. Fry joined the army during the Mexican War as a first lieutenant in the 1st Voltigeurs on February 24, 1847, and took part in the drive on Mexico City. He was discharged from the service in August 1848. Following the war, he went to California (he was a forty-niner) and established a law practice in Sacramento. In October 1856, he was a colonel and later brigadier general in William Walker's filibuster expedition to Nicaragua, which was defeated by a coalition of Central American countries. Fry returned to California but moved to Tallassee, Alabama, in 1859. His wife's family owned cotton mills in the Tallassee area, and he learned the family business.

After Alabama seceded, Birkett Fry joined the Confederate Army, became colonel of the 13th Alabama, and was sent to Virginia. He fought in the Peninsula Campaign and was wounded five times in the Battle of

F

Seven Pines. He took part in the Seven Days Battles. His regiment was not present at the Battle of Second Manassas and was only lightly engaged at South Mountain but was involved in heavy fighting around the Sunken Road during the Battle of Sharpsburg. Colonel Fry was seriously wounded in the right arm. He returned to duty in March 1863 and fought at Chancellorsville, where he was wounded again.

The 13th Alabama went into the Battle of Gettysburg with 308 men and suffered casualties of about 80 percent. After General James J. Archer was captured on July 1, 1863, Birkett Fry assumed command of the brigade. On July 3, he was called upon to spearhead J. Johnston Pettigrew's division during George Pickett's Charge. As his brigade advanced, Fry was struck in the right shoulder by a shell fragment but refused to relinquish command. As the disintegrating Confederate advance reached the Angle, a bullet hit the colonel in the thigh, fractured it, and knocked him down. After the Confederates retreated, Fry was taken prisoner.

Colonel Fry was sent to Johnson's Island, Ohio, on September 28. He was part of a special prisoner exchange in April 1864 and rejoined the Army of Northern Virginia in time to command two brigades (his own old brigade and Seth Barton's) at Cold Harbor. He was promoted to brigadier general on May 14, 1864.

General Fry fought at Drewry's Bluff on May 16 (where his performance did not satisfy General Robert Ransom) and led his brigade during the early stages of the Siege of Petersburg but was forced to go on sick leave on June 28. On September 14, 1864, he was assigned to a command in the District of Georgia, with headquarters at Augusta. From March 21, 1865, until the collapse of the Confederacy, Fry commanded the District of North Georgia.

In May 1865, convinced that the war was lost, General Fry paroled 2,200 of his men and fled to Cuba. He did not return to the United States until 1868, whereupon he became a businessman in Tallassee, Alabama. In 1881, Fry moved to Richmond, Virginia, where he became president of a cotton mill. Here he died of diarrhea and a hemorrhage of the bowels on January 21, 1891. He was sixty-eight years old. General Fry is buried in Oakwood Cemetery, Montgomery, Alabama.

G

GANO – GRIMES

G.

RICHARD MONTGOMERY GANO was born in Bourbon County, Kentucky, on June 17, 1830, the son and grandson of preachers. Richard Gano also became a Church of Christ preacher noted for his kind, suave, gentle, and persuasive manner and preaching. First, however, he enrolled in Bacon College at the age of twelve. He transferred to Bethany College, Virginia (later West Virginia), a year later and then the Louisville Medical Institute, graduating in 1849.

Dr. Gano practiced medicine in Bourbon County, Kentucky, and Baton Rouge, Louisiana. He settled in Grapevine Prairie, Texas, where he farmed, raised livestock, and practiced medicine. Comanches threatened his area (northeast Tarrant County) in 1859, so he organized posses from local citizens and smashed their raiding parties. For this, he was awarded a sword by the community. In 1860, they elected him to the legislature.

In 1861, Richard Gano raised a mounted rifle company, the Grapevine Volunteers, and was elected its captain. His command was assigned to John Hunt Morgan's 2nd Kentucky Cavalry Regiment, with Gano commanding Company G. In July 1862, he participated in Morgan's first Kentucky raid and in August was involved in his Louisville & Nashville Railroad raid. He was promoted to major on July 4 and was given command of a squadron. Morgan officially declared that he could not speak too highly of Richard Gano.

Gano rose rapidly and took part in all of Morgan's major successes in 1862. In February 1863, Richard Gano took charge of the 1st Brigade of Morgan's cavalry division. His brigade was left in the McMinnville, Tennessee, sector when Morgan galloped off on his disastrous Ohio Raid. General Morgan was captured, and most of his command was destroyed.

After the Tullahoma Campaign, Colonel Gano fell ill and returned to Texas. On September 1, Governor Francis Lubbock gave him command of an 1,800-man cavalry brigade organizing at Bonham. He led it to Arkansas and took part in defeating U.S. General Frederick Steele's

Camden Expedition in 1864 but was severely wounded in the arm in a skirmish near Camden, Arkansas, on April 14.

After he recovered, Gano led an unsuccessful foray against Fort Smith, Arkansas, in June 1864, but he surprised and smashed the 6th Kansas Cavalry at Massard Prairie on July 27. Encouraged by his victory, Gano pushed into the Indian Territory, where he led the 5th Texas Cavalry Brigade and Stand Watie's Indian cavalry in the Second Battle of Cabin Creek (September 19). Here, he and Watie overran the Union supply line, captured 130 wagons, 740 mules, and more than $2 million worth of supplies. General Edmund Kirby Smith, the commander of the Trans-Mississippi Department, called it "one of the most brilliant raids of the entire war."

Colonel Gano was given command of a brigade in General Samuel Maxey's cavalry division in September 1864 and led it until March 1865. Although he had served as an acting brigadier general since early 1864, Richard Gano was not formally promoted until March 18, 1865, with a date of rank of March 17. He later remarked that he fought in seventy-two engagements during the war and was successful in all but four. He had five horses shot out from under him during the conflict. Three of them were killed.

Richard M. Gano was one of those rare people who are successful at everything they attempt. Ordained as a minister in the Disciples of Christ (also known as the Christian Church or Church of Christ) by his father in 1866, he held many gospel meetings, personally baptized four thousand people, and helped establish several churches in northern Texas and Kentucky over thirty years.

A successful rancher, his spread covered fifty-five thousand acres, and he was a leader in breeding cattle, horses, sheep, and hogs. He was a millionaire by the early 1880s. He was also active in the Prohibition movement and the United Confederate Veterans.

Richard Montgomery Gano died of uremic poisoning in Dallas on March 27, 1913, at the age of eighty-two. He is buried in Oakland Cemetery, Dallas.

G

FRANKLIN KITCHELL GARDNER was born in New York City on January 29, 1823, the son of a career army officer. Franklin enrolled in West Point in 1838 and graduated in 1843 as a brevet second lieutenant of infantry.

Shortly after, he married into the rich and powerful Mouton family of Louisiana. Future Confederate General Alfred Mouton was his brother-in-law. Lieutenant Gardner was sent to Texas just before the Mexican War broke out. He fought at Fort Brown and Monterrey, where he won a brevet to first lieutenant for bravery. Transferred to General Winfield Scott's army, he earned a brevet to captain during the drive on Mexico City.

Gardner later served in New York, Missouri, Arkansas, Pennsylvania, Minnesota, Wisconsin, the Wyoming Territory, and the Pacific Northwest, among other places. He also fought Seminoles in Florida and Mormons in Utah. He became a captain (full rank) in 1855.

Gardner "went south" in 1861 as a lieutenant colonel of Louisiana state troops. He became a captain in the Confederate Army and assistant adjutant general to Jubal Early on September 11, 1861. He was an aide-de-camp to General Braxton Bragg at Shiloh. After reorganizing the army's cavalry for General G. T. Beauregard, he was promoted to brigadier general on April 12, 1862, to rank from April 11, despite having been arrested for public drunkenness early in the war. He led an infantry brigade in the Kentucky Campaign and the subsequent retreat to Tennessee. On December 20, 1862, he was promoted to major general (to rank from December 13) and was sent to command Port Hudson, the southern anchor of the Confederacy's hold on the Mississippi River.

Gardner was an excellent commander whose abilities have not been fully appreciated by historians. He smashed U.S. Admiral David Farragut's ocean-going fleet when it tried to run the batteries at Port Hudson on March 14, 1863. He then faced Union ground forces under General Nathaniel Banks, who outnumbered him more than thirty thousand to seven thousand. Gardner intended to evacuate the place, but President Jefferson Davis ordered it held.

The siege began on May 25. The Yankees launched their first major assault on May 27 and lost 1,995 men. Gardner suffered 235 casualties. They attacked again on June 14 and lost another 1,792 men. Gardner lost only 45. The Confederates had to be starved into submission.

As the days wore on and food, ammunition, and hope diminished, Gardner instilled his fighting spirit into his men, who idolized him. Gardner only capitulated after Vicksburg did. Of the 6,500 starving men he surrendered on July 9, fewer than 3,000 were able to stand up at the official surrender ceremony. Gardner's surrender marked the end of the Confederate hold on the Mississippi River, and all of the food, supplies, equipment and manpower west of the Mississippi were now lost to the Southern Confederacy.

Franklin Gardner was imprisoned for more than a year, mostly on Johnson's Island. His original promotion to major general was never confirmed by the Senate. He was renominated on June 6, 1864, and was confirmed June 10. He was exchanged in July 1864.

Gardner was named commander of the District of the Gulf in the Department of Mississippi and Eastern Louisiana on July 26, 1864, and worked under his brother-in-law, General Richard Taylor, a post he held for the rest of the war. He was paroled in Meridian on May 11.

After the war, Gardner returned to the family plantation in Vermillionville (now Lafayette), Louisiana. He died there on April 29, 1873, at the age of fifty. He was buried in the cemetery of St. John's Catholic Cathedral in Lafayette.

WILLIAM MONTGOMERY GARDNER was born on June 8, 1824, in the Sand Hills, not far from Augusta, Georgia. He attended Georgetown College in the District of Columbia but left there in 1842 to attend West Point, from which he graduated in 1846.

An infantry officer, Gardner fought in the Battle of Monterrey. Transferred to General Winfield Scott's army, he took part in the Siege of Veracruz. He was severely wounded in the groin at Contreras and was critically wounded in the chest in the Battle of Churubusco. Doctors were afraid to remove the bullet, which remained in him until the day he died. He was brevetted first lieutenant for gallantry at Contreras and Churubusco.

After the Mexican War, he fought Indians in California and the Pacific Northwest.

Gardner resigned his commission on January 19, 1861, and was commissioned a major in the Confederate Regular Army in February. In May, he was assigned to the 8th Georgia Infantry Regiment as a lieutenant colonel, second in command to Colonel Francis S. Bartow.

Stationed in the Shenandoah, the regiment took part in the evacuation of Harpers Ferry and on July 18 was ordered to Manassas, where it arrived on July 20. Colonel Bartow was given command of a brigade, and Gardner assumed command of the regiment. In battle on July 21, a minié ball shattered Gardner's leg, a near-fatal wound that left him permanently maimed and essentially bedridden (at his home in Georgia) for two years.

The War Department nevertheless promoted him to full colonel (effective the day he was shot), and President Jefferson Davis appointed him brigadier general on November 14, 1861. On October 6, 1863, he returned to limited active duty and was given command of the District of Middle Florida, and he fought in the Battle of Olustee (Ocean Pond) on February 20, 1864.

He worked as a commandant of military prisoners until he was recalled to active field duty near the end of the war, taking command of three thousand infantrymen and fourteen guns. On April 12, 1865, near the town of Salisbury, North Carolina, his ad hoc battle group was smashed by U.S. General George Stoneman's cavalry. About half of Gardner's men were captured, as well as all his artillery.

After the war, General Gardner's wounds were so debilitating he was unable to work. He lived in Augusta and Rome, Georgia, and at his children's homes in Memphis. He died at a son's home in Memphis on June 16, 1901. He was seventy-seven years old. He is buried in Elmwood Cemetery, Memphis, Tennessee.

SAMUEL GARLAND, JR., was born in Lynchburg, Virginia, on December 16, 1830. He was educated at a private classical school and at Randolph Macon College, which he entered at age fourteen. In 1846, he transferred to the Virginia Military Institute, from which he graduated in 1849. He did postgraduate work in legal studies at the University of Virginia, was admitted to the bar, and set up a law practice in Lynchburg.

After John Brown's attack on Harpers Ferry, Garland helped organize the Lynchburg Home Guard, a militia company, and was elected its captain. He opposed secession, but after Virginia left the Union, he and his company joined the 11th Virginia Infantry Regiment, and Governor John Letcher appointed Garland its colonel. While he prepared his regiment for war, an influenza epidemic struck Lynchburg. His wife died on June 12, followed by their only child, a four-year-old son, on July 31.

Meanwhile, Colonel Garland led his regiment into action at Blackburn's Ford on July 18 during the First Manassas Campaign. He fought with such fearlessness and contempt for danger that some thought he had a death wish. Three days later, Garland's regiment played a minor role in the First Battle of Bull Run. He took part in the Battle of Dranesville on December 20 before being transferred to the Peninsula. Colonel Garland was shot in the elbow early in the Battle of Williamsburg but refused to leave the field.

Garland became a brigadier general on May 23, 1862, and was given Jubal Early's former brigade. He fought in the Battle of Seven Pines and in the Seven Days Battles and particularly distinguished himself at Gaines' Mill on June 27, where he got behind the Federal flank and

G.

captured many prisoners. He also had two horses shot from under him in this campaign.

Samuel Garland's brigade remained in the Richmond area during the Second Manassas Campaign. He rejoined General Robert E. Lee for the Maryland Campaign and was given the mission of holding part of South Mountain. No attack was expected initially, but the Yankees found a misplaced Confederate order and discovered Lee's plans, so they struck in overwhelming force. Garland was ordered to hold Fox's Gap at all costs. Outnumbered more than three to one, Garland fought stubbornly until a Union bullet knocked him off his horse. His staff carried him to a nearby house and laid him on the front porch, where he died shortly after. D. H. Hill officially lamented that the action cost the Confederacy a "pure, gallant, and accomplished Christian soldier, General Garland, who had no superiors and few equals in the service."

Brigadier General Samuel Garland, Jr., was buried in Presbyterian Cemetery, Lynchburg, Virginia, beside his wife and son. He was thirty-one years old.

RICHARD BROOKE GARNETT was born on November 21, 1817, at the family's Rose Hill estate in Essex County, Virginia. He was a cousin of future Confederate General Robert S. Garnett, as well as Robert M. T. Hunter, a U.S. senator and Confederate secretary of state. He grew up with the former, with whom he is often mistaken.

Richard and his cousin Robert both attended West Point and both graduated in 1841. (Richard Garnett entered the academy in 1836 but was set back a year.) He was commissioned in the infantry and fought Seminoles in Florida before being sent west, where he became a noted Indian fighter. During the Mexican War, he held a staff position in New Orleans.

Richard Garnett was promoted to captain in 1855 and saw duty throughout the West, including Texas, Wyoming, the Dakotas, and

California, where he was when the South seceded. Garnett strongly opposed secession but nevertheless resigned his commission on May 17, 1861, and joined the Confederate Army as a major of artillery. He was transferred to Cobb's Legion (a Georgia unit) on August 31, 1861, as a lieutenant colonel. Due in part to the shortage of qualified officers, he was promoted to brigadier general on November 14.

Garnett was given command of the Stonewall Brigade in late 1861. Garnett was handsome, friendly, and popular with the troops, who considered him competent and likeable. Stonewall Jackson, however, did not like him, and he tended to be hard on officers he did not like. (Perhaps he learned that Garnett had an illegitimate half-Indian son in Wyoming.) As early as December 1861, Jackson complained to Secretary of War Judah P. Benjamin that Garnett lacked discipline. The climax of their poor relationship occurred on March 23, 1862, during the Battle of Kernstown, when Garnett's men ran out of ammunition and he retreated without permission. Stonewall Jackson relieved Garnett of his command, placed him under arrest, and ordered that he be court-martialed. The court never met because military events intervened. The weight of the evidence, however, suggests that Garnett did the right thing. Robert E. Lee must have thought so. After the Battle of Second Manassas, he instructed Jackson to release Garnett from arrest and on September 5 made Garnett acting commander of George Pickett's brigade for the invasion of Maryland.

Garnett redeemed his reputation in the Maryland Campaign. In the Burnside's Bridge sector at Antietam, he beat back several attacks from numerically superior Union forces. When Pickett was advanced to division commander, Lee made Garnett permanent commander of the brigade.

General Garnett took part in the Battle of Fredericksburg and the unsuccessful Siege of Washington, North Carolina. At Gettysburg on July 3, 1863, he was ill with fever and hobbled because he'd been kicked by his own horse. As the Rebels prepared for Pickett's Charge, the forty-five-year-old Garnett was too sick and injured to go into action on foot.

Still, over the protests of his fellow officers, he led his brigade forward on horseback, knowing this made him a prime target.

Twenty yards from the famous "copse of trees" that marked the Union line, Richard Garnett disappeared into a storm of shot, shell, and smoke. Moments later his riderless horse emerged, its saddle covered with blood. Richard Garnett's body was never identified. It was likely buried in a mass grave at the battle site until 1872, when many of the Confederate dead from Pickett's Charge were reinterred in Hollywood Cemetery, Richmond, Virginia. His sword was discovered in a Baltimore pawn shop in 1893.

General Garrett has a cenotaph in Hollywood Cemetery.

ROBERT SELDEN GARNETT, JR., was born on the family plantation, Champlain, in Essex County, Virginia, on December 16, 1819. He was the cousin of Confederate General Richard B. Garnett.

Robert entered West Point in 1837 and graduated in 1841 as a second lieutenant of artillery. He served on the Canadian border, as a West Point tactics instructor, as a recruiter, and as a staff officer with General John E. Wool in Troy, New York.

In 1846, Garnett accompanied his regiment to Texas, where it joined Zachary Taylor's Army of Occupation. Garnett was adjutant of an artillery battalion in the battles of Palo Alto and Resaca de la Palma. Afterward, he became Taylor's aide. He distinguished himself in the battles of Monterrey and Buena Vista, for which he was brevetted captain and major.

Garnett accompanied Taylor to Louisiana after the war. He went to California in 1849 and while there sketched what would later be adopted as the California state seal. He also served in Florida, the Indian Territory, and Texas. Colonel Robert E. Lee, the superintendent of West Point, arranged for Garnett to be appointed commandant of cadets (1852–54). Promoted to major in 1855, Garnett later served at Fort

Steilacoom in Washington Territory. His young wife and son died of fever within six days of each other in 1858. A heartbroken Garnett took a leave of absence in Europe and did not return to the United States until March 1861.

After the Old Dominion seceded, Garnett resigned his commission and joined the Provisional Army of Virginia. He was appointed adjutant general on April 25 and served on General Lee's staff until early June, when he was sent to Staunton to assume command of the Department of Northwestern Virginia. He was named a brigadier general in the Confederate Army on June 6, 1861.

Robert S. Garnett was not at all happy about his new assignment. He knew the counties that later became West Virginia were pro-Union, the roads were horrible, there was no logistical infrastructure, and he was badly outnumbered. He had 4,500 men, while U.S. General George McClellan had more than 20,000. Predictably, General Garnett's Army of the Northwest was defeated at Rich Mountain and was forced to retreat. Garnett fought several small delaying actions to slow the Union's pursuit. On July 13, 1861, while directing the rear guard, Richard S. Garnett was killed by a Union volley. He was the first Confederate general killed during the Civil War. He was forty-one years old.

Union soldiers found Garnett's body and had it delivered to his family in Baltimore. He was buried in the Green-Wood Cemetery, Brooklyn, with his wife and child.

ISHAM WARREN GARROTT was born in 1816 in central North Carolina. He attended the University of North Carolina (1837–40), where he studied law. He moved to Greenville, Alabama, and then to Marion, Alabama, where he formed a law partnership with James Phelan, Sr., a future Confederate senator from Mississippi. Isham Garrott served in the Alabama legislature as a Whig (1845–50) but was a presidential elector for Southern Democrat John C. Breckinridge in 1860.

After Alabama seceded, he and Edmund W. Pettus raised the 20th Alabama Infantry Regiment. Garrott was elected its colonel on September 16, 1861.

Garrott's regiment spent the winter of 1861–62 defending Mobile. In February 1862, it was sent to Knoxville and then took part in the defense of Chattanooga and the invasion of Kentucky as part of General Edward D. Tracy's brigade. In December, it was sent to Mississippi, to help defend Vicksburg from General Grant's forces. When Grant landed south of Vicksburg in late April 1863, Tracy's brigade was sent to reinforce the Grand Gulf–Port Gibson sector. After a forced march of forty-four miles, it joined Confederate General John S. Bowen for the Battle of Port Gibson. General Tracy was killed early in the struggle, and command devolved upon Garrott. He did a superb job as a brigade commander, but the Confederates, who were outnumbered five to one, were eventually defeated in heavy fighting.

Despite Garrott's outstanding performance, he was succeeded as brigade commander in early May by Brigadier General Stephen Dill Lee, the artillery commander of the Army of Mississippi, who was also a man of exceptional ability and who had a much stronger military background.

Garrott returned to the command of his regiment, the 20th Alabama, which fought well during the Battle of Champion Hill (May 16) and the Siege of Vicksburg, which began on May 18. Fort Garrott, a major defensive work on the Confederate perimeter, was named after him.

Colonel Garrott frequently visited the front lines, talking with and encouraging his men. His talents as an energetic, persistent, and untiring commander were recognized, and he was promoted to brigadier general on May 28, 1863. His former law partner, Senator Phela, was almost certainly behind his unusually rapid promotion, as Garrott was only a brigade commander for about a week.

Garrott never learned of that promotion. On June 17, 1863, he borrowed a rifle to go after some Union sharpshooters. As he took aim, he was shot dead. He fell without uttering a word. He was forty-six or forty-seven years old. Isham Garrott was buried at Lonewood, the Finney Plantation in Vicksburg. His body is now under what has become Finney

Street, between Drummond Street and Cherry Street in Vicksburg. He has a cenotaph in the Confederate section of Cedar Hill Cemetery (the Old City Cemetery) in Vicksburg.

LUCIUS JEREMIAH GARTRELL was born in Washington, Georgia, on January 7, 1821. His father was a wealthy planter. Lucius attended Randolph-Macon College and Franklin College, later the University of Georgia in Athens. He was admitted to the bar in 1842 and set up a law practice in Washington.

Gartrell was solicitor general for the North Georgia Judicial Circuit from 1843 to 1847, when he was elected to the Georgia legislature. In 1856, he was elected to the U.S. House of Representatives, serving from March 4, 1857, to January 23, 1861.

Lucius Gartrell was an outspoken advocate of secession. When Georgia seceded, he resigned his seat in Congress and organized the 7th Georgia Infantry in Atlanta in May 1861. He was elected colonel and led it during the Battle of First Manassas as part of General Francis Bartow's brigade.

Gartrell was elected to the Confederate Congress in November 1861 and held a seat there from 1862 to 1864, where he was a strong supporter of Jefferson Davis's administration. He declined to run for reelection and was appointed a brigadier general in the Confederate Army on August 22, 1864. He returned to Georgia, raised a brigade, and attempted to halt William Sherman's March to the Sea, but with little success. In late 1864, his brigade made a tenacious stand that allowed Confederate General William J. Hardee's Savannah garrison to escape encircling Union forces.

General Gartrell was wounded near Coosawhatchie, South Carolina, in January 1865. He was transported to Augusta to recover and was apparently still there when the war ended.

After the surrender, Gartrell moved to Atlanta and built a reputation as the best criminal attorney in the state. He was a member of the

Georgia Constitutional Convention in 1877 and ran for governor in 1882 but was defeated by former Confederate Vice President Alexander H. Stephens. General Gartrell died in Atlanta on April 7, 1891. He was seventy years old. He is buried in Oakland Cemetery, Atlanta.

MARTIN WITHERSPOON GARY was born in Cokesbury, South Carolina, on March 25, 1831. Young Martin was educated at Cokesbury Academy and enrolled in South Carolina College in 1850, but was expelled in 1852 for his part in the "Great Biscuit Rebellion" against the school's terrible food and the requirement that students dine at the college. He transferred to Harvard, from which he graduated in 1854. He returned to South Carolina, read law, was admitted to the bar, and established a practice in Edgefield.

Gary was a fervent secessionist. He was elected to the South Carolina legislature in 1860, but when South Carolina seceded, he joined Hampton's Legion as a captain in the infantry. He fought in the Battle of First Manassas and became deputy commander of the legion (under Captain James Connor) after Colonel Wade Hampton was wounded and Lieutenant Colonel Benjamin Johnson was killed. Later that year, he was elected lieutenant colonel and commander of the legion's infantry battalion. In 1862, the legion was reorganized and lost its cavalry and artillery. Gary was promoted to colonel and commander of the legion.

Colonel Gary's men fought in the Peninsula Campaign and the Seven Days Battles and at Second Manassas (where it smashed the 5th New York) and Sharpsburg, where they suffered heavy casualties. Sent to the rear to rebuild, they were part of the Richmond garrison and did not participate in the Gettysburg Campaign. Gary's soldiers returned to action in the fall of 1863, fighting at Chickamauga, Chattanooga, and Knoxville.

In March 1864, Gary was given command of a cavalry brigade. He was promoted to brigadier general on May 19, 1864. Gary's brigade

·G

fought in several actions during the Siege of Petersburg and raided U.S. supply lines. When Robert E. Lee surrendered at Appomattox, General Gary and two hundred of his men cut their way out of the Union encirclement and joined Jefferson Davis's escort as he fled south. The last Confederate cabinet meeting took place in Gary's mother's house in Cokesbury.

After the war, General Gary resumed his law practice at Edgefield. He joined the struggle for home rule and proved to be a very effective stump speaker. He worked with white paramilitary groups and the Red Shirts, an organization dedicated to suppressing the black vote in South Carolina. He apparently was involved in voter fraud. When Hampton ran for governor in 1876, the total number of votes he received in Edgefield County exceeded the number of registered voters. This was critical, as Hampton won by only 1,100 votes.

General Gary was elected to the state senate from Edgefield County in 1876, but he and General Hampton had a political falling out. Gary fiercely opposed Hampton's policy of magnanimity toward black South Carolinians, and Hampton and his political allies (including fellow former-Confederate-general-turned-U.S.-senator Matthew Calbraith Butler) twice blocked Gary's election to the U.S. Senate. Hampton also prevented Gary from running for governor in 1880. Gary left politics and returned to Cokesbury, where he practiced law. He died in Cokesbury on April 9, 1881, at the age of fifty. He is buried in Tabernacle Cemetery, Cokesbury.

RICHARD CASWELL GATLIN was born in Kinston, North Carolina, on January 18, 1809. After attending the University of North Carolina, Gatlin gained admission into West Point and graduated in 1832. He served as an infantry officer in the Seminole War and in the Mexican War, fighting in the defense of Fort Brown and in the Battle of Monterrey, where he was wounded. He was brevetted for his conduct in these battles.

Later, Gatlin was stationed in Missouri, Louisiana, Florida again, the Kansas frontier, the Indian Territory, Arkansas, and the Dakotas. He accompanied Albert Sidney Johnston's expedition to Utah and was then stationed at Fort Craig, New Mexico, in 1860 and Fort Smith, Arkansas, in 1861. He was promoted to major in February 1861.

Arkansas state forces took Gatlin prisoner on April 23, 1861. After he was paroled, he resigned his commission and offered his services to his native state. The governor of North Carolina appointed him adjutant general of the state with the rank of major general of militia. Shortly after, he accepted a commission as a colonel in the Confederate Army and on August 15 was promoted to brigadier general. Appointed commander of the Department of North Carolina, he had the impossible task of defending the state's coast, including the Outer Banks, with few troops, little artillery, and no navy. The Confederacy was threatened at many points, and his requests for reinforcements were ignored. The Yankees easily captured the weakly defended Hatteras Inlet area in late August 1861 and took Roanoke Island on February 8, 1862, and New Bern on March 14.

Gatlin was unfairly castigated by the newspaper editors and general public. He was relieved of his command on March 19, ostensibly for reasons of health. He resigned his Confederate commission in September 1862 but continued to serve as North Carolina adjutant and inspector general until the end of the war.

Following the surrender, Gatlin moved to Sebastian County, Arkansas, and became a farmer until 1881. He then retired to Fort Smith. General Richard C. Gatlin died at Mount Nebo, Arkansas, on September 8, 1896. He was eighty-seven years old. He is buried in Fort Smith National Cemetery, Arkansas.

SAMUEL JAMESON GHOLSON was born near Richmond, Kentucky, on May 19, 1808. He moved with his father to Franklin County, Alabama, in 1817. Educated at local schools, he studied law and was admitted to the bar in 1829. The following year, he moved to Mississippi and entered a law practice at Athens. He was a member of the state legislature in 1835, 1836, and 1839 and served in the U.S. House of Representatives from the end of 1836 to early 1838. President Martin Van Buren appointed Gholson U.S. district court judge for the Northern and Southern Districts of Mississippi on February 9, 1839. He resigned that position on January 10, 1861, the day after Mississippi seceded from the Union.

Though he had been a major general in the Mississippi militia, Gholson enlisted as a private in the 14th Mississippi Infantry Regiment. He was subsequently elected captain of a company and was rapidly promoted to major and colonel. He was captured when Fort Donelson surrendered on February 16, 1862. He was exchanged in August, in time to fight at Iuka and Corinth, where he was wounded in the left thigh. It took him months to recover.

In April 1863, Mississippi Governor John J. Pettus appointed him major general of Mississippi State Troops and sent him to northeastern Mississippi. On General Nathan Bedford Forrest's recommendation, Gholson was given command of a Confederate cavalry brigade, which he led against General William T. Sherman west of Jackson, Mississippi, on July 7, 1863. Gholson was badly wounded again but by early 1864 had returned to the field commanding a brigade of state troops under General Forrest. Gholson was promoted to brigadier general on May 6, 1864.

General Gholson was seriously wounded in a skirmish near Egypt, Mississippi, on December 28, 1864, and lost his left arm. His combat career was over. He was paroled at Meridian, Mississippi, in May 1865.

Gholson resumed his law practice. In 1865, he was elected to the Mississippi House of Representatives, which promptly elected him speaker of the house. He served until March 1867, when Congress passed the first Reconstruction Act, radical Reconstruction began, and former Confederates were expelled from government positions. He worked to restore home rule until the carpetbagger regime was ousted in 1876. He was reelected to the state legislature in 1878.

General Samuel J. Gholson died October 16, 1883, in Aberdeen, Mississippi, at the age of seventy-five. He is buried in Odd Fellows Rest Cemetery, Aberdeen.

RANDALL LEE GIBSON was born on September 10, 1832, at Spring Hill, his mother's family estate in Versailles, Kentucky. He was educated by a private tutor at his father's plantation, Live Oak, in Terrebonne Parish, Louisiana. He graduated from Yale in 1853 and went to law school at the University of Louisiana (now Tulane), graduating in 1855. Gibson spent the next few years traveling in Europe, served as a U.S. attaché in Madrid, and farmed in Louisiana.

After Louisiana seceded from the Union, Gibson served as an aide-de-camp to Governor Thomas O. Moore. On May 8, 1861, he became a captain in the 1st Louisiana Artillery. On August 13, he was named colonel of the 13th Louisiana Infantry. He fought at Shiloh, Farmington, the Siege of Corinth, and Perryville during General Braxton Bragg's Kentucky Campaign. The regiment suffered so many casualties in 1862 that it had to be consolidated with the 20th Louisiana, with Colonel Gibson commanding the new regiment. The 13th/20th Louisiana took part in the Second Battle of Murfreesboro, the Tullahoma Campaign, and the Battle of Chickamauga, where it suffered more than 40 percent casualties.

Randall Gibson was promoted to brigadier general on January 11, 1864. He led a brigade in the Atlanta Campaign (where he distinguished himself) and in the Tennessee Campaign of 1864, during which he fought at Franklin and Nashville. In early 1865, he was sent to Mobile. His defense of Spanish Fort (March 27–April 8, 1865) was brilliant. With 2,500 men, Gibson held off 30,000 Federals for more than a week; then, during the night of April 8, as the fort was all but surrounded and about to fall, he escaped with his entire command.

General Gibson surrendered at Cuba Station, Alabama, on May 8, 1865, and was paroled at Meridian, Mississippi, on May 14. He returned to Louisiana, where his plantation lay in ruins, and he struggled to restore his finances by practicing law in New Orleans.

In 1874, he was elected to the U.S. House of Representatives as a Democrat and served from 1875 to 1883. The state legislature elected him to the U.S. Senate in 1882, and he served there from 1883 until his death. Senator Gibson and philanthropist Paul Tulane were primarily responsible for saving the University of Louisiana (now Tulane), by making it a privately endowed university.

Randall Lee Gibson died on December 15, 1892, in Hot Springs, Arkansas, at the age of sixty. He is buried in Lexington Cemetery, Lexington, Kentucky. The town of Tigerville, Louisiana, was renamed Gibson in his honor.

·G

JEREMY FRANCIS GILMER was born on February 23, 1818, in Greensboro, North Carolina. He attended West Point and graduated with the class of 1839. Gilmer was commissioned into the engineers—the most prestigious branch of the service. He spent the next twenty-six years in a variety of engineering assignments, mostly in the South. He was chief engineer for the U.S. Army in New Mexico during the Mexican War.

Gilmer was stationed in San Francisco when he resigned his commission on June 29, 1861. He did not reach Savannah, Georgia, until October 1, because of an attack of rheumatic fever and the need to avoid Federal authorities who might arrest him. Gilmer was then swiftly commissioned a major of engineers and named chief engineer of the Army of Tennessee.

Gilmer fought in the Battle of Shiloh, where he was severely wounded. On July 1, 1862, he was promoted to lieutenant colonel and ordered to report to General Robert E. Lee. Gilmer hoped for field duty with the Army of Northern Virginia, but Lee placed him in charge of constructing defenses around Richmond and Petersburg. Despite his disappointment, he was an effective administrator, was promoted to colonel in October 1862, and was named chief of the Engineer Bureau. He held this post for the rest of the war.

Gilmer used his influence with President Jefferson Davis and Secretary of War James A. Seddon to ensure that all field armies had engineer companies.

On August 25, 1863, Gilmer received a special promotion to major general, bypassing the rank of brigadier general altogether. He was simultaneously named second-in-command to General G. T. Beauregard's Department of South Carolina, Georgia, and Florida while retaining his responsibilities in Richmond and helping improve the defenses of Charleston, Atlanta, Savannah, and Mobile. Gilmer was the most outstanding military engineer in Confederate service.

After the war, Gilmer settled in Savannah and spent eighteen years as president and chief engineer of the Savannah Gas and Light Company. He was also a member of the board of directors of the Georgia Central Railroad and the Banking Company of Georgia and was a trustee of the Independent Presbyterian Church. Jeremy Gilmer died in Savannah on December 1, 1883, at age sixty-five. He was buried in Laurel Grove Cemetery (North), Savannah.

VICTOR JEAN BAPTISTE GIRARDEY was born on June 26, 1837, in Lauw, Alsace, France. His family immigrated to Georgia in 1842. An orphan by age sixteen, he nevertheless completed his education in New Orleans and was a second lieutenant in the Louisiana Militia in 1861. He entered Confederate service as a second lieutenant in the 1st Louisiana Infantry Battalion, the original Louisiana Tigers.

On October 12, 1861, he became aide-de-camp to General Albert G. Blanchard. Promoted to captain on June 21, 1862, Girardey became assistant adjutant general on Brigadier General Ambrose Wright's staff. He fought in the Seven Days Battles, Sharpsburg, Chancellorsville, and Gettysburg. He won several commendations for his gallantry and courage. In the Confederate victory at the Battle of Manassas Gap (also known as the Battle of Wapping Heights) on July 23, 1863, he briefly commanded a regiment when its colonel was wounded.

Girardey fought in the Overland Campaign of 1864, during which he was transferred to Major General William Mahone's divisional staff on May 24, 1864. On July 30, during the Battle of the Crater, Union engineers detonated four tons of black powder under Confederate trenches and blew a huge hole in the Rebel lines. Mahone's division was rushed to the endangered sector, and Captain Girardey led two brigades to their assembly areas, formed them for a counterattack, led them in the assault, and sealed the breakthrough. The Union forces in the crater were slaughtered. General Robert E. Lee was so impressed by Girardey's performance that, on August 3, he promoted him from captain to brigadier general—the only such promotion made in the history of the Southern Confederacy. His rank was backdated to July 30.

Girardey was given command of General Ambrose Wright's old brigade. On August 16, during the Second Battle of Deep Bottom, Girardey was leading the defense of Fussell's Mill on the Darbytown Road when he was shot in the head. He died instantly.

Victor Girardey was buried in Magnolia Cemetery in Augusta, Georgia. He was twenty-seven years old.

STATES RIGHTS GIST (pronounced "Guest") was born on September 3, 1831, in Union, South Carolina. "States" (as he was called) graduated from South Carolina College and attended Harvard Law School for a year, returned home, read law, was admitted to the bar, and set up a law practice. His older cousin, William Henry Gist, was governor of South Carolina from 1858 to 1860. As a brigadier general of militia, States became a full-time advisor to Governor Gist in April 1860.

Francis W. Pickens succeeded William Gist as governor on December 14, 1860. South Carolina seceded on December 20. In January 1861, Pickens appointed States Rights Gist as state adjutant and inspector general. His main responsibilities were to acquire weapons and mobilize the state's manpower. He was present when artillery from the South Carolina Militia opened fire on Fort Sumter.

Gist joined the Confederate Army as a volunteer aide to Brigadier General Barnard Bee. He served in the Battle of First Manassas. When the commander of the 4th Alabama was mortally wounded and his second-in-command was wounded, General G. T. Beauregard appointed Gist acting commander of the regiment. Gist performed well. He was also wounded that day, but not seriously, and remained on the field until the enemy fled. General Bee, however, was mortally wounded at Bull Run, and Gist was then appointed his replacement as acting brigade commander.

Following Manassas, States Gist returned to South Carolina and organized and equipped Palmetto state units until March 20, 1862, when he was appointed a brigadier general in the Confederate Army, commanding forces east of James Island and eventually on the island itself. In December, he directed the regiments sent to relieve Wilmington, North Carolina.

In May 1863, Gist was ordered to assume command of a brigade and go to Mississippi. He took part in the First Battle of Jackson in May and the Second Battle of Jackson in July.

Gist and his men were sent to join the Army of Tennessee in Georgia that summer and performed well in the Battle of Chickamauga. For part of the battle, he commanded a division. He also fought at Missionary Ridge (commanding General William H. T. Walker's division) and led his brigade in the Atlanta Campaign.

General Gist's last campaign ended on November 30, 1864, during the Battle of Franklin when he was mortally wounded. He was thirty-three years old.

Gist was buried in the yard of William White's home near the battlefield. In 1866, his remains were reinterred in Trinity Episcopal Cathedral Cemetery in downtown Columbia, South Carolina.

ADLEY HOGAN GLADDEN was born on October 28, 1810, in Fairfield County, South Carolina. He became a cotton broker in Columbia, South Carolina, in 1830 but left his business to fight in the Second Seminole War in Florida. After he returned home, President John Tyler appointed him postmaster of Columbia.

Gladden joined the U.S. Army for the Mexican War and served in the Palmetto Regiment as a major. His regimental commander and second-in-command were killed trying to take the Mexican fieldworks at Churubusco, so Gladden assumed command of the regiment. He was promoted to lieutenant colonel shortly after. He and his men stormed the Belén Gate in the Battle of Mexico City, where Gladden was severely wounded.

After the war, Gladden moved to New Orleans and returned to the cotton business until South Carolina seceded. On January 25, 1861, he became lieutenant colonel of the 1st South Carolina Infantry Regiment, but he resigned soon thereafter to become a member of the Louisiana Secession Convention. After Louisiana seceded, he was named colonel of the 1st Louisiana Infantry Regiment. He was sent to Pensacola, Florida, and was promoted to brigadier general on September 30, 1861. From December 22, 1861, to January 27, 1862, he was commander of the Army of Pensacola.

General Braxton Bragg wanted to form a brigade that would set an example of discipline and excellence and asked General Gladden to command it. Gladden was transferred to Mobile on January 27, 1862, and remained there until March 9, commanding this brigade. He was sent to Corinth in March and led his brigade in the Battle of Shiloh. There, on April 6, 1862, while attacking U.S. General Benjamin Prentiss's division, he was struck by a shell fragment, and his arm was amputated on the battlefield. The general failed to rally from the operation and died on April 12. General G. T. Beauregard lamented losing the services of a man of his "soldierly aptitudes and experience."

General Gladden was buried in Magnolia Cemetery, Mobile, Alabama.

ARCHIBALD CAMPBELL GODWIN was born in 1831 in Nansemond County, Virginia, and raised in Portsmouth, Virginia. He grew into a tall man—he stood six feet six—and was considered handsome. He left home at age nineteen and went to California to make his fortune. He succeeded, developing business interests in mining, livestock, lumber, milling, retail trade, real estate, and a luxury hotel, and he owned 640 acres. In 1860, he reportedly came within a single vote of winning the Democratic nomination for governor of California.

When the war began, he rented his property or deeded it to friends and rushed to Virginia, where he offered his services to Confederate President Jefferson Davis, who commissioned him as a major and named him assistant provost marshal at Libby Prison in Richmond. He was then sent to North Carolina to construct a prison stockade in Salisbury. On July 6, 1862, Godwin organized the prison guards as a regiment (the 57th North Carolina), with Godwin as its colonel, with a date of rank of July 17. Godwin and his men were soon sent to Richmond, to defend the city in case of a Yankee attack. They spent the summer training and drilling.

In early November 1862, the 57th North Carolina joined the Army of Northern Virginia. It fought at Fredericksburg, where Godwin was ordered to attack Union forces occupying a railroad cut in front of Confederate general John B. Hood's division. Despite heavy enemy fire, his regiment struck with parade-ground precision and threw the Northerners out. Godwin's regiment held the railroad the rest of the day, despite losing 250 of its 800 men.

In May 1863, the 57th fought at Chancellorsville, where Godwin was slightly wounded. He fought in the Second Battle of Winchester and was on the extreme Confederate left flank at Gettysburg. The acting commander of General Robert Hoke's brigade, Colonel Isaac Avery, was mortally wounded on Cemetery Hill on July 2. As senior colonel, Godwin assumed command of the brigade and led it for the remainder of the battle and in the retreat to Virginia. He took part in the Bristoe Campaign. His brigade and H. T. Hays's Louisiana Brigade formed a bridgehead at the Rappahannock in the fall of 1863. On November 7, the Federals attacked in overwhelming force, and Godwin's brigade collapsed. The colonel and most of his men were captured. They were sent to the infamous Johnson's Island prison in the middle of Lake Erie.

Godwin was still highly thought of by his superiors. At the special urging of General Jubal Early, he was exchanged in the summer of 1864 and rejoined his brigade, which now totaled only eight hundred men. He served with Early's Army of the Valley and was promoted to brigadier general on August 5, 1864.

On September 19, he fought in the Third Battle of Winchester. While Godwin was conferring with Captain John Beard, the commander of his old regiment, a Union artillery shell exploded above their heads. A shell fragment struck General Godwin in the head, killing him instantly. He was thirty-two or thirty-three years old. He is buried in the Stonewall Cemetery in Winchester, Virginia.

JAMES MONROE GOGGIN was born on October 23, 1820, in Bedford County, Virginia. He entered West Point on July 1, 1838, but resigned before graduating. He relocated to Texas and joined the republic's army as a first lieutenant. He also began buying real estate in Waller County, northwest of Houston.

Goggin moved to California in 1848, got a job as a special agent for the U.S. Postal Service, and began establishing post offices and mail routes in northern California and southern Oregon. Later, he moved to Memphis, where he became a cotton broker.

When the war began, Goggin joined the Confederate Army as a major in the 32nd Virginia Infantry Regiment and fought in the early stages of the Peninsula

Campaign. In April 1862, he transferred to the staff of Lafayette McLaws and became his assistant adjutant general and de facto chief of staff. He took part in the Seven Days Battles and the battles of Second Manassas, Sharpsburg, Fredericksburg, Chancellorsville, Gettysburg, Chickamauga, and Knoxville. When General James Longstreet sacked McLaws and replaced him with Joseph B. Kershaw, Goggin remained as assistant adjutant general; no one doubted his abilities.

Goggin served in the Overland Campaign, Cold Harbor, the early part of the Siege of Petersburg, and the defense of the Shenandoah Valley. On October 13, 1864, during the Battle of Cedar Creek, Confederate General James Conner's leg was shattered and had to be amputated. Kershaw placed Goggin in command of Conner's brigade. Goggin was given a promotion to brigadier general (temporary rank) on December 4, 1864. The appointment was cancelled shortly after, and Goggin returned to Kershaw's staff as a major.

James M. Goggin served as Kershaw's assistant adjutant general until April 6, 1865, when Kershaw, Goggin, and most of the division were captured in the Battle of Sayler's Creek. He was paroled as a major.

After the surrender, Goggin returned to Waller County but later relocated to Austin. He died there on October 10, 1889, and is buried in Oakwood Cemetery, Austin, Texas.

GEORGE WASHINGTON GORDON was born on October 5, 1836, in Pulaski, Tennessee. He grew up in Mississippi and Texas but returned to Tennessee in the 1850s and graduated from the Western Military Institute in Nashville in 1859. Then, he worked for the Nashville & Northwestern Railroad and later became a surveyor. He joined the Confederate Army in May 1861 as first lieutenant and drillmaster for the 11th Tennessee Infantry Regiment. He was promoted to captain in July.

The regiment spent most of 1861 and much of 1862 engaged in minor skirmishes in East Tennessee. Gordon was promoted to lieutenant colonel on May 27, 1862. He was captured in the Battle of Tazewell, Tennessee, south of the Cumberland Gap, in August. He was exchanged in November.

Gordon was promoted to colonel of the 11th Tennessee in December 1862. He fought in the Second Battle of Murfreesboro (December 31, 1862, to January 2, 1863), where he was again captured. Exchanged in the spring, he took part in the Tullahoma Campaign, Chickamauga, Chattanooga, Missionary Ridge, and the Atlanta Campaign, including the Battle of Kennesaw Mountain. During a skirmish at Vining's Station near Marietta on July 4, 1864, his brigade commander, Alfred Vaughan, Jr., lost his leg to a Union artillery shell. Gordon took command of the brigade and was promoted to brigadier general on August 15, 1864.

After Atlanta fell, Gordon led his brigade into Tennessee as part of Confederate General John Bell Hood's disastrous Franklin-Nashville Campaign. On November 30, 1864, during the Battle of Franklin, Gordon was wounded and captured. Sent to Fort Warren in Boston Harbor, he was paroled on July 24, 1865.

The war over, Gordon studied law at Cumberland University, was admitted to the bar, and practiced law in Pulaski and Memphis. He also joined the Ku Klux Klan. In 1867, he became first Grand Dragon for the Realm of Tennessee, second in rank only to Grand Wizard Nathan Bedford Forrest. He wrote the *Prescipt*, which governed the activities of the secret organization. Gordon ended his membership after Forrest officially disbanded the organization in 1869.

In 1883, Gordon won a gubernatorial appointment to serve as one of Tennessee's railroad commissioners. From 1885 to 1889, he worked for the U.S. Department of the Interior as a special Indian agent in Arizona and Nevada. From 1889 to 1907, he was superintendent of the Memphis city schools.

In 1906, General Gordon was elected to the U.S. House of Representatives. He served from March 4, 1907, until his death in Memphis on August 9, 1911. He was seventy-four years old and was the last Confederate general to sit in Congress. He was also the commander-in-chief of the United Confederate Veterans at the time. Gordon's obituary noted that he was a "gentle, courteous man," a man "without pretense," and "the last of the illustrious list." He is buried in Elmwood Cemetery, Memphis.

JAMES BYRON GORDON was born in Wilkesboro, North Carolina, on November 2, 1822. He was educated in local schools and studied at Emory and Henry College in Virginia but left after two years. He returned home, worked the family farm, and went into the mercantile business. He was elected to the North Carolina legislature in 1850 and served several terms as a commissioner of Wilkes County.

Gordon enlisted in the army as a private on May 9, 1861, but was quickly promoted to first lieutenant. When the Wilkes County Guards were redesignated Company B, 1st North Carolina Infantry Regiment, Gordon became a captain and company commander. Shortly after, the 1st North Carolina Cavalry Regiment was formed, and Gordon became its major.

The 1st North Carolina fought in more than fifty engagements during the war and was regarded as one of the best cavalry units in the conflict. Initially sent to Virginia, it was sent back to eastern North Carolina in March 1862, where it skirmished against Ambrose Burnside's forces. Meanwhile, Gordon was promoted to lieutenant colonel. The regiment returned to Virginia in June and fought in all the major engagements of Jeb Stuart's cavalry. Gordon was frequently mentioned for his courage and leadership and was one of General Stuart's favorite subordinate commanders.

In July 1863, Gordon became commander of the 1st North Carolina Cavalry, and rebuffed U.S. General George Meade's forces at Hagerstown, Maryland. Gordon was promoted to colonel on August 11 and was acting commander of General Wade Hampton's brigade during the Battle of Jack's Shop on September 22, 1863.

In September 1863, General Robert E. Lee created an exclusively North Carolinian cavalry brigade with Gordon as commander. He was promoted to brigadier general on September 28.

Gordon continued to be in the thick of the combat, fighting in minor actions at Bethsaida Church (October 10), Bull Run (October 16), the Buckland Races, and the Mine Run fighting. He had a horse shot out from under him at Parker's Station.

In March 1864, General Gordon helped foil the raid on Richmond, led by U.S. General Judson Kilpatrick and Colonel Ulric Dahlgren. In May 1864, Gordon's cavalry fought in the Overland Campaign, the Battle of the Wilderness, and the Battle of Spotsylvania and clashed with U.S. General Phil Sheridan's cavalry at Meadow Bridge north of Richmond on May 12. Here, a Union minié ball struck Gordon in the arm, and though the wound did not appear to be serious, it proved fatal. General James Gordon died in Richmond on May 18, 1864. He was forty-one years old. He was buried with full military honors at St. Paul's Episcopal Churchyard in Wilkesboro, North Carolina. Gordon was an excellent brigade commander.

JOHN BROWN GORDON was born in Upson County, Georgia, on February 6, 1832. Influenced by his father, a Baptist preacher, he was a strong Christian all his life. He attended the University of Georgia, read law in Atlanta, and passed the bar. Gordon did not prosper as an attorney and joined his father in a profitable coal mining operation.

Immediately after Fort Sumter fell, Gordon raised a company, the Raccoon Roughs, of which he was elected captain. The company was assigned to the 6th Alabama Infantry Regiment and, on May 14, 1861, he was elected major. He took to soldiering like a duck to water. He looked like a soldier: tall (six feet), slender, dark black hair and beard, and piercing gray eyes; he was also a brilliant orator and a master at commanding people's respect. Sent to Virginia, he was promoted to lieutenant colonel in late 1861 and was unanimously elected colonel on April 28, 1862.

Gordon's first major action was the Battle of Seven Pines, where he performed extremely well and temporarily replaced the wounded Robert Rodes as the brigade commander here and in the Seven Days Battles. In July, Rodes returned, and Gordon reverted back to command of the 6th Alabama. The regiment fought at Turner's Gap and Sharpsburg (September 17, 1862), where Gordon held a vital position on the Sunken Road (Bloody Lane). Gordon was wounded five times in the battle and took months to recuperate.

He returned to the Army of Northern Virginia on March 30, 1863, and on April 11 was assigned to command a brigade in General Jubal Early's division, distinguishing himself in the Battle of Chancellorsville (April 30 to May 6). On May 11, 1863, on Robert E. Lee's recommendation, Gordon was promoted to brigadier general, to rank from May 7.

On July 1, during the first day of the Battle of Gettysburg, Gordon delivered an attack which was called "as brilliant as any charge of the war." With 1,200 men, he killed or wounded 1,200 to 1,500 Yankees and captured about 1,800—all in less than an hour. He suffered 380 casualties. Gordon urged immediate pursuit but was overruled by General Richard Ewell. This decision was one of the turning points of the war. The Northerners rallied and reinforced Cemetery Hill that night, and the Confederates never were able to capture it.

General Grant's Overland Campaign began on May 4, 1864. Gordon continued to display great tactical acumen. On May 7, Robert E. Lee gave Gordon temporary command of Early's division. On May 12, Gordon launched a determined attack into "the center of hell itself" and sealed off the Union's "Bloody Angle" breakthrough. He was promoted to major general on May 14, 1864.

On May 22, General Lee reorganized his army so that Gordon would have a permanent divisional command. Gordon distinguished himself at Cold Harbor and in the Shenandoah Valley Campaign of 1864. Early gave Gordon command of the II Corps on October 18, although he was never promoted to lieutenant general, as some authors assumed.

Gordon spent most of the rest of the war in the trenches around Petersburg. On March 25, 1865, he suffered his worst defeat when his surprise attack on Fort Stedman failed.

On April 2, General Grant broke Gordon's lines at several points. Lee ordered Richmond and Petersburg evacuated, and the Confederate capital fell the following morning. On April 9, the remnants of the Army of Northern Virginia surrendered at Appomattox.

After the war, Gordon supported his family by establishing a rice plantation in Brunswick in southern Georgia. When this failed, he went into several other businesses, and his fortunes fluctuated wildly.

Gordon opposed Radical Reconstruction and even joined the Ku Klux Klan. He ran for governor of Georgia in 1868 but lost narrowly. After the carpetbagger regime was overthrown, the legislature elected Gordon to the U.S. Senate, where he worked from 1873 to 1880 and 1891 to 1897. He also served a term as governor (1886–90). He retired from politics in 1897.

Gordon was the founding commander in chief of the United Confederate Veterans, a position he held until his death. His book *Reminiscences of the Civil War* was published in 1904.

Major General John Brown Gordon died while visiting a son in Miami, Florida, on January 9, 1904, at age seventy-one. He is buried in Oakland Cemetery, Atlanta, Georgia.

JOSIAH GORGAS was born in Running Pumps, rural south-central Pennsylvania, on July 1, 1818. He grew up in poverty, and his father moved the family frequently. Young Josiah apprenticed at a newspaper in Lyons, New York, and studied law. He entered West Point in 1837, graduated in 1841, and was commissioned in the Ordnance Department.

Gorgas served at the Watervliet Arsenal near Troy, New York, and the Detroit Arsenal before spending a year in Europe, studying foreign ordnance. He served in Mexico under General Winfield Scott and took part in the battles of Veracruz and Cerro Gordo.

After a tour of duty in Pennsylvania and at Fort Monroe, Virginia, he was transferred to the Mount Vernon Arsenal north of Mobile, Alabama. When the South seceded, Gorgas struggled with the decision as to whether to go with her. He resigned his commission on March 21, 1861. One result of his decision was permanent estrangement from his family in Pennsylvania.

General G. T. Beauregard recommended that Gorgas be appointed chief of ordnance for the Confederacy, and President Jefferson Davis concurred. It was one of the best appointments he ever made.

Gorgas faced a Herculean task. When he arrived in Richmond in June, the Confederacy had only 159,000 small arms and a thousand cannons, mostly old and obsolete. Gorgas immediately sent representatives to Europe to trade cotton for ordnance, munitions, and raw materials, including gunpowder, copper, tin, lead, and saltpeter. He organized a fleet of blockade runners to carry these supplies to Southern ports. He also worked tirelessly to increase the South's industrial capacity and did so. When the war began, the South had no foundries except the Tredegar Iron Works in Richmond and no rifle works except a few small arsenals. Gorgas organized cannon foundries, iron works, and shot and shell plants, as well as the largest powder works in North America at Augusta, Georgia. He was also highly innovative. His agents used limestone from caves in the Appalachians to make saltpeter, and Southern women were encouraged to save the contents of their chamber pots, from which saltpeter could be leached. Bells, particularly church bells, were melted down for bronze. Gorgas also created the Nitre and Mining Bureau and the Bureau of Foreign Supplies. General Joseph E. Johnston later commented, "He created the ordnance department out of nothing." Gorgas entered the Confederate Army as a major. He was promoted to brigadier general on November 10, 1864.

Without a doubt, Gorgas was highly successful. When General Robert E. Lee surrendered, his army had no food, but every man had seventy-five rounds of ammunition in his cartridge box.

Following the war, Gorgas struggled financially until 1869, when he became a headmaster and then vice-chancellor at the University of the South. He remained there until 1878, when he became president of the University of Alabama. A series of strokes, however, incapacitated him, and he served as president for less than a year. The board of trustees took care of him, allowing him and his family to live in what had been known as the Pratt House—now a museum called the Gorgas House—and created for him a largely honorary position as school librarian, stipulating that the position would go to his wife should he die. He passed away on May 15, 1883, at age sixty-four. He is buried in Evergreen Cemetery, Tuscaloosa, Alabama.

DANIEL CHEVILETTE GOVAN was born on July 3, 1827, in Northampton County, North Carolina, but was raised in Marshall County, Mississippi. He was educated by private tutors and at South Carolina College but returned home in 1848 without graduating. He and his cousin, Ben McCulloch, went to California as forty-niners but experienced only minor success in the goldfields. He served briefly as deputy sheriff in Sacramento. He returned home in 1852, and in December 1853 married a daughter of James Hervey Otey, a well-known Episcopal clergyman. He and his wife moved to Helena, Arkansas, in 1854, where he acquired a modest plantation in Phillips County.

When the war began, Daniel Govan raised a company of infantry and was appointed captain in the Arkansas state troops. His company was incorporated into Confederate service as Company F, 2nd Arkansas Infantry. On June 5, Govan was elected lieutenant colonel of the 2nd Arkansas Infantry Regiment. On January 28, 1862, Govan was promoted to colonel and regimental commander.

Colonel Govan took part in the Battle of Shiloh, the Siege of Corinth, the retreat to Tupelo, and the Battle of Perryville. Later, he fought in the Second Battle of Murfreesboro, after which St. John R.

Liddell (his brigade commander), Patrick Cleburne (his division commander), and William J. Hardee (his corps commander) all recommended he be given a brigade and promoted to brigadier general.

In August 1863, Braxton Bragg made Govan temporary commander of Liddell's brigade. In September, he led the brigade into fierce fighting at Chickamauga, where it suffered heavy casualties and left Govan, who was by nature quiet and introspective, deeply troubled.

Returning to command of his regiment, he fought at Missionary Ridge, taking five hundred prisoners and performing well in a Confederate defeat.

As the army settled into winter quarters at Dalton, Georgia, St. John Liddell was transferred and recommended that Govan replace him as brigade commander. Daniel Govan was promoted to brigadier general on December 29, 1863.

Govan's Arkansas Brigade took part in the Atlanta Campaign. "We slept on our arms, lulled to sleep (if we slept at all) to the sound of the bullet, and awoke in the morning saluted by artillery," he recalled. Sometimes the fighting was hand-to-hand. Casualties were appalling.

On September 1, 1864, when Joseph H. Lewis's and Govan's understrength brigades were attacked near Jonesboro by three U.S. divisions. Govan was among those taken prisoner. On September 9, Confederate authorities arranged a "special exchange" of two thousand prisoners. The Arkansas Brigade was back on duty by the end of the month.

Govan and his men took part in the Tennessee Campaign of 1864, including the Battle of Franklin. On the afternoon of December 16, during the Battle of Nashville, General Govan fell when a bullet struck him in the throat. He could not rejoin the Army of Tennessee until April 1865, when he was given a brigade of two regiments, but he saw no more combat. General Joseph E. Johnston surrendered the army on April 26.

General Liddell called Govan "an unpretending and reliable gentleman, zealous in the cause, deliberate and cool in judgment. . . ." He was also respected by his men, who regarded him as a true Christian gentleman. He was a fine regimental and brigade commander.

After the war, Govan became a farmer near Marianna, Arkansas. He refused to run for public office, although he apparently helped direct the Helena, Arkansas, Ku Klux Klan. In 1894, he moved to Washington state because President Grover Cleveland appointed him Indian agent at the Tulalip Agency. He was also active in the United Confederate Veterans. General Govan died of pulmonary edema at the home of a daughter in Memphis, Tennessee, on March 12, 1911. He was eighty-three years old. He is buried in Hill Crest Cemetery, Holly Springs, Mississippi.

ARCHIBALD GRACIE III was born on December 1, 1832, in New York City to a wealthy Manhattan family whose business interests included cotton exports from Mobile, Alabama. Archibald III's grandfather built Gracie Mansion, a Federal-style building that is the official residence of the mayor of New York. He attended the University of Heidelberg, Germany, before he was admitted to West Point in 1850, graduating with the class of 1854. He was appointed a second lieutenant and was stationed in the Washington Territory. He resigned his commission in 1857 and joined one of his father's business firms, which was located in Mobile. Gracie later became president of the Barings Bank of Mobile.

As the war approached, Gracie joined the Washington Light Infantry, a Mobile militia company, and became its captain. It seized the Federal arsenal at Mount Vernon, Mobile County, just before Alabama's secession. He entered Confederate service as a member of the 3rd Alabama Infantry but in June was chosen to be major of the 11th Alabama. In March and April 1862 he commanded a company of sharpshooters that fought with General John B. Magruder in the Siege of Yorktown.

Gracie then returned to Alabama and recruited the 43rd Alabama Infantry Regiment, which elected him colonel. In July 1862, he was given command of a brigade near Chattanooga, Tennessee, and suppressed a pro-Union uprising in Scott County.

Gracie was promoted to brigadier general on November 4, 1862. He participated in the Tullahoma Campaign of 1863, the Battle of Chickamauga, and the Battle of Bean's Station (December 14, 1863) during the Knoxville Campaign. There, he was shot in the arm and temporarily lost the use of his little and ring fingers. After he recovered, he joined General G. T. Beauregard in front of Petersburg.

Archibald Gracie served in the trenches before Petersburg from July to December 1864. On December 1, Gracie's birthday, his second child, a daughter, was born. He was granted leave to see the baby, beginning on December 3. On December 2, however, he was observing Union lines with a telescope when an artillery shell exploded in front of him. He was killed instantly. He was thirty-two.

His family recovered his body after the war. He is buried in Woodlawn Cemetery, Bronx, New York City.

HIRAM BRONSON GRANBURY was born on March 1, 1831, in Copiah County, Mississippi, the son of a Baptist preacher. Originally, his name was spelled *Granberry*, but he changed it to *Granbury* for some unknown reason. He was educated at Oakland College in Rodney, Mississippi (which is now a ghost town). In the 1850s he immigrated to Waco, Texas, and gained admission to the bar. He was chief justice of McLennan County from 1856 to 1858.

When the war began, he recruited the Waco Guards, which became part of the 7th Texas Infantry Regiment. In November 1861, after it was stationed at Hopkinsville, Kentucky, Granbury was elected major of his regiment.

The 7th Texas was rushed to Fort Donelson in early 1862 and surrendered with the garrison on February 16, 1862. He was imprisoned at Fort Warren in Boston Harbor.

Major Granbury was traded back to the Confederacy on August 27, 1862, in exchange for two Union lieutenants. Two days later, he was promoted to colonel and earmarked to command the 7th Texas Infantry Regiment. It was, however, not reactivated until January 1863.

Granbury and his men were sent to northern Mississippi, where they helped check Grant's Bayou Expeditions. After Grant landed south of Vicksburg, the 7th Texas fought in the battles of Raymond and Jackson. It escaped the Vicksburg encirclement and was part of General Joseph E. Johnston's Army of Relief during his perfunctory attempt to rescue the besieged fortress.

The 7th Texas was transferred to the Army of Tennessee, and Granbury fought in the Battle of Chickamauga, where he was wounded. He recovered quickly enough to fight in the Siege of Chattanooga and the Battle of Missionary Ridge on November 25. During this mêlée, Brigadier General James A. Smith was badly wounded, and Granbury took charge of his brigade. He led it in the retreat from Chattanooga and particularly distinguished himself at Ringgold Gap on November 27. He was promoted to brigadier general on March 5, 1864, to rank from February 29.

General Granbury led his Texas brigade in the Atlanta Campaign and the Franklin-Nashville Campaign. At the Battle of Franklin on November 30, John Bell Hood launched a desperate and almost suicidal attempt to overwhelm the well-fortified Union army. Granbury was killed about eighty yards from the Yankee works. He was buried near the field. On November 30, 1893, twenty-nine years after his death, he was reinterred in Granbury City Cemetery in Granbury, Texas, a town named in his honor.

HENRY GRAY, JR., was born in Laurens County, South Carolina, on January 19, 1816. He attended South Carolina College and graduated in 1834. He was admitted to the bar but soon moved to Mississippi, where he practiced law and became district attorney of Winston County.

Henry Gray was elected to the legislature in 1846 but only served one term. During this period, he became a close friend of Jefferson Davis. Gray made an unsuccessful run for Congress as a Whig in 1850. In 1851, he moved to Bienville Parish, northwestern Louisiana, where he had purchased 332 acres of land. He was an elector of President James Buchanan in 1856 and was elected to the Louisiana House of Representatives. In 1860, he ran for U.S. senator but lost by one vote in the Louisiana legislature.

When Mississippi seceded, Gray enlisted as a private in a Mississippi regiment. Jefferson Davis promoted Gray to colonel and asked him to form a regiment in Louisiana. He recruited the 28th Louisiana Infantry, which was mustered into Confederate service on May 2, 1862. It saw action in the bayou country, and Gray rose to brigade commander. On April 14, 1863, he was wounded in the fighting around Bayou Teche.

Colonel Gray was a small man, "not prepossessing in appearance," and did not have the look of a mighty warrior, but he was considered fearless. He was an effective leader, with a good tactical sense, but also sociable and humble, and he did not like military display.

Gray played a prominent role in the Red River Campaign of 1864. In the decisive Battle of Mansfield (April 8), his brigade (three regiments) lost five regimental commanders (killed or mortally wounded) and suffered roughly 40 percent casualties but routed the enemy. Gray was in the middle of the fray, but, somewhat remarkably, he was untouched. He and his men broke the Union line and ended the Northern attempt to capture northwest Louisiana and the Red River Valley. Gray then participated in the pursuit, including the Battle of Pleasant Hill, until the Union army escaped across the Atchafalaya River.

After the Red River Campaign ended, Gray and his brigade marched to Arkansas. They were camped at Camden, Arkansas, when Henry Gray learned that he had been elected to the Confederate Congress to represent his congressional district in Louisiana. He didn't even know he had been a candidate, but he dutifully took his seat on December 28, 1864.

On March 17, 1865, Gray was promoted to brigadier general and returned to the field.

After the war, he returned to Louisiana and was elected to the state legislature, but he retired from public life after a single term. Gray's only son had died in 1864, and he was soon a widower as well. Depressed and isolated, Henry Gray became something of a recluse. He died December 11, 1892, in a daughter's house in Coushatta, Louisiana, at age seventy-six. He is buried in Springville Cemetery, Coushatta.

JOHN BRECKINRIDGE GRAYSON was born on October 18, 1806, at Cabell's Dale, the Breckinridge family estate in Fayette County, Kentucky. Grayson graduated from West Point in 1826. He was commissioned in the artillery and spent the first nine years of his career serving in Southern forts. In 1835, he was sent to Florida and fought in the Second Seminole War. In 1836, he was posted to New Orleans and remained there for eleven years.

In 1847, Grayson joined Winfield Scott's army for the invasion of Mexico and fought in all the major battles from Veracruz to the capture of Mexico City. He was brevetted major for bravery and meritorious conduct at Contreras and Churubusco and subsequently lieutenant colonel for his actions at Chapultepec.

After the Mexican War, Grayson was stationed at Detroit (1848–55) and in the New Mexico Territory (1855–61). He resigned his commission as a major on July 1, 1861, and "went south."

President Jefferson Davis appointed Grayson a brigadier general in the Provisional Army on August 15. He was named commander of the Department of Middle and Eastern Florida, with headquarters at Fernandina. Soon after he arrived, however, he developed tuberculosis and pneumonia and was relieved of duty for reasons of health. He failed to rally and died in Tallahassee on October 21, 1861. He was buried in St. Louis Cemetery Number 1 in New Orleans.

G·

MARTIN EDWIN GREEN was born in Fauquier County, Virginia, on June 3, 1815. In 1836, he moved to Lewis County, Missouri, where he and his brothers operated a steam sawmill. Martin became a prominent Democrat and was elected judge of the Lewis County Court.

In the summer of 1861, Green (an outspoken secessionist) formed a Confederate cavalry command in northeast Missouri. After taking part in several minor skirmishes, he joined Sterling Price's army. Here Green's Missouri Cavalry Regiment was formed, and Green was elected its colonel. He aided in the capture of the Federal garrison at Lexington, Missouri, in September 1861. He fought at the Battle of Pea Ridge in March 1862. He and his men crossed the Mississippi River and operated in Mississippi in April 1862.

Green was promoted to brigadier general on July 21, 1862, and was given command of a brigade of Missouri and Arkansas regiments. He fought at the Battles of Iuka, Corinth, and Hatchie's Bridge in northern Mississippi. Green's brigade then became part of John S. Bowen's division and earned a reputation as an excellent combat unit.

Martin Green and his men fought tenaciously in the Battle of Port Gibson and at Champion Hill, where they temporarily threw back U.S. General Ulysses Grant's main advance. They were, however, too badly outnumbered to exploit their success. After Federal forces defeated General John Pemberton's Army of Mississippi, Green and his depleted brigade fell back into the fortress of Vicksburg.

The Siege of Vicksburg began on May 18, 1863. By June, Green's brigade was holding an important portion of the main siege line. On June 25, General Green was slightly wounded. He returned to the front on June 27. Later that day, he was observing the Union line through a pair of binoculars when a Yankee sharpshooter put a bullet in his head. He died instantly. He was forty-eight years old.

Martin Edwin Green was buried within the fortress of Vicksburg; the exact location was forgotten in the chaos and confusion after the city fell. He has a cenotaph in the Confederate section of Cedar Hill Cemetery (Old City Cemetery) in Vicksburg.

THOMAS GREEN was born on June 8, 1814, in Buckingham County, Virginia, but moved with his family to Tennessee in 1817. He received a degree from East Tennessee College at Knoxville in 1834. He then studied law but never stood for the bar, because the Texas Revolution began, and he left immediately to join the volunteers. On April 21, 1836, during the Battle of San Jacinto, he helped fire the famous "Twin Sisters," the only two cannons General Sam Houston had that day. This obviously impressed Houston, who promoted him to lieutenant a few days later. In early May, he was promoted to major but resigned his commission on May 30 because the war was over. He returned to Tennessee.

In 1837, the congress of the Republic of Texas gave Green a large amount of land between Houston and Austin. This enticed Green to relocate to Texas permanently. He became clerk of the House of Representatives of the Republic of Texas (1837–41) and was a member of the Fourth Congress of the Republic in 1839. Green became clerk of the Texas Supreme Court in 1841 and held this office for twenty years.

Green remained involved with the Texas army from 1837 to 1861, fighting against Comanches and Mexicans. He also commanded a company of Texas Rangers and, during the Mexican War, took part in the capture of Monterrey.

In 1861, after Texas seceded from the Union, Green was elected colonel of the 5th Texas Cavalry Regiment and participated in the invasion of the New Mexico Territory. In 1862, he led Confederate forces to victory at the Battle of Valverde. (His superior, General Sibley, was present; but he was so inebriated that he almost fell off of his horse, and Green took de facto command of the Rebel forces.) Later, Green led his men on a hard retreat back to Texas. On January 1, 1863, he was involved in General John B. Magruder's recapture of Galveston from the Federals.

In the spring of 1863, Green was named commander of the 1st Cavalry Brigade of Richard Taylor's Army of Western Louisiana. He was involved in the fighting along Bayou Teche, where he demonstrated brilliance as an independent cavalry commander. He was promoted to brigadier general on May 20, 1863.

On June 24, Green captured a U.S. garrison at Brashear City (now Morgan City), Louisiana. His forces suffered about thirty casualties, as opposed to four hundred Northerners killed, wounded, or captured. He routed a superior Union force at Koch's Plantation (Cox's Plantation) on July 13 and captured another isolated Federal detachment at Stirling's Plantation in September. On November 3, at the Battle of Bayou Bourbeux (also known as the Battle of Grand Coteau or Boggy Creek), he overran a Union camp. Overall, in the Bayou Campaign of 1863, he inflicted five casualties on the Yankees for every man he lost.

There is no doubt that Thomas Green was a brilliant cavalry commander and a kind gentleman—when he was sober. This became less common in 1864. He had a drinking problem, and alcohol unleashed his temper. He performed well in the retreat up the Red River and in the Battle of Mansfield but was apparently intoxicated on April 9, during

the Battle of Pleasant Hill, when he sent two of his cavalry brigades into an ambush. They extracted themselves, but only after suffering heavy casualties.

On April 12, an obviously inebriated General Green was trying to organize a cavalry attack on some Union ironclads when he was struck by an iron ball from a heavy naval gun. It tore off the top half of General Green's skull, killing him instantly. He was forty-nine years old. His body was taken back to Texas and buried in the family plot at Oakwood Cemetery in Austin.

ELKANAH BRACKIN GREER was born on October 11, 1825, in Paris, Tennessee. In 1846, he joined Colonel

Jefferson Davis's 1st Mississippi Rifle Regiment and fought at Monterrey and Buena Vista. He moved to Marshall, Texas, in 1848. He was a merchant, planter, and lawyer, as well as superintendent of the Southern Pacific Railroad in Marshall.

A strong states' rights Democrat, Greer became national commander of the Knights of the Golden Circle (KGC), a secret organization that advocated the establishment of a slaveholding empire encompassing the South, Mexico, the West Indies, and parts of Central America. He attended the Democrat convention of 1860 as a delegate, but he, like many Southern Democrats, walked out rather than accept Stephen Douglas and his platform. After Lincoln was elected president, Greer urged Texas to secede, which it did on February 1, 1861.

Greer joined the Confederate Army in May 1861 and raised the South Kansas–Texas Cavalry Regiment, which was later redesignated the 3rd Texas Cavalry Regiment. It was operational by June. Elected colonel, he joined Ben McCulloch's Army of the West, leading his regiment in the battles of Wilson's Creek, Missouri, and Chustenahlah, Indian Territory. The latter battle was a lopsided Confederate victory that forced nine thousand pro-Union Indians to flee to Kansas during a bitter winter. About two thousand of them died on the way. This march became known as the Trail of Blood on Ice.

At Pea Ridge, Greer was severely wounded in the arm, and though he could no longer command troops in the field, he advanced to the rank of brigadier general on October 4, 1862, and was named chief of the conscription bureau of the Trans-Mississippi Department. In 1864, he also commanded the department's reserve corps, but he held no more field commands after Pea Ridge.

After the war, Greer returned to Marshall, where he resumed his previous careers as a planter and a merchant. He remained friends with Jefferson Davis and was part of a reception committee for him when the former president visited Marshall in 1875.

General Elkanah Greer died while visiting his sister at DeValls Bluff, Arkansas, on March 25, 1877. He was fifty-one years old. He is buried in Elmwood Cemetery, Memphis, Tennessee, next to his parents.

JOHN GREGG was born on September 28, 1828, in Lawrence County, Alabama. He was educated at the LaGrange College (present-day University of North Alabama), from which he graduated in 1847. LaGrange later hired him as a professor of mathematics. He studied law in Tuscumbia before moving to Fairfield, Texas, where he set up a law practice. He was elected district judge at the age of twenty-eight and served from 1855 to 1860. He was one of the founders of the *Freestone County Pioneer*, the first newspaper in the county. It editorialized in favor of states' rights.

John Gregg advocated secession after Lincoln was elected president. As a delegate to the secession convention, he helped take Texas out of the Union on February 1, 1861.

Gregg was elected to the Provisional Confederate Congress but resigned his seat in August 1861 to join the Confederate Army. He returned to Texas and recruited the 7th Texas Infantry Regiment. He was elected its colonel in September.

His regiment first saw action at Fort Donelson on February 12, 1862. It surrendered with the rest of the garrison on February 16, 1862. Gregg was a prisoner of war at Fort Warren, in Boston Harbor, until he was exchanged on August 15. He was promoted to brigadier general on August 29, 1862. John Gregg was not qualified for this promotion by training or experience, but he nevertheless proved to be a superb brigade commander and a tenacious warrior noted for his boldness and courage.

Gregg's new brigade was sent to Mississippi, where it performed well in the Battle of Chickasaw Bluffs and in rebuffing Grant's forces in his Bayou Expeditions.

After Grant landed south of Vicksburg and pushed northeast, Gregg found himself on the Confederate extreme southern flank. General Joseph E. Johnston stripped the Army of Mississippi of its cavalry, so General Gregg was denied adequate reconnaissance. On May 12, 1863, thinking he outnumbered the Yankees and had the chance to smash the Union extreme right, Gregg struck the Union forces near Raymond with four thousand men. He was actually attacking General James McPherson's XVII Corps, which had nearly twenty thousand men. So fierce was Gregg's assault that the Yankees thought *they* were outnumbered. Still, the Federals rallied and defeated the Confederates, but Gregg escaped with his brigade intact. He later fought at the First Battle of Jackson and was part of Johnston's Army of Relief after Vicksburg was surrounded.

Gregg's brigade was then sent to Georgia and fought at Chickamauga. On September 20, he was shot in the neck, severely wounded, and initially left for dead. He was finally taken to a field hospital and gradually recovered.

By now, Gregg's reputation as a commander was so good that General James Longstreet appointed him commander of John Bell Hood's Texas Brigade, which General Robert E. Lee often used as his shock troops. Gregg distinguished himself in the Battle of the Wilderness and was repeatedly praised by his superiors in every battle from the Wilderness to the Siege of Petersburg. On October 7, 1864, a Union soldier armed with a Spencer repeating rifle shot him in the neck again. This time it killed him. He was thirty-six years old.

General Gregg was buried in Hollywood Cemetery in Richmond. Later, his wife took his body back to Mississippi and buried him in Odd Fellows Rest Cemetery, Aberdeen, Mississippi.

MAXCY GREGG was born on August 1, 1814, in Columbia, South Carolina. His father was the mayor of Columbia. Maxcy Gregg attended South Carolina College and graduated at the top of his class in 1836. He studied law and was admitted to the bar in 1839.

Gregg was noted for his wide education and sharp intellect, although he labored with the handicap of partial deafness. He was considered an authority on ornithology, botany, and astronomy. He even constructed an observatory at his home. He was a bachelor all his life.

In 1846, Gregg volunteered for service in the Mexican War and became a major in the 12th U.S. Infantry, but the war ended before he could reach the field.

Maxcy Gregg was a strong Fire-Eater and an early advocate of secession. He wrote a book, *An Appeal to the State Rights Party of South Carolina* (1858). He was a member of the 1860 Secession Convention that led South Carolina out of the union. On January 25, 1861, the convention appointed him colonel of the 1st South Carolina Volunteer Infantry, a six-month regiment that took part in the bombardment of Fort Sumter. The regiment was sent to Virginia, but most of the men's enlistments expired before the Battle of First Manassas. Gregg returned home, reformed his regiment as the 1st South Carolina Infantry, and led it back to Virginia, where it was stationed at Suffolk.

On December 14, 1861, Maxcy Gregg was promoted to brigadier general. His brigade fought well in the Seven Days Battles, despite suffering heavy casualties. An army reorganization put Gregg under the command of Stonewall Jackson, with whom he feuded. He once called Jackson "tyrannical and unjust."

Gregg and his men were lightly engaged at Cedar Mountain but were involved in fierce hand-to-hand combat at the Battle of Second Manassas. They fought from daylight to dark and repulsed six major attacks. Toward the end of the day, with their ammunition spent, some of his men resorted to throwing rocks; others used knives, swords, bayonets, and pistols. By the time the smoke cleared, one-third of Gregg's men were casualties; he had been conspicuous for his coolness under fire, roaming the line to encourage his men.

The South Carolinians fought at Sharpsburg, and General Gregg was slightly wounded. On December 13, 1862, at the Battle of Fredericksburg, the brigade was in reserve when U.S. General George Meade's division struck an unprotected section of Stonewall Jackson's line between James Henry Lane's brigade and James Archer's brigade. The Yankees broke through, took Gregg's brigade by surprise, and routed it. While the general was rallying his men, a bullet went through his side and into his spine. Taken to a field hospital, the doctors told him his wound was mortal. Stonewall Jackson visited him on his deathbed and found him awake but in great agony. The two reconciled. Jackson asked him to turn his mind to God. Gregg mumbled his thanks. He was, however, not a believer.

General Maxcy Gregg died on December 15, 1862. He was forty-eight years old. His body was brought back to South Carolina and buried in Elmwood Memorial Gardens, Columbia, with full military honors.

RICHARD GRIFFITH was born in Philadelphia, Pennsylvania, on January 11, 1814. He graduated from Ohio University at Athens, Ohio, in 1837, and moved to Vicksburg around 1840. There, he worked as a school-teacher. During the Mexican War, he was the adjutant of the 1st Mississippi Rifle Regiment and became close friends with its commander, Colonel Jefferson Davis. He settled in Jackson, Mississippi, after the war, where he was a bank cashier and a U.S. marshal, and he was also twice elected treasurer of the state of Mississippi. In addition, he was a brigadier general in the Mississippi Militia.

When the Civil War began, Griffith was appointed colonel of the 12th Mississippi Infantry Regiment in May 1861. It was sent to Virginia and arrived on the Manassas battlefield the night after the battle. Griffith was placed in charge of a brigade of four Mississippi regiments and was promoted to brigadier general on November 12, 1861. He was transferred to John B. Magruder's division on the Virginia Peninsula in April 1862.

After participating in the Peninsula Campaign, Griffith's men fought in the Seven Days Battles. Here, on June 29, 1862, Griffith took part in the Battle of Savage's Station. He was pursuing the retreating Union troops when a Union shell exploded. About half the shell wound up in Griffith's body. Knowing that his wound was fatal, the general said, "If only I could have led my brigade through this battle, I would have died satisfied." He was taken to Richmond, where he died later that day. Jefferson Davis described him as "the gallant soldier, the useful citizen, the true friend, the Christian gentleman. . . . He had served with distinction in foreign war, and, when the South was invaded, was among the first to take up arms in defense of our rights." He was the first general from Mississippi killed in action.

Griffith was a good commander and was very popular with his men. Some of them formed a musical/singing group, "The McLaws Minstrels." They performed at a theater in Fredericksburg and charged a modest fee, which was used to erect a monument in the Mississippi State Capitol for Richard Griffith. He is buried in Greenwood Cemetery, Jackson, Mississippi.

BRYAN GRIMES, JR., was born on November 2, 1828, at Grimesland, his family's plantation in Pitt County, North Carolina. Educated at an academy in nearby Washington, North Carolina, and at an excellent private school in Hillsborough, he entered the University of North Carolina in 1844 at age fifteen. He graduated in 1848. The following year, his father gave him Grimesland, which included more than one hundred slaves.

Grimes was a delegate to the North Carolina Secession Convention and voted for secession. He entered the Confederate Army as a major in the 4th North Carolina Infantry Regiment on May 16, 1861.

Major Grimes took part in the Battle of First Manassas and was promoted to lieutenant colonel on May 1, 1862. He fought in the Battle of Seven Pines and was severely injured when his horse was wounded and fell on top of him. He was promoted to colonel and commander of the 4th North Carolina on June 19, 1862. He fought in the Seven Days Battles.

On September 5, 1862, during the early days of the Maryland campaign, his mount kicked him so hard that the doctors actually considered amputating his leg. He was sent back to Shepherdstown in an ambulance. After he returned to active duty, he was given temporary command of a brigade in Stonewall Jackson's corps. He performed well in the Battle of Fredericksburg, where his men repulsed a major Union attack on December 13.

Colonel Grimes reverted to regimental command before the Battle of Chancellorsville, where he was wounded in the foot on May 3, 1863.

It was one of four wounds he sustained during the war. During the Battle of Gettysburg, his regiment was the first to enter the streets of the town on July 1. It formed part of the army's rear guard during the retreat to Virginia.

By now, Grimes's leadership abilities were recognized by all the senior commanders in the Army of Northern Virginia. He was given permanent command of a brigade of North Carolinians and was promoted to brigadier general on May 19, 1864. That fall, he was transferred to Jubal Early's Army of the Valley. He was wounded in the leg at the Battle of Cedar Creek, the same battle in which General Stephen D. Ramseur was killed. When Grimes returned to duty on December 9, he was named permanent commander of Ramseur's old division, which he led for the rest of the war.

On February 15, 1865, Bryan Grimes was promoted to major general—the last officer in the Army of Northern Virginia to reach that rank. He fought until the end of the war. On the morning of April 9, he led the Army of Northern Virginia's last attack. General Robert E. Lee surrendered later that day.

Grimes returned to North Carolina after the war and rebuilt his former prosperity as a successful planter. General Grimes was returning home from a convention in Beaumont when he was murdered by a hired killer named William Parker near Bear Creek, about five miles from Grimesland, on August 14, 1880. The killer had, apparently, been hired to prevent Grimes from testifying in a trial. Grimes was fifty-one years old. Bryan Grimes was buried in the family cemetery at Grimesland. Parker was found not guilty of the assassination, but years later he drunkenly boasted about getting away with Grimes's murder and was lynched.

H

· HAGOOD – HUNTON ·

H·

JOHNSON HAGOOD was born on February 21, 1829, in Barnwell, South Carolina, the son of a planter. He graduated from the South Carolina Military Academy (now The Citadel) in 1847 first in his class and became a planter.

On January 27, 1861, Hagood was elected colonel of the 1st South Carolina Infantry and took part in the reduction of Fort Sumter. He led his regiment in the Battle of First Manassas, after which he and his command returned to South Carolina. He was commissioned a colonel in the Confederate Army and led the 1st South Carolina Infantry Regiment, which became the core of a new brigade that he commanded. Hagood led his brigade (2,900 men) in the successful Battle of Secessionville (June 16, 1862), in the defense of James Island, and in repulsing the Union assaults in the Second Battle of Battery (or Fort) Wagner on Morris Island (July 18, 1863). His gallantry and fine performance at Secessionville resulted in his promotion to brigadier general on July 21, 1862. Hagood was a talented officer, both in the field and in military administration, and in addition to his brigade command and his responsibility for defending Charleston, he was in charge of the Second Military District of South Carolina (1862–64) and the Seventh District (1864).

On May 4, 1864, General Grant launched his Overland Campaign. Before long, General Robert E. Lee was losing five hundred men a day defending Virginia from the Federals. To replace these losses, significant forces were transferred from North and South Carolina to Virginia, including Hagood's brigade. It fought in the battles of Drewry's Bluff and Cold Harbor and the Siege of Petersburg until December 1864. The brigade was then sent to the relief of Fort Fisher, North Carolina, which fell on January 15, 1865, and Wilmington, North Carolina, which fell on February 22. Hagood fought in the Battle of Bentonville, but he was not present at the surrender, where his brigade was commanded by the senior colonel. There is no record of General Hagood's ever being paroled.

After the war, Hagood returned to his plantation. He was a reserved man, but he felt compelled to enter politics after the war. He served in the South Carolina General Assemby (1865–66) and ran for Congress in 1868 but was defeated. He actively campaigned for Wade Hampton when he ran for governor in 1876. Hampton added Hagood to his ticket as state comptroller, and he was elected. He was reelected in 1878.

In 1880, General Hagood was elected governor and served from December 1, 1880 to December 1, 1882. He did not seek reelection in 1882. The Citadel was reopened during his administration.

Hagood was president of the Association of Graduates of The Citadel from 1877 to 1898. During his semiretirement, he wrote a manuscript, which was later edited by Ulysses R. Brooks and published as *Memoirs of the War of Secession* in 1910.

General Hagood died at his plantation home on January 4, 1898. He was sixty-eight years old. He was buried in the Church of the Holy Apostles Episcopal Cemetery, Barnwell. The Citadel honored him by briefly shutting down, and the entire corps of cadets, along with its officers and faculty, attended his funeral.

WADE HAMPTON III, was born in Charleston, South Carolina, on March 28, 1818, the child of a wealthy family. Hampton was homeschooled by a private tutor and graduated from South Carolina College. He passed the bar exam but never practiced; instead, he managed some of his father's plantations in South Carolina and Mississippi. He served in the South Carolina legislature from 1852 to 1858, when he took his seat in the South Carolina State Senate. He served there until 1861.

As a legislator, Hampton expressed misgivings about slavery and opposed secession but went with his state when it succeeded. He was forty-three years old and had the largest fortune in the state but nevertheless opted for field duty. He recruited and equipped Hampton's Legion and became its colonel. The Legion fought in the Battle of First

Manassas, where he reinforced the wavering Confederate line at a key moment and enabled Stonewall Jackson's brigade to reach the field. When he charged a Union battery, he received a glancing blow on the head from a Northern bullet, rendering him *hors de combat*. He quickly recovered and was given command of an infantry brigade, which he led in the Peninsula Campaign. He was promoted to brigadier general on May 23, 1862.

Hampton was severely wounded in the foot on May 31. He was seriously wounded five times during the war. He was commanding an infantry brigade under Stonewall Jackson at the end of the Seven Days Battles.

In July, General Robert E. Lee created a cavalry division under J. E. B. Stuart. It consisted of two cavalry brigades. Lee selected Wade Hampton to command of one of them. Hampton proved to be fearless, bold, and brilliant. He personally killed about a dozen Yankees in close combat. He, Nathan Bedford Forrest, and Richard Taylor were the only three non–West Pointers to reach the rank of lieutenant general. Hampton was allowed to conduct several raids on his own, and they were always successful.

Hampton received three saber wounds at Gettysburg. When he returned to camp four months later, he was a cavalry division commander. He was promoted to major general on August 3, 1863. General Stuart was mortally wounded on May 11, 1864. Robert E. Lee appointed Hampton corps commander on August 11.

Remarkably, General Hampton did not lose a single battle for the rest of the war. At the Battle of Trevilian Station (June 11–12, 1864), despite being outnumbered 9,000 to 6,000, he and Confederate General Fitzhugh Lee crushed the Union cavalry of Generals Phil Sheridan and George Armstrong Custer, who were trying unsuccessfully to destroy the Virginia Central Railroad. In September, he conducted his famous Beefsteak Raid behind Union lines. With 3,000 cavalrymen, led by what Hampton called "several certified Texas cattle thieves," he captured 2,685 cattle and more than 300 Yankees. Hampton lost 61 men, of whom 10 were killed.

In January 1865, Hampton was sent to South Carolina to join the Army of Tennessee. He was promoted to lieutenant general on February 14, 1865. He rode with General Joseph E. Johnston's army until he surrendered on April 26. Before the capitulation, Hampton seriously considered committing suicide.

Hampton returned to South Carolina and began to try to partially rebuild his lost fortune, with limited success. He worked for home rule for South Carolina and for an end to the incredibly corrupt Radical Reconstruction regime. Immensely popular, he won a disputed election for governor and served from December 14, 1876. He was reelected in 1878. Meanwhile, he lost his right leg as the result of a hunting accident in late 1878, but this did not affect his energy.

Governor Hampton refused to run for the U.S. Senate, but the legislature elected him anyway. He resigned as governor and served in the Senate from March 4, 1879 to March 3, 1891. He was defeated for reelection in 1890 by an ally of "Pitchfork Ben" Tillman, who had come to dominate South Carolina politics. President Grover Cleveland appointed Hampton railroad commissioner, an office he had from 1893 to 1897.

Wade Hampton died in Columbia, South Carolina, on April 11, 1902, at age eighty-four. He is buried in Trinity Episcopal Cathedral Cemetery, Columbia.

ROGER WEIGHTMAN HANSON was born on August 27, 1827, at Winchester, Kentucky, the son of a successful attorney. He joined the 4th Kentucky Infantry Regiment in 1846 and was elected lieutenant. Sent to Mexico, he was cited for bravery at the Battle of Cerro Gordo. After he returned home, he studied law and fought a duel in which he was shot in the leg just above the knee. He limped for the rest of his life. His troops nicknamed him "Bench Leg" during the Civil War. They also called him "Old Flintlock."

After spending a year in California, Hanson returned home and was elected to the Kentucky legislature, serving

from 1853 to 1857. He opened a law office and was quite prosperous. He ran for Congress in 1857 but was defeated by the son of Henry Clay. In 1860, he was a presidential elector for John Bell.

Hanson supported Kentucky's neutrality in 1861. On August 19, he was named colonel of the Kentucky State Guard. After both Northern and Southern forces entered the state, Hanson opted for the Confederacy. He organized the 2nd Kentucky Infantry Regiment in Lexington and on September 3, 1861, became its colonel.

The 2nd Kentucky was sent to Fort Donelson in early 1862. The Rebel garrison was loosely surrounded on February 15 when the 2nd Kentucky regiment launched a magnificent counterattack. Confederate Generals John B. Floyd, Simon B. Buckner, and Gideon Pillow, however, failed to take advantage of it. They surrendered the garrison the next day.

Hanson was held at Fort Warren, Massachusetts, as a prisoner of war. On August 15, 1862, he was exchanged. Hanson was promoted to brigadier general on December 13, 1862, based largely on his gallantry at Fort Donelson. His new command was from Kentucky and was called the "Orphan Brigade" because its state was occupied by the Federals and its men could not go home.

Roger Hanson only fought one battle as a general. On January 2,

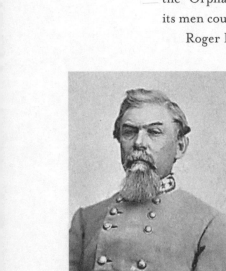

1863, he was mortally wounded in the Second Battle of Murfreesboro while leading an attack. He died two days later (January 4) at age thirty-five. The *Confederate Military History* commented on Hanson thusly: "Endeared to his friends by his private virtues and to his command by the vigilance with which he guarded its interest and honor, he was, by the universal testimony of his military associates, one of the finest officers that adorned the service of the Confederate States." He is buried in Lexington Cemetery, Lexington, Kentucky.

WILLIAM JOSEPH HARDEE was born in Wytheville, Virginia, on October 12, 1815, the son of a prominent planter. He entered West Point in 1834, graduated in 1838, and was assigned to the 2nd Dragoons. He was sent to Florida to fight the Seminoles.

Hardee spent a year in France studying tactics. During the Mexican War, he was captured at Carricitos Ranch but was quickly exchanged. He was then court-martialed for his command decisions at Carricitos Ranch but was acquitted. Hardee was brevetted to major for his bravery at Veracruz and to lieutenant colonel for valor at San Augustín. He was also wounded in a skirmish at La Rosita. After the war, Hardee commanded Texas soldiers and Texas Rangers.

Posted to Washington, D.C., he wrote the new infantry tactics manual for the U.S. Army. *Rifle and Light Infantry Tactics: For Exercise and Manœuvres of Troops When Acting as Light Infantry or Riflemen* (commonly called Hardee's *Tactics*) became the standard drill manual for both sides during the Civil War.

Hardee was commandant of cadets at West Point (1856–60) and was briefly lieutenant colonel of the 1st U.S. Cavalry. Hardee resigned his commission on January 31, 1861, after Georgia seceded and was commissioned a colonel of cavalry in the Confederate Army on March 28, 1861.

Colonel Hardee briefly commanded Forts Morgan and Gaines in Alabama. He was promoted to brigadier general on June 17, 1861, and was named commander of the Upper District of Arkansas (northeast Arkansas). Hardee's ability to solve supply and logistical problems earned him the nickname "Old Reliable."

On October 7, 1861, Hardee was promoted to major general and division commander. He led the III Corps at Shiloh (April 6–7, 1862), where he was wounded in the arm. Later that spring, he took part in the Siege of Corinth. On October 8, 1862, he fought at the Battle of Perryville and was promoted to lieutenant general two days later.

Now commanding the II Corps of Braxton Bragg's Army of Tennessee, Hardee fought at the Second Battle of Murfreesboro, where he launched a massive, successful surprise attack on the Union right flank and captured several Federal batteries before they could fire a shot.

Hardee hurled the Yankees back three miles, took more than three thousand prisoners, captured twenty-eight guns, and almost drove the Union Army of the Cumberland from the field, but, as often happened, General Bragg lost his nerve and withheld support for Hardee's attack, allowing the Yankees to rally and eventually win a marginal victory.

After the Tullahoma Campaign, Hardee conspired against Braxton Bragg, which led to his being exiled from the Army of Tennessee. He briefly commanded Confederate forces in eastern Mississippi. Sent back to Tennessee, he fought in the Siege of Chattanooga, including the disastrous defeat at Missionary Ridge. Braxton Bragg resigned as army commander on December 2, 1863, and was replaced by General Hardee, who declined permanent command. On December 16, he was superseded by Joseph E. Johnston.

General Hardee commanded a corps during the Atlanta Campaign, first under Johnston and then under John Bell Hood. After Hood's reckless, ill-planned, and badly executed attacks in front of Atlanta, Hardee correctly considered Hood to be incapable of successfully leading an army, so he requested a transfer. He was given command of the Department of South Carolina, Georgia, and Florida. While Hood invaded Tennessee with the main army and suffered a major disaster at Nashville, Hardee opposed Sherman's March to the Sea with woefully inadequate forces. He evacuated Savannah on December 20, 1864.

As Sherman turned north and launched his Carolina Campaign, Hardee was superseded in overall command by G. T. Beauregard and then by Joseph E. Johnston. He fought at the Battle of Bentonville and surrendered with the rest of the Army of Tennessee at Durham Station on April 26, 1865.

After the war, he moved to Selma, Alabama, to assume the presidency of the Selma and Meridian Railroad, which he held from 1866 to 1868. After that, he worked in the warehousing and insurance businesses. He died at Wytheville, Virginia, on November 6, 1873, at the age of fifty-eight. He is buried in Old Live Oak Cemetery, Selma.

WILLIAM POLK "GOTCH" HARDEMAN was born in Williamson County, Tennessee, on November 4, 1816. His father moved west and was one of the founders of the Republic of Texas. Young Hardeman attended the University of Nashville and then moved to Matagorda County, Texas, with his family. He immediately joined the resistance to Mexican dictator Antonio López de Santa Anna. In 1837, Hardeman joined the Texas Rangers and did frontier duty with Erastus "Deaf" Smith. He fought Comanches, bandits, and Mexican raiders and also took part in raids into Mexico in 1843.

During the Mexican War, Hardeman participated in operations around Monterrey and in the Battle of Buena Vista acted as a member of Ben McCulloch's Guadalupe Valley Raiders, who scouted for General Zachary Taylor.

Following the Mexican War, Hardeman operated his plantation in Guadalupe County for fifteen years. He owned as many as thirty-one slaves. After Lincoln was elected president, Hardeman joined the Texas Secession Convention and voted in favor of leaving the Union. When the Civil War began, he formed a company of eight hundred men. They were soon designated Company A of the 4th Texas Cavalry, and in May 1861 Hardeman became their captain. He took part in the New Mexico Campaign and was wounded twice in the Confederate victory at Valverde, where he led a successful charge against a Union battery. He was promoted to major immediately afterward and to lieutenant colonel on March 28, 1862. In April, Hardeman defended the supply depot at Albuquerque. The Federals attacked Hardeman with greatly superior forces, but he checked them every time and saved the Confederate artillery.

Hardeman was promoted to colonel in January 1863 and transferred to the Army of Western Louisiana, in which he served under General Tom Green. He briefly commanded a brigade in December 1863 and led the 4th Texas Cavalry in General Richard Taylor's highly successful Red River Campaign, including at the battles of Mansfield and Pleasant Hill and the subsequent pursuit of the U.S. Army of the Gulf across Louisiana.

Colonel Hardeman assumed command of a brigade of mounted Texans in October 1864. He was promoted to brigadier general on March 17, 1865. The Confederate Army's Trans-Mississippi Department surrendered the last Confederate significant ground forces on May 26, 1865, although most of its men had gone home before that.

General Hardeman fled to Mexico at the end of the war but soon returned home and resumed his previous occupation as a planter. In 1874, he became sergeant at arms of the Texas House of Representatives, followed by a job as inspector of railroads. He was also one of the founders of the Agriculture and Mechanical College of Texas, which became Texas A&M University. Finally, he became superintendent of public buildings and grounds at Austin, which included supervising the Texas Confederate soldiers' home. A veteran of four wars, William Polk Hardeman died of Bright's disease on April 8, 1898, in Austin. He was eighty-one years old. He is buried on Republic Hill in Texas State Cemetery, Austin.

NATHANIEL HARRISON HARRIS was born in Natchez, Mississippi, on August 22, 1834. He graduated from the University of Louisiana (now Tulane) law school and set up a practice with his brother in Vicksburg, Mississippi. When the war began, he organized the Warren Rifles and was elected its captain. The unit was incorporated into the 19th Mississippi Infantry Regiment as Company C in June 1861.

In July, Harris and his men were stationed in the Shenandoah and were sent to Manassas on July 21, but the battle was over when they arrived. They were sent to the Virginia Peninsula, where they fought in the Siege of Yorktown. Harris received high praise for his gallantry in the Battle of Williamsburg on May 5, in which he was wounded and after which he received a promotion to major. He also took part in the Battle of Seven Pines and the Seven Days Battles, in which he was wounded during the Battle of Frayser's Farm on June 30. He received a third wound during the Battle of Second Manassas on August 30. Harris commanded the regiment at Sharpsburg, where he was wounded yet again. After that, he was promoted to lieutenant colonel.

In December 1862, he fought at the Battle of Fredericksburg and on April 2, 1863, was promoted to colonel. He led the 19th Mississippi in heavy fighting at Chancellorsville and Gettysburg.

Harris's brigade commander, Carnot Posey, was wounded during the Battle of Bristoe Station, and as the senior surviving colonel, Harris assumed command of the brigade. Posey died on November 13, 1863. Nathaniel Harris succeeded him as permanent commander and was promoted to brigadier general on January 20, 1864.

General Harris, though portly, was a solid and dependable combat officer, described by one of his men, a Captain Foote, as "devoid of fear, and aggressive." He particularly distinguished himself in the battles of Fort Gregg and Fort Whitworth (April 2, 1865), in which his brigade checked twenty-five thousand Yankees despite multiple attacks and allowed General Robert E. Lee to successfully evacuate Petersburg. General Harris surrendered at Appomattox on April 9, along with the rest of the Army of Northern Virginia.

Nathaniel Harris resumed his law practice at Vicksburg after the war and became president of the Mississippi Valley and Ship Island Railroad but still struggled financially. He relocated to Aberdeen, South Dakota, where he worked for the U.S. Land Office. He died in Malvern, Worcestershire, England, on August 23, 1900, while on a business trip. He was sixty-six years old. His body was cremated (as he requested), and the ashes were buried in Green-Wood Cemetery, Brooklyn, New York, where his grandparents had lived. He never married.

JAMES EDWARD HARRISON was born April 24, 1815, in Greenville County, South Carolina. His brother

Thomas also became a Confederate brigadier. He was a second cousin of General Wade Hampton, III.

The Harrison family moved to Alabama shortly after James's birth and in 1829 relocated to Monroe County, Mississippi. James became prominent in local community affairs and was twice elected to the Mississippi State Senate. In 1857, he settled near Waco, Texas. Because Harrison was fluent in Choctaw and Creek, he was appointed an Indian commissioner. He was a delegate to the secession convention, and when Texas left the Union, he entered the Confederate Army as a major in the 1st Texas Infantry Battalion and was promoted to lieutenant colonel when it expanded into the 15th Texas Infantry Regiment. He became regimental commander in January 1863.

Harrison spent his entire Confederate career in the Trans-Mississippi Department, mostly in minor operations. He saw combat in the First Bayou Teche Campaign in Louisiana (April and May 1863), which resulted in the fall of Alexandria. During the summer, he moved to the Mississippi River, where he harassed Union shipping and outposts. The regiments overran a Union force at Stirling's Plantation on September 29.

The 15th Texas became part of Prince Camille Armand Jules Marie de Polignac's brigade in October 1863. It skirmished with enemy forces at Vidalia and Harrisonburg before rejoining General Richard Taylor's main force for the Red River Campaign. At Mansfield and Pleasant Hill, the regiment helped smash the Union Army of the Gulf. When Polignac succeeded the late General Alfred Mouton as divisional commander, Harrison succeeded Polignac as brigade commander. The brigade was involved in the last attempt to cut off the fleeing Yankees in the Battle of Yellow Bayou (May 18, 1864) but was unsuccessful.

On December 22, 1864, James E. Harrison was promoted to brigadier general. He and his brigade were stationed in Louisiana until March 1865. Then they returned to Texas, where they remained until the surrender of the Trans-Mississippi Department on May 26.

After the war, General Harrison returned to Waco. He was active in local civic affairs and was a trustee of Baylor University until his death, which occurred in Waco on February 23, 1875. He was fifty-nine years old. He is buried in First Street Cemetery, Waco.

THOMAS HARRISON was born in Jefferson County, Alabama, on May 1, 1823. His older brother, James E. Harrison, was also a Confederate general. In 1843, Thomas moved to Brazoria County, Texas. He studied law and set up a practice in Waco. Later, he returned to Mississippi, set up a practice in Aberdeen, and joined Jefferson Davis's 1st Mississippi Rifle Regiment when the Mexican War started. After the battles of Monterrey and Buena Vista, he returned to Houston, Texas, and served a term in the legislature. He was back in Waco in 1855 and ran for Congress in 1857 but lost a close race.

In 1860, Harrison was a captain and company commander in the Texas Rangers and chased Indian marauders in northern Texas. When the Civil War began, Harrison was elected captain of a militia company that served in West Texas. His company captured Camp Cooper and its Union garrison on the Clear Fork of the Brazos River. Sent east, it became part of Benjamin F. Terry's Texas Rangers (the 8th Texas Cavalry), which was organized in Houston in August 1861. Harrison was promoted to major in early 1862.

The Rangers fought at the Battle of Shiloh, where they distinguished themselves. They also fought at the Siege of Corinth and were part of Nathan Bedford Forrest's cavalry in the First Battle of Murfreesboro, where they played a major role in a resounding Confederate victory. Their colonel, John Wharton, was wounded, and Harrison assumed temporary command of the regiment and was promoted to lieutenant colonel.

The 8th Texas became shock troops for the Army of Tennessee, routinely operating behind enemy lines. They took part in the Kentucky Campaign and the Battle of Perryville.

When Wharton was promoted to brigadier general on November 18, 1862, Harrison was promoted to colonel and succeeded him as commander of the 8th Texas. He led it in the Second Battle of Murfreesboro, where he was wounded in the hip on January 1, 1863. He also directed the 8th in the Tullahoma Campaign, the Battle of Chickamauga, the Knoxville Campaign, the Atlanta Campaign, the Savannah Campaign (Sherman's March to the Sea), and the Carolinas Campaign, in which he commanded a cavalry brigade.

Harrison was not a popular commander. He was a strict disciplinarian and believed in corporal punishment. One soldier called him "a small, nervous, irascible man." Lieutenant Frank Batchelor found him "addicted to getting drunk," saying, "[He] does it when battle is pending & has thus lost the confidence of his men & injured our effectiveness against the enemy."

Thomas Harrison was wounded in the Battle of Monroe's Crossroads on March 10, 1865. He was convalescing from his wounds when he received notification that he had been promoted to brigadier general on January 14, 1865. Harrison formally surrendered on May 31, 1865, in Mason, Mississippi.

General Harrison returned home to Waco and was elected district judge. He was removed from office by the carpetbagger regime in 1867.

He continued to practice law and was a Democratic presidential elector in 1872.

Thomas Harrison died in Waco, Texas, on July 14, 1891, at age sixty-eight. He is buried in Oakwood Cemetery, Waco.

ROBERT HOPKINS HATTON was born in Ohio on November 2, 1826. Sources differ as to whether his birthplace was Youngstown or Steubenville. In any case, his family soon relocated to Tennessee, where he attended public schools and later Cumberland University in Lebanon, where he earned his baccalaureate degree in 1847. He remained at Cumberland as a tutor and attended law school until 1849. He was headmaster of the Woodland Academy in Sumner County (1849–50) before gaining admission to the bar in 1850. He set up a law practice in Lebanon and in 1854 was named a trustee of Cumberland University, a position which he held until his death.

Hatton entered politics as a Whig. He was elected to the Tennessee House of Representatives in 1855 and served until 1857, when he made an unsuccessful run for governor. In 1858, after the Whig Party collapsed, he ran for Congress as a member of the Opposition Party (made up of former Whigs) and was elected. He served from March 4, 1859 to March 3, 1861.

Robert Hatton opposed secession but, after Lincoln called for seventy-five thousand volunteers to suppress the "rebellion," he reversed his position. He helped form the Lebanon Blues, which became part of the 7th Tennessee Infantry, of which Hatton was elected colonel on May 26, 1861. It trained at Camp Trousdale in Sumner County and was sent to western Virginia in July 1861. The regiment first saw action at Cheat Mountain, where the Rebel forces were defeated. It was involved in skirmishing against the enemy until winter arrived.

Hatton and his men were transferred to the main army in the spring of 1862. He fought in the Peninsula Campaign, where he distinguished himself. He was given command of a Tennessee brigade and on May 23 was promoted to brigadier general. Just eight days later, on May 31, 1862, he was shot in the head while leading his brigade in the Battle of Seven Pines (Fair Oaks). His body was returned to Tennessee for burial, but because middle Tennessee was now in Union hands, he was buried in Knoxville. In 1866, after the war, he was reburied in Cedar Grove Cemetery, Lebanon, Tennessee.

JAMES MORRISON HAWES was born on January 7, 1824, in Lexington, Kentucky, to a politically influential family. He was admitted to West Point in 1841, graduated in 1845, and was assigned to the 2nd Dragoons.

Hawes fought in the Mexican War, including the Siege of Veracruz and the battles of Contreras, Churubusco, and Molino del Rey and was brevetted first lieutenant. After Mexico, he became an assistant instructor at West Point, where he taught cavalry tactics, infantry tactics, and mathematics. In 1850, he was sent to the Cavalry School at Saumur, France, to learn advanced tactics. He returned to the United States in 1852 and was stationed on the Texas frontier. This was followed by service in Albert Sidney Johnston's Utah Expedition and a tour of duty in "Bleeding Kansas."

When war broke out, Hawes (now a captain) resigned his commission on May 9, 1861, and became a captain in the 2nd Kentucky Cavalry. He was promoted to major on June 16 and to colonel of state troops on June 26. He later resigned this position to become a major in the Confederate States Army. At the request of Albert Sidney Johnston, James Hawes was promoted to brigadier general on March 5, 1862, and was given command of the cavalry in the Western Department. He fought at Shiloh, after which he was given command of an infantry brigade under John C. Breckinridge. In October 1862, he assumed command of a cavalry brigade in the Trans-Mississippi Department and led raids in Arkansas. In 1863, he commanded an infantry brigade in John G. Walker's Texas Division and fought in the battles of Milliken's Bend and Young's Point, Louisiana, in May and June.

James Hawes's father, Richard, was now the second Confederate Governor of Kentucky (the first had been killed at Shiloh), but this position of political prominence seemed to bring James Hawes no favors. On February 11, 1864, James Hawes was relieved of his command at his own request (possibly because of a dispute with General Edmund Kirby Smith, commander of the Trans-Mississippi Department). Five days later, General Richard Taylor, the commander of the Army of Western Louisiana, reported to Kirby Smith that he had made a "minute inspection" of Hawes's brigade and had "never seen any troops in finer condition." He went on, "Hawes' brigade is in splendid order. A change would be very unfortunate." He requested Kirby Smith rescind the order. This Kirby Smith would not do. Instead, General

Hawes was placed in charge of the garrison and fortifications of Galveston Island. He remained in this backwater assignment until the end of the war. He saw no further action.

General Hawes's home in Paris, Kentucky, was destroyed in the war. In 1866, Hawes relocated to Covington, Kentucky, and went into the hardware business. He died of cerebritis on November 22, 1889, at his home in Covington. He was sixty-five years old. General Hawes was buried in Highland Cemetery, Fort Mitchell, Kentucky.

ALEXANDER TRAVIS HAWTHORN was born on January 10, 1825, in Conecuh County, Alabama, the son of a Baptist preacher. He attended Evergreen Academy, Mercer University, and Yale University (1846–47), where he studied law. He returned to Alabama and volunteered for service in the Mexican War. Elected lieutenant in his company, Hawthorn was sent to Mexico but was assigned the task of guarding General Winfield Scott's line of communications from the main army to the coast. After the war, he settled in Camden, Ouachita County, Arkansas, where he established a law office.

After some years in Camden, Hawthorn and his wife moved to New Orleans, where he owned a mercantile business. When Arkansas seceded, however, he returned to that state and joined the 6th Arkansas Infantry Regiment. He was elected its lieutenant colonel. The regiment was sent to Kentucky. On October 10, 1861, the regiment's colonel was killed in a riding accident. Hawthorn replaced him as commanding officer.

The 6th Arkansas Infantry saw action at the Battle of Rowlett's Station near Woodsonville, Kentucky, on December 17, and then at Shiloh (April 6–7, 1862), where the 6th and its sister regiments surprised U.S. General Sherman, overran his camp, and threw his legions back in confusion. By all accounts, the 6th and its commander performed extremely well.

In May 1862, the twelve-month enlistments of the various Confederate regiments expired, leading to an army-wide reorganization, including an election of new officers. Colonel Hawthorn decided not to stand for reelection. He briefly commanded a brigade of Alabama, Tennessee, and Arkansas soldiers during the summer of 1862 but, after the Siege of Corinth, returned to Arkansas without a command. He was selected to lead the 39th Arkansas Infantry, which he commanded in the battles of Prairie Grove and Helena, the Little Rock Campaign of 1863, and the subsequent retreat into southwestern Arkansas. Hawthorn particularly distinguished himself at Helena.

Alexander Hawthorn was promoted to brigadier general on February 18, 1864. He was assigned to Thomas J. Churchill's division, which took part in the Red River Campaign in Louisiana, including the Battle of Pleasant Hill (April 9), where it suffered heavy casualties. Following the Union defeat in the Red River Campaign, the division was sent to Arkansas, where Union General Frederick Steele was driving on the Confederate state capital of Washington. By the time Hawthorn's troops arrived, Steele had retreated to Camden. Hawthorn's brigade fought in the Battle of Jenkins' Ferry, which ended with General Steele's retreating to Little Rock. This all but ended the Civil War in Arkansas.

Hawthorn remained in southern Arkansas for the rest of the conflict. After the surrender, he moved to Brazil, where he lived until 1874. He returned to the United States and took up residence in Atlanta, where he pursued a brief business career. In 1880, he moved to Marshall, Texas, and became an ordained Baptist minister.

Reverend Hawthorn died in Dallas, Texas, on May 31, 1899. He was seventy-four years old. He is buried in Greenwood Cemetery, Marshall, Texas.

HARRY THOMPSON HAYS was born on April 14, 1820, in Wilson County, Tennessee. His older brother was John Coffee "Captain Jack" Hays, a famous lawman memorialized in the Texas Rangers Hall of Fame. Harry

Hays studied law at St. Mary's College in Baltimore, after which he settled in New Orleans. Admitted to the bar, he established a successful law
practice. He joined the 5th Louisiana Cavalry Regiment and served in
the Mexican War, after which he returned to New Orleans.

On June 5, 1861, Hays entered the Confederate Army as colonel of
the 7th Louisiana Infantry Regiment. He fought in the Battle of First
Manassas and Stonewall Jackson's Valley Campaign. At Port Republic,
the 7th Louisiana lost nearly 50 percent of its men, killed or wounded,
including Harry Hays, who was shot in the shoulder and knocked unconscious by a shell burst.

In June, General Richard Taylor was transferred to the Trans-Mississippi Department. Hays was picked to succeed him as brigade commander and was promoted to brigadier general on July 25, 1862.
However, since he was still recovering from his wounds, Hays missed
the Seven Days Battles and the Battle of Second Manassas. He fought
in the Battle of Sharpsburg, where half his brigade was killed, wounded,
or captured.

General Hays's brigade became known as the "Louisiana Tigers," a
nickname originally owned by Major Chatham Roberdeau Wheat's Irish
battalion but soon applied to the entire brigade. The Tigers fought at
Fredericksburg and Chancellorsville. At Gettysburg, as night was falling
on July 1, 1863, Hays and his men advanced up Cemetery Hill, captured
several Union guns, and held part of the position, until they were forced
to withdraw because Generals Richard Ewell and Jubal Early did not
reinforce them.

On November 7, 1863, Hays's brigade and Colonel Archibald Godwin's North Carolina brigade defended a bridgehead on the north bank
of the Rappahannock when they were attacked by U.S. General John
Sedgwick's VI Corps. The bluecoats took the Rebels by surprise and
overwhelmed them. About 1,600 Confederates were captured, including
General Hays, who only partially redeemed himself by escaping his
Union captors.

In March 1864, 500 of the 699 Louisianians captured at Rappahannock Station were exchanged and returned to duty. The Louisiana

Tigers continued their tradition of hard fighting during the Overland Campaign. On May 9, during the Battle of Spotsylvania Court House, Hays was seriously wounded by a shell fragment. After he recovered, he was transferred to the Trans-Mississippi Department, where he was given command of a division. He surrendered in May 1865.

Following the surrender, Harry Hays returned to New Orleans and spent a year as sheriff of Orleans Parish. After he suppressed the New Orleans race riot of July 1866, during which about fifty people, mostly African Americans, were killed, Federal troops removed him from office.

General Hays returned to his law practice. He died of Bright's disease on August 21, 1876, in New Orleans. He was fifty-six years of age. He is buried in Lafayette Cemetery Number 1, New Orleans.

LOUIS HÉBERT (pronounced ay-BEAR) was born on March 13, 1820, in Iberville Parish, Louisiana, into one of the oldest aristocratic Creole families in the state. He was a cousin and foster-brother of Paul O. Hébert, a future Confederate general. Louis attended West Point and graduated third in the class of 1845.

Hébert was selected for the Army Corps of Engineers. He was stationed at Fort Livingston, Louisiana, on Grand Terre Island, but resigned his commission on February 15, 1846, to return home and run the family's sugar plantation. From 1855 to 1860 he was a member of the Louisiana legislature and chief engineer of the state.

Hébert opposed secession but offered his services to the governor when Louisiana left the Union. He was commissioned colonel of the 3rd Louisiana Infantry on May 11, 1861. It soon had the reputation of being a well-drilled and well-equipped regiment. It joined Ben McCulloch's infantry brigade (later division) and first saw action on August 10 at Wilson's Creek, where Hébert overran a battery of five Union guns.

The tables were turned on March 7, 1862. During the Battle of Pea Ridge, he fell victim to a sudden Union attack and was captured. Hébert was exchanged on March 20 and promoted to brigadier general on May 26, 1862. He was given a brigade in General Lewis H. Little's division of General Sterling Price's corps in northern Mississippi. He fought in the Battle of Iuka, distinguished himself, and captured nine guns. Hébert took temporary command of a division after General Little was killed that day. The next morning, after the Federals were reinforced, General Price was compelled to retreat.

Following the Confederate defeat at Corinth, Hébert took part in the defense of Vicksburg. Hébert's brigade dug in on the south side of the Graveyard Road, the easiest natural approach to the city. He held this critical position despite massive Federal attacks and heavy casualties on May 19 and 22, 1863.

On June 25, The Yankees detonated 2,200 pounds of high explosives beneath the Louisiana Redan. Before the explosion, however, General Hébert had figured out what the Yankees were up to and moved most of the 3rd Louisiana into a second line of trenches behind the Redan. The Rebel line remained intact, and Northerners were cut to ribbons when they attacked.

Louis Hébert was a fine tactical commander, but not even he could save Vicksburg. He surrendered, along with the rest of the garrison, on July 4, 1863. After he was exchanged on October 13, he was placed in charge of the heavy artillery in and around Fort Fisher and named chief engineer for the Confederate War Department in North Carolina. He held this position until the end of the war.

When Hébert returned to Louisiana, his plantation was in ruins, and his wealth was gone. He edited a newspaper, *Iberville South*, and taught at several private schools. After he became president, Ulysses S. Grant (a former West Point classmate) gave Hébert valuable engineering contracts connected to Louisiana and Texas rivers and bayous. He was thus able to restore much of his antebellum fortune.

General Louis Hébert passed away on January 7, 1901, in St. Martin Parish. He was eighty years old. As his West Point obituary noted, Hébert died as he had lived—"the highest type of educated soldier and the cultured southern gentleman."

He was buried in the Hébert Family Cemetery, Cecilia, Louisiana, in St. Martin Parish. In 2002, his body was reinterred in St. Joseph Catholic Church in Cecilia.

PAUL OCTAVE HÉBERT was born in Plaquemine, Iberville Parish, Louisiana, on December 12, 1818. He was the descendent of a line of wealthy, aristocratic, Creole sugarcane planters. His first cousin was Louis Hébert, who also became a Confederate general. He finished first in his class at Jefferson College in 1836 and at West Point in 1840. Upon graduation, he went from student to engineering faculty member in one day.

In 1845, Hébert resigned his commission because the governor of Louisiana had appointed him chief engineer for the state. Hébert rejoined the army in March 1847 to fight in the Mexican War. He was commissioned a lieutenant colonel and fought at Contreras, Churubusco, Molino del Rey, Chapultepec, and Mexico City. He was brevetted full colonel for gallant and meritorious conduct at Chapultepec and Mexico City. He returned to New Orleans in July 1848 and entered the world of politics.

Paul Hébert ran for the state senate in 1849 but lost by nine votes. In 1852, he was a delegate to the Louisiana Constitutional Convention to approve a new state constitution and was elected governor.

Hébert served as governor from January 22, 1853 to January 30, 1856. He was a highly successful governor, pushing through improvements in education, railroad development, hospitals (including fighting an outbreak of yellow fever), and waterworks. He also started a state library and established the Louisiana Seminary of Learning in Alexandria (later Louisiana State University). After his term ended, Hébert, though only thirty-seven years old, retired to his plantation and never again ran for public office.

On February 5, 1861, he was named colonel and commander on the 1st Louisiana Artillery (later Heavy Artillery) Regiment, which defended New Orleans. He was promoted to brigadier general of militia on April 1 and to brigadier general in the Confederate States Army on August 17, 1861. He was appointed commander of the Department of Texas on August 14 and assumed command on September 16, 1861, superseding Henry E. McCulloch.

For all his earlier successes, Hébert's record as a Confederate general was mediocre at best. He was unpopular with the Texans, who thought him aristocratic and snobbish. Governor Francis Lubbock stated that Hébert was "somewhat bewildered by the magnitude of the task assigned him" and was unable to formulate any definite policies.

Jefferson Davis dismissed him from his Texas post on October 10, 1862, for the harsh measures he took to enforce conscription laws. Hébert then held backwater assignments for the rest of the war: commander of the Subdistrict of North Louisiana and commander of the District of Eastern Texas. He did not participate in any major battles in the Civil War.

After the surrender, Paul Hébert returned to his sugar plantation. He took seats on the board of state engineers in 1873 and on the Board of U.S. Engineers for the Mississippi River Commission in 1874. (President U. S. Grant knew him from West Point and admired him.)

Former Governor Paul O. Hébert died of cancer in New Orleans on August 29, 1880. He was sixty-one years old. He is buried in St. Raphael Cemetery, Bayou Goula, Iberville Parish, Lousiana.

BENJAMIN HARDIN HELM was born in Bardstown, Kentucky, on June 2, 1831. He was educated at the Elizabethtown Seminary and the Kentucky Military Institute in Frankfort. He entered the U.S. Military Academy at West Point and graduated in the class of 1851. He was assigned to the 2nd Cavalry Regiment on the

Texas frontier but returned to Kentucky and resigned his commission in 1852. He enrolled in law school at the University of Louisville and then Harvard, from which he graduated in 1853. He passed the bar and practiced his profession in Elizabethtown and later Louisville. He was elected to the Kentucky legislature in 1855 and served one term. Helm was appointed assistant adjutant general of the state militia in 1860.

In 1856, Helm married Emilie Pariet Todd (called "Pariet"). She was the half-sister of Mary Todd Lincoln, Abraham Lincoln's wife. Pariet brought Ben Helm into Lincoln's family circle, and Abraham Lincoln liked the future Confederate general.

At the outbreak of the Civil War, Kentucky tried to remain neutral. President Lincoln offered Helm a position as paymaster of the Union Army with the rank of colonel. Helm declined the offer.

Kentucky's effort at neutrality collapsed in early September 1861. Helm, meanwhile, organized the 1st Kentucky Cavalry Regiment, which was posted at Bowling Green. He was promoted to brigadier general in the Confederate Army on March 14, 1862, and three weeks later was named commander of a partially formed brigade, consisting of Kentucky, Alabama, and Mississippi troops.

General Helm and his men were sent to Yazoo City, Mississippi, to protect the Confederate ironclad *Arkansas*, which was then under construction. After the gunboat was completed, Helm's command was sent to Vicksburg, where it took part in the first siege (1862). It fought in the Battle of Baton Rouge, where Helm was injured when his horse fell on him.

The 1st Kentucky Infantry Brigade, which was known as the "Orphan Brigade," was commanded by Roger W. Hanson. He was mortally wounded in the Second Battle of Murfreesboro and died on January 4, 1863. His division commander, General John C. Breckinridge, selected Helm to replace him.

The Orphan Brigade was considered one of the better units in the Western Theater. Under Helm, it became part of the Army of Relief and took part in General Joseph E. Johnston's half-hearted attempt to rescue Vicksburg in the summer of 1863. Sent back to the Army of Tennessee, it fought in the Battle of Chickamauga (September 19–20, 1863). At 9:30 a.m. on September 20, Breckinridge's division was ordered forward to strike the Union's left flank. The fighting was extremely heavy. In less than an hour, the Orphan Brigade lost a third of its men. During this attack, a sniper from the 15th (U.S.) Kentucky Infantry shot General Helm in the chest. Bleeding profusely, he was carried to a field hospital, where he died the next day. He was thirty-two years old.

Abraham Lincoln learned of Helm's death on September 22. He was visibly shaken and at first refused to believe it. He later declared that this was the worst day of the war for him.

General Helm's remains were buried in Atlanta. More than twenty years later, they were reinterred in Helm Cemetery, Elizabethtown, Kentucky.

HENRY "HARRY" HETH (pronounced "Heath") was born in Black Heath, Chesterfield County, Virginia, on December 16, 1825, the son of the owner of a coal mine and former navy captain. Harry attended West Point and graduated last in his class in 1847. Commissioned in the infantry, he was sent to Mexico but arrived after the fighting ended. After he returned to the United States, he fought Indians on the Western frontier and distinguished himself in the Battle of Ash Hollow (September 3, 1855) against the Lakota (eastern Sioux) in present-day Nebraska. He was promoted to captain in 1855. In 1858, he wrote the army's first manual on marksmanship, *A System of Target Practice*, which was used for many years. Heth served as a quartermaster for much of his U.S. Army career.

Virginia seceded on April 17, 1861. On April 25, Heth resigned his commission and four days later was appointed acting quartermaster of the Provisional Army of Virginia with a rank of lieutenant colonel. He worked directly for Robert E. Lee, and the two soon became good friends. Heth was one of the few officers whom Lee called by his first name.

On June 17, Heth was named commander of the 45th Virginia Infantry Regiment, which he led in the unsuccessful campaign in western Virginia. Colonel Heth's men were mountain farmers who didn't like their commander. They considered him an arrogant Tidewater aristocrat and unsparing disciplinarian, and he considered them illiterate and ignorant.

On January 6, 1862, Harry Heth was promoted to brigadier general. He fought a significant delaying action in the mountains, preventing Union forces from reaching the Shenandoah Valley and falling on Stonewall Jackson's rear. He commanded a small division in the Kentucky Campaign that autumn. He was nominated for the rank of major general on October 10, 1862, but the Senate would not confirm him.

In March 1863, Robert E. Lee had Heth transferred from eastern Tennessee to Virginia, where he assumed command of a brigade in A. P. Hill's division. Heth was wounded at Chancellorsville.

He was promoted to major general on May 23 to rank from May 24. This time his nomination was confirmed by the Senate, and he became a permanent divisional commander.

On July 1, Heth touched off the Battle of Gettysburg by leading his division toward the town, despite General Lee's order to avoid a general engagement.

Harry Heth did not handle his division well that day, and he ended up in the hospital with a fractured skull from a rifle bullet that knocked him out. He was not able to exercise active command again until July 7.

Heth's performance during the war was uneven and disappointing, with his gravest mistake occurring on the night of May 5–6, 1864, during the Battle of the Wilderness. Generals Heth and Cadmus Wilcox failed to order their men to dig in or to strengthen their positions. They did not even bother to replenish their troops' ammunition, because they expected General Lee to order a withdrawal. But Lee had no intention of withdrawing, and at dawn Grant attacked with two corps, and the unready Rebel divisions of Heth and Wilcox were crushed. Heth later recalled, "[Robert E. Lee] never forgave Wilcox or me for this awful blunder."

Heth partially redeemed himself as the Overland Campaign of 1864 unfolded. He also fought in the battles of Spotsylvania, North Anna, and Cold Harbor and in the Siege of Petersburg. He surrendered at Appomattox on April 9, 1865.

Overall, Heth was a general who never really lived up to his potential. After the war, Harry Heth worked in the insurance business in Richmond. He later became a surveyor for the government and was employed by the Office of Indian Affairs. He was debilitated by a stroke several months before he died on September 27, 1899, at the age of seventy-three, in Washington, D.C. His official cause of death was chronic interstitial nephritis and cardiac hypertrophy. He is buried in Hollywood Cemetery, Richmond.

EDWARD HIGGINS was born in Norfolk, Virginia, in 1821 (exact date unknown). He had a lifelong interest in the sea and became a midshipman in the U.S. Navy on January 23, 1836. In those days of slow promotion, he did not reach the rank of lieutenant until 1849, but he became an expert on heavy artillery and heavy naval guns. He resigned his commission in 1854 and became a steamship agent in the mail service from New Orleans to New York.

The day the Rebels fired on Fort Sumter, Edward Higgins joined the Confederate Army as a captain in the 1st Louisiana Artillery (later Heavy Artillery) Regiment. He supervised the construction of the defenses on Ship Island, off the Mississippi coast. Higgins was commissioned a lieutenant colonel in the 21st Louisiana Infantry Regiment (which was really a heavy artillery unit) on February 13, 1862. It was stationed at Fort Jackson and Fort St. Philip on the Mississippi River; the twin forts were designed to protect New Orleans from an attack by the Federal deep-sea fleet.

On April 18, 1862, the forts were attacked by a large Union fleet, which managed to run past the batteries on April 24. It reached New

Orleans the next day, and the isolated forts surrendered on April 28. Edward Higgins was among the prisoners.

Higgins was exchanged on October 16, 1862. He learned that he was promoted to full colonel on September 26. He was assigned to command the river batteries at Vicksburg and took part in the Battle of Chickasaw Bluffs, in which he successfully commanded an ad hoc brigade. He commanded the 1st Louisiana Heavy Artillery Regiment during the defense of Vicksburg, which fell on July 4, 1863, after a forty-seven-day siege.

Colonel Higgins was a prisoner of war until October 13, when he was exchanged. He was promoted to brigadier general on October 29, 1863, at the request of Major General Dabney Maury, who was in charge of defending Mobile. Higgins was placed in command of the bay and harbor defenses of Mobile. He seems to have done a good job, but he was relieved of his command on February 18, 1865, for reasons not made clear by the records, although his fractious personality no doubt had much to do with it. He went to Macon, Georgia, and was unemployed for the rest of the war.

After the surrender, Higgins returned to Norfolk, where he worked in the insurance and import business. He moved to California in 1872 to be an agent for the Pacific Mail Steamship Company. General Higgins died in San Francisco on January 31, 1875, at age fifty-three or fifty-four. He was buried in Mount Calvary Cemetery, San Francisco. Later, the coffins from this cemetery were reinterred in Holy Cross Catholic Cemetery, Colma, California.

AMBROSE POWELL HILL, called "Powell" or "A. P.," was born on Greenland, his father's plantation near Culpeper, Virginia, on November 9, 1825. He was admitted to West Point in 1842 but had to miss a year (1844) due to illness. (He had contracted gonorrhea from a prostitute and continued to suffer the effects of this disease his entire life.)

Powell Hill was sent to Mexico, but he arrived too late to fight in the major battles of the Mexican War. Afterward, he did garrison duty on the Atlantic coast. He took part in some minor skirmishing in the Third Seminole War in Florida (1855–58).

Anticipating Virginia's secession, Lieutenant Hill resigned his commission on March 1, 1861. He was appointed colonel of the 13th Virginia Infantry Regiment on May 22, 1861. He did not see action at Bull Run but was promoted to brigadier general on February 26, 1862, and was given command of a brigade. He distinguished himself in the retreat up the peninsula in the spring of 1862 and in the Battle of Williamsburg. This led to his promotion to major general on May 26, 1862. He was the youngest officer of this rank in the Confederate Army.

Hill dubbed his new command the "Light Division," and it became one of the most celebrated units in the war. It marched rapidly, encumbered with little other than weapons, cartridge boxes, and haversacks.

General Hill established a reputation for boldness, aggressiveness, and fearlessness. He also was fractious, had a fierce temperament, and was quick to take offense. After the Seven Days Battles, he became involved in a dispute with General James Longstreet, who had Hill placed under arrest for insubordination. Hill responded by challenging Longstreet to a duel.

General Robert E. Lee restored Hill to command and placed the Light Division under General Stonewall Jackson. Hill and Jackson feuded constantly, and Hill was arrested more than once, but at least there were no more challenges to duels.

His problems with his superiors did not affect A. P. Hill's performance on the battlefield. He played a major role in one victory after another, including Cedar Mountain, Second Manassas, and Harpers Ferry. His most famous action was at Sharpsburg, where he and his division arrived just in time to save Lee's army on September 17, 1862.

A. P. Hill did not perform well at Fredericksburg but resumed his previous success at Chancellorsville and played a major role in routing the enemy on May 2, 1863. After nightfall, Stonewall Jackson was wounded, and Hill assumed command of Jackson's II Corps—but not for long. He was wounded in the calves of both legs and had to be carried to the rear.

After Jackson died, A. P. Hill was given command of the newly formed III Corps. He was promoted to lieutenant general on May 24, 1863.

General Hill's performance at Gettysburg was undistinguished. The worst day of the war for Powell Hill was October 14, 1863, when he launched a hasty attack without reconnaissance against the U.S. II Corps at the Battle of Bristoe Station. He ran into an ambush and lost 1,400 men as casualties.

Hill performed well in the Battle of the Wilderness, hurling back several of Grant's attacks. He temporarily stepped down as corps commander due to illness, and when he returned to fight at the Battle of North Anna, General Lee reprimanded him for launching piecemeal attacks. Hill returned to form at the Battle of Cold Harbor, where he slaughtered the attacking Federals. The South lost six hundred men, as opposed to Grant's seven thousand casualties.

During the Siege of Petersburg, Hill's corps defended Lee's right flank and fought in several important battles. Grant finally broke the thin Confederate line on April 2, 1865. Hill, accompanied by a single soldier, rode to the front, where a Union straggler shot him through the heart. He died instantly. He was thirty-nine years old.

Hill's body was recovered and buried in Chesterfield County. In February 1867, his remains were reinterred in Hollywood Cemetery, Richmond. He is now (2021) buried beneath the Ambrose Powell Hill Monument in Richmond, which was dedicated in 1892. In accordance with his last will and testament, he was buried standing up.

Although he often clashed with his superiors, he was unfailingly courteous and respectful to his men. Hill was a great division commander and a mediocre corps commander; he has been called the most lovable of Lee's generals.

BENJAMIN J. HILL was born near McMinnville, Tennessee, on June 13, 1825, and grew up on his father's farm. His father died when he was nine years old. After being educated at local schools, he borrowed money to attend Irving College, from which he graduated. Hill started out in the mercantile business as a clerk, moved up to store manager, and became a successful merchant. He was a Tennessee state senator from 1855 to 1861.

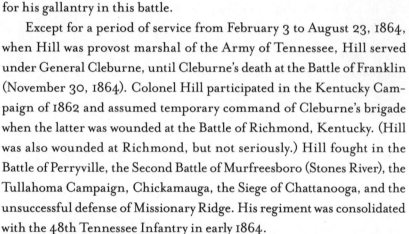

After Tennessee seceded, Governor Isham Harris appointed Hill colonel of the 5th Tennessee Volunteers Regiment of the Provisional Army of Tennessee. He was commissioned a colonel in September 1861 when his regiment was accepted for Confederate service as the 35th Tennessee Infantry. It formed part of General Patrick Cleburne's brigade at Shiloh. Hill was commended for his gallantry in this battle.

Except for a period of service from February 3 to August 23, 1864, when Hill was provost marshal of the Army of Tennessee, Hill served under General Cleburne, until Cleburne's death at the Battle of Franklin (November 30, 1864). Colonel Hill participated in the Kentucky Campaign of 1862 and assumed temporary command of Cleburne's brigade when the latter was wounded at the Battle of Richmond, Kentucky. (Hill was also wounded at Richmond, but not seriously.) Hill fought in the Battle of Perryville, the Second Battle of Murfreesboro (Stones River), the Tullahoma Campaign, Chickamauga, the Siege of Chattanooga, and the unsuccessful defense of Missionary Ridge. His regiment was consolidated with the 48th Tennessee Infantry in early 1864.

Benjamin Hill was promoted to brigadier general (temporary rank) on November 30, 1864. Despite his career as an infantry officer, he was transferred to William H. "Red" Jackson's cavalry division of General Nathan Bedford Forrest's cavalry corps. Hill and his men worked with William Bate's infantry division in destroying the railroad and blockhouses between Murfreesboro and Nashville. He took part in the retreat after the Battle of Nashville (December 15–16, 1864), and in General Forrest's defense against U.S. General James Wilson's Raid (March–April 1865). He was paroled at Chattanooga on May 16, 1865.

After the war, General Hill returned to McMinnville and the mercantile business. He also set up a law practice and became president of the McMinnville and Manchester Railroad.

General Benjamin J. Hill died January 5, 1880, at McMinnville, Tennessee, and was buried there in Old City Cemetery. He was fifty-four years old.

DANIEL HARVEY HILL was born on July 12, 1821, in York, South Carolina. He was not related to A. P. Hill. His father died in 1825, and he grew up in genteel poverty. His mother raised him as a strong Presbyterian, and he became a strict and deeply religious man, noted for his intelligence, sarcasm, and dry sense of humor. He also tended to be overly pessimistic and opinionated and feuded often with his colleagues, superiors, and subordinates. He was a slim man of average height with striking blue eyes and a chronic spinal problem that perhaps helps explain his irascibility.

D. H. Hill entered West Point in 1838 and graduated in 1842. He was assigned to the 1st U.S. Artillery Regiment and was stationed to posts on the East Coast, ranging from Maine to Charleston, South Carolina.

In the Mexican War, he served under both General Zachary Taylor and General Winfield Scott. He saw action at the Battle of Monterrey and distinguished himself in the drive on Mexico City. He was brevetted captain for his bravery at the battles of Contreras and Churubusco and brevetted major for his performance at Chapultepec.

On February 28, 1849, First Lieutenant Hill resigned his commission to pursue a career in academia. Over the next twelve years, he became a professor of mathematics at Washington College, chair of the department at Davidson College, and superintendent of the North Carolina Military Institute in Charlotte (1859–61).

When North Carolina seceded, Governor John W. Ellis asked Hill to organize the state's first camp of instruction at Raleigh. He became colonel of the 1st North Carolina Infantry, which he led to victory at the Battle of Big Bethel on May 19, 1861. It was the first major clash between Union and Confederate forces. Hill was slightly wounded in the knee. He was promoted to brigadier general on July 10, 1861.

General Moxley Sorrel called Hill "about the bravest man ever seen," but noted too that he had a "marked and peculiar character." With his staff, Hill was easygoing and frequently led Bible classes and prayer meetings. But Hill also had an uncontrollable impulse to criticize other officers, especially his superiors. At various times, he feuded with Robert Toombs (who challenged him to a duel), John B. Magruder, J. E. B. Stuart, Josiah Gorgas, James Longstreet, Leonidas Polk, Braxton Bragg, and even Robert E. Lee.

D. H. Hill was given command of a division on March 25, 1862, and was promoted to major general on March 26. He fought in the Peninsula Campaign, at Seven Pines, and in the Seven Days Battles. He suffered four minor wounds in eight days. In keeping with his religious nature, he credited God with his deliverance. Later, he commanded the Department of North Carolina, took part in the invasion of Maryland, and performed well in the battles of South Mountain and Sharpsburg. Hill's division was in reserve during the Battle of Fredericksburg. In January 1863, he was sent back to North Carolina.

When Lee moved north to invade Pennsylvania, the War Department made Hill temporary commander of the Department of Richmond, but not for long. On July 11, President Jefferson Davis promoted him to lieutenant general (temporary rank) and ordered him to report to General Braxton Bragg in Georgia, where he would assume command of a corps.

Due to confusion and a muddled chain of command, D. H. Hill's performance during the Battle of Chickamauga left much to be desired. His downfall, however, came after the battle, when he joined a cabal of generals who advocated replacing Bragg as commander of the Army of Tennessee. The effort failed, and Bragg relieved D. H. Hill of his command. Hill reverted to the rank of major general on October 15, 1863.

General Hill spent the rest of the war in backwater assignments—when he was employed at all. He surrendered with Joseph E. Johnston on April 26, 1865.

In 1866, D. H. Hill settled in Charlotte, North Carolina, and established a periodical, *The Land We Love*. He wrote numerous articles on the war, most notably for *Battles and Leaders of the Civil War*, a compilation of articles published by *Century Monthly*. He refused to bend his knee to the "Northern Baal" and devoted the rest of his life to educating young people in the South. From 1877 to 1884, he was president of Arkansas Industrial University (later the University of Arkansas). From 1885 to 1899, he was president of the Middle Georgia and Agricultural College at Milledgeville (later the Georgia Military College). In his last years, he developed stomach cancer. He never once complained about the pain.

General Daniel Harvey Hill died in Charlotte, North Carolina, on September 24, 1889, at age sixty-eight. He is buried in Davidson College Cemetery, Davidson, North Carolina.

THOMAS CARMICHAEL HINDMAN, JR., was born in Knoxville, Tennessee, on January 28, 1828. His family moved to Alabama in 1833, and in 1841 to Ripley, Mississippi, where his father purchased a plantation.

In 1843, Hindman graduated with honors from the Lawrenceville Classical Institute in Lawrenceville, New Jersey, where he had been a boarding student, and returned to Ripley, where he read law. When war broke out with Mexico, Hindman volunteered immediately and was named second lieutenant in the 2nd Mississippi Infantry Regiment. It was sent to northern Mexico but arrived after the Battle of Buena Vista had virtually ended the war in that sector. He was discharged in 1848.

Hindman, who was a member of the Sons of Temperance, was elected to the Mississippi legislature in 1853, but he moved to Helena, Arkansas, where he opposed the anti-Catholic, anti-immigrant Know-Nothing Party. He was elected to Congress in 1858 and 1860.

After Abraham Lincoln was elected president in November 1860, Hindman resigned his seat in Congress and became a passionate secessionist. On May 6, 1861, the Arkansas state legislature voted sixty-nine to one to leave the Union. Hindman hoped it would appoint him to the Confederate Congress, but that did not happen. Undeterred, he recruited the 2nd Arkansas Infantry Regiment and was appointed a colonel in the Confederate States Army on June 21, 1861. He joined the Army of Central Kentucky and was soon given command of a brigade. He was promoted to brigadier general on September 28, 1861.

Hindman's first major action was the Battle of Shiloh on April 6, 1862, where he distinguished himself with his coolness under the heaviest fire and his good judgment. The battle ended for him when an artillery shell killed his horse and he was injured in the ensuing fall. He was only *hors de combat* for a few days, however.

On April 14, 1862, Hindman was promoted to major general. He commanded the II Corps of G. T. Beauregard's Army of Mississippi during the Siege of Corinth. The following month, he returned to Arkansas as the commander of the Trans-Mississippi Department, with headquarters in Little Rock.

Not surprisingly, Hindman focused on defending Arkansas rather than Louisiana. He enacted a series of harsh measures to check the Federal invaders, including burning cotton and cotton fields, declaring martial law, enforcing conscription, requisitioning supplies, organizing guerrilla warfare, and enforcing strict discipline on the troops. Largely because of Hindman's delaying tactics, the Yankees' invasion was checked, but he made some powerful enemies in the process. The Confederate government yielded to political pressure and in August 1862 replaced Hindman with the incompetent Theophilus Holmes. Hindman retained command of the District of Arkansas.

On December 7, 1862, at the Battle of Prairie Grove, Hindman's customary aggressiveness failed him. The battle was a tactical draw, but it proved a strategic victory for the Yankees, because Hindman, who was low on food and ammunition, was forced to retreat, leaving northwest Arkansas to the Federals.

In July 1863, General Hindman was appointed commander of a division in the Army of Tennessee. He fought at Chickamauga, where he was severely wounded in the neck. The general assessment was that Hindman performed poorly in the run-up to the battle but very well in the battle itself.

Hindman fought at the Battle of Missionary Ridge and led his division in the Atlanta Campaign until July 4, 1864, where he was badly wounded and partially blinded. Incapable of further field service, he relocated to San Antonio, Texas. He was still recovering when the Confederate armies capitulated. Hindman moved to Mexico and became a coffee planter.

He returned to Arkansas in the spring of 1867 and worked to end the corrupt rule of the Radical Republicans in Arkansas. At 9:30 p.m. on September 27, 1868, General Hindman was shot at his home in Helena while reading a newspaper to his children. He died the following morning, September 28, 1868, at age forty. His assassins were never found.

Thomas C. Hindman was buried in Evergreen Cemetery (which was later renamed Maple Hill Cemetery) in Helena, Arkansas, not far from the grave of his friend, Pat Cleburne.

GEORGE BAIRD HODGE was born on April 8, 1828, in Fleming County, in northeast Kentucky. He was appointed to the U.S. Naval Academy at Annapolis in 1845 and graduated from an abbreviated course as a midshipman. He took part in the Mexican War and saw action in the Siege of Veracruz. He was an acting lieutenant when he resigned his commission in 1850.

Hodge became a lawyer and set up his practice in Newport, Kentucky. He was an unsuccessful candidate for the U.S. House of Representatives in 1852 but was elected to the Kentucky legislature as a Democrat in 1859. Hodge was a firm believer in states' rights but opposed secession. He was a presidential elector for his good friend, John C. Breckinridge, in 1860.

When Kentucky's neutrality collapsed in September 1861, Hodge enlisted in the Confederate Army as a private. He was soon elected to the Provisional Confederate Congress and simultaneously served as a captain on the staff of General John C. Breckinridge.

Hodge fought at Shiloh and was promoted to major for gallantry on May 6, 1862. In early 1862, he was elected to represent Kentucky in the First (Regular) Confederate Congress. He split his time for the next two years, serving in the legislative branch when Congress was in session and serving in the field as an officer when it was not. He was promoted to colonel on May 6, 1863.

Hodge was given command of a brigade of cavalry under Nathan Bedford Forrest. The "Wizard of the Saddle," however, was not satisfied with his performance and, in one of his famous tempers, relieved Hodge of his command and had him prosecuted on charges of incompetence and cowardice. The court-martial, however, acquitted him.

President Jefferson Davis appointed Hodge to the rank of brigadier general on November 20, 1863, but his nomination was rejected by the Senate. Congressman Hodge's term expired on February 17, 1864, and he did not seek reelection but opted instead for full-time military service. He was named inspector general of the District of East Louisiana and Mississippi and was reappointed brigadier general on August 2, 1864, only to have his nomination to general rejected by the Senate on February 8, 1865. Meanwhile, Hodge commanded a cavalry brigade under Joseph Wheeler, who commended him for his performance.

In the final days of the Confederacy, Davis reportedly appointed Hodge brigadier general for the third time. The legitimacy of this appointment was questioned, as it never received senatorial confirmation. The third appointment was not found in the *Official Records*, but Hodge was still commanding 2,500 men on March 9 and was listed as a brigadier general at Jackson, Mississippi, on April 3. His department commander, Lieutenant General Taylor, ordered "General Hodge" to assume command of the forces south of the Homochitto on April 6. Hodge was paroled at Meridian, Mississippi, on May 10, 1865, as a brigadier general.

After the War for Southern Independence, George Hodge returned to Newport, Kentucky, and rebuilt his law practice. He was a presidential elector for Horace Greeley in 1872 and a member of the Kentucky Senate from 1873 to 1877. Shortly after his term expired, Hodge moved to Florida and became a successful orange grower. He died on August 1, 1892, in Longwood, Orange County, Florida, at age sixty-four. George B. Hodge was buried in Seminole, Florida, but his body was moved to Evergreen Cemetery, Southgate, Kentucky, in 1903.

JOSEPH LEWIS HOGG was born on September 13, 1806, in Morgan County, Georgia. He and his parents moved to Tuscaloosa County, Alabama, where his father became a successful plantation owner. Joseph studied law, moved to Texas in 1839, and established a law practice near Nacogdoches. He was elected to the House of Representatives of the Republic of Texas, serving from 1843 to 1844, and was elected to the first state senate in 1845. He resigned in 1846, after the Mexican War broke out. He lost his election for colonel of the 2nd Texas Mounted Rifles but remained in the regiment as a private and fought in the battles in and around Monterrey.

After the Mexican War, Hogg ran a successful law practice and worked with the railroad industry. In 1861, he was a delegate to the Texas Secession Convention and voted to leave the Union. He ran for the Confederate Congress but was defeated. He was elected captain of the Lone Star Defenders, which was soon redesignated Company C, 3rd Texas Cavalry. Texas Governor Edward Clark, however, promoted him to colonel and gave him the task of recruiting troops in East Texas. He was a successful recruiter and was appointed a brigadier general in the Confederate Army on February 12, 1862.

One of his sergeants described Hogg as "a fine specimen of the best type of Southern manhood—tall, slender, straight as an Indian and exceedingly dignified in his manner." Another of his men found him "rather an irritable man" whose "suspicions were easily aroused." General G. T. Beauregard did not think highly of him and had him arrested for allegedly endangering a trainload of supplies.

General Hogg was never tried. He developed dysentery and died on May 16, 1862, at the age of fifty-five. He was buried near Mount Holly School but was reinterred in Fort Robinette Cemetery, Corinth, Mississippi, in 1918. One of his sons, James Stephen Hogg, was the first native-born Texan to be governor of the state, serving from 1891 to 1895.

ROBERT FREDERICK HOKE was born in Lincolnton on May 27, 1837, into a prominent and wealthy North Carolina family. Future Confederate General Stephen D. Ramseur, who was born four days after Hoke, was his cousin and childhood playmate. He was also related to future generals John Forney, William Henry Forney, and Robert D. Johnston.

Hoke grew into a handsome man, standing six feet tall, with dark hair and eyes. He was known throughout his life for his modesty. He dropped out of the Kentucky Military Institute at age sixteen to run the family's industrial and manufacturing enterprises, which included a cotton gin, a blacksmith shop, a brass foundry, and the first cottonseed oil mill in the United States. The businesses were secure enough by 1860 for Hoke to go to Washington, D.C., where he studied law and worked at the Census Bureau.

Robert Hoke opposed secession but, like many in the upper South, changed his mind when President Abraham Lincoln asked for volunteers to crush the "rebellion." He joined the Confederate Army as a second lieutenant in the 1st North Carolina Infantry Regiment and fought in the Battle of Big Bethel, where D. H. Hill commended him for his "coolness, judgement and efficiency."

On November 27, Hoke was named major in the 33rd North Carolina Infantry, which was forming in Raleigh. His regimental commander was Lawrence Branch, and C. M. Avery was lieutenant colonel. When Branch was promoted to brigadier general on January 17, 1862, Avery became colonel, and Hoke advanced to lieutenant colonel. On March 14, 1862, the regiment saw action at the Battle of New Bern, and Colonel Avery was captured by the Federals.

On May 4, 1862, the 33rd North Carolina was sent to Virginia. Under Hoke's leadership, the regiment fought in the Seven Days Battles. Hoke was promoted to colonel on August 5.

Colonel Avery was exchanged in the fall of 1862 and reassumed command of the 33rd. Hoke was given command of the 21st North Carolina. His regiment was transferred to Isaac Trimble's brigade, but because Trimble was still recovering from wounds received at the Battle of Second Manassas, Hoke, as senior regimental commander, assumed command of the brigade, which he led at Sharpsburg (Antietam) and Fredericksburg, where he sealed off the only Union breakthrough by launching a superb counterattack. Hoke was promoted to brigadier general on January 19, 1863, and was given permanent command of Trimble's brigade. He led it in the Battle of Chancellorsville, where, on the afternoon of May 4, 1863, a minié ball shattered his shoulder. It took him the rest of the year to recover.

General Hoke returned to duty in January 1864. He and his brigade were sent to North Carolina, where they fought in General George Pickett's unsuccessful attempt to recapture New Bern from the Federals. Hoke then led his brigade against the Union garrison at Plymouth, North Carolina, and in a battle lasting from April 17 to April 20, captured the place, along with more than 2,800 men, 40 pieces of artillery, and a huge quantity of supplies. He lost only 20 men killed in this action—the most complete victory the Confederacy ever achieved in North Carolina. He received a promotion to major general on April 23, to rank from April 20.

Robert Hoke now commanded a new division of six brigades. It was soon ordered to the Petersburg sector in Virginia, where Hoke performed with his usual competence. He particularly distinguished himself at Cold Harbor, where he checked several Union attacks. He and his men remained in the siege lines around Petersburg until December 1864. Then they were sent to defend North Carolina from Sherman. Hoke fought in the defense of Fort Fisher, in the Carolinas Campaign, and in the Battle of Bentonville. He surrendered with the rest of the Army of Tennessee at Bennett Place, North Carolina, on April 26, 1865.

After the war, Major General Robert Hoke became a highly successful businessman. He died of diabetes in Raleigh on July 3, 1912. He was seventy-five years old. He was buried in Oakwood Cemetery, Raleigh, with full military honors. Hoke County, North Carolina, is named in his honor.

THEOPHILUS HUNTER HOLMES, who was called "Granny" by his men, was born on November 13, 1804, in Clinton, North Carolina. He acquired a plantation but failed as a manager, so he asked his father, an influential politician, to get him an appointment to West Point, which he did. He graduated in 1829. Jefferson Davis, a close personal friend, graduated the year ahead of Holmes.

Commissioned in the infantry, Lieutenant Holmes served in a variety of posts on the Western frontier and in Florida during the Second Seminole War. His overall performance was hampered by the fact that he was hard of hearing. He was, nevertheless, promoted to captain in 1838.

Holmes fought in the Mexican War and led an assault group in the storming of Monterrey, where he won lavish praise from Colonel Jefferson Davis. He was awarded a brevet to major for valor. He received a regular promotion to major in 1855. He fought against the Navajos in the southwest and later served as superintendent of the U.S. Army's Recruiting Service. He resigned his commission on April 22, 1861, and returned to North Carolina. He was offered a colonel's commission in the Confederate Army.

Holmes was initially responsible for North Carolina's coastal defenses. On June 5, 1861, President Davis appointed him brigadier general, gave him command of a brigade, and placed him in charge of the Department of Fredericksburg, Virginia. He saw fighting at the Battle of First Manassas and was promoted to major general on October 7, 1861.

General Holmes returned to his home state to lead the Department of North Carolina. He did a good job reorganizing the state's forces but showed a lack of aggression in combating the Federals. He took part in the Seven Days Battles, in which his performance was mediocre, and General Robert E. Lee replaced him with D. H. Hill. Even so, President Davis still had confidence in him and named him commander of the Trans-Mississippi Department with a promotion to lieutenant general effective October 10, 1862.

In the Trans-Mississippi, Holmes was inefficient, jealous, and resentful, and he refused to cooperate with the Army of Mississippi in the defense of Vicksburg. This was his most important duty, and he failed miserably. He was also partially responsible for the Confederate disaster at Arkansas Post (January 9–11, 1863), which was the largest surrender of Confederate troops west of the Mississippi until the end of the war. President Davis relieved him of command in March 1863 and replaced him with Edmund Kirby Smith, who appointed Holmes commander of the Department of Arkansas. On July 4, 1863, Holmes made a belated attempt to take some of the pressure off Vicksburg by launching an attack on the Union garrison at Helena, Arkansas. Holmes's attacks were poorly coordinated, in large part due to his unclear orders, and he was defeated by numerically inferior Federal forces. Realizing that he was whipped, the general deliberately exposed himself to enemy fire, seeking death on the battlefield, but he was not killed.

Kirby Smith asked Davis to replace Holmes with a younger and more energetic officer on January 29, 1864. When he heard of this request, Holmes resigned in anger on February 28 and returned to North Carolina, where he was placed in charge of the state's reserve forces. He held this post until the end of the war.

Holmes spent his twilight years operating a small farm near Fayette-ville, North Carolina. He died in Fayetteville on June 21, 1880. He was seventy-five years old. He is buried in MacPherson Presbyterian Church Cemetery, Fayetteville.

JAMES THADEUS HOLTZCLAW was born on December 17, 1833, in McDonough, Georgia, but was raised in Chambers County, Alabama. He was educated at the local Presbyterian school, the East Alabama Insti-tute in Lafayette. In 1853, he declined an appointment to West Point and chose instead to study law under famous secessionist and Fire-Eater William Lowndes Yancey, who became a close personal friend. He was admitted to the bar in 1855.

In early 1861, he was a lieutenant in the Montgomery True Blues, a local militia unit. He took part in the cap-ture of the Pensacola Navy Yard and in May 1861 entered Confederate service as a lieutenant in what became the 18th Alabama Infantry Regiment. He was promoted to major in August and to lieutenant colonel in December.

The 18th Alabama was heavily engaged at Shiloh on April 6, 1862. Among the wounded was James Holtzclaw, who took a bullet to the right lung. Doctors initially thought he would die, but Holtzclaw made a remarkable recovery and returned to duty in three months.

All of the field officers of the 18th Alabama were killed or wounded at Shiloh. The regiment was stationed at Montgomery when Holtzclaw returned, and he was quickly promoted to colonel. The regiment was sent to Mobile and remained there until April 1863, when it joined the Army of Tennessee. It took part in the Tullahoma Campaign, the Battle of Chicka-mauga, and the Siege of Chattanooga. Holtzclaw served as acting commander of Henry Clayton's brigade in the Battle of Lookout Mountain.

Holtzclaw was involved in several battles during the Atlanta Cam-paign and became the permanent brigade commander after Henry

Clayton was promoted to divisional command. Holtzclaw was promoted to brigadier general on July 7, 1864.

General Holtzclaw participated in General John Bell Hood's Tennessee Campaign and was wounded in the ankle during the Battle of Franklin. He continued to lead his brigade, fought in the Battle of Nashville, and was part of the rear guard in the subsequent retreat from Tennessee.

In January 1865, Holtzclaw was transferred to the Department of the Gulf. He was given command of a division and fought in the Mobile Campaign, where he commanded the Spanish Fort garrison. After the city fell on April 12, he retreated into the interior of Alabama and surrendered at Meridian, Mississippi, on May 10.

After the war, General Holtzclaw resumed his law practice in Montgomery. He was prominent in local political circles and interested himself in the railroad business. He also served on the Alabama Railroad Commission.

James T. Holtzclaw died at home in Montgomery, Alabama, on July 19, 1893, several months shy of his sixtieth birthday. He is buried in Oakwood Cemetery, Montgomery.

JOHN BELL HOOD was born in Owingsville, Kentucky, on June 29, 1831, the son of a country doctor. He was raised near the town of Mount Sterling in the Bluegrass region of central Kentucky. Hood grew into an amiable, young, blond giant of a man. He used the assistance of his uncle, a U.S. congressman, to secure an appointment to West Point.

After a mediocre academic career, Hood graduated with the class of 1853, was commissioned in the infantry, and was sent to the Western frontier. In July 1857, near Devil's River, Texas, a Comanche brave shot an arrow through his left hand. He recovered quickly.

Hood resigned his commission on April 16, four days after the Rebels fired on Fort Sumter, and entered into Confederate service as a captain of cavalry. He was soon promoted to major and on September 30, 1861, became lieutenant colonel of the 4th Texas Infantry Regiment. He was the regimental commander by October.

Louis T. Wigfall, the brigade commander, resigned to take his seat in the Confederate Senate on February 20, 1862, and Hood succeeded him in command. From then on, the brigade was known as "Hood's Brigade" or "Hood's Texas Brigade." He was promoted to brigadier general on March 3, 1862, and under his leadership, the brigade became an elite combat unit. It fought extremely well in the retreat up the Virginia Peninsula and in the Seven Days Battles. Hood personally led the final charge in the Confederate victory at Gaines' Mill.

On July 26, 1862, Hood became an acting division commander. At the Battle of Second Manassas, he led the attack on the Union's left flank that routed the Federal forces. At Sharpsburg, General Hood's division lost almost half its men in some of the heaviest fighting of the war but held its line and inflicted heavy casualties in turn. General Stonewall Jackson was impressed and recommended Hood be promoted. Hood became a major general on October 10, 1862.

Hood's division was lightly engaged at Fredericksburg and was part of General James Longstreet's Suffolk Expedition. The division rejoined the main army for the Gettysburg Campaign. Here, on July 2, 1863, John Bell Hood devised a plan to get around the Union's left flank. Had Longstreet approved this maneuver, the South might have won the battle, but he did not. Hood was compelled to launch a frontal attack on Little Round Top, where an artillery shell exploded over his head and crippled his left arm, which he was unable to use the rest of his life.

General Hood resumed command of his division in September 1863 and fought at the Battle of Chickamauga (September 19–20, 1863), where he led the decisive breakthrough against the U.S. Army of the Cumberland. He was seriously wounded in the process, and his right leg had to be amputated four inches below his hip. He was sent back to Richmond to recover. He was promoted to lieutenant general on February 1, 1864, to rank from September 20, 1863.

During his recuperation, General Hood went on several carriage rides with President Jefferson Davis, and the two become personal friends. On February 24, 1864, Davis assigned "Sam" Hood ("Sam" was a nickname Hood had acquired at West Point) to Joseph E. Johnston's Army of Tennessee.

During the Atlanta Campaign, Johnston showed his usual timidity and retreated more or less constantly. President Davis, who could not afford to lose that city, relieved Johnston on July 17 and replaced him with John Bell Hood, who was promoted to full general (temporary rank) on July 18. At age thirty-three, Hood was the youngest commander on either side to command an army—and also one of the worst.

Hood hurled his legions into suicidal charges against Sherman's defensive positions. Sherman threw back Hood's reckless assaults, inflicting casualties the South could not afford, and then forced Hood to abandon Atlanta. It fell on September 2.

Hood sidestepped Sherman's armies and struck at their supply lines, with limited success. Hood's maneuvers left no Confederate army in front of General Sherman, who began his infamous March to the Sea on November 16. Hood countered by invading Tennessee, but on November 30 he was defeated in the Battle of Franklin, and his army was routed at Nashville on December 15–16 and barely escaped complete destruction. It was no longer an effective fighting force.

John Bell Hood resigned his command on January 23, 1865, and asked to be transferred to the Trans-Mississippi Department. The end came too quickly for him to reach Louisiana. He was paroled at Natchez, Mississippi, on May 31.

Hood settled in New Orleans in 1865 and became a cotton broker and president of the Life Association of America, an insurance company. He was initially quite successful and enjoyed a happy marriage to Anna Marie Hennen in 1868, fathering eleven children over the next ten years (with three sets of twins).

An outbreak of yellow fever, however, destroyed his business and cut through his family, killing his eldest daughter, his wife, and himself. John Bell Hood died on August 30, 1879. He was forty-eight years old. He was initially buried in Lafayette Cemetery, New Orleans, but was later reinterred in the Hennen family tomb in Metairie Cemetery, New Orleans.

BENJAMIN HUGER was born in Charleston, South Carolina, on November 22, 1805, and grew up on Rice Hope, his family's plantation. He was admitted to West Point in 1821 and graduated in 1825.

Huger initially served as a topographical engineer (1825–28) and then took a leave of absence to visit Europe. In 1832, he transferred to the ordnance branch and over the course of his U.S. Army career was often in command of important arsenals.

He distinguished himself in the Mexican War as General Winfield Scott's chief of ordnance and was one of the few officers to receive three brevets. After he returned to the United States, he commanded the arsenals at Fort Monroe and Harpers Ferry. In 1860, he was in command of the Charleston Arsenal.

Huger resigned his commission on April 22, 1861—ten days after the Rebels fired on Fort Sumter. The Confederate War Department commissioned him as a lieutenant colonel and assigned him to command the Department of Norfolk on May 24. He was promoted to brigadier general on June 17, 1861, and to major general on December 13, 1861.

Roanoke Island, North Carolina, was part of Huger's area of responsibility. He failed to reinforce it, and it was overwhelmed by 13,000 Federals on February 8. The South lost 2,600 men and 30 guns. The Union forces suffered fewer than 300 casualties.

The loss of Roanoke Island sent shock waves throughout North Carolina and southeastern Virginia, and the region's faith in Huger was forever shattered. The Federals continued to gain ground, and General Joseph E. Johnston ordered Huger to abandon Norfolk on April 27 and to salvage as much equipment as he could. Huger evacuated Norfolk and nearby Portsmouth on May 9 but left so much equipment behind for the occupying Federals that the Confederate Congress began an investigation.

Meanwhile, General Huger reorganized his command (nine thousand men) as a division and joined the main army near Richmond. He fought in the Battle of Seven Pines, where Joseph E. Johnston made him the scapegoat for General James Longstreet's failures on the first day of battle. Johnston liked Longstreet and didn't like Huger, who was self-important, inarticulate, and overweight and did not look like a soldier. Huger demanded a court of inquiry, arguing that he was unfairly blamed for the Confederate defeat, but this was denied to him; and it has to be said that his overall performance during the Seven Days Battles was not good. He was slow, unnecessarily delayed by Federal resistance, and at Malvern Hill on July 1, 1861, he lost control of his division,

General Robert E. Lee fired Benjamin Huger on July 12. The following month, Huger was transferred to the Trans-Mississippi Department as inspector of artillery and ordnance. In July 1863 he was promoted to commander of ordnance in the department, and he held this post until the end of the war. General Huger was a fine ordnance officer, artilleryman, and military engineer, but his talents simply did not extend to commanding a division of combat infantry. His son, Frank Huger, distinguished himself as an artillery commander and rose to the rank of colonel.

After the war, Benamin Huger became a farmer in North Carolina and then in Virginia, though without much success. He died in Charleston, South Carolina, on December 7, 1877. He was seventy-two years old. General Huger was buried in Green Mount Cemetery, Baltimore, Maryland.

WILLIAM YOUNG CONN HUMES was born on May 1, 1830, in Abingdon, Virginia. His father made and lost a fortune, so Humes borrowed money to complete his education. He enrolled at the Virginia Military Institute in 1848 and graduated in 1851. He went to work as a teacher, paid off his debts, moved to Knoxville, Tennessee, to study law, and in 1858 moved to Memphis where he set up shop as a lawyer. He was there when the war began.

Humes became a first lieutenant in the 1st Confederate Regular Artillery effective March 16, 1861, and was promoted to captain in June. He was placed in charge of the artillery on Island Number 10, where he was captured when it fell to U.S. forces on April 7, 1862.

Captain Humes was imprisoned on Johnson's Island, Ohio, in Lake Erie, and was exchanged in September 1862. He was promoted to major and named chief of artillery of General Joe Wheeler's cavalry in March 1863. He fought in virtually all of Wheeler's battles for the rest of the war. He was wounded in the foot at Farmington, Tennessee, on October 7, 1863. He recovered quickly, was given command of a cavalry brigade, and was promoted to brigadier general on November 16, 1863. He took part in the Tullahoma Campaign, Chickamauga, and the Siege of Chattanooga, including the battles of Lookout Mountain and Missionary Ridge. In 1864, he fought in the Atlanta Campaign and led a division in Wheeler's disastrous raid into Tennessee in October 1864.

During the winter of 1864–65, Humes's understrength division resisted Sherman's March to the Sea, but with little success. On March 10, 1865, he fought in the Confederate victory at Monroe's Crossroads, where he was wounded in the leg. He was back in the saddle at Bentonville and surrendered with Joseph E. Johnston's army on April 26. Some sources suggest that he was promoted to major general in March 1865, but the records do not bear that out. His tombstone gives his rank as brigadier general.

After the war, Humes returned to Memphis and resumed his law practice. He later moved to Huntsville, Alabama. General Humes died in Huntsville in 1883 at age fifty-three. His body was returned to Memphis, where it was interred in Elmwood Cemetery.

BENJAMIN GRUBB HUMPHREYS was born on August 26, 1808, at Heritage, his father's plantation along Bayou Pierre in Claiborne County, Mississippi Territory. Humphreys was admitted to West Point

in 1825 but was expelled from the academy, along with about twenty other cadets, for his part in the Eggnog Riot on December 24–25, 1826. (Basically, it was a drunken Christmas party that got out of hand.) Cadet Jefferson Davis also took part in the riot, although he was not court-martialed.

Humphreys returned home and helped his father run the plantation. In the 1830s, the younger Humphreys was elected to the Mississippi House of Representatives. He served in the state senate as a Whig from 1839 to 1844. In 1846, he relocated to Sunflower County, established a plantation at Roebuck Lake, and continued to farm until 1861.

Humphreys opposed secession, but in 1860 he organized the Sunflower Guards, a militia company, in case war came. Mississippi seceded on January 9, 1861. Humphreys became a captain in the 21st Mississippi on May 18, 1861, and was elected colonel on September 11.

The 21st Mississippi was mustered into Confederate service at Manassas, Virginia, in October, and was an important part of what later became the Army of Northern Virginia, fighting at Sharpsburg, Fredericksburg, and Chancellorsville.

At Gettysburg, Humphreys pushed through the Peach Orchard on July 2, 1863, captured a battery of Massachusetts artillery, drove to the foot of Cemetery Ridge, and succeeded the mortally wounded General William Barksdale as brigade commander. He was promoted to brigadier general on August 12, 1863. The Mississippi Brigade was part of the main Confederate breakthrough at Chickamauga on September 20. It participated in the Siege of Knoxville (including the unsuccessful attack on Fort Sanders), the battles of the Wilderness and Spotsylvania, and the early stages of the Siege of Petersburg. It was transferred to General Jubal Early's Army of the Shenandoah in late August 1864.

General Humphreys was seriously wounded in the Battle of Berryville in early September. He was reassigned to duty in southern

Mississippi following his recovery and remained there until the end of the war.

Humphreys was elected governor on October 2, 1865. The Radical Republicans instituted Congressional Reconstruction in March 1867. Humphreys firmly and courageously opposed it. He was reelected governor in 1868 but was deposed from the office by Federal troops on June 15, 1868, for failure to support Federal Reconstruction policies.

Following his removal from office, General Humphreys retired from politics. He worked in the insurance business in Jackson, Mississippi, until 1877, when he retired to his plantation in Leflore County, near Greenwood, Mississippi. He died on December 20, 1882, in Jackson, at the age of seventy-four. General Humphreys is buried in Wintergreen Cemetery, Port Gibson, Mississippi. He has a cenotaph in the Confederate section of that cemetery, but his remains are located in the family plot, about ten yards to the right of the main entrance. Humphreys County, Mississippi, is named after him.

EPPA HUNTON II, was born in Warrenton, Virginia, on September 22, 1822, and was educated at New Baltimore Academy. Hunton taught school while simultaneously studying law. He was admitted to the bar in 1843 and set up a law office in Brentsville, Virginia.

Eppa Hunton became a fervent secessionist and was a delegate to the secession convention. After Virginia left the Union, he was appointed colonel of the 8th Virginia Infantry Regiment, which fought at Manassas and Ball's Bluff, where the fighting was heavy and Colonel Hunton ordered a bayonet charge that routed the Federals. His regiment, which had gone into action with 400 men, took 710 prisoners and captured all of the enemy's artillery. Colonel Hunton also led the regiment in the Peninsula Campaign and the Seven Days Battles until General George Pickett was wounded, after which Hunton acted as brigade commander.

Meanwhile, the Federals burned Hunton's home, and his family had to take refuge in Lynchburg.

Eppa Hunton led the brigade in the Battle of Second Manassas and did well, but he was nevertheless replaced by Richard Garnett early in the Maryland Campaign, and Hunton reverted to the command of the 8th Virginia. He led it at South Mountain, Sharpsburg, and Fredericksburg. In the spring of 1863, Hunton's regiment was in North Carolina collecting supplies. At Gettysburg, the "Bloody 8th" had only 200 men present, and 190 of them, including Colonel Hunton (who was ill and then wounded), became casualties on July 3, 1863, during Pickett's Charge. With General Richard B. Garnett missing, presumed dead, after the charge, Hunton succeeded him as brigade commander. This time, the appointment was permanent. He was promoted to brigadier general on August 9, 1863.

General Hunton's brigade was used to guard Richmond during the Wilderness and Spotsylvania campaigns but then rejoined the main army and fought in the Battle of Cold Harbor and the Siege of Petersburg. The unit was down to fewer than 1,500 men on April 1, 1865, when it was routed in the Battle of Five Forks. Hunton and the surviving remnants of his command fought in the Battle of Sayler's Creek (April 6), where they were surrounded by Union cavalry and infantry. With no chance of escape, General Hunton surrendered.

Eppa Hunton was imprisoned at Fort Warren, Massachusetts, where he was paroled on July 24. Hunton returned home and resumed his law practice. He moved to Warrenton and bought a house in 1867.

General Hunton was a vocal opponent of Radical Reconstruction. He was elected to the Virginia Senate but was not allowed to take his seat. As Congressional Reconstruction in Virginia crumbled, however, he ran for Congress in 1872 and was elected over an abolitionist from Massachusetts. He served from 1873 to 1881. He declined to run for reelection in 1880. He concentrated on his legal practice and was quite successful.

In 1892, the legislature selected Hunton to fill the late John Barbour's unexpired term in the U.S. Senate. He served until March 4, 1895. He eventually moved to Richmond, where there were more opportunities for Eppa Hunton III, his son and law partner. In his last years, he wrote his autobiography and was active in the United Confederate Veterans. Eppa Hunton died in Richmond on October 11, 1908, at the age of eighty-six. He is buried in Hollywood Cemetery, Richmond.

I

• IMBODEN – IVERSON •

JOHN DANIEL IMBODEN (pronounced IM-boden) was born on February 16, 1823, in Staunton, Virginia. He was educated at the Staunton Academy and Washington College, but he did not graduate. He nevertheless became a teacher at the Virginia School for the Deaf and Blind in Staunton while he studied law. He was admitted to the bar in 1844.

Imboden was twice elected to the Virginia House of Delegates, serving from 1850 to 1853 and from 1855 to 1857. He did not win reelection in 1857. After John Brown's terrorist attack on Harpers Ferry in 1859, Imboden helped form the Staunton Light Artillery, partially at his own expense. He was elected its captain in late 1859. The unit had 107 men and four 6-pounder bronze cannons. Imboden and his men took part in the capture of the Harpers Ferry Arsenal on April 17, 1861.

The Staunton Light Artillery was mustered into Confederate service on July 1, 1861, and fought in the Battle of First Manassas. During the battle, Imboden's left ear drum was perforated, causing him to lose all hearing in that ear.

The battery returned to the Shenandoah, where it formed part of Stonewall Jackson's command during the Valley Campaign of 1862. Afterward, Imboden left the artillery and set about organizing the 62nd Virginia Mounted Infantry, which was also known as the 1st Partisan Ranger Regiment. He was promoted to colonel on September 9, 1862.

Over the next several months, Imboden successfully raided the Baltimore and Ohio Railroad, Yankee supply lines, and several small encampments, capturing thousands of horses and cattle. As a result, Imboden was promoted to brigadier general on January 28, 1863.

During the Gettysburg Campaign, Imboden's brigade covered General Robert E. Lee's left flank as he moved his army north through the Shenandoah and into Maryland and Pennsylvania. The brigade also helped cover Lee's retreat and checked a major Union cavalry raid near Williamsport, Maryland. General Lee praised Imboden's performance.

That fall and the following spring, Imboden fought in the Shenandoah, including at New Market and Cedar Creek. He was then stricken with typhoid fever and was unable to perform any further field service.

General Imboden's brigade was never considered any more than a third-class cavalry force and suffered heavily from desertion in 1864, but the general seemed to have a talent for getting the most out of a mediocre team. He returned to active duty on January 2, 1865, and spent the rest of the war commanding the Camp Millen Prison, another prisoner-of-war camp at Aiken, South Carolina, and other prison camps. He was paroled at Augusta, Georgia, on May 3.

After the surrender, Imboden moved to Richmond and then Abingdon, Virginia, in the southwest corner of the state, where he worked on developing Virginia's iron ore and coal resources. He also founded the town of Damascus, Virginia, which became a lumber center. He authored several articles and books on the war and also contributed to the writing of the *The War of the Rebellion: A Compilation of the Official Records of the Union and Confederate Armies* and *Century Monthly's Battles and Leaders of the Civil War*.

John D. Imboden died in Damascus on August 15, 1895, at the age of seventy-two. He is buried in Hollywood Cemetery, Richmond, Virginia.

ALFRED IVERSON, JR., was born in Clinton, Georgia, on February 14, 1829. His father was a judge, a congressman, and a U.S. senator. He was also a strong opponent of secession.

Alfred Iverson, Jr., attended the Tuskegee Military Institute, but he left the school in 1846 at age seventeen so he could join the army and fight in the Mexican War. His father raised and equipped a Georgia volunteer cavalry regiment, which Alfred Iverson, Jr., joined. He distinguished himself in Mexico and was commissioned a second lieutenant. After the war, he became a lawyer, but in 1855 he returned to the Regular Army, securing a commission as a first lieutenant of cavalry.

He served in "Bleeding Kansas" and later fought against the Kiowas and Comanches.

When the Southern states seceded, Iverson resigned his U.S. Army commission and accepted a commission from Jefferson Davis, an old friend of his father, as colonel of the 20th North Carolina. The regiment joined the Army of Northern Virginia in June 1862. It fought in the Seven Days Battles, where Iverson distinguished himself at Gaines' Mill by leading a charge and capturing a Union battery. He was severely wounded in the attack but recovered in time to participate in the Maryland Campaign. The 20th fought at South Mountain and the Battle of Sharpsburg, where the regiment bolted, but Iverson rallied his men and lead them back into the battle. Colonel Duncan McRae, the acting brigade commander, was seriously wounded and was replaced by Alfred Iverson.

On November 1, 1862, Iverson was promoted to brigadier general. Iverson's brigade was in reserve at Fredericksburg and fought in the Battle of Chancellorsville, where it was part of General Stonewall Jackson's legendary flank march. Iverson himself was wounded when a spent shell struck him in the groin.

At Gettysburg on July 1, 1863, General Robert Rodes ordered a poorly coordinated, hasty attack on Union forces northwest of the town. Iverson chose not to lead the attack and sent his regiments forward without reconnaissance. They walked straight into an ambush and lost 900 of their 1,350 men. Iverson suffered a nervous breakdown and was no longer fit to command. General Rodes sent him to the rear and attached the remnants of his unit to Stephen Ramseur's brigade. During the retreat to Virginia, General Lee (who had witnessed Iverson's behavior at Gettysburg) relieved Iverson of his command. Iverson was sent back to Georgia in October. His father's political influence helped gain him command of state forces in the vicinity of Rome, Georgia. Eventually, General Iverson was given command of a cavalry brigade in General Joe Wheeler's cavalry corps, which he led well in the Atlanta Campaign. In late July, Union General George Stoneman launched a raid into the Confederate rear with 2,500 men. With only 1,300 men, Iverson defeated him at Macon on July 29 and crushed him at Sunshine Church on July 31, dispersing his command and taking more than 500 prisoners to add to the 200 he captured at Macon. Among the prisoners was Stoneman, the highest-ranking Union prisoner captured in battle during the war.

Iverson opposed Sherman's March to the Sea and was commander of the garrison at Greensboro. As the end of the war approached, he was unable to maintain discipline among the troops, and his command was characterized by plundering and desertion. His record as a Confederate commander was definitely a mixture of fine successes and dismal failures.

After the war, Alfred Iverson tried his hand at business in Macon and then moved to Florida, where he became a successful orange grower near Kissimmee. Late in his life, he moved to Atlanta to live with his daughter's family. He died there on March 31, 1911, at age eighty-two. He is buried in Oakland Cemetery.

I

J

· JACKSON – JORDAN ·

ALFRED EUGENE "MUDWALL" JACKSON was born in Davidson County, Tennessee, on January 11, 1807. He attended Washington College and Greeneville College, two Presbyterian schools which later merged and are now Tusculum University. After graduation, he became a farmer, a produce wholesaler, a miller, and a manufacturer. He also established an extensive boat and wagon network to market his goods from North Carolina to Louisiana.

Alfred Jackson joined the Confederate Army as a major on September 11, 1861. General Felix Zollicoffer named Jackson his quartermaster, a post he held until the general was killed at Mill Springs on January 19, 1862. Jackson then became paymaster for General Edmund Kirby Smith. He was appointed brigadier general on October 29, 1862, but this appointment was canceled. He was reappointed on February 9, 1863, and this time he was confirmed. He assumed command of a brigade in the Department of East Tennessee in April 1863. Later, Jackson operated in the Trans-Allegheny Department.

Jackson's brigade was a mixed formation, including cavalry, infantry, and Cherokee scouts. It usually numbered 1,500 to 2,000 men. East Tennessee was mostly pro-Union, and Jackson was constantly occupied pursuing Confederate deserters (often recent draftees) and fighting pro-Union guerrillas and bushwhackers. His men took part in several minor battles and skirmishes in East Tennessee, western North Carolina, southwestern Virginia, and eastern Kentucky. It also conducted raids on Union outposts.

The Trans-Allegheny Department was a backwater theater of operations during the Civil War, and the men on both sides lacked discipline. In May 1864, General Braxton Bragg reported that Jackson's brigade was in "miserable order." It was nevertheless useful in the region in which it operated. It took part in the defense of Saltville, Virginia, and the East Tennessee and Virginia Railroad, and guarded the rear area of General James Longstreet's corps during the winter of 1863–64. On September

30, 1864, Jackson's brigade was at its best when it gobbled up the entire 100th Ohio Infantry Regiment in the Battle of Telford Station.

Alfred Jackson fell ill in late 1864 and was assigned light staff duties under John C. Breckinridge's Department of East Tennessee and West Virginia. He was in this position when the war ended.

Jackson was impoverished by the war. Initially, he became a tenant farmer in Virginia and cultivated the fields with his own hands. In November 1865, however, he was issued a special pardon by President Andrew Johnson because of kindnesses Jackson had shown Johnson's family in Tennessee during the war. This pardon allowed him to recover part of his antebellum property. He returned to Jonesborough, Tennessee (near Johnson City, on the North Carolina line), and worked to rebuild his fortune. General Alfred Jackson died in Jonesborough on October 30, 1889, at the age of eighty-two. He is buried there in City Cemetery.

HENRY ROOTES JACKSON was born on June 24, 1820, in Athens, Georgia. His father, who tutored him, was a professor at the University of Georgia. He attended Yale University, where he graduated with honors in 1839. He returned to Georgia, studied law in Columbus, passed the bar exam, and set up a legal practice in Savannah. He possessed a brilliant legal mind and was named the U.S. District Attorney of Georgia at age twenty-three. He wrote a book of poetry, *Tallulah and Other Poems*, which was published in 1850 and was well received by critics.

When the Mexican War broke out, Jackson helped form and became colonel of the 1st Georgia Infantry Regiment, which he commanded from 1846 to 1848. The regiment was sent to Mexico but never saw combat.

After he returned from the war, he accepted an appointment as a judge on the state superior court. He resigned in 1853 to become chargé d'affaires and later resident minister in Vienna, Austria (1853–59). He was a delegate to the Democratic convention in Charleston in 1860 but walked out with dozens of other Southern delegates who refused to support Stephen Douglas. He took part in the Georgia Secession Convention of 1861 and supported leaving the Union.

Jackson accepted a Confederate judgeship but resigned when the war began. He joined the Confederate Army as a brigadier general, with his appointment dated June 4, 1861. He fought in western Virginia, including at Cheat Mountain, but his brigade was disbanded shortly after.

Henry Rootes Jackson resigned his commission on December 2, 1861, and returned to Georgia, where he was appointed major general of militia. On September 21, 1863, as the Yankees approached Georgia, Jackson was reappointed as a brigadier general in the Confederate Army. Given a brigade, he fought in the Atlanta Campaign and took part in General John Bell Hood's invasion of Tennessee. He was captured in the Battle of Nashville and was a prisoner of war at Fort Warren, Massachusetts. He was paroled on July 8, 1865.

After the war, Jackson returned to Georgia, reestablished his law practice, and served as ambassador to Mexico (1885–86). Later, he was a director of the Central Railroad and Banking Company of Georgia. He was president of the Georgia Historical Society from 1875 until his death.

General Henry R. Jackson died at Savannah, Georgia, on May 23, 1898, at the age of seventy-seven. He was buried in Bonaventure Cemetery, Savannah.

JOHN KING JACKSON was born on February 8, 1828, in Augusta, Georgia. He was educated at the Richmond Academy, Georgia, and South Carolina College, from which he graduated with honors in 1846. He then read law, was admitted to the bar, and practiced in his hometown from 1848 to 1861. He also joined the state militia and was a lieutenant colonel commanding a militia battalion when Georgia seceded.

In April 1861, Jackson became a lieutenant colonel in the 5th Georgia Infantry Regiment. A month later, he was elected colonel. On October 9, 1861, the 5th Georgia fought at the Battle of Santa Rosa Island, a failed attempt to wrest Fort Pickens from the Federals in Florida. Jackson was nevertheless promoted to brigadier general on January 14, 1862.

In February 1862, he was sent to Grand Junction, Tennessee, where he organized his brigade, and then to Corinth, Mississippi. Jackson performed well in the Battle of Shiloh. His brigade guarded the railroad bridges and the Army of Tennessee's line of communications from Chattanooga to Murfreesboro during General Braxton Bragg's Kentucky Campaign. It rejoined the main army in December and fought in the Second Battle of Murfreesboro.

After stops at Bridgeport, Alabama, and Chattanooga, Jackson and his brigade were ordered to defend the railroad from Atlanta to Tullahoma. He participated in the Tullahoma Campaign and the Battle of Chickamauga, where his brigade suffered more than 60 percent casualties.

Jackson's brigade took part in the Siege of Chattanooga and the Battle of Missionary Ridge, where it slowed but could not stop the Union advance.

Jackson fought in the Atlanta Campaign until July 3, 1864, when he and two of his regiments were ordered to report to General Samuel Jones in Charleston. Jones sent him to Lake City, Florida, where he remained until September 29, 1864, when Jackson and his men were transferred to Savannah. They defended the town from Sherman. After the city fell on December 21, 1864, Jackson was sent to South Carolina, where he organized supply depots for the Army of Tennessee. He was later sent to North Carolina for the same purpose. Finally, he was transferred to his hometown of Augusta. He was still there when General Joseph E. Johnston surrendered on April 26, 1865. Jackson was paroled on May 17.

After the war, Jackson resumed his profession as an attorney. He represented several banks that were trying to obtain financial relief from the Georgia legislature. He was engaged in this project when he died of pneumonia in Milledgeville, Georgia, on February 27, 1866, at age thirty-eight. He was buried in Magnolia Cemetery, Augusta.

THOMAS JONATHAN "STONEWALL" JACKSON was born on January 21, 1824, in Clarksburg, Virginia (now West Virginia). His friends called him "Tom." His father, who was an attorney, but not a prosperous one, died of typhoid fever in 1826, and Jackson grew up in poverty. When his mother's health began to fail, she sent Thomas and his sister to live with their half-uncle, Cummins Jackson, who owned a grist mill (Jackson's Mill).

Cummins Jackson provided for Thomas physically but not emotionally. He also spent a difficult year with an aunt and her husband but later ran away. Stonewall's childhood was so bad that he refused to speak of it in later years. The only person he was close to was his sister, Laura.

In 1842, Jackson was admitted to West Point, but his self-education was deficient. He barely passed his entrance exam, and as he started his studies at West Point, few believed he would graduate. Cadet Jackson, however, was determined to be the hardest-working student at the academy. He spent virtually all his spare time studying or reading the Bible. He graduated in 1846, ranking seventeenth out of fifty-nine students in his class.

Jackson became an artillery officer and distinguished himself in the Mexican War. He earned a promotion to first lieutenant and brevets to captain and major.

After the Mexican War, Major Jackson fought in the Second Seminole War. In August 1851, he became a professor of natural and experimental philosophy and instructor of artillery at the Virginia Military Institute.

Jackson was neither a good teacher nor a popular one. His stiff, distracted manner and high-pitched voice prompted the cadets to call him "Tom Fool." But his artillery course was equal to any in the New World, and Jackson very much enjoyed living and teaching in Lexington, Virginia.

Jackson was an eccentric. He had a touch of narcolepsy and frequently fell asleep in church. He suffered from dyspepsia, vitreous floaters (to the point that he worried about going blind), and was, on top of that, a hypochondriac who periodically went on bizarre diets as part of his obsession with his health. Sometimes his diet consisted mostly of buttermilk and corn bread; at other times, it was stale bread and cold water, with meat once a month. When he adopted a diet, he stuck with it, even bringing his own food to dinner parties, and he had strange food-based superstitions, such as the belief that if pepper contacted his tongue, he would temporarily lose the use of his right leg.

Jackson believed in walking five miles a day. He also invented a form of exercise that resembled modern aerobics, but the fact that he performed these exercises in uniform on his way to class contributed to his reputation as an eccentric.

His first wife died in childbirth in 1854 and was buried with their son, who was stillborn. He remarried to Mary Anna Morrison in July 1857. They had a very happy domestic life, marred only by the death of their first child in 1858.

Major Jackson was a Union man until April 15, 1861, when Lincoln called for seventy-five thousand volunteers to suppress the "rebellion." Virginia seceded two days later, and Jackson was named a colonel of Virginia militia. Initially, he was tasked to act as drillmaster for the hundreds of new recruits who flocked to the colors.

On April 27, Virginia Governor John Letcher gave Jackson command of the Southern forces at Harpers Ferry. After capturing most of the rolling stock of the Baltimore and Ohio Railroad, he was promoted to brigadier general in the Confederate Army on June 17, 1861.

Jackson became famous on July 21, during the Battle of First Manassas, where he commanded a brigade and earned the name "Stonewall" after South Carolina General Barnard Bee exclaimed, "Look, men, there is Jackson standing like a stone wall! Let us determine to die here, and we will conquer. Rally behind the Virginians!" Jackson was wounded in the left hand early in the battle. A physician wanted to amputate the hand, but Jackson refused. In the end, he suffered only a small loss of bone, and was fully recovered by October 7, 1861, when he was promoted to major general and given command of a division.

Stonewall Jackson's career was marked by one brilliant victory after another—too many to be described in depth here. Jackson was promoted to lieutenant general on October 10, 1862. Shortly after, on November 23, 1862, Julia Laura Jackson was born in Charlotte, North Carolina. She was Jackson's only child to live into adulthood. He saw her briefly in April 1863, when she and her mother visited his headquarters.

Stonewall Jackson's justly famous flanking attack at Chancellorsville on May 2, 1863, broke the Northern offensive and allowed 58,000 Rebels to defeat 134,000 Yankees. Unfortunately, Jackson was accidentally shot by his own men as he returned to Southern lines after nightfall. Two bullets shattered his left arm, and another struck his right hand. Dr. Hunter McGuire was forced to amputate Jackson's left arm.

Dr. McGuire at first assumed that Jackson would fully recover, but the general developed pneumonia and died on May 10, 1863. He was thirty-nine years old.

Stonewall Jackson's death was a tragedy for the Confederacy. Many historians have speculated that if Jackson had been with General Robert E. Lee at Gettysburg, the South would have won that battle and perhaps the war.

Jackson is buried in Stonewall Jackson Memorial Cemetery, Lexington, Virginia.

WILLIAM HICKS "RED" JACKSON was born in Paris, Tennessee, on October 1, 1835. He was educated at West Tennessee College (present-day Union University) and West Point, from which he graduated in 1856. He was assigned to the Mounted Rifles Regiment at Fort Bliss and fought Kiowas and Comanches in New Mexico Territory and western Texas. He resigned from the army on May 16, 1861, to join the Confederacy.

Jackson was commissioned a captain of artillery and became an aide to General Gideon Pillow. He fought in the Confederate victory at Belmont, Missouri. In early 1862, he was appointed colonel of the 1st (later 7th)

Tennessee Cavalry, serving in the Army of Mississippi. He commanded a cavalry brigade in the Second Battle of Corinth.

Jackson was promoted to brigadier general on December 29, 1862, and was given command of a cavalry division of three thousand men in early 1863. Sent to the Army of Tennessee, Jackson's division served under General Earl Van Dorn's cavalry corps until early June, when he was ordered to join the Army of Relief in Jackson, Mississippi.

General Jackson remained in eastern Mississippi after Vicksburg fell and commanded General Leonidas Polk's cavalry during Sherman's Meridian Expedition. Here he experienced little success, and Meridian fell on February 14, 1864.

That summer, Jackson's division joined General Joe Wheeler's cavalry corps in Georgia, where it again clashed with Sherman's forces. After Atlanta fell, Jackson's division was transferred to Nathan Bedford Forrest's cavalry corps and participated in General John Bell Hood's disastrous invasion of Tennessee. Jackson fought at Franklin and Nashville and helped cover Hood's retreat to Mississippi.

Jackson's worst campaign was also his last. Pursuing a Union cavalry column, he failed to join Forrest, whose corps was crushed in the Battle of Selma on April 2.

William H. Jackson was a general who compiled a very mixed record as a division commander. Perhaps this explains why he was never promoted to major general.

After the war, General Jackson returned to Tennessee to manage Belle Meade, his father-in-law's cotton plantation near Nashville. "Red" Jackson became one of the most successful horse breeders and traders in the United States. His operations, however, were severely damaged in the financial panic of 1893.

General Jackson and his wife were noted for their generosity, friendliness, and hospitality. Jackson died at Belle Meade on March 30, 1903. He was buried in the mausoleum in the plantation's cemetery. The family sold Belle Meade in 1906, and his remains, along with those of other members of the family, were reinterred in Mount Olivet Cemetery, Nashville.

WILLIAM LOWTHER JACKSON, a second cousin of Stonewall Jackson, was born in Clarksburg, Virginia (now West Virginia), on February 3, 1825. He overcame poverty, studied law, and was admitted to the bar in 1847. He set up his law practice in Harrisville, Virginia, where he became a prosperous lawyer. He became the district's commonwealth attorney and was twice elected to the legislature, serving from December 1850 to 1852. Jackson then served as second auditor for the state and superintendent of the state library fund. He was elected lieutenant governor of Virginia in 1857 and served until January 1860. Henry A. Wise was the governor.

Jackson was a large man, weighing about 200 pounds in a day when the average male weighed about 143 pounds. He had thick, dark red hair, and piercing blue eyes. He was known as a "gentleman of great personal popularity," even with members of the opposing Republican Party, and a forceful speaker, if not an eloquent one.

The legislature elected Jackson circuit judge in 1860. When the war began, Judge Jackson—a strong supporter of slavery and secession—resigned from the bench and immediately enlisted in the Confederate Army as a private. Prominent friends intervened to get him a commission, and he was soon lieutenant colonel of the 31st Virginia Infantry, which fought in the disastrous Western Virginia Campaign of 1861. Though the campaign was a failure, Jackson turned his disorderly rabble of a regiment into well-drilled, well-disciplined soldiers who would perform well in every major battle fought by the Army of Northern Virginia.

He was on Stonewall Jackson's staff as a volunteer aide during the Valley Campaign of 1862, the Seven Days Battles, and the battles of Second Manassas, Sharpsburg, and Fredericksburg.

With West Virginia annexed to the Union, the Confederate Congress authorized William Jackson to create a cavalry regiment behind enemy lines in the area. He recruited what became the 19th Virginia Cavalry and was promoted to colonel on April 17.

Colonel Jackson took part in the Jones-Imboden Raid (April–May 1863), which smashed the Baltimore and Ohio Railroad in West Virginia and gained a few hundred recruits. He fought in minor actions in West Virginia and western Virginia in 1863–64 and was given command of a cavalry brigade. He took part in the Valley Campaign of 1864 and was especially prominent in General Jubal Early's drive on Washington. Most of the time, however, Jackson's brigade did not fight as a unit, but was scattered throughout the Valley on patrols, as scouts, and in foraging operations and other roaming duties.

William L. Jackson was promoted to brigadier general on December 19, 1864. At the end of the war, he disbanded his brigade, fled west, and emigrated to Mexico. He returned to West Virginia but found that the Radical Republican legislature had passed a law forbidding former Confederates from practicing law in the state. Jackson moved to Louisville, Kentucky, where he set up a law office. Later, he again became a circuit judge. He died in Louisville of Bright's disease on March 26, 1890, at age sixty-five. He was buried in Cave Hill Cemetery, Louisville.

ALBERT GALLATIN JENKINS was born on his father's plantation, Greenbottom, in Cabell County, Virginia (now West Virginia), on November 10, 1830. He received an excellent private education and enrolled in Jefferson College in Canonsburg, Pennsylvania, at age fourteen. He graduated four years later (1848) and then studied law at Harvard. He was admitted to the bar in 1850 and set up a law practice in Charleston, (West) Virginia.

Jenkins was elected to the U.S. Congress in 1856. He served from March 4, 1857, until the war began. He then returned home and raised a company of mounted men, which he dubbed the "Border Rangers." On May 29, 1861, it was incorporated into the Confederate Army, with Jenkins as captain.

Albert Jenkins fought in a number of minor battles in western (West) Virginia and performed well. That autumn, the Border Rangers were absorbed into the 8th Virginia Cavalry, of which Jenkins was elected lieutenant colonel on September 24. He was promoted to colonel in November.

That winter, Jenkins was elected to the First Confederate Congress and took office on February 18, 1862. He was appointed brigadier general on August 5, 1862, resigned his seat the next day, and returned to the field.

The high point of Jenkins's military career occurred in August and September 1862, when he led a raid into western (West) Virginia and Ohio. With 550 men, he destroyed much of the Baltimore and Ohio Railroad, turned into the Kanawha Valley, traveled through thirty miles of roadless wilderness, and won the Battle of Buckhannon on August 30. On September 2, he fell on the 11th West Virginia Infantry at Spencer Court House, captured the entire regiment, and headed northwest, where he crossed the Ohio River into Ohio. He briefly occupied the town of Racine, treated its citizens well as a matter of duty and diplomacy, and recrossed into western Virginia. After a ride of five hundred miles, he had inflicted more than one thousand casualties on the Yankees and temporarily recaptured parts of western Virginia for the Confederacy.

General William Loring, Jenkins's superior, was finally defeated and expelled from the Kanawha Valley in October. General Robert E. Lee asked that Jenkins and his men be assigned to the Shenandoah Valley, where they spent the winter of 1862–63.

Jenkins took part in the Gettysburg Campaign, where he formed a cavalry screen for Richard Ewell's II Corps. He was wounded at Gettysburg on July 2. He did not recover for months.

After the Pennsylvania debacle, General Lee decided that Jenkins's command did better when it served closer to home. Accordingly, he transferred it to the Department of Western Virginia and Tennessee.

Jenkins returned to duty in late 1863 as commander of the Department of Western Virginia. On May 9, 1864, in the Battle of Cloyd's Mountain, his 2,400 men were attacked by 6,100 Yankees.

General Jenkins was decisively defeated. As the Yankees overwhelmed the Confederate center, he tried to rally his troops but was wounded and captured.

Jenkins's arm was amputated by Union surgeons. He failed to rally from the operation and died on May 21, 1864, at the age of thirty-three. He was initially buried in New Dublin Presbyterian Cemetery. After the war, he was reinterred in Spring Hill Cemetery, Huntington, West Virginia.

MICAH JENKINS was born on December 1, 1835, on Edisto Island, South Carolina, the son of a wealthy cotton planter. He entered the South Carolina Military Academy in 1851 (at the age of fifteen) and graduated first in his class of 1854. He and a fellow graduate established King's Mountain Military School, and he worked there until the outbreak of the war. He was confirmed at the Yorkville Episcopal Church in 1855 and was a deeply religious man who carried a Bible and a prayer book with him everywhere, even into battle.

After John Brown's terrorist attack on Harpers Ferry, Jenkins raised a company of volunteer militia, the Jasper Guards, of which he was elected captain. They became the Jasper Light Infantry in 1860 and formed the nucleus of the 5th South Carolina Infantry Regiment when it was organized the following year. The regiment totaled 1,200 men, and Jenkins was elected colonel.

The 5th South Carolina was sent to Virginia and fought in the Battle of First Manassas. Jenkins became an acting brigade commander during the Peninsula Campaign, fighting at Williamsburg and Seven Pines, where he was wounded in the knee. "General Jenkins was magic," one of his men recalled. "He could come nearer to making his men work like machinery than any other man I saw. . . . We fought five fresh lines that evening and whipped every one."

Colonel Jenkins also fought in the Seven Days Battles. At Frayser's Farm, his aide was killed at his side, his horse was shot twice, his reins were cut in two by bullets, his sword was struck three times, he received three flesh wounds from Union shrapnel, and his right arm was badly wounded by a Union shell. After he recovered, Micah Jenkins was promoted to brigadier general on July 22, 1862.

That same month, Jenkins's brigade was assigned to James Longstreet's I Corps. General Jenkins was severely wounded in the abdomen during the Battle of Second Manassas and did not return to duty for several weeks. He then fought in the Battle of Fredericksburg, where his brigade was only lightly engaged.

In 1863, Jenkins and his men fought in the Siege of Suffolk (April–May 1863). When General Robert E. Lee invaded Pennsylvania, Jenkins's brigade was assigned to defend Richmond. It then rejoined Longstreet's corps and went with it to Tennessee. Longstreet named Jenkins—whom he considered one of the best young officers in the army—acting divisional commander of John Bell Hood's division after Hood had assumed a corps command and had been wounded. Jenkins's promotion infuriated General Evander Law, who believed the position should have been his. The acrimony between the two generals forced President Jefferson Davis to personally intervene. In early February 1864, he promoted Charles Field to major general and gave him command of the division. Jenkins reverted to the command of his brigade.

On May 6, 1864, during the Battle of the Wilderness, members of the 12th Virginia mistook Jenkins's men for Yankees and unleashed a volley into them. Longstreet was critically wounded, a staff officer and an orderly were killed, and a minié ball struck Jenkins in the forehead and lodged in his brain. General Jenkins died six hours after he was shot. He was twenty-eight years old.

Micah Jenkins was buried in Summerville, South Carolina. Seventeen years later, he was reburied in Magnolia Cemetery in Charleston, where he still lies.

ADAM RANKIN "STOVEPIPE" JOHNSON was born in Henderson, Kentucky, on February 8, 1834, the son of a medical doctor. He began working at a drugstore when he was twelve but left this job in 1854

to move to Texas, where he became a surveyor on the Western frontier, an Indian fighter, and a stagecoach driver.

When the war began, Johnson returned to Kentucky and enlisted in the Confederate Army as a private and a scout for Nathan Bedford Forrest. He rose to chief of scouts and was with Forrest when he escaped from Fort Donelson in February 1862. The loss of this fortress resulted in the loss of Kentucky and middle Tennessee. Johnson responded by returning to the Bluegrass State and recruiting a regiment, the 10th Kentucky Partisan Rangers, behind Union lines.

Johnson's exploits became legendary. On July 18, 1862, he forced two thousand pro-Union local defense troops to evacuate Newburgh, Indiana, by creating fake cannons (made of stovepipes mounted on wagon wheels) and threatening to reduce the town to rubble if it did not surrender. It did. Johnson had a dozen men with him at the time.

Newburgh was the first Northern town captured by the Rebels, and Johnson's feat was a major news story in the South and even in Europe, winning him the nickname "Stovepipe." Federal forces that otherwise could have been fighting Confederate armies had to be redeployed to guard the Ohio River.

General Braxton Bragg promoted Johnson to colonel in August 1862. Johnson continued to raid behind Union lines and earned a second nickname as the "Swamp Fox of the Confederacy." As a brigade commander, he took part in John Hunt Morgan's Ohio Raid. After Morgan's disastrous defeat at the Battle of Buffington Island on July 19, Johnson broke off from the rest of Morgan's division, crossed to the south side of the Ohio with 350 men, and escaped with his command. Morgan was forced to surrender on July 26.

On August 21, 1864, one of Johnson's own men accidentally shot him in a skirmish near Princeton, Kentucky. He was blinded for life and captured. Apparently not aware that he was blind, the War Department promoted Johnson to brigadier general on September 6, 1864, to rank from June 1.

General Johnson was imprisoned at Fort Warren, Massachusetts, but was exchanged near the end of the war. He applied to return to active duty, but the war ended before his request could be considered.

Johnson refused to let his blindness handicap him. He was noted for his cheerfulness, his sharp mind, and his industriousness. He formed several businesses, worked to develop the water resources of the Colorado River, and founded the city of Marble Falls, Texas. He also wrote a memoir, *The Partisan Rangers of the Confederate States Army*, which was published in 1904.

Stovepipe Johnson died at Burnet, Texas, on October 20, 1922, at eighty-eight. He is buried in Texas State Cemetery, Austin, at the foot of Republic Hill, not far from the graves of Albert Sidney Johnston and Stephen F. Austin.

BRADLEY TYLER JOHNSON was born on September 29, 1829, in Frederick, Maryland. He graduated from the College of New Jersey (Princeton) in 1849, read law in Frederick, completed his legal studies at Harvard, and was admitted to the bar in 1851. He dabbled in politics and was elected the state's attorney for Frederick County and chairman of the Maryland Democratic Party. As a delegate to the Baltimore Democratic Convention of 1860, he strongly supported John C. Breckinridge for president and joined with other Southern delegates in walking out when the party chose Stephen Douglas as its nominee.

When the war began, he organized and equipped a company at his own expense. On May 22, 1861, he became a captain of the Maryland Volunteers and took a major role in organizing the 1st Maryland Infantry. He was rapidly promoted to major (June 17), lieutenant colonel (July 21), and colonel, commanding the regiment (March 18, 1862). Johnson led the 1st Maryland in Stonewall Jackson's celebrated Valley Campaign of 1862.

Stonewall Jackson was impressed by Johnson's performance and recommended that he be promoted to brigadier general on more than one occasion. His recommendations, however, were not acted upon, because no Maryland brigade existed for Johnson to command, though Johnson was widely recognized as a fine regimental commander. He fought in the Seven Days Battles, the Battle of Second Manassas (where he was an acting brigade commander), and the Maryland Campaign.

He was finally appointed brigadier general on June 28, 1864, initially at temporary rank. He was not confirmed at full rank until February 20, 1865. He fought in General Jubal Early's Shenandoah Valley Campaign of 1864 and played a role in the burning of Chambersburg, Pennsylvania.

Heavy casualties led to the consolidation of General Early's cavalry, and Johnson—a Marylander—was the odd man out. He was named commandant of the post at Salisbury, North Carolina, which included a prisoner-of-war camp. Here, Johnson did everything he could to mitigate the suffering of the prisoners.

After the surrender, Johnson practiced law in Richmond. He served in the Virginia Senate from 1875 to 1877. Around 1879, he moved to Amelia, Virginia, although he frequently returned home to Maryland. He wrote numerous historical articles, two biographies (one on George Washington and one on Joseph E. Johnston), and the Maryland portion of the *Confederate Military History*.

Bradley Tyler Johnson died on October 5, 1903, in Amelia, Virginia, at the age of seventy-four. He is buried in Loudon Park Cemetery, Baltimore.

BUSHROD RUST JOHNSON was born in Belmont County, Ohio, on October 7, 1817. His family were Quakers (pacifists) and strong abolitionists, and his uncle even worked on the Underground Railroad. Bushrod gained admission to West Point in 1836 and graduated in 1840. Commissioned in the infantry, he fought in the Seminole and Mexican Wars. He was placed in the quartermaster department at Veracruz while his regiment drove on Mexico City. Johnson was forced to resign his commission on October 27, 1847, after he was caught attempting to sell contraband goods and offering a bribe to a superior officer.

Johnson secured an appointment as a professor of natural philosophy and chemistry at the Western Military Institute in Georgetown, Kentucky, and later at the Military College of the University of Nashville. When war came, he was named colonel of engineers in the Tennessee Provisional Army on June 28, 1861, and served as state mustering officer at Camp Trousdale.

Johnson was a quiet man, friendly and affable, but also, as a colleague at the University of Nashville recalled, "retiring, reserved and diffident, slow and cautious of speech." Though some doubted his leadership capabilities, he secured a nomination to brigadier general on January 24, 1862.

General Albert Sidney Johnston sent him to Fort Donelson, where, during the night of February 15–16, 1862, Generals John B. Floyd, Gideon J. Pillow, and Simon B. Buckner decided to surrender; Johnson was left out of the deliberations. In the chaotic situation immediately after the surrender, several unparoled Confederates simply walked out of the fort and made their way to Rebel lines. One of them was General Johnson. He was given command of a brigade in the Army of Mississippi, which he led at the Battle of Shiloh until he suffered a concussion from a Union artillery shell that exploded near him.

General Johnson led a brigade during the Kentucky Campaign of 1862, including the Battle of Perryville, where he did well. He also fought in the Second Battle of Murfreesboro and the Battle of Hoover's Gap in the Tullahoma Campaign.

During the Battle of Chickamauga, Johnson commanded a provisional division and performed brilliantly. He accompanied General James Longstreet to Knoxville, where Longstreet's I Corps was defeated in the Battle of Fort Sanders.

Johnson was then selected to command a division in General G. T. Beauregard's Department of North Carolina and Southern Virginia.

He took part in the Bermuda Hundred Campaign and successfully blocked the Union advance on Petersburg at Swift Creek on May 9, 1864. He was promoted to major general on May 21, 1864.

Johnson spent nine months in the siege lines around Petersburg and performed lethargically in the Battle of the Crater. Later, his division formed the major part of Richard Anderson's IV Corps. Both of these commanders had lost faith in eventual victory, and the defeatist attitude of one commander reinforced the defeatist attitude of the other. Their attitudes were reflected in their performance. On April 6, 1865, during the retreat to Appomattox, Anderson's corps, together with General Richard Ewell's command, was swamped by the Federals at Sayler's Creek. Both Anderson and Johnson fled the battlefield. After he learned some of the details of this debacle, Robert E. Lee relieved both generals of their commands on April 8. Without a command, Bushrod Johnson remained with the Army of Northern Virginia to Appomattox, where it surrendered the next day.

After the war, General Johnson returned to academia and in 1870 became co-chancellor of the University of Nashville, along with Edmund Kirby Smith. Johnson then established a preparatory school, which failed financially and was forced to shut its doors. A somewhat despondent Johnson returned to the North, where he became a farmer near Brighton, Illinois. His health declined, and he was partly paralyzed near the end of his life. He passed away on September 12, 1880, at age sixty-two. He was buried in Miles Station Cemetery near Brighton. In August 1975, he was reinterred next to his wife in Nashville City Cemetery, Nashville, Tennessee.

EDWARD "ALLEGHENY" JOHNSON was born on the plantation of Salisbury, Chesterfield County, Virginia, on April 16, 1816. His family moved to Kentucky shortly after. He attended West Point and graduated in 1838. He served in the West, fought in the Seminole Wars, and then returned to the Western frontier. He

distinguished himself in the Mexican War, where he was brevetted twice (to captain and major), was wounded at least once, and was awarded a sword by the Virginia legislature for his bravery. He returned to the Western frontier after Mexico and served in the Dakota Territory, California, and Kansas and in the Utah Expedition. He was promoted to captain (regular rank) in 1851.

Johnson was heavy, rough-looking, often rude and a lifelong bachelor. He was nevertheless quite a ladies' man. Due to his wound from Mexico, one of his eyes winked uncontrollably. Women often thought he was flirting with them, even when he wasn't. He was, however, noted for his love—of taffy.

Captain Johnson became a strong secessionist. He "went south" and was appointed colonel of the 12th Georgia on July 2, 1861. He was sent to the Allegheny Mountains of western Virginia, where he served under Robert E. Lee, who gave him command of a brigade. On December 13, he occupied the summit of Allegheny Mountain when he was attacked by a brigade under Union General Robert H. Milroy. With a musket in one hand and a club in the other, he led a counterattack and drove the Yankees down the mountain, personally killing or wounding several in the process. For this victory, he received the nom de guerre "Allegheny" and was promoted to brigadier general on December 13, 1861.

Johnson joined Stonewall Jackson in the Valley Campaign. On May 8, 1862, during the Confederate victory at McDowell, he was shot in the ankle. It took him a year to recover. He was promoted to major general on February 28, 1863, probably because General Lee thought highly of him.

When Lee reorganized the Army of Northern Virginia after the Battle of Chancellorsville, Johnson was given command of Stonewall Jackson's old division. At Gettysburg, late in the day on July 1, he missed an opportunity to attack Culp's Hill before the Yankees could reinforce it and dig in. Many historians have blamed General Richard Ewell and General Johnson for losing the Battle of Gettysburg. Johnson did try to take Culp's Hill on July 2 and 3 but was unsuccessful. During the battle, he was wounded, and his horse was shot out from under him.

Johnson played a prominent role in the Mine Run campaign, in which Lee's army (forty-eight thousand men) checked a Union army of eighty-one thousand men. He also fought well in the Battle of the Wilderness, and Lee considered making him an acting corps commander, replacing the wounded James Longstreet, but eventually elevated Richard H. Anderson instead.

During the Battle of Spotsylvania Court House, Johnson's division held a dangerously exposed salient called the Mule Shoe. Here, on May 12, 1864, Johnson was attacked by an entire corps. The majority of his division was killed or captured in hand-to-hand fighting. General Johnson was among the prisoners.

Allegheny Johnson was exchanged on August 3, 1864. He was then sent to command a division in the final struggle for Atlanta. Later, he fought in the battles of Franklin and Nashville, where he was captured again on December 16. He was paroled on July 22, 1865.

Although he definitely misfired at Gettysburg, Johnson was generally a reliable brigade and division commander. After the war, he returned to Chesterfield County and became a farmer. He died in Richmond on February 22, 1873, at age fifty-six. He was buried in Hollywood Cemetery, Richmond. His grave marker is a cenotaph.

ALBERT SIDNEY JOHNSTON was born on February 2, 1803, in Maysville, Kentucky, the son of a Connecticut physician. He attended Transylvania University in Lexington, where he met Jefferson Davis, a fellow student who was studying law. They became lifelong friends.

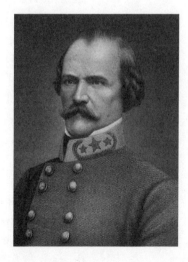

Johnston graduated from West Point in 1826. Commissioned a second lieutenant of infantry, he fought in the Black Hawk War (1832). He resigned in 1834 to take care of his wife, who had tuberculosis. She died in the summer of 1835. The following year, he moved to Texas, enlisted in its army, and on August 5, 1836, was commissioned a colonel and made adjutant general of the Army of the Republic of Texas.

Albert Sidney Johnston was a man of commanding appearance. He was tall (six feet one), well-built, and handsome. He had broad shoulders, a massive chest, and a firm, square jaw. He was strong and energetic, with a simple and direct manner, and was noted for his ramrod-straight military bearing. Simply put, he *looked* like a general, and on December 22, 1836, Texas president Sam Houston promoted him to senior brigadier general in command of the Texas army.

In late 1838, Johnston was named secretary of war for the Republic of Texas. In his new post, Johnston imposed discipline on the army and waged a successful campaign against the Indians of northern Texas. After his term expired in February 1840, he lived in Kentucky for a few years, then moved back to Texas and settled at his China Grove Plantation in Brazoria County. He rejoined the U.S. Army as colonel of the 1st Texas Rifle Regiment when the Mexican War began. Johnston fought at the battles around Monterrey and at Buena Vista, where he showed incredible courage.

After Antonio López de Santa Anna's forces in northern Mexico had been decisively defeated, Johnston returned to his plantation, where he experienced hard times financially. In December 1849, he returned to the U.S. Army when President Zachary Taylor recommissioned him as a major. For the next eleven years he served on the Western frontier, first as a paymaster and then as a cavalry officer, becoming colonel of the newly forming 2nd U.S. Cavalry in 1855. He later served in Kansas (Fort Riley) during the "Bleeding Kansas" era. In November 1857, he assumed command of U.S. forces that were ordered to install Alfred Cummings as governor of Utah, a move opposed by the Mormon colonists. He was brevetted brigadier general for his services in Utah.

Johnston commanded the Department of the Pacific (1860–61) but resigned his commission after he learned that Texas had seceded. He joined the pro-Confederate Los Angeles Mounted Rifles in California and rode across the desert to the Confederate Territory of Arizona, where he arrived on July 4.

Meanwhile, on May 30, 1861, Jefferson Davis had appointed him to the rank of full general. He was the second highest-ranking general in the Southern Army, outranked only by Samuel Cooper. On September 10, he was given command of the Department of the West, which encompassed all Confederate forces west of the Allegheny Mountains except the coastal areas.

Johnston struggled with huge logistical difficulties, especially in terms of men, arms, and ammunition. He had fewer than forty thousand men—many of them poorly armed—to cover a massive front. He faced ninety thousand Federals under U.S. Generals Ulysses Grant, William Sherman, and George Thomas. Yet by raids and aggressive patrolling, Johnston convinced Sherman that the Rebel main force (called the Army of Central Kentucky) badly outnumbered the Yankees. Sherman was so harassed by the Confederates that he suffered a mental and emotional breakdown and had to be relieved.

Sooner or later, most bluffs are called. On January 19, 1862, Confederate General Felix Zollicoffer was defeated and killed in the Battle of Mill Springs. That defeat unhinged Johnston's right flank. The fall of Fort Henry and the surrender of Fort Donelson broke his left flank. He was forced to abandon Kentucky and most of Tennessee, including Nashville.

Johnston decided to concentrate his forces at Corinth, Mississippi, then advance north, launch a surprise attack on Grant's Army of the Tennessee at Shiloh Church, and destroy it. His plan almost worked. The Confederate attack of April 6, 1862, achieved complete surprise. Johnston pushed Grant back toward Pittsburg Landing and into his last line of defense.

Albert Sidney Johnston seemed to be everywhere during the battle. At one point, he saw a group of severely wounded Yankees. He ordered his personal surgeon to tend to them. This was a fatal mistake. At about 2:30 p.m., while he was leading a charge against the Peach Orchard, a bullet struck him behind the right knee. It nicked the popliteal artery and his boot filled with blood. Johnston did not realize how seriously he was injured. Finally, his volunteer aide, Isham Harris, noted that Johnston was pale and about to faint. Harris and some staff officers pulled him from his horse and carried him to a small ravine. By this time, the general was unconscious. They sent for a doctor, but by the time one arrived, Albert Sidney Johnston was dead. He was fifty-nine years old. He was the highest-ranking officer on either side to be killed in action during the Civil War.

Ironically, when they examined the body, they found a tourniquet in his pocket.

Jefferson Davis later cited Johnston's death as the turning point of Confederate fortunes during the war.

How good a general was Albert Sidney Johnston? He died so early in the war that it is hard to tell. But that he was a hero of the first order cannot, in my opinion, be questioned.

General Johnston was initially buried in New Orleans. After the war, he was reinterred in Texas State Cemetery in Austin, where the Lone Star State buries its heroes.

GEORGE DOHERTY JOHNSTON was born in Hillsborough, North Carolina, on May 30, 1832. In 1834, his father (also named George) moved the family to Greensboro, Alabama, but died unexpectedly two weeks later. George was raised and homeschooled by his aunt, who was also his legal guardian. He attended Howard College and graduated in law at Cumberland University in Lebanon, Tennessee. He was admitted to the bar and established a law practice in Marion, Alabama, in 1855. He was elected mayor in 1856 and also served in the legislature (1857–58).

On April 6, 1861, George Johnston was commissioned as a second lieutenant in the 4th Alabama Infantry Regiment and fought in the Battle of First Manassas. Johnston was commissioned a major in the newly formed 25th Alabama Infantry on January 8, 1862. Stationed initially at Mobile, the regiment was sent north and fought at Shiloh. After the regimental commander was wounded, Johnston assumed command of the 25th. He was promoted to lieutenant colonel, and Johnston led the regiment during Braxton Bragg's invasion of Kentucky and in the Second Battle of Murfreesboro, where Johnston was wounded. After he recovered, he took part in the Tullahoma Campaign. Finally, on September 14, 1863, he was promoted to colonel.

Colonel Johnston fought in the Battle of Chickamauga, the Siege of Chattanooga, the Battle of Missionary Ridge, and the Atlanta Campaign, distinguishing himself in the Battle of Atlanta on July 22. He was promoted to brigadier general on July 26. Two days later, during the Battle of Ezra Church, George Johnston was seriously wounded when a bullet went through his leg.

Johnston spent most of General John Bell Hood's Tennessee Campaign on crutches. After Brigadier General William Quarles was wounded during the Battle of Franklin, Johnston assumed command of his brigade and led it in the Battle of Nashville. It formed part of Hood's rear guard as he retreated to Alabama and Mississippi.

Johnston took part in every major engagement of the Army of Mississippi/Tennessee from Shiloh to Bentonville. When General Joseph E. Johnston decided to surrender, George Johnston refused and joined General Richard Taylor in Alabama. Apparently, he was never paroled.

After the war, Johnston resumed practicing law in Alabama. In 1868, he moved to Tuscaloosa, where he was commandant of cadets at the University of Alabama. Later, he was superintendent of the South Carolina Military Academy and the U.S. Civil Service Commissioner during President Grover Cleveland's second term.

Johnston returned to Tuscaloosa and was elected to the state senate. He died in Tuscaloosa on December 8, 1910, at the age of seventy-eight. He was buried there in Greenwood Cemetery.

JOSEPH EGGLESTON "JOE" JOHNSTON was born at Longwood House (Cherry Grove) near Farmville, Virginia, on February 3, 1807. He grew up in Abingdon in far southwest Virginia and was educated at home and in the Abingdon Academy. He graduated from West Point in 1829.

Johnston was assigned to the 4th U.S. Artillery Regiment. He resigned his commission in 1837 but rejoined the army in 1838. Ironically, he first saw combat in Florida as a civilian employee of the Topographical Bureau, in between his army stints, during the Second Seminole War.

Joe Johnston was a friendly, if parsimonious, junior officer who was popular with his men. He was, however, fussy, overly ambitious, and very jealous of his prerogatives. He sought to advance himself, even if it meant unfairly elbowing aside men with greater claim to promotion than he, and he was not afraid to use political influence for his own interests. He did, however, radiate an air of dignity and self-assurance. He certainly was not afraid of hard work, his courage was beyond question, and—according to Dabney Maury, who knew him well—he studied military history and biography more thoroughly than anyone in the country.

When the Mexican War broke out, he was attached to the staff of General Winfield Scott's Army of Mexico and fought from Veracruz to Mexico City. He was severely wounded twice and was brevetted lieutenant colonel. He was named second-in-command of the newly formed U.S. Regiment of Voltigeurs, a unit of light infantry or skirmishers. He fought at Contreras, Churubusco, and Chapultepec, where he was again wounded and brevetted colonel of volunteers.

After a period of occupation duty in Mexico, he continued to labor as a topographical engineer. He also constantly bombarded his superiors for higher rank and took the untenable position that his brevet (honorary) colonelcy entitled him to the regular rank of full colonel.

John B. Floyd, Johnston's cousin by marriage, became secretary of war in 1857. In a ruling that reeked of nepotism, he recognized Johnston as a full colonel. This was an unprecedented action. No other brevet colonels were so favored, and it clearly demonstrated that Johnston was prepared to use favoritism and politics to advance his own career. On June 10, 1860, the quartermaster general of the army died. Ignoring better qualified candidates, Secretary Floyd picked Johnston to succeed him. He was promoted to brigadier general (staff rank) on June 28.

Johnston enjoyed his new rank but not his new position. He disliked paperwork and did such a poor job that he became the subject of a Congressional investigation.

Virginia seceded on April 17, 1861. Johnston resigned his commission on April 22 and was named a major general in the Provisional Army of Virginia the next day. He was promptly placed in charge of the Confederate forces in the Shenandoah Valley and was named brigadier general in the Confederate Regular Army on May 14. By July, Johnston's Army of the Shenandoah numbered twelve thousand men. He was ordered to Manassas at 1:00 a.m. on July 18. He responded rapidly and played a major role in the Confederate victory in the First Battle of Bull Run on July 21. President Jefferson Davis, who was on the field of battle, wanted to pursue the Union Army after it was routed, but Johnston advised against it, and Davis did not overrule him—a huge blunder. Davis later said it was the worst mistake he made during the war.

Joseph E. Johnston was touchy about any criticism, and he did not like to be supervised. He was also poor at communicating. He was promoted to full general on August 31, 1861, but with a date of rank of July 4, 1861. Johnston was grossly offended to rank only fourth on the list of seniority among Confederate generals. He wrote President Davis a churlish letter, opening a wound that never healed, because Davis, like Johnston, was a man who never forgot an insult (real or imagined).

The Union Army of the Potomac landed on the Virginia Peninsula in the spring of 1862. Johnston shifted to the southeast to meet it and retreated from Yorktown to positions six miles from Richmond. Union soldiers were able to hear church bells ringing in the Confederate capital.

Wanting to push back U.S. General George McClellan from the gates of Richmond, Johnston launched a counterattack at Seven Pines on May 31, 1862. It was his first major battle as a general. His orders were fundamentally flawed: too complex and inadequately explained. The result was confusion. The battle deteriorated into a series of brigade and regimental actions. Johnston's counteroffensive was checked at a cost of more than six thousand Confederate casualties.

Late in the day, Johnston ventured too close to the front. A Union musket ball slammed into his shoulder. A moment later, an enemy artillery shell exploded, hurling shrapnel into his chest and thigh. Johnston was so seriously wounded that his convalescence took six months. He was replaced by Robert E. Lee.

When General Johnston returned to duty, President Davis gave him command of the Department of the West, which included all Confederate forces between the Mississippi River and the Appalachian Mountains, excluding some coastal regions. He assumed command on December 4, 1862, and held it until December 16, 1863.

Johnston's two major commanders were General Braxton Bragg of the Army of Tennessee and General John C. Pemberton of the Army of Mississippi. Bragg was controversial and unpopular, but Johnston endorsed him enthusiastically and even transferred almost all of Pemberton's cavalry to Bragg. Pemberton was thus deprived of reconnaissance as General Grant advanced on Jackson, Mississippi.

On May 18, 1863, Pemberton's Army of Mississippi was surrounded at Vicksburg, a position Johnston had wanted Pemberton to abandon. As a commander, Johnston was cautious, almost invariably preferring to give up key positions and even vital cities rather than risk losing a battle. President Davis, however, wanted Vicksburg held, and ordered Johnston to form an "Army of Relief" to rescue it. Johnston's efforts to save Vicksburg were perfunctory at best. Vicksburg surrendered on July 4. Johnston blamed Davis for interfering in his command and Pemberton for following the orders of the Confederate president; they blamed Johnston, as did Secretary of War James Seddon, for not supporting the Army of Mississippi. Despite this acrimony, when Braxton Bragg resigned his command on December 2, 1863, after his defeat at Missionary Ridge, President Davis chose Joseph E. Johnston to replace him.

Johnston proved better in this role, and the Atlanta Campaign, which began on May 4, 1864, is considered Johnston's flawed tactical masterpiece. As Sherman advanced, Johnston fell back slowly, avoided encirclement, and inflicted heavy casualties on the Yankees. Johnston even won a significant defensive victory at Kennesaw Mountain on June

27. Unfortunately, this campaign was also Sherman's masterpiece. He outflanked Johnston several times and forced him to give up 110 miles of easily defended mountainous territory in just two months. The Confederate army commander desperately needed Forrest's cavalry (which was denied him) to raid Sherman's lengthy supply lines, was unable to organize a major attack against Sherman's turning movements, and made the mistake of being uncommunicative with the president, refusing to assure him that he would defend Atlanta rather than abandon it. Jefferson Davis sacked Johnston on July 17, 1864.

Joseph E. Johnston's historic reputation benefited greatly from the fact that he was succeeded by John Bell Hood, who was as reckless as Johnston was cautious. Hood launched a series of poorly conceived attacks that left the Army of Tennessee with too few men to defend Atlanta, which fell on September 2, 1864. Hood then invaded Tennessee, with disastrous results.

On January 31, 1865, President Davis named Robert E. Lee general-in-chief of the Confederate Army (a new position, created by the Confederate Congress to limit President Davis's military responsibilities). Lee, with Davis's acquiescence, appointed Johnston commander of the Army of Tennessee on February 22.

Johnston attempted to smash part of Sherman's army at the Battle of Bentonville on March 19–21 but was unsuccessful. Johnston surrendered at Bennett Place near Durham, North Carolina, on April 26. General Sherman gave him generous terms.

After the war, Johnston eventually became quite successful in the insurance business. This gave him time to write his memoirs, *Narrative of Military Operations*, which was published in 1874. Johnston portrayed himself as a military genius and blamed every failure on President Davis or other generals. The book was dishonest, hateful, and self-serving in the extreme and made Johnston appear small and petty. Sales were poor, and the publisher lost money.

Johnston moved to Richmond and was elected to Congress in 1878 but disliked making speeches and did not run for reelection in 1880. President Grover Cleveland appointed him commissioner of railroads in 1885. He lost his job after President Cleveland was defeated for reelection in 1888.

General Johnston retired to his home on Connecticut Avenue in Washington, D.C. He never forgot the generous terms Sherman gave him at Bennett Place and would not allow anyone to criticize his erstwhile opponent in his presence. On February 19, 1891, he served as an honorary pallbearer at Sherman's funeral. Despite the weather, which was cold and wet, he refused to put on his hat. He caught a cold, which developed into pneumonia that killed him, although this might be romantic legend. He did not die until March 21, and his death certificate states that he died of heart failure, after an illness of three weeks. In any event, he was buried in Green Mount Cemetery, Baltimore, Maryland. He was, and will remain, one of the most controversial figures of the Civil War and—in this author's opinion—the most overrated of all of the Confederate generals.

ROBERT DANIEL JOHNSTON was born on March 19, 1837, in Lincoln County, North Carolina. He was a first cousin of Confederate Generals William H. and John H. Forney. He graduated from the University of North Carolina in 1858, studied law at the University of Virginia, was admitted to the North Carolina bar, and started a practice.

When North Carolina seceded, Johnston was a second lieutenant in the Beattie's Ford Rifles, a county militia unit. He and four of his brothers joined the Confederate Army. (One of them, James Forney Johnston, later became a governor and United States senator from Alabama.) Daniel became a captain and company commander in the 23rd North Carolina Infantry on July 15, 1861. He became lieutenant colonel of the regiment on April 16, 1862. Sent to Virginia, he first saw combat at the Battle of Williamsburg on May 5. He was wounded in the face and neck at the Battle of Seven Pines but nevertheless became temporary commander of his regiment. He fought at South Mountain (where he was officially cited for bravery), Sharpsburg, Chancellorsville, and Gettysburg, where he was wounded again. At Chancellorsville, he briefly assumed command of the 12th North Carolina after all its field-grade officers became casualties.

The 23rd North Carolina was part of General Alfred Iverson's brigade, which was slaughtered at Gettysburg. After General Robert E. Lee sacked Iverson, Johnston was the senior surviving officer of the brigade. He became brigade commander, was promoted to brigadier general on September 1, 1863, and did much to restore the morale of the unit. He distinguished himself again in the Wilderness and was severely wounded during the Battle of Spotsylvania Court House. After he recovered, he fought at Cold Harbor, in the Siege of Petersburg, in the Shenandoah Valley Campaign of 1864, and at Petersburg again. In March 1865, Johnston was on detached duty to defend a sector of the Roanoke River and to round up deserters. He thus missed the Appomattox Campaign. Johnston was paroled at Charlotte, North Carolina, the following month.

After the war, Johnston remained in Charlotte and practiced law. In 1887, he moved to Alabama, where he assumed the presidency of the First National Bank of Birmingham. He was very successful, made many wise business investments, and was involved in mining promotions.

General Robert Daniel Johnston died at the home of a son on February 1, 1919, in Winchester, Virginia. He was eighty-one years of age. He is buried in Stonewall Jackson Cemetery, Winchester.

DAVID RUMPH "NEIGHBOR" JONES was born on April 5, 1825, in Orangeburg County, South Carolina, but his family moved to central Georgia when he was a child. He enrolled at the U.S. Military Academy in 1842 and graduated in 1846. Jones was assigned to the 2nd U.S. Infantry in upstate New York. Jones and his regiment, however, were soon involved in the Mexican War, fighting from Veracruz to Mexico City. He was brevetted first lieutenant and captain for his bravery and gallant service.

After a brief period of occupation duty in Mexico, Jones sailed via Cape Horn to California in 1848, where he skirmished with Indians and protected forty-niners. In 1851, he returned to West Point as a tactics instructor.

Jones was tall, stately, and gregarious. His outgoing personality earned him the nickname "Neighbor."

Captain Jones resigned his commission on February 15, 1861, and on March 6, 1861, joined the Confederate Army as a major and commissary for the forces near Charleston, South Carolina. Shortly after, he was named chief of staff to General G. T. Beauregard. He was with the general during the bombardment of Fort Sumter on April 12 and 13.

Beauregard was quick to recognize Jones's abilities and designated him for promotion. On June 17, 1861, David Jones was named brigadier general and was given command of a brigade, which played a minor role at the Battle of First Manassas.

In February 1862, Jones was given command of a division in General John B. Magruder's command on the Virginia Peninsula. He was appointed major general on March 10.

Jones was an effective commander in the Battle of Yorktown, the retreat up the peninsula, and the Seven Days Battles. Throughout his career, he was cool in combat and showed excellent judgment. He drove the Yankees from the Thoroughfare Gap on August 27, 1862, helped rout the Federals at the Battle of Second Manassas, defended South Mountain during the Maryland Campaign, and played an important role in the Battle of Sharpsburg.

Neighbor Jones suffered from a heart ailment for years. The stress of war naturally made it worse. Shortly after Sharpsburg, he asked to be relieved for reasons of health. He was succeeded by his former West Point classmate, George Pickett. David R. Jones went on furlough at Richmond, where he died of a massive heart attack on January 20, 1863. He was thirty-seven years old. He was buried in Hollywood Cemetery, Richmond, Virginia.

JOHN MARSHALL JONES was born on July 26, 1820, in Charlottesville, Virginia. He attended West Point and graduated in 1841. During his cadetship, he was nicknamed "Rum" because of his fondness for alcoholic beverages. He was commissioned a second lieutenant in the infantry and served on the Western frontier until he became a tactics instructor at West Point (1845–52).

Jones was promoted to captain in 1855. He spent the period from 1855 to 1858 in a variety of posts and forts across the country and then took part in the Utah War in 1858. He remained there until 1860.

Rum Jones resigned his commission on May 27, 1861, and joined the Confederate Army as a captain of artillery. He was promoted to lieutenant colonel on September 4, 1861, and became an assistant adjutant general on the staff of Joe Johnston's Army of the Potomac. He transferred to Stonewall Jackson's staff in time to fight in Jackson's famous Valley Campaign of 1862. He remained with Jackson during the Seven Days Battles and the battles of Second Manassas, Fredericksburg, and Chancellorsville. He bypassed the rank of colonel, was promoted straight to brigadier general on May 15, 1863, and was given command of a brigade in Edward "Allegheny" Johnson's division. Such promotions were rare and usually accompanied by howls of protest from colonels. But it speaks well of John M. Jones that no such protests were recorded at his promotion.

Jones served in the Pennsylvania Campaign and took part in Allegheny Johnson's assault on Culp's Hill until a bullet in the thigh rendered him *hors de combat*. General Robert E. Lee praised him as "a good commander."

Rum Jones returned to fight in the Mine Run Campaign on the Rapidan River, where he was severely wounded in the Battle of Payne's Farm on November 27, 1863. He returned to duty later that winter.

The Overland Campaign began on May 4, 1864, and the Battle of the Wilderness began the next day. Jones's brigade was heavily attacked by the U.S. V Corps, and elements of his unit wavered and panicked. John Marshall Jones desperately tried to rally his men but was killed by the Federals. He was forty-three years old. His aide, Lieutenant Robert Early, a nephew of Jubal Early, was also killed.

General John Marshall Jones was buried in Maplewood Cemetery in Charlottesville.

JOHN ROBERT JONES was born in Rockingham County, Virginia, on March 12, 1827, the son of Irish immigrants. He was raised in Harrisonburg, Virginia, where he attended private schools. He was admitted to the Virginia Military Institute in 1845 and graduated in 1848. He became a teacher in Virginia and then principal of the military school in Urbana, Maryland. He took another teaching job in Florida just before the war.

In early January 1861, he commanded a Florida militia company that helped seize the Federal Arsenal at Apalachicola. A few weeks later, Jones returned to Rockingham, Virginia, and raised the Rockingham Confederates, which, after the Battle of First Manassas (July 21, 1861), became Company I of the 33rd Virginia Infantry. On August 21, 1861, Jones was elected lieutenant colonel and second-in-command of the 33rd.

The regiment was part of the Stonewall Brigade. It fought in the Battle of Kernstown (March 23, 1862), where Jones was commended for his gallantry by Stonewall Jackson.

The 33rd Virginia held elections in the spring of 1862, and Jones was successively defeated for colonel, lieutenant colonel, and major, but Stonewall Jackson then promoted him to brigade commander. He became a brigadier general on June 25, 1862. Five days later, during the Battle of White Oak Swamp, Jones was wounded in the knee by a piece of shrapnel. Sent to Richmond to recuperate, he contracted typhoid fever, which delayed his recovery several weeks. He rejoined Jackson's corps in Frederick, Maryland, during the first week of September 1862, where Jackson gave him command of his own former division—including the Stonewall Brigade.

It was not immediately apparent to Jackson or anyone else, but Jones's wounding, illness, and hospitalization had changed him. At Sharpsburg, a Union shell exploded over his head, leaving him, in his own words, so "stunned and injured ... that [he] was rendered unfit for duty, and retired from the field," causing some of his fellow officers wonder at his behavior. Then, at Fredericksburg, Jones's brigade moved forward, but Jones remained in the woods, hiding behind a tree. Suspicions of cowardice became accusations, and he was court-martialed on March 17, 1863. Jones was acquitted on April 18.

At Chancellorsville, Jones claimed that an ulcerated leg made him unfit for duty, and he again went to the rear while his men moved forward. General Robert E. Lee relieved him of his command. Jones submitted his resignation, but on July 4, 1863, he was captured in Maryland by a Union patrol. He spent the rest of the war in prison. The Confederate authorities made no attempt to secure his release.

After the war, Jones returned to Harrisonburg, Virginia, and became a successful businessman, selling farm implements and machinery. He served on the local school board and on the vestry of the Episcopal Church in Harrisonburg. He occasionally used his personal funds to buy farm machinery for poor local farmers who could not afford to pay.

Jones and his wife had no children, but he did have two babies by Malinda Rice, an African American, in 1875 and 1877. Shortly after his first wife's death, Jones remarried, but his second wife divorced him a year later on grounds of adultery. After this, Jones fathered two more biracial children.

J. R. Jones acknowledged his four children but was ostracized by his friends and neighbors. General Jones died on April 1, 1901, at age seventy-four. He paid for his eldest daughter's education (through college) and left his estate to his sons. Jones is buried in Woodbine Cemetery, Harrisonburg.

SAMUEL JONES was born at Woodfield, his family's plantation in Powhatan County, Virginia, on December 17, 1819. He graduated from West Point in 1841 and was commissioned a second lieutenant of artillery. Initially, he was posted to Houlton, Maine, during the border dispute with Canada. He missed the Mexican War, because from 1846 to 1851 he was an assistant professor of mathematics and an instructor of artillery and infantry tactics at West Point.

Lieutenant Jones was transferred to the staff of the Judge Advocate in Washington, D.C. On April 27, 1861, Jones, who had been promoted to captain, resigned his commission. In May, he joined the Confederate Army as a major of artillery.

In June 1861, Jones was promoted to colonel and chief of artillery and ordnance of the Confederate Army of the Potomac (a predecessor to the Army of Northern Virginia). He fought at the Battle of First Manassas and performed so well that the next day (July 22, 1861) he was promoted to brigadier general. He replaced Colonel Francis S. Barlow, who was killed at Bull Run, as brigade commander.

Jones was named commander of the Pensacola District on January 22, 1862, and was promoted to major general on March 10. On September 23, he was named commander of the Department of Western Virginia, where he defended the Virginia and Tennessee Railroad and the critical salt mines in southwestern Virginia. In September 1863, Jones was transferred to Charleston to replace G. T. Beauregard as the commander of the Department of South Carolina, Georgia, and Florida.

General Jones did a good job defending Charleston, preventing the U.S. Navy from entering the harbor and rebuffing a major Union infantry assault against Fort Sumter. He was superseded as department commander by Lieutenant General William J. Hardee in October 1864, but he retained command of the Department of South Carolina.

After Savannah fell on December 21, 1864, Samuel Jones was appointed commander of the Department of South Georgia and Florida. It was an isolated zone with no railroad or telegraphic communications with the rest of the Confederacy and few troops. The Federals, however, limited themselves to probes from Union-held Jacksonville. That meant that Jones's men spent most of their time fighting outlaw gangs rather than the Yankees. Jones held this post until the end of the war. He surrendered at Tallahassee on May 10, 1865. Tallahassee and Austin, Texas, were the only Confederate state capitals never captured during the war.

After the war, General Jones tried his hand at farming. In 1873, he became president of the Maryland Agricultural College (now the University of Maryland, College Park). He revised the curriculum, emphasizing science over classics, and established six departments (languages, mathematics, English, natural science, moral philosophy, and agriculture). In 1875, the board of directors, unsupportive of the changes, asked for his resignation. From 1875 to 1887, the former Confederate general worked in the adjutant general's office in Washington, D.C.

Samuel Jones was considered an accomplished gentleman who held to the highest ideals of conduct in both his professional life and his private life. He died on July 31, 1887, at Bedford Springs, Pennsylvania, at age sixty-seven. He is buried in Hollywood Cemetery, Richmond. He wrote a book, *The Siege of Charleston and the Operations on the South Atlantic Coast in the War among the States*, which was published posthumously.

WILLIAM EDMONDSON "GRUMBLE" JONES was born near the middle fork of the Holston River in Washington County, Virginia, on May 9, 1824. He graduated from Emory and Henry College in 1844 and then attended West Point, from which he graduated in 1848.

He was assigned to the Regiment of Mounted Rifles and spent his entire tour of duty with them, fighting Indians or serving on garrison duty in the Pacific Northwest.

In 1852, Jones returned home on a furlough, during which he married seventeen-year-old Eliza Margaret "Pink" Dunn, who was known for being beautiful, sweet, and "uncommonly brilliant." A few weeks later, they boarded the steamship *Independence* to return to his unit. Off the coast of Texas, the ship was wrecked, and Pink was literally swept from his arms and drowned. Jones was never the same after that. He became "eccentric [and] cantankerous," with "a razor sharp tongue . . . caring little for pretense and appearance." During this period, he was nicknamed "Grumble" by his peers because of his quarrelsome attitude, fierce temper, legendary ability to curse, and love of complaining. He never remarried.

Jones resigned his commission in 1857 and returned to Virginia as a farmer and virtual recluse. When Virginia seceded, the veteran Indian fighter was elected captain of the Washington Mounted Rifles, a local militia company. In May 1861, he was promoted to major in the 1st Virginia Cavalry. He fought in the Battle of First Manassas (July 21, 1861) and became colonel of the 1st Virginia Cavalry Regiment in August.

Grumble Jones was a harsh taskmaster. When the Confederate Congress passed a law allowing enlisted men to elect their officers, Jones was not elected. He transferred to the 7th Virginia Cavalry and became its commander during the Valley Campaign of 1862. After Turner Ashby was killed in action in June 1862, Colonel Jones succeeded him as commander of the Laurel Brigade.

After Stonewall Jackson's Valley campaign of 1862, Jones's brigade was transferred to J. E. B. Stuart's cavalry division (later a corps). Stuart disliked Jones personally but nevertheless called him "the best outpost officer in the army." He also considered Jones the most difficult man in the service. Jones and his command performed well at Orange Court House (where he was wounded), Cedar Mountain, the Battle of Second Manassas, and Sharpsburg. Stonewall Jackson recommended Jones for promotion, while J. E. B. Stuart tried to block it.

But General Robert E. Lee concurred with Jackson. Jones was promoted to brigadier general on September 19, 1862, and took command of the cavalry of the Valley District on December 29. Jones soon justified Jackson's faith in him. In the spring of 1863, he led a raid into western Virginia, smashed several Union formations, and returned having lost only twelve men.

Jones's brigade was attached to Stuart's corps for the Gettysburg Campaign. Stuart gave Jones's brigade only secondary missions, but it was nevertheless heavily engaged at Fairfield, Pennsylvania, on July 3, where it both protected a large Confederate wagon train and crushed the 6th U.S. Cavalry Regiment. The Yankees suffered 240 casualties; the Laurel Brigade, only 34.

In September 1863, the longstanding enmity between Jones and Stuart erupted into public view when Jones gave Stuart a piece of his mind. Stuart placed Jones under arrest for using disrespectful language to a superior, and he was court-martialed in Richmond. General Robert E. Lee, however, quietly intervened, as he often did in such disputes between his generals. Jones was found guilty on October 9, 1863, and transferred to the Trans-Allegheny Department—out of Stuart's area of responsibility.

Once again, Grumble Jones performed brilliantly, leading successful raids into East Tennessee and defeating a Union attempt to capture Saltville. In May 1864, Jones assumed command of the cavalry in the Shenandoah Valley and was ordered to defend Lynchburg against a Union thrust.

On July 5, 1864, Jones clashed with the Federals at Piedmont. He had about five thousand men (some of them infantry) to oppose about twice as many Yankees. Uncharacteristically, Jones left a large gap in his lines. The Northerners spotted it, pierced it, and routed Jones's forces. The general was shot in the head while trying to rally his men and died instantly. He was forty years old.

General Jones was buried by the enemy on the field. He was later reinterred at (Old) Glade Spring Presbyterian Church Cemetery, next to his wife.

THOMAS JORDAN was born on September 30, 1819, in Luray, Virginia. He was educated in local schools and gained admission to West Point, where his roommate was William T. Sherman. Jordan graduated in 1840 and was commissioned in the infantry. Initially assigned to Fort Snelling, Minnesota, he was sent to Florida to fight in the Second Seminole War.

Lieutenant Jordan was on frontier duty in the American West from 1843 to 1846. He fought in the Mexican War, during which he was promoted to captain in 1847 and joined the quartermaster branch. Jordan was in charge of all quartermaster arrangements for the evacuation of Mexico, including the land and sea transport of thirty-five thousand men, which brought him a special commendation from General David E. Twiggs.

Captain Jordan later served in Florida and the Indian Territory. In 1860, he was transferred to Washington, D.C. Anticipating war, he set up an effective pro-Southern spy organization in the nation's capital.

On May 21, 1861, Jordan resigned and joined the Confederacy as a captain. In June, he was promoted to lieutenant colonel and assigned to General G. T. Beauregard's staff. By July, he was Beauregard's adjutant general and chief of staff.

On March 29, 1862, at General Beauregard's suggestion, Albert Sidney Johnston named Jordan adjutant general of the Army of Mississippi (later the Army of Tennessee). He distinguished himself at Shiloh and was promoted to brigadier general on April 14, 1862.

Jordan served as General Braxton Bragg's adjutant general and chief of staff during the Kentucky campaign in the summer and fall of 1862. The two did not get along, and in 1863, General Jordan rejoined Beauregard in Charleston, South Carolina, as his chief of staff of the Department of South Carolina, Florida, and Georgia. In May 1864, he was appointed commander of the 3rd Military District of South Carolina—the only command he held during the war. He was apparently unemployed due to illness after August 1864.

After Charleston fell in February 1865, Jordan rejoined Beauregard in an unofficial capacity and was part of the Army of Tennessee, commanded by Joseph E. Johnston, when it surrendered on April 26, 1865.

After the war, Thomas Jordan proved that he was as fine a writer as he was a staff officer. He became editor of the Memphis *Appeal* newspaper, wrote articles for magazines, and, along with J. P. Pryor, coauthored *The Campaigns of Nathan Bedford Forrest and of Forrest's Cavalry*, which was published in 1868 and is still in print.

Later that year, the restless General Jordan accepted the post of chief of staff to the Cuban Mambi liberation army, where he again performed well, but the numbers were against him. Seeing that defeat was inevitable, Jordan resigned his commission and returned to the United States in an open boat in 1870. This ended his military career.

The former Confederate staff officer moved to New York City and became editor of the *Financial and Mining Record*.

Jordan had admired Jesuit missionaries for years but did not openly profess a religious creed until 1893, when he received the sacrament of baptism from the Society of Jesus at the Church of St. Francis Xavier. He was later confirmed by the Archbishop of New York.

General Thomas Jordan died on November 27, 1895, in New York City at age seventy-six. He was buried in Mount Hope Cemetery, Hastings-on-Hudson, New York.

K

KELLY – KIRKLAND

JOHN HERBERT KELLY was born in Carrollton, Pickens County, east-central Alabama, on March 31, 1840. He received an appointment to West Point at age seventeen, thanks to an uncle who was a congressman.

Kelly resigned from the military academy on December 29, 1860, and went to Montgomery, Alabama, which soon became the capital of the Confederacy. Here he was commissioned an artillery second lieutenant in the Confederate Regular Army and was sent to Fort Morgan, Alabama. He was promoted to captain on October 5 and was assigned to the staff of William J. Hardee, who was commanding forces in Arkansas. He was then sent to Pocahontas, Arkansas, where he helped organize the 14th Arkansas Infantry Regiment. He was promoted to major on September 23, 1861.

In early 1862, Major Kelly was named commander of the 9th Arkansas Infantry Battalion, which he led at Shiloh. He distinguished himself by leading a charge, ignoring enfilade fire from Union infantry and capturing an enemy battery. For his gallantry and general efficiency, he was promoted to colonel on May 5, 1862, and became commander of the 8th Arkansas Infantry Regiment on May 3.

Colonel Kelly led the 8th at Perryville and Murfreesboro, where he was wounded in the left arm. He was involved in the Tullahoma Campaign and fought at Chickamauga, where he commanded a large brigade and his horse was shot out from under him. He so impressed his superiors in this battle that he was recommended for promotion by Colonel John S. Preston and Generals Pat Cleburne and St. John R. Liddell. Cleburne personally told Secretary of War James Seddon that he knew no better officer in the army than Kelly. He was promoted to brigadier general on November 16, 1863. He was twenty-three years old.

Called the "Boy General of the Confederacy," Kelly was entrusted with the command of a cavalry division in Joseph Wheeler's corps. Attached to Cleburne's command, he played a major role in the Confederate victory at Pickett's Mill on May 27, 1864. Sherman tried to turn the Confederate right and lost 1,600 men in thirty minutes. The Southerners suffered 500 casualties. On September 2, 1864, while leading a charge near Franklin, Tennessee, General Kelly was shot in the chest by a Union infantryman. He was taken to the house of William H. Harrison but was too badly wounded to travel farther. The Rebels had no choice but to leave him, and he was captured by the enemy on September 3. John H. Kelly died the next day, September 4, 1864. He was twenty-four years old. Local residents bought him a coffin and new clothes, except for his uniform coat, which he was wearing when he fell.

General Kelly was buried in the gardens of the Harrison House, just south of Franklin, on the same day he died. In 1866, his body was removed to Magnolia Cemetery in Mobile, Alabama, where it lies today.

JAMES LAWSON KEMPER was born on June 11, 1823, at Mountain Prospect Plantation in Madison County, Virginia, the son of a successful merchant. He was educated at Old Field School, which was located on his father's plantation to educate local children, including James's lifelong friend, A. P. Hill. During the winters, he boarded at Locust Dale Academy. He graduated from Washington College when he was nineteen. He returned home, read law, and returned to Washington College, where he earned a master's degree in June 1845. He was admitted to the bar in 1846.

When the Mexican War broke out, Kemper secured a captain's commission in the 1st Virginia Infantry, which arrived in northern Mexico just after the Battle of Buena Vista and did not see action. He was discharged in 1848. He returned home and opened a law office in Madison County.

James Kemper was known for his hard work rather than being social. Politically, he was a Jacksonian Democrat. He was elected to the Virginia House of Delegates in 1853, became a brigadier general in the militia, and was among those who called for a secession convention in December 1860. Virginia left the Union on April 17, 1861.

Kemper was elected speaker of the house of delegates in 1861 and served until 1863, but he spent most of that time with the Confederate Army. He was commissioned colonel of the 7th Virginia Infantry in May 1861 and led it in the Battle of First Manassas. Later assigned to A. P. Hill's brigade, he fought in the Peninsula Campaign, including the Battle of Williamsburg. Kemper moved up to brigade commander on May 26, 1862, when Hill took charge of the Light Division. Kemper fought in the Battle of Seven Pines and was promoted to brigadier general on June 3, 1862.

During the Seven Days Battles, his brigade spearheaded the attack in the Battle of Frayser's Farm on June 30 and broke the Union line. Kemper then assumed command of a division.

In the Battle of Second Manassas, Kemper's division was part of General Longstreet's attack of August 30, which routed and nearly destroyed John Pope's Army of Virginia. Shortly after, Kemper was succeeded by Brigadier General David R. Jones. Reverting to the command of his old brigade, he fought in the Maryland Campaign and the Battle of Sharpsburg.

After an army reorganization, Kemper's brigade became part of George Pickett's new division. It was in reserve at Fredericksburg, was sent on detached duty, and then rejoined the main army after Chancellorsville.

Kemper's men arrived at Gettysburg late on July 2, 1863. They took part in Pickett's Charge, where Kemper rode his horse. A conspicuous target, he was shot in the thigh and abdomen and was captured. An assault party from the 1st Virginia rescued him, although Kemper thought he was mortally wounded. He was captured again during the Confederate retreat from Pennsylvania. On September 19, 1863, he was exchanged.

General Kemper was too badly injured to return to the field, so he was given command of Virginia's reserve forces. He was promoted to major general on September 19, 1864. He was paroled at Danville on May 2, 1865.

After the surrender, General Kemper returned to Madison and, in partnership with General John D. Imboden, became a bankruptcy attorney. Kemper reentered politics and ran for Congress in 1872 but lost. He ran for governor in 1873 and was handily elected.

Kemper's election ended Republican rule in Virginia. He was governor from January 1, 1874 to January 1, 1878. The big issue he faced was the state's war debt. He was an honest, fair, and frugal governor.

James Kemper lived in near constant pain from the wounds he suffered at Gettysburg. After his gubernatorial term ended, Kemper sold his Madison County property and retired to a place overlooking the Rapidan River near Orange County courthouse with his six surviving children. He named his new home "Walnut Hills." Meanwhile, complications from an old bullet wound—which was inoperable—caused paralysis on his left side. He died on April 7, 1895, at the age of seventy-one. The general is buried in the Kemper Family Cemetery, Orange, Virginia.

JOHN DOBY KENNEDY was born in Branham Heights, near Camden, South Carolina, on January 5, 1840, the son of a Scottish immigrant. John attended South Carolina College from 1855 to 1857 but apparently dropped out in order to get married.

Kennedy was a successful planter, and in 1860 his personal estate was valued at $335,000 ($10,513,107 in 2020 money). He owned sixty slaves. Meanwhile, he read law and was admitted to the bar in January 1861 but went to war instead of opening a law office.

Kennedy enlisted as a private but in April 1861 was elected captain of Company E, 2nd South Carolina Infantry. He was badly wounded in the Battle of First Manassas. After he recovered, he was elected colonel of the 2nd South Carolina. He fought in the Seven Days Battles but was ill after Savage's Station. Kennedy returned to duty in time for the Maryland Campaign, where he was involved in the capture of Harpers Ferry. He was severely wounded in the Battle of Sharpsburg when a bullet struck his Achilles tendon. He nevertheless returned to duty in time to fight at

Fredericksburg, where his regiment supported Thomas R. R. Cobb's brigade on Marye's Heights.

Colonel Kennedy fought at Chancellorsville and Gettysburg, where he was seriously wounded while charging a Union battery near the Peach Orchard. He rejoined his regiment, now engaged in the Siege of Knoxville, where he was again wounded. He was back on active duty for the Battle of the Wilderness. Here, he was wounded for the fifth time and almost died from a loss of blood. He was medically unfit to return to duty until around September. He was sent to the Shenandoah Valley, where he was given command of a badly depleted South Carolina brigade, which he led at Cedar Creek. John Kennedy was promoted to brigadier general on December 22, 1864.

Kennedy's brigade returned home to oppose Sherman in the Carolinas Campaign. It served with the Army of Tennessee until the surrender at Bennett Place on April 26, 1865.

In all, Kennedy was wounded six times during the war and was hit by fifteen spent balls. After the war, he became a farmer until, finally, after a delay of sixteen years, General Kennedy set up his law office in 1877.

He had been elected to Congress in December 1865 but was denied his seat because he would not take the "oath of allegiance."

Still, Kennedy was elected to the state legislature in 1878 and was elected lieutenant governor in 1880. In 1882, he ran for governor, but failed to secure the Democratic nomination. He retired from elective politics but in 1886 accepted the post of consul general to Shanghai, China. He returned home to Camden, where he again took up the practice of law.

John Doby Kennedy died of a stroke in Camden, South Carolina, on April 14, 1896, at age fifty-six. He is buried there in Quaker Cemetery.

JOSEPH BREVARD KERSHAW, who was of Scottish and Huguenot ancestry, was born on January 5, 1822, in

Camden, Kershaw County, South Carolina. He was part of the old South Carolina planter aristocracy.

Kershaw went to school in Camden and later the Cokesbury Conference School in the Abbeville area. He started his career as a clerk for a dry goods firm in Charleston but hated it. He returned home, read law, was admitted to the bar at age twenty-one, and set up a law office in Camden.

He and his law partner shut down their practice in 1846 in order to join the Palmetto Regiment and fight in the Mexican War. Kershaw was elected first lieutenant in the DeKalb Rifle Guards before he fell ill and was forced to return home. He resumed his law practice, entered the political arena, and was elected to the state legislature in 1852 and 1854. He was a member of the South Carolina Secession Convention in Charleston and was on Morris Island during the bombardment of Fort Sumter. He organized the 2nd South Carolina Infantry Regiment and was elected its colonel on May 22, 1861.

The 2nd South Carolina was sent to Virginia as part of Milledge L. Bonham's brigade. During the Battle of First Manassas, the 2nd and 8th South Carolina were detached to Stonewall Jackson at Henry House Hill and played a significant role in routing the Union Army. After General Bonham resigned to take his seat in the Confederate Congress, Kershaw assumed command of the brigade. He was promoted to brigadier general on February 1, 1862.

At Fredericksburg on December 13, he assumed command of the vital stonewall position on the sunken road at Marye's Heights after Thomas R. R. Cobb was killed. He repulsed the last two Yankee attacks. At Chickamauga, he served as acting commander of General Lafayette McLaws's division and helped destroy the right wing of the Union Army of the Cumberland. For the Siege of Knoxville, he reverted back to the command of his old brigade.

General Robert E. Lee did not normally promote people who were not professional soldiers to division command, but he made a few exceptions, such as John Gordon, Wade Hampton, and Joseph Kershaw, who was appointed to replace McLaws as division commander and became a major general on June 2, 1864.

Kershaw's division fought at Cold Harbor, served in the Shenandoah Valley, and defended against the siege of Richmond until Grant broke through and the Confederate capital was evacuated during the night of April 2–3, 1865.

Kershaw's division joined General Richard Ewell's ragtag command for the retreat to the west, but it was cut off at Sayler's Creek on April 6. Joseph Kershaw was among the prisoners.

After he was released from the prison at Fort Warren, Massachusetts, Kershaw resumed his law practice. He was deeply involved in the Masonic movement (he became Grand Master of the Freemasons of South Carolina and the struggle to restore home rule. He was reelected to the legislature and became president of the South Carolina Senate. In 1877, he was elected judge of the 5th Circuit Court of South Carolina, a post he held until 1893, when he resigned due to failing health. He was briefly postmaster of Camden but died there on April 12, 1894, at the age of seventy-two. He is buried in Quaker Cemetery, Camden.

WILLIAM WHEDBEE KIRKLAND was the only U.S. Marine to serve as a Confederate general. He was born on February 13, 1833, at his family's Mount Ayr estate in Hillsborough, North Carolina. In 1852, William obtained an appointment to West Point but was expelled for disciplinary reasons in 1855. Secretary of the Navy James C. Dobbin, however, offered him a commission in the Marine Corps, which he accepted.

The Marines sent Kirkland to China. His service record and his 1859 marriage to the niece of William J. Hardee, respected Army officer and future Confederate general, helped redeem him.

Kirkland resigned his commission in August 1860 and in March 1861 was commissioned a captain in the Confederate Army. He helped form the 11th (later 21st) North Carolina Infantry and in June was elected its first colonel. His regiment's discipline and drill exceeded that of most other volunteer regiments—a reflection, perhaps, of Kirkland's Marine Corps training. Kirkland fought in the Battle of First Manassas and Jackson's Valley Campaign up to the First Battle of Winchester, where he was shot through both thighs. He was out of action for months.

In late 1862, Kirkland returned to duty as General Patrick Cleburne's chief of staff. He returned to the Army of Northern Virginia and command of his old regiment after the Battle of Chancellorsville. The regiment fought at Gettysburg as part of Jubal Early's division.

After General J. Johnston Pettigrew was mortally wounded, Kirkland replaced him. He led the brigade in the retreat from Pennsylvania and was promoted to brigadier general on August 29, 1863. During the Battle of Bristoe Station, he was shot through the arm, and his ulna bone was fractured. He was sent to Savannah to recover. He was back in command of a North Carolina brigade for the battles of the Wilderness, Spotsylvania, and Cold Harbor, where he was again wounded in the right thigh.

He recovered to take command of James Martin's brigade in the trenches outside Petersburg, (after Martin's health had collapsed.) He took part in the heavy fighting around Fort Harrison in October 1864.

Kirkland's brigade returned to North Carolina in late 1864 to defend Fort Fisher and Wilmington, which fell on February 22, 1865. On March 10, 1865, at the Battle of Wyse Fork, he cut off a Union brigade and took more than one thousand prisoners.

As the Confederates slowly retreated, General Joseph E. Johnston, the commander of the Army of Tennessee, was informed that the Federals were planning to attack Kirkland's brigade. "Let them attack!" Johnston snapped. "I know of no brigade in the Southern Army I would sooner they would attack." He knew who would win that battle.

The Federals did attack. Kirkland's men fired concentrated volleys, and the invaders fell back with severe losses.

General Kirkland and his men fought in the Battle of Bentonville and then retreated to the west. The Army of Tennessee was unable to feed them, and a good many men deserted. William W. Kirkland had only three hundred men left when General Johnston surrendered. They received their paroles at High Point on May 1, 1865.

After the war, Kirkland lived in Savannah. Not finding success as a businessman, he moved to New York City, where he worked in the post office. General Kirkland spent the last years of his life in a soldiers' home in Washington, D.C. He died there on May 12, 1915, at the age of eighty-two. He was buried in Elmwood Cemetery, Shepherdstown, West Virginia.

L

LANE – LYON

JAMES HENRY LANE was born on July 28, 1833, at Mathews Court House, Virginia. He became known for his high moral character, his integrity, and his hard work. He was educated locally and at the Virginia Military Institute (VMI), where he studied under Stonewall Jackson. Lane graduated second in the class of 1854.

Lane enrolled in the University of Virginia but returned to VMI as a professor of mathematics. He became principal of Upperville Academy in 1858. The following year, he was chair of the Department of Mathematics and Military Tactics at the West Florida Seminary (now Florida State University) in Tallahassee. Lane was appointed professor of natural philosophy and instructor in military tactics at the North Carolina Military Institute in Charlotte.

Lane opposed secession, but he volunteered for Confederate service when North Carolina left the Union. On May 11, 1861, he was elected major of the 1st North Carolina Infantry.

Major Lane fought in the Confederate victory at Big Bethel in Virginia, which earned him a promotion to lieutenant colonel on September 1, 1861. He was sent back to North Carolina, where he organized the 28th North Carolina Infantry. It was sent to the New Bern sector but arrived too late to prevent the capture of the city. It was sent to Virginia in May 1862.

Colonel Lane fought in the Seven Days Battles (where he was wounded twice), at Cedar Mountain, the Battle of Second Manassas, Chantilly, Harpers Ferry, and Sharpsburg, where his commander, Lawrence O. Branch, was killed. As senior colonel, he took command of the brigade. He was promoted to brigadier general on November 1, 1862.

Lane proved to be a fine brigade commander. His brigade served in Stonewall Jackson's corps in the battles of Fredericksburg and Chancellorsville, where Lane's brother and Stonewall Jackson were both killed. Lane's brigade became part of William Dorsey Pender's division of A. P. Hill's III Corps in May 1863. Lane and his men fought at Gettysburg, and when Pender was wounded, Lane briefly succeeded him, until he was superseded by Isaac Trimble.

Lane's men were part of Pickett's Charge on July 3, 1863. After General Trimble was cut down, Lane assumed command of the division. Lane's brigade suffered almost 50 percent casualties. The commander himself was wounded and had a horse shot out from under him.

He reverted to brigade command and fought in all of the major battles of the Army of Northern Virginia. He surrendered at Appomattox on April 9.

After the war, General Lane founded schools in Concord, North Carolina, and Richmond, Virginia. In 1872, Lane became the first commandant of cadets and professor of civil engineering and commerce at Virginia Agricultural and Mechanical College (now Virginia Tech). In 1880, he had an argument with the college president. It became violent, and both men were forced to resign.

From 1881 to 1907, James Lane was professor of civil engineering at Alabama Polytechnic Institute (now Auburn University). He became department chair in 1883 and did a wonderful job. During his tenure at Alabama Tech, the engineering department won international awards and honors, and he helped turn the school into a leading educational institution.

On June 7, 1907, General Lane retired as Emeritus Professor of Civil Engineering. On the morning of September 21, he suffered a stroke and died that afternoon. He was seventy-four years old. He was buried in Pine Hill Cemetery, Auburn.

WALTER PAYE LANE was born in County Cork, Ireland, on February 18, 1817. His family immigrated to the United States in 1821 and settled in Ohio. Walter Lane moved to Texas in 1835, just before the Texas Revolution began. He was wounded by a Mexican lancer during the Battle of San Jacinto, where he was given a battlefield commission to second lieutenant. He was nineteen years old at the time. Lane then became a privateer aboard the *Thomas Toby* and raided commerce along the Mexican coast until October 1837, when a storm wrecked the ship.

On October 8, 1838, he participated in the Battle Creek Fight. About three hundred Waco, Kickapoo, Tehuacana, and Caddo Indians attacked about twenty-five white surveyors. The battle lasted twenty-four hours, and about thirty Indians and all but four surveyors were killed. Lane was wounded, but he and the surviving whites escaped.

Lane lived in San Augustine County from about 1838 to 1843, when he moved to San Antonio and joined the Texas Rangers. With the outbreak of the Mexican War, he joined the 1st Texas Mounted Rifle Regiment and was elected first lieutenant. He fought in the Battle of Monterrey, where his horse was shot out from under him. After that, he was promoted to major and given command of a battalion. Later in the war, he was shot through the leg.

After the Mexicans surrendered, the adventuresome Lane went to California during the Gold Rush and spent four years as a miner and a merchant in Shasta City and Nevada City. He went to Peru in the 1850s (again as a prospector), but around the year 1853 he returned to Texas, where he joined his brother, Judge George Lane, and opened a store. After the Gadsden Purchase of 1854, he went to southern Arizona to prospect for gold. He became a rancher and worked in the mercantile business in Marshall, Texas.

When the Civil War began, Lane raised a cavalry company and joined the 3rd Texas Cavalry as a lieutenant colonel in July 1861. He fought at Wilson's Creek, Missouri; Chustenahlah, Indian Territory; Pea Ridge, Arkansas; and Corinth, Mississippi. By May 1863, the 3rd Texas was dismounted. When the soldiers' enlistments expired, Lane refused to run for reelection. He returned to Texas and recruited the 1st Texas Partisan Ranger Regiment, which fought at Prairie Grove, Arkansas, but Lane missed this battle because of illness. He rejoined the regiment for the Louisiana Campaigns of 1863 and fought in the successful raids on the at Atchafalaya and at Donaldsonville.

In 1864, Lane and his men opposed the Union Army of the Gulf as it advanced up the Red River. He was seriously wounded in the Rebel victory at Mansfield on April 8, 1864. He was taken back to Texas, where he recovered. He rejoined his regiment near Hempstead, Texas, and was promoted to brigadier general on March 17, 1865.

Lane returned to Marshall after the war and restarted his mercantile business. He also served as a U.S. deputy marshal and was active in the Texas Veterans Association. After Reconstruction, he and his brother Judge George Lane formed the White Citizens Party, which was pledged to keep blacks and Republicans out of Marshall (the city) and Harrison County.

Walter P. Lane never married. He died on January 28, 1892, at the age of seventy-four. He is buried in Marshall Cemetery.

EVANDER MCIVER LAW was born on August 7, 1836, in Darlington, South Carolina. He attended the South Carolina Military Academy (now called The Citadel) and graduated in 1856. In his senior year, he was also an assistant professor of *Belles lettres*. After graduation, he taught at Kings Mountain Military Academy in Yorkville, South Carolina, and simultaneously studied law. In 1860, he moved to Alabama, where he was the cofounder of the Tuskegee Military School and taught history and writing. As the war approached, he formed a company, comprised mostly of his high school students, called the Alabama Zouaves. It was posted to Pensacola and took part in the seizure of the Federal naval yards and the forts on the mainland.

Law's company was accepted into Confederate service as part of the 4th Alabama Infantry. Law was elected captain and on May 2 was promoted to lieutenant colonel. He fought in the Battle of First Manassas, where he was severely wounded and lost the use of his left elbow. Shortly after, he assumed command of the 4th Alabama and was promoted to colonel on October 28, 1861.

The following year, Law led his regiment in the retreat from York-town (the Peninsula Campaign) and in May 1862 assumed command of a brigade in General Longstreet's division. Colonel Law fought in the Seven Days Battles and the Battle of Second Manassas, where he was wounded twice but refused to leave the field. As part of John Bell Hood's division, his regiments were involved in some of the fiercest fighting in the Battle of Sharpsburg (Antietam). The casualties were so heavy that, at the end of the battle, three of Law's regiments were commanded by captains and one by a lieutenant.

Evander Law was promoted to brigadier general on September 26, 1862. He was the youngest general in the Army of Northern Virginia at the time. He also excelled at Fredericksburg, where his horse was shot from under him.

Law's command, which was dubbed the "Alabama Brigade," fought in the Suffolk Campaign and in the Little Round Top sector at Gettysburg, where it suffered heavy casualties. On July 3, Law defended General Robert E. Lee's far right flank against a Union cavalry charge by Judson Kilpatrick.

Hood's division played a major role in the Battle of Chickamauga, where Hood was so badly wounded that his leg was amputated. Law assumed command, and Longstreet expressed his "admiration and satisfaction" with Law's performance—just before he named Micah Jenkins permanent commander of the division. Confederate President Jefferson Davis thought Jenkins was the wrong choice, preferred Law, and settled the matter by appointing a compromise candidate, General Charles W. Field, to command.

An annoyed Longstreet had Law arrested twice during this ongoing dispute, charging him with insubordination. Though General Samuel Cooper, the ranking officer in the Confederate Army, and General Robert E. Lee had Law restored to command, Law was technically, at Longstreet's orders, under arrest during the Battle of the Wilderness on May 6, 1864, when Jenkins was killed and Longstreet was seriously wounded. Law did not resume full command of his brigade until shortly before the Battle of Cold Harbor in June 1864, during which he was badly wounded with a bullet that injured his left eye and fractured his skull.

After he recovered, Law was transferred to Wade Hampton's command, where he was given a cavalry brigade. He fought in the Siege of Petersburg and the Carolinas Campaign. When General Matthew Butler was wounded in the Battle of Bentonville, Law took command of his division. Generals Joseph E. Johnston and Wade Hampton recommended that Law be promoted to major general, which he was on March 20, 1865. By now, however, the Confederate Senate had met for the last time, so his appointment was never confirmed. He surrendered with the Army of Tennessee on April 26, 1865.

Law returned to South Carolina after the war, where he administered his father-in-law's estate and extensive agricultural holdings and railroad interests. In the early 1870s, he moved to Alabama, where he helped organize the Alabama Grange. He settled in Florida in 1881, where he opened the South Florida Military College at Bartow, which he modeled after The Citadel. He remained superintendent until 1903.

Evander Law died on October 31, 1920, at the age of eighty-four. He was buried in Oak Hill Cemetery, Bartow, Florida. Evander McIver Law was the last Confederate with a rank of major general or higher to, in Stonewall Jackson's famous phrase, "cross over the river and rest in the shade of the trees."

ALEXANDER ROBERT LAWTON was born in Beaufort County, South Carolina, on November 5, 1818. He entered West Point at the age of sixteen, graduated in 1839, and was commissioned a second lieutenant in the artillery. He was stationed in northern New York and Vermont. In 1840, his regiment was moved to the boundary line between Maine and New Brunswick, Canada, during a border dispute.

Lawson resigned his commission on December 31, 1840, and graduated from Harvard Law School in 1842.

He settled in Savannah, where he set up a law office. He was soon involved in state politics and railroad administration.

Alexander Robert Lawton was an alderman in Savannah (1853–55) and served in the Georgia House of Representatives (1855–56) and in the Georgia Senate (1859–60). By late 1860, he was a colonel, commanding the 1st Georgia Infantry (state troops) and, on January 3, 1861, seized Fort Pulaski with volunteer militia units. On April 13, 1861, the day Fort Sumter surrendered, he was commissioned a brigadier general in the Confederate Army. He was named commander of the District of Georgia. Lawton was transferred to Richmond as a brigade commander in late 1861.

General Lawton was assigned to Stonewall Jackson's command in the Shenandoah Valley. He fought in the Valley Campaign of 1862, the Seven Days Battles, the Battle of Second Manassas, and the Maryland Campaign of 1862. He commanded General Richard Ewell's division in the Battle of Harpers Ferry and the Battle of Sharpsburg, where he was badly wounded.

General Lawton returned to active duty in the fall of 1863 but was not well enough to take to the field. Considered a highly competent officer, he was appointed Quartermaster General of the Confederate Army. Although he was energetic and resourceful, he was unable to solve the problems of the department, including material shortages and poor railroads. He held this post until the end of the war.

After the surrender, Lawton resumed his law practice. In 1870, he was again elected to the legislature, serving until 1875. He was a delegate to Georgia's Constitutional Convention in 1876 and ran an unsuccessful campaign for the U.S. Senate in 1880. He also became president of the Augusta and Savannah Railroad. General Lawton was an early investor in the development of Mount Airy in northeast Georgia and built his home, Lawton Place, in Mount Airy.

In 1882, Lawton was elected president of the American Bar Association. From 1887 to 1889, he served as U.S. envoy extraordinary and minister plenipotentiary to the Austro-Hungarian Empire.

Alexander and Sarah Lawton celebrated their Golden Wedding Anniversary in 1895. He died July 2, 1896, in Clifton Springs, New

York. He was seventy-seven years old. General Lawton is buried in Bonaventure Cemetery, Savannah.

DANVILLE LEADBETTER was born on August 26, 1811, in Leeds, Maine. He was educated by private tutors and at Anson Academy, prepared for a career in law, and worked as a deputy law clerk. He was considered both handsome and intelligent. He was admitted to West Point in 1832 and graduated in 1836.

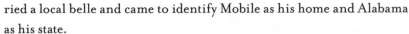

Leadbetter was commissioned a second lieutenant in the artillery but transferred to the Corps of Engineers and served as both an artillery officer and an engineer. He held assignments in the West, New York, and New England before he was sent to Mobile, Alabama, in 1852. Promoted to captain, he supervised the customs house in Mobile, the repair of Fort Morgan, and the construction of Fort Gaines in Mobile Bay. While here, he married a local belle and came to identify Mobile as his home and Alabama as his state.

Leadbetter resigned his commission on December 31, 1857, became chief engineer of Alabama, and built the Sand Island Lighthouse. In March 1861, he was commissioned a major in the Confederate Army. He was ordered to Richmond and by August was acting chief of the Engineer Bureau and, among other projects, worked to improve the defenses of Yorktown. He was promoted to lieutenant colonel in October and transferred to Mobile in November.

Leadbetter designed or improved several forts on the Alabama coast, including four forts on Mobile Bay, erecting ramparts, redoubts, parapets, and entrenchments. He did a fine job. Mobile did not fall until April 12, 1865, three days after General Lee surrendered.

Recognized as one of the best military engineers in the country, Danville Leadbetter was held in high esteem by the War Department and was promoted to brigadier general on February 27, 1862. He was transferred to the District of East Tennessee and briefly commanded a brigade. In the autumn of 1863, he was named chief engineer of the Department of Tennessee. He became chief engineer of the Army of Tennessee shortly after.

General Leadbetter constructed the defenses in front of Knoxville and Chattanooga for General Braxton Bragg in 1862, but Bragg was maneuvered out of both cities without a major battle. After the Battle of Chickamauga was won and the Siege of Chattanooga began, Leadbetter was sent back to East Tennessee to advise General James Longstreet during the Siege of Knoxville in 1863. After two days of reconnoitering Union lines, Leadbetter recommended he attack Fort Sanders. The result was a Confederate defeat on November 29. Leadbetter was severely criticized by E. Porter Alexander for the advice he gave Longstreet at Knoxville. He was, however, still held in high esteem by such diverse officers at Braxton Bragg, Joseph E. Johnston, Dabney H. Maury (the commander at Mobile), and G. T. Beauregard. It is safe to say, however, that his performance at Knoxville was the low point of Leadbetter's career.

Danville Leadbetter briefly served as chief engineer for Joseph E. Johnston. He was sent back to the District of the Gulf in late April 1864 and remained there until the end of the war.

After Mobile fell, Leadbetter escaped to Mexico. He then traveled to Canada, where he died in Clifton (now known as New London), Prince Edward Island, on September 26, 1866. He was fifty-five years old. General Leadbetter was buried in Magnolia Cemetery, Mobile.

EDWIN GRAY "NED" LEE was born on May 27, 1836, the son of a prominent Shepherdstown, Virginia, attorney. Edwin was also a second cousin of Robert E. Lee. Ned's exact birthplace is not certain. He attended William and Mary College (1851–53), Benjamin Hallowell's school for young men in Alexandria (1853–56), and John White Brockenbrough's law school (1857–59), where he received his law degree.

In 1856, Lee married Susan Pendleton, the daughter of the Reverend (later Brigadier General) William N. Pendleton. The couple had no children.

Ned entered Confederate service in April 1861 as a second lieutenant. He was soon promoted to first lieutenant and became an aide-de-camp to Stonewall Jackson at Harpers Ferry. By now a captain, he took part in the Battle of First Manassas on July 21.

On July 26, Edwin Lee was promoted to major of the 33rd Virginia Infantry Regiment, which was part of the Stonewall Brigade. He fought in the Romney Expedition, the Valley Campaign of 1862, and the Seven Days Battles. He was promoted to lieutenant colonel on July 25, 1862, and to colonel and commander of the 33rd Virginia on August 28. He fought at Cedar Mountain, Groveton, the Battle of Second Manassas, Chantilly, Harpers Ferry, and Sharpsburg. By then the regiment was down to two hundred men.

Colonel Lee was captured at Sharpsburg. He was paroled nine days thereafter at the behest of U.S. General George B. McClellan but did not rejoin the regiment immediately due to ill health. Lee returned to the 33rd briefly for the Battle of Fredericksburg, but then, on doctor's advice, he resigned because of problems with his lungs.

By late 1863, Edwin Lee had at least partially recovered. He applied for active duty, was recommissioned colonel on November 12, and performed staff duties in Richmond and later in the Shenandoah Valley. On May 17, 1864, he was named commandant of Staunton, Virginia. On September 23, 1864, he was promoted to brigadier general.

On November 28, 1864, Ned Lee was granted a six-month leave of absence to restore his failing health, but apparently this was just a cover story. It seems he was actually on a mission for the Confederate Secret Service. He and his wife ran the blockade in December and were in Canada when the war ended.

The Confederate Senate confirmed Lee's appointment as a brigadier general on February 3, 1865, but for some reason reconsidered the measure and rejected the appointment on February 24.

Ned and Susan Lee lived in Montreal, Canada, until the spring of 1866. They allocated funds to needy former Confederates in exile. He also looked after Rebels in Canadian prisons. He returned to the United States and was a witness at the trial of John Surratt, an accomplice in the Lincoln assassination.

Edwin Gray Lee died of lung disease at Yellow Sulphur Springs, Virginia, on August 24, 1870, at the age of thirty-four. He is buried in Stonewall Jackson Memorial Cemetery in Lexington, Virginia.

FITZHUGH LEE was born on November 19, 1835, at Clermont, near Alexandria, Virginia. He was a nephew of Samuel Cooper and Robert E. Lee and a cousin of future Confederate generals George Washington Custis Lee and W. H. F. "Rooney" Lee.

"Fitz" Lee graduated from West Point with the class of 1856 and was assigned to the 2nd U.S. Cavalry on the frontier. In 1859, in Nescutunga, Texas, Fitz Lee suffered a nearly fatal wound in a skirmish with Comanches. He was transferred back to West Point in May 1860 as an instructor of cavalry tactics.

On May 21, 1861, Fitz Lee resigned his commission. He was appointed first lieutenant of cavalry, Confederate States Army, and was assigned to the staff of Joseph E. Johnston, with whom he served in the Battle of First Manassas. He was promoted to lieutenant colonel of the 1st Virginia Cavalry on September 29.

Many Confederate regiments were allowed to elect their own officers during the Civil War. Fitz Lee ran against "Grumble" Jones and defeated him for colonel and commander of the 1st Virginia. Meanwhile, Fitzhugh formed a close, personal friendship with J. E. B. Stuart, the commander of the cavalry in the Confederate Army of the Potomac (soon to become the Army of Northern Virginia).

Fitz Lee quickly distinguished himself as a cavalry commander during Stuart's famous "Ride around McClellan." After taking part in the Seven Days Battles, Fitz Lee was promoted to brigadier general on July 24, 1862.

Lee's cavalry brigade took part in almost every major action involving the Army of Northern Virginia. Lee particularly distinguished himself in the Battle of Kelly's Ford (March 17, 1863), where he was in command of 400 Confederates. He captured 150 Federals and lost only 14 men. At Chancellorsville, Fitz Lee's reconnaissance revealed that the Union right flank was exposed, allowing Stonewall Jackson to make his famous flanking attack of May 2. The only major cavalry action Lee missed was Brandy Station. At the time, he was incapacitated by inflammatory rheumatism. He was laid up for a month.

On August 3, 1863, Lee was promoted to major general. The government in Richmond, meanwhile, upgraded Stuart's command to a cavalry corps with two divisions. Wade Hampton commanded one, and Fitz Lee the other.

On September 19, 1864, during the Third Battle of Winchester, Lee received a serious wound which put him out of action for most of the rest of the year. In early February 1865, after Wade Hampton's cavalry was sent to South Carolina, Fitzhugh Lee assumed command of all the cavalry of the Army of Northern Virginia. Unlike Hampton, however, he was not promoted to lieutenant general.

When his uncle, General Robert E. Lee, capitulated at Appomattox on April 9, 1865, Fitzhugh Lee cut his way out and reached Lynchburg but then had second thoughts. He returned to Appomattox and surrendered on April 12.

After the war, Fitz Lee went to Stafford County, Virginia, where he took up farming. He gradually increased his wealth to include a grist mill and a stud farm. In 1885, he was elected Virginia's governor by a narrow margin.

Fitz Lee served as governor of Virginia from January 1, 1886, to January 1, 1890. He advocated a number of progressive reforms—from improving education, including for black Virginians, to promoting industry, agriculture, and railroads in the state—but failed to get much support from the legislature for more spending. He ran for the U.S. Senate in 1893 but was defeated. He never sought public office again.

Lee was named consul general to Cuba in 1896. After war was declared with Spain, President William McKinley appointed him major general and commander of the U.S. VII Corps, but the Spanish collapsed quicker than expected, and the VII Corps saw no combat. Fitz Lee retired as a U.S. brigadier general on March 2, 1901. He lived in semi-retirement in Charlottesville after that.

Fitzhugh Lee died during a visit to Washington, D.C., on April 28, 1905. He was sixty-nine years old. He was buried in Hollywood Cemetery in Richmond.

GEORGE WASHINGTON CUSTIS LEE was born on September 16, 1832, at Fort Monroe, Virginia, where his father, Robert E. Lee, was stationed. "Custis" or "Boo," as he was called, was Lee's oldest child. From his youngest days, he idolized his father. When Custis was about seven, Robert E. Lee said of Custis, "It behooves me to walk very straight, when my son is already following in my tracks." He always would.

"Boo" was educated in private boarding schools, which emphasized mathematical studies. Custis was admitted to West Point in 1850 and graduated in 1854, ranking first in his class.

Custis Lee was commissioned in the Corps of Engineers and served in San Francisco Bay, California; Georgia; Florida; and Washington, D.C., during his years in the U.S. Army. When Virginia seceded, he resigned his commission as first lieutenant on May 2, 1861, and joined the Virginia State Troops, which were commanded by his father, as a major of engineers. That summer, he was transferred to Confederate service as a captain of engineers. He was initially involved in constructing fortifications for the defenses of Richmond.

Confederate President Jefferson Davis promoted him to colonel and made him a military aide. He was on Davis's staff from August 31, 1861, to June 25, 1863. In 1862, he was temporarily placed in charge of the construction engineers at Drewry's Bluff.

Custis Lee was a quiet and self-effacing but astute military advisor, and Jefferson Davis liked him. Lee was promoted to brigadier general on June 25, 1863, but the president refused to transfer him to a field command. Custis Lee commanded the Richmond Local Defense Forces from June 25, 1863, to March 1865. In this post, he saw action against U.S. Generals Ulysses Grant and Benjamin Butler in 1864 and performed well. He was given command of Chaffin's Bluff, across the river from Drewry's Bluff and about eight miles south of Richmond. He was promoted to major general on October 20, 1864.

In March 1865 Custis helped organize the final Confederate defense of Richmond, mobilizing clerks, ordnance personnel, mechanics, staff officers, and others. After Robert E. Lee's line was broken on April 2, Custis joined General Richard Ewell's forces, which evacuated the capital that night, heading for Appomattox. The Confederate units were cut off at Sayler's Creek on April 6, and Custis Lee was among the prisoners. He was paroled almost immediately, however, because his mother was ill.

After the war, Custis followed his parents to Lexington, where Robert E. Lee was president of Washington College. Custis was appointed professor of engineering at the Virginia Military Institute; simultaneously, he designed the Lee Chapel at Washington College.

Upon his father's death in October 1870, Custis was appointed president of Washington College, a position he held until his retirement in 1897. Shortly after assuming the presidency, Custis was confirmed in the Episcopal Church. He had not taken much interest in religion until 1870, but afterward, he paid a great deal of attention to the church. He remembered it liberally in his will.

His students remember Custis for "his gentleness and kindliness mixed with his dignity and even austereness. . . ." He told one student, "Son, have all the fun you can. I have never had any fun in my life."

Custis Lee was not a successful administrator. It was not in his nature to ask other people for money, even for the college, and under his leadership, enrollment fell from a high of 410 under Robert E. Lee to 96. After leaving Lexington in 1897, General Lee moved into Ravensworth Mansion in Fairfax County, which was part of the estate of Rooney Lee, who had died in 1891. He was happy there, where he was often found reading in the ample library or exercising in the garden or taking carriage drives in the neighborhood.

In December 1911, Lee slipped on the stairs and fractured his hip. Even though he never walked again and was confined to a wheelchair, he never complained. General Custis Lee died on February 18, 1913, in Annandale, Virginia. He was eighty years old. He was interred in the Lee Crypt in the Lee Chapel and Museum, Lexington, Virginia.

ROBERT EDWARD LEE was born in Stratford Hall, Westmoreland County, Virginia, on January 19, 1807. He was the son of Henry Lee III, known as "Light-Horse Harry," the chief of George Washington's cavalry. Unfortunately, Light-Horse Harry was poor at business and finances, and Robert E. Lee grew up in genteel poverty. As a result of this upbringing, Robert was always parsimonious with money, with both his own and public funds. He was largely homeschooled. Later, he attended the Alexandria Academy for three years, where he learned to read Greek and Latin. He could read the latter for the rest of his life, despite not studying it after age seventeen.

"Robert was always good," his father wrote in 1817. He attended the Episcopal Church in Alexandria (later known as Christ Church) with his mother and learned the Episcopal catechism. He was molded by his mother, who was a strong Christian; so was her son. (Franklin D. Roosevelt once commented that Lee was the most Christlike American who ever lived.) Hers was a simple belief in a merciful God, and she transmitted this belief to her son. John Esten Cooke later wrote of Lee, "The soldier was great, but the man himself was greater." Robert E. Lee was a Christian gentleman-soldier of the Old School.

Lee attended West Point and graduated second in the class of 1829, with no demerits in four years. He is the only cadet in the history of the U.S. Military Academy to accomplish this feat.

Lee had a brilliant career in the U. S. Army. He fought in the Mexican War, where he earned three brevets, which was roughly equal to winning the Congressional Medal of Honor today. His substantive rank, however, remained captain.

Robert E. Lee had many successful assignments. He served as superintendent of the U.S. Military Academy at West Point from 1852 to 1855, was second-in-command of Albert Sidney Johnston's 2nd Cavalry Regiment, and saw action on the Western frontier of Texas, protecting settlers from attacks by Comanches and Apaches. After his father-in-law, George Washington Parke Custis, died in 1857, Lee was named executor of the estate, and he was forced to take three long furloughs to deal with the estate, which was a mess, physically and financially.

Lee's attitude toward slavery has been beaten to death by historians, but suffice it to say, he believed that slavery was evil and should be abolished; his only preference was that abolition be achieved gradually by Christian persuasion—and with adequate provision for the freed slaves— and not by violence and social upheaval. (This was a view held by many Virginians of his class.) Lee had no slaves of his own. Mr. Custis's slaves belonged to the estate, not to Lee. He only inherited responsibility for them, which included manumitting them within five years of Custis's death.

In October 1859, Lee suppressed a terrorist attack at Harpers Ferry quickly and efficiently. The leader turned out to be the radical abolitionist John Brown, who was hanged on December 2.

Lee was opposed to secession, which he called "nothing but rebellion." His first loyalty, however, was to Virginia. He would not fight against his own kith and kin and commented sadly, "[A] Union that can only be maintained by swords and bayonets . . . has no charm for me." After President Abraham Lincoln called for seventy-five thousand volunteers to suppress the Southern "rebellion," General Winfield Scott suggested that Lincoln offer Lee command of the U.S. Army. Lincoln did so through an intermediary. Lee politely turned it down. That same day, April 17, Virginia seceded. After a struggle with his conscience, Lee resigned his commission on April 20, and within a matter of days he was named major general and commander of the Provisional Army of Virginia. He was appointed full general in Confederate service on August 31, 1861.

After an unsuccessful attempt to coordinate three independent generals in western Virginia in 1861, Lee performed brilliantly for most of the remainder of the war. He commanded a department in South Carolina, Georgia, and Florida and was military advisor to the president from March 13 to May 31, 1862. After Joseph E. Johnston was wounded, Lee replaced him as commander of the main Southern Army, which he redesignated the Army of Northern Virginia.

Lee's gentleness belied his nature as a commander. He made bold strategic and tactical moves that author Burke Davis called "breath-taking." He added, "The kindly face, fatherly beard and gentle manner have concealed too long one of the fiercest of the great captains."

One of Lee's men put it best when he commented, "He loved us like a father and led us like a king."

His list of victories is too long to describe here, but Theodore Roosevelt, Winston Churchill, Franklin D. Roosevelt, Dwight D. Eisenhower, John F. Kennedy, Gerald Ford, Ronald Reagan, and Donald Trump are just a few of the statesmen who have praised Lee as one of America's greatest military commanders and heroes. He suffered his worst setback at Gettysburg in July 1863, of course, and was finally forced to surrender to overwhelming numbers on April 9, 1865, but his role in American history was far from over. Lee's outstanding military accomplishments, his upright moral conduct, and his devotion to restoring the Union and rebuilding the South made him a symbol of American heroism that transcended the battle lines, stood for reconciliation, and inspired many as the American model of the Christian soldier-gentleman.

From late 1865 until his death, General Lee served as president of Washington College in Lexington, Virginia. By all accounts he was an excellent president. His health, however, was compromised by the war. He died at 9:15 a.m. on October 12, 1870, at the age of sixty-three. He is buried in the Lee Crypt in the Lee Chapel and Museum, Lexington, Virginia.

STEPHEN DILL LEE was born in Charleston, South Carolina on September 22, 1833. His father was a man of limited means, and although his childhood was happy, Stephen's formal schooling was necessarily limited. His admission to West Point in 1850 provided him with an education he could not otherwise afford.

He graduated in 1854, was commissioned in the artillery, and was posted to bases in Texas, Florida, Kansas, Nebraska, and the Dakota Territory. He resigned his commission on February 20, 1861, and returned to South Carolina.

Lee was immediately appointed a captain of artillery in the state forces. He served on the staff of G. T. Beauregard and took part in the Battle of Fort Sumter. Shortly after, he was elected commander of the light battery in the Hampton Legion and directed his artillery units with great success. He was promoted to major on November 1, 1861, and to full colonel on July 9, 1862.

Lee was promoted to brigadier general on November 6, 1862, and transferred to the Army of Mississippi as chief of artillery. He was twenty-nine years old. In December 1862, he commanded an ad hoc division in the Battle of Chickasaw Bayou, where he repelled Sherman's main attack, inflicting 1,900 Union casualties to only 200 for the Confederates.

On May 1, 1863, General Edward D. Tracy was killed in action in the Battle of Port Gibson, and General John C. Pemberton selected Stephen Lee to replace him. Lee was heavily engaged at the Battle of

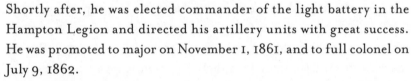

Champion Hill, where he had three horses shot out from under him and was slightly wounded in the shoulder. During the retreat from the Big Black River, he was hit again, and a spent bullet left his arm bruised from the elbow to the shoulder.

Lee fought in the Siege of Vicksburg and became a prisoner of war on July 4, 1863. Lee was exchanged and, on the recommendation of General Pemberton, was promoted to major general on August 3, 1863. He was assigned to Joseph E. Johnston, who thought highly of Stephen Lee and gave him the task of organizing a cavalry division. Lee operated in eastern Mississippi and (briefly) in northern Alabama under General Joe Wheeler. He opposed Sherman's Meridian Expedition and was named commander of the Department of Mississippi, Alabama, and Eastern Louisiana on May 9, 1864. He was promoted to lieutenant general on June 23, 1864—the youngest officer of this grade in the history of the Confederacy.

On July 14, he combined with General Nathan Bedford Forrest and fought at Tupelo, where they suffered a rare defeat. (Forrest did not wish to attack, but Lee insisted on it.) On July 17, 1864, General John Bell Hood replaced General Joseph E. Johnston as commander of the Army of Tennessee. At Hood's request, Stephen Lee was named commander of Hood's old corps.

After the fall of Atlanta on September 2, 1864, Lee participated in the Tennessee campaign, fighting at Spring Hill (where he was wounded), Franklin, and Nashville, where the army was crushed and routed. During the retreat, on December 17, a shell fragment from a Union cannon lodged in the heel of his foot. He continued to direct his corps until nightfall, when he turned command over to Carter Stevenson. He did not return to duty until April 1865.

On February 8, 1865, Lee married a Christian lady who was serving as a Confederate Army nurse. Stephen Lee had not been particularly religious before marrying her, but he became a Baptist afterwards.

S. D. Lee was a courageous man. One survivor later wrote that only D. H. Hill was Stephen Lee's equal in composure under fire. Lee was not a colorful leader like Stonewall Jackson or Nathan Bedford Forrest, and he was not a great general like Robert E. Lee, but he was courageous and highly competent. General Sherman called him "the most enterprising [general] in all their army."

Lee surrendered with Joseph E. Johnston on April 26, 1865. He settled in his wife's hometown of Columbus, Mississippi, where he labored unsuccessfully as a planter for ten years before becoming an insurance salesman. The fact that he was an affable, friendly man and a thorough gentleman helped him achieve success in the insurance business, though he soon gave it up for other ventures.

Lee ran for the state senate in 1877 and won a heated election. He became the first president of the Mississippi Agricultural and Mechanical College, which is now Mississippi State University, in 1880. He resigned in 1899 to serve on the commission that organized the Vicksburg Military Park. He served as president of the Mississippi Historical Society and was a charter member of the United Confederate Veterans. He served as commander-in-chief of the United Confederate Veterans from 1904 until his death. He also assisted Confederate survivors who were undergoing difficult times financially.

General Lee suffered a cerebral hemorrhage and died in Vicksburg on May 28, 1908, at age seventy-four. He is buried in Friendship Cemetery, Columbus, Mississippi.

WILLIAM HENRY FITZHUGH "ROONEY" LEE, the third child and second son of Robert E. Lee, was born in Arlington, Virginia, on May 31, 1837. Robert E. Lee nicknamed him "Rooney" to distinguish him from his second cousin, Fitzhugh Lee. Rooney grew up to stand six feet, four inches tall and weigh 240 pounds. General Lee joked that Rooney was too large to be a man but too small to be a horse.

Army regulations prohibited brothers from attending West Point together, so with his elder brother Custis already enrolled at the military academy, Rooney attended Harvard. Rooney's friend and classmate Henry

Adams described him as "[t]all, largely built, handsome, genial, with liberal Virginia openness towards all he liked." He also had "the Virginia habit of command," Adams noted, "and took leadership as his natural habit. No one cared to contest it," possibly because he was the college's bare-knuckles boxing champion. He was, for a time, "the most popular and prominent" student in his class.

General Winfield Scott commissioned him directly into the army as a second lieutenant of cavalry in 1855. He took part in the Utah Expedition of 1857 but became bored with the service and resigned his commission on May 31, 1857. He married and settled down to farm at White House, an estate on the Pamunkey River he had inherited from his grandfather, George Washington Parke Custis.

Rooney Lee joined the Confederate Army as a captain of cavalry on May 10, 1861. He seemed to have inherited his grandfather Light-Horse Harry Lee's cavalry skills, and he rose rapidly in rank. Rooney was promoted to major in the 9th Virginia Cavalry later that month, to lieutenant colonel on January 18, 1862, and to colonel and regimental commander on April 28, 1862. He fought in all of the major campaigns of the Army of Northern Virginia in 1862, as well as in the Chancellorsville Campaign in 1863.

He also played a major role in the Confederate victory in the Battle of Brandy Station. Unfortunately, he was shot in the thigh and severely wounded during the action. Taken to Hickory Hill, his wife's family home, to recover, he was captured by a Union patrol on June 26, 1863, and spent eight months in Union prisons. He was finally exchanged on February 25, 1864. By the time of his release, his wife was dead, his children were dead, and his plantation house was burned to the ground. He nevertheless continued to act with dignity and without hatred toward his opponents.

J. E. B. Stuart advanced him to division commander, and he was promoted to major general on April 23, 1864. He fought at the Wilderness, Spotsylvania Court House, and North Anna. He patrolled the extreme right flank of the Army of Northern Virginia during the Siege of Petersburg, was part of Wade Hampton's famous Beefsteak Raid, and helped check a major Union advance in the Battle of Boydton Plank Road (October 27–28, 1864). He screened the Confederate evacuation of Petersburg on April 2–3, 1865, and surrendered with his father at Appomattox Court House on April 9.

After the war, Rooney rebuilt White House Plantation, remarried, and then moved to Ravensworth Plantation in 1874. In 1875, he was elected to the Virginia Senate, where he served through 1879. In 1886, he was elected to the U.S. House of Representatives, serving from 1887 to 1891.

Rooney was always cheerful and friendly. He often picked wildflowers on his way to Congress and gave them to his colleagues—even Republicans. Like his father, he was an advocate of reconciliation.

Congressman William Henry Fitzhugh "Rooney" Lee died at the Ravensworth Plantation house on October 15, 1891. He was fifty-four years old. He is entombed in the Lee Chapel in Lexington, Virginia.

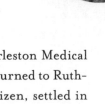

COLLETT LEVENTHORPE was born on May 15, 1815, in Exmouth, Devon, England. He was educated at Winchester College and by private tutors. In 1832, when he was seventeen years old, he was commissioned an ensign in the 14th Regiment of Foot (the "Buckinghamshires") by King William IV and spent a decade in the British Army, serving in Ireland, the British West Indies, and Canada. A captain of grenadiers by 1842, he sold his commission and returned to England. He studied medicine for a time but did not finish his training. Instead, he went to work for a British trading firm. On a business trip to Asheville, North Carolina, in 1843, he met the love of his life, Louisa Bryan (1827–1908) of Rutherfordton, North Carolina. To win her hand, he needed an occupation, so Leventhorpe attended Charleston Medical College, finished with top honors, and immediately returned to Rutherfordton and married Louisa. He became a U.S. citizen, settled in Rutherfordton, practiced medicine, and was regarded as a leader in the

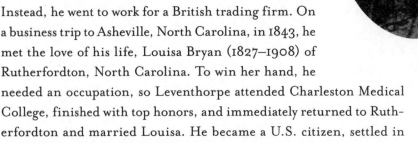

community. Leventhorpe was a handsome man, standing about six feet five, with a straight military bearing. He was known as a kind and gentle man. Later he was known as a brave one.

When North Carolina left the Union, Leventhorpe offered his services to his adopted state. On October 25, 1861, he was commissioned colonel of the 34th North Carolina Infantry, which he turned into a well-trained regiment. He was posted on the Roanoke River to guard against incursions from Union naval forces.

On April 2, 1862, he was named colonel of the 11th North Carolina. He and his regiment clashed with a Union force at Whitehall (White Hall) on the Neuse River. The Yankees attacked with four regiments and poured a fierce fire onto his positions, but the 11th returned volley for volley and eventually drove their numerically superior foes from the field.

In the spring of 1863, Leventhorpe's regiment took part in the failed operations around Plymouth, North Carolina. By then, the 11th had the reputation of being the best-drilled unit in the Confederate Army. Other regiments competed in drilling contests, but the 11th was so good that it was barred from competition. It took part in the aborted siege of Washington, North Carolina, and was then transferred to the Army of Northern Virginia. On July 1, 1863, Colonel Leventhorpe was seriously wounded in General J. Johnston Pettigrew's successful charge on McPherson Ridge during the Battle of Gettysburg. His left arm was splintered, and his hip was shattered. Several days later, the ambulance in which he was riding was captured. Union surgeons found that the wounded arm was gangrenous, and they wanted to amputate it. Dr. Leventhorpe refused and asked the surgeons to cauterize it with nitric acid. He endured the procedure without anesthetics. He later remarked that he "would have died, rather than let an enemy see that a Confederate Officer could not endure anything without a complaint." His arm discharged bone fragments for three months after the operation.

The colonel was exchanged on March 10, 1864, and was appointed brigadier general of North Carolina State Troops by Governor Zebulon

Vance. Commanding one of the two home guard brigades, he operated on the Roanoke River and the Petersburg and Weldon Railroad until the end of the war.

General Robert E. Lee called him the best officer in the district and on January 20, 1865, recommended his promotion to brigadier general in the Confederate States Army. President Jefferson Davis signed his commission on Feburary 18, 1865, to rank from February 3, and ordered him to serve under General Braxton Bragg in the defense of Wilmington. He thus became the sole former English subject to become a Confederate general, if only briefly. Leventhorpe declined the appointment on March 6, preferring to remain a state general, perhaps because of the effects of his war wounds. Instead of giving him command of a field brigade as originally planned, Bragg placed him in charge of Raleigh. After the North Carolina capital fell on April 13, Leventhorpe and his remaining troops headed for Greensboro. He was there when Johnston surrendered.

After the war, General Leventhorpe worked in the shipping business in New York City and the mining business in North Carolina. He and his wife eventually settled at Holly Lodge in the Happy Valley area, near Lenoir, North Carolina.

Leventhorpe enjoyed writing poetry and collecting paintings and antiques. He died at his wife's sister's home in Yadkin Valley, North Carolina, on December 1, 1889, at the age of seventy-four. General Leventhorpe is buried in Chapel of Rest Cemetery, Happy Valley, North Carolina.

JOSEPH HORACE LEWIS was born on October 29, 1824, near Glasgow, Kentucky. He was educated in local public schools and at Centre College in Danville, Kentucky. He graduated in 1843, after which he studied law, was admitted to the bar in 1845, and set up a practice in Glasgow.

Lewis was elected to the Kentucky legislature as a Whig in 1850. He was twice reelected and served until

1855. He ran for Congress in 1856 and 1860 but was defeated both times. Meanwhile, he became a colonel in the state militia.

When the Civil War began, Kentucky tried to do the impossible and remain neutral. Lewis supported the Confederacy and established a camp near Cave City to recruit and train volunteers. When the 6th Kentucky Infantry was organized on November 1, 1861, he became its colonel.

The 6th was part of the famous Orphan Brigade (the 1st Kentucky Brigade). It fought at Shiloh, took part in the retreat to Corinth, the Battle of Baton Rouge, the Second Battle of Murfreesboro (where the brigade suffered more than 50 percent casualties), the defense of Vicksburg (during which it escaped encirclement), the Second Battle of Jackson, and the Battle of Chickamauga, where the brigade commander, Ben Helms, was killed in action. Joseph Lewis—who was repeatedly praised by General John C. Breckinridge—was selected to replace him. He was promoted to brigadier general on September 30, 1863.

Lewis led the Orphan Brigade in the Siege of Chattanooga, the Battle of Missionary Ridge, and the Atlanta Campaign. After Atlanta fell, the much-reduced brigade was converted into a mounted rifle unit. It opposed William Sherman's March to the Sea and took part in the Carolinas Campaign. As the Confederacy crumbled, it became part of President Jefferson Davis's escort. Lewis and his men surrendered at Washington, Georgia, May 6–7, 1865.

After the war, Lewis returned to Glasgow, where he resumed his law practice. He was reelected to the state legislature in 1868 and won a special election to Congress in 1870. He was reelected and served from May 10, 1870, to March 3, 1873. He was not a candidate for reelection.

General Lewis returned to Glasgow and his law practice in 1873. He was elected judge of the Kentucky Court of Appeals in 1874 and was continually reelected until he retired in 1898.

After leaving the bench, Joseph H. Lewis moved to a farm in Scott County, Kentucky. He died on July 6, 1904, in Georgetown, Kentucky, at the age of seventy-nine. General Lewis is buried in Glasgow Municipal Cemetery.

WILLIAM GASTON LEWIS was born in Rocky
Mount, North Carolina, on September 3, 1835, but grew
up in Chapel Hill. He attended the University of North
Carolina, studied engineering, and graduated in 1855,
when he was nineteen. He taught at the University of
North Carolina (1855–56) and in Jackson County, Florida (1856–57), and worked for the U.S. Survey Corps
(1857–59), before returning to North Carolina as assistant engineer for the Wilmington and Weldon Railroad.

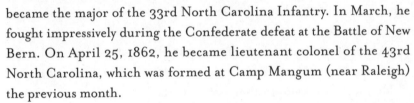

When the Civil War began, Lewis joined the 1st
North Carolina Infantry Regiment as a third lieutenant
and fought in the Battle of Big Bethel in Virginia. He
returned to North Carolina and, on January 17, 1862,
became the major of the 33rd North Carolina Infantry. In March, he
fought impressively during the Confederate defeat at the Battle of New
Bern. On April 25, 1862, he became lieutenant colonel of the 43rd
North Carolina, which was formed at Camp Mangum (near Raleigh)
the previous month.

The 43rd North Carolina was sent to Virginia and took part in the
Seven Days Battles. After this victory it was made part of the Drewry's
Bluff garrison south of Richmond. Sent to Goldsborough, North Carolina, in December, it participated in the attempt to recapture New Bern
and Washington, North Carolina, in March and April 1863. Sent back
to the Army of Northern Virginia in May, it fought at Brandy Station,
Beverly Ford, the Second Battle of Winchester, and other actions during
the Pennsylvania Campaign. It was heavily engaged during the Battle of
Gettysburg, especially in the successful attempt to take the railroad cut
on July 1 and the unsuccessful attack on Culp's Hill on July 3. During
this fight, the regiment's commander was severely wounded, and Lieutenant Colonel Lewis replaced him.

After Gettysburg, William G. Lewis and his regiment fought in the
Bristoe Campaign and along the Rappahannock. The regiment returned
to North Carolina. Lewis took part in recapturing Plymouth (April
17–20, 1864) and temporarily commanded a brigade. Sent back to

·L

Virginia, the 43rd joined Colonel Bryan Grimes's brigade on May 21 and fought in the final stages of the Battle of Spotsylvania Court House. Lewis commanded Robert Hoke's old brigade during the Battle of Cold Harbor. He was promoted to brigadier general (temporary rank) on May 31, 1864. He also fought in the engagement at Drewry's Bluff in June.

General Lewis accompanied General Stephen D. Ramseur's division to the Shenandoah Valley and, on July 20, 1864, was severely wounded during the minor Battle of Stephenson's Depot in Virginia. He was out of action until September.

General Lewis rejoined the Army of Northern Virginia after he recovered. He formed part of Robert E. Lee's rear guard during the retreat to Appomattox. On April 7, 1865, he was wounded and captured at Farmville. He was paroled a few days later. Although without military experience before the war, William G. Lewis proved to be a highly capable commander.

After the surrender, Lewis returned to his profession of civil engineering and worked as a construction engineer for the Wilmington and Weldon Railroad among other assignments. He was also a member of the state board of education.

On January 7, 1901, General William Gaston Lewis died suddenly and unexpectedly of pneumonia at his home in Goldsboro (the spelling had changed in 1869), at age sixty-five. He was buried in Willow Dale Cemetery, Goldsboro, North Carolina.

ST. JOHN RICHARDSON LIDDELL was born on September 6, 1815, at Elmsley, his family's plantation near Woodville, Mississippi. His father, a planter and a probate judge, saw to it that "John," as he was called, obtained the best education possible. He entered the University of Virginia and disliked it intensely. He enrolled at West Point in the summer of 1833. He was, however, an emotional man of violent temperament, and he was expelled on February 19, 1835, for bad conduct and poor grades. He returned to Mississippi but moved to Louisiana in 1837 and established his own plantation, Llanada, just below Trinity (near the present-day town of Jonesville).

He and his family were involved in a long-standing feud with the family of Charles Jones. In 1852, Liddell shot and killed two members of the Jones faction. He was arrested and tried for murder but pled justifiable homicide and was found not guilty. Charles Jones and John Liddell agreed to a formal peace treaty in 1857, but hard feelings lingered.

When Louisiana seceded, Liddell joined the Confederate Army and secured a commission on the staff of his close friend and former West Point classmate William J. Hardee. Liddell was promoted to colonel on September 15. He joined the staff of General Albert Sidney Johnston in January 1862 and went to Richmond for him, where he discussed strategy with Jefferson Davis, but Liddell missed the Battle of Shiloh because of illness. He served on General G. T. Beauregard's staff during the retreat to Corinth.

On June 10, 1862, Hardee formed a new brigade of Arkansas regiments and gave the command to Liddell. He was promoted to brigadier general on July 12. He fought in all of the major battles on the Western Front until the end of 1863, when Liddell asked to be transferred to Louisiana, where his family was in danger from Yankees, anti-Confederate guerrillas, and outlaws. The War Department honored his request.

Back home, John Liddell was given command of the northeast Louisiana area. His command consisted of seven hundred men in four fourth-class cavalry regiments. General Richard Taylor ordered him to harass the enemy in the Pineville-Alexandria sector. This Liddell did to the best of his ability, but he had no artillery and lacked enough strength to make much of an impact. As a result, Taylor (who disliked Liddell personally) relieved him of his command.

Meanwhile, General Dabney Maury at Mobile was clamoring for veteran infantry officers. The War Department in Richmond sent him Liddell. He reported for duty in July 1864, and Maury gave him responsibility for the Confederate defenses on the eastern side of Mobile Bay and command of about 2,700 of his 6,500 men.

In early April 1865, Union General Edward R. S. Canby attacked Mobile with more than thirty thousand men. Liddell held off the overwhelming forces for nine days, but on April 9, the Yankees attacked with thirty-five regiments (sixteen thousand men) along a three-mile front. Liddell was captured when Fort Blakely fell that evening. Mobile fell on April 12.

After he was paroled, Liddell returned to a devastated land. Carpetbaggers plundered Louisiana with high taxes, and Liddell faced high inflation rates, a shortage of labor, low cotton prices, and a shortage of money. He was forced into bankruptcy in December 1868. Formerly wealthy, he was now unable to pay for his children's education. Fortunately, friends took care of that.

On February 14, 1870, Liddell was eating dinner on a steamboat when Charles Jones and his two sons entered the dining room and shot him seven times. He died instantly. He was fifty-four years old. General St. John R. Liddell was buried in Llanada Plantation Cemetery near Jonesville, Louisiana, where he lies today.

An angry mob of about thirty men caught Charles Jones and one of his sons and shot them to death on February 27.

ROBERT DOAK LILLEY was born on January 28, 1836, in Greenville, Virginia. He graduated from Washington College and became a salesman of surveying instruments his father had invented. He was in Charleston, training people on one of his father's instruments, when G. T. Beauregard fired on Fort Sumter. He quickly returned to Virginia and recruited an infantry company, the Augusta Lee Rifles, and was elected its captain. The Rifles were incorporated into the 25th Virginia as Company C, and Lilley was elected its captain.

The regiment was sent to western Virginia, where it fought in the Battle of Rich Mountain and much of the 25th Virginia was captured. Captain Lilley, however, followed Jed Hotchkiss, the famous mapmaker, and escaped with part of his company.

The following year, Lilley took part in Stonewall Jackson's Valley Campaign and the Seven Days Battles. On August 9, 1862, the 25th Virginia was attacked by strong Union forces at Cedar Mountain. It fell back in disorder. Captain Lilley personally grabbed the regimental colors, rallied the panicked soldiers, led a sharp counterattack, and restored the line. From this point, he was considered fearless in an army known for its fearlessness. He was also commended for bravery in the Battle of Second Manassas.

After fighting at Sharpsburg and Fredericksburg, Lilley was promoted to major in January 1863. The 25th Virginia was stationed in the Shenandoah Valley during the Chancellorsville Campaign but took part in the invasion of Pennsylvania. At Gettysburg, Lilley commanded his brigade's skirmish line. This led to his promotion to lieutenant colonel after the battle.

In late 1863 and 1864, Lilley fought in the Mine Run Campaign and the battles of the Wilderness and Spotsylvania Court House, after which he was promoted to colonel and regimental commander. He was with General Jubal Early during the invasion of Maryland and actually entered Washington, D.C. He fought in the Shenandoah Valley Campaign of 1864, during which he was placed in command of Early's old brigade. On May 31, 1864, he was promoted to brigadier general.

On July 20, 1864, during the Battle of Stephenson's Depot, he was shot in the arm and leg. As he lay helpless on the battlefield, a poisonous moccasin snake crawled over him but did not bite him. Lilley was eventually picked up by Northern soldiers and made a prisoner of war. The leg wound was not serious, but Union surgeons had to amputate his shattered arm. Four days later, when the Yankees abandoned Winchester, they left Lilley behind, and he was rescued by Confederate forces. No longer able to exercise field command, he was placed in charge of the reserve forces in the Shenandoah, a position he had until the end of the war.

Following the surrender, Robert E. Lee, the president of Washington College, recommended he be appointed the college's financial agent. He held this job the rest of his life. On November 9, 1886, while attending a session of the Virginia Synod of the Presbyterian Church in Richmond, he suffered a major stroke. He died November 12, 1886, in Richmond at age fifty. General Robert D. Lilley was buried in Thornrose Cemetery, Staunton, Virginia, not far from the grave of Jed Hotchkiss.

LEWIS HENRY LITTLE was born in Baltimore, Maryland, on March 19, 1817, the son of a former congressman. He graduated from West Point and was commissioned as a second lieutenant in the 5th U.S. Infantry Regiment in 1839. He fought in the Mexican War and was awarded a brevet promotion to captain for gallantry and meritorious conduct in the Battle of Monterrey. The 5th Infantry also fought at Molino del Rey, Chapultepec, and the capture of Mexico City. Little was promoted to captain (substantive rank) in 1847. After the Mexicans surrendered, Little was stationed on the Western frontier.

Little resigned his U.S. Army commission on May 7, 1861. He was appointed a major of artillery in the Confederate Army that same month. He was promoted to colonel in the Missouri State Guard on May 18, 1861. In August, he was a Confederate Army colonel and assistant adjutant general (and de facto chief of staff) to Major General Sterling Price. He served in the unsuccessful attempt to bring Missouri into the Confederacy in 1861.

By early March 1862, Little was commander of the 1st Missouri Brigade in Sterling Price's division. He fought in the Battle of Pea Ridge (or Elkhorn Tavern), March 7–8, 1862. He was in the heaviest of the fighting, during which he showed dash, competence, and initiative, and by the end of the battle, as casualties mounted and his responsibilities grew, he was the de facto commander of Price's division.

Regarded as an excellent officer and a good disciplinarian, Colonel Little was promoted to brigadier general on April 12, 1862. That same month, he crossed the Mississippi River, along with most of Earl Van Dorn's Army of the West. He served in the Siege of Corinth, where he came down with malaria. He never fully recovered.

On September 19, 1862, General Price attacked U.S. General William Rosecrans at Iuka. At 5:45 p.m., while talking with General Sterling Price, General Louis Hébert, and Colonel John W. Whitfield, a minié ball struck Little in the forehead and killed him instantly. He was forty-five years old.

General Little was buried by torchlight in Iuka that night. He was reinterred in Green Mount Cemetery, Baltimore, Maryland, after the war.

THOMAS MULDRUP LOGAN, the son of a local judge, was born in Charleston, South Carolina, on November 3, 1840. He graduated from South Carolina College in Columbia in 1860 at the head of his class, joined the Washington Light Infantry, and took part in the firing on Fort Sumter. Commissioned a second lieutenant in the Confederate Army later that month, he joined the Hampton Legion in May and was elevated to first lieutenant. He fought in the Battle of First Manassas, after which he was promoted to captain. He took part in the Seven Days Battles, where he was wounded in the foot at Gaines' Mill on June 27, 1862. He fought in the Battle of Second Manassas and was cited for "great bravery" in the Battle of Sharpsburg (September 17, 1862). He was promoted to major to rank from that date. He was advanced to the rank of lieutenant colonel in December.

The Legion's artillery was transferred to Micah Jenkins's brigade in 1863. It took part in the Suffolk operation and did not return to the I Corps until after Gettysburg. Logan went west with General James Longstreet and fought at Chickamauga, the Siege of Chattanooga (in its early stages), and the Siege of Knoxville before returning to Virginia. He was promoted to colonel on May 19, 1864. He was wounded again during the Battle of Riddell's Shop on June 13, 1864, and saw action at the Siege of Petersburg.

In late 1864, he was selected to command a brigade under Wade Hampton in South Carolina. He was promoted to brigadier general (temporary rank) on December 1, 1864, at age twenty-four, but the Confederate Senate refused to confirm it, so he reverted to the rank of colonel. For a short time, however, he was the youngest general in the Confederate Army. He was reappointed brigadier on February 15, 1865 (full rank), and he was confirmed a week later. He fought in the Battle of Bentonville and surrendered with the rest of the Army of Tennessee on April 26. He was paroled at Greensboro, North Carolina, on May 1.

After the war, General Logan studied law and went to work in the railroad industry. He was the principal organizer of the Southern Railway and a business associate of John D. Rockefeller. He also became chairman of the Virginia Democratic Party's executive committee and was later a leader in the "Gold Democrat" Party, although he never sought public office.

Thomas M. Logan died in his New York City apartment on August 11, 1914, at age seventy-three. He was buried in Hollywood Cemetery, Richmond, Virginia.

LUNSFORD LINDSAY LOMAX was born on November 4, 1835, at Newport, Rhode Island, where his father, a career army officer, was stationed.

Lunsford was able to secure an appointment to West Point and graduated with the class of 1856. As a second lieutenant of cavalry, he served in the Nebraska and Kansas Territories. On April 25, 1861, Lomax (now a first lieutenant) resigned his commission and was quickly appointed a captain in the Virginia Militia. He became an assistant adjutant general on the staff of Joseph E. Johnston.

After the Battle of First Manassas, Lomax was transferred to the West and served on the staffs of Ben McCulloch and Earl Van Dorn. He set up a system of scouts and partisan rangers in West Tennessee which materially contributed to the Southern cause. This led to his promotion to lieutenant colonel. He also fought at Pea Ridge, Farmington, Corinth, the First Siege of Vicksburg (1862), and Baton Rouge. On February 8, 1863, Lomax assumed command of the 11th Virginia Cavalry Regiment. He was promoted to full colonel that same day.

Lomax set up partisan ranger units in the Shenandoah Valley. These units provided scouts and information for regular Confederate units and engaged in telegraph wiretapping and raids. The most famous were Mosby's Rangers, named after John Singleton Mosby, the "Gray Ghost of the Confederacy."

Lomax led his regiment on raids into West Virginia, Brandy Station, Winchester, Rector's Crossroads, Gettysburg, and Buckland. He was promoted to brigadier general on July 23, 1863.

Lomax's brigade was placed in General Fitzhugh Lee's division and fought at Culpeper Court House, Brandy Station, the Wilderness, Cold Harbor, Yellow Tavern, Ream's Station, Trevilian Station, and other engagements. In 1864, General Lomax was named commander of Jubal Early's cavalry in the Shenandoah Valley. On October 9, 1864, during the Battle of Woodstock, he was captured, but three hours later he personally overwhelmed his guard and escaped.

Considered a gallant and cool leader, he was promoted to major general (temporary rank) on August 10, 1864. He was later confirmed at full rank (February 20, 1865).

In the last days of the war, General Lee relieved Jubal Early of his command. He was replaced by General Lomax as commander of the Valley District on March 29, 1865. After Lee surrendered on April 9, Lomax assembled his forces at Lynchburg and rode south, where he joined Joseph E. Johnston's Army of Tennessee. He surrendered his division at Greensboro shortly after Johnston capitulated on April 26.

After the war, Lunsford Lomax returned to Caroline County, Virginia, and farmed for more than twenty years. From 1886 to 1891, he was the president of Virginia Agricultural and Mechanical College (now Virginia Tech) at Blacksburg. He was then employed by the U.S. War Department, where he helped edit the *Official Records of the Union and Confederate Armies in the War of the Rebellion*. He was also commissioner of Gettysburg National Military Park.

Lunsford Lindsay Lomax died in Washington, D.C., on May 28, 1913, at age seventy-seven and is buried in Warrenton Cemetery, Warrenton, Virginia.

ARMISTEAD LINDSAY LONG was born on September 13, 1825, in Campbell County, Virginia. He attended the U.S. Military Academy at West Point and graduated in the class of 1850. Commissioned a second lieutenant of artillery, he was stationed at Fort Moultrie, South Carolina; New Mexico; Fort McHenry, Maryland; Kansas Territory; Nebraska Territory; Indian Territory; Fort Monroe, Virginia; and the Augusta Arsenal, Georgia.

He was in Washington, D.C., as aide-de-camp to his father-in-law, Brigadier General Edwin V. Sumner, when the war began. Long resigned his commission on June 10, 1861, and was named major of artillery in the Confederate Army. As chief of artillery on the staff of W. W. Loring in western Virginia, he became close friends with Robert E. Lee. In the fall of 1861, he joined General Lee's staff when Lee was the commander of the Department of South Carolina, Georgia, and Florida. Lee appointed Long military secretary and promoted him to colonel. Long followed Lee to Virginia in 1862, when Lee became commander of the Army of Northern Virginia.

Long was an excellent staff officer, as well as a fine artillery officer, as he demonstrated at Fredericksburg and Chancellorsville. Although he was reluctant to part with Long, General Lee decided after Gettysburg that he would be even more valuable as chief of artillery of the II Corps. Long was promoted to brigadier general on September 21, 1863.

General Long commanded the II Corps artillery during the Bristoe Campaign and the Mine Run Campaign. Sent to the Shenandoah Valley in the spring of 1864, he directed General Jubal Early's artillery during his drive on Washington and his Valley Campaign of 1864. Long was praised for his "unfailing judgment" and his "steadfast gallantry and unfaltering courage."

Long remained with Early until his army was destroyed in the Battle of Waynesboro on March 2, 1865. He then returned to Richmond and rejoined the II Corps (now under General John B. Gordon) and remained with it until it surrendered at Appomattox.

After the war, Long served as the chief engineer of the James River and Kanawha Canal Company. Tragically, in 1870, he went totally blind. He nevertheless wrote a well-received biography of General Lee that was published in 1886, along with a variety of historical articles. Despite spending the last twenty years of his life in total darkness, he never complained.

His wife was appointed postmistress of Charlottesville by President Ulysses Grant, which allowed the family to survive financially. General Long died on April 29, 1891, in Charlottesville. He was sixty-five years old. He was buried in Maplewood Cemetery, Charlottesville.

·L

JAMES "PETE" LONGSTREET, who was called "Old Pete" by his men, was born on January 8, 1821, in the Edgefield District of South Carolina. His parents owned a plantation near Gainesville in northeast Georgia, and Longstreet regarded this as his home.

Longstreet grew into a big man: six feet, two inches in height and powerfully built. His father nicknamed him "Peter," after the rocklike apostle in the Bible, whose virtues he wanted his son to emulate. Young Longstreet enjoyed exercise, hunting, fishing, horseback riding, swimming, drinking whiskey, and playing cards, which was considered somewhat immoral in the antebellum South. He often dressed poorly, was not very refined, and used coarse or vulgar language, though never in the presence of ladies.

He was educated in a good preparatory school and at West Point, from which he graduated in 1842 as a second lieutenant of infantry.

Longstreet's early assignments took him to Jefferson Barracks, Missouri; western Louisiana; Florida; and Texas. The Mexican War began in April 1846. Longstreet fought in the battles of Palo Alto, Resaca de la Palma, and Monterrey in northern Mexico. He did well.

Sent to General Winfield Scott's army, Longstreet fought in all of the major engagements from Veracruz to Chapultepec, where he led a charge and caught a musket ball in the thigh.

After he recovered, Longstreet enjoyed a varied career as a recruiter, regimental adjutant, chief regimental commissary, company commander, post commander, and paymaster.

Major Longstreet resigned his commission on May 9, 1861, and was appointed lieutenant colonel of infantry in the Confederate Regular Army. He was promoted to brigadier general, Provisional Army, on June 17. He fought in the Battle of First Manassas, where his brigade was lightly engaged. He was given a division and promoted to major general on October 7.

Longstreet's division fought in the Peninsula Campaign and in the Battle of Seven Pines, where he performed poorly. Longstreet's efforts were much more successful in the Seven Days Battles, where he established himself as one of General Robert E. Lee's top lieutenants. He was given command of the I Corps, which he led for the rest of the war, except when he was recovering from wounds. He was promoted to lieutenant general on October 9, 1862.

James Longstreet was ambitious and yearned for an independent command, which he received in the spring of 1863 when he was named commander of the Department of North Carolina and Southern Virginia. But, after unsuccessfully besieging Suffolk and missing the Battle of Chancellorsville, he rejoined the main army in time for the Battle of Gettysburg. On July 2, 1863—the critical day—Longstreet's performance as a field commander was sluggish at best. His conduct at Gettysburg has been the subject of criticism and controversy ever since.

On July 3, Longstreet repeatedly asked General Lee not to launch Pickett's Charge, but to no avail. In his memoirs, Longstreet painted a dramatic scene where he firmly warned a stubborn Lee of the disaster that awaited him if he persisted. None of the witnesses to the alleged confrontation remembered it. But he was right: Pickett's Charge was a disaster.

After Gettysburg, Longstreet's corps was sent west. At Chickamauga, it scored a major breakthrough, but Longstreet was unable to convince General Braxton Bragg to launch an aggressive pursuit of the Federals.

Longstreet again received an independent command but suffered a defeat at Knoxville, after which he sacked Generals Lafayette McLaws (a good friend from West Point days), Evander Law, and Jerome B. Robertson, making them scapegoats for his failure. Soldiers in the ranks, however, seemed to assign the blame to Longstreet, whom they nicknamed "Peter the Slow." Longstreet submitted his resignation on December 30, 1863. The War Department refused to accept it.

Returning to the Army of Northern Virginia, Longstreet redeemed himself in the Battle of the Wilderness by launching a brilliant surprise attack on the Union flank. After the war, his opponent, General Winfield Scott Hancock, told Longstreet, "You rolled me up like a wet blanket!" Unfortunately, Longstreet was accidentally shot by his own men. He was out of action until September 1864. He then took command of the forces north of the James, and after A. P. Hill's death on April 2, 1865, he commanded both I Corps and III Corps before the Confederate surrender at Appomattox.

Longstreet assembled one of the best staffs in the Confederate Army, and as a corps commander, he generally performed well—sometimes even brilliantly—but as an independent commander, he was a failure.

After the war, he moved to New Orleans and became a scalawag and a Republican and worked for the carpetbagger regime (A "scalawag" was a Southerner who collaborated with the carpetbagger regime. Scalawags were looked upon like French collaborators in World War II who cooperated with the Nazis. Many of them met the same fate.). In 1875, fearing for his safety and that of his family, Longstreet returned to Gainesville, Georgia. In 1877, he converted to Catholicism.

While he became unpopular with many of his former Confederate comrades, Longstreet was very popular with Republican presidents and was named U.S. ambassador to the Ottoman Empire by President Rutherford B. Hayes and U.S. Commissioner of Railroads by Presidents William McKinley and Theodore Roosevelt.

In 1896, he finished his autobiography, *From Manassas to Appomattox: Memoirs of the Civil War in America*, which did little to silence his critics, like Jubal Early and Fitzhugh Lee, because it came across as self-serving and not entirely accurate.

General Longstreet's last years were plagued by bad health and partial deafness. He died in Gainesville, Georgia, on January 2, 1904. Had he lived six more days, he would have been eighty-three. He is buried in Alta Vista Cemetery in Gainesville.

L.

WILLIAM WING LORING was born in Wilmington, North Carolina, on December 4, 1818. His family moved to St. Augustine, Florida Territory, when he was four. He volunteered for the Florida Militia at age fourteen and fought the Seminoles. He was promoted to second lieutenant in 1837.

Loring enrolled in Georgetown College, Washington, D.C., in 1839 but dropped out the following year. He returned to Florida, studied law, and was admitted to the bar in 1842. He was elected to the legislature in 1843 but was defeated when he ran for the Florida State Senate in 1845.

In 1846, Loring joined the newly formed Regiment of Mounted Rifles as a captain thanks to an influential law partner. By 1847, he was a major. Loring fought in several battles in Mexico, was brevetted twice (to colonel), and was wounded three times. At

Chapultepec, a bullet shattered his left arm. Surgeons amputated it. Even so, he remained in the army, serving in the West, fighting Comanches, Apaches, and Kiowas. He was promoted to colonel (permanent rank) in 1856 and was the youngest man of that rank in the U.S. Army. He commanded the Mounted Rifle Regiment (which later became the 3rd Cavalry) from 1856 to 1859. He was in New Mexico when the South seceded.

W. W. Loring resigned his commission on May 13, 1861, and was named brigadier general in the Confederate Army on May 20, 1861. He was placed in command of the Army of the Northwest in western Virginia, which was reinforced to a strength of 11,500 men, but he would not cooperate with other generals. Partially as a result, the Western Virginia Campaign of 1861 failed.

When he was assigned to Stonewall Jackson's command in late 1861, Jackson filed court-martial charges against him. President Jefferson Davis rescued Loring's career by appointing him commander of the Department of Southwestern Virginia—out of Jackson's area of command. Loring was promoted to major general on February 15, 1862.

Loring performed well in his new assignment. He invaded what became West Virginia and seized Charleston in September 1862, but was forced to retreat six weeks later. A week after that, General Samuel Cooper relieved him of his command because Loring was feuding with Governor John Letcher, with whom Loring could never establish a working relationship. Robert E. Lee had had enough and declared that there was no place in his army for W. W. Loring.

On November 27, 1862, Loring was sent to Mississippi as second-in-command to General John C. Pemberton, the commander of the Army of Mississippi. On January 2, 1863, Loring assumed command of the 1st Division of the Army of Mississippi.

Loring took an instant disliking to Pemberton, both personally and professionally. He was not a loyal subordinate, but he successfully defended Fort Pemberton, which was constructed to defeat Grant's Yazoo Pass Expedition.

After Grant landed south of Vicksburg, Loring's division was ordered to join the main army. Loring hated Pemberton so badly, it appears, that he was willing for Pemberton to lose a battle if it meant he would lose his job—or at least two staff officers present at Champion Hill thought so. Distinguished historians Michael B. Ballard and James R. Arnold have made similar suggestions.

It is hard to imagine any general performing any worse than Loring did during the Battle of Champion Hill on May 16, 1863. Always fractious, he was insubordinate and ignored Pemberton's orders. Had Loring obeyed them, the Confederates might have won the battle. Pemberton made a stand east of Big Black River, in large part to keep open an escape route for Loring's division. But Loring, without telling Pemberton, had taken his division off the field, moving to the south. Loring's refusal to follow orders or communicate with Pemberton resulted in the first rout of a Confederate army. While inflicting fewer than two hundred casualties on the Federals, Loring was forced to abandon all his guns and wagons, and about two thousand of his men were captured.

That summer Loring joined General Joseph E. Johnston's Army of Relief south of Jackson, Mississippi, in a failed attempt to save Vicksburg from falling to the Federals. In February 1864, he was involved in the unsuccessful defense of Meridian and eastern Mississippi. Then he and his division were dispatched to northwest Georgia to join the Army of Tennessee.

During the Atlanta Campaign, he performed well but was passed over for commander of the III Corps. He was wounded at Ezra Church on July 28 and could not return to duty until after Atlanta fell. He took part in the invasion of Tennessee, fighting at both Franklin and Nashville. Only remnants of his division escaped, but they returned to the East and fought in the Carolinas Campaign, including the Battle of Bentonville. He was with Joseph E. Johnston's army when it surrendered at Bennett Place on April 26.

After the war, Loring joined the Egyptian Army and spent several years in the service of the Khedive of Egypt. He returned to the United States in 1878 and wrote a book, *A Confederate Soldier in Egypt*. It was published in 1884. In Florida, he ran for a U.S. Senate seat but was defeated.

He then moved to New York City, where he died on December 30, 1886, at age sixty-eight. He was buried in Loring Park, St. Augustine, Florida.

Although he had his moments of glory and was certainly technically proficient in the mounted infantry, W. W. Loring's performance in the Civil War was highly disappointing. His personal deficiencies clearly outweighed his positive military attributes. It would have been better for the Confederacy if Jefferson Davis had let Stonewall Jackson court-martial him in 1862.

MANSFIELD LOVELL was born in Washington, D.C., on October 20, 1822, the son of the surgeon general of the U.S. Army. Lovell was orphaned when he was fourteen. He was admitted to West Point at age fifteen and graduated in 1842.

Lieutenant Lovell joined the 4th U.S. Artillery and established himself as a promising young officer. He fought with General Zachary Taylor in northern Mexico and was wounded at Monterrey. During the drive on Mexico City, he became chief of staff to General John A. Quitman. He was wounded again in the Battle of Chapultepec. He was brevetted captain for his courage and gallantry.

After the war, Lovell's assignments were uneventful, and he resigned from the army in 1854 to take a position with an iron-works firm. In 1857, he became deputy street commissioner of New York City, serving under his old classmate G. W. Smith, another future Confederate general.

In 1861, Lovell resigned his job and joined the Confederacy. On the recommendation of General Joseph E. Johnson, who remembered Lovell from their service together in the 4th Artillery, Lovell was appointed as a major general on October 7, 1861. He was never a brigadier.

Lovell was given the assignment of defending New Orleans. He had an extremely difficult—if not impossible—task. The Crescent City was one of the least defensible cities in North America. To make matters worse, the naval forces in the area would not cooperate with him, and his appeals to Richmond for help were ignored. A Union fleet under Admiral David Farragut reached New Orleans on April 25, 1862, and after prolonged negotiations, the city was firmly in Northern hands by April 29.

General Lovell was strongly criticized for losing the South's largest city. He was nevertheless given command of a division in Earl Van Dorn's Army of Mississippi. He fought in the Second Battle of Corinth, where his performance was hesitant, slow, and unsatisfactory. Shortly after, John C. Pemberton was named commander of the army and sent Lovell home to await orders that never came.

Jefferson Davis let Lovell take the blame for the loss of New Orleans. Lovell demanded a court of inquiry and finally got one beginning on April 4, 1863. Except for two minor criticisms, the court completely exonerated him and praised his "great energy" and "untiring industry." Still, he received no further assignments from the War Department in Richmond, despite the fact that Generals Joe Johnston and John Bell Hood both requested his services. From May until September 1864, he was deputy commander of the Georgia militia.

General Robert E. Lee was among those who thought Lovell deserved commendation rather than condemnation for his defense of New Orleans. After Lee became general-in-chief of the Confederate armies on January 31, 1865, he approved General Joseph E. Johnston's request to employ Lovell, who was on his way to join the Army of Tennessee when Johnston surrendered on April 26.

After the war, Lovell farmed a rice plantation near Savannah, Georgia, but when a storm destroyed his first crop, he returned to New York with his family. He worked as a civil engineer and, under the general supervision of former Union General John Newton, cleared obstructions from the East River.

Major General Mansfield Lovell died in New York City on June 1, 1884, at age sixty-one. He is buried in Woodlawn Cemetery, Bronx, New York.

MARK PERRIN LOWREY was born in McNairy County, Tennessee, on December 29, 1828, the son of English and Irish immigrants. He received no formal education, and his father died of yellow fever when he was young. He moved to Mississippi in 1843 and became a bricklayer. He enlisted as a private in the 2nd Mississippi Infantry Regiment in 1847 and went to Mexico but saw no combat.

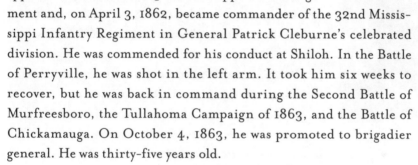

Lowrey became a Southern Baptist preacher in 1853, working mainly around the village of Kossuth in northern Mississippi. He also joined the Mississippi Militia and was a captain when the war started. He was appointed colonel of the 4th Mississippi Militia Regiment and, on April 3, 1862, became commander of the 32nd Mississippi Infantry Regiment in General Patrick Cleburne's celebrated division. He was commended for his conduct at Shiloh. In the Battle of Perryville, he was shot in the left arm. It took him six weeks to recover, but he was back in command during the Second Battle of Murfreesboro, the Tullahoma Campaign of 1863, and the Battle of Chickamauga. On October 4, 1863, he was promoted to brigadier general. He was thirty-five years old.

Lowrey became known in the Army of Tennessee as the "fighting preacher." He checked every attack launched on his brigade at Missionary Ridge and performed well at Ringgold Gap, where Cleburne defeated U.S. General Joseph Hooker and saved the army's wagon train. During the retreat from Dalton to Atlanta, Lowrey distinguished himself in the Battle of Pickett's Mill, where Cleburne's division checked U.S. General Oliver O. Howard's entire corps. Lowrey fought in all the battles and campaigns around Atlanta, as well as in General John Bell Hood's Tennessee Campaign, where he fought at Franklin and Nashville. General Cleburne called Lowrey the bravest man in the Confederate Army.

On the retreat from Tennessee, General Lowrey's health started to fail, and he resigned his commission on March 14, 1865. After the war, Lowrey returned to Mississippi, where he studied the Bible and preached

413

the gospel. In 1873, he founded and taught at the Blue Mountain Female Institute, which later became Blue Mountain College, near Tupelo.

On February 27, 1885, while purchasing a train ticket in Middleton, Tennessee, he suddenly dropped dead. He was fifty-six years old. General Mark P. Lowrey was buried in Blue Mountain Cemetery, Blue Mountain, Mississippi.

ROBERT LOWRY was born on March 10, 1829, in Chesterfield County, South Carolina. While still a boy, he was sent to live with his uncle, Judge James Lowry, in Raleigh, Smith County, Mississippi. His early education was limited, but under the tutorage of his uncle, he read law and was admitted to the bar in 1859. He set up his practice in Brandon. Lowry soon rose to prominence and was elected to the Mississippi House of Representatives.

When the war began, Lowry enlisted as a private in the 6th Mississippi Infantry Regiment but was elected its major in August 1861. He fought in the Battle of Shiloh, where he was wounded twice. His regimental commander was also seriously wounded and resigned for reasons of health on May 23, 1862. Lowry was elected colonel that same day.

Lowry led his regiment at Corinth, in the battles around Vicksburg, and at Port Gibson, where he was praised by General Martin Green for his coolness under fire and his promptness in carrying out every order. The 6th Mississippi was attached to General Lloyd Tilghman's brigade at Champion Hill, escaped encirclement in Vicksburg, and then became part of General Joseph E. Johnston's Army of Relief.

In early 1864, Lowry suppressed a minor anti-Confederate uprising in Jones County, Mississippi. In the spring, Colonel Lowry and his regiment were sent to Georgia. They fought in the Atlanta Campaign and repulsed two major attacks at Kennesaw Mountain. After Atlanta fell, Lowry took part in the Tennessee Campaign. On November 30, 1864, during the Battle of Franklin, General John Adams was killed, and Lowry assumed command of the brigade. After fighting in the

Battle of Nashville and the retreat to Tupelo, Mississippi, Robert Lowry was promoted to brigadier general on February 4, 1865.

Remaining in the Army of Tennessee, Lowry fought in the Carolinas Campaign, including the Battle of Bentonville. He and his men surrendered at Bennett Place, near Durham, on April 26, 1865.

General Lowry returned to Mississippi in 1865 and was promptly elected to the state senate. He ran for state attorney general in 1869, but the state was still under Radical Republican Reconstruction rule, and he was defeated. In 1881, the Democratic Party's gubernatorial nomination was deadlocked. Lowry was selected as a compromise candidate. He was elected governor on November 8, 1881, and was reelected in 1885 without opposition. A conservative and free market–inclined "Bourbon Democrat," Lowry's administration was marked by rapid economic growth. After his second term expired, Lowry settled in Jackson, and coauthored a history of Mississippi.

Lowry ran for the U.S. Senate in 1901 but was defeated. He retired from politics and died in Jackson, Mississippi, on January 19, 1910, at age of eighty. He is buried in Brandon Cemetery, Brandon, Mississippi.

HYLAN BENTON LYON was born on February 22, 1836, in Eddyville, Kentucky, in Caldwell County, which is now Lyon County. His father was a wealthy plantation owner but died when Hylan was no more than five. He was then raised by a guardian, who saw to it that Lyon was well educated. He attended the Masonic University of Kentucky and Cumberland College and gained admission to West Point at age sixteen. He graduated in 1856 and was commissioned in the artillery. He was posted to Florida during the Third Seminole War and subsequently fought Indians in the Washington Territory and Montana. He also served in California.

Lyon resigned his commission on April 30, 1861, and joined the Confederate Army as a first lieutenant of artillery. He raised a company for the 3rd Kentucky Infantry, but it was converted into a battery in the 1st Kentucky Artillery Battalion on

September 30, 1861. He transferred to the 8th Kentucky Infantry as its lieutenant colonel on January 24, 1862. He led the regiment at Fort Donelson but was taken prisoner when it surrendered on February 16, 1862. After seven months in Northern prisons, he was exchanged on August 15, 1862.

Hyland Lyon was promoted to colonel of the rebuilt 8th Kentucky on October 7, 1862. As part of the Army of Mississippi, he led it in the Battle of Coffeeville, which was won by the South. Lyon escaped encirclement at Champion Hill and managed to reach Jackson with 250 men. Later he was transferred to the Army of Tennessee, where General Braxton Bragg appointed him commander of two cavalry regiments in Joe Wheeler's cavalry corps. He took part in the Siege of Knoxville under General Longstreet. When Lyon was sent back to Chattanooga, Bragg made him temporary commander of all artillery taking part in the siege. He managed to save most of it in the ensuing retreat.

Colonel Lyon rejoined the cavalry in 1864, under General Nathan Bedford Forrest, who thought highly of him. On June 14, 1864, Lyon was promoted to brigadier general. He commanded a brigade under Forrest and directed the Rebel artillery when it destroyed Sherman's supply base at Johnsonville on November 4, 1864.

Lyon succeeded Adam Johnson as commander of the District of Western Kentucky in September 1864 and led cavalry raids to distract Union attention during General John Bell Hood's invasion of Tennessee. After Hood was defeated at Nashville, Lyon rejoined Forrest in northern Mississippi. In January 1865, Lyon was sleeping in a private home when he was surprised by Union cavalry. He was captured but managed to escape.

After the war, Lyon went to Mexico with former Tennessee Governor Isham G. Harris. A year later, he returned to Eddyville, Kentucky, and took up farming. Eventually, he established a profitable mercantile business and later became warden of the Kentucky State Penitentiary.

General Hylan B. Lyon died on April 25, 1907. He was seventy-one years old. He is buried in River View Cemetery, Eddyville.

M

MACKALL – MOUTON

WILLIAM WHANN MACKALL was born on January 18, 1817, in Georgetown, District of Columbia, but lived in Wilna, Maryland, from around the age of six until he left home for West Point. He graduated from the U.S. Military Academy in 1837. An artillery officer, he was sent to Florida, where he fought in the Second Seminole War. At River Inlet, he was ambushed and severely wounded on February 11, 1839.

After tours of duty at Plattsburgh, New York, and on the Maine frontier, Mackall was a staff officer in Mexico. He fought at Monterrey, where he was brevetted captain. Transferred to General Winfield Scott's army, he received a brevet promotion to major for gallantry at Contreras and Churubusco. He was wounded in action at Chapultepec shortly before the Mexicans surrendered.

Mackall was a superb staff officer and served as an adjutant general throughout the 1850s. In 1861, he was offered a promotion to lieutenant colonel, but instead he resigned his U.S. Army commission and made his way south, where he accepted an appointment as a lieutenant colonel in the Confederate Army on September 9, 1861. He joined General Albert Sidney Johnston's staff as assistant adjutant general. On February 27, 1862, he was appointed brigadier general. Johnston gave him command of Island Number 10 in the Mississippi River of Tennessee, where he was captured on April 7, 1862. He was imprisoned at Fort Warren in Boston Harbor until August 15, 1862, when he was exchanged and sent to the Department of Tennessee. In December 1862 he was transferred to the Department of the Gulf, where he served with General Simon B. Buckner improving the defenses of Mobile.

In April 1863, General Mackall was appointed chief of staff to General Braxton Bragg. Mackall was unhappy in this position (he did not like working for his former West Point classmate) and asked to be transferred. Bragg nevertheless praised him for "capacity, professional acquirements, and urbanity."

Mackall was sent to General Leonidas Polk's Department of Mississippi and Eastern Louisiana, where he commanded a brigade. Polk recommended his promotion to major general, but his recommendation was not acted upon.

In January 1864, William Mackall became chief of staff to General Joseph E. Johnston, who was now commanding the Army of Tennessee. After Johnston was sacked by President Jefferson Davis on July 17, Mackall declined to serve under General John Hood. Mackall received no further assignments from the War Department in Richmond, so he moved to Macon, Georgia, and served as a volunteer commander of Georgia forces. On April 20, he was present, along with Generals G. W. Smith and Howell Cobb, when they surrendered Macon.

After the war, Mackall settled in Fairfax County, Virginia, where he was a farmer and real estate speculator. General William W. Mackall died at Langley, one of his farms in Fairfax County, on August 19, 1891, at age seventy-four. He was buried in Lewinsville Presbyterian Cemetery, McLean, Fairfax County, Virginia.

WILLIAM MACRAE (sometimes spelled "McRae") was born on September 9, 1834, in Wilmington, North Carolina. Young William's family was prosperous, and he received a good private education. He was always interested in railroads, and he moved to Philadelphia at age sixteen to learn how to build locomotives; he went on to study civil engineering. MacRae was an assistant engineer for the Carolina Central Railroad when the war began. He joined the Monroe Light Infantry as a private. It became Company B of the 15th North Carolina in May 1861, and MacRae was elected captain on June 11, 1861.

The 15th was sent to Virginia and became part of General John B. Magruder's command. It took part in the Peninsula Campaign, where William MacRae was promoted to lieutenant colonel on May 2, 1862. It subsequently fought in the Seven Days Battles, the Battle of Second Manassas, and at Crampton's Gap. On

September 17, during the Battle of Sharpsburg, MacRae obtained the command of Thomas R. R. Cobb's brigade, even though he was only a lieutenant colonel. The brigade was down to a strength of 250 men; MacRae nevertheless repulsed three Union charges. When he fell back, only 50 of his men were still standing, and his ammunition was exhausted. He was promoted to full colonel on February 27, 1863.

MacRae's regiment was given the task of guarding the Charleston and Savannah Railroad in early 1863. It also fought in the Battle of Bachelor's Creek near New Bern and returned to General Robert E. Lee's army after Gettysburg. It fought at Bristoe Station on October 14, 1863.

In 1864, MacRae fought in the Overland Campaign. On June 23, he was given a temporary promotion to brigadier general and command of William W. Kirkland's brigade after that officer was wounded. He took part in the Siege of Petersburg. During the Battle of Ream's Station, he launched a surprise attack that overran part of the U.S. II Corps and captured more than two thousand men, along with nine guns. He was commended by General Lee and formally promoted to brigadier general (permanent rank) on November 4.

William MacRae surrendered at Appomattox on April 9, 1865. He was wounded only once (shot through the jaw), but his sword had been broken twice by shot and shell, and on several occasions his clothes had been penetrated by bullets or shell fragments.

After the war, General MacRae returned to the railroad business and in January 1866 was named general superintendent of the Wilmington and Manchester Railroad and later of the Macon and Brunswick Railroad. In 1873, he became general superintendent of the Western and Atlantic Railroad of Georgia.

William MacRae's health declined in the 1870s. He developed lung disease and was finally forced to retire. He went to Florida to take advantage of the warmer climate but decided to return home to Wilmington to die. He did not make it. General William MacRae passed away in a hotel in Augusta, Georgia, on February 11, 1882. He was only forty-seven years old. He is buried in Wilmington's Oakdale Cemetery. He never married.

JOHN BANKHEAD MAGRUDER, probably the most theatrical of the Confederate officers, was born on May 1, 1807, in Port Royal, Virginia. He was admitted to West Point in 1826 and graduated in 1830. He was a very flamboyant, hyperactive, extroverted, intelligent, well-educated, well-read, graceful, charming, and flash-ily dressed man who took full advantage of the pleasures of life. For these reasons, he was nicknamed "Prince John." He stood six feet tall and was considered by more than one observer to be the handsomest man in the Confederacy. He spoke with a lisp, which was his only physical flaw.

Magruder loved pomp and ostentatious dress, but he knew how to motivate and inspire the troops under his command, and he used his colorful personality to the best effect, often visiting them in the field and joking with them.

Assigned to the infantry, he transferred to the artillery in August 1831 and spent most of his career there. He served in Mexico under Generals Zachary Taylor and Winfield Scott and commanded a light artillery battery in Gideon Pillow's division. He took part in the drive on Mexico City, earned two brevets, and was slightly wounded near the Mexican capital.

Magruder resigned his commission on April 20, 1861, three days after Virginia seceded. He was placed in charge of defending the Virginia Peninsula east of Richmond. Union General Benjamin Butler blundered into his defenses on June 10 and was defeated in the Battle of Big Bethel. The South was elated by this early triumph, and for a time Magruder became the principal military hero of the South after G. T. Beauregard. He was promoted to brigadier general on June 17 and major general on October 7, 1861.

By March 17, 1862, Magruder commanded 13,500 men. Union General George McClellan began shipping troops to the peninsula that day until his force numbered 130,000 men. Magruder, however, deceived McClellan into thinking that the Confederates had many more troops. Instead of attacking en masse, McClellan laid siege to Yorktown. General Joseph E. Johnston later wrote that Magruder's actions on the peninsula saved Richmond and allowed the Confederate government time to prepare its defenses.

At the Seven Days Battles, General Robert E. Lee reprimanded him. Magruder moved his men slowly, and his attacks on Malvern Hill were piecemeal and poorly coordinated. Afterward, President Jefferson Davis transferred him to the Trans-Mississippi Department, which received many of Lee's rejects. Magruder was essentially in professional exile for the rest of the war.

Magruder commanded the District of Texas, New Mexico, and Arizona (and between August 1864 and March 1865, the District of Arkansas). He had one shining moment of glory: on New Year's Day 1863, he launched a surprise attack on the Union forces at Galveston and bagged most of the garrison.

For the most part, though, Magruder was an administrator. He executed his duties ably and was generally well liked by the citizens of the Lone Star State.

After the war, Magruder traveled to Mexico and became a major general in the Imperial Army. Magruder returned to Houston in 1867, where he was still quite popular. He went on the lecture circuit and proved to be an engaging and popular speaker. He developed heart problems, however, and died on February 18, 1871, in Houston, Texas, at the age of sixty-three. Initially buried in the Episcopal Cemetery in Houston, he was reinterred in Trinity Episcopal Cemetery, Galveston.

WILLIAM MAHONE was born on December 1, 1826, in Monroe, Southampton County, Virginia. His family moved several times in the 1830s and ended up in Jerusalem (later Courtland), Virginia, the county seat, in 1840, where his father bought a tavern. William learned to drink, gamble, use tobacco, and curse prodigiously. He was given the nickname "Little Billy" because he was physically small. He stood five feet six and weighed about one hundred pounds. During the war, his men joked that Mahone was every inch a soldier—but there weren't many inches to him.

He was educated locally and attended the Virginia Military Institute in Lexington in 1844 on a state scholarship, which was rare in those days. He graduated in 1847 with a degree in civil engineering.

Mahone became a teacher at the Rappahannock Academy in Caroline County in northeastern Virginia until he found work on the Orange and Alexandria Railroad. He moved his way up in the railroad business until he was president of the Norfolk and Petersburg Railroad. On April 17, 1861, Virginia seceded. William Mahone was an ardent secessionist and was commissioned as a lieutenant colonel of the 6th Virginia Infantry, winning promotion to colonel on May 2, 1861, and to brigadier general on November 16, 1861.

Mahone remained in the Norfolk-Tidewater area until early May 1862, when he was ordered to Drewry's Bluff. His brigade, part of Benjamin Huger's division, joined the main army for General Joseph E. Johnston's attack on Seven Pines. It performed well. It also fought in the Seven Days Battles and in the Battle of Second Manassas, where Mahone was shot in the chest. He was out of action for two months.

General Mahone returned to the army in time for the Battle of Fredericksburg, but his brigade was not engaged. His brigade fought in the Battle of Chancellorsville and at Gettysburg but was mostly held in reserve and only suffered a few casualties. On July 3, Mahone's brigade was detached to guard the artillery batteries and did not take part in Pickett's Charge.

During the Battle of the Wilderness, General James Longstreet was wounded. General Richard Anderson succeeded him as commander of the I Corps, and Mahone replaced Anderson as divisional commander. He performed brilliantly in this role. He was promoted to major general (temporary rank) on June 1, with a date of rank of May 31, but he did not want temporary rank, so he turned it down on June 7. He continued to command Anderson's old division as a brigadier general.

Mahone was confident that he was an outstanding divisional commander—and indeed he was. He fought skillfully in the Overland Campaign and the Siege of Petersburg. At dawn on July 30, 1864, the Yankees detonated four tons of gunpowder under Rebel lines and blew them sky high. The North had a chance to seize Petersburg, without which the Rebel capital of Richmond could not be held. The Union commanders were slow to take advantage of their opportunity. William Mahone, on the other hand, moved with almost incredible speed, closed in on "The Crater" with three brigades, and sealed off the Union breakthrough. For his outstanding performance in the Battle of the Crater, General Robert E. Lee promoted him to major general on the field. His promotion was made official on August 3.

General Mahone fought in the trenches throughout most of the Siege of Petersburg. He remained with the main army during the retreat to Appomattox and surrendered with General Lee on April 9, 1865.

After the war, William Mahone became one of the South's leading railroad tycoons and worked for a peaceful return to home rule in Virginia. In 1878, he ran for the Democratic nomination for governor but was defeated. In 1879, he helped set up the Readjuster Party, a populist coalition of moderate Republicans, blacks, and dissident Democrats, and was elected to the U.S. Senate in 1880.

William Mahone held office from March 4, 1881, to March 4, 1887. He was defeated for reelection by the Democrat nominee in 1886. This effectively destroyed Mahone's electoral career. He continued to live in Washington, D.C., and was there when he suffered a major stroke and died a week later on September 8, 1895. He was sixty-eight years old. General William Mahone was buried in Blandford Cemetery, Petersburg, Virginia.

JAMES PATRICK MAJOR was born in Fayette, Missouri, on May 14, 1836. He attended the U.S. Military Academy and graduated with the class of 1856. He was sent to the famous 2nd U.S. Cavalry on the Texas frontier. On October 1, 1858, he fought Comanches at the Battle of Wichita Village, where he personally killed three braves in one-on-one combat.

Major resigned his commission as a second lieutenant on March 21, 1861. He returned to Missouri, where he was named lieutenant colonel in the state guard and fought at Wilson's Creek. Afterward, he served on the staffs of David Twiggs and Earl Van Dorn.

In the summer of 1862, three Union flotillas steamed to Vicksburg, Mississippi, and opened fire on the place. Van Dorn appointed Major acting chief of artillery, and he played a significant role in the successful defense of the fortress.

Transferred to the Trans-Mississippi Department in 1863, James Major commanded a Texas cavalry brigade during the Bayou Teche Campaign in southern Louisiana until June 28, when he was wounded near Donaldsonville. General Richard Taylor, the commander of the Army of Western Louisiana, recommended Major be promoted to brigadier general. He received his promotion on July 21, 1863.

Following his recovery, Major commanded the garrison at Galveston for several months. On March 17, 1864, he was given command of a division of Texas cavalry and ordered to Louisiana. He fought in the Red River Campaign. His was a veteran unit of skilled cavalrymen, including a good many former Texas Rangers. Many of his men had fought outlaws, Mexicans, Comancheros, bandits, Apaches, and other Indians. Most of the Union cavalrymen they faced were infantrymen who were just recently mounted. Major's men had little trouble defeating them repeatedly; but when Major's men fought dismounted at Mansfield and Pleasant Hill, their advantages were fewer.

Major took part in the Battle of Monett's Ferry (April 23, 1864), where the U.S. Army of the Gulf escaped an encirclement, as well as the Siege of Alexandria. He and his men sank a handful of Union vessels on the Red River and pursued the defeated Union Army until it escaped across the Atchafalaya. Following that, the war basically shut down in Louisiana, and Major was transferred to Texas, where he commanded a cavalry brigade. He was paroled at New Iberia, Louisiana, on June 11, 1865.

After the war, General Major lived briefly in France before returning to Louisiana to begin a career as a planter. He died in Austin, Texas, on May 7, 1877, while on a business trip. He was forty years old. James Patrick Major is buried in Ascension of Our Lord Catholic Cemetery, Donaldsonville, Louisiana.

GEORGE EARL MANEY was born on August 24, 1826, in Franklin, Tennessee, the son of a circuit judge. He grew up in Nashville and was well grounded in politics. He graduated from the University of Nashville in 1845 at age nineteen.

Maney joined the Army when the Mexican War began. He took part in General Winfield Scott's drive to Mexico City as a dragoon and was discharged as a first lieutenant.

He returned home in 1848, read law, and passed the bar exam in 1850. He set up a law practice in Franklin and was quite successful. He was subsequently elected to the Tennessee legislature, in which he served three terms.

Before Tennessee's secession, which he supported, Maney joined the Rock City Guards, a Nashville militia unit. In early May 1861, he became a captain in the 11th Tennessee Infantry Regiment. On May 8, 1861, he was elected colonel of the 1st Tennessee Infantry. It served in northwestern Virginia, fought in the Battle of Cheat Mountain, and was part of Stonewall Jackson's Romney Expedition, where Maney was the only officer in General W. W. Loring's division to win Jackson's praise.

Maney and his regiment were recalled to Tennessee after the fall of Fort Henry and Fort Donelson. He commanded a brigade in the Battle of Shiloh and on April 6 led a charge that General Benjamin

Cheatham praised as "one of the most brilliant, as it was certainly one of the most decisive, movements of the day." He was promoted to brigadier general on April 16, 1862.

General Maney continued to perform well in the battles of Perryville, Second Murfreesboro, Chickamauga, Lookout Mountain, and Missionary Ridge. He was praised by Lieutenant Colonel James D. Porter as "[a]ttentive to every detail, a good disciplinarian, careful of the wants of his men, skillful and courageous in battle, implicitly relied upon. . . ."

Maney was wounded in the arm in the Battle of Ringgold Gap (November 27, 1863) during General Braxton Bragg's retreat from Chattanooga. After his recovery, he took part in the retreat from Dalton to Atlanta, including the Battle of Kennesaw Mountain. Near Jonesboro, on August 31, 1864, Maney was wounded again. He was captured and quickly exchanged but did not immediately return to field duty because of his wound. He rejoined the Army of Tennessee for the Carolinas Campaign, including the Battle of Bentonville. He surrendered with the rest of Johnston's army on April 26, 1865.

General Maney returned home to resume his legal practice. In 1868, he became president of the Tennessee and Pacific Railroad, a job he held until 1877. He had considerable influence in Nashville, even though he was a Republican. He was elected to the state senate and helped restore the civil rights (including the right to vote) of many former Confederates.

George Maney moved to Washington, D.C., after Reconstruction and worked as a lobbyist. He served as ambassador to Colombia (1881–82), resident minister to Bolivia (1882–83), and resident minister and later envoy extraordinary and minister plenipotentiary to Uruguay and Paraguay (1889–94).

On February 9, 1901, he was walking down the sidewalk with a friend in the nation's capital when he suddenly became very ill. The friend helped him into a restaurant, where he lost consciousness. A physician was summoned, but General George Maney died just as the doctor arrived. He is buried in Mount Olivet Cemetery, Nashville, Tennessee.

ARTHUR MIDDLETON MANIGAULT (pronounced MAN-i-GO) was born in Charleston (or nearby South Island), South Carolina, on October 26, 1824, into a wealthy Huguenot family. He enrolled at the College of Charleston but did not graduate.

In 1846, he was commissioned first lieutenant in the Palmetto Regiment, which was part of General Winfield Scott's army, and fought in the Mexican War from the Siege of Veracruz onward. In September 1847, his regiment stormed the Garita de Belén, the main gate into Mexico City. Manigault later said the Mexican Campaign was the happiest period of his life.

He returned to South Carolina and became a planter but was also deeply involved in military preparations for the impending Civil War. He raised a company of mounted riflemen, supervised the construction of batteries in Charleston Harbor, and served on General G. T. Beauregard's staff as an inspector general and aide, with the rank of lieutenant colonel. He was present for the bombardment of Fort Sumter (April 12–13, 1861) and was then elected colonel of the 10th South Carolina Infantry Regiment. Later that year, he was appointed commander of the state's 1st Military District.

In April 1862, he and his regiment were sent to the Army of Mississippi. Manigault commanded a brigade during the Siege of Corinth, in the Kentucky Invasion, and in the Second Battle of Murfreesboro. He was promoted to brigadier general on April 26, 1863. He was a fine brigade commander, and it was said he would have been promoted earlier but for the fact that his prominent family had political enemies in the Confederate War Department.

Manigault's brigade fought in the Tullahoma Campaign and the Battle of Chickamauga, the Siege of Chattanooga, the Battle of Missionary Ridge, the retreat to Georgia, the retreat from Dalton to Atlanta, and in General John Bell Hood's counterattacks in front of Atlanta. He was wounded in the Battle of Resaca.

At the Battle of Franklin, Manigault was wounded in the head, and was unable to return to duty before the war ended.

After the war, General Manigault returned to his rice plantation on South Island. He was elected adjutant general of South Carolina in 1880 and served in that position until his death on August 17, 1886. The cause of his death was declared to be the lingering effects of the head wound he suffered at Franklin. He was sixty-one years old. Arthur Middleton Manigault is buried in Magnolia Cemetery, Charleston.

JOHN SAPPINGTON MARMADUKE was born on March 14, 1833, near Arrow Rock, Missouri. He spent his early years working on the family farm. He attended local schools, then spent 1850 to 1852 at Yale University before transferring to Harvard. He quit after less than a year in order to accept an appointment to West Point, where he graduated with the class of 1857.

Lieutenant Marmaduke took part in the Utah War and was stationed in the New Mexico Territory when the war began. He resigned his commission on April 17, 1861, and was appointed colonel of the 1st Missouri Rifle Regiment of the Missouri State Guard. Shortly after, he resigned his colonelcy and obtained a lieutenant's commission in the Confederate Army. He was assigned to William J. Hardee's command in Arkansas. Here he was promoted to lieutenant colonel and placed in charge of the 1st Arkansas Cavalry Battalion on September 19, 1861. Transferred to Kentucky, he was promoted to colonel on January 28, 1862, and given command of the 18th Arkansas (3rd Confederate) Infantry Regiment. He led it in the Battle of Shiloh, where he was seriously wounded on April 7. It took him months to recover.

After he recuperated, Colonel Marmaduke was sent back to Arkansas, where he was given command of the 4th Cavalry Division of Thomas C. Hindman's Army of the Trans-Mississippi. He was promoted to brigadier general on November 15, 1862. He fought a nine-hour battle at Cane Hill on November 28. Superior numbers finally prevailed, and Marmaduke was forced to retreat, although he did so in good order. He also fought at Prairie Grove, and General Hindman praised Marmaduke warmly for his part in the battle. Afterward, Marmaduke led his men in several successful raids. He also led a Confederate cavalry attack in the unsuccessful Battle of Helena, Arkansas, on July 4.

After the Battle of Reed's Bridge (August 26, 1863), an incident occurred that General Marmaduke regretted for the rest of his life. He criticized General Lucius Walker's conduct during the battle in a way that Walker took as an accusation of cowardice. Marmaduke denied that was his intent but did not withdraw the criticism. Shortly after dawn on September 6, 1863, seven miles below Little Rock on the north side of the Arkansas River, he met Walker on the field of honor. Marmaduke shot Walker and mortally wounded him. General Sterling Price ordered Marmaduke arrested, but General Theophilus H. Holmes (who had been ill) resumed command of the District of Arkansas on September 25 and swept the entire incident under the rug.

Marmaduke went on another raid into Missouri in late 1863 but returned in time to take part in the Camden Expedition, the Arkansas portion of the Red River Campaign. Here, he commanded a cavalry division. He successfully defended Washington, Arkansas, and compelled Union General Frederick Steele and his U.S. VII Corps to undergo a siege at Camden. Steele was forced to send a foraging expedition under Colonel James M. Williams to keep his corps supplied. It included 1,300 men and 198 wagons. On April 18, 1864, Marmaduke ambushed Williams's column at Poison Spring, eighteen miles west of Camden, and destroyed it. The Battle of Poison Spring was the largest Confederate victory in Arkansas during the war, and Marmaduke's casualties were light.

Marmaduke took part in Sterling Price's Great Missouri Raid of 1864. It was not successful, and Marmaduke, who commanded the cavalry, was captured near Mine Creek, Kansas, on October 25. He was imprisoned on Johnson's Island in Ohio. He was promoted to major general on March 17, 1865, and confirmed the next day, even though he was a prisoner of war. He was the last Confederate officer confirmed to the rank of major general. He was paroled July 24, 1865.

After the war, Marmaduke settled in the Carondelet suburb of St. Louis. He was the state's railroad commissioner from 1875 to 1880. As a champion of the small farmer, he ran for governor in 1880 but failed to win the Democratic nomination. He ran again in 1884. He advocated regulation of the railroads, support for farmers and education, criticized carpetbaggers, condemned the brutality of Union troops in Missouri during the war, and praised those who had served the Confederacy, including Bill Quantrill and his guerrillas. He won this election and took office on January 2, 1885.

Despite his partisan rhetoric during the campaign, he governed in a manner that he hoped would unify Missourians, and in his short term, he was successful and popular. In late 1887, Governor Marmaduke contracted pneumonia and died in office on December 28, 1887, at the age of fifty-four. He was buried in Woodland-Old City Cemetery in Jefferson City, Missouri.

HUMPHREY MARSHALL was born on January 13, 1812, in Frankfort, Kentucky, into a distinguished family. He received an appointment to West Point and graduated with the class of 1832. He was commissioned in the cavalry and saw action in the Black Hawk War. He resigned his commission in 1833 to return home and study law. He was admitted to the bar that same year.

Humphrey Marshall practiced law in Frankfort and later Louisville from 1833 to 1846. He was active in the militia. In 1846, Marshall became colonel of the 1st Kentucky Cavalry, which was sent to northern Mexico. During the Battle of Buena Vista, he heroically charged and defeated a much larger force of Mexican cavalry.

Marshall returned home and soon entered the political arena. He was a moderate by the standards of the day and an effective speaker. He was elected to Congress in 1848 as a Whig and served from 1849 to 1852, when he resigned to become U.S. ambassador to China. He returned to Kentucky in 1854, joined the American or Know-Nothing Party, and was elected to Congress again, serving from 1855 to 1859. He did not run for reelection. He supported John C. Breckinridge for president in 1860.

Marshall was an advocate of Kentucky neutrality in 1861. The Union Army occupied much of the state in September and October, and Abraham Lincoln's minions were arresting and holding prominent Southern sympathizers, who were denied recourse to habeas corpus. Marshall left Kentucky and "went south" to avoid being arrested. Shortly after, he was indicted for treason.

President Jefferson Davis made him a brigadier general on October 30, 1861. He hardly looked the part. Humphrey Marshall stood a little less than six feet and weighed more than three hundred pounds. He was not in the physical shape to command, but he appears to have thought himself a military genius and resigned every time he was ordered to report to a senior officer. He constantly sent letters to Robert E. Lee and Jefferson Davis offering military and political advice. Lee always treated him politely, but Davis became irritated. Marshall was verbose, ambitious, brusque, annoying, and supremely self-confident.

In late 1861, Marshall went to eastern Kentucky, where he raised a force of more than two thousand men. He and his men, however, were defeated in the Battle of Middle Creek on January 10, 1862, and retreated into southwestern Virginia, where Marshall was named commander of Southern forces. In May 1862, he fought and soundly defeated a Union expedition at Princeton Court House, Virginia (now West Virginia), It was the high point of Marshall's military career.

During General Braxton Bragg's Kentucky Campaign of 1862, it was hoped that Marshall would rally Kentuckians to the standard, but he was unsuccessful. Public sympathy was generally with the South, but it was tepid.

Unable to secure an important command, General Marshall resigned again on June 17, 1863. He practiced law in Richmond,

Virginia, until May 2, 1864, when he was elected to the Confederate Congress. He no longer had any real role in the Southern war effort.

After Richmond fell in 1865, Marshall fled to Texas and eventually moved to New Orleans. In 1868, he returned to Louisville and practiced law. He was no longer politically active.

Humphrey Marshall died at his residence in Louisville on March 28, 1872. He was sixty years old. He was buried in Frankfort Cemetery, Kentucky.

JAMES GREEN MARTIN was born on February 14, 1819, in Elizabeth City, North Carolina, the son of a prominent shipbuilder and planter. Young James was educated at St. Mary's Boys' School in Raleigh, admitted to West Point in 1836, and graduated in 1840. Commissioned in the artillery, Martin was stationed on the New England coast, mostly in Maine. During the Mexican War, he was a battery commander. At Churubusco, his right arm was shattered by a grapeshot and had to be amputated. He was brevetted major on August 20. His men later affectionately nicknamed him "Ol' One Wing."

After he recovered, James Martin was stationed at Fort Monroe, Virginia; the Schuylkill Arsenal in Pennsylvania; Governor's Island, New York; and Fort Snelling, Minnesota. He was sent to Utah in 1858 and was appointed Albert Sidney Johnston's quartermaster. After peace was established with the Mormons, he was stationed at Fort Riley, Kansas. He resigned his commission on June 14, 1861, and returned to North Carolina. He was soon appointed a captain of cavalry in the Confederate Army.

In September 1861, Ol' One Wing was appointed major general of militia and adjutant general of North Carolina, with headquarters in Raleigh. The governor could not have made a better appointment. Always noted for his energy, by January 1862, Martin had forty-one regiments in the field or ready to take it, raising twelve thousand men more than his quota. He set up manufacturing plants for military equipment, and what North Carolina couldn't produce it would try to import, as he convinced the state to buy a small fleet of blockade runners. It was said that, thanks to Martin, North Carolina produced more troops during the first year of the war than any other state and that they were the best equipped.

In the fall of 1863, the Confederate War Department ordered him to form and command a brigade. He was a strict disciplinarian and initially was not particularly popular with his men, but they entered battle well drilled and well trained. Ordered to Virginia, Martin and his men fought in the successful defense of Drewry's Bluff on May 16, 1864, and helped bottle up U.S. General Benjamin Butler's Army of the James on the Bermuda Hundred peninsula. Martin's courage in these attacks was so conspicuous that his troops hoisted him to their shoulders, crying "Hooray for Old One Wing!"

His brigade fought in the Battle of Cold Harbor, but during the Siege of Petersburg, Martin's health failed him, and he was sent to Asheville, North Carolina, to command the District of Western North Carolina—a less strenuous assignment. When he left the Army of Northern Virginia, General Robert E. Lee said, "General Martin is one to whom North Carolina owes a debt she can never repay."

Martin commanded his district until the end of the war. He surrendered his command at Waynesville, North Carolina, on May 9, 1865, after General Joseph E. Johnston's capitulation. This ended the last organized Confederate resistance in the state.

With his property and profession gone, James Martin started over from scratch. He decided to study law and was admitted to the bar in 1866. He practiced successfully in Asheville from then until his death, which occurred in Asheville on October 4, 1878. He was fifty-nine years old. He was buried in Riverside Cemetery, Asheville.

WILLIAM THOMPSON MARTIN was born in Glasgow, Kentucky, on March 25, 1823. He attended Centre College in Danville, Kentucky, and graduated in 1840 but moved to Vicksburg, where his parents lived, in 1842. He studied law with his father and passed the bar in 1844. He set up a law office and was elected district attorney for Adams County that same year (at age twenty-two) and served until 1860.

Natchez was a tough river town in the 1840s. Gambling and prostitution flourished, as did drinking, fighting, and brawling. Martin didn't mind "mixing it up" with unsavory characters and brought them into line, physically and legally. On at least one occasion, he severely beat a thug with his cane. On another occasion, one of the rowdies bit off one of his fingers.

Politically, Martin was a strong Whig and opposed secession, but when Mississippi left the Union on January 9, 1861, he went with her and organized the Adams County (Cavalry) Troops. He was elected its captain on July 8, 1861. On October 24, 1861, Martin was promoted to major and given command of the newly formed Jeff Davis Legion, which included his troop and cavalry companies from Mississippi and Alabama. On February 13, 1862, he was promoted to lieutenant colonel. The Legion became part of J. E. B. Stuart's cavalry division and participated in Stuart's first ride around George McClellan. Martin fought in the Seven Days Battles and was promoted to full colonel in July. He took part in the Maryland Campaign and in the retreat from South Mountain, covering the rear of the Rebel infantry. William T. Martin served as General Robert E. Lee's personal aide during the Battle of Sharpsburg, which led to his promotion to brigadier general on December 2, 1862.

In 1863, Martin was deployed in the West and given command of a cavalry division. He performed exceedingly well in the Tullahoma Campaign and at Chickamauga, but his division suffered devastating losses in General Joe Wheeler's unsuccessful October Raid. Martin's relationship with Wheeler was superficially cordial, but he regarded Wheeler with distrust because "Fighting Joe" was a notoriously lax disciplinarian, a poor administrator, and sometimes a bad tactician. Martin was promoted to major general on November 10, 1863.

Martin directed the cavalry attached to General Longstreet's corps during the unsuccessful Siege of Knoxville in November and December 1863. Longstreet lamented the cavalry's failures and asked that Wade Hampton replace Martin. General Martin, in turn, said that his cavalry had been left in tatters because of Wheeler's October Raid and because Wheeler had deliberately withheld desperately needed wagons and replacement troops.

In February 1864, Martin's division returned to Wheeler's cavalry corps and fought in the Atlanta Campaign. They had another falling out in August 1864, and Wheeler relieved James Martin of his command for disobeying an order.

General Martin was transferred to the command of the Subdistrict of Northwest Mississippi—a definite demotion. He spent the rest of the war trying to protect the area from outlaws, enforcing the Confederate draft, and rounding up deserters. He was paroled at Meridian on May 11, 1865.

Martin was one of the better cavalry commanders in the Army of Tennessee. His tactical judgment was certainly sound, but he could not overcome the lack of discipline in Wheeler's corps all by himself.

Martin joined the Democratic Party and worked for the return of home rule and the expulsion of the carpetbagger regime in Mississippi.

He served as a delegate to the constitutional conventions of 1865 and 1890 and in the Mississippi Senate from 1882 to 1894. He acted as president of the Jackson and Columbus Railroad, during which he oversaw the completion of the line between Natchez and Jackson. President Theodore Roosevelt named him postmaster of Natchez in 1905.

General William T. Martin died in Natchez, Mississippi, on March 16, 1910. He was eighty-six years old. He is buried in Natchez City Cemetery.

DABNEY HERNDON MAURY was born on May 21, 1822, in Fredericksburg, Virginia, the descendent of an old Virginia family. Called "Dab" by his friends, Maury was educated at a classical school in Fredericksburg. He graduated from the University of Virginia in 1841 (where he studied law) and attended West Point, graduating in the famous class of 1846 that produced nineteen Civil War generals.

Lieutenant Maury was assigned to the cavalry branch and fought in the Mexican War at Veracruz and Cerro Gordo, where he was severely wounded and almost lost an arm. He was brevetted first lieutenant for gallantry. After the war, he was best known for writing *Tactics for Mounted Rifles* (1859), a textbook that was still in use four decades later. He was a captain in New Mexico when Virginia seceded. He resigned his U.S. Army commission, joined the Provisional Army of Virginia, and on August 28, 1861, became lieutenant colonel of the 20th Mississippi Infantry (then in Virginia). He was sent to Arkansas in early 1862 and joined General Earl Van Dorn's staff as assistant adjutant general.

Maury distinguished himself in the Battle of Pea Ridge and was promoted to brigadier general on March 12. Transferred to Mississippi, Maury assumed command of a brigade in Sterling Price's Army of the West. He covered the retreat of the army after its defeat at Iuka. Brigadier General Henry Little was killed at Iuka, and Maury was given command of his division, which he led in the Second Battle of Corinth. When Van Dorn retreated, Maury again covered the rear. He fiercely defended Hatchie's Bridge, which allowed the army to escape. He was promoted to major general on November 4.

Maury was part of General John C. Pemberton's Army of Mississippi when it checked Grant's Mississippi Central Railroad Offensive in December 1862. He fought at Steele's Bayou in early 1863 and in the defeat of Grant's Yazoo Pass Expedition. On April 15, he was sent to Knoxville as commander of the Department of East Tennessee.

General Maury was transferred to the command of the District of the Gulf in May 1863. His main task was to defend Mobile, which he did tenaciously. After a bitter struggle, the Federals captured the outer defenses of Mobile Bay in August 1864. In March 1865, he faced U.S. General Edward Canby's army of forty-five thousand men with a garrison of nine thousand. He inflicted heavy casualties upon the Yankees but was forced to evacuate the city on April 12, 1865—three days after Robert E. Lee surrendered. He retired slowly to Meridian, Mississippi, where he surrendered on May 4.

Dab Maury returned to Fredericksburg and founded a classical school for boys and turned himself into an historian. In 1868, he established the Southern Historical Society, providing a treasure trove of papers for students of the Civil War. Maury was a happy, affable man and wrote a charming autobiography, *Recollections of a Virginian in the Mexican, Indian, and Civil Wars*, published in 1894.

During President Grover Cleveland's first administration, Maury served as U.S. ambassador to Colombia. During a visit to his son's home in Peoria, Illinois, General Maury died on January 11, 1900. He was seventy-seven years old. He was buried in the Confederate Cemetery, Fredericksburg, Virginia.

SAMUEL BELL MAXEY was born in Tompkinsville, Kentucky, on March 30, 1825. He attended West Point and graduated in the famous class of 1846. For one year, his roommate was Stonewall Jackson.

Maxey was commissioned a second lieutenant of infantry and sent to Mexico with General Winfield Scott's army in 1847. He fought from the siege of Veracruz to the capture of Mexico City. He was brevetted to first lieutenant for his services at Contreras. After the war, he was posted to Jefferson Barracks, Missouri, but he found garrison duty boring. He resigned from the army in 1849, studied law, and set up a law practice in Albany, Kentucky, with his father, General Rice Maxey. They moved to Paris, Lamar County, Texas, in 1857.

Sam Maxey had a talent for making friends, even among political enemies. In Paris, he was elected district attorney shortly after he arrived. A Whig by conviction, he supported secession after Abraham Lincoln became president. He was elected captain of the Lamar Rifles and was sent to the Indian Territory. He requested permission to form a Confederate regiment. The War Department in Richmond agreed, and the 9th Texas Infantry was created shortly after. The 9th Texas trained at Camp Benjamin (near Bonham) and left for Kentucky on New Year's Day, 1862.

Maxey was promoted to brigadier general on March 4, 1862. He was sent to East Tennessee, where he led a brigade and successfully attacked Union forces at Bridgeport and Battle Creek, earning official praise from General Braxton Bragg.

Maxey was transferred to command a brigade at Port Hudson in early 1863. He was then sent to Jackson, Mississippi, where he fought in the last Vicksburg Campaign and later served in the Army of Relief under General Joseph E. Johnston. He and his brigade were sent to Mobile in August.

In December 1863, President Jefferson Davis ordered him to the Indian Territory. He completely reorganized the Confederate forces there, which grew to eight thousand men, conducted raids, and prevented the Yankees from invading Texas. He joined General Sterling Price in Arkansas in April 1864, where he took part in the Camden Expedition. His performance in the Battle of Poison Spring was described as "brilliant."

After General Frederick Steele's U.S. VII Corps retreated to Little Rock, Maxey returned to command of the Indian Territory, then took a command in Texas and surrendered to U.S. General Edward R. S. Canby in Paris, Texas, in July 1865.

Sam Maxey resumed his law practice after the war. He ran for Congress in 1872 but lost. He was elected to the U.S. Senate by the Texas legislature in 1875 and was subsequently reelected, serving until 1887, when the Texas legislature replaced him with John H. Reagan, the former postmaster general of the Confederacy.

General Maxey returned to Paris and practiced law. He traveled to Eureka Springs, Arkansas, for treatment of a gastrointestinal disease and died there on August 16, 1895, at the age of seventy. He is buried in Evergreen Cemetery, Paris, Texas.

JOHN MCCAUSLAND, JR., was born on September 13, 1836, in St. Louis, Missouri, the son of an Irish immigrant. McCausland attended the Virginia Military Institute and graduated first in the class of 1857. After attending the University of Virginia (1857–58), he returned to VMI as a professor of mathematics.

When the war began, he formed the Rockbridge Artillery and then handed command over to William N. Pendleton. At Robert E. Lee's request, McCausland then organized the 36th Virginia (2nd Kanawha) Infantry Regiment in the Kanawha Valley. He became a colonel in the Virginia Militia on May 3, 1861, and a colonel in the Confederate Army on July 16, 1861, the day his regiment was incorporated into Confederate service.

McCausland took part in the unsuccessful Western Virginia Campaign in 1861. He was sent to Tennessee with General John B. Floyd, fought at Fort Donelson, and escaped with Floyd via steamboat when Floyd deserted his post. After President Jefferson Davis sacked Floyd the following month, McCausland and his men returned to the Department of Southwest Virginia, where they served in several minor operations. He was so fierce in combat that his men nicknamed him "Tiger John."

He fought in the Battle of Cloyd's Mountain on May 9, 1864. After General Albert G. Jenkins was mortally wounded, McCausland took charge of the outnumbered Confederates and directed the retreat. He was promoted to brigadier general on May 18 and was placed in charge of a cavalry brigade. He was considered a hero after he saved Lynchburg from U.S. General David Hunter's marauders. McCausland ambushed Union supply trains, burned bridges, attacked the crews sent to rebuild them, and delayed Hunter until fresh Rebel brigades could reinforce Lynchburg.

John McCausland led his brigade in the Valley Campaign of 1864. In retaliation for Hunter's vandalism, McCausland burned Chambersburg, Pennsylvania, to the ground. The fire left three thousand people homeless.

After Confederate General Jubal Early's defeat at Waynesboro on March 2, 1865, "Tiger John" McCausland joined the Army of Northern Virginia, which was besieged at Petersburg. He fought in the Battle of Five Forks (April 1, 1865) and in the retreat to Appomattox. He cut his way out from a Yankee encirclement and took his brigade to Lynchburg, where he disbanded it. He was paroled at Charlestown, West Virginia, on May 22.

After the war, McCausland fled to Mexico and Europe because he faced charges of arson for his burning of Chambersburg. (No Federal officers were indicted for anything they did in the South.) He returned home in 1867 and, with money he inherited from his father, purchased six thousand acres in Mason County, West Virginia—on the Ohio border—and became a farmer.

McCausland kept a low profile—and President Ulysses Grant eventually quashed the arson charges against him—but Tiger John remained unreconstructed. Near the end of his life, he declared that he would rather see his sons dead than in a blue uniform.

John McCausland, Jr., died at Grape Hill, near Point Pleasant, West Virginia, on January 22, 1927. He was ninety years old and was the last surviving Confederate general except for Felix H. Robertson of Texas. Most of his farm—now known as Smithland Farm—is presently owned by the state of West Virginia and is a living history museum.

WILLIAM MCCOMB was born on November 21, 1828, in Mercer County, Pennsylvania, the son of a flour mill owner. He moved to Montgomery County, Tennessee, around 1854 and set up a large flour mill at Price's Landing on the Cumberland River. He went with his adopted state after Fort Sumter was fired upon and in May 1861 enlisted as a private in the 14th Tennessee Infantry. He was promoted to second lieutenant and regimental adjutant that same month. He fought in the Cheat Mountain Campaign in western Virginia and in

the Romney Expedition and was elected major on April 26, 1862. He took part in the Battle of Seven Pines and the Seven Days Battles and was wounded at Gaines' Mill on June 27. He was promoted to lieutenant colonel on August 15, 1862, and to colonel on September 2. He had advanced rapidly because the officers above him kept getting killed in action. He almost joined them on September 17, when he was severely wounded at Sharpsburg. He was wounded again in May 1863 during the Battle of Chancellorsville. Colonel McComb did not recover in time to participate in the invasion of Pennsylvania.

In August 1863, McComb was back on active duty. He led the 14th Tennessee in the Overland Campaign of 1864 and at the Siege of Petersburg. He was promoted to brigadier general on January 20, 1865, and led his brigade until Appomattox, where he surrendered with the rest of General Robert E. Lee's army on April 9. By this time, his old regiment, the 14th Tennessee, was down to its last forty men. It had had more than nine hundred when the war began. McComb was undoubtedly courageous and "steadfast to the last," as General Lee said of his survivors at Appomattox.

After the war, McComb lived in Alabama and Mississippi. He finally settled in Gordonsville, Virginia, where built a plantation and farmed for almost fifty years. General William McComb died on July 21, 1918, in Gordonsville. He was eighty-nine years old. He is buried in Mechanicsville Baptist Church Cemetery, Boswell's Tavern, Virginia, near Gordonsville.

JOHN PORTER McCOWN was born on August 19, 1815, in Sevier County, Tennessee. He attended West Point, from which he graduated in 1840. He was commissioned a second lieutenant, assigned to the artillery branch, and fought against Indian tribes on the Canadian border in 1840 and 1841.

McCown became a noted ornithologist. He named the McCown's longspur, which the North American Classification Committee of the American Ornithological

Society renamed in 2020 because McCown "fought for slavery," which shows how little the committee knew about the war.

McCown fought in the Mexican War, including the battles at Palo Alto, Resaca de la Palma, Monterrey, Veracruz, and Cerro Gordo, where he was brevetted captain for his courage and gallantry.

After the war, McCown served along the Rio Grande frontier and was promoted to captain in 1851. He fought in the Third Seminole War in Florida in 1856–57 and the Utah War in 1858. He was then on garrison duty in the Nebraska and Dakota Territories until May 17, 1861, when he resigned his captaincy. He was promoted to full colonel in the Confederate Army that same day. He took part in General Leonidas Polk's occupation of Columbus, Kentucky, and on September 7 was given command of a brigade under Gideon Pillow.

McCown was promoted to brigadier general on October 12, 1861, and commanded McCown's Artillery Corps, which included seventeen artillery battalions. It fought in the Battle of Belmont against General Grant on November 7.

When Polk evacuated Columbus, he ordered McCown to reinforce the garrisons of New Madrid and Island Number 10 with five thousand men and several guns. From March 3, 1862, General McCown commanded and defended the two posts against U.S. General John Pope's Army of the Mississippi (eighteen thousand men). He was promoted to major general on March 11, 1862, to rank from March 10, and directed the evacuation of the New Madrid positions during the night of March 13–14. He was criticized for abandoning too many guns and supplies and was replaced by William W. Mackall, who surrendered Island Number 10 on April 8.

General G. T. Beauregard later called McCown's command of New Madrid and Island Number 10 "the poorest defense made" of any fortified post in the entire war. Nevertheless, McCown was appointed commander of a division in the Army of the West and fought in the Siege of Corinth. When Generals Braxton Bragg and Edmund Kirby Smith decided to invade Kentucky, Bragg sent McCown's division to Chattanooga. McCown fought in the Second Battle of Murfreesboro

(December 31, 1862, to January 2, 1863). After the Confederate defeat, McCown was among a group of generals who tried to get Braxton Bragg removed from command. Bragg retaliated against McCown by reiterating criticism of his defense of New Madrid and Island Number 10 and accusing him of disobeying orders and delaying the Confederate attack at Murfreesboro on the morning of December 31. He relieved McCown of his command on February 27, 1863, and had him court-martialed. On March 16, McCown was found guilty and suspended from command for six months.

The court-martial effectively ruined McCown's career. He held no further major commands. General McCown was paroled at Salisbury, North Carolina, on May 12, 1865. After the war, he became a schoolteacher in Knoxville, Tennessee. He moved to Magnolia, Arkansas, in 1868 and became a farmer and a respected member of the community.

He died from pneumonia in Little Rock on January 22, 1879, at the age of sixty-three. His body was returned to Magnolia, where it was buried in the city cemetery.

M

BENJAMIN "BEN" MCCULLOCH was born on November 11, 1811, in Rutherford County, Tennessee. McCulloch's father was a wanderer and took the family to North Carolina, East Tennessee, Alabama, and West Tennessee. In Tennessee, they were neighbors with Sam Houston and Davy Crockett.

In 1836, Ben McCulloch joined Sam Houston's Texas Army and fought at San Jacinto, where he commanded one of the army's "Twin Sisters" artillery pieces. Houston was so delighted by McCulloch's performance that he promoted him to first lieutenant.

After the Texas Revolution, McCulloch worked as a surveyor in Gonzales and Seguin and then joined the Texas Rangers. In 1839, his fame as an Indian fighter helped him win an election to the Texas House of Representatives. He continued his service as a Texas Ranger, too, and distinguished himself in a decisive victory against marauding Comanches at the Battle of Plum Creek on August 11–12, 1840. That same year, his left arm was partially crippled in a duel.

After Texas was admitted to the Union in 1845, McCulloch was elected to the first state legislature. When the Mexican War began, McCulloch raised a company of Texas Rangers and became chief of scouts in Zachary Taylor's army. He led his company in the Battle of Monterrey, and his long-distance reconnaissance and timely reports were credited with saving the army at the Battle of Buena Vista.

In 1849, he took part in the California Gold Rush. He did not "strike it rich" but was elected sheriff of Sacramento County (1849–52). President Franklin Pierce appointed McCulloch U.S. marshal for eastern Texas, a post which he held from 1853 to 1861.

After Texas seceded on February 1, 1861, Ben McCulloch was commissioned a colonel by the Texas government and was authorized to demand the surrender of all United States posts within the borders of the Republic of Texas. (The Confederate States of America was not formed until February 8, 1861.) General David Twiggs (who would himself soon enter Confederate service) surrendered the Federal arsenal and other U.S. property at San Antonio on February 16. President Jefferson Davis appointed McCulloch a brigadier general in the Confederate Army on May 11.

General McCulloch was assigned to command Confederate troops in the Indian Territory and Arkansas, and he led troops in the Battle of Wilson's Creek, Missouri, on August 10, 1861.

Partially because Generals Ben McCulloch and Sterling Price could not cooperate, Jefferson Davis appointed Earl Van Dorn commander of the Trans-Mississippi Department and of the Army of the West. McCulloch was given command of a division, which he led in the Battle of Pea Ridge. On the morning of the first day of the battle (March 7, 1862), Benjamin McCulloch advanced boldly against the Union skirmish line and was shot through the heart. He died instantly. General McCulloch was fifty years old.

Ben McCulloch was very popular with his men, and though he lacked formal military training, experience and study made him a good commander. He was initially buried on the battlefield but is now interred on Republic Hill in Texas State Cemetery, Austin. He was one of thirty men inducted into the Texas Ranger Hall of Fame in Waco, Texas.

HENRY EUSTACE MCCULLOCH was born in Rutherford County, Tennessee, on December 6, 1816, the younger brother of future Confederate general Ben McCulloch. He went to Texas with Ben in 1835 and only missed going to the Alamo with Davy Crockett because his brother contracted the measles. While he was sick, Ben persuaded Henry to return to Tennessee.

By 1838, Henry was back in Texas and, like his brother, developed a reputation as an Indian fighter. Henry joined the Texas Rangers in 1840 and fought Indians, outlaws, and Mexican troops and was wounded in the Battle of Plum Creek (August 12, 1840). He was elected sheriff of Gonzales County in 1843. In 1844, he moved to Seguin and became a merchant. He spent the Mexican War commanding a volunteer company, guarding the West Texas frontier from Indian attack.

Henry McCulloch was a polite gentleman who was popular with his neighbors and colleagues. He was elected to the Texas House of Representatives in 1853. Two years later, he was elected to the state senate. In 1860, he was appointed a U.S. marshal by President James Buchanan.

In March 1861, one month after Texas's secession from the Union, the Confederate Congress commissioned Henry McCulloch as a colonel. He organized and led the 1st Texas Mounted Rifle Regiment (about 1,300 men). Its main duty was stifling Indian uprisings and guarding the Western frontier. On May 9, 1861, he captured the entire 8th U.S. Infantry Regiment near San Lucas Springs, northwest of San Antonio. He was promoted to brigadier general on May 11.

Early in 1862, he was given command of Texas troops stationed in Arkansas. He proved to be a fine regimental training officer and drill instructor. On September 6, 1862, he was handed a newly formed Texas Division in Little Rock, but divisional responsibilities were too much for him; he was soon superseded by Major General John G. Walker, a hero of the Battle of Sharpsburg, and McCulloch took command of the division's 3rd Brigade.

Sent to Louisiana in April 1863, McCulloch fought at the Battle of Milliken's Bend on June 7. His men inflicted heavy casualties on the Federals—who lost 652 men to only 185 for the Confederates—but failed to finish them off. The Federals (mostly badly equipped African Americans) were pushed back to the levee on the Mississippi River, but the Confederates feared the U.S. gunboats behind them. For this failure, General Richard Taylor, commander of the Army of Western Louisiana, relieved Henry McCulloch of his command. McCulloch was then placed in charge of the Western Subdistrict of the District of Texas, where he dealt with Indians, deserters, draft dodgers, and outlaws.

Despite a war record that was not entirely stellar, McCulloch remained a well-known Texas figure after the war. In 1876, he was named superintendent of the Deaf and Dumb Asylum (later the Texas School for the Deaf) in Austin. It was meant as a political sinecure, but he was a poor administrator, and a legislative investigation forced him to resign in 1879.

McCulloch returned to Seguin, where he retired. He enjoyed receiving visitors, corresponding about the war, and public speaking. He was a Mason and a trustee in the local Methodist church.

Henry Eustace McCulloch died in Rockport, Texas, on March 12, 1895, at the age of seventy-eight. He was given a full Masonic funeral and was buried in San Geronimo Cemetery in Seguin.

SAMUEL MCGOWAN was born on October 19, 1819, in the Laurens District of South Carolina. He attended a private school and South Carolina College, from which he graduated in 1841. He read law, was admitted to the bar, and began practicing in Abbeville. When the Mexican War broke out, he enlisted as a private in the Palmetto Regiment. He was promoted to captain and served as quartermaster on the staffs of Generals John A. Quitman, William J. Worth, and David E. Twiggs. Despite his staff rank, he took part in the storming of Chapultepec and the capture of the Belén Gate.

After the Mexican War, McCowan returned to his law practice and was elected to the South Carolina legislature six times, serving from 1850 to 1861. As regional tensions heightened, he became a militia brigade commander, serving under G. T. Beauregard, and was involved in the Battle of Fort Sumter (April 12–13, 1861). After the enlistments of his brigade expired, McGowan joined the staff of General Milledge L. Bonham and fought in the Battle of First Manassas. He returned home, helped recruit the 14th South Carolina Infantry, and became the regiment's lieutenant colonel on September 9, 1861. After serving on coastal duty in South Carolina, McGowan returned to Virginia with his regiment in April 1862 (he became colonel of the 14th South Carolina on April 11, 1862) and remained with the Army of Northern Virginia throughout the war. The regiment fought in the Seven Days Battles, during which, on June 27, he was slightly wounded by Union canister fire during the Battle of Gaines' Mill.

Sam McGowan's regiment fought in the Battle of Second Manassas, where he was wounded in the thigh. He was back in command at Sharpsburg. On December 13, during the Battle of Fredericksburg, General Maxcy Gregg was mortally wounded. McGowan took command of the brigade and was promoted to brigadier general on January 17, 1863.

General McGowan received his most serious wound of the war at Chancellorsville, when a minié ball slammed into his leg below the knee. Doctors were able to save the leg, but the general could not return to active duty until February 1864.

Sam McGowan led his brigade in the Battle of the Wilderness and at Spotsylvania, where he was near the apex of the Mule Shoe Salient. He and his 1,300 men battled thousands of Yankees for eighteen hours—sometimes in hand-to-hand combat—and the brigade held its position. He led his brigade throughout the Siege of Petersburg and surrendered at Appomattox on April 9, 1865.

Samuel McGowan was considered one of the best brigade commanders in the Confederate Army. Superior in every respect, he only had one weakness as a military commander: he frequently stopped a bullet in flight.

McGowan returned home in 1865 and was promptly elected to the U.S. House of Representatives, but the Radical Republicans would not allow him to take his seat. He resumed his law practice and worked to rid South Carolina of its corrupt carpetbagger government. He was reelected to the legislature in 1878 and on December 11, 1879, was elected associate justice of the South Carolina Supreme Court. He held this office until he retired in 1894.

Highly respected in his community, General Samuel McGowan died August 9, 1897, in Abbeville, South Carolina. He was seventy-seven years old. He is buried in Upper Long Cane Cemetery, Abbeville.

JAMES MCQUEEN MCINTOSH was born at Fort Brooke, near what is now Tampa, Florida, in 1828. The exact date is not known. McIntosh was admitted to the U.S. Military Academy at West Point and graduated dead last in the class of 1849. He was assigned to the infantry and served on the Western frontier. He transferred to the cavalry and was promoted to captain in 1857. He fought in several skirmishes with Kiowas and Comanches.

In 1861, McIntosh was stationed at Fort Smith, Arkansas, near the Indian Territory. He resigned his commission when Florida left the Union and was commissioned a captain of cavalry in the Confederate Army. Shortly after Fort Sumter, he became colonel of the 2nd Arkansas Mounted Rifles. He went to Missouri with General Ben McCulloch and fought in the Battle of Wilson's Creek on

August 10, 1861, where he was courageous to the point of recklessness, placing himself at maximum danger on the front line, though this only added to his already-high popularity with his troops. In late 1861, General Earl Van Dorn placed him in command of a cavalry brigade.

After pro-Union Indians under Muscogee (Creek) Chief Opothleyahola defeated Confederate Colonel Douglas Cooper on November 19, 1861, they threatened to conquer what later became Oklahoma. Colonel McIntosh was sent to the Indian Territory to prevent this. On December 26, in the Battle of Chustenahlah, he routed the enemy, who retreated to Kansas and did not threaten Confederate Indian Territory for the rest of the war. McIntosh was promoted to brigadier general on January 24, 1862.

On March 7, 1862, during the Battle of Pea Ridge, General Ben McCulloch was killed and replaced by McIntosh. He put himself at the head of his old regiment and rushed an enemy battery. He was shot through the heart and died instantly. He commanded the division less than fifteen minutes.

Along with the body of General McCulloch, McIntosh was carried to Fort Smith, where he was buried in the National Cemetery. He was thirty-three or thirty-four years old.

His younger brother, John B. McIntosh (1829–88) became a Union brigadier general and lost a leg at Winchester in September 1864.

LAFAYETTE MCLAWS was born on January 15, 1821, in Augusta, Georgia. He was educated in public schools and at the University of Virginia before being admitted to the U.S. Military Academy in 1838. He graduated in 1842. He fought in the Mexican War, taking part in the defense of Fort Brown, as well as in the Battle of Monterrey and the Siege of Veracruz.

After the war, McLaws was sent back to the frontier and later took part in the Utah Expedition of 1857.

After that, he was engaged in escorting Mormons to California and protecting them.

Following Georgia's secession, McLaws (now a captain) resigned his commission on March 23, 1861. Initially a Rebel major, he was promoted rapidly: first to colonel and commander of the 10th Georgia Infantry (June 17), then to brigadier general (September 25), and last to major general (May 23, 1862).

McLaws fought in the Peninsula Campaign, the Seven Days Battles, and the Maryland Campaign and played a major part in the capture of Harpers Ferry and 12,000 Federals. At Sharpsburg, he caught U.S. General John Sedgwick's left flank and smashed his division. The Yankees lost 2,200 men in fewer than thirty minutes and retreated in disarray. This was probably the high point of the war for General McLaws.

During the Battle of Fredericksburg, McLaws's division held part of Marye's Heights and slaughtered several Union attacks. At Chancellorsville, however, Robert E. Lee was disappointed that McLaws did not move more aggressively to cut off the Federal VI Corps, which escaped across the Rappahannock. During the Battle of Gettysburg, McLaws took part in General James Longstreet's assault on the Union left and played a major role in crushing U.S. General Daniel Sickles's III Corps.

McLaws accompanied General Longstreet's I Corps to the Western Theater in 1863. Longstreet needed scapegoats for his failed attack at Fort Sanders on November 29. One of them was Lafayette McLaws, whom he relieved of his command on December 17 and charged with neglect of duty. McLaws demanded a court-martial. It was granted, and General McLaws was found innocent of the major charges, but General Lee denied McLaws command of his former division.

As a commander, McLaws was capable but not brilliant—and certainly too slow and conservative for Lee's purposes, so he was given a backwater assignment as commander of districts in Georgia and South Carolina. He fought against Sherman's March to the Sea and against Union forces at the battles of Averasborough (Averasboro) and Bentonville. He surrendered with General Joseph E. Johnston on April 26, 1865.

After the war, McLaws pursued a variety of business interests, from insurance to part ownership of a canal company, and worked for the government as a tax collector and, briefly, as a postmaster. He died in Savannah, Georgia, on July 24, 1897. He was seventy-six years old. He was buried in Laurel Grove Cemetery (North), Savannah.

EVANDER MCNAIR was born on April 15, 1820, near Laurel Hill, North Carolina, the son of Scottish immigrants. Shortly after he was born, his parents moved to Simpson County, Mississippi. He received a spotty education in local schools and farmed with his father. In 1843, he formed his own mercantile business, McNair and Company. He left the firm in 1846 to enlist as a private in Colonel Jefferson Davis's 1st Mississippi Rifles. He fought at Monterrey and Buena Vista and rose to the rank of sergeant.

After the war, McNair returned to the mercantile business, this time in Brandon, Mississippi. He moved to Washington, Arkansas, in 1858.

Despite being a Whig by political conviction, McNair embraced Confederate service and raised a battalion of seven infantry companies that soon became the 4th Arkansas Infantry Regiment. On August 17, 1861, he was elected colonel. He fought at Wilson's Creek and at Pea Ridge, where he took command of a brigade after General Ben McCulloch was killed and Louis Hébert was captured. He crossed the Mississippi River with Earl Van Dorn and joined Edmund Kirby Smith for the invasion of Kentucky. Still commanding a brigade, Colonel McNair fought in the Battle of Richmond, Kentucky, where he turned the enemy's right flank, routing the Federals. On November 4, 1862, Evander McNair was promoted to brigadier general "for gallantry and bravery on the battlefield."

On December 31, 1862, at the Second Battle of Murfreesboro, he took part in General John P. McCown's brilliant attack, which pushed the Federals back three or four miles and nearly won the battle for the

South. He was sent to Mississippi to join General Joseph E. Johnston's Army of Relief outside Vicksburg. He and his men also fought against Sherman in the Second Battle of Jackson.

At Chickamauga on September 20, 1863, McNair's brigade took part in General James Longstreet's highly successful attack, which helped sweep half the Union Army of the Tennessee from the field. During this breakthrough, however, McNair was shot in the thigh. It took some time for General McNair to recover. He was then transferred to the Trans-Mississippi Department, where he participated in General Sterling Price's unsuccessful Missouri Raid. He surrendered with the Trans-Mississippi Department at the end of the war.

General McNair returned to the mercantile business, settling in Magnolia, Mississippi, after brief stops in Arkansas and New Orleans. He died November 13, 1902, at Hattiesburg, Mississippi, in the home of a son-in-law. He was eighty-two years old. He is buried in the Magnolia Cemetery, Magnolia, Mississippi.

DANDRIDGE MCRAE was born in Baldwin County, Alabama, on October 10, 1829, the son of an attorney and plantation owner. Dandridge was educated by a private tutor and attended South Carolina College, from which he graduated in 1849. His father died the same year, and he returned home to manage the plantation.

In 1853, McRae moved to Searcy, Arkansas, studied law, and was admitted to the bar in 1854. He was elected circuit clerk for White County in 1856. He held this office until the war began.

After Lincoln was elected president, Dandridge McRae organized a volunteer militia company, the "Arkansas Guards," which was part of the 21st Arkansas Militia Regiment. After helping capture the Little Rock Arsenal, McRae returned to White County, where he organized the Border Rangers, a volunteer cavalry troop. He was elected captain.

When the war began, Governor Henry M. Rector appointed him colonel and inspector general for the Arkansas Militia. Shortly after, he was authorized to raise a regiment but initially could field only four companies instead of the required ten. The companies were mustered into Confederate service as the 3rd Arkansas Infantry Battalion on July 15, 1861. McRae became its lieutenant colonel. The battalion became part of Ben McCulloch's division.

McRae fought at the Battle of Wilson's Creek, Missouri, and General McCulloch praised him for his coolness under fire. In November 1861, McRae's battalion expanded and became the 21st Arkansas Infantry Regiment. The War Department had inadvertently created two 21st Arkansas regiments, so they called themselves the "21st Arkansas (McRae's)" and "21st Arkansas (Cravens's)," after the names of their commanding officers (the latter commanded by Colonel Jordan E. Cravens). McRae's regiment fought in the Battle of Pea Ridge in March 1862 and at the Siege of Corinth. McRae was then ordered to raise another regiment. He created the 28th Arkansas Infantry.

McRae was promoted to brigadier general on November 5, 1862, and led his new brigade in the Battle of Prairie Grove (December 7, 1862). After the Battle of Helena on July 4, 1863, Brigadier General James Fleming Fagan accused McRae of willful failure to provide assistance during an attack. The result was a court of inquiry. While waiting for the court to convene, McRae took part in the battles of Marks' Mills and Jenkins' Ferry in April 1864.

On December 29, 1864, the court of inquiry finally found McRae not guilty of any misconduct. McRae, however—apparently disgusted by the long-drawn-out proceedings—resigned his commission in November 1864. He returned to Searcy, Arkansas, to resume the practice of law, which he continued until 1881.

McRae was called "a gentle man, with a great capacity for love and understanding." He was also an active Mason and briefly a member of the Ku Klux Klan during the Reconstruction Era. In 1881, McRae became deputy secretary of state of Arkansas and "a one-man state chamber of commerce." He continued to work hard for his state until

1897, when he had a stroke. His mind remained alert, but his body deteriorated rapidly. General Dandridge McRae died in Searcy, Arkansas, on April 23, 1899, at the age of sixty-nine. He was buried in Oak Grove Cemetery, Searcy.

HUGH WEEDON MERCER was born on November 27, 1808, in Fredericksburg, Virginia. He attended West Point, graduated in 1828, and was assigned to the artillery and stationed in Savannah. In fact, he spent most of his time in the service in Georgia. He resigned his commission on April 30, 1835, and married a Savannah native. He became a bank cashier at Planters Bank in Savannah and an artillery officer in the local militia.

After Georgia left the Union, Hugh Mercer was named a colonel in the Confederate Army and commander of the 1st Georgia Regiment. On October 29, 1861, he was promoted to brigadier general.

General Mercer spent the bulk of the war commanding a three-regiment brigade in Savannah, which was not attacked until late 1864. He simultaneously commanded the District of Georgia.

When the Atlanta Campaign began in May 1864, Mercer was sent to the Army of Tennessee, where he was given command of a brigade in W. H. T. Walker's division and fought at Dalton, Marietta, and Kennesaw Mountain and in the Battle of Atlanta. When General Walker was killed in action on July 22, Mercer took command of his division and led it until after Atlanta fell.

Mercer was an old man by the standards of Confederate generals in 1864 (only eight of the thirty-three cadets he graduated with in 1828 served in the Civil War), and active campaigning was hard on him. Unable to meet the physical demands of active campaigning, he was sent back to Savannah, where he served under William J. Hardee. As Sherman approached the city, Mercer was given command of the 10th Infantry Battalion of Georgia State Troops. He returned to Savannah after the

THE ENCYCLOPEDIA OF CONFEDERATE GENERALS

city fell and was imprisoned at Fort Pulaski (which he once commanded) and on Cockspur Island. He was paroled on May 13, 1865.

By 1866, General Mercer was back in the banking business in Savannah. From 1869 to 1872, he lived in Baltimore and worked as a commission merchant. His health, however, continued to deteriorate. In 1872, he traveled to the spa town of Baden-Baden, Germany, and died there on June 9, 1877, at age sixty-eight. He was buried in Bonaventure Cemetery, Savannah.

WILLIAM MILLER was born in Ithaca, New York, on August 3, 1820, but his family moved to Louisiana when he was an infant. He attended Louisiana College and served with General Zachary Taylor's army in Mexico. The U.S. government awarded him forty acres of land in Santa Rosa County, Florida, for his services, so he moved to Florida, studied law, passed the bar exam, and set up a law practice in Santa Rosa County, in the extreme northwestern part of the state. He also went into the timber and lumber businesses and owned a sawmill.

When the war began, Miller formed the 3rd Florida Infantry, a six-company battalion, of which he was the commander, with the rank of major (later lieutenant colonel). The battalion spent a year drilling and protecting Pensacola and Confederate blockade runners. It was consolidated with the 1st Florida Infantry Battalion (which had been depleted at Shiloh in April 1862) to form the 1st Florida Infantry Regiment, under Miller's command. It took part in the Kentucky Campaign of August through October 1862. After John C. Brown was wounded in the Battle of Perryville (October 8), Colonel Miller assumed command of his brigade. Miller himself was wounded, but only slightly. After the retreat to middle Tennessee, he reverted to regimental command, and the 1st Florida was consolidated with the 3rd Florida Infantry Regiment, with Miller as commander. Miller led the 1st/3rd Florida in the Second Battle of

Murfreesboro (December 31, 1862, to January 2, 1863), where Miller was badly wounded and part of his thumb was blown away.

Miller's recuperation took months. When he was able to return to limited duty, he was named director of the Confederate Conscription Bureau in Florida. He was promoted to brigadier general on August 2, 1864, and on September 8 was placed in charge of Florida's reserve forces. On September 29, he was named commander of the District of Florida.

In March 1865, Union forces attempted to capture Tallahassee. They were met by 1,000 ragtag troops under the command of General Miller, who blocked them from crossing the St. Marks River at the Natural Bridge east of the capital. Miller selected a strong position and dug in. The Yankees launched three attacks on March 6 and were defeated each time in a battle that lasted twelve hours. The Yankees lost 148 men. Miller lost 3 men killed and 23 wounded.

General Miller surrendered his remaining forces at Tallahassee in May 1865. He proved to be a highly competent, resourceful commander—and a brave one.

After the war, he returned to northwestern Florida, the lumber business, and farming. He settled in the Point Washington community of Walton County and served two terms in the Florida House of Representatives and one in the state senate.

Late in life, Miller was considered a bit of an eccentric, gracious and "kind-hearted as long as his temper was not ruffled," but crotchety and prodigiously profane when it was.

General William Miller died on August 8, 1909, in Point Washington, Florida, at age eighty-nine. Initially, he and his wife were buried in Port Washington Cemetery, but in 1922, the United Daughters of the Confederacy called attention to the neglected nature of their graves. They had the Millers exhumed and reinterred in St. John's Cemetery in Pensacola, Florida.

YOUNG MARSHALL MOODY was born on June 23, 1822, in Chesterfield County, Virginia. His father was a wealthy man. Moody moved

to Alabama in 1842 and worked as a teacher and a merchant. He was clerk of the court of Marengo County, Alabama, from 1856 to 1861. Moody was a Mason and attended the Methodist Church.

When the Civil War began, he became a captain in the 11th Alabama. Archibald Gracie was the regiment's major. The regiment was sent to Virginia and was on duty along the Potomac but saw no significant action as of the spring of 1862, when Gracie and Moody returned to Alabama. They raised the 43rd Alabama Infantry Regiment in Mobile. The men elected Gracie colonel and Moody lieutenant colonel. In July 1862, the regiment was deployed against Tennessee Unionists at Fort Cliff and scattered them with little difficulty. The regiment also took part in the Kentucky invasion but was not engaged in either of the significant battles (Richmond or Perryville).

Archibald Gracie was promoted to brigadier general on November 4, 1862, and Young M. Moody became a colonel and commander of the 43rd. The regiment spent the winter of 1862–63 at Cumberland Gap and most of 1863 in East Tennessee. It fell back in front of U.S. General Ambrose Burnside's IX Corps and abandoned Knoxville on September 2, 1863. It then headed southwest to join the main army.

Moody and his men took part in the Battle of Chickamauga (September 18–20, 1863), where the regiment was attached to General James Longstreet's corps. In its first major combat action, the 43rd Alabama traded volleys with U.S. General George Thomas's veteran soldiers. The regiment fell back when it ran out of ammunition. It lost sixteen men killed and eighty-three wounded.

After Chickamauga, the regiment was sent to reinforce Longstreet in the Knoxville sector. On December 14, it fought in the Battle of Bean's Station, where it delivered a successful attack.

In April 1864, the 43rd was sent to Virginia as part of General G. T. Beauregard's department. In May, it helped defeat U.S. General Phil Sheridan's cavalry raid on Richmond and then reinforced the defenders of Drewry's Bluff, where on May 16 it took part in the flank-ing attack that repulsed the Federals. In that action, Colonel Moody was severely wounded in the right ankle and did not return to duty until fall.

The regiment moved into the Petersburg trenches in June and fought in the trenches for the next nine months. Young M. Moody assumed command of the brigade on December 2, 1864, after General Gracie was killed by a shell burst. He directed it for the rest of the war and was promoted to brigadier general on March 4, 1865.

When Petersburg fell, Moody's brigade joined the retreat to Appo-mattox. Suffering from illness, General Moody traveled with the army's wagon train and was captured on April 8 near Appomattox. He was allowed to rejoin Robert E. Lee's army for the formal surrender the next day.

After the war, Moody settled in Mobile, Alabama, and became a businessman. During a business trip to New Orleans, he came down with yellow fever and died on September 18, 1866. He was forty-four years old. He was buried in a large wall tomb on Myrtle Avenue in Green-wood Cemetery, New Orleans.

General Moody was a fine regimental commander and a steady brigade commander. Of him, General Joseph Wheeler wrote, "He was a man of soldierly bearing, six feet in height, slender and erect; of very gentle disposition, and loved by the men of his command."

JOHN CREED MOORE was born on February 28, 1824, at Red Ridge in Hawkins County, Tennessee. He attended Emory and Henry College in Virginia before being admitted to West Point in 1845. He graduated with the class of 1849 and was commissioned in the artillery. He was sent to Florida and fought the Seminoles. After serving in the New Mexico and Nebraska Territories, Moore resigned his commission in 1855. He became a professor at Shelby College in Kentucky.

The Confederate States of America was founded on February 8, 1861. Moore was quick to side with the Confederacy and was commissioned a captain of artillery on March 24, 1861. He was assigned to Fort Jackson, Louisiana, and then to Galveston, Texas, where he was ordered to construct defensive fortifications. While there, he adopted Texas as his home state and organized and trained the 2nd Texas Infantry. He was promoted to colonel on September 2, 1861.

Moore and his regiment fought at Shiloh (April 6–7, 1862), where they helped envelop and destroy Union General Benjamin Prentiss's division. Moore was then given a brigade and promoted to brigadier general on May 26, 1862, over the objections of General William J. Hardee, who despised him. As part of the Army of Mississippi, Moore led his command in the Siege of Corinth. In the Second Battle of Corinth (October 3–4, 1862), he led his brigade over the Union fortifications and into hand-to-hand combat in the town, before he was finally forced to retreat. Moore's brigade had advanced further than any other Confederate unit that day.

General Moore took part in checking the Union's efforts to battle its way into Vicksburg from October 1862 to April 1863. In May 1863, his men were part of the Vicksburg garrison and played a major role in thwarting U.S. General Ulysses Grant's massive assault of May 22.

One of his soldiers at Vicksburg called the redheaded, red-bearded and red-faced Moore a "brave and gallant officer, but not a Christian." Nominally an Episcopalian, Moore was noted for being hot-tempered, and one of his men recalled, "It was only a short time until I had strong suspicions that I had joined a regiment of devils."

Moore held his line throughout the siege and surrendered with the rest of the garrison on July 4, 1863.

After General Moore was paroled, he collected the remnants of his command at Demopolis, Alabama, and joined Braxton Bragg's army in the battles of Lookout Mountain and Missionary Ridge. His corps commander was William J. Hardee, with whom he had a long-running feud. He requested a transfer. General Dabney Maury, the Confederate commander of Mobile, had been impressed with John Moore when they had served together in Mississippi, and he asked that Moore be assigned to his command, but President Jefferson Davis denied his request. As a result, on February 3, 1864, General Moore resigned his commission in the Provisional Army. He retained his rank of lieutenant colonel in the Regular Army of the Confederacy and was transferred to Savannah as commander of the arsenal there. Moore accepted a demotion of two grades in rank just to get away from Hardee. In September 1864, he was named commander of the arsenal at Selma, where he remained for the rest of the war.

After the surrender, Moore returned to Texas and taught mathematics at the Coronal Institute. He later became superintendent of schools at Mexia and East Dallas and taught at Galveston, Kerrville, Osage, and Coryell City. He died on December 31, 1910, in Osage, Texas, at age eighty-six and was buried in Osage Cemetery.

PATRICK THEODORE MOORE was born in Galway, Ireland, on September 22, 1821. He moved with his family to Canada in 1835 and later to Boston. Moore came to Richmond when he was twenty-nine years old, and the city became his home. He worked as a merchant and served in the militia.

On April 21, 1861, just days after Virginia seceded, he was promoted to colonel and named commander of the 1st Virginia Militia Regiment. On July 1, 1861, he became colonel of the 1st Virginia Infantry Regiment of the Confederate Army and was attached to General James Longstreet's brigade.

On July 18, 1861, three days before the Battle of First Manassas, Moore was engaged in a skirmish against the Yankees at Blackburn's Ford. He was seriously wounded in the head and incapacitated for field duty. He served as a volunteer aide to General Joseph E. Johnston in the Peninsula Campaign and at Seven Pines and to General Longstreet during the Seven Days Battles, even though he was only partially recovered. Generals G. T. Beauregard and Longstreet made it clear in their reports that they thought highly of Moore, but he could never again stand the strain of active campaigning.

For the rest of 1862 and all of 1863, Colonel Moore performed court-martial duty. In 1864, he helped organize Virginia's reserve forces, under the supervision of General James Kemper. On May 18, 1864, he became commander of the 1st Virginia Reserve Brigade and was assigned to General Richard S. Ewell's Richmond local defense forces. He was promoted to brigadier general on September 20, 1864.

General Moore did not accompany his brigade when General Robert E. Lee evacuated Richmond during the night of April 2–3, 1865. He was paroled at Manchester, Virginia (now part of Richmond), on April 30, 1865.

Patrick Moore lost everything during the war. He started over and opened an insurance agency in the former capital of the Confederacy. He died in Richmond on February 19, 1883, at age sixty-one and was buried in Shockoe Hill Cemetery, Richmond.

M·

JOHN HUNT MORGAN was born in Huntsville, Alabama, on June 1, 1825. His family moved to Lexington, Kentucky, when John was four. He grew up on a farm and was educated in local schools.

John Morgan attended Transylvania College but was suspended two years later for dueling with a fraternity brother. In 1846, he enlisted as a private for the Mexican War, rose to first lieutenant of cavalry, and fought at Buena Vista. After the war, he returned home and went into the hemp manufacturing business.

John Morgan was a womanizer and a gambler, but he was also generous, charming, and charismatic. He seduced a slave and had at least one biracial son. In 1857, he raised an independent militia company, the Lexington Rifles, at his own expense and drilled it frequently. He did not initially support secession, but when Kentucky's neutrality collapsed in September 1861, he went to Tennessee and raised the 2nd Kentucky

Cavalry Regiment. He became its colonel on April 4, 1862, and led it in the Battle of Shiloh.

In July, with fewer than 900 men, Morgan led his first raid into Kentucky. He dispersed 1,500 Union home guard troops, captured 1,200 regular Union troops (and paroled them), made off with hundreds of excellent horses, raided 17 towns, destroyed Federal property worth millions of dollars, and burned several railroad bridges, all while suffering only 90 casualties and actually increasing the size of his force. When he returned to Southern lines, he had 1,200 men.

On December 7, Morgan fought in the Battle of Hartsville, Tennessee. With 1,300 men, he forced a Union infantry brigade of 2,100 men to surrender and captured a large wagon train. General Joseph E. Johnston called the raid "brilliant." General Braxton Bragg recommended Morgan for promotion to brigadier general on December 11, 1862, and President Jefferson Davis signed the promotion orders on December 14.

Morgan went on his most famous raid from June 11 to July 26, 1863. It covered more than one thousand miles. He captured and paroled six thousand Federals during the raid. Thinking he would get help from Copperheads (anti-Lincoln Northerners), Morgan disobeyed General Bragg's orders and crossed the Ohio at Brandenburg, Kentucky, on July 8. The help Morgan expected to receive from the Copperheads never materialized, and he was forced to surrender near West Point, Ohio, on July 26. It was the northernmost advance of regular Confederate forces in the war.

John Morgan and his officers were sent to the Ohio Penitentiary at Columbus, from which Morgan and six comrades escaped. Two of these men were recaptured; the rest made it to Southern lines.

General Morgan was not universally popular—Confederate authorities were quietly investigating Morgan for criminal behavior and banditry—but he was given another command and raided Kentucky in June 1864. It was a failure.

Though the quality of his cavalry had declined, he still had ambitious plans and plotted to capture Knoxville, Tennessee. A Union sympathizer spotted him as he spent the night in a private home at Greeneville,

Tennessee; the Union sympathizer informed Federal cavalry of his location. By early morning September 4, 1864, Federals had surrounded the house. Morgan—having sworn that he would never be captured again—made a run for it. A Union cavalryman shot him in the back, killing him instantly. He was thirty-nine years old.

John Hunt Morgan is buried in Lexington Cemetery, Lexington, Kentucky, near the grave of his brother-in-law and good friend, Brigadier General Basil Duke.

Morgan was an excellent cavalry officer and raider by the standards of 1861 and 1862. He was, however, far too rash, impulsive, and unstable. Like Joe Wheeler, and unlike Nathan Bedford Forrest, he didn't measure up to the standards required in 1863 and 1864, after the Union cavalry became much better than it had been.

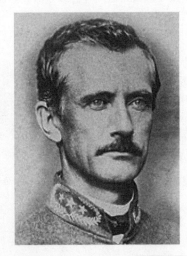

JOHN TYLER MORGAN was born on June 20, 1824, in Athens, Tennessee. He was a sickly youth and was initially homeschooled by his mother and occasionally by a private tutor. Many of his early playmates were Indian children, and he became familiar with their culture. His family moved to Calhoun County, Alabama, when he was nine. His attended a local school, read law, and was admitted to the bar in 1845 without having attended college.

Morgan moved to Selma in 1855, where he set up a law practice. He was known as a fine attorney and an excellent debater. He also became a fire-eating secessionist.

In April 1861, Morgan enlisted as a private in the Cahaba Rifles, which later became part of the 5th Alabama Infantry. It trained at Pensacola and was then sent to Virginia, where it fought at the Battle of First Manassas. The regimental commander, Robert Rodes, was promoted to brigade commander in October, and Morgan moved up to lieutenant colonel shortly after. He fought at the Siege of Yorktown in April 1862.

The following month, John Morgan returned to Alabama to recruit a partisan ranger regiment. On August 11, 1862, the 51st Alabama Partisan Rangers (later redesignated the 51st Alabama Cavalry) was activated, with Morgan as its colonel. It had a strength of 1,300 men. The regiment served under Nathan Bedford Forrest, Joe Wheeler, and W. W. Allen. It fought in the Second Battle of Murfreesboro and was often used to cover General Braxton Bragg's lines of communication. On June 14, 1863, John T. Morgan was offered command of Rodes's old brigade but turned it down to stay with his regiment. On July 27, during the Tullahoma Campaign, it fought in the disastrous Battle of Shelbyville, where it lost half its men. He was then given command of a brigade in General William T. Martin's division of Joe Wheeler's corps and led it in the Battle of Chickamauga. He was promoted to brigadier general on November 16, 1863.

Morgan's brigade accompanied General James Longstreet to Knoxville. It operated in East Tennessee in the winter of 1863–64 and performed poorly. At one time, it was routed and dispersed by Union cavalry. Morgan was given a new brigade, which he led in the Atlanta Campaign. Later, he opposed Sherman's March to the Sea. He was then sent to Demopolis, Alabama, and tried to organize black troops for Confederate service in Mississippi and Alabama. He was engaged in this endeavor when the South surrendered.

After the war, Morgan returned to Selma, resumed the practice of law, and worked to restore home rule. He was elected to the U.S. Senate in 1876 and was reelected five times, serving until his death. He believed in American imperialism, such as the acquisition of Hawaii, the building of a Central American canal, and a much-enlarged Navy and Merchant Marine. In domestic policy, he supported segregation, restrictions on black voting rights, and the encouragement of black emigration to American overseas holdings. He was widely regarded as extremely knowledgeable, an impressive speaker, and a cultivated man, fluent in Latin and fond of music and art. He was a Knight Templar in the Masonic Order and a member of the Methodist Episcopal Church.

General John Tyler Morgan died in Washington, D.C., on June 11, 1907, at age eighty-two. He is buried in Live Oak Cemetery, Selma, Alabama.

JEAN-JACQUES-ALFRED-ALEXANDRE "ALFRED" MOUTON was born on February 18, 1829, in Opelousas, Louisiana. His father was Alexandre Mouton, governor of Louisiana. Alfred entered the U.S. Military Academy in 1846. He was a native French speaker, and West Point was his first experience in an English-speaking institution. He had to master not only a difficult curriculum, but also what for him was a foreign language as well. He did so and graduated in 1850 but resigned his commission in September. He returned to South Louisiana and helped run his father's huge sugarcane plantation, which employed two hundred slaves. Alfred proved to be a successful manager. He also joined the Louisiana Militia, became a brigadier general in 1856, and was renowned as a local hero for his work in cracking down on criminal gangs. He was a tough-looking and big man, standing more than six feet tall, weighing 210 pounds, and sporting a thick, dark, full beard.

When the Civil War began, Mouton organized an infantry company in Lafayette Parish. On October 5, 1861, he was elected colonel of the 18th Louisiana Infantry. He fought at Shiloh (April 6–7, 1862), and was severely wounded leading a charge. On April 16, 1862, while still recuperating in the hospital, he was promoted to brigadier general and named commander of a Louisiana brigade. He was then temporarily commander of the forces of Western Louisiana before coming under the command of General Richard Taylor.

In 1864, Mouton fought in the Red River Campaign. On April 8, 1864, General Taylor launched a shattering counteroffensive against the Union forces near Mansfield. He chose Mouton to lead the first attack.

Mouton drew his sword and gave the order: "Let us charge them right in the face and throw them into the valley!"

Taylor remembered Mouton's charge as "magnificent." It broke the Union front and turned the entire campaign in the Confederates' favor, but the costs were high. Among the casualties was General Mouton. He pushed too far forward, and as the 48th Ohio fired its last organized volley, five bullets hit him in the chest. He slid off his horse and died without saying a word. He was thirty-five years old. For the rest of the battle, "Mouton!" was the battle cry of the Confederate Army.

Alfred Mouton was buried on the battlefield at Mansfield. He was reinterred in his family's burial plot at St. John's Cemetery in Lafayette, Louisiana.

N

· NELSON – NORTHROP ·

ALLISON NELSON was born in Fayette County (today's Fulton County), Georgia, on March 11, 1822, the son of a Chattahoochee River ferry operator. When the Mexican War began, Nelson organized the Kennesaw Rangers, a volunteer company, and became its captain. It did not, however, see any combat. Returning to civilian life, he read law, was admitted to the bar, and in 1848 was elected to the legislature. During an 1851 attempt by Cuba to be free of Spanish rule, he was appointed a brigadier general by rebel leader General Narciso López, but the revolt was unsuccessful, Nelson saw no combat, and López and many of his followers were executed by the Spanish.

Nelson was elected mayor of Atlanta as a Democrat in 1854. He was inaugurated on January 26, 1855, but resigned on July 6 after a dispute with the city council. He lived briefly in Kansas during the border troubles, where he supported the pro-slavery forces, and in 1856 moved to Meridian, central Texas, where he distinguished himself as an Indian fighter and served as an Indian agent under Lawrence Sullivan "Sul" Ross. He was elected to the legislature in 1859.

When Texas seceded, Nelson was largely responsible for raising the 10th Texas Infantry Regiment in Waco. In 1862, the 10th was sent to Arkansas, where General Thomas C. Hindman was pleased with what he saw and praised Nelson and his regiment. Nelson further impressed his superiors when he foiled a plot by Arkansas troops to stage a mass desertion. He executed several ringleaders and increased discipline among the troops.

Lieutenant General Theophilus H. Holmes, the commander of the Trans-Mississippi Department, recommended Nelson for promotion. Nelson became a brigadier general on September 12, 1862, and was given command of a division. Unfortunately, General Nelson fell victim to a typhoid epidemic sweeping through the Southern regiments. He died in Austin, Arkansas, on October 7, 1862, at the age of forty. He was buried in Mount Holly Cemetery, Little Rock.

In announcing his death, Holmes wrote, "He is an irreparable loss to me."

Camp Hope was renamed Camp Nelson in his honor and is now a Confederate cemetery, where about 1,500 former soldiers are buried.

FRANCIS REDDING TILLOU NICHOLLS was born in Donaldsonville, Ascension Parish, Louisiana, on August 20, 1834. He attended Jefferson Academy in New Orleans and West Point, from which he graduated in 1855 at age twenty, and was commissioned a second lieutenant of artillery.

Nicholls was sent to Florida during the Third Seminole War. He was at Fort Yuma, California, when he resigned effective October 1, 1856. He returned home, studied law, was admitted to the bar, and practiced law in Napoleonville.

Nicholls opposed secession but went with his state when the die was cast. He and his brother mustered the Phoenix Guards, which became Company K of the 8th Louisiana Infantry Regiment. Nicholls was named its lieutenant colonel. He was a strong disciplinarian.

Nicholls fought in the Battle of First Manassas and in Stonewall Jackson's Valley Campaign. At the First Battle of Winchester, on May 25, 1862, he was shot in the left arm, which had to be amputated.

When Jackson turned south to deal with other Federal forces, Nicholls had to be left behind. He was captured on or about June 1. Probably because of his wound, he was paroled rather than imprisoned. He was exchanged on September 21. He had been promoted to colonel on September 10, while still a prisoner.

Robert E. Lee knew Nicholls from West Point and chose him to command a Louisiana brigade. Nicholls was promoted to brigadier general on October 14, 1862, although he could not return to duty until January 1863. He led his brigade in the Battle of Chancellorsville and formed part of Jackson's famous flanking attack of May 2. As the Yankees fled before him in "wild disorder," one of their artillery shells, Nicholls recalled, "passed through my horse's belly & came out the other side and took my foot off thoroughly & completely."

Nicholls was no longer able to exercise field command. He went to Lynchburg, Virginia, to recuperate and from August 1863 to May 1864 commanded the Lynchburg district. In July 1864, he was ordered to the Trans-Mississippi Department as commander of its volunteer and conscript bureau.

The Trans-Mississippi surrendered on May 26, 1865, and Nicholls was paroled on June 18. He returned to his law practice and became a strong advocate of home rule in Louisiana. In 1876, his friends nominated "all that [was] left of General Nicholls" for governor on the Democratic ticket. The election was close and contested by the carpetbaggers, but he was inaugurated on April 24, 1877, and served until January 14, 1880.

Governor Nicholls battled for honest government—which in Louisiana is an exercise in frustration. In 1887, he decided to run for governor again and was easily reelected. He served from 1888 to 1892. When he left the governor's mansion, he became chief justice of the Louisiana Supreme Court, a post he held until 1911. Simultaneously, he was the owner of the prosperous Ridgefield Plantation near Thibodaux, which harvested sugarcane.

General Francis R. T. Nicholls, a hero of his state, died at Ridgefield Plantation on January 4, 1912, at the age of seventy-seven. He is buried in St. John's Episcopal Cemetery, Thibodaux. Nicholls State University in Thibodaux is named after him.

LUCIUS BELLINGER NORTHROP was born on September 8, 1811, in Charleston, South Carolina. He was appointed to the U.S. Military Academy, became good friends with Cadet Jefferson Davis (class of 1828), and graduated in 1831.

Northrop was commissioned in the dragoons. He fought in the Second Seminole War. Sent to the Indian

Territory, he accidentally shot himself in the knee and spent more than
seven of the next eight years on medical leave. With the approval of the
War Department, he used some of this time to study at the Jefferson
Medical School in Philadelphia.

The army finally dropped him from the roles in January 1848. He
practiced medicine in Charleston until 1861, when President Jefferson
Davis appointed him commissary general of the Confederate Army with
the rank of colonel. It was arguably the worst appointment he made
during the Civil War.

Northrop's tasks were herculean. They included providing food and
forage for the Southern armies and, beginning in 1863, food for Union
prisoners of war as well. His many problems included hoarding, inflation, the near collapse of the railroad system, shortages of wagons and
teams, dishonest agents, price fixing, the loss of territory (especially
agriculturally rich territory), and every other problem you can imagine
in a newly established republic of independent-minded states in the
midst of a giant war. His efforts to feed Union prisoners were stifled by
Ulysses S. Grant's refusal to continue exchanging prisoners. All of these
problems might have defeated a capable man, but this Northrop was not.
Although personally incorruptible, his job required flexibility, tact,
patience, and resourcefulness, but Northrop was petty, rigid, and pessimistic and suffered from, as Professor James I. Robertson noted, a
"blind devotion to bureaucracy."

Northrop's failures were major contributing factors to the Confederate defeat. For example, the failure of the Commissary Department
led to the near collapse of the South's cavalry. In 1864, J. E. B. Stuart's
horses were fed two to three pounds of grain per day. Union horses
received twenty-two to twenty-three pounds per day. Northrop was convinced his methods were right and were only thwarted by the stupidity of
generals in the field. President Jefferson Davis steadfastly refused to
replace Northrop—even as Confederate armies starved.

Incredibly, Jefferson Davis promoted him to brigadier general on
November 26, 1864. Davis did not, however, submit this nomination to
the Senate, where it certainly would have been rejected. Most of the

senators, in fact, supported an extraordinary measure—an impeachment resolution against the commissary general!

Matters came to a crisis when Davis sought to appoint John C. Breckinridge secretary of war. Breckinridge agreed to accept the post only if Northrop were removed. General Robert E. Lee also wanted a change in the commissary department. Finally, Davis yielded, and Northrop was forced to resign on February 15, 1865. But it was too late. Appomattox was only seven weeks away.

After the war, Lucius Northrop settled on a farm near Charlottesville, Virginia, where he lived in obscurity. In 1890, a stroke left him partially paralyzed. He was moved into the Maryland Line Confederate Soldiers' Home in Pikesville, Baltimore County, Maryland, and died there on February 9, 1894, at the age of eighty-two. He was buried in New Cathedral Cemetery, Baltimore.

With the possible exception of Braxton Bragg, Lucius Northrop was the most hated man in the Confederacy. He contributed more to the fall of the Southern Confederacy than did many Union generals.

N·

O'NEAL

EDWARD ASBURY O'NEAL was born on September 20, 1818, in Madison County, Alabama Territory, the son of an Irish immigrant and a South Carolina Huguenot. Edward was educated at Green Academy and LaGrange College (now the University of Alabama), from which he graduated in 1836. He studied law in Huntsville, was admitted to the bar in 1840, and set up a practice in Florence. From 1841 to 1845, he was solicitor of the Fourth Judicial Circuit.

Edward O'Neal was a strong believer in the rule of law and the right of secession. He raised an infantry company when the Civil War began, expanded this command into three companies, and was commissioned as a captain in the Confederate Army on June 4, 1861. His companies were incorporated into the 9th Alabama, and O'Neal was elected major on June 26. In July, the 9th was sent to Winchester, where it became part of Edmund Kirby Smith's brigade. It missed the Battle of First Manassas due to a railroad accident.

O'Neal was promoted to lieutenant colonel on October 21, 1861, and to colonel on March 24, 1862. He fought in all the major battles of the Army of Northern Virginia in 1862 and 1863. At Seven Pines, his horse was shot out from under him, and he was wounded by a shell fragment. He was painfully wounded in the thigh at Sharpsburg and was wounded again at Chancellorsville.

Robert E. Lee praised O'Neal's performance at Chancellorsville, recommended his promotion to brigadier general, and had that recommendation approved on June 6, 1863. Lee, however, had second thoughts, and he did not forward the promotion order to O'Neal. O'Neal did not do well as a brigade commander at Gettysburg, and General Lee recalled his recommendation. O'Neal's promotion was cancelled by President Jefferson Davis, and O'Neal returned to command of the 26th Alabama.

Edward O'Neal and his men took part in the indecisive Bristoe and Mine Run campaigns of 1863. In early 1864, he and his depleted regiment were sent to Alabama to rest and recruit and later to guard prisoners. On May 14, however, they were ordered to Dalton, Georgia, and fought in the Atlanta Campaign.

After General John Bell Hood replaced Joseph E. Johnston as commander of the Army of Tennessee on July 17, 1864, Colonel O'Neal was relieved of his command. He was on detached duty for the rest of the war and, at the end of the conflict, was arresting deserters in northern Alabama.

After the war, O'Neal returned to Florence, Alabama, resumed his law practice, and worked for a return to home rule. He was elected governor of Alabama on August 7, 1882, and was inaugurated on December 1. He was reelected in 1884 and held office until December 1, 1886. He returned to Florence, where he died on November 7, 1890, at age seventy-two. He is buried in Florence Cemetery.

Edward Asbury O'Neal was undoubtedly a fine regimental commander but did not distinguish himself as a brigade commander, except at Chancellorsville. He was, however, an outstanding governor. The memory of his successful administration was a major contributing factor to his son's election to the same post in 1911, twenty-one years after his death.

P

PAGE – PRYOR

RICHARD LUCIAN PAGE, who was nicknamed "Ramrod" and "Bombast" Page, was born on December 20, 1807, in Clarke County, Virginia, a first cousin of Robert E. Lee. Richard Page opted for a naval career and became a midshipman in 1824. He had many and varied assignments.

When the Mexican War broke out, he was a lieutenant commander and executive officer of the frigate USS *Independence*, the flagship of the American squadron that fought at Veracruz. Page was also commander of the sloop-of-war USS *Germantown* in the East India Squadron for two years. He was on duty as an ordnance officer at Norfolk, Virginia, when the Civil War began. He resigned from the U.S. Navy on April 18, 1861, after thirty-seven years of service and became an aide to Virginia Governor John Letcher. His first job was to organize the Virginia Navy. When Virginia joined the Confederacy, he was commissioned as a commander and later captain in the Confederate Navy.

Richard Page took part in the unsuccessful Battle of Port Royal as an assistant to Commodore Josiah Tattnall aboard the gunboat CSS *Savannah*. He then returned to Norfolk and supervised the evacuation of machinery and equipment from the naval yard in May 1862. He established the ordnance and construction depot at Charlotte, North Carolina, which he managed with great efficiency. It became one of the most important ordnance centers in the entire South.

On March 1, 1864, Captain Page was transferred to the Confederate Army as a brigadier general and was placed in command of the outer defenses of Mobile Bay. He set up his headquarters at Fort Morgan, which the Northerners attacked in August. On August 8, the Federals called upon him to surrender. U.S. Admiral David Farragut and his attached army units totaled ten thousand men and more than two hundred guns. Page had four hundred men and twenty-six operational guns. Under constant bombardment, he nevertheless held out for more than two weeks.

On August 22, the bombardment became furious. Fort Morgan was hit by three thousand shells in twelve hours. Many of the Confederate guns were knocked out and walls were breached. On the morning of August 23, Richard Page determined he had no further chance of a successful defense, so he ran up the white flag. He broke his sword over his knee rather than surrender it to the Federals. "The defense of Fort Morgan under the command of General Page is one of the most celebrated instances of heroism in the history of the war," an admiring Jed Hotchkiss wrote later.

The former naval captain was imprisoned at Fort Delaware on Pea Patch Island, Delaware. He was released in September 1865. He returned to Norfolk and became superintendent of the city's public schools from 1875 to 1883.

General Richard Lucian Page died at Blue Ridge Summit, Pennsylvania, on August 9, 1901. He is buried in Cedar Grove Cemetery, Norfolk.

JOSEPH BENJAMIN PALMER was born on November 1, 1825, in Rutherford County, Tennessee. Palmer attended Union University, read law, and was admitted to the bar in 1848. He set up a law office in Murfreesboro and was very successful. He was elected to the state legislature in 1849 and reelected in 1851. He was elected mayor of Murfreesboro in 1855 and served until 1859.

Palmer opposed secession but, like many Americans in 1861, believed his primary allegiance was to his state. He organized a company of infantry and was elected its captain in May. The following month it was combined with other companies to form the 18th Tennessee Infantry. By unanimous vote, Joseph Palmer was elected its colonel. The regiment fought at Fort Donelson, which was surrendered by the Confederates on February 16, 1862. Palmer became a prisoner of war and was sent to Fort Warren, Massachusetts, where he remained until exchanged on August 15, 1862. The 18th Tennessee was reformed, and Palmer was reelected its colonel.

His next major action was near his home in the Second Battle of Murfreesboro. On January 2, 1863, he was an acting brigade commander and was wounded three times. He was unable to return to duty for four months. He took part in the Tullahoma Campaign and the Battle of Chickamauga, where he was wounded in the shoulder and almost bled to death. He did not return to duty until the Atlanta Campaign. Meanwhile, the 18th Tennessee was combined with the 26th Tennessee to form the 18th/26th Tennessee Infantry Regiment, with Palmer as its colonel. In mid-August, General John C. Brown was given command of William Bate's division, and Palmer found himself leading a brigade. On September 1, 1864, he was wounded yet again in the Battle of Jonesboro.

After he recovered, he returned to commanding a brigade and on November 15, 1864, was at last promoted to brigadier general. He led his brigade in General John Bell Hood's Franklin-Nashville Campaign, although it did not fight in either battle; instead, it was detached to General Nathan Bedford Forrest and besieged Murfreesboro. After the Army of Tennessee was routed at Nashville, Palmer's brigade was part of the rear guard. During the Carolinas Campaign, General Joseph E. Johnston consolidated his Tennessee troops into four regiments and placed them under Palmer's command. He fought and was wounded in the Battle of Bentonville and surrendered with Johnston on April 26. He was paroled in Greensborough on May 1.

General Palmer resumed his law practice in Murfreesboro after the war. Finished with public life, he was content to work at his profession and enjoy peacetime. He died in Murfreesboro on November 4, 1890, at age sixty-five. He is buried in Evergreen Cemetery.

MOSBY MONROE PARSONS was born on May 21, 1822, in Charlottesville, Virginia. His family moved to Cole County, Missouri, when he was thirteen and relocated to Jefferson City two years later. Parsons studied law, passed the bar exam in 1846, and then went to the war in Mexico. He emerged from that conflict as a captain and was cited for gallantry at the Battle of the Sacramento River in northern Mexico. He also took part in the conquest of California.

Parsons returned to Missouri after the war and set up a law practice. He became U.S. District Attorney for Western Missouri and, in 1856, was elected to the legislature. He became a state senator in 1858 and served until 1861. He was also a brigadier general and commander of the 6th Missouri State Guard Division.

Parsons joined the South when the war began and led his small division in the battles of Carthage, Wilson's Creek, and Pea Ridge. He was commissioned as a brigadier general in the Confederate Army on November 5, 1862, and led an infantry brigade at the Battle of Prairie Grove, Arkansas, on December 7.

General Parsons and his men took part in the unsuccessful Battle of Helena on July 4, 1863. A division commander in 1864, he was part of Richard Taylor's Army of Western Louisiana in the Battle of Pleasant Hill (April 9, 1864), which was a marginal Confederate victory. After that, Parsons's men were sent to Arkansas, where they took part in the successful efforts to check the Union's Camden Expedition. He fought at Marks' Mills, where a large Union detachment was destroyed, and at Jenkins' Ferry on April 30. Parsons took part in Sterling Price's unsuccessful thrust into Missouri and eastern Kansas in the fall of 1864.

After the Confederacy fell, Parsons moved to Mexico. On or about August 17, 1865, bandit-soldiers loyal to Benito Juárez murdered him, his brother-in-law (Captain Austin M. Standish), former Confederate Congressman Aaron H. Conrow, and two other companions. He was forty-three years old. His body was buried in an unmarked grave and is now lost. He has a cenotaph in Riverview Cemetery, Jefferson City, Missouri.

ELISHA FRANKLIN "BULL" PAXTON was born in Rockbridge County, Virginia, on March 24, 1828. He attended the James H. Paxton

School (owned by a cousin) and Washington College in Lexington. In 1847, he enrolled at Yale and graduated in 1849. He then attended the University of Virginia Law School in Charlottesville. After graduating at the top of his class, he returned to Lexington and practiced law. He was quite successful and eventually became president of the first bank in Rockbridge County, but failing eyesight forced him to give up his legal career, and he became a farmer at Thorn Hill.

Paxton was called "Bull" because of his physique. He was above average height and was known for his great physical strength, as well as his outspoken views. A fervent secessionist, Paxton clashed with Virginia Military Institute Professor Thomas J. Jackson—the future Stonewall—who was a strong Union man. The issue caused a breach in their friendship that was not healed until the Civil War, when Jackson apologized and admitted that Paxton was right all along.

Bull Paxton was a "straight arrow," morally speaking. He never drank, and his strong religious convictions became even stronger during the war. After Abraham Lincoln was elected president, Bull Paxton joined the Rockridge Rifles and was elected first lieutenant. The Rifles became part of the 4th Virginia Infantry Regiment of the 1st Virginia Brigade, which later became famous as the Stonewall Brigade. It fought in the Battle of First Manassas, where Paxton demonstrated "conspicuous gallantry" and was wounded. After that victory, the Rockridge Rifles were attached to the 27th Virginia Infantry. Paxton was elected major of this regiment in October 1861. He was not reelected, however, because he was heavy-handed and lacked tact.

Stonewall Jackson made Paxton one of his aides. He took part in all of Jackson's battles. In the summer of 1862, he was assistant quartermaster of the II Corps and on August 15 was named assistant adjutant general.

On September 23, 1862, Jackson recommended him for immediate promotion to brigadier general and commander of the Stonewall

Brigade. Bull Paxton did not seek this promotion, and it meant passing over several senior officers, but President Jefferson Davis made the appointment on November 15, effective November 1. Paxton led his new command in the Battle of Fredericksburg, where he "handled his troops with skill and promptness" and was officially praised by General William B. Taliaferro, his division commander. Fredericksburg Campaign historian and park ranger Frank O'Reilly was less impressed, stating that Paxton "mismanaged the brigade, caused needless casualties by halting under cannon fire, and missed an opportunity to surround and capture two Union regiments."

During the Battle of Chancellorsville, Paxton's brigade held the important Germanna Junction. Jackson delivered his famous flanking attack on May 2, 1863. Early on the morning of May 3, Paxton went forward to renew the attack. He was shot through the chest and died almost instantly. He was thirty-five years old.

Paxton was buried at Guinea Station, near where Jackson lay dying. Later, he was reinterred in Stonewall Jackson Memorial Cemetery at Lexington, only a few feet from his legendary commander.

WILLIAM HENRY FITZHUGH PAYNE was born in Midland, Fauquier County, Virginia, on January 27, 1830. He attended the Virginia Military Institute for a year but left to study law at the University of Virginia. He was admitted to the bar and in 1851, at the age of twenty-one, entered into a law partnership in Warrenton. In 1856, he was elected commonwealth attorney in Fauquier County.

As soon as his state seceded, Payne joined the Provisional Army of Virginia and took part in the occupation of Harpers Ferry. He was promoted to captain of the Black Horse Cavalry on April 26, 1861, which became the 4th Virginia Cavalry in September 1861. William Payne became its major on September 17.

As part of Fitzhugh Lee's brigade of J. E. B. Stuart's cavalry, Payne fought in the Peninsula Campaign. He commanded the regiment in the Battle of Williamsburg (May 5, 1862). It was a fierce battle, and Payne was captured, presumed dead. General Stuart reported that Payne received "a very severe, and [he] fear[ed], mortal wound in the face." But Payne survived and was exchanged on August 15.

In September 1862, he was promoted to lieutenant colonel and named acting commander of the 2nd North Carolina Cavalry, which defended Warrenton, where three thousand wounded Confederates were housed.

In February 1863, he returned briefly (until March 20) to the 4th Virginia Cavalry as acting commander. Payne's next assignment was temporary command of the 2nd North Carolina Cavalry. Its permanent commander, Colonel Sol Williams of North Carolina, returned on June 6 but was killed three days later at the Battle of Brandy Station, and Payne resumed command of the regiment.

On June 30, 1863, Payne fought in the cavalry action at Hanover, Pennsylvania. He was badly wounded—slashed by a Union saber and pinned beneath his dead horse—and captured. He was sent to Johnson's Island, Ohio, and not exchanged until May 8, 1864.

When he returned to duty, Colonel Payne led a cavalry brigade and fought at the battles of Second Winchester, Fisher's Hill, and Cedar Creek. He was promoted to brigadier general on November 1, 1864.

Payne was given another brigade and was sent to Richmond. He took part in the defense of Petersburg and on April 1, 1865, was badly wounded during the Battle of Five Forks. He evaded capture for two weeks, until the bluecoats caught him near Warrenton on the night of April 14–15. He was sent to Johnson's Island but was released on May 29.

After the war, he remained unreconstructed, declaring, "I am a true Confederate today as I was when I first rode from Warrenton to Manassas. I think the greatest calamity that has befallen the country is the wreck of the Confederacy." He resumed practicing law and served in the Virginia legislature in 1879 and 1880.

In the 1890s, Payne became general counsel for the Southern Railway Company and lived in Washington, D.C. He died there on March 29, 1904, at the age of seventy-four. His body was buried in Warrenton Cemetery.

WILLIAM RAINE PECK was born in Jefferson County, Tennessee, on January 31, 1818. In the 1840s he moved to Milliken's Bend in Madison Parish, Louisiana, to take advantage of the cotton boom. He was quite successful and soon had a sizable plantation.

He was nicknamed "Big Peck" because he was six feet six and weighed 330 pounds. He was an ardent secessionist and, as a delegate to the Louisiana Secession Convention, voted to leave the Union. On July 7, 1861, he enlisted as a private in the 9th Louisiana Infantry Regiment, which was posted to the Shenandoah Valley.

On April 24, 1862, the 9th Louisiana Infantry Regiment was reorganized, and Peck was elected lieutenant colonel under Colonel Leroy A. Stafford. The regiment fought in all the important battles of Stonewall Jackson's Valley Campaign, as well as at Cedar Mountain, Bristoe Station, Second Manassas, Chantilly, Harpers Ferry, and Sharpsburg.

When Stafford took charge of the brigade, Peck assumed command of the 9th Louisiana. At Fredericksburg, it was held in reserve but still lost twelve men to Union artillery fire. At Chancellorsville, it fought at Marye's Heights and Salem Church. It helped storm Star Fort during the Second Battle of Winchester on June 13, 1863, and captured the Union artillery.

Leroy Stafford again took command of the regiment during the invasion of Pennsylvania and led it at Gettysburg. When Stafford finally received his promotion to brigadier general on October 8, 1863, "Big Peck" was promoted to colonel and permanent regimental commander.

Colonel Peck led his regiment in the Bristoe Campaign and was part of the debacle at Rappahannock Station on November 7, when most of the regiment was captured, but Peck managed to escape.

In March 1864, the Confederates captured at Rappahannock Station were exchanged and returned to their regiments. They fought in the Wilderness, where General Stafford was mortally wounded. After his death, the 1st and 2nd Louisiana Brigades were consolidated into a single brigade under Harry Hays. General Hays was seriously wounded at Spotsylvania on May 10. Two days later, Peck led the brigade at the Mule Shoe, where it fought for sixteen hours.

After taking part in the Battle of Cold Harbor, Peck and his brigade joined General Jubal Early in his push on Washington. Peck received especially high praise from General John B. Gordon for his part in the Battle of Monocacy. He was seriously wounded when a shell fragment hit his right thigh during the Third Battle of Winchester. It was his only wound of the war. He could not return to active duty until December, when his brigade was about a third of the size his regiment had been in 1861. It was sent to Richmond with the remnants of the II Corps in December 1864. On February 18, 1865, William R. Peck finally received his promotion to brigadier general. His brigade surrendered at Appomattox Court House on April 9. He was paroled in Vicksburg on June 6.

William R. Peck returned to his plantation in Louisiana, but his health was shattered by four years of arduous service. He died of congestive heart failure near Milliken's Bend on January 22, 1871. He was fifty-two years old. He is buried in the family plot in the Old Methodist part of Westview Cemetery, Jefferson City, Tennessee.

JOHN PEGRAM was born on January 24, 1832, in Petersburg, Virginia. His family were planters, and he grew up as a strong Episcopalian, a Christian gentleman who did not drink or use foul language and was always ready to help those who needed it.

Pegram attended West Point and graduated in 1854 as a cavalry offi-cer. He was stationed on the frontier mostly, although he was sent to Europe (1858–59) to observe the war between Italy and Austria. He was in New Mexico when Virginia seceded.

Pegram became a lieutenant colonel and commander of the 20th Virginia Infantry Regiment in western Virginia in June 1861. He was attacked by a larger force at Rich Mountain on July 11. Perhaps half the Confederates escaped. Colonel Pegram was wounded; he was finally captured on July 13, the first Confederate field grade officer to be taken prisoner in the war. He was sent to Fort Warren, Massa-chusetts, in Boston Harbor until January 24, 1862, when he was released on parole and was eventually exchanged. He was promoted to colonel and headed west as an engineer officer under General G. T. Beauregard and later Braxton Bragg and Edmund Kirby Smith in East Tennessee. He took part in the invasion of Kentucky, including the Battle of Richmond. He was promoted to brigadier general on November 7, 1862, and was given command of a small cavalry brigade in the Army of East Tennessee. He did not perform well in this assignment or in the Second Murfreesboro Campaign. On March 31, 1863, he was defeated at Somerset, Kentucky, by a force half his size. On May 1, Union General O. B. Willcox surprised Pegram and drove him across the Cumberland River.

During the Battle of Chickamauga, he commanded a small, dis-mounted division in Nathan Bedford Forrest's cavalry corps and acquit-ted himself well. He was then sent to Virginia, where he was given an infantry brigade in Jubal Early's division. He led his unit in the Overland Campaign, from the Rapidan to the James. He particularly distinguished himself on May 5, 1864, during the second day of the battle of the Wil-derness, where he defeated several Federal attempts to turn General Richard Ewell's flank.

Pegram fought at Cold Harbor and then in the Shenandoah Valley Campaign of 1864. He was often praised for his leadership and personal bravery, as well as his piety. After General Robert Rodes was killed during the Third Battle of Winchester, Pegram took command of a division but was never promoted to major general.

After Cedar Creek, his division went into the Petersburg trenches. On January 19, 1865, he married Hetty Cary, who was charming and was reputedly the most beautiful woman in America. The couple honeymooned at Pegram's headquarters, near the Rebel front lines.

On February 6, Pegram's division was heavily attacked by a large Union force at Hatcher's Run. General Pegram, at the head of his division, was shot in the chest. He died a few moments later in the arms of Colonel Henry Kyd Douglas. He was thirty-three years old. He was buried in Hollywood Cemetery, Richmond. As a cavalry brigade commander, he was a failure, with a poor grasp of tactics. Commanding infantry, however, he was much better. His tragic death was mourned by Robert E. Lee and throughout Virginia.

JOHN CLIFFORD "JACK" PEMBERTON was born in Philadelphia, Pennsylvania, on August 10, 1814. His father was a successful businessman. Jack received a classical education and retained a lifelong fondness for reading Greek and Latin. He was tall, handsome, slender, and erect, in excellent physical shape. Socially, he was congenial but occasionally arrogant.

Jack Pemberton enrolled in the University of Pennsylvania and ranked at the top of his class but dropped out to enter West Point in 1833. He graduated in 1837 and was assigned to the 4th U.S. Artillery. He was stationed everywhere from Florida to New Jersey, from the upper peninsula of Michigan to Fort Monroe, Virginia, and other posts in between. He fought in the Mexican War, distinguished himself at Resaca de la Palma, won a brevet to captain in the Battle of Monterrey, and also fought at Churubusco and Molino del Rey, where he was brevetted major. He was wounded in the hand outside Mexico City but suffered no permanent damage.

Pemberton married a Virginian and by 1861 looked upon himself as a Virginian. He resigned his commission on April 24. Two days later, Governor John Letcher commissioned him as a lieutenant colonel in the Provisional Army of Virginia. He became a major in the Confederate Army on June 15. Two days later, he was promoted to brigadier general, skipping the ranks of lieutenant colonel and colonel altogether. He was Robert E. Lee's deputy commander in the Department of South Carolina, Georgia, and Florida. When President Jefferson Davis ordered Lee to Richmond, Pemberton became department commander. He was promoted to major general on February 13, 1862, to rank from January 14. He did a good job, but he could not get along with the South Carolina aristocracy, so President Davis relieved him on August 29, 1862, and on October 1, Davis named him commander of the Army of Mississippi. He was promoted to lieutenant general on October 10.

The department was a mess from the Confederate point of view. Pemberton completely reorganized it and showed considerable administrative skill in doing so. He also defeated U.S. General Ulysses Grant's efforts to capture the key city of Vicksburg, on the Mississippi River, five separate times. Unfortunately, General Joseph E. Johnston took away Pemberton's cavalry, which meant Pemberton was blind to the enemy's movements when Grant made his sixth attempt to capture the city.

Grant defeated Pemberton's forces at Port Gibson, Raymond, Jackson, and in the decisive battle of Champion Hill. Part of Pemberton's army was routed on the Big Black River, and he was forced to endure a siege at Vicksburg, beginning on May 18, 1863. Joseph E. Johnston was put in charge of the Army of Relief, which was supposed to rescue the garrison, but he made virtually no effort to do so. Pemberton's force was starved into submission, and he surrendered on July 4.

Historians have portrayed Grant as a genius for his siege of Vicksburg and Pemberton as a blithering idiot for losing the city. But Grant had tremendous advantages, including outnumbering Pemberton's force more than two to one, and Grant had a navy, which Pemberton didn't. Grant's last effort to take Vicksburg was indeed brilliant, but Pemberton was a much better commander than many historians have portrayed him.

Jack Pemberton was exchanged but received no further commands. Finally, on April 19, 1864, Lieutenant General Pemberton accepted a demotion to lieutenant colonel so that he could return to the field with the Richmond Defense Artillery Battalion. In January 1865, he was named inspector of artillery for the War Department. He surrendered in North Carolina in April 1865.

Pemberton started over as a farmer in Virginia but gave it up after a decade of struggle. He moved to Penllyn, Pennsylvania, near Philadelphia, where he died on July 13, 1881. He was sixty-six years old. Just before he passed away, he told his wife and children, "Except for leaving you, I am not sorry my time has come." General John C. Pemberton is buried in an isolated corner of Laurel Hill Cemetery, Philadelphia.

The son of a planter, **WILLIAM DORSEY PENDER** was born on February 6, 1834, at Pender's Crossroads near Tarboro, Edgecombe County, North Carolina. "Dorsey," as he was called, graduated from West Point with the class of 1854. He was assigned to the artillery but transferred to the cavalry the following year. He served in New Mexico and California and fought Indians in Washington and Colorado.

On March 21, 1861, Captain Pender resigned his commission in the U.S. Army and was appointed a captain of artillery in the Confederate States Army. On May 16, he was elected colonel of the 3rd North Carolina Infantry. In August, he assumed command of the 6th North Carolina Infantry Regiment at Manassas, replacing Charles F. Fisher, who was killed at Bull Run.

Pender led the 6th North Carolina in the Peninsula Campaign. During the Battle of Seven Pines, his well-drilled regiment performed brilliantly. President Jefferson Davis witnessed the regiment in action and was so impressed that he prematurely promoted Pender by exclamation: "General Pender, I salute you!" Three days later (June 3), Davis made it official, promoting Pender to brigadier general and giving him command of J. J. Pettigrew's brigade of the Light Division. (Pettigrew was shot and bayoneted at Seven Pines and was not expected to live, but he did.)

Dorsey Pender looked like a general. He was energetic, tall, and handsome, and, as Daniel Harvey Hill, Jr., recalled, "[h]is manner was both dignified and modest." He took part in the Seven Days Battles and was wounded in the arm at Frayser's Farm. He also fought at the Battle of Second Manassas, where he received a minor head wound from a shell fragment, and at Chantilly, where he was wounded again, but only slightly. He later participated in the battles at Harpers Ferry, Sharpsburg, and Fredericksburg, where he was wounded in the left arm. At Chancellorsville on May 2, he was part of Stonewall Jackson's famous flanking attack; he was again wounded in the arm by a bullet that killed the officer standing in front of him. The wound was painful, but the bullet was spent, so it was not serious.

After Stonewall Jackson and A. P. Hill were wounded, Pender took command of the Light Division, and when Jackson died, Lee recommended that Pender be made permanent commander of the division, calling him "an excellent officer, attentive, industrious and brave," and saying, "[He] has been conspicuous in every battle, and I believe wounded in almost all of them." He was promoted to major general on May 27, 1863.

On July 1, Dorsey Pender led his division at Gettysburg and drove the enemy from Seminary Ridge. On the second day, while riding down his line before an attack on Cemetery Hill, a shell fragment struck him in the leg. Pender was evacuated to Staunton, Virginia.

His wound did not seem serious at first, but it became infected, and though surgeons tried to deal with the complications and amputated his leg, he died a few hours later. He was only twenty-nine years old. His last words were as follows: "Tell my wife that I do not fear to die. I can confidently resign my soul to God, trusting in the atonement of Jesus Christ. My only regret is to leave her and our two children. I have always tried to do my duty in every sphere in which Providence has placed me." His death was disastrous for the South, as he was a man of virtually unlimited potential and was probably the best divisional commander in the Army of Northern Virginia when he was wounded.

General Dorsey Pender was buried in Calvary Church Cemetery, Tarboro, North Carolina. Pender County, North Carolina, was named in his honor.

WILLIAM NELSON PENDLETON was born in Richmond, Virginia, on December 26, 1809. He grew up on his father's plantation in Caroline County in eastern Virginia. He attended West Point and graduated in the class of 1830.

Second Lieutenant Pendleton was assigned to the 4th U.S. Artillery Regiment and was stationed at Fort Moultrie, South Carolina; Fort Hamilton, New York; and Fort Monroe, Virginia. He resigned his commission on October 31, 1833, to become a minister of the gospel. In 1853, he was installed as the rector of Grace Episcopal Church in Lexington, Virginia.

Pendleton was a Union man until President Abraham Lincoln called for volunteers to suppress the "rebellion." Even though he was already fifty-one years old, he joined the Rockbridge Artillery and was elected its captain on May 1, 1861. He performed so well at Bull Run that he was named chief of artillery of the Army of the Potomac by President Jefferson Davis. General Joseph E. Johnston promoted Pendleton to colonel, and he was advanced to brigadier general on March 26, 1862.

William Nelson Pendleton was unquestionably a better man than he was a general. He was also a poor chief of artillery. In 1861–62, the Army of the Potomac (later the Army of Northern Virginia) had a large central artillery reserve. During the Seven Days Battles, Pendleton was unable to concentrate his guns effectively. When General Robert E. Lee reorganized the army, he dispersed his artillery to the various corps and divisions and rarely used a large central reserve of guns.

Although Pendleton was a poor tactical commander, he was a good administrator. He also spent a great deal of time preaching, and not just to artillery units. He was a major factor in the great religious revival that swept the army during the winter of 1862–63 and thereafter. The men seemed to appreciate him as a preacher—even though he tended to be long-winded and bombastic—because he was trying to save their souls, but they did not like him as a commander. One Confederate soldier wrote in a Richmond newspaper, "By the way Pendleton is Lee's weakness. [Pendleton] is like the elephant, we have him & we don't know what on earth to do with him, and it costs a devil of a sight to feed him." During the last two years of the war, Lee kept him in the rear, where he was involved in administrative matters and commanded only the reserve ordnance.

Pendleton didn't do anything of merit on the battlefield after the Battle of First Manassas that deserves special praise—that is, until the retreat to Appomattox, when he made a gallant defense at Rice's Station (April 6, 1865) and Farmville (April 7). Pendleton was with the army at Appomattox Court House.

After the surrender, he returned to Lexington and was instrumental in persuading Robert E. Lee to accept the presidency of Washington College. After Lee accepted, the two men worked together on a number of civic, religious, and educational projects.

General Pendleton was a true believer in the Lost Cause, which he regarded as noble. He also tried to shield General Lee's reputation from any responsibility for the South's defeat. General Pendleton died in Lexington on January 15, 1883, at the age of seventy-three. He is buried in Stonewall Jackson Memorial Cemetery beside his son, Sandie, a lieutenant colonel who was killed in action in 1864.

ABNER MONROE PERRIN was born on February 2, 1827, in the Edgefield District of South Carolina. When the Mexican War began, he enlisted in the 12th U.S.

Infantry Regiment and was sent to Veracruz but arrived too late to participate in any major battles. He was discharged in July 1848, with the rank of captain.

After he returned home, Perrin studied law, was admitted to the bar, set up a legal practice, and speculated in land. By 1860, he was a wealthy man.

After South Carolina left the Union, Perrin became captain of the Edgefield Rifles, which became part of the 14th South Carolina Infantry. It was posted to Pocotaligo to guard against Union gunboats. He fought at the Battle of Port Royal Ferry on January 1, 1862.

In April 1862, the 14th South Carolina was attached to the Army of Northern Virginia and fought in all its major battles. Perrin took command of the regiment after the Battle of Fredericksburg and was promoted to colonel in January 1863. When General Samuel McGowan was wounded at the Battle of Chancellorsville, Perrin assumed command of the South Carolina Brigade.

As part of William Dorsey Pender's division at Gettysburg on July 1, 1863, the brigade was heavily engaged in the capture of Seminary Ridge. It lost almost 600 of its 1,600 men that day and was not involved in any heavy fighting on July 2 or 3, although it did engage in skirmishing both days. During the retreat from Gettysburg, Perrin repulsed a serious Union cavalry attack at Falling Waters on July 14. He was promoted to brigadier general on September 10 and was later given command of Cadmus Wilcox's old brigade after Wilcox was promoted to division commander.

Perrin was a brave and capable man, but he was also ambitious. Before the Battle of the Wilderness began, he said, "I shall come out of this fight a live major general or a dead brigadier." At the Battle of Spotsylvania, on May 12, 1864, Perrin, mounted on horseback, led a counterattack against the Federals. He was shot seven times and died instantly. He was thirty-seven years old.

General Abner Monroe Perrin is buried in Confederate Cemetery in Fredericksburg, Virginia.

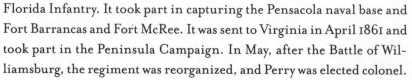

EDWARD AYLESWORTH PERRY, a descendant of one of the earliest settlers of New England, was born in Richmond, Massachusetts, on March 15, 1831. His father was a prosperous farmer. "E. A.," as he was sometimes called, attended local schools, the Lee Academy, and Yale University. He visited the South, liked what he saw, and in 1853 settled in Greenville, Alabama. He taught school, studied law, and was active in civic affairs and in the Methodist Church.

Perry moved to Pensacola in 1857 and joined a law firm. When the Civil War began, he sided with his adopted state and raised an infantry company, the Pensacola Rifle Rangers, which became Company A, 2nd Florida Infantry. It took part in capturing the Pensacola naval base and Fort Barrancas and Fort McRee. It was sent to Virginia in April 1861 and took part in the Peninsula Campaign. In May, after the Battle of Williamsburg, the regiment was reorganized, and Perry was elected colonel.

E. A. Perry led the 2nd Florida in the Battle of Seven Pines (where it suffered heavy casualties) and in the Seven Days Battles, where Colonel Perry was wounded. He was out of action for the rest of the summer but was promoted to brigadier general on August 28. He was back on duty during the Battle of Sharpsburg. He also fought at Fredericksburg and Chancellorsville but fell ill with typhoid fever and missed the Gettysburg Campaign. He returned to fight in the Bristoe Campaign and at the Battle of the Wilderness, where, on May 6, 1864, he was so badly wounded that he had to relinquish command. He tried to return to duty during the Siege of Petersburg but was finally transferred to the Invalid Corps and spent the rest of the war in Alabama.

After the war, General Perry returned to his law practice in Florida, fought to end Radical Reconstruction, and was an outspoken proponent of home rule. In 1884, the Florida Democratic Party convention broke into factions and needed a candidate for governor who could reunite them. Perry was selected on the sixth ballot. In the general election, he defeated a coalition of Republicans and dissident Democrats by a vote of 32,087–27,845.

E. A. Perry's administration gave Confederate veterans a small monthly pension, established the state board of education, and gave the state a constitution that stood for more than six decades. The general wealth of Florida increased from $60 million to more than $87.5 million, and the treasury had a positive balance when he left office.

General Perry was in poor health for some time before he left the governor's mansion in January 1889. He went visiting friends in Texas in hopes of recovering. Instead, he had a stroke on October 5, 1889. He died in Kerrville, Texas, on October 15, at the age of fifty-eight. He was buried in St. John's Cemetery, Pensacola.

WILLIAM FLANK PERRY was born in Jackson County, Georgia, on March 12, 1823. His parents moved to Chambers County, Alabama, when he was ten. He became schoolteacher and administrator in Talladega. In 1853, he moved to Tuskegee, read law, and was admitted to the bar in 1854. Instead of setting up a law practice, he was elected to the newly established office of state superintendent of education. He was reelected twice but resigned in 1858 to accept the presidency of the East Alabama Female College of Tuskegee (now Huntingdon College).

On May 6, 1862, William Perry enlisted as a private in the 44th Alabama Infantry. On May 16, he was elected major. He quickly became known for his sterling character, high standards of discipline, and coolness under fire.

The regiment was sent to Richmond in June, was lightly engaged in the Seven Days Battles, and fought at the Battle of Second Manassas (after which Perry was promoted to lieutenant colonel), the Siege of Harpers Ferry, and the Battle of Sharpsburg (after which he was promoted to colonel).

The regiment was in reserve during the Battle of Fredericksburg. It took part in the Suffolk Campaign, where two of its companies were captured, and the Pennsylvania Campaign. At Gettysburg, it battled at Little Round Top and captured a section of Federal artillery. Perry was wounded.

As part of General Longstreet's command, the regiment fought in the Battle of Chickamauga, where Perry was cited for his bravery, and in the Knoxville Campaign. The 44th Alabama then returned to Virginia. At the Battle of the Wilderness, Perry had two horses shot out from under him and fought well. His regiment continued to fight stubbornly at Spotsylvania Court House (where Perry was again commended), Cold Harbor, and Petersburg, where Colonel Perry was often an acting brigade commander. He was wounded again in the Second Battle of Deep Bottom in mid-August 1864. Despite recommendations from General James Longstreet and others, Perry was not promoted to brigadier general until February 21, 1865. He fought until the end and surrendered at Appomattox Court House on April 9.

After the war, General Perry became a planter for a couple of years. He then returned to education. He moved to Kentucky and was a professor of English and philosophy at Ogden College for many years, beginning when the school was founded in 1877.

William Flank Perry died on December 7, 1901, in Bowling Green, Kentucky, at the age of seventy-eight. He was buried in Fairview Cemetery, Bowling Green.

JAMES JOHNSTON PETTIGREW, who was called by his middle name, was born on July 4, 1828, at Bonarva, the family's plantation on Lake Scuppernong in Tyrrell County, North Carolina. People recognized early that young Johnston was gifted and extraordinary. He enrolled in the University of North Carolina at age fifteen and graduated at the head of his class in 1847, excelling not only in academics but in boxing and fencing. His commencement was

· P

attended by President James K. Polk (an alumnus) and noted scientist Commodore Matthew Fontaine Maury, the "father of oceanography," who offered Pettigrew an assistant professorship as an astronomer at the National Observatory on the spot. He accepted, but after less than a year, he resigned in order to become a lawyer. He studied in Baltimore and passed the bar. He also learned five languages so that he could spend two years (1850–52) traveling the globe.

He then practiced law in Charleston and became known as the best attorney in the city. He was elected to the South Carolina legislature in 1856 but was defeated for reelection in 1858. In 1860, Pettigrew was named colonel and commander of the 1st South Carolina Militia Regiment (the 1st South Carolina Rifles) in Charleston, despite having no military experience. When Pettigrew's regiment was not immediately accepted into Confederate service, he went to Richmond and enlisted in the Hampton Legion as a private, despite being offered commissions as a captain and a major. On July 11, 1861, however, he was elected colonel of the 12th (later 22nd) North Carolina Infantry. President Jefferson Davis personally promoted Pettigrew to brigadier general on February 26, 1862 (i.e., he did not solicit recommendations from Pettigrew's senior officers).

Pettigrew fought in the Peninsula Campaign and was almost killed in the Battle of Seven Pines on May 31, 1862. He was hit in the throat, arm, and shoulder by minié balls, bayoneted in the leg, left for dead, and reported as killed in action. The Yankees captured the still unconscious general the next day. He was exchanged on August 15, 1862.

General Pettigrew was given a brigade of North Carolinians in the fall of 1862. In the spring of 1863, he defended Richmond against General George Stoneman's cavalry raid.

Pettigrew's men loved him. He was willing to converse with them on practically any subject and, though a strict disciplinarian, he was considered just and impartial.

In June, Pettigrew's brigade was assigned to Henry Heth's division of A. P. Hill's III Corps. It took part in the invasion of Pennsylvania, and Pettigrew assumed command of the division when Heth was wounded in the head. Johnston Pettigrew played a major role in pushing the Yan-kees off McPherson Ridge on July 1.

On July 3, 1863, Pickett's Charge included not just Pickett's division, but also Pettigrew's division and Isaac Trimble's (formerly William Dorsey Pender's) division. Pettigrew led his men against the center of the Union line, where it suffered heavy casualties. Pettigrew was wounded in the arm (painfully but not seriously) and had his horse shot out from under him. He continued to lead his men on foot. The brigades suffered staggering losses. Pettigrew's brigade of three thousand men lost well more than half its strength at Gettysburg, and most of Pettigrew's staff officers were either killed, wounded, or captured.

On July 14, 1863, the remnants of Pettigrew's brigade fought a rear-guard action at Falling Waters, (West) Virginia, where Pettigrew was shot and badly wounded. He was transported to Edgewood Manor, a planta-tion home in Bunker Hill, (West) Virginia, where he died early on the morning of July 17, 1863. His last words were to a staff officer: "It is time to be going," he said. A Louisiana bishop recalled, "In a ministry of near thirty years, I have never witnessed a more sublime example of Christian resignation and hope in death." He was thirty-five years old.

Johnston Pettigrew was a genius of the first order. His death was a major loss for the Army of Northern Virginia and to the Confederacy. His remains were buried in the Pettigrew family ceme-tery at Bonarva.

P

EDMUND WINSTON PETTUS was born in Athens, Alabama, on July 6, 1821. His father was a planter, and his brother was John J. Pettus, Jr., who went on to become governor of Mississippi (1854 and 1859–63). Edmund was well educated in local schools and at Clinton College in Tennessee. He read law in Tuscumbia, Alabama, was admitted to the bar in 1842, and was elected solicitor for the Seventh Judicial District of Alabama.

Edmund Pettus established a law office in Gaines-ville, Alabama, but left his practice to fight in the

Mexican War as a lieutenant. After the war, he went to California, where he fought Indians.

Pettus returned to Alabama by 1853 and resumed practicing law. He was an enthusiastic supporter of secession and regarded slavery as a benevolent institution. When Alabama seceded, he and Isham W. Garrott raised the 20th Alabama Infantry Regiment. Garrott was elected colonel and Pettus became its major on September 9, 1861. He was promoted to lieutenant colonel on October 8.

The 20th Alabama was stationed in East Tennessee in the summer of 1862 but saw little action until the Second Battle of Murfreesboro (December 31, 1862, to January 2, 1863), where Pettus was captured. He was quickly exchanged and, with General Edward D. Tracy's brigade, was transferred to the Army of Mississippi. Pettus fought well in the Battle of Port Gibson, was captured, escaped, and rejoined his regiment for the Battle of Champion Hill, where he was cited for his gallantry by Stephen Dill Lee, his brigade commander. He was with the army as it retreated into Vicksburg.

The Siege of Vicksburg began on May 18, 1863. On May 22, U.S. General Ulysses Grant launched his second major attack on the city and secured a dangerous foothold in the Confederate line. General Stephen D. Lee delegated Pettus to destroy it. With about forty men from Colonel Thomas Neville Waul's Texas Legion, he did just that. Despite a hail of musket and artillery fire, Pettus and his men managed to kill or capture every Yankee who had broken through the Confederate defenses. He took one hundred prisoners and three Yankee battle flags. "A more gallant feat than this charge has not illustrated our arms during the war," an admiring General Carter L. Stevenson, his division commander, reported. For his immense courage and gallantry, Pettus was promoted to full colonel on May 28, although his rank (for the moment) was too high for the position he occupied.

Colonel Pettus assumed command of the 20th Alabama after Colonel Garrott was killed in action on June 17. He surrendered with the remainder of the garrison on July 4, 1863.

Pettus was officially exchanged on September 12 and appointed brigadier general and brigade commander on September 18, succeeding Stephen Dill Lee, who had also been promoted.

Edmund Pettus and his brigade fought in the Siege of Chattanooga, the defense of Atlanta, and the Carolinas Campaign. He was wounded in the leg at Bentonville in March 1865 and surrendered at Salisbury, North Carolina, on May 2.

General Pettus returned to Alabama and resumed his law practice at Selma. He was a champion of home rule and sought to banish the carpetbaggers. To that end he became Grand Dragon of the Alabama Ku Klux Klan. Despite his popularity in Alabama, he did not seek public office until 1896 when, at the age of seventy-five, he ran for the U.S. Senate and ousted the incumbent. He served from March 4, 1897, until his death.

Senator Pettus died in Hot Springs, North Carolina, on July 27, 1907, at age eighty-six. He was the last Confederate general to serve in the U.S. Senate. He was buried in Live Oak Cemetery, Selma, Alabama.

Despite his regrettable postwar association with the Ku Klux Klan, his career as a Confederate general can only be rated as outstanding.

GEORGE EDWARD PICKETT was born on January 16, 1825, in Richmond, Virginia. His father owned a plantation but lost it due to financial mismanagement. Pickett attended West Point and graduated in 1846, ranking at the very bottom of his class. Commissioned in the infantry, he was soon on his way to Mexico.

Pickett distinguished himself in the Mexican War. He earned a brevet to first lieutenant on August 20, 1847, for his "gallant and meritorious conduct" in the battles of Contreras and Churubusco and an honorary captaincy for scaling the wall at Chapultepec.

After the fall of Mexico City, he was a company commander at Fort Bliss, Texas, and in Washington Territory. Captain Pickett resigned his commission on June 25, 1861, and was appointed a major in the Confederate States Army. On July 23, he was promoted colonel and placed in charge of the Rappahannock Line under the command of General Theophilus H. Holmes. Pickett was elevated to brigadier general on February 28, 1862, and given command of a brigade in General James Longstreet's division.

Pickett was a colorful commander and a dandy, with his immaculate uniform, long hair, and perfumed beard. His brigade first saw action in the Peninsula Campaign of 1862. He was commended for his performance in the Battle of Williamsburg and on the second day of the Battle of Seven Pines, where he held his ground despite repeated attacks from numerically superior forces. During the Battle of Gaines' Mill (June 27), he was shot in the shoulder and severely wounded.

Pickett returned to duty after the Battle of Sharpsburg. Longstreet gave him command of a division, and he was promoted to major general on October 10. He played a minor role in the Confederate victory at Fredericksburg in December.

George Pickett took part in Longstreet's unsuccessful Suffolk Campaign. He is most famous today because of what happened at Gettysburg on July 3, 1863, when he spearheaded Robert E. Lee's attack on the Union center. Pickett's Charge is considered the turning point of the war by many historians. Certainly it was a disaster. Blasted by artillery, Pickett's division alone suffered 2,600 casualties out of 5,500 men engaged, and Pettigrew's and Trimble's divisions suffered similar carnage. Total Southern losses were about 6,500, while the Yankees lost fewer than 2,000 men. General Pickett never forgave Robert E. Lee for ordering this attack.

After Gettysburg, Pickett began rebuilding his division in North Carolina. His division suffered heavily from desertion. In January 1864, Lee ordered him to retake New Bern, but he failed miserably.

Pickett's division returned to Virginia in May 1864. It played a major role in G. T. Beauregard's successful efforts to bottle up Benjamin Butler's Army of the James in the Bermuda Hundred peninsula. Pickett remained in the trench lines opposite General Butler (and later General Edward Ord) until March 1865. He was then transferred to Lee's far right flank, with orders to defend the critical railroad junction at Five Forks at all costs. He was miles away, attending a shad bake, on April 1, 1865, when Union General Phil Sheridan attacked with his Army of the Shenandoah, along with the V Corps and the cavalry corps of the Army of the Potomac. The Confederates never had a chance, but they might have done much better if their commander had been present. The Rebel forces were crushed.

U.S. General Ulysses Grant broke Robert E. Lee's lines the next day, and Richmond fell on April 3. After the disaster at Sayler's Creek on April 6, in which Pickett escaped but many of his men did not, Robert E. Lee issued orders relieving Richard Anderson, Bushrod Johnson, and George Pickett of their commands. Pickett, however, apparently never received the word. He continued in command of the remnant of his division until the surrender on April 9. He was paroled on April 12, 1865.

After the war, there was talk of arresting and trying Pickett as a war criminal for shooting twenty-two deserters in North Carolina. Fearing prosecution, he fled to Canada with his family. General Grant did not want Pickett prosecuted and squashed the investigation in 1866.

Following his return to the United States, General Pickett worked as a farmer and an insurance agent in Norfolk, Virginia. He lived in straitened circumstances and declining health until July 30, 1875, when he passed away in Norfolk of liver disease. He was fifty years old. He is buried in Hollywood Cemetery, Richmond.

ALBERT PIKE was born in Boston on December 29, 1809. His father was a cobbler. He attended public schools in Byfield, Newburyport, and Framingham, acquired a good classical education, and understood Hebrew, Latin, and Greek. Pike was admitted to Harvard at age sixteen but dropped out because he could not continue paying the tuition. Instead, he taught himself and became a schoolteacher. He also wrote for literary journals; some of this work was later collected and published in book form as *Prose Sketches and Poems, Written in the Western Country* (1834) and *Hymns to the Gods and Other Poems* (1872).

Pike left Massachusetts in 1831, went west, and settled in Arkansas. He married in 1834, and his wife was wealthy enough that he was able to purchase the *Arkansas Advocate* newspaper (for which he had been a staff writer) and to study law. He sold the newspaper and focused on developing a lucrative practice. He learned several Indian languages and dialects, as his clients included tribes and nations of the Indian Territory.

In the Mexican War, he served with the Arkansas Mounted Infantry, was promoted to captain, and took part in the decisive victory at Buena Vista. After the war, he returned to his law practice, dabbled in politics, and continued to represent Indians. He was a Whig before the party collapsed in 1854; then he joined the Know-Nothing Party because it was strongly anti-Catholic and so was Pike. He also opposed slavery and secession, while simultaneously accepting that secession was constitutional and that states' rights were paramount.

After Arkansas seceded, the state named Pike its commissioner to the Indian Territory and authorized him to negotiate with the various tribes. On August 15, 1861, he was appointed brigadier general. He brought the Creeks, Seminoles, Choctaws, Chickasaws, and some of the Cherokees into alliances with the Confederacy.

General Pike's only battle was Pea Ridge (March , 7–8, 1862), where he led a force of Indians, who proved somewhat ineffective, as they were unable to sustain their forward progress. They stopped to take scalps and panicked when brought under artillery fire, with which they were not familiar. After the Confederates were defeated at Pea Ridge, he and his men returned to the Indian Territory.

Albert Pike could not get along with his superior officers, one of whom filed charges against him, and he resigned his commission on July 12, 1862. He remained a contentious figure, but in 1864 he was appointed to the Arkansas Supreme Court.

After the Confederate surrender, Pike fled to Canada. President Andrew Johnson pardoned him on August 30, 1865, and he returned to Arkansas before moving to Memphis in 1867, where he joined a law partnership and edited the *Memphis Appeal*. He moved to Washington, D.C., in 1870 and practiced law there until 1880, when he retired from the legal profession.

Albert Pike was a prominent Mason. Late in life, he learned Sanskrit and translated several works from that language. He also published a book, *Indo-Aryan Deities and Worship as Contained in the Rig-Veda*.

General Pike died on April 2, 1891, at the Scottish Rite Temple in Washington, D.C. He was eighty-one years old. He was buried in Oak Hill Cemetery in Washington, but in 1944 his body was removed and placed in a crypt in the House of the Temple, also in Washington.

Albert Pike was a genius, a fine writer, a great poet, and an outstanding scholar and lawyer. He was not, however, a very good general.

GIDEON JOHNSON PILLOW was born in Williamson County, Tennessee, on June 8, 1806, the son of a man who was both a wealthy attorney and a renowned Indian fighter. Gideon attended the University of Nashville, from which he graduated in 1827. He established a law office in Columbia, Tennessee, and found quick success.

During the Mexican War, President James K. Polk appointed him a brigadier general of volunteers. He was promoted to major general on April 13, 1847. Five days later, he was wounded in the arm at the Battle of Cerro Gordo. In September 1847, he was wounded in the leg at Chapultepec.

While Gideon Pillow performed well during the Mexican War, his battle reports (leaked to the newspapers) were wildly exaggerated; he appeared to take credit for General Winfield Scott's victories at Contreras and Churubusco. This led to a huge controversy. Scott later wrote that Pillow was "amiable and possessed of some acuteness," but added, "[He was] the only person I have ever known who was wholly indifferent in the choice between truth and falsehood, honesty and dishonesty."

After being discharged from the army, Gideon Pillow returned to his law practice and became involved in politics. Pillow was a moderate Democrat, in favor of reconciling North and South and opposed to nullification and secession. He failed twice to secure a vice presidential nomination (in 1852 and 1856) and once to win his party's nomination for a U.S. Senate seat (1857).

Pillow was much more successful in business, which went well beyond his law practice and included land speculation. He was one of the wealthiest men in Tennessee by 1860. After Tennessee left the Union, Governor Isham G. Harris appointed him senior major general and commander of the Provisional Army of Tennessee. On July 9, 1861, he was appointed a brigadier general in the Confederate States Army.

General Pillow did well during the Battle of Belmont (November 7, 1861). At Fort Donelson, he commanded the Confederate left wing, which included seven small infantry brigades and Nathan Bedford Forrest's cavalry. Pillow directed his command "with skill and ability," according to Colonel James D. Porter, and Pillow's attack on February 15, 1862, pushed U.S. General Ulysses Grant's right flank to the edge of annihilation. General Simon B. Buckner, however, failed to attack as planned, and General John B. Floyd panicked and ordered the Rebel regiments to withdraw.

During the night of February 15–16, Buckner urged the garrison commander, Floyd, to surrender. Pillow opposed the idea, but Floyd opted to take Buckner's bad advice. Generals Floyd and Pillow then abandoned their commands and escaped, effectively ruining their careers.

Pillow assumed command of a division in General Albert Sidney Johnston's army, but only briefly. President Jefferson Davis suspended Pillow for "grave errors in judgment" at Fort Donelson. Pillow resigned his commission on October 21, 1862. Jefferson Davis, however, gave him one more chance. He rescinded Pillow's resignation and gave him command of a brigade in John C. Breckinridge's division of the Army of Tennessee on December 10. Pillow, however, did not arrive until January 2, 1863, the third day of the Battle of Stones River, where he performed poorly. Gideon Pillow received no more important assignments and spent the rest of the war in backwater posts. He ended the war as Commissary General of Prisoners (1865). He was captured at Union Springs, Alabama, on April 20 and was paroled in May.

Despite his advanced age, Gideon Pillow became a farmer on land in Maury County, Tennessee, and on property he retained in Arkansas. Like most Southern farmers of that era, he struggled financially. General Pillow died in Helena, Arkansas, on October 8, 1878, and was buried in Elmwood Cemetery, Memphis.

PRINCE CAMILLE ARMAND JULES MARIE DE POLIGNAC was one of the most colorful Confederate generals. He was born in Millemont, Seine-et-Oise, France, on February 16, 1832. His mother was an English aristocrat, and his father, Prince Jules Auguste Armand Marie de Polignac, was a royalist conservative who was variously an ambassador to London, prime minister of France, and a political prisoner or exile.

Prince Camille, the future Southern general, wanted to be a soldier from childhood. He graduated with honors in mathematics from Collège Stanislas de Paris in 1852 (where he also studied music). He applied for the French military academy, L'École Polytechnique, but was rejected. Devastated, he joined the 3rd Chasseurs (light cavalry) as a private in 1853. He had immense self-confidence and was sure he could rise through the ranks, which he did. He fought in the Crimean War (1854–56) and was commissioned a second lieutenant in the 4th Regiment, Chasseurs d'Afrique, in 1855. He resigned from the service in 1859 and eventually came to the New World, where he met several important Southern leaders, including G. T. Beauregard. When the war began, Polignac joined Beauregard's staff and took part in the Battle of First Manassas.

The prince was a slim man of average height, with deep blue eyes and auburn hair. He was a meticulous dresser; his English was perfect, spoken with a British accent, not a French one; and his debonair, aristocratic manners charmed many Southern belles. He was a favorite of Varina Howell Davis, first lady of the Confederacy, and was a frequent visitor to Brockenbrough Mansion, the Confederate White House.

In April 1862, after the Battle of Shiloh, Beauregard gave Polignac command of the 18th Louisiana. To Polignac's surprise, the men of the regiment refused to accept him, and he was replaced.

In August 1862, after serving on the staff of General Braxton Bragg, Lieutenant Colonel Polignac received a second chance to lead a regiment, becoming acting commander of the 5th Tennessee. He showed incredible courage during the Battle of Richmond and won the enlisted men's respect, but it was not enough. The officers demanded new elections. Polignac lost and found himself back on Bragg's headquarters staff.

In November 1862, Polignac returned to Richmond. A noted bon vivant, he took Richmond society by storm and successfully lobbied for promotion. He became a brigadier general on January 10, 1863. That spring, he was transferred to the Trans-Mississippi Department, where his old friend General Edmund Kirby Smith gave him command of the 2nd Texas Brigade in General Richard Taylor's Army of Western Louisiana. The brigade was soon in open rebellion against the Frenchman, to the point that Taylor met with the leading dissenters and offered them a deal. They would accept Polignac as commander for one battle. If after that battle they still wanted him replaced, Taylor would relieve him. If they did not accept Taylor's offer and still rebelled against Polignac, it would mean severe repercussions for them personally. This was a threat—and everyone took a threat from Dick Taylor seriously. The Texans decided to accept the deal.

In an unimportant skirmish near Vidalia, Louisiana (February 7, 1864), Polignac's performance impressed the Texans, who accepted Polignac as their commander. Camille de Polignac led his brigade in the retreat up the Red River and at the impressive victory at Mansfield, in which he was slightly wounded. After General Alfred Mouton was killed, he assumed command of the division. He fought in the Battle of Pleasant Hill, in the Siege of Alexandria, and in the pursuit across the

Atchafalaya. On June 14, 1864, he was promoted to major general. He was so proud of his performance in the Battle of Mansfield that Polignac named his only son Victor Mansfield.

Polignac was sent on a diplomatic mission to France in early 1865. The Confederacy fell shortly thereafter, and he never returned to the South. Independently wealthy, he lived on his family's estate and studied mathematics for the next five years. During the Franco-Prussian War (1870–71), Polignac was commissioned a major in the French Army. Here, the experience he had gained in the Confederate Army was immediately apparent. He was one of the few French officers capable of defeating the Germans. In less than a year, he was promoted to major general. He was a corps commander when Paris surrendered.

Polignac retained a love of the South and the Confederacy, which he instilled in his children. For them, the South was synonymous with courage, generosity, hospitality, and a noble lost cause: the right of free and independent states to leave a union that no longer served their interests.

In 1883, he bought Podwein, a large estate in the Austrian Alps. He spent his remaining years studying mathematics and playing the violin. His wife, an accomplished pianist, usually accompanied him.

Prince Camille de Polignac died on November 15, 1913, at his daughter's home in Paris. He was eighty-one years old. He was buried with his first wife's family in a large vault in the Hauptfriedhof, Frankfurt am Main, Germany. He was the last Confederate major general to pass away.

LEONIDAS POLK was born on April 10, 1806, in Raleigh, North Carolina, the son of Colonel William Polk, a wealthy man who moved his family to Tennessee when Leonidas was a child. Young Leonidas entered the University of North Carolina in 1821 but left in 1823 to attend West Point, where he became good friends with one Cadet Jefferson Davis. Polk graduated in 1827.

During his last year at the Academy, Polk became a Christian and joined the Episcopal Church. He resigned his commission in December 1827 to attend Virginia Theological Seminary. He was ordained as a deacon in 1830 and a priest in 1831.

In 1832, Leonidas Polk moved to Maury County, Tennessee, and became a planter. By 1850, he owned 215 slaves. He also served as an Episcopal priest. He was appointed Missionary Bishop of the Southwest in 1838 and was very active. Bishop Polk was also the leading founder of the University of the South in Sewanee, Tennessee.

Polk was elected Bishop of Louisiana in 1841, where he set up a vast sugarcane plantation called Leighton on Bayou Lafourche. At its peak, it employed four hundred slaves, but it failed in 1854 due to several factors, including a cholera epidemic that killed more than one hundred black people. The plantation's failure put Polk in debt.

Leonidas Polk supported states' rights and secession. When President Jefferson Davis called upon him to join the Southern war effort, he did so, saying it was "a call of Providence." He was appointed major general on June 25, 1861. His presence lent a great deal of prestige to the Confederate Army, but he was promoted too high, too soon. He was an eloquent preacher and a brave man and was highly respected throughout the Confederacy, but he was a mediocre tactical commander at best—and sometimes not even that. He did not understand logistics and never would, his grasp of strategy was weak, and his stubbornness and pettiness did great harm to the Southern cause.

On September 3, 1861, Polk entered Kentucky and seized the town of Columbus. He thus violated Kentucky's neutrality and brought the state into the war. Columbus was a location of no strategic importance, but Paducah—at the junction of the Mississippi and Ohio Rivers—was strategically vital. Ulysses S. Grant took it on September 6.

On November 7, Polk defeated Grant at Belmont, Missouri, just across the Mississippi River from Columbus. Even though it was a minor victory of little importance, the Southern press greatly magnified its significance and redeemed Polk's reputation.

Polk abandoned Columbus on March 2, 1862. He fought in the Battle of Shiloh, where he commanded the I Corps, and took part in the Siege of Corinth under General G. T. Beauregard. He marched west with Braxton Bragg's army for the invasion of Kentucky. His performance was at best mediocre, and he was disappointingly slow at Perryville. He was nevertheless promoted to lieutenant general on October 11, 1862.

Polk fought in the Second Battle of Murfreesboro, the Tullahoma Campaign, and the Chickamauga Campaign. On September 13, 1863, Polk ignored Bragg's order to attack an isolated Federal detachment and allowed it to escape. (Bragg and Polk never got along.) Polk was again slow in the Battle of Chickamauga and was unable to attack when he was ordered to. General Bragg reprimanded him for dilatory tactics and relieved the bishop of his command.

In December 1863, after the Confederates were routed at Missionary Ridge, President Davis relieved Braxton Bragg, gave General Joseph E. Johnston command of the Army of Tennessee, and gave Leonidas Polk command of what was dubbed "the Army of Mississippi."

In February 1864, General Sherman launched an offensive in eastern Mississippi. Polk failed to concentrate his troops in time to block the Union advance, and Sherman captured Meridian, the objective of the campaign, with little difficulty.

In May 1864, Sherman invaded Georgia with three armies. Polk was named commander of the III Corps of the Army of Tennessee. On June 14, 1864, Polk was on a scouting mission at Pine Mountain, near Marietta, Georgia, with Generals Joseph E. Johnston and William J. Hardee. Sherman spotted the cluster of officers and ordered that his artillery fire on them. A shell fired from a three-inch gun struck Polk's left arm, ripped through his chest, exited through his right arm, and exploded against a tree. Bishop Leonidas Polk was nearly cut in half. He died instantly. He was fifty-eight years old.

Although he was a poor commander, Polk was beloved by his men. Lieutenant General Leonidas Polk was buried at St. Paul's Church in

Augusta, Georgia. In 1945, he and his wife were reinterred in Christ Church Cathedral, New Orleans.

LUCIUS EUGENE POLK, a nephew of Lieutenant General Leonidas Polk, was born in Salisbury, North Carolina, on July 10, 1833, but grew up on the family plantation near Columbia, Tennessee. He graduated from the University of Virginia in 1852 and settled on a plantation near Helena, Arkansas, shortly after. When the war began, he enlisted as a private in the Yell Rifles, a unit that was soon absorbed into Patrick Cleburne's 15th Arkansas Infantry Regiment. Lucius Polk became a first lieutenant and fought well in the Battle of Shiloh, where he received the first of several wounds. On April 11, he was commissioned colonel of the 15th Arkansas. Shortly after, the 13th and 15th Arkansas Infantry Regiments were combined, and Polk was elected commander.

Polk was severely wounded at Richmond, Kentucky, where he was "scalped" by a minié ball. which left a permanent scar on his head. After the army returned to Tennessee, he returned to command of the 13th/15th for a brief period but was then given command of Cleburne's old brigade. Lucius Polk was promoted to brigadier general on December 13, 1862.

Physically, Polk had long, curly, black hair and, as Sam Watkins recalled, "a gentle and attractive black eye that seemed to sparkle with love rather than chivalry, and were it not for a young moustache and goatee that he usually wore, he would have passed for a beautiful girl. In his manner he was as simple and guileless as a child, and generous almost to a fault."

General Polk took part in the Second Battle of Murfreesboro and the Tullahoma Campaign. He returned to the Army of Tennessee and fought at Chickamauga and Chattanooga and in the Atlanta Campaign. In June 1864, during the Battle of Kennesaw Mountain, Georgia, a cannon ball struck the horse Polk was riding; the shrapnel killed

P.

members of his staff and badly injured him. He never fully recovered from these wounds and retired from the army "with the admiration and regret of officers and men, who so well knew his worth," as Confederate veteran John M. Harrell wrote later.

The crippled general returned to his family's plantation in Tennessee and took up life as a planter. During the Reconstruction era, he once stared down the Ku Klux Klan and prevented them from attacking a black man who worked for him. Late in life, General Polk entered Tennessee politics. He was a delegate to the Democratic National Convention in Chicago in 1884 and was elected to the Tennessee Senate in 1887. Lucius Eugene Polk died on December 1, 1892, in Columbia. He was fifty-nine years of age. He is buried in St. John's Church Cemetery, Ashwood, Tennessee.

CARNOT POSEY was born in Wilkinson County, Mississippi, on August 5, 1818. His father was a planter. Carnot was educated in local schools before attending the University of Virginia in Charlottesville, where he studied law. He returned to the family plantation and established a law practice in Woodville, the seat of Wilkinson County.

Jefferson Davis was also from Wilkinson County. When the Mexican War began, Carnot Posey joined his 1st Mississippi Rifles as a first lieutenant. He fought in the battles in and around Monterrey and at Buena Vista, where he was wounded. He returned home and resumed his practice of law. President James Buchanan appointed him U.S. District Attorney for the Southern District of Mississippi in 1858. After the Confederacy was formed, President Davis reappointed Posey to the same position, but he resigned after the Rebels fired on Fort Sumter.

On May 21, 1861, Posey was elected captain of the Wilkinson Rifles. On June 4, he was named colonel of the 16th Mississippi Infantry Regiment, which was mustered into Confederate service at Corinth on

June 8. It was sent to Virginia in August 1861 and served with Stonewall Jackson in the Valley Campaign.

Colonel Posey led the 16th Mississippi in the Seven Days Battles and became acting commander of W. S. Featherston's brigade on August 20. He led it at the battles of Second Manassas and Sharpsburg. During the Battle of Fredericksburg, Posey's brigade turned back a major Union attack. Posey was promoted to brigadier general on January 18, 1863, to rank from November 1, 1862.

The brigade was lightly engaged at Chancellorsville, spending most of the battle in reserve at Salem Church. It was transferred to Richard Anderson's division. At Gettysburg, it was part of Anderson's July 2 attack, which was described as "feeble" and "disjointed." Posey's brigade was held in reserve with the artillery on July 3.

After the retreat to Virginia, Carnot Posey fought in the Battle of Bristoe Station on October 14, 1863. He was struck in the thigh by a shell fragment. The wound was not thought to be life-threatening. He was taken to the University of Virginia, which housed wounded Confederate soldiers, and placed in Room 33 on the West Lawn, which was the same room he had occupied as a law student. His wound became infected, and despite the efforts of his friend and physician, Dr. John Davis, to save him, he died on November 13, 1863. He was forty-five years old. He was buried in the Davis family plot in the University of Virginia Cemetery.

JOHN SMITH PRESTON was born on April 20, 1809, at Salt Works, his family's large estate near Abingdon, Virginia. He graduated from Hampden-Sydney College in 1824 and studied law at the University of Virginia and Harvard. After passing the bar, he established a practice in Abingdon.

Preston settled in Columbia, South Carolina, where he opened a law office and built a sugar plantation. A Democrat, he was elected to the South Carolina Senate, serving from 1848 to 1856. He spent the years 1856 to

1860 traveling and living abroad. After he returned home, he was chairman of the South Carolina delegation to the Democratic National Convention in 1860.

John Preston was a fine lawyer and an excellent orator, in addition to being a strong secessionist. After South Carolina left the Union, the secession convention appointed Preston commissioner to Virginia. His task was to guide the Old Dominion toward secession. Preston's speech to the Virginia Secession Convention on February 19, 1861, brought the entire convention to its feet with wild applause. He convinced the delegates that Virginia should join the South if President Abraham Lincoln issued a call to arms, as Preston knew he would.

Preston was appointed lieutenant colonel and assistant adjutant general on the staff of General G. T. Beauregard. He was present when the Rebels fired on Fort Sumter and at the Battle of First Manassas, where he was officially commended for his efficiency.

Already in his fifties when the war began, Lieutenant Colonel Preston was considered physically unfit for extended field service and was instead often posted as a commandant to camps for prisoners of war or conscripts. On April 23, 1863, he was promoted to colonel and on June 10, 1864, he became a brigadier general in the Provisional Army of the Confederacy. He was superintendent of the Bureau of Conscription in Richmond, from July 30, 1863, until the city fell to the Federals in April 1865.

After the war, General Preston escaped to England. He did not return to the United States until 1868. He was an unrepentant defender of the Confederacy for the rest of his life. He had told the Virginians in 1861, "[T]he people of South Carolina have declared . . . that they have always retained their sovereignty and independence; that they, with their confederates, did delegate certain powers to a common agent; that . . . this compact has been violated, and the Government established under it has become destructive of the purposes for which it was established; and it is, therefore, their right to abolish that Government, so far as it concerns them, and institute another." To him, that was the Southern cause, and he never wavered in his belief that it was just. General John Smith Preston died on May 1, 1881, in Columbia, South Carolina. He was seventy-two years old. He is buried in Trinity Episcopal Cathedral Cemetery.

WILLIAM PRESTON III, was born in Louisville, Kentucky, on October 16, 1816. He was educated at a Jesuit school, St. Joseph's College, in Bardstown, Kentucky. He attended Yale in 1835 and graduated from Harvard Law in 1838. Preston returned home and set up a law practice.

During the Mexican War, Preston was appointed a lieutenant colonel of the 4th Kentucky Infantry. He was part of General Winfield Scott's Great Long Walk on Mexico City.

After the war, Preston returned home to his law practice in Kentucky. He entered the political world in 1849 when he became a delegate to the state constitutional convention. He was elected to the state house of representatives in 1850. Next, he was elected to the state senate, serving from 1851 to 1853.

After Congressman Humphrey Marshall (another future Confederate general) resigned his seat in 1852, Preston was elected to fill the vacancy. He was reelected later that year and served from December 6, 1852, to March 3, 1855. In 1854, Marshall ran for his old seat and defeated Preston. In 1858, President James Buchanan named Preston envoy extraordinary and minister plenipotentiary (ambassador) to Spain. He resigned this position when the Civil War began.

General Albert Sidney Johnston (who had been married to Preston's sister until her death from tuberculosis) appointed him as a colonel on his staff. On April 6, 1862, General Johnston was mortally wounded at Shiloh. He died in Preston's arms.

William Preston was promoted to brigadier general on April 14, 1862. He took command of a brigade in John C. Breckinridge's division and served in the First Siege of Vicksburg (1862) and the Battle of Baton Rouge. Sent to middle Tennessee, he led his command in the Second

Battle of Murfreesboro, taking part in the charge of January 2, 1863. On April 28, he was ordered to replace Humphrey Marshall as the commander of the Department of Southwest Virginia and East Tennessee. He headquartered at Abingdon and commanded a brigade in Simon B. Buckner's Army of East Tennessee. At the Battle of Chickamauga (September 19–20, 1863), General Preston directed a division.

As a regimental and brigade commander, Preston was noted for his "chivalrous courage," but he was unsuited to divisional command. In 1864, President Jefferson Davis made use of Preston's diplomatic experience by appointing him ambassador to Mexico.

After the war, Preston traveled to England and Canada. He returned to the United States in 1866 and resumed the practice of law. He was elected to the legislature in 1867 and was a delegate to the Democratic National Convention in 1880. He spent most of his time, however, attending to his very successful law practice. He retired comfortably and died in Louisville on September 21, 1887. He was seventy years old. General William Preston was buried in Cave Hill Cemetery, Louisville.

STERLING PRICE was born on September 20, 1809, close to Farmville in Prince Edward County, Virginia, into a family of Welsh descent. He attended Hampden-Sydney College, studied law, and worked at a local court before moving with his family to Missouri in 1831. In 1832, Sterling moved to Keytesville, Missouri, where he began a business career that included faming and a general store.

In 1835, Price ran for the state legislature. He was elected and served from 1836 to 1838 and from 1840 to 1844, when he was speaker of the state house. In 1844, he was elected to the U.S. House of Representatives and served from March 4, 1845, to August 12, 1846. He resigned to fight in the Mexican War.

Sterling Price raised the 2nd Missouri Mounted Cavalry Regiment and was sent to Santa Fe, where he took command of the Territory of

New Mexico. As military governor, he put down the Taos Revolt—an effort by Mexicans and Indians to overthrow U.S. rule in northern New Mexico—in January 1847. On July 20, 1847, President Polk promoted Price to brigadier general. He also appointed Price military governor of Chihuahua that same month. He led the Army of the West, which had only three hundred men, in the Battle of Santa Cruz de Rosales on March 16, 1848, where he defeated a Mexican force of nine hundred men. It was the last battle of the Mexican War. Price was discharged from the army in late 1848 and returned to Missouri, where he established a tobacco plantation on Bowling Green prairie.

General Price was elected governor of Missouri in 1852 and served from January 3, 1853, to January 5, 1857. After he left the governor's office, he served as Missouri Bank Commissioner from 1857 to 1861.

Sterling Price was a political moderate who strongly opposed secession and wanted Missouri to stay neutral in any North-South conflict. That, however, became impossible after pro-Union forces under Captain Nathaniel Lyon seized Camp Jackson from a pro-Confederate state militia on May 10, 1861. Missouri Governor Claiborne Fox Jackson, who favored the Confederacy and had refused President Abraham Lincoln's request that Missouri raise troops to suppress the South, was outraged by Lyon's action and saw it as a threat to Missouri's sovereignty and his authority. Sterling Price agreed. On May 18, 1861, Governor Jackson appointed Sterling Price a major general to raise and command a new Missouri State Guard to expel Union military forces from the state. On August 10, Price and Confederate General Ben McCulloch concentrated 12,000 men at Wilson's Creek and smashed Lyon's army of 5,500. Lyon, who had been promoted to brigadier general on May 17, was among the dead.

Price and McCulloch were unable to agree on strategy, so McCulloch returned to Arkansas, and Price advanced into northern Missouri, where the Rebels defeated Union forces at the Siege of Lexington (September 13–20, 1861) and captured three thousand men. Price later exchanged these prisoners of war for the pro-Confederate militiamen who had been captured at Camp Jackson.

Federal forces, however, kept pouring into the state—so many that Price had to abandon most of Missouri. Moreover, his rivalry with Ben McCulloch was so acrimonious that President Jefferson Davis had to appoint General Earl Van Dorn commander of the Army of the West, giving him authority over both McCulloch and Price.

On March 7, 1862, Van Dorn engaged U.S. General Samuel Curtis's Army of the Southwest at the Battle of Pea Ridge. Ben McCulloch was killed the first day of the battle, and Price—who was appointed a major general in the Confederate States Army on March 6—was wounded. Price, however, continued in command and pushed Curtis back to Elkhorn Tavern. On March 8, the Federals counterattacked, forcing Van Dorn to withdraw from the field.

Price and his men crossed the Mississippi River with Van Dorn and fought in the defeats at Iuka and Second Corinth. General Price then secured a transfer and became commander of the District of Arkansas. On September 10, 1863, Little Rock fell despite his attempts to defend it, and in the spring of 1864, he was outnumbered nearly two to one and defeated by U.S. General Frederick Steele's VII Corps at the Battle of Prairie D'Ane (April 9–13). Price then served under General Edmund Kirby Smith's command at the Battle of Jenkins' Ferry (April 30, 1864), which ended the Federals' Red River Campaign.

On September 19, 1864, Price, with Kirby Smith's permission, invaded Missouri. Price crossed the Arkansas-Missouri border with 12,000 horsemen and 14 guns. He failed to capture any major objectives and suffered devastating defeats at the Battle of Westport (October 23) and at the Battle of Mine Creek (October 25), which was the second largest cavalry battle of the war. After a few more minor engagements, Sterling Price escaped to Texas. Missouri was now firmly in Union hands, and by the time he returned to southwestern Arkansas, General Price had only 3,500 men left.

At the end of the war, rather than surrender, Sterling Price went to Mexico, joining the Confederate colony at Carlota. When that failed, he returned to Missouri. He died of cholera on September 29, 1867, in St. Louis. Price remained a Missouri hero. His funeral, which ended in his burial at Bellefontaine Cemetery, was the largest St. Louis had ever seen.

ROGER ATKINSON PRYOR was born on July 19, 1828, near Petersburg, Virginia, the son of a preacher. Pryor graduated from Hampden-Sydney College in 1845 and attended law school at the University of Virginia, from which he graduated in 1848. He worked on the editorial staffs of newspapers in Washington, D.C., and Richmond, Virginia. President Franklin Pierce named him U.S. Commissioner to Greece (1854–57). When he returned home, he established *The South*, a daily newspaper in Richmond. Pryor strongly advocated Southern rights, secession, and slavery. Even though he owned no slaves himself, Pryor saw the institution as an economic necessity.

Pryor was elected to fill an unexpired term of the late Congressman William O. Goode in 1859. A "fire-eating secessionist" and a passionate orator, he was involved in several duels. Pryor went to South Carolina in early April and was a witness to the firing on Fort Sumter (an action he supported). He was offered the "honor" of firing the first shot in the War for Southern Independence, but he declined it.

Pryor was reelected to Congress, but Virginia's secession made that irrelevant, and he served instead in the Confederate Provisional Congress. He also joined the Confederate Army as a volunteer aide to General G. T. Beauregard.

On April 20, 1861, the 3rd Virginia Infantry Regiment was organized at Portsmouth, and Pryor was named its colonel. It was assigned to the Virginia Peninsula, and three of its companies fought at Big Bethel in June. From July 1861 to April 1862, it was posted at Norfolk. On April 16, 1862, Pryor was promoted to brigadier general and was given command of a brigade in General James Longstreet's division.

General Pryor fought in the Peninsula Campaign, Seven Pines, the Seven Days Battles, Second Manassas, and the Siege of Harpers Ferry.

At Sharpsburg, he briefly commanded Richard Anderson's division after Anderson was wounded. Pryor performed poorly, allowing his division to be outflanked and retreating in disorder. General Robert E. Lee broke up Pryor's brigade, sent its regiments to other commands, and sent Pryor to southeast Virginia to organize a new brigade. On January 30, 1863, in the Battle of Deserted House, south of the Blackwater River, Pryor suffered a minor defeat, although he performed creditably.

Pryor remained in this backwater assignment south of the James until August 26, 1863, when he resigned his commission. He promptly enlisted as a private and served as a special courier and spy for the 3rd Virginia Cavalry. On November 28, 1864, he was captured. Confined in Fort Lafayette, New York, as a suspected spy, Pryor renounced the Confederate cause and received a parole from Abraham Lincoln on February 25, 1865.

After the war, Pryor moved to New York and eventually became a law partner with Benjamin F. "Beast" Butler, the former Union general. Pryor embraced the Northern way of life, declared he was glad the Union won the war, and made derogatory remarks about the South.

In 1890, he was appointed judge of the New York Court of Common Pleas, a post he held until 1894, when he advanced to justice of the New York Supreme Court. He retired in 1899.

Roger A. Pryor died in New York City on March 14, 1919. He was ninety years old. He is buried in Princeton Cemetery, Princeton, New Jersey.

P

QUARLES

WILLIAM ANDREW QUARLES was born on July 4, 1825, in Louisa County, Virginia. His family relocated when he was five years old to rural Christian County, Kentucky, and subsequently to Clarksville, Tennessee. He was homeschooled until his late teens, when he enrolled at the University of Virginia. He was forced to drop out, however, because of his father's death.

Quarles managed the family's estate while studying law. He was admitted to the bar in 1848 and established a law office in Clarksville. In 1852, he was a Democratic Party presidential elector for Franklin Pierce. In 1858, he became the state's bank inspector, served briefly as a circuit court judge, and ran unsuccessfully for Congress. He was more successful as the president of the Memphis, Clarksville, and Louisville Railroad Company, where he supervised the construction of railroad lines in the Volunteer State and the Blue Grass State.

After Tennessee's secession, he helped organize the 42nd Tennessee Infantry Regiment at Camp Cheatham. He was commissioned a colonel on November 20, 1861. On February 13, 1862, the 42nd Tennessee was ordered to Fort Donelson. It experienced three days of heavy combat. Quarles was highly praised for his courage and coolness under fire. After the garrison surrendered on February 16, Quarles was imprisoned on Johnson's Island, Ohio. He was exchanged in August 1862 and immediately resumed command of his regiment.

Quarles and his men were stationed at Port Hudson, Louisiana, and then Jackson, Mississippi. The regiment was part of General Joseph E. Johnston's Army of Relief during the Siege of Vicksburg. On August 25, 1863, Quarles was promoted to brigadier general and was given command of a brigade of four Tennessee regiments, including the 42nd. It was sent to the Army of Tennessee but arrived after General Braxton Bragg's disastrous defeat at Missionary Ridge. It then fought in the Atlanta Campaign.

On May 27, 1864, General Quarles distinguished himself in the Battle of Pickett's Mill, where he was severely wounded. He returned to take part in the Tennessee Campaign. He received another serious wound at the Battle of Franklin on November 30. When the Confederate Army abandoned Franklin, General Quarles was left behind and captured. He spent the rest of the war in Union prisoner-of-war camps. He was paroled at Nashville in May 1865.

William Quarles returned to Clarksville and resumed his law practice. He was a member of the Methodist Episcopal Church in Clarksville, a trustee of the Tennessee Orphans Society, and a Mason. He was a presidential elector for Horace Greeley in 1872 and ran for the U.S. Senate in 1874 but was defeated. Later he was twice elected to the Tennessee Senate, serving from 1875 to 1877 and from 1887 to 1889.

Brigadier General William A. Quarles died on December 28, 1893, at age sixty-eight. He was buried in Flat Lick Cumberland Presbyterian Church Cemetery in Herndon, Kentucky. General Quarles was a solid brigade commander and a model American citizen-soldier.

R

RAINS – RUST

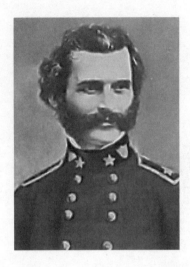

GABRIEL JAMES RAINS was born on June 4, 1803, near New Bern, Craven County, North Carolina. He was admitted to West Point in 1822, graduated in 1827, and was commissioned in the infantry. Rains served primarily in the West, mainly in the Indian Territory. He was promoted to first lieutenant in 1834 and captain in 1837.

He first saw action against the Seminole Indians in Florida in 1839, where he commanded a company at a forward outpost called Fort King. Rains showed tactical skill, including an innovative use of land mines, in defending the fort but was so badly injured by an Indian attack that he was reported as killed. Luckily, he recovered and was brevetted major for his actions at Fort King.

He was at Fort Brown, Texas, in 1846, when the Mexican War began. The fort was surrounded by a greatly superior Mexican force. The Texas officers voted on whether to surrender. Rains had the deciding vote. He opted to fight, and the Texans held the fort. He subsequently fought in the American victory at the Battle of Resaca de la Palma. Rains was then transferred to recruiting duty. In 1849–50, he fought in the Second Seminole War and was promoted to major in 1851. The following year, Gabriel Rains was transferred to California, where he fought Indians. He was promoted to lieutenant colonel in 1860.

When the South seceded, Rains was commissioned a colonel in the Confederate Regular Army and was promoted to brigadier general in the Provisional Army on September 23, 1861.

Rains's first assignment was to command a division of General John B. Magruder's Department of the Peninsula, where he continued his experiments with land mines. By April 1862, Rains's unit became a brigade in D. H. Hill's division. When he retreated from Yorktown, he scattered land mines behind him and killed or wounded many Northerners. Land mines had not been used on this scale, and U.S. General George B. McClellan was quick to denounce the use of land mines as improper, calling them "murderous and barbarous."

According to Northern newspapers, mines were placed in wells, in bags of flour, around houses, and wherever Rains or his men thought the Yankees might detonate them. General James Longstreet wrote to Rains on May 11, 1862, and asked that he cease deploying land mines (then called "torpedoes") because they were not recognized as a proper method of war. General D. H. Hill, on the other hand, disagreed. "In my opinion, all means of destroying our brutal enemies are lawful and proper," he declared. The question ended up on the desk of Secretary of War George Randolph. He ruled that mines could be used to stop pursuit, defend a breastwork, or sink a ship, but not for the sole purpose of killing enemy soldiers.

Rains led his brigade in the battles of Williamsburg (May 5) and Seven Pines (May 31), where he was wounded. On June 18, he was transferred to the defenses of the James and Appomattox Rivers. He also briefly commanded the Confederate defenses of the Cape Fear River sector in North Carolina. On December 16, 1862, he was placed in charge of the Bureau of Conscription in Richmond. Here he formulated plans to defend Confederate ports using "torpedoes" (mines). He presented his ideas to President Jefferson Davis, who was very impressed. On May 25, 1863, he ordered Rains to put his plans into effect. He did so at Vicksburg, Charleston, and Mobile. On June 17, 1864, he was formally named chief of the newly formed Torpedo Bureau, a post he held until the end of the war. He established torpedo factories at Richmond, Wilmington, Mobile, Charleston, and Savannah. His devices were widely used by the end of the war and were very successful. His torpedoes sank an estimated fifty-eight Union vessels.

General Rains lived in Augusta, Georgia, after the war, where he worked as a chemist. Later, he moved to Charleston, South Carolina, where he was employed as a civilian clerk in the U.S. Army's Quartermaster Department. Gabriel J. Rains died on August 6, 1881, in Aiken, South Carolina, at age seventy-eight. He is buried in St. Thaddeus Cemetery, Aiken.

· R

JAMES EDWARD RAINS was born in Nashville, Tennessee, on April 10, 1833, the son of a Methodist minister who also ran a small saddle shop. He received a loan of $400 to attend Yale Law School, from which he graduated in 1854, finishing second in his class.

After he graduated, he became headmaster of the Millwood Institute in Cheatham County and associate editor of the *Daily Republican Banner*, whose editor was Felix Zollicoffer, another future Confederate general. He was elected Nashville City Attorney in 1858.

Rains, like many Southerners, was opposed to secession but followed his state when it left the Union. He enlisted in the Hermitage Guards, a local company that became part of the 11th Tennessee Infantry. He was elected colonel on May 10, 1861. By July, the 11th Tennessee had 880 men, but they were armed with a mere 175 rifles and 710 flintlocks. Still, the regiment was accepted into Confederate service in August and sent to East Tennessee under General Zollicoffer's command.

During the winter of 1861–62, Rains commanded the garrison at Cumberland Gap and defended it against Union attacks. His garrison strength grew to four thousand men, and in April 1862 he was superseded in command by Brigadier General Carter Stevenson. The Federals finally turned the Cumberland Gap position on June 18, 1862, but Rains's role in its defense and his conduct in the subsequent Kentucky Campaign were so well regarded that he was promoted to brigadier general on November 4, 1862.

On December 31, 1862, during the Second Battle of Murfreesboro (Stones River), Rains led his men in an attack on a Union battery. He was at the head of his brigade when he was shot through the heart by a minié ball. He died instantly. His last words were: "Forward, my brave boys, forward!" The South had lost another fine brigade commander.

General Rains was initially buried on the battlefield. Rains's father, wife, and three-year-old daughter went to the headquarters of U.S. General William Rosecrans and asked the Northern commander for

R ·

General Rains's body. Rosecrans allowed it to be transported through Union lines, and it was interred in Nashville City Cemetery. In 1888, Rains's remains were reinterred in the Confederate section of Mount Olivet Cemetery, Nashville.

STEPHEN DODSON RAMSEUR was born in Lincolnton, North Carolina, on May 31, 1837. He did not use his first name, and his friends called him "Dod." He was a second cousin of Generals John H. Forney and William H. Forney. He attended Davidson College before entering the U.S. Military Academy, from which he graduated in the class of 1860. He was commissioned in the artillery.

Lieutenant Dodson was an intensely religious man who believed that slavery was a divinely ordained institution, and as such, he disliked abolitionists and believed that the South had every right to secede from a Union that might threaten its way of life. He resigned his U.S. Army commission on April 6, 1861, and was commissioned a major of the North Carolina State Troops, taking command of the Ellis Light Artillery. He was then posted to Smithfield, Virginia, just south of the James River, and was commissioned a captain in the Confederate States Army. He saw action as an artillery commander at the outset of the Peninsula Campaign.

On April 12, 1862, Ramseur was elected colonel of the 49th North Carolina Infantry Regiment and led it in the Seven Days Battles, including a charge up Malvern Hill, during which he was severely wounded in the right arm. He was unable to return to duty for several weeks. On October 27, 1862, General Robert E. Lee recommended him for promotion, and on November 1, 1862, Ramseur became a brigadier general. He led a brigade at the Battle of Fredericksburg (December 11–15, 1862).

On May 2, 1863, in the Battle of Chancellorsville, Ramseur's brigade led Stonewall Jackson's famous flanking attack. At Gettysburg on July 1, Ramseur again displayed the aggression that General Lee so

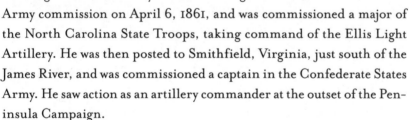

·R

admired in him by hitting the Union right flank and forcing them out of the town. He was upset that the Confederate pursuit was halted at the foot of Cemetery Hill. Even so, he received commendations for his performance from Generals Robert Rodes and Richard Ewell. Ramseur's brigade basically sat idle for the next two days and then joined the retreat to Virginia.

During the Battle of Spotsylvania Court House, on May 12, 1864, Ramseur's horse was shot from under him, and a minié ball ripped through his arm. On May 19, Ramseur led a brilliant attack on the Union flank. He was promoted to divisional commander on May 27 and to major general (temporary rank) on June 1. He first commanded his division in the Battle of Cold Harbor, where he was again successful.

Ramseur was then sent to the Shenandoah Valley, where, serving under General Jubal Early, he helped rescue the garrison at Lynchburg, invaded Maryland, fought in the Battle of Monocacy, and threated Washington, D.C. He did not handle his division as well during the Third Battle of Winchester on September 19, 1864, which was the low point of his military career. Many of his troops were captured, and the survivors retreated through the town in disarray and confusion.

On October 19, his badly depleted division fought the Federals at Cedar Creek, and he mounted a gallant defense against a Yankee counterattack. Two horses were shot from beneath him, and he was mortally wounded. When the Rebels retreated, they had to leave Ramseur behind. He died the next day, October 20, at Philip Sheridan's headquarters in Meadow Mills, Virginia. His last message was to his wife: "I die a Christian and hope to meet her in heaven." He was twenty-seven years old.

The day before he was fatally wounded, Ramseur received word that his only child, a daughter, had been born on October 16.

General Stephen Dodson Ramseur was buried in St. Luke's Episcopal Church Cemetery, Lincolnton, North Carolina.

GEORGE WYTHE RANDOLPH was born on March 10, 1818, in Virginia, at Monticello, the home of his grandfather, Thomas Jefferson. Randolph was also a descendant of Pocahontas.

Randolph attended preparatory schools in Massachusetts and Washington, D.C., and then became a midshipman in the U.S. Navy in 1831, at age thirteen. On a voyage to the Mediterranean, he contracted tuberculosis, but it went into a long remission. He returned to the United States in 1837, enrolled at the University of Virginia (while still in the Navy), studied law, resigned from the Navy in 1839, and was admitted to the bar in 1840. He established a law practice in Charlottesville before moving to Richmond and practicing law there. He was active in the Virginia Historical Society and became a civic leader.

In 1859, Randolph was so alarmed by John Brown's attack on Harpers Ferry that he organized the Richmond Howitzers, a light artillery unit equipped with short-range guns, and, with the approval of Virginia's governor, led it to Charles Town, Virginia (now West Virginia), to provide security during Brown's trial and subsequent execution.

In 1861, George Randolph was elected as a delegate to the Virginia Secession Convention. He served on the convention's military committee and helped prepare the commonwealth for war. He was appointed a major of militia, and his Richmond Howitzers were attached to John B. Magruder's Army of the Peninsula. As summer approached, George Randolph was promoted to colonel and chief of artillery for Magruder's Command. He fought in the Battle of Big Bethel on June 10 and, anticipating Union General George B. McClellan's landing on the peninsula, designed the Confederate defenses at Yorktown. In February 1862, Colonel Randolph was named director of artillery for the Department of Norfolk. He was promoted to brigadier general on February 16, 1862.

On March 18, 1862, President Jefferson Davis appointed Randolph secretary of war, replacing Judah P. Benjamin, who resigned after being censured by the Confederate Congress following the loss of Roanoke Island. The difficulties Randolph faced were mammoth, and he was unable to improve cooperation between state governors or between prickly generals.

His efforts to institute centralized economic planning failed, and he was frustrated by Jefferson Davis's micromanagement and strategic vision that made Virginia the focus of the Confederate war effort. Perhaps triggered by the stress of his position, Randolph's tuberculosis returned, his health deteriorated, and he resigned as secretary of war on November 15, 1862.

George Randolph was unemployed for the rest of the war, although he did not formally resign his army commission until December 18, 1864, a month after he had run the Union blockade to Europe. He spent the rest of the conflict in England and France. He returned to the United States in September 1866. He died at Edgehill, in Albemarle County, Virginia, of tuberculosis and pneumonia on April 3, 1867. He was forty-nine years old. He is buried on the grounds of what is now Monticello National Park, near Charlottesville, Virginia.

George W. Randolph was not a success as secretary of war. In fairness to him, it must be pointed out that Jefferson Davis was, for all practical purposes, his own secretary of war, and the person who held the secretary's portfolio was little more than a glorified clerk. I doubt if anyone could have done much better. George Randolph's major mistake as secretary of war was taking the job in the first place.

MATT WHITAKER RANSOM was born on October 8, 1826, in Warren County, North Carolina. He attended Warrenton Academy and the University of North Carolina, where he studied law; he graduated in 1847. He was admitted to the bar, practiced law in Warrenton, and was regarded as a personable, outgoing, and popular young man. He was a presidential elector for Winfield Scott in 1852. The following year, the Democrat-controlled state legislature elected him state attorney general, even though he was a Whig.

In 1858, with the Whigs no longer a party, Matt Ransom was elected to the legislature as a Democrat. He was reelected and served until 1861. Ransom was strongly pro-Union until Lincoln issued his call for seventy-five thousand troops to crush the "rebellion." Like tens of thousands of other Southerners, he immediately became a secessionist and enlisted in the Confederate Army as a private. On June 3, 1861, when the 1st North Carolina Infantry Regiment was organized at Warrenton, he was commissioned a lieutenant colonel. He subsequently became lieutenant colonel of the 35th North Carolina Infantry Regiment when it was organized in November 1861.

The regiment first saw action near New Bern on March 14, 1862, and it was a disaster. It retreated in disorder, New Bern fell, and the Rebels fell back to Kinston.

On April 21, the 35th North Carolina was reorganized. The soldiers held elections and elected Matt Ransom colonel. The regiment was ordered to Virginia on June 19. It saw action in the Seven Days Battles and repulsed a rare Union night attack on June 25. Ransom distinguished himself in the attack on Malvern Hill, during which he was wounded twice and was carried from the field. He recovered quickly, took Loudon Heights (overlooking Harpers Ferry) on September 14, and fought at Sharpsburg, where he repulsed three strong infantry attacks in the Dunker Church–West Woods sector. He saw action again at Fredericksburg.

The 35th North Carolina was then sent to Wilmington, and Matt Ransom promoted to brigadier general on June 13, 1863.

Ransom's brigade held positions near Suffolk during the Gettysburg Campaign and in late July defeated a Union advance on Weldon, North Carolina. Ransom defeated another enemy advance at Suffolk on March 9, 1864, and took part in the Confederate victory at Plymouth, North Carolina, in April. In June 1864, he joined General G. T. Beauregard south of Petersburg and helped prevent the Yankees from capturing the city. After the Battle of the Crater, Ransom's brigade held part of the Crater Line. Ransom and his men later served north of the James in the defense of Richmond, and in March 1865 they fought in the Battle of Fort Stedman, where General Robert E. Lee praised Ransom's performance. Ransom and his brigade took part in the Appomattox Campaign and surrendered with the rest of the army on April 9, 1865.

After the war, the Ransom family settled in Weldon, where he became a farmer and resumed his law practice. The North Carolina state legislature elected him to the U.S. Senate in early 1872, following the ouster of a corrupt carpetbagger incumbent. A forceful and eloquent speaker, Ransom was popular and served as a U.S. senator until he was finally defeated for reelection in 1894. President Grover Cleveland appointed Ransom ambassador to Mexico in 1895, a post he held until 1897, when he retired from public life. He returned to his North Carolina estate, Verona, and was a highly successful planter.

General Matt Whitaker Ransom passed away in Garysburg, North Carolina, on October 8, 1904. He was seventy-eight years old. He was buried in the Ransom family cemetery on his Verona Plantation, near Jackson, North Carolina.

ROBERT RANSOM, JR., was born on February 12, 1828, in Bridle Creek, the family plantation in Warren County, North Carolina. His older brother was future Confederate General Matt Ransom. He was educated by private tutors and at West Point, from which he graduated in 1850. A cavalryman, he served in New Mexico, Arizona, Colorado, Utah, and Texas. Early in his career, Robert Ransom contracted cholera. Although he survived, his health was never quite the same.

In the autumn of 1854, he was transferred to West Point as a cavalry instructor. In 1855, he was assigned to the 1st Cavalry and spent two years as the regimental adjutant. He was sent to Fort Leavenworth in 1857, took part in an expedition against the Sioux, and tried to keep the peace in "Bleeding Kansas." After a tour of recruiting duty in Arkansas, he was promoted to captain in January 1861.

After he learned of North Carolina's secession, Ransom resigned his commission and was commissioned a captain of cavalry in the

R·

Confederate Army. He helped form the 1st North Carolina Cavalry and became its colonel. Sent to Virginia, it quickly established a reputation as an elite unit of horsemen, and Ransom was promoted to brigadier general on March 6, 1862. After the fall of New Bern later that month, he and his men were sent to protect eastern North Carolina.

Ransom considered the ensuing campaign to be some of his best work. He was able to stabilize the chaotic situation and, although the enemy continued to hold the coastal areas around Albemarle Sound, they were never able to exploit their foothold.

In June 1862, the Federals pushed to within six miles of Richmond. Ransom was recalled to Virginia and given command of six North Carolina infantry regiments. Despite their inexperience, they performed well in the Seven Days Battles. In the Maryland Campaign, Ransom and his men fought in the Siege of Harpers Ferry and at Sharpsburg. In the Battle of Fredericksburg, he commanded an all–North Carolina ad hoc division, where some of the heaviest fighting took place.

After Fredericksburg, Ransom was sent south again to contain the Yankees, who were trying to cut the strategically critical Wilmington and Weldon Railroad. On May 26, 1863, Robert Ransom was promoted to major general. He was recalled to Virginia and ordered to take command of the Richmond area. After two months, however, he was forced to step down because of illness. He returned to active duty in October 1863, when he was given command of the District of Southwest Virginia and East Tennessee. He was ordered back to Richmond and fought in the victory at Drewry's Bluff on May 16, 1864. He then helped General G. T. Beauregard bottle up U.S. General Benjamin Butler's Army of the James in the Bermuda Hundred peninsula.

In June 1864, Robert Ransom was placed in charge of General Jubal Early's cavalry in the Shenandoah Valley. In August, however, he again fell ill. The War Department continued to employ him in limited duty assignments, but he was basically unemployed for the rest of the war. He surrendered at Warrenton, North Carolina, on May 2, 1865.

After the war, Ransom lived in Wilmington, North Carolina, where he was an agent for a freight company and sold railroad supplies until

1875, when he became a farmer. Apparently unsuccessful in agriculture, he gave it up in 1879. His health continued to be shaky at best, and he now suffered from rheumatism. He finally took a job with the U.S. government as an assistant to the civil engineer in New Bern. He died there on January 14, 1892, at age sixty-three. He was buried in Cedar Grove Cemetery, New Bern.

ALEXANDER WELCH REYNOLDS was born sometime between 1815 and 1817, somewhere in northwest Virginia, possibly in what is now West Virginia. He was an ambitious man of indifferent education and questionable morals. Historians Weymouth T. Jordan, Jr., and John D. Chapla have noted that "[a]mid the numerous, mostly self-inflicted misfortunes that plagued his life, Alexander Welch Reynolds reliably displayed the cerebral agility of a trial lawyer, the aplomb, confidence, and ethics of a cardsharp, and a Houdini-like ability to escape ultimate disaster. . . . [His] certifiable moral infirmities included avarice and opportunism; dissemblance, prevarication, and manipulation; and penchants for drinking, gambling, and the occasional debauch."

Thanks to his mother's political connections, Reynolds entered West Point in 1833 at age seventeen. Reynolds had to repeat his junior year but graduated in 1838 and was commissioned in the infantry. He was stationed in Florida, where he fought the Seminoles. Subsequently, he did frontier duty and served in Iowa and Wisconsin, as well as recruiting duty in Philadelphia.

Alexander Reynolds transferred to the Quartermaster's Department in 1847. He briefly served in Mexico, but in a noncombat role. From 1849 to 1851, he was stationed in New Mexico. Here, he became one of the richest men in the territory, mainly because of "fraudulent schemes financed from his quartermaster accounts." He also did a tour of duty in the Indian Territory.

R·

Captain Reynolds was dismissed from the service for embezzlement in 1855 but was restored to active duty in 1858 thanks to the help of Vice President John C. Breckinridge and Secretary of War John B. Floyd. He was posted to the Lone Star State, where he absconded with more than $50,000 during the confusion wrought by the Texas secession crisis.

Reynolds joined the Confederate Army as a captain of infantry. He was commissioned colonel of the 50th Virginia Infantry in July 1861 and joined Floyd's brigade in West Virginia. That same month, U.S. forces pushed the Confederates out of the Kanawha Valley. Reynolds played a key role in checking the Union pursuit on the Gauley River and was nicknamed "Old Gauley" as a result.

In April 1862, he and his regiment were ordered to join General Edmund Kirby Smith at Knoxville. He was given command of a brigade, which in December 1862 was sent to Vicksburg during the Battle of Chickasaw Bluffs. Colonel Reynolds was trapped in Vicksburg with the rest of the Army of Mississippi and surrendered with the garrison on July 4, 1863. He was exchanged in October and promoted to brigadier general on September 17 (to date from September 14). He was sent to General Braxton Bragg's Army of Tennessee and given command of a newly formed brigade. All his regiments were relatively inexperienced, and during the rout of the Confederate forces at Missionary Ridge, Reynolds's regiments were, according to General Bragg, the first to give way and could not be rallied.

Alexander Reynolds continued to command his reduced brigade and fought in the Atlanta Campaign. On May 27, 1864, he was badly wounded in the Battle of New Hope Church. When he returned to active duty, it was as assistant inspector general of the District of Georgia, a post he held until the South surrendered. He was paroled in Atlanta on May 8, 1865.

In 1869, Reynolds accepted a commission in the forces of the Khedive of Egypt (as did several other former American officers). What followed were a succession of personal tragedies, including the deaths of his wife and son. Moreover, the Khedive owed him money, and Alexander Reynolds owed his creditors. Reynolds moved into a low-rent boarding house in Alexandria, Egypt. He died there on May 26, 1876. He was around sixty years old. The location of his remains is unknown.

DANIEL HARRIS REYNOLDS was born near Centerburg, Ohio, on December 14, 1832, the son of a farmer. He was a restless youth. He attended Ohio Wesleyan University in Delaware, Ohio, and briefly taught school in Ohio. In 1854, he moved to Louisa County, Iowa, where he read law; to Somerville, Tennessee, where he continued his legal studies and was admitted to the bar; and finally to Lake Village, Arkansas, where he settled down and set up a law practice. His legal career was a success, and he also invested in property, although he would not buy slaves.

By early 1861, Daniel Reynolds was a strong advocate of secession. When the war came, he joined the Arkansas State Troops on May 25, 1861, as a captain of the Chicot Rangers. Ordered to Little Rock, Reynolds and his company were mustered into Confederate service as Company A, 1st Arkansas Cavalry, on June 14, 1861. The regiment served in Missouri and fought in the Battle of Wilson's Creek, where it suffered heavy casualties. It was then sent to the Indian Territory, where he fought pro-Union Cherokees. The regiment returned to Arkansas that spring in time to fight in the Battle of Pea Ridge. In April 1862, it became, for all practical purposes, an infantry regiment (dismounted cavalry)—much to the annoyance of its men. Daniel Reynolds, meanwhile, climbed the promotion ladder. He was advanced to major on April 14, 1862, and to lieutenant colonel on May 1, 1862.

Reynolds and his regiment were sent to General G. T. Beauregard's Army of Mississippi and saw action in the Siege of Corinth and the retreat to Tupelo. The regiment then marched to east Tennessee, where it joined General Edmund Kirby Smith for the Kentucky Campaign of 1862, and fought in the Battle of Richmond, where it helped turn the enemy's right flank and rout the Yankees.

On May 10, 1863, the 1st Arkansas Cavalry (Dismounted) was ordered to join General Joseph E. Johnston's Army of Relief during the Vicksburg Campaign. After Vicksburg fell, the regiment fought in the Battle of Chickamauga, where it joined General James Longstreet's forces that broke through the Federal lines, but with heavy losses. The regiment's commander was killed by a cannon ball, so Reynolds assumed command. He was praised for his leadership by General Bushrod Johnson, his divisional commander, and was promoted to colonel on November 17, 1863, to date from September 20, 1863.

Reynolds's regiment then was sent back to Mississippi, took part in the Meridian Campaign, and marched to Mobile. On March 5, 1864, Daniel H. Reynolds was promoted to brigadier general and given command of the Arkansas brigade. In May 1864, when the Atlanta Campaign began, the brigade was ordered to Dalton, Georgia, with General Leonidas Polk's corps and remained with the Army of Tennessee for the rest of the war, fighting throughout the Atlanta, Tennessee, and Carolina campaigns. Reynolds was slightly wounded in the Battle of Franklin.

He fought his last battle at Bentonville, North Carolina, on March 19, 1865. This was one too many battles for Daniel Reynolds: a cannon ball killed the horse he was riding and hit him, taking off his left leg above the knee. He handled his disability with great stoicism.

General Reynolds was paroled at Charlottesville, Virginia, on May 29, 1865. He went to Baltimore, acquired a wooden prosthetic leg, and used it for the rest of his life. He returned to Lake Village in Chicot County and resumed his law practice.

Reynolds was elected to the Arkansas Senate in 1866 but was removed from office by the military in 1867 under the Reconstruction Acts. In 1874, he ran for a seat in the constitutional convention but lost. He never sought public office again. He did, however, become a successful speculator in real estate. At one point, he owned sixty thousand acres in Chicot County.

General Daniel H. Reynolds died in Lake Village, on March 14, 1902, at age sixty-nine. He was buried in Lake Village Cemetery.

ROBERT VINKLER RICHARDSON was born in Granville County, North Carolina, on November 4, 1820. His family moved to Tennessee when he was a child. Little is known about his early education. He was admitted to the bar in 1847 and started a practice in Memphis. He was a successful attorney, and by 1860 he was worth $39,000 ($1,140,199 in 2020 dollars). He was a brigadier general in the Tennessee Militia by 1861.

Richardson fought in the Battle of Shiloh and in September was authorized by the War Department to form his own partisan regiment in West Tennessee. He recruited the 1st Tennessee Partisan Rangers behind Union lines and led it in dozens of small raids against Yankee garrisons and outposts. Despite his lack of military training, he was promoted to colonel on February 19, 1863.

In West Tennessee, Richardson basically fought his own war. His harassment tactics were quite effective, and the Northerners sent several expeditions to destroy his forces, but to no avail.

There was friction between Robert Richardson and the regular Confederate authorities, because they could not control the partisans, who were not above an occasional atrocity or reprisal. To better control and coordinate operations, the 1st Partisan Rangers Regiment was redesignated the 12th Tennessee Cavalry, placing it under regular Confederate Army control—at least theoretically.

In late 1863, Nathan Bedford Forrest assumed command of the Confederate forces in northern Mississippi, which totaled fewer than 400 men. To assist him, General Joseph E. Johnston ordered Richardson to join Forrest. Because it was reported that Richardson had at least 2,000 men, President Jefferson Davis promoted him to brigadier general on December 3, 1863, and he was confirmed by the Senate on January 25, 1864. When Richardson showed up in Okolona, Mississippi, however, he only had 240 men, and a quarter of them were unarmed. (Most of Richardson's partisans had refused to leave West Tennessee.) An unhappy Jefferson Davis recalled and cancelled

Richardson's promotion on January 27, 1864. Robert V. Richardson was a Confederate general from December 3, 1863, to January 27, 1864. He was a colonel for the rest of the war.

Richardson commanded the West Tennessee Brigade in 1864. He fought in Forrest's spectacular victory at Okolona in February. On March 5, he joined Brigadier General Sul Ross in his attack on the Union garrison at Yazoo City. They captured most of the town, including the supply depot, although part of the garrison held out in a citadel that was too strong to attack.

On March 12, 1864, Richardson was relieved of his command, after Colonel John Green of the 12th Tennessee Cavalry preferred charges against him. (The *Official Records* do not reveal what the charges were.) Forrest dissolved Richardson's brigade and sent his regiments to other commands. On October 21, Richardson returned to command of the 12th Tennessee Cavalry. He remained in Mississippi when Forrest joined the Army of Tennessee in late 1864. He was paroled at Citronelle, Alabama, on May 4, 1865.

Richardson went abroad after the war but soon returned to Memphis, where he engaged in civil engineering and levee and railroad construction. On January 5, 1870, in Clarkton, Missouri, he was shot by an unknown assassin. He died the next day. He was forty-nine years old. His murderer was never found.

General Robert V. Richardson is buried in Elmwood Cemetery, Memphis, Tennessee.

ROSWELL SABINE RIPLEY was born on March 14, 1823, in Worthington, Ohio. He attended St. Lawrence Academy in Potsdam, Ohio. Although Ripley was not a diligent student and used profanity "to an awful degree," he nevertheless gained admission to West Point in 1839. Ripley graduated in 1843 and was commissioned a brevet second lieutenant of artillery.

During the Mexican War, Ripley served under General Zachary Taylor at the Battle of Monterrey, then under General Winfield Scott, and fought in all the major battles from Veracruz to the capture of Mexico City. He was brevetted captain and major in the process. After the war, he took a leave of absence and wrote a two-volume history, *The War with Mexico*, which was published in 1849. It was the first history of the war to hit the bookstores, and it did quite well.

Ripley fought in the Second Seminole War as an infantry company commander. In 1852, he was posted to Fort Moultrie, where he married into a prominent South Carolina family. He resigned from the service in early 1853 and spent the next several years managing his wife's estates.

South Carolina seceded on December 20, 1860. Governor Francis Wilkinson Pickens appointed Ripley major of ordnance on December 27. The following month, he was promoted to lieutenant colonel and commander of the 1st South Carolina Artillery Battalion at Fort Moultrie. He took part in the bombardment of Fort Sumter. He was named a lieutenant colonel in the Confederate Army in May 1861 and was promoted to brigadier general on August 13, 1861. He was initially in charge of the Department of South Carolina and its coastal defenses.

As a young officer, Ripley had a reputation for being affable and gregarious. But with age, he had become quarrelsome and irascible, and early in the war, he clashed with Governor Pickens and Generals Robert E. Lee, John C. Pemberton, and G. T. Beauregard, among others.

On December 11, 1861, the Great Fire of Charleston broke out and destroyed much of the city. It would have been worse, except for Ripley, who quickly blew up buildings between the fire and the Catholic Orphan Asylum, the Roper Hospital, and many homes, thus establishing a firebreak. He also sent his reserve regiments to help the firemen. He was forever popular in Charleston for these actions.

Sent to Virginia in the spring of 1862, Ripley performed poorly during the Seven Days Battles and at South Mountain during the Maryland Campaign, where his brigade got lost in the thick brush near Turner's Gap and did not fire a shot all day. At Sharpsburg, he was shot in the neck and severely wounded. He was transferred back to Charleston on October 7, 1862, and returned to managing its coastal defenses.

Ripley's plan for defending Charleston was brilliant. He formed "circles of fire," through which enemy warships would have to pass on the main shipping channel to the city. The Union Navy could not run past his batteries.

In September 1864, Ripley was the subject of an investigation by General Samuel Cooper concerning his drinking, his rudeness, and an affair he apparently had with a Mrs. Mason, who was said to be beautiful. Ripley had some supporters, including South Carolina Governor Milledge Luke Bonham, but not enough of them. On November 22, Ripley was replaced by Major General Robert Ransom. Beauregard wanted to court-martial him.

As the Confederacy entered its death throes, he joined General Joseph E. Johnston's Army of Tennessee. After the war, he lived in England. He struggled financially, failed in business, filed for bankruptcy, and was briefly arrested for debt. He returned to the United States in 1874.

In the United States, Sabine Ripley was financially dependent on friends in England until he invented a large cannon and a device for metallurgical furnaces. He moved to France in the early 1880s and worked on improving ammunition for a breech-loading cannon. All this enabled him to overcome his financial struggles.

On March 29, 1887, two weeks after his sixty-fourth birthday, he suffered a fatal stroke in a New York hotel. He was still popular in Charleston, and the citizens of that city gave him an impressive funeral. He is buried Magnolia Cemetery, Charleston.

Roswell Sabine Ripley was an excellent organizer and a fine artillery commander, but not a good infantry commander, and his difficult personality put unfortunate limits on his effectiveness.

JOHN SELDEN ROANE was born on January 8, 1817, in Wilson County, Tennessee, the son of a storekeeper. He was educated in local schools and at Cumberland

College, Princeton, Kentucky. He settled in Pine Bluff, Arkansas, in 1837. He read law under his brother and was admitted to the bar.

Roane entered politics in 1840 as a Democrat and was elected the first prosecuting attorney for the new Second Judicial District. He was elected to the legislature in 1842 and 1844 and became speaker. In 1846, during the Mexican War, he raised a company of mounted riflemen, which became part of the 1st Arkansas Mounted Rifles. Roane was elected lieutenant colonel of the regiment and fought in the Battle of Buena Vista. Here the regiment performed poorly, and its commander, Archibald Yell, was killed. Roane succeeded him as colonel.

Colonel Roane returned to Pine Bluff, where he acquired his own plantation and continued practicing law. When Arkansas's governor resigned on January 10, 1849, the Democratic Party caucused and nominated Roane for governor. He faced a little-known Whig in a special election on March 14, 1849. Roane won 3,486 votes to 3,322.

Roane supported internal improvements and hoped to use tax revenue from the sale of Federal lands to solve Arkansas's fiscal problems. Instead, the legislature acted irresponsibly, spent the money on pet projects, and lowered taxes, while the crisis deepened. Frustrated, Roane did not seek reelection in 1852. He served as governor from April 19, 1849, to November 15, 1852, then he returned to Pine Bluff and never sought public office again.

Roane opposed secession, while conceding that states had the right to secede. Though he followed his state when Arkansas left the Union, he did not join the Confederate Army until March 20, 1862, when he accepted a commission as a brigadier general and oversaw the defense of Arkansas. General Thomas C. Hindman and Roane fought the Federals at the Battle of Prairie Grove, Arkansas, on December 7, 1862, where Roane commanded a brigade that was poorly equipped, demoralized, and poorly led and that was held in reserve for most of the battle, which was a Confederate defeat.

General Theophilus Holmes, commander of the Trans-Mississippi Department, considered John Roane "a useless commander," and Roane was not well liked by his men or superiors. He spent the rest of the war in rear area assignments in Arkansas, Louisiana, and Texas. He was paroled at Shreveport on June 11, 1865.

He returned to Pine Bluff after the war and began rebuilding his shattered fortunes. Brigadier General John Selden Roane died in Pine Bluff on April 8, 1867, at the age of fifty. He was buried in Oakland and Fraternal Historic Cemetery Park, Little Rock.

WILLIAM PAUL ROBERTS was born on July 11, 1841, in Gatesville, Gates County, North Carolina. He was educated in local schools and at a small, private school in Harrellsville. He was a teacher when the war began. On June 10, 1861, at age nineteen, he enlisted in the 19th North Carolina Infantry. His company became part of the 2nd North Carolina Cavalry in August. He was promoted to third lieutenant on August 30 and to second lieutenant on September 30.

The 2nd North Carolina was on duty in eastern North Carolina (mainly on picket duty around Pamlico) until September 1862, when it was transferred to Robert E. Lee's army and fought in the Maryland Campaign. William P. Roberts was promoted to first lieutenant on September 13, 1862.

Roberts and his regiment took part in the Fredericksburg, Suffolk, and Gettysburg campaigns. Roberts was promoted to captain on November 18, 1863, and major on February 18, 1864. On June 23, 1864, he became commander of the regiment. He was promoted to colonel on August 19, to date from June 23, bypassing the rank of lieutenant colonel altogether.

In the Second Battle of Ream's Station (August 25, 1864), more than two thousand Yankees were captured, and total Confederate losses were less than nine hundred. Roberts distinguished himself in this operation, where he led a bold dismounted charge, overran a critical Federal trench, and took many prisoners.

On February 21, 1865, twenty-three-year-old William Paul Roberts was promoted to brigadier general—the youngest general officer in the history of the Confederate Army. In recognition of his valor and leadership, Robert E. Lee presented him with his own gauntlets. Roberts was given command of a small brigade.

On April 1, 1865, Roberts's brigade fought in the Battle of Five Forks. Roberts had the mission of maintaining contact between the Confederate defenses in Petersburg and General George Pickett's left flank at Five Forks—a distance of seven miles. His brigade was so thinly spread that it had no chance against a determined enemy attack. As the Confederate lines collapsed, Roberts rallied what troops he could and led them in the final retreat to Appomattox. On April 9, he surrendered his entire command: five officers and eighty-eight men.

After the war, Roberts represented Gates County in the constitutional conventions of 1868 and 1875 and was elected to the legislature in 1876. He was elected state auditor in 1880 and reelected in 1884. President Cleveland appointed him consul to Victoria, British Columbia, in 1889. Roberts eventually returned to Gates County and took up farming. He died March 27, 1910, in Norfolk, Virginia, at age sixty-eight. General William Paul Roberts is buried in Gatesville Cemetery, Gatesville, North Carolina.

BEVERLY HOLCOMBE ROBERTSON was born on June 5, 1827, on The Oaks, a plantation in Amelia County, Virginia. He was educated locally and attended West Point, from which he graduated with the class of 1849. Assigned to the 2nd Dragoons (heavy cavalry), he was sent to the Western frontier, where he fought Apaches, Lakota Sioux, Utes, Comanches, and Navajos. He was commended for gallantry and bravery more than once and became known as a skilled Indian fighter.

At one time in his antebellum career, he was engaged to Flora Cooke, the daughter of Colonel (and future

R·

Union general) Philip St. George Cooke. Eventually they called off their engagement, and Flora married J. E. B. Stuart.

Beverly Robertson "went south" in 1861 and accepted an appointment as a captain of cavalry in the Confederate States Army. In the autumn of 1861, he formed the 4th Virginia Cavalry Regiment and on September 4 became its colonel. He fought in the Valley Campaign with Stonewall Jackson and became his cavalry commander after Turner Ashby was killed in action. He was promoted to brigadier general on June 9, 1862, and defended the Shenandoah Valley during the Seven Days Battles. He reorganized the valley cavalrymen into a brigade and imposed discipline on them—something which was sorely lacking in Ashby's day.

On July 28, the Cavalry Division of the Army of Northern Virginia was formed under Jeb Stuart. Stuart disliked Robertson, but Robertson continued to perform good service. He led the raid that captured the headquarters wagon of U.S. General John Pope at Catlett's Station. He also fought at the Battle of Cedar Mountain and in the Battle of Second Manassas, where on August 30 he led a brilliant cavalry charge against John Buford's brigade, capturing three hundred men. He was ordered to North Carolina on September 5 to organize and train new cavalry regiments.

On December 16, 1862, Robertson won his most impressive victory in the Battle of White Hall. He faced more than 20,000 enemy soldiers with 212 men. He prevented the enemy from crossing the Neuse River and possibly saved Goldsboro.

Robertson returned to Virginia in the spring of 1863 with a small brigade. He played an important part in the Confederate victory at Brandy Station, and even Jeb Stuart praised the performance of his men.

In June 1863, General Robert E. Lee launched his second invasion of the North. While Stuart disappeared into the Union rear, Robertson remained with the main army. He was engaged in several skirmishes and small battles, and his brigade was reduced to three hundred men.

After Lee retreated to Virginia, Robertson criticized Stuart harshly for leaving Robert E. Lee blind at Gettysburg and asked to be transferred out of Stuart's command. An angry Stuart immediately approved the request, and Robertson was named commander of the 2nd District of South Carolina, which was responsible for guarding the coast between Savannah and Charleston. He defeated the Federal attempt to take John's Island in July 1864 and joined General William J. Hardee in opposing Sherman's March to the Sea. On November 19, he was wounded in a skirmish at West Buckhead Church, Georgia. He remained commander of the 2nd District until it was abandoned in February 1865. He covered Hardee's retreat from Charleston, fought in the Carolinas Campaign, and ended the war as part of Joseph E. Johnston's Army of the Tennessee in North Carolina.

General Robertson settled in Washington, D.C., after the war, where he operated a successful insurance and real estate business.

Beverly Robertson died on November 12, 1910, in Washington, D.C., at the age of eighty-three. He was buried in Rock Castle Farm Cemetery (the Robertson family cemetery) in Gills, Amelia County, Virginia.

FELIX HUSTON ROBERTSON was born on March 9, 1839, in Washington-on-the-Brazos, Washington County, Texas. He was the only native-born Texan to serve as a Confederate general in the war. His father was Jerome B. Robertson, who also became a Confederate general. Felix enrolled in West Point in 1857 and would have graduated with the class of 1861 had the war not intervened. He resigned from the military academy, was commissioned a second lieutenant of artillery in the Confederate States Army, and took part in the bombardment of Fort Sumter, where he commanded a mortar battery. He joined the staff of General A. H. Gladden in Pensacola, Florida, before being given command of an artillery battery.

Robertson was considered one of the best artillery officers in the Confederacy and distinguished himself at Shiloh and in the Second Battle of Murfreesboro. He was promoted to major of artillery on July 1 and was given command of an artillery battalion.

Robertson's command was attached to James Longstreet's corps during the Battle of Chickamauga. He was promoted to lieutenant colonel in January 1864 and then assigned to Joe Wheeler's corps as its artillery commander. Felix Robertson fought well in the Atlanta Campaign. Wheeler made him his chief of staff and a brigade commander. He was promoted to brigadier general (temporary rank) on July 26, 1864.

General Robertson was not an easy man to serve with or under. He was a harsh disciplinarian, strongly opinionated (with not-always-popular opinions), and his Indian-like appearance earned him the nickname "Comanche Robertson."

Robertson took part in numerous raids and skirmishes while working under General Wheeler. After the Battle of Saltville (October 2, 1864) in southwestern Virginia, several Union prisoners were executed, mainly from the 5th U.S. Colored Troops Cavalry. Northern propaganda sheets referred to the incident as the "Saltville Massacre." General Robert E. Lee ordered John C. Breckinridge, the department commander, to prefer charges against Robertson and bring him to trial. Robertson escaped court-martial only because of the chaotic military situation.

General Robertson later rejoined Wheeler and opposed Sherman's March to the Sea. He commanded a brigade at Buckhead Creek near Augusta on November 29, 1864, when he was badly wounded in the elbow.

On February 22, 1865, his nomination to brigadier general was rejected by the Confederate Senate, and in any event his injuries were such that he could not return to active duty before the war ended. On April 20, 1865, Felix Robertson was captured by Federal forces near Macon, Georgia.

After the war, he settled in Waco, Texas, studied law, was admitted to the bar, and established a profitable legal practice. He also invested in railroads and real estate with his father. He was active in the United Confederate Veterans and was for a time the commander of the Texas Division. He ran for mayor of Waco in 1902 but was defeated and never again sought public office.

· R

Felix Huston Robertson died in Waco on April 20, 1928, at the age of eighty-nine. He was buried in Oakwood Cemetery, Waco.

JEROME BONAPARTE "POLLY" ROBERTSON, the son of a Scottish immigrant, was born on March 14, 1815, in Woodford County, Kentucky. His father died in 1819, and his mother, who was almost destitute, apprenticed Jerome to a hatter when he was eight years old. Despite many challenges and privations, Robertson was determined to be a success in life. He studied medicine at Transylvania University and graduated in 1835. He joined a company of Kentucky volunteers and went to Texas to aid in the revolution against Mexico. His men arrived, however, after Antonio López de Santa Anna was defeated. Robertson nevertheless served in the Army of the Republic of Texas as a captain. He settled in Washington-on-the-Brazos, where he established a medical practice. He also developed a reputation as an Indian fighter. Every year for six consecutive years he was involved in a campaign against Indians or Mexicans. Robertson also served as mayor of Washington-on-the-Brazos (1839–40) and town postmaster (1841–43). He was elected to the state house of representatives in 1847 and to the state senate in 1849.

Jerome Robertson was a delegate to the Texas Secession Convention in 1861 and signed the secession resolution. He immediately raised a company to fight for the Confederacy. Elected captain, his command became part of the 5th Texas Infantry Regiment (part of what became John Bell Hood's famous Texas Brigade) in October 1861. Robertson was promoted to lieutenant colonel (October 10).

The 5th Texas participated in the Peninsula Campaign and fought in the Battle of Seven Pines, after which Robertson succeeded James Archer as commander of the regiment. On June 3, 1862, he was promoted to colonel.

The Texas Brigade distinguished itself in the Seven Days Battles (in which Robertson was slightly wounded), the Battle of Second Manassas, and the Maryland Campaign. During the Battle of South Mountain (September 14), an exhausted and overworked Colonel Robertson collapsed and had to be carried off the field.

Robertson recovered by November 1, when John Bell Hood was promoted to major general and permanent division commander. That same day, Jerome Robertson was promoted to brigadier general and commander of the Texas Brigade.

General Robertson's men respected him as a fine tactical commander. They were also amused and pleased by how solicitous he was of their welfare. That earned him the nickname of "Aunt Polly" or "Polly."

Robertson fought at Fredericksburg, Suffolk, and Gettysburg, where he was wounded on July 2, 1863, and had to give up command.

In September, a recuperated Robertson distinguished himself at Chickamauga, but his performance at Knoxville earned him the censure of his division commander, Micah Jenkins, and General James Longstreet, who filed court-martial charges against him for dereliction of duty. In retrospect, it appears that Robertson was made a scapegoat for the failure of Longstreet's Knoxville Campaign, and President Jefferson Davis and Secretary of War James Seddon dismissed the charges, although Robertson was not restored to command. One of Longstreet's staff officers wrote to his mother and said that, although Robertson was not "considered a good officer," he had been unjustly treated and was "more sinned against than sinning."

The War Department granted Robertson's request for a transfer to Texas, and he was named commander of the state reserve forces. He was essentially sent into professional exile. He was still in this backwater post when the war ended.

It seems clear that Jerome Robertson was a better regimental leader than a brigade commander, but while he didn't perform brilliantly in East Tennessee, his treatment by Longstreet was neither fair nor just.

After the war, Robertson returned to the practice of medicine in Independence, Texas. He was appointed superintendent of the Texas Bureau of Immigration in 1874. He relocated to Waco in 1879, where he worked in the railroad industry. He was also active in the Masons and the United Confederate Veterans.

General Jerome Robertson died on January 7, 1890, at age seventy-four. He was initially buried in Independence, Texas, next to his first wife and his mother. In 1894, his son, former Confederate General Felix Robertson, had all three bodies moved to Oakwood Cemetery in Waco.

PHILLIP DALE RODDEY was born in Moulton, Alabama, on April 2, 1824, although some sources list his birth year as 1826. His father was a saddler who was murdered when Philip was four years old, and his mother never remarried. A single mother with three children, Mrs. Roddey struggled financially, and Phillip Roddey received a sketchy education. He apprenticed as a tailor and worked hard to help support his mother and two sisters.

Roddey was "[a] clever young man with ambition and an inviting personality," notes historian Arley McCormick. "His notoriety, popularity, and genteel southern manner" secured his favor in the region and folks referred to him as 'Buttermilk Phil.'" In August 1849, at age twenty-six, he was elected sheriff of Lawrence County. He left office three years later to work in the steamboat business, first as a clerk, then as a manager, and finally as an owner. His boat operated mainly in the Tennessee River but made occasional trips to New Orleans.

Like many in northern Alabama, he was not a secessionist but followed his state out of the Union. Roddey raised a cavalry company, the Tishomingo Rangers, burned his steamboat to keep it from falling into Yankee hands, joined the Army of Central Kentucky (later the first Army of Mississippi), and commanded Braxton Bragg's escort at the Battle of Shiloh. Bragg told General Sterling Price that Roddey had "shown himself to be an officer of rare energy, enterprise and skill in harassing the enemy and procuring information of his movements." "Captain Roddey," he concluded, had his "entire confidence."

As Bragg moved west in the prelude to his invasion of Kentucky, Roddey was given command of another cavalry company in addition to his own. With them, he captured 123 Yankees in a single raid. Bragg could not have been more pleased.

Roddey fought at Iuka and the Second Battle of Corinth. That November, Captain Roddey recruited his own regiment, the 4th Alabama Cavalry. In the spring of 1863, Roddey was named commander of the District of Northern Alabama. He was instrumental in forcing U.S. Colonel Abel Streight's raiders to surrender to General Nathan Bedford Forrest at Lawrence Plantation on May 3, 1863. Roddey then returned to northwest Alabama and captured Florence from the Federals on May 28. He was promoted to brigadier general on August 3, 1863.

Although he fought at Chickamauga and Chattanooga, Roddey spent most of the war defending northern Alabama and launching successful raids behind enemy lines. He fought in Forrest's incredible victory at Brices Cross Roads, the Battle of Harrisburg, and the subsequent pursuit of U.S. General A. J. Smith. He also fought in the disastrous Battle of Selma, where Forrest was overwhelmed and Roddey's brigade was shattered, and he barely escaped capture by swimming across the Alabama River at night. He surrendered to Federal forces at Pond Spring on May 17.

After the war, Phillip Roddey worked briefly registering students at the University of Alabama, then began a business career in New York City and became involved in a notorious scandal that found him accused of adultery, bigamy, and fraud.

General Roddey moved to London around 1882 and lived in the Westminster Palace Hotel. He died from uremia in a London hospital on July 20, 1897, at age seventy-three. Known as the "Defender of North Alabama," Phillip Roddey is buried in Greenwood Cemetery, Tuscaloosa, Alabama.

ROBERT EMMETT RODES was born in Lynchburg, Virginia, on March 29, 1829. He attended the Virginia Military Institute, graduated in 1848, and stayed on as an assistant professor, teaching tactics,

physical science, and chemistry. He applied for a full professorship in 1850 and left the institute when he was not chosen for the position. The job went to his future commander, Stonewall Jackson.

Rodes worked in railroad construction in Alabama and became chief engineer of the Alabama and Chattanooga Railroad. He was married in Tuscaloosa in 1857, and Alabama became his home.

On May 11, 1861, he was named colonel of the 5th Alabama Infantry. The regiment trained at Pensacola and was sent to Virginia but missed the Battle of First Manassas. General G. T. Beauregard was nevertheless impressed by Colonel Rodes and recommended his promotion to brigadier general. The recommendation was approved on October 21. His new brigade was designated the 1st Alabama, part of D. H. Hill's division.

Rodes's brigade fought in the Peninsula Campaign, including the Battle of Williamsburg and the Battle of Seven Pines, where General Rodes was wounded in the arm on May 31 and had to leave the field. He was back in action during the Seven Days Battles (June 26 to July 1, 1861), but his wound had not healed, and he had to turn over his command to Colonel John B. Gordon on June 29.

Rodes was back in command at the Battle of South Mountain, where his men put up a stiff defense at Turner's Gap. He defended the Sunken Road during the Battle of Sharpsburg, turning back several Federal assaults and remaining at his post, despite being wounded again.

In January 1863, Rodes's division commander, D. H. Hill, was transferred to North Carolina, and Stonewall Jackson named Rodes as Hill's replacement (though Rodes was not Jackson's first choice). Rodes was the first non–West Pointer to become a division commander in the Army of Northern Virginia.

Rodes spearheaded Jackson's famous May 2 flank attack during the Battle of Chancellorsville and routed the U.S. XI Corps. Jackson was mortally wounded that night and was succeeded by A. P. Hill, who was wounded soon after. Rodes assumed temporary command of the II Corps until he was superseded by J. E. B. Stuart. On his death bed, Stonewall Jackson recommended Rodes's promotion to major general. It was approved on May 7, with an effective date of May 2.

General Rodes led his division during the Pennsylvania Campaign, fought at Gettysburg, and retreated with the army to Virginia to fight in the Bristoe Campaign of 1863, the Mine Run Campaign, and the Overland Campaign of 1864.

General Rodes helped Jubal Early chase the Yankees out of the Shenandoah Valley and into Maryland. He was part of the drive to the outskirts of Washington and the subsequent retreat to Winchester. Here, on September 19, 1864, during the Third Battle of Winchester, he was killed in action when a fragment from a Yankee shell struck him in the back of the head. He died within a few hours. Jubal Early lamented that Rodes "was a most accomplished, skillful and gallant officer, upon whom [he] placed great reliance."

General Robert Rodes's body was returned to the town of his birth, where he was buried.

LAWRENCE SULLIVAN "SUL" ROSS was born on September 27, 1838, in Bentonsport, Iowa Territory, the son of a noted Indian fighter who had killed Chief Big Foot. He moved with his family to the Republic of Texas in 1839 and eventually settled in Waco.

Sul Ross entered Baylor University (then in Independence, Texas) and completed a two-year program in one year. He then enrolled in Wesleyan University in Florence, Alabama. He fought Comanches during his summer breaks and was so effective that Captain Earl Van Dorn and his officers signed a petition asking Winfield Scott, the general-in-chief of the U.S. Army, to offer Ross a direct commission. Scott made the offer, but Ross elected to complete his education. He graduated from Wesleyan in 1859.

After Texas seceded on February 1, 1861, Ross enlisted as a private in his brother's militia company. In the middle of August, they left for Missouri and joined what became the 6th Texas Cavalry. Ross was elected major and led successful scouting missions for Ben McCulloch, with whom he had served in Texas. He fought in the unsuccessful Battle of Pea Ridge.

The 6th Texas was dismounted on April 15 and was sent to Corinth, Mississippi. On May 14, 1862, the 6th Texas held elections and chose Sul Ross as its commander. It fought in the First Battle of Corinth (April 29 to May 30) and the Second Battle of Corinth (October 3–4). Ross commanded a brigade in the Battle of Hatchie's Bridge on October 5, where the Yankees tried to cross the river via frontal assault with seven thousand men. They were slaughtered. The battle lasted for three hours, and Ross repulsed three separate assaults.

The 6th Texas Cavalry was remounted shortly after and joined William H. "Red" Jackson's Cavalry Brigade. It took part in the victory at Thompson's Station (May 5, 1863). In July, Stephen Dill Lee organized a new cavalry brigade in eastern Mississippi and picked Ross to command it. Sul Ross was promoted to brigadier general on December 21, 1863.

There were a great many battles and skirmishes in Mississippi from 1864 through the spring of 1865. Most of them were too small to rate more than a footnote in the history of the war, if that; however, that did not make them any less lethal for the participants. Ross's brigade endured 112 consecutive days of skirmishes and suffered 25 percent casualties.

Ross and his Texans were sent to Georgia as part of Joe Wheeler's cavalry corps during the Atlanta Campaign. Sul Ross was captured at Brown's Mill on July 30. "Fighting Joe" Wheeler quickly counterattacked, defeated the Union raiders, took more than 1,200 prisoners, and freed 300 Confederates, including Ross.

After the fall of Atlanta, Sul Ross joined Nathan Bedford Forrest for the Franklin-Nashville Campaign. During this operation, he captured 550 prisoners while losing 12 killed, 70 wounded, and 5 missing or captured. When the Army of Tennessee marched east from Mississippi to North Carolina in February 1865, Ross's brigade was left behind to guard what was left of Confederate Mississippi. Ross, meanwhile, asked for a furlough, which was approved in March. The Confederate armies surrendered while he was at home. During the Civil War, he fought in 135 engagements and had five horses shot from under him.

Lawrence Sullivan Ross was only twenty-six years old when the war ended. He initially took up life as a farmer and owned more than a thousand acres of farmland by 1875. The ending of Reconstruction allowed Ross to enter public service, and he was elected sheriff of McLennan County in December 1873. He deputized his brother and like-minded men, and they immediately began to suppress outlaws in the county. It was reported that they arrested seven hundred people in two years.

General Ross resigned as sheriff in 1875 and returned to farming until 1880, when he was elected to the state senate. In 1886, Ross ran for governor as a Democrat and was overwhelmingly elected. His administration focused on land reform, regulating monopolies, and reducing tariffs. He was easily reelected and served from 1887 to 1891. He refused to run for a third term, although there is a consensus among historians that he would have won reelection easily. Instead, he became president of Texas A&M University. He brought the school financial stability, massively improved its facilities, increased its enrollment, and reduced the cost of tuition.

Sul Ross was highly popular among the students. Apparently, none of them ever heard him curse or saw him angry. He was a Mason and a member of the United Confederate Veterans, serving as commander of the Texas Division several times. He also served a term as commander-in-chief of the national organization.

Ross passed away (probably of a heart attack) on January 3, 1898, at his home in College Station, Texas, at age fifty-nine. He was buried in Oakwood Cemetery, Waco. Sul Ross University in Alpine, Texas, is named after him.

THOMAS LAFAYETTE "TEX" ROSSER was born on Catalpa Hill, a farm in Campbell County, Virginia, on October 15, 1836. The

family relocated to Panola County, Texas, where his father acquired a 640-acre farm. Rosser was educated at Mount Enterprise School in Rusk County and at West Point, which he entered in 1856. Because of the sectional crisis, he resigned only two weeks before he would have graduated.

Rosser traveled to Montgomery, Alabama, then capital of the new Confederacy, and was commissioned a first lieutenant of artillery. He instructed the Washington Artillery, a New Orleans battalion, and commanded one of its batteries at the Battle of First Manassas. A few weeks later, he shot down one of U.S. General George B. McClellan's observation balloons, which earned him a promotion to captain on September 17, 1861. Sent to the Virginia Peninsula, he was badly wounded at the Battle of Mechanicsville but was swiftly promoted from lieutenant colonel to colonel, commanding the 5th Virginia Cavalry. He fought in the Second Manassas Campaign and quickly established for himself a reputation as a skillful and daring cavalryman. He fought at Crampton's Gap and at Sharpsburg.

On March 17, 1863, Rosser was seriously wounded during the Battle of Kelly's Ford. He recovered in time for the Pennsylvania Campaign, fought at Gettysburg, and on September 9, 1863, was given command of the Laurel Brigade (Turner Ashby's old command). He was promoted to brigadier general on September 28, 1863.

Thomas L. Rosser served in the Overland Campaign of 1864 and became commander of General Jubal Early's cavalry in the Shenandoah Valley in October. Although he continued to perform well, the tide had turned irresistibly against the South. Rosser was promoted to major general on November 1, 1864. He led two successful raids into West Virginia, served at Petersburg, and was hosting a shad bake, with General George Pickett in attendance, when the enemy struck and destroyed half of Pickett's division at Five Forks (April 1, 1865) before the Confederate commanders could recover. He redeemed himself at High Bridge (April 6), where he defeated General Theodore Read and captured his entire

R·

command. The next day, Rosser rescued General Robert E. Lee's wagon train and captured Union General John I. Gregg at Farmville (April 7). On April 9, when he learned that Robert E. Lee was planning to surrender, Rosser broke out and headed for Staunton. He attempted to resurrect Lee's army but, finally realizing that further resistance was futile, he surrendered on May 4, 1865.

After the war, Rosser held several railroad and engineering jobs until 1886, when he bought a plantation near Charlottesville, Virginia. During the Spanish-American War, he was appointed brigadier general, but the war ended before he could see combat.

Rosser was a gallant raider and cavalry officer. He was wounded seven times during the war but remained a lifelong friend of Union General George Custer, his roommate at West Point and occasional battlefield opponent. General Thomas L. Rosser died in Charlottesville, Virginia, on March 29, 1910. He was seventy-three years old. He was buried in Riverview Cemetery, Charlottesville.

DANIEL RUGGLES was born on January 31, 1810, in Barre, a small town in central Massachusetts. He followed in his family's military tradition and attended West Point, from which he graduated in 1833.

Lieutenant Ruggles served in the Wisconsin Territory, in the Seminole War (1839–40), and along the Canadian border. He was with General Zachary Taylor at Palo Alto and Resaca de la Palma and was transferred to General Winfield Scott's Army of Mexico, where he fought from Veracruz to Mexico City. He was breveted twice for bravery and promoted to captain on June 18, 1846.

Ruggles served mostly in Texas for the next ten years and was part of Albert Sidney Johnston's Utah Expedition in 1858. He reported sick in 1859 and was still on a leave at the outbreak of the Civil War. After thirty-two years of service, Captain Ruggles resigned his commission on May 7, 1861, and joined the

Confederate Army. He had married into an old Virginia family (his wife was a niece of Founding Father George Mason), and he did not believe that the South should be held in the Union against her will. Moreover, he hated abolitionists. He owned no slaves himself—and indeed became a critic of the planter class—but he believed "half-civilized" blacks were the beneficiaries of slavery, not its victims.

He was appointed colonel of the Provisional Army of Virginia in May 1861 and on August 6, 1861, was promoted to brigadier general of the Confederate States Army. Initially stationed in Florida, New Orleans, and North Alabama, after the fall of Fort Henry and Fort Donelson, he was given command of the 1st Division of Braxton Bragg's II Corps and fought at the Battle of Shiloh. He assembled sixty-two guns—then the largest artillery concentration in American history—and blasted Union General Benjamin Prentiss's division into submission. Nevertheless, Prentiss had held up the Confederates long enough to save U.S. General Grant's army, and the next day the Northerners pushed the outnumbered Rebels off the field. Ruggles served well throughout the engagement, at one point seizing the battle flag of the 17th Louisiana and leading a counterattack.

During the retreat to Corinth, Mississippi, he won a small victory at Farmington. He could not get along with his corps commander, Mansfield Lovell, so the army commander, G. T. Beauregard, sent him to Grenada as commander of the Gulf Coast Supply Depots.

Ruggles commanded a small division in the Battle of Baton Rouge on August 5, 1862. He again performed well, but this was his last major command of the war. Daniel Ruggles was considered too old for combat commands, though I believe he was underestimated in his time and by later historians. He always performed well, and it appears that his chief handicap to command was not his age, but his prickly personality and the fact that he could not get along with anyone.

After briefly commanding Port Hudson, he was given the task of defending northeast Mississippi. He had only three thousand men under his command, and most of them were fourth-class state troops. Still, he did a good job of minimizing the damage inflicted by aggressive Union cavalry probes. In late June 1863, for example, Ruggles's forces on the Tallahatchie routed eight hundred Federals in the Battle of Rocky Ford.

After the fall of Vicksburg, Ruggles was confined to administrative duties in Alabama and Mississippi—when he was not simply unemployed. Jefferson Davis appointed him commissary general for prisoners of war on March 30, 1865.

Following the Confederate surrender, Daniel Ruggles moved first to Texas and then to Virginia, where he farmed and became a real estate agent in Fredericksburg. General Ruggles died there on June 1, 1897 at age eighty-seven. He is buried in the Confederate Cemetery in Fredericksburg.

ALBERT RUST was born in Fauquier County, Virginia, in 1818. In 1837, he moved to the Western frontier and settled on the banks of the Ouachita River in southern Arkansas and built a store.

Rust studied law, gained admission to the bar, and was elected to the state legislature, in which he served from 1842 to 1848 and again from 1852 to 1854.

He ran for Congress in 1846 and lost but ran again and won in 1854. As a Southern Democrat, Rust advocated expanding slavery into the territories. Horace Greeley, the editor of the *New York Tribune*, furiously editorialized against Rust, who responded by attacking Greeley with his cane—on two separate occasions. The Democrats did not renominate Rust in 1856.

But Rust mended his political fences and was reelected to Congress in 1858. He did not seek reelection in 1860. Rust supported Democrat Stephen A. Douglas for president and opposed secession, but like hundreds of thousands of other Southerners, he changed his mind after President Abraham Lincoln called for troops to invade the South on April 15, 1861.

Albert Rust was named a delegate to the Provisional Confederate Congress in 1861. On July 5, he was commissioned colonel and

· R

commander of the 3rd Arkansas Infantry Regiment. He was sent to western Virginia in the fall of 1861, where he served under General Robert E. Lee. At the Battle of Cheat Mountain (September 12–15), he and General Samuel Anderson were fooled into thinking that they were badly outnumbered and withdrew their forces, when in fact they held overwhelming numerical superiority. Their lack of nerve led to a Confederate defeat.

That winter, the 3rd Arkansas took part in the Romney Expedition, where Rust performed better, earning the praise of Stonewall Jackson. Rust was promoted to brigadier general on March 4, 1862, and transferred to Arkansas, which was stripped of most of its troops later that month, when General Earl Van Dorn's Army of the West was dispatched to Mississippi.

In Arkansas, Union General Samuel Curtis's Army of the Southwest (ten thousand men), operating out of Batesville, moved to clear the White River area of Confederate forces. Rust tried to stop him in the Battle of Cotton Plant (also called the Battle of Hill's Plantation) on July 7, 1862, but was routed. Rust lost more than one hundred men, as opposed to six killed and fifty-seven wounded for the Federals, and the Confederate defeat would have been much worse had the Union Army and Navy properly supported each other.

Albert Rust joined Earl Van Dorn in northern Mississippi and fought in the Second Battle of Corinth (October 3–4, 1862). The next spring, he was transferred back to Arkansas. Rust had become increasingly outspoken in his criticisms of the Confederate government and even made numerous pro-Union statements. Many people now questioned his loyalty, and it was certainly obvious that he was not a good general. He was quietly put on the shelf.

After the war, Rust settled in the Little Rock area and became a Republican. He died in Little Rock on April 4, 1870. His grave was unmarked and must be regarded as lost, but he has a cenotaph in Mount Holly Cemetery, Little Rock.

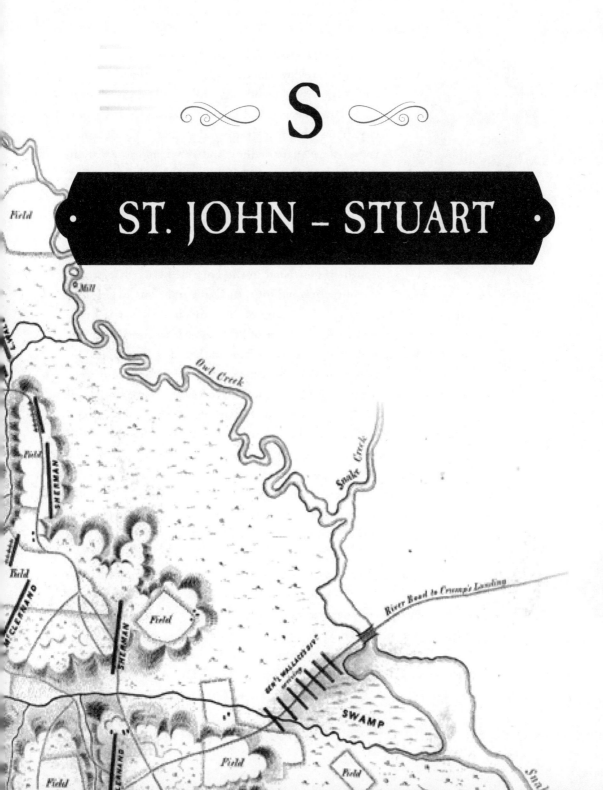

S

ST. JOHN – STUART

Field

Mill

Owl Creek

Snake Creek

SHERMAN

Field

McCLERNAND

Field

SHERMAN

Field

GEN'L WALLACE DIV

River Road to Crump's Landing

SWAMP

CLERNAND

Field

Field

Field

Snake

ISAAC MUNROE ST. JOHN was born in Augusta, Georgia, on November 19, 1827. His parents moved to New York City when he was a child, and he was educated at the Poughkeepsie Collegiate School and Yale University, from which he graduated in 1845. He became a lawyer, a newspaper editor, and a civil engineer with the Baltimore and Ohio (B&O) Railroad from 1848 to 1855. He relocated to South Carolina and from 1855 to 1861 and was chief construction engineer for the Blue Ridge Railroad Company.

When the war began, St. John cast his lot with the South. He enlisted in the Fort Hill Guards of South Carolina in April 1861. By October, he was an engineer in General John B. Magruder's Army of the Peninsula. He was Magruder's chief engineer during the Siege of Yorktown (1862) until April 18, when he was named chief of the Nitre Bureau (later the Nitre and Mining Corps). Nitre (or niter) is the mineral form of potassium nitrate, also known as saltpeter, and is a critical ingredient in the manufacture of gunpowder. St. John proved to be highly efficient at producing this vital substance, as well as other metals and supplies necessary to the Southern war effort. As the Union blockade tightened, St. John discovered that the limestone caves in the southern Appalachian Mountains contained saltpeter. It could thus be said that he outflanked the Northern blockade. Naturally, this led to promotions: to major of artillery (September 26, 1862), lieutenant colonel (May 26, 1863), and colonel (June 15, 1864).

On February 15, 1865, the Confederate House of Representatives officially called for the removal of Lucius Northrop from his post as commissary general for subsistence, and President Davis finally accepted his resignation. The next day, by a special vote, Congress gave the post to St. John, along with a promotion to brigadier general, to date from February 14, 1865. Lucius Northrop had done a miserable job, but Isaac St. John's appointment came too late to make any difference for the

S

survival of the Confederacy. He surrendered in Thomasville, Georgia, on or about June 1, 1865.

After the war, he worked as a civil engineer, mainly for railroads. Brigadier General Isaac M. St. John, a brilliant engineer and staff officer, died on April 7, 1880, at White Sulphur Springs, West Virginia. He was fifty-two. He is buried in Hollywood Cemetery, Richmond.

JOHN CALDWELL CALHOUN SANDERS (his name is occasionally misspelled as "Saunders") was born in Tuscaloosa, Alabama, on April 4, 1840, and grew up in Clinton, Alabama. In early 1861, after Alabama seceded, he left the University of Alabama, where he had been a student, to join the Confederate Guards, which later became Company E of the 11th Alabama Infantry Regiment. Sanders was elected captain of the company on June 11, 1861.

The 11th Alabama fought in the Battle of Seven Pines and the Seven Days Battles, including at Frayser's Farm (June 30), where Captain Sanders was wounded in the leg by a shell fragment. When he returned to duty on August 11, he was the senior surviving officer. He assumed command of the regiment and led it at the Battle of Second Manassas. He was promoted to colonel on September 11, 1862.

Sanders fought at the Siege of Harpers Ferry and the battles of Sharpsburg, Fredericksburg, Chancellorsville, and Gettysburg, where he was wounded in the knee by a minié ball. After he recovered, he served as acting commander of Abner Perrin's brigade in the Bristoe and Mine Run campaigns and then resumed his role as commander of the 11th Alabama in the spring of 1864.

Sanders led his regiment during the Overland Campaign of 1864 until General Perrin was killed at Spotsylvania on May 12. Sanders again assumed command of the brigade. He was promoted to brigadier general (temporary rank) on May 31. A competent brigade commander,

·S

he performed satisfactorily at the Battle of Cold Harbor and the Siege of Petersburg.

On August 21, while leading an attack along during the Battle of Globe Tavern, a minié ball ripped through his thighs, severing both femoral arteries. He calmly ordered his adjutant to take him to the rear. He bled to death within a few minutes. John C. C. Sanders was twenty-four years old.

The Alabamians were saddened by his loss. "He was stern but kind," one of them recalled, "and always looked after the comfort and safety of his men, and as the war progressed he grew continually in their estimation." He was also known to have a sterling moral character.

Sanders's body was initially interred in a vault in Hollywood Cemetery, Richmond, Virginia. Eventually his family took him back to Alabama and buried him in Greenwood Cemetery, Montgomery. The exact location of his body has been lost, although a granite marker to his memory was erected in the cemetery in 1971.

ALFRED MOORE SCALES was born on November 26, 1827, in Reidsville, North Carolina, the son of a medical doctor. He was educated at a boys' preparatory school and the University of North Carolina at Chapel Hill, where he studied law. He was admitted to the bar in 1852 and in the 1850s was twice elected to the North Carolina House of Representatives and once to the U.S. Congress. He then worked as clerk of the court of equity of Rockingham County and was a presidential elector for John C. Breckinridge in 1860.

Five days after President Abraham Lincoln called for seventy-five thousand troops to suppress the "rebellion," Scales enlisted in the Rockingham Guards as a private. The Guards became Company H of the 13th North Carolina Troops on April 30, and they elected Scales their captain. North Carolina seceded on May 20, 1861, and the regiment was soon on its way to Virginia. He became a colonel and commander of the regiment on

November 14, 1861. The 13th North Carolina fought on the Virginia Peninsula and in the Seven Days Battles. Scales demonstrated great courage, and on the last day of the Seven Days Battles, he collapsed from exhaustion and almost died. It took him months to recover.

Colonel Scales returned to his regiment in November 1862 and fought at the battles of Fredericksburg and Chancellorsville, where the regiment formed part of Stonewall Jackson's famous flanking attack and suffered 216 casualties out of about 500 engaged. One of them was Scales, who was shot through the thigh but kept on advancing until he collapsed from a loss of blood.

On June 13, 1863, while still home on medical leave, Alfred Scales was promoted to brigadier general. At Gettysburg, he led William Dorsey Pender's former brigade (Pender having been promoted to division command) and on July 1 was severely wounded on Seminary Ridge by a shell fragment. He was evacuated to Virginia in the same ambulance that carried the wounded Dorsey Pender.

After Scales recovered from his latest wound, he rejoined the Army of Northern Virginia and fought in the Overland Campaign and the Siege of Petersburg. One of his old wounds acted up in 1865, and he took a leave of absence to let it heal. He was at home in North Carolina when Lee surrendered. He apparently was never paroled, but he did apply for amnesty on June 22, 1865, and was pardoned on June 18, 1866.

Scales returned to his law practice and was very successful. In 1874, he was elected to Congress and was reelected four times, serving from March 4, 1875, to December 30, 1884, when he resigned because he was elected governor of North Carolina.

Scales was governor from 1885 to 1889. His term was rather uneventful. His health was not good after his term expired. He spent his remaining years living in Greensboro, where he was president of Piedmont Bank. He also served as an elder in the First Presbyterian Church of Greensboro.

General Alfred M. Scales died in Greensboro, North Carolina, on February 8, 1892, at age sixty-four. He was buried in Green Hill Cemetery, Greensboro.

THOMAS MOORE SCOTT was born in Athens, Georgia, in 1829. Little is known of his early life and education, except that he lived in both Georgia and Louisiana.

In the late 1850s, Scott was a farmer in Claiborne Parish, North Louisiana, near Homer. He joined the Claiborne Rangers in 1861 and was elected captain. The company left Homer on July 1, 1861, and underwent training at Camp Moore, Louisiana. The Rangers became part of the 12th Louisiana Infantry Regiment. Thomas Scott was elected colonel on August 13.

Initially, the 12th Louisiana was assigned to the defense of the Mississippi River. It first saw action at Island Number 10 near New Madrid, Missouri, during the bombardment of March 1862. It was then transferred to Fort Pillow. After operating against Grant in northern Mississippi, Scott and his men were transferred to Port Hudson in late 1862. They were assigned to William Loring's division during the campaigns against Vicksburg and were cut off from the main army during the Battle of Champion Hill. Most of the regiment thus avoided being trapped in Vicksburg, although it lost its wagons during the escape. The 12th Louisiana was part of Joseph E. Johnston's Army of Relief during the Siege of Vicksburg and at the Second Battle of Jackson.

During the fall and winter of 1863–64, Scott and his men remained in Mississippi. They were at Meridian in early 1864 and later retreated to Demopolis and Montevallo, Alabama. In the spring of 1864, Scott was ordered to Georgia, along with Leonidas Polk's corps, for the Atlanta Campaign. Shortly after the start of Sherman's drive on the city, Scott was promoted to brigade commander. His unit consisted of five Alabama regiments and his own 12th Louisiana, which suggests someone in authority (probably Joe Johnston) thought highly of him. He was promoted to brigadier general on May 10, 1864.

General Scott fought in the battles of Resaca, Marietta, Kennesaw Mountain, Lost Mountain, Bethel Church, and Atlanta. Casualties were high. After Atlanta fell on September 2, Scott accompanied General John Bell Hood into Tennessee. At Franklin, on November 30, 1864, he was one of seven seriously wounded Confederate generals; six others were killed.

Thomas M. Scott disappears from the record at this point. Apparently, he did not recover in time to see further action, and no record of his parole or pardon was found. After the war, he returned to Louisiana and became a sugar planter.

Scott's wife died in New Orleans in 1866. After that, he took to drinking heavily and essentially drank himself to death. He died in Sample Coffee Shop in New Orleans on April 21, 1876.

General Thomas M. Scott was buried in Greenwood Cemetery, New Orleans. As of 2007, his tombstone (if there was one) was gone, and his burial site was just a pile of small rocks. He now (as of 2020, that is) has a Confederate headstone.

WILLIAM READ "DIRTY NECK BILL" SCURRY

was born in Gallatin, Sumner County, Tennessee, on February 10, 1821. He moved to Texas in 1839 and received a land grant in the San Augustine area. He was admitted to the bar in 1840 and became a district attorney the following year. He represented Red River County in the Congress of the Republic of Texas (1844–45), where he advocated Texas's joining the Union.

In 1846, when the Mexican War broke out, he enlisted as a private in the 2nd Texas Mounted Rifle Regiment. Promoted to major on July 4, 1846, he distinguished himself in the Battle of Monterrey. After the war, he practiced law in Clinton, Texas, and was co-owner and editor of the Austin *State Gazette*, which he sold in 1854.

Scurry became a wealthy planter in the 1850s and owned dozens of slaves, but he came to view slavery as wrong. One night, he had an attack of conscience. He stayed up all night, pacing and debating with

·S

himself. The next morning, he freed his slaves—a tremendous material sacrifice for him, because they were worth more than a million dollars in today's money.

Though now opposed to slavery, Scurry had become a pro-secession Democrat. That made him a political opponent of Sam Houston, who saddled Scurry with the nickname "Dirty Neck (or Dirty Shirt) Bill." Bill Scurry was a member of the Texas Secession Convention and voted in favor of leaving the Union. In July 1861, he joined the Confederate Army as lieutenant colonel in the 4th Texas Cavalry. He distinguished himself in the New Mexico Campaign of 1861–62 and was de facto commander of the Confederate Army of New Mexico during the Battle of Glorieta Pass, where he was wounded but refused to leave the field. Scurry was promoted to full colonel effective March 28, 1862 and to brigadier general on September 12, 1862. He was sent to southeast Texas, where on January 1, 1863, he played a key role in helping General John B. Magruder recapture Galveston.

In October 1863, Scurry was named commander of the 3rd Brigade of John George Walker's Texas Division, the Greyhounds. Captain E. P. Petty said of Scurry, "I am well pleased with him. He is a fighter and those who follow him will go to the Cannon's mouth."

General Scurry took part in the Red River Campaign and fought in the decisive victory at Mansfield, as well as at Pleasant Hill. After this, the Texas Division was sent north to deal with the U.S. VII Corps. On April 30, 1864, Confederate General Edmund Kirby Smith launched an ill-advised attack at Jenkins' Ferry. General Scurry was wounded in the leg but refused to leave the field. Had he done so, surgeons might have been able to save his life, but Scurry was afraid that his absence would have a deleterious effect on the morale of his men. By the time he was taken to the rear, it was too late, and he died from a loss of blood. He was forty-three years old.

Scurry's body was taken back to Texas and buried on Republic Hill in Texas State Cemetery, Austin, Texas, where the Lone Star State inters its heroes. Scurry County, Texas, is named in his honor.

CLAUDIUS WISTAR SEARS was born in Peru, Massachusetts, on November 8, 1817. His father was a doctor. Claudius attended the U.S. Military Academy and graduated in 1841. Sears was assigned to the 8th U.S. Infantry and fought against the Seminoles in Florida but resigned after one year of service. He took a teaching position at an Episcopal military school in Mississippi and became a mathematics instructor at St. Thomas's Hall in Holly Springs in 1844. In 1845, he became a professor of mathematics and civil engineering at the University of Louisiana (now Tulane) in New Orleans. Sears later moved back to St. Thomas's Hall, where he became commandant of cadets and ultimately president of the institution.

Claudius Sears was a strong Democrat and secessionist. He joined the Confederate Army in May 1861 as a private in the 17th Mississippi. He was elected captain of Company G on June 5. He fought in the Battle of First Manassas, the Battle of Ball's Bluff, the Peninsula Campaign of 1862, the Battle of Seven Pines, the Seven Days Battles, and the Maryland Campaign, including the Battle of Sharpsburg. Sent to northern Mississippi, he took part in the Mississippi Central Campaign, during which he commanded the 46th Mississippi Infantry Regiment, and the Battle of Chickasaw Bluffs. He was promoted to colonel on December 11, 1862.

Colonel Sears was a fine commander and fought in the trenches at Vicksburg. He surrendered with the garrison on July 4, 1863.

In October 1863, he was exchanged and given command of a rebuilt 46th Mississippi under the command of General William Edwin Baldwin. Sent to Mobile, he became brigade commander when Baldwin was killed in a riding accident on February 19, 1864. Sears was promoted to brigadier general on March 1, 1864.

Sears's regiment joined the Army of Tennessee at Resaca on May 16 and was almost continuously engaged from then until September. Sears was wounded in the Battle of Adairsville on May 19 but returned to take part in the battles around Atlanta.

·S

General Sears was part of General John Bell Hood's Tennessee Campaign, in which he fought at Franklin and in the Third Battle of Murfreesboro. Sent to rejoin the main army at Nashville, he held a dangerous salient when it was overrun by a massive Union attack. Sears was sitting on a horse observing the battle through his binoculars when a cannonball struck his leg, tore it off, and killed his horse. Sears was evacuated, but the Confederate front collapsed, and he was captured near Pulaski, Tennessee, on December 27. He remained in prison camps for the rest of the war. He was paroled at Nashville, Tennessee, on June 23, 1865.

General Sears acquired a wooden leg that squeaked loudly on wooden floors. He resumed his teaching career and was a mathematics and civil engineering professor at the University of Mississippi from 1865 to 1889, when he retired. He died two years later, on February 15, 1891, at the age of seventy-three. He was buried in St. Peter's Cemetery, Oxford.

PAUL JONES SEMMES was born on Montford's Plantation in Wilkes County, northeast Georgia, on June 4, 1815. He was a cousin of Raphael Semmes, the commander of the CSS *Alabama*. Paul J. Semmes was educated at the University of Virginia, became a banker and planter in Wilkes County, and from 1837 to 1840, served as commander of the 1st Georgia Militia Brigade. He moved to Columbus, Georgia, where he prospered in business and became one of the most respected people in the city.

Throughout his life, he retained his interest in military affairs. In Columbus, he rejoined the Georgia Militia and was a member from 1846 to 1861, reaching the rank of colonel. When the Civil War approached, Governor Joseph E. Brown appointed him quartermaster general for the state. On April 25, 1861, fewer than two weeks after the Rebels fired on Fort Sumter, he was promoted to brigadier general, Georgia Militia.

S

On May 7, Semmes was elected colonel of the 2nd Georgia Infantry Regiment. It was ordered to Richmond on July 24, arriving there on July 29.

Paul Semmes was promoted to brigadier general and brigade commander on March 11, 1862. He fought at Williamsburg and Seven Pines and in the Seven Days Battles, helped defend Crampton's Gap during the Battle of South Mountain, was heavily engaged at Sharpsburg, and had his men arrayed on Marye's Hill at Fredericksburg. During the Battle of Chancellorsville, he fought Union General Joseph Hooker, then wheeled and met the forces of Union General John Sedgwick at Salem Church.

At Gettysburg, on July 2, 1863, Semmes led his brigade, as General Robert E. Lee reported, "with the courage that always distinguished him," when he was mortally wounded in the fighting for the Round Tops. He was transported back to Martinsburg, (West) Virginia, where he died on July 10, 1863. Among his last words were "I consider it a privilege to die for my country." He was forty-eight years old. Robert E. Lee recalled that he "died as he had lived, discharging the highest duty of a patriot with devotion that never faltered and courage that shrank from no danger."

General Semmes was first buried at Martinsburg, but his final resting place is in the Linwood Cemetery, Columbus, Georgia.

RAPHAEL SEMMES was born in Charles County, Maryland, near Washington, D.C., on September 27, 1809. He was a cousin of Confederate General Paul Jones Semmes. Orphaned at an early age, Raphael was raised by an uncle and grew up in Georgetown, Washington, D.C. He was educated at Charlotte Hall Military Academy and on April 1, 1826, became a midshipman in the U.S. Navy. He remained in the U.S. Navy more than thirty-four years. He studied law in his off-duty hours.

Semmes was posted to Mobile in 1842 and made Alabama his permanent onshore home. During the Mexican War, he fought in the Siege of Veracruz and served inland with General Winfield Scott's army. When Mexico City fell, Semmes was a volunteer aide to Brigadier General William J. Worth.

After the war, Semmes returned to Mobile and took an extended leave of absence, during which he practiced law and wrote two books about the war. He was promoted to commander in 1855 and in 1856 was stationed at Washington, D.C.

A strong supporter of states' rights who considered Alabama his home, he resigned his commission in the U.S. Navy on February 15, 1861, and accepted a commission as a commander in the Confederate Navy. On April 18, he was given command of the *Havana*, a former packet steamer, which he converted into a commerce destroyer, the CSS *Sumter*. It was not a sturdy vessel, but, nevertheless, in a matter of months, Semmes captured eighteen Union merchant ships, which he either burned or released on bond. Three Union warships blockaded the *Sumter* at Gibraltar, where Semmes had taken her for repairs, in January 1862. He and his officers eventually escaped, abandoning the vessel, and made their way to England. From there, Semmes traveled to the Azores, where he took command of another commerce raider, the *Alabama*.

Semmes was promoted to captain on August 21, 1862. From August 1862 to June 1864, Semmes and his men turned themselves into legends. They ranged across the Atlantic and Indian Oceans and the Gulf of Mexico, capturing sixty-four enemy ships. One they converted into a satellite raider. They also fought and sank the U.S. warship *Hatteras*. For more than a year, Semmes did not set foot on dry land.

The *Alabama* was finally sunk by the USS *Kearsarge* off the coast of Cherbourg, France, on June 19, 1864. Raphael Semmes, who was wounded in the hand, and forty-one of his men were picked up by a British yacht and three French boats and taken to London, where they were hailed as heroes, and Semmes published another book, *The Cruise of the* Alabama *and the* Sumter.

From England, Captain Semmes traveled to Cuba, then to the Texas coast, and finally overland to Richmond, Virginia, arriving in January 1865. On February 10, 1865, he was promoted to rear admiral, and eight days later was named commander of the James River Squadron, which guarded the river approach to the Confederate capital. On April 2, with Richmond on the brink of falling to the Federals, Semmes scuttled his squadron and formed a naval brigade to join with the Confederate Army. President Jefferson Davis appointed Admiral Semmes brigadier general (temporary rank) on April 5. His force linked up with Joseph E. Johnston's Army of the Tennessee and was with it when General Johnston surrendered at Bennett Place near Durham Station, North Carolina, on April 26, 1865. Semmes was a fine lawyer, and he insisted on being paroled as both a brigadier general and a rear admiral; this way, he could not be charged with piracy after the war.

Powerful Northern shipping interests and insurance companies had lost a great deal of money because of him and wanted him hanged. They used their influence to have him arrested for treason, piracy, and mistreating prisoners on December 15, 1865. The Radical Republican lawyers, however, could not find a way around his parole, so they released him on April 7, 1866.

After the war, Semmes was briefly a professor and a newspaper editor before returning to Mobile to practice law. He also wrote a book, *Memoirs of Service Afloat, During the War Between the States*. It was published in 1869 and popularized the term "War Between the States."

In 1871, the citizens of Mobile presented him with a home, which became known as the Raphael Semmes House. He lived there until his death on August 30, 1877, from food poisoning. He was buried in the Catholic Cemetery of Mobile. He was sixty-seven years old.

JACOB HUNTER SHARP was born in Pickensville, Alabama, on February 6, 1833. His family moved to Lowndes County, Mississippi, when he was a child. Jacob

·S

was educated in private schools, attended the University of Alabama for a year, and then returned to Mississippi and read law. He passed the bar exam and opened a practice in Columbus.

When Mississippi seceded, Jacob Sharp joined the Tombigbee Rangers in 1861 and was elected captain. The Rangers later became Company A of the 44th Mississippi Infantry Regiment, which was part of J. R. Chalmers's "High Pressure" Brigade. The regiment first saw action in the Battle of Belmont, where it attacked Union gunboats. It also fought at the Battle of Shiloh, where Captain Sharp was commended for his gallantry.

Sharp was again commended for his courage at Munfordville, where Confederate General Braxton Bragg captured a garrison of 4,148 men at a cost of 285 casualties. (It was perhaps Bragg's best performance of the war.) The regiment later took part in the Battle of Perryville, where it was lightly engaged.

Sharp was promoted to colonel and given command of the 44th Mississippi after the Second Battle of Murfreesboro (Stones River). He continued to distinguish himself in virtually all the battles of the Army of Tennessee. On May 14, 1864, early in the Atlanta Campaign, Sharp's brigade commander, General William F. Tucker, had his arm shattered at Resaca. Sharp led the "High Pressure" Brigade for the rest of what one historian called "the Hundred Days' battles." He was promoted to brigadier general on July 26, 1864. His performance was excellent.

Sharp continued to impress in the Battle of Franklin—where his men charged the Northern works after dark, fought hand-to-hand in the trenches, and captured three battle flags before they were beaten back—and at the Battle of Nashville. The brigade then retreated across the Tennessee River and was furloughed until February 14, 1865, when it reassembled in Meridian, Mississippi. Sharp and his men fought in the Carolinas Campaign, including the Battle of Bentonville. They surrendered with General Joseph E. Johnston on April 26, 1865; however, there is no record of General Sharp's parole.

After the war, Jacob Sharp returned to Columbus, practiced law, and contested Reconstruction as head of the Lowndes County Ku Klux Klan.

After home rule was reestablished, he was elected to the state legislature in 1886, 1888, 1890, 1892, 1900, and 1902, and served one term as speaker of the state house (1886–88). He ran for state treasurer of Mississippi in 1903 but was defeated.

From 1879, General Sharp was the owner and editor of the Columbus *Independent* newspaper and served a term as president of the Mississippi Press Association.

General Jacob H. Sharp died on September 15, 1907, in Columbus, Mississippi. He was seventy-four years old. He was buried in Friendship Cemetery, Columbus.

JOSEPH ORVILLE "JO" SHELBY was born in Lexington, Kentucky, on December 12, 1830. His family was one of the wealthiest and most influential in the state. He was educated at home and at Transylvania University. At age nineteen, he moved to Waverly, Lafayette County, Missouri, near Kansas City, where he purchased a rope factory and became a hemp planter. He also entered the steamboat business, opened a sawmill, and became wealthy in his own right.

During the "Bleeding Kansas" crisis of the mid-1850s, Shelby joined the pro-Southern side and organized a company of cavalry, the Blue Lodge. After General G. T. Beauregard fired on Fort Sumter in April 1861, Shelby formed the Lafayette County Mounted Rifles in support of Missouri Governor Claiborne Fox Jackson, who favored the Confederacy. Shelby was appointed captain in the Missouri State Guard in June and led his command in the Battle of Carthage, which was a minor Southern victory. From the beginning he proved to be a daring and enterprising commander. He fought at Wilson's Creek and Pea Ridge, where he especially distinguished himself, and took part in the Siege of Corinth. Next, he returned to Missouri and formed his own regiment, the 5th Missouri Cavalry, and formally became its colonel in June 1862. After successfully bringing his regiment back to

Arkansas, he was given command of a brigade, which consisted mostly of inexperienced recruits.

Jo Shelby fought at the Battle of Helena (July 4, 1863), where he had two horses shot out from under him, was badly wounded after a bullet shattered his wrist, and finally had to leave the field.

Shelby soon became a famous raider. After leaving Arkadelphia, Arkansas, on September 22, he inflicted 600 casualties on the enemy; severely damaged Union infrastructure; destroyed 10 Yankee forts; seized 600 modern rifles, 400 wagons, and 6,000 horses and mules; deprived the Federals of a massive amount of supplies and equipment; and prevented Arkansas-based Union troops from reinforcing General William Rosecrans, who was besieged in Chattanooga, Tennessee. Shelby's losses were about 100 men. By the time Shelby returned to Confederate lines on October 3, 1863, he and his men had traveled 1,500 miles. Shelby's giant raid restored Confederate morale in Arkansas, and he was promoted to brigadier general on December 15, 1863.

During U.S. General Frederick Steele's Camden Expedition in 1864, Shelby wreaked havoc on the Union rear, helped destroy his supply trains in the Battle of Marks' Mills, and played a significant role in defeating the Federal invasion.

Shelby commanded a division in Sterling Price's Missouri Raid, in which he captured several small Union garrisons and saved most of Price's wagons when they retreated to Texas through Kansas and the Indian Territory. He also distinguished himself in the battles of Little Blue River and Westport. He returned to Arkansas in December.

General Shelby's men adored him, and about one thousand of them followed him to Mexico after the war. His plan to join the army of the Emperor Ferdinand Maximilian failed because the emperor refused to accept the Confederate forces, but he did grant them land in what was called the "New Virginia Colony" near Veracruz. After Maximilian was overthrown and executed, the land grant was revoked by the new Mexican government, so Shelby returned to Missouri in 1867 and became a farmer.

Shelby's adjutant was John Newman Edwards. He was later editor of the *Kansas City Times* and a prolific writer who was largely responsible for creating the legend of Jesse James and, to a certain extent, the legend of Jo Shelby. His book *Shelby and His Men: Or, the War in the West* was published in 1867 and sold many copies. It was one of the first "Lost Cause" books and as history should be handled with care. In *Shelby and His Men*, the general appears to be a combination of superhero and Sir Galahad. But many people, especially in Missouri, accepted it as gospel.

Shelby was enormously popular in his state but refused all political office (which he could easily have won) until 1893, when President Grover Cleveland appointed him U.S. marshal for the Western District of Missouri. He retained this position until his death, which occurred in Adrian, Missouri, on February 13, 1897. He was sixty-six years old. General Shelby is buried in Forest Hill Cemetery, Kansas City, Missouri.

CHARLES MILLER SHELLEY was born on December 28, 1833, in Sullivan County, Tennessee. His father moved the family to Alabama when he was three. He appreticed as an architect and builder in Selma and by 1860 had a brickmaking and plastering business.

In February 1861, Charles Shelley joined the Confederate Army as a lieutenant in the Talladega Artillery. On May 11, 1861, he became a captain in the 5th Alabama, which was organized at Camp Jeff Davis in Montgomery.

The regiment took part in the Battle of First Manassas, where it was lightly engaged. In early 1862, Shelley returned to Alabama and helped recruit and organize the 30th Alabama Infantry Regiment. He was elected its colonel on March 22, 1862.

The 30th was sent to the Cumberland Gap and took part in the Kentucky Campaign of 1862. In December 1862, it was transferred to northern Mississippi, where it was heavily engaged in the battles of Port

Gibson and Champion Hill in May 1863. Stephen Dill Lee, his brigade commander, singled out Colonel Shelley as a hero at Champion Hill.

The regiment retreated into the fortress of Vicksburg, where it helped repulse U.S. General Ulysses Grant's frontal assaults of May 19 and 22, 1863. It was engaged in near continuous skirmishing until July 4, when the fortress surrendered.

Shelley was soon exchanged and joined the rebuilt 30th Alabama. The regiment took part in every major engagement of the Army of Tennessee from Chattanooga to Bentonville. Shelley was an acting brigade commander during the Battle of Jonesboro, performed well, and was promoted to brigadier general on September 17, 1864. After the fall of Atlanta, he commanded a brigade in General John Bell Hood's Tennessee Campaign. At Franklin, the brigade lost 670 men out of 1,100 engaged. The general himself was not seriously injured, but his horse was shot out from under him, and several bullets pierced his uniform. Confederate General Alexander P. Stewart was lavish in his praise of Shelley's adroit tactical maneuvering, which he credited with saving his entire corps. General Hood's report also made special mention of Shelley.

General Shelley fought at Nashville and in the subsequent retreat to Mississippi. He then marched the remnants of his command to North Carolina, where he fought in the Army of Tennessee's last campaign. He surrendered with General Joseph E. Johnston at Bennett Place on April 26, 1865, and was paroled at Greensboro on May 1.

Despite his humble beginnings, limited formal education, and total lack of military training in 1861, Charles Miller Shelley proved to be both a fine commander and a popular one. After the surrender, he returned to Selma and was elected sheriff of Dallas County.

General Shelley was elected to Congress and served from 1877 to 1885. He then moved to Birmingham and promoted industrial development.

Charles M. Shelley died of stomach cancer in Birmingham on January 20, 1907, at age seventy-three. He was buried in Oak Hill Cemetery, Talladega.

FRANCIS ASBURY SHOUP was born on March 22, 1834, in Franklin County, Indiana; he was the oldest of nine children. He attended Indiana Asbury (now DePauw) University and then West Point, from which he graduated in the class of 1855. Commissioned a brevet second lieutenant of artillery, he served in Florida and South Carolina before his parents died in early 1860. He resigned his commission and returned home to Indiana to take care of his brothers and sisters. He studied law and was admitted to the bar later that year.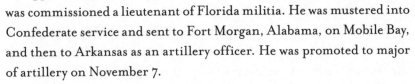

Shoup supported states' rights, believed that secession was legal, and admired the Southern people. As the war approached, he moved to St. Augustine, Florida, and was commissioned a lieutenant of Florida militia. He was mustered into Confederate service and sent to Fort Morgan, Alabama, on Mobile Bay, and then to Arkansas as an artillery officer. He was promoted to major of artillery on November 7.

Shoup commanded an artillery battalion of twenty-one guns at Shiloh (April 6–7, 1862). He did so well that General G. T. Beauregard appointed him chief of artillery of the Army of Mississippi on April 10. On June 8, he was promoted to colonel and sent to Arkansas, where he served on the staff of General Tom Hindman and later General Theophilus Holmes. He was promoted to brigadier general on September 12. On December 7, 1862, he commanded a division at the Battle of Prairie Grove. In April 1863, he was sent to Alabama as chief of artillery for the Department of the Gulf. On May 3, General John C. Pemberton named him commander of the Louisiana Brigade at Vicksburg, where Shoup defended Graveyard Road, and successfully repulsed U.S. General Ulysses Grant's assaults on May 19 and 22. Pemberton surrendered Vicksburg on July 4, and Shoup was exchanged on October 13.

In late March 1864, Shoup was transferred to Georgia, where he was named chief of artillery of the Army of Tennessee. He commanded the Rebel artillery until July 24, when he became chief of staff for General John Bell Hood and served in that position until December 1864.

·S

On February 21, 1865, Shoup became chief of staff of the Department of South Carolina, Georgia, and Florida, and strongly advocated recruiting black soldiers to fight for the Confederacy, offering them their freedom in exchange, but as with other such proposals, it was never implemented to any important degree. After General Joseph E. Johnston surrendered, Shoup was paroled at Greensboro on May 2, 1865.

After the war, Shoup was a professor of mathematics at the University of Mississippi (1865–68). In 1868, he became an Episcopal priest and the following year accepted a position at the University of the South in Sewanee, Tennessee. Shoup later did parish work in New York, Tennessee, and New Orleans. He returned to the classroom at Sewanee in 1883 and remained a professor there until his death on September 4, 1896. He was sixty-two years old. He is buried in the University of the South Cemetery, Sewanee.

General Shoup's great-grandson was General David M. Shoup, who earned the Congressional Medal of Honor during World War II and was later commandant of the Marine Corps from 1960 to 1963.

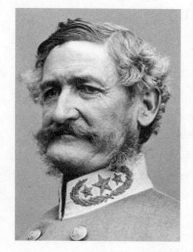

HENRY HOPKINS SIBLEY was born in Natchitoches, Louisiana, on May 25, 1816. He was admitted to West Point in 1833, graduated in 1838, and was commissioned a second lieutenant of dragoons. He fought Seminoles in the Everglades, and, during the Mexican War, he distinguished himself fighting from Veracruz to Mexico City, earning a brevet promotion to major.

Sibley was an innovative officer. In 1855, he invented the Sibley Tent, which housed twelve. It was adopted by the U.S. Army and the British Army, and he received a patent for it in 1856. It was based on a design of a tepee used by the Plains Indians. He also invented the Sibley Tent Stove, which was designed to heat it. A modified version of the stove was still being used by the U.S. Army in World War II.

He was promoted to major on May 16, 1861, and "went south" the same day. He was appointed colonel in the Confederate Regular Army. In June, Sibley met with President Jefferson Davis and urged him to conquer New Mexico. Davis approved the idea and promoted Sibley to brigadier general on June 17, 1861.

Placed in charge of a West Texas cavalry brigade, Sibley promptly dubbed his command the Army of New Mexico and invaded the territory. He intended to establish a supply base here and advance north into Colorado to capture the territory's gold and silver mines. Ultimately, he hoped to capture Southern California's ports and thus break the Northern blockade of the Confederacy. Sibley did not, however, have even a fraction of the men he needed for such a grandiose plan, which was at best unrealistic and at worst logistically impossible.

Sibley's campaign in New Mexico was a disaster, and he revealed himself to be an alcoholic, often too drunk to lead his men, who soon viewed their commanding general with contempt. They nicknamed him the "Walking Whiskey Keg."

In early July 1862, he was officially charged with being drunk on duty, cowardice, and misappropriation of goods. President Davis, however, dismissed the charges and sent Sibley and his Arizona Brigade of almost four thousand men to New Iberia, Louisiana, to join the forces of General Richard Taylor. Taylor appreciated the reinforcements, but not their lack of discipline or their general. After Sibley committed several blunders during the Bayou Teche Campaign, Taylor relieved him of his command on April 23, 1863. Moreover, he filed charges against Sibley, and in August a general court-martial censured him. Theophilus Noel, a reporter for the *Richmond Inquirer* and the New Orleans *Picayune*, stated that Sibley's "love of liquor exceeded that for home, country, or God."

Sibley spent the rest of the war either unemployed or in positions of minimum responsibility, such as directing wagon trains. He was pardoned in Shreveport, Louisiana, on June 8, 1865.

After the war, Henry H. Sibley hired out as a mercenary, and from December 1869 to September 30, 1873, was a brigadier general of

·S

THE ENCYCLOPEDIA OF CONFEDERATE GENERALS

artillery in the Egyptian Army and military advisor to Isma'il Pasha, the Khedive of Egypt, and was placed in charge of Egypt's coastal fortifications. He was sent home for alcoholism and indebtedness.

From 1874, he lived with his daughter in Fredericksburg, Virginia. By 1883, he was practically an invalid. General Sibley died in poverty on August 23, 1886, at the age of seventy. He is buried in the Confederate Cemetery in Fredericksburg, Virginia.

JAMES PHILLIP SIMMS was born on January 16, 1837, in Covington, Georgia, and, except for the war years, remained there practically his entire life. Little is known of his childhood or early education except that he studied law and was admitted to the bar.

Simms entered Confederate service on October 21, 1861, as a second lieutenant in the 6th Georgia Militia Regiment. By April 1862, he was a first lieutenant in the 42nd Georgia. He transferred to the 53rd Georgia and was promoted to captain on August 20.

James Simms fought in the Seven Days Battles and the Maryland Campaign and at Fredericksburg, mostly as part of Lafayette McLaws's division. On September 24, 1862, Simms was promoted to major and on October 8 became colonel and commander of the 53rd Georgia.

Colonel Simms and his men distinguished themselves in the Battle of Salem Church (part of the Battle of Chancellorsville), capturing the colors of the 2nd Rhode Island. At Gettysburg, Simms's regiment was heavily engaged around Rose Hill and the Wheatfield. The 53rd Georgia took part in the early stages of the Siege of Chattanooga and in the Siege of Knoxville. Simms led one of the attacks on Fort Sanders and was wounded. It took him some weeks to recover, but he was back in command of the regiment during the battles of the Wilderness, Spotsylvania Court House, and North Anna, as well as the Siege of Petersburg.

On August 6, 1864, Simms and his men were sent to the Shenandoah Valley with Joseph Kershaw's division. Simms became acting brigade commander on September 20, 1864, when General Goode Bryan resigned for medical reasons. Simms performed well at the Battle of Cedar Creek on October 19 and was promoted to brigadier general on December 8, 1864.

Simms's brigade returned to the trenches around Petersburg and remained there until Union General Ulysses S. Grant finally broke Robert E. Lee's line on April 2, 1865. Simms and his command joined the retreat to Appomattox until April 6, 1865, when most of the brigade was captured at Sayler's Creek, including General Simms. He was imprisoned at Fort Warren, Massachusetts, until July 24, 1865, when he was released.

James P. Simms returned to Covington and resumed his law practice. He was elected to the legislature in 1865 but lost his seat to the carpetbaggers in 1867. After home rule was restored, he was reelected in 1877. General Simms died in Covington on May 30, 1887, at age fifty. He is buried there in Southview Cemetery.

Simms was like many of Robert E. Lee's brigadiers during the last year of the war: he obtained his rank through attrition. Still, even if Simms lacked superior military training, innate martial gifts, or tactical or strategic brilliance, he was steady, competent, reliable, and courageous. Every army needs officers like General Simms.

WILLIAM YARNEL SLACK was born in Mason County, Kentucky, on August 1, 1816. His father was a potter who moved his family to Missouri in 1819. William received his education from local schools, read law in Columbia, Missouri, and was admitted to the bar in 1837. Slack moved to Chillicothe in Livingston County in March 1839.

Slack was a member of the Missouri legislature (1842–43) and a delegate to the constitutional convention in 1845. When the Mexican War broke out, he helped organize a company of Livingston County volunteers, who elected him captain. Assigned to Sterling

Price's regiment, he fought in the Taos Revolt in 1847 and took part in the occupation of Santa Fe.

After the war, Captain Slack returned home, practiced law quite successfully, entered business, and became one of the wealthiest and most influential citizens in Livingston County. He was a strong Southern Democrat and supported slavery. In 1861, as Missouri divided into pro-Union and pro-Confederate factions, Governor Claiborne F. Jackson, the leader of the secession movement, appointed Slack commander of the 4th Missouri State Guard Division with the rank of brigadier general, effective May 18, 1861.

General Slack assembled his command at Chillicothe and joined Sterling Price, now the commander in chief of the Missouri State Guard, at Lexington in June.

With his lean, stern appearance and firmly set jaw, Slack looked like a tough and capable warrior. In his case, looks were not deceiving. He was one of Price's best commanders. He fought in the Confederate victory at Carthage, where he commanded seven hundred men. He also distinguished himself at Wilson's Creek on August 10, 1861, where he was seriously wounded. He was officially commended for his "gallant conduct" during this victory.

Slack resumed command of his division on October 11 and took part in the campaigning in southwestern Missouri during the winter of 1861–62. Meanwhile, the Missouri State Guard was absorbed into the Confederate Army, and Price named him commander of the 2nd Missouri Brigade on January 23, 1862.

Professor Hal Bridges of the University of Arkansas has noted of him as a commander, "Slack revealed rare qualities: utter fearlessness on the battlefield, and the ability to inspire enduring loyalty in his men."

On March 7, 1862, during the Battle of Pea Ridge, General Slack was shot through the right hip, almost exactly where he was shot at Wilson's Creek. An aide took him to a house near the battlefield; later he was moved to a house seven miles away. He died there on the morning of March 21, 1862. He was forty-five years old. President Jefferson Davis appointed Slack brigadier general on April 12, 1862, and his nomination was confirmed by the Senate five days later. Because they did not normally grant posthumous promotions, it is highly doubtful that either Davis or the Confederate Senate knew he was dead.

General Slack was buried eight miles east of the Pea Ridge battle site. In 1880, his body was reinterred in Fayetteville Confederate Cemetery in Fayetteville, Arkansas.

JAMES EDWIN SLAUGHTER was born in June 1827 in Culpeper County, Virginia, on his father's estate, which later became the battlefield of Cedar Mountain, also known as Slaughter's Mountain. Both his mother and father were descended from the First Families of Virginia. President James Monroe was James Slaughter's great-uncle.

Slaughter enrolled in the Virginia Military Institute at Lexington in 1845 but resigned on July 6, 1846, to accept a commission as a second lieutenant in the newly formed 1st Voltigeurs Regiment. He was soon on his way to Mexico. Lieutenant Slaughter fought at Contreras, marched across the Pedregal, and took part in the battles of Churubusco, Molino del Rey, and Chapultepec and the capture of Mexico City.

The Voltigeurs Regiment remained in Mexico City on occupation duty until mid-1848, when it was disbanded. Lieutenant Slaughter was transferred to the 1st U.S. Artillery Regiment and served with it until 1861, when he became a first lieutenant of artillery in the Confederate Regular Army.

In July 1861, he was promoted to captain and served with General Braxton Bragg at Pensacola as an assistant inspector general. From November 6, 1861, to March 13, 1862, he was a major, the assistant adjutant general, and the de facto chief of staff of the Army of Pensacola. During this period, he played a key role in defending Pensacola and bombarding Fort Pickens. General G. T. Beauregard, the department commander, was so pleased with Slaughter's performance that he strongly

S

recommended Slaughter's promotion to brigadier general. The appointment was granted on March 11, 1862, to date from March 8.

Slaughter was assistant inspector general for General Albert Sidney Johnston at the Battle of Shiloh and in May was named chief of the inspector general's department of the Army of Mississippi and took part in the Kentucky Campaign, which ended in the indecisive Battle of Perryville. He was then transferred to Mobile and, from October 1862 to April 1863, was a brigade commander and later artillery commander for the District of the Gulf, which headquartered at Mobile.

He contracted severe laryngitis in November 1862. For a full year, he could not speak above a whisper and was limited in his duties. His surgeon recommended he be transferred to a drier climate, and General Slaughter was named chief of artillery for the District of Texas, New Mexico, and Arizona on April 20, 1863, serving under General John B. Magruder. He also later served as Magruder's chief of staff and was appointed as commander in charge of defending East Texas, though for several months he was sick and not present for duty.

Slaughter commanded Confederate forces in the Battle of Palmito Ranch (May 12–13, 1865), where he smashed a Union column driving on Brownsville. Slaughter suffered no fatal casualties, only five or six wounded and three captured. The Yankees lost about thirty killed and more than one hundred captured. The Battle of Palmito Ranch had no strategic or operational significance and was only important because it was the last battle of the Civil War.

Shortly after that engagement, General Slaughter crossed the border into Mexico rather than surrender. He remained in Mexico for several years working as a civil engineer. When he returned to the United States, he lived in Mobile and was its postmaster before moving to New Orleans.

Brigadier General James E. Slaughter died while on a visit to his extended family in Mexico City on New Year's Day, 1901. He was seventy-three years old. He was buried in the Mexico City National Cemetery, along with unidentified American soldiers killed in the 1846–48 conflict. General Slaughter never married.

EDMUND "TED" KIRBY SMITH was born in St. Augustine, Florida, on May 16, 1824. His father sent him to a West Point preparatory school in northern Virginia, and he entered West Point in 1841. Overcoming weak vision (which almost got him dismissed), he graduated in 1845, earning the nickname "Seminole" because he was from Florida and had a swarthy complexion. He was commissioned in the infantry.

Kirby Smith fought in the Mexican War with Generals Zachary Taylor and Winfield Scott and was brevetted first lieutenant for his actions at Cerro Gordo and to brevet captain for his conduct at Contreras and Churubusco.

After the Mexican surrender, Kirby Smith strongly considered resigning from the army and becoming a Christian minister. But he remained in the service, joined the cavalry on the Texas frontier, and gained a reputation as an Indian fighter. He was promoted to captain in 1855 and to major in 1861.

Kirby Smith resigned his commission on April 6, 1861. He was immediately offered a lieutenant colonelcy in the Confederate Army. He was promoted to brigadier general on June 17, 1861, and given command of the 4th Brigade of the Army of the Shenandoah.

Five minutes after taking the field at the Battle of First Manassas, on July 21, 1861, he was badly wounded and could not return to active field duty until October, when General Joseph E. Johnston appointed him a division commander, and he was promoted to major general. On February 5, 1862, Kirby Smith became a commander of the Army of East Tennessee (briefly dubbed the Army of Kentucky) and took part in the Kentucky Campaign of 1862. He distinguished himself in the Battle of Richmond (August 29–30, 1862), where he led the last charge and routed a numerically superior Union force, inflicting 5,353 casualties on the Federals (most of whom were captured) while suffering losses of only 451 men. Though the Kentucky Campaign ultimately failed, in large part because of a lack of coordination

S

between the forces of Braxton Bragg and Kirby Smith, Smith was promoted to lieutenant general on October 9, 1862. He was only thirty-eight years old.

After briefly commanding a corps in Bragg's army, Smith was appointed commander of the Trans-Mississippi Department on January 14, 1863, a post he held for the rest of the war. He was promoted to full general on February 19, 1864.

Edmund Kirby Smith looked older than he was. He was tall and had a thick, black beard, graying hair, and a receding forehead. He wore spectacles, which made him look scholarly. He was a man of immense energy and was affable and exhibited good manners; however, as an aide noted, he possessed no "remarkable intellectual endowments." He was not a successful commander in this department. He failed to cooperate with John C. Pemberton against Ulysses S. Grant in the Vicksburg Campaign, and he was partly responsible for the fall of the city. He did try to attack Grant's supply line at Milliken's Bend (June 7, 1863), but by the time Kirby Smith moved, it was far too late.

Kirby Smith also failed to cooperate with the fractious Richard Taylor, the commander of the Army of Western Louisiana—although this was probably more Taylor's fault than Smith's. Kirby Smith did withhold two Arkansas divisions from Taylor during the Battle of Mansfield, refused to give him the floating bridge companies he so desperately needed, and—after Taylor's incredible victory at Mansfield—stripped him of three of his four infantry divisions and sent them to Arkansas, where they accomplished little. This arguably allowed General Nathaniel Banks to escape, while Kirby Smith made a futile and unsuccessful attempt to destroy Frederick Steele's VII Corps.

Following the escapes of Banks and Steele, the war in the Trans-Mississippi Department was basically over. Kirby Smith was a decent administrator, but there was little he could do to help the Confederate forces east of the Mississippi River. General Simon B. Buckner, his chief of staff, surrendered the department on May 26, 1865. Kirby Smith fled into exile in Mexico and later Cuba. He returned to the United States in 1866.

Kirby Smith became an educator, serving first as president of the Western Military Academy, then as chancellor of the University of Nashville (1870–75), and finally as professor of mathematics at the University of the South in Sewanee, Tennessee, from 1875 until his death on March 28, 1893, at the age of sixty-eight. He was the last full general on either side to pass away. He is buried in the University of the South Cemetery, Sewanee, Tennessee.

GUSTAVUS WOODSON SMITH was born in Georgetown, Kentucky, on November 30, 1821, into a family of prosperous farmers. He entered West Point at age sixteen and graduated in 1842. He was commissioned in the engineers and was named an assistant on the construction of fortifications for the harbor of New London, Connecticut, and later as acting assistant professor of engineering at West Point. He commanded an engineer company with General Winfield Scott from Veracruz to Mexico City and was brevetted first lieutenant after Cerro Gordo and captain after Contreras.

Smith resigned his commission in 1854 and became a civil engineer. He was named street commissioner for New York City in 1858. He was active in Democratic Party politics in New York and worked ardently against the election of Republican Abraham Lincoln in the presidential election of 1860. He feared that Lincoln's election would lead to secession.

In the spring of 1861, Smith visited friends in Kentucky. While there, he learned that the Lincoln regime intended to arrest him, so he submitted his resignation as street commissioner and "went south." He was commissioned as a major general in the Confederate Army on September 19, 1861, and given command of the II Corps in Joseph E. Johnston's Army of the Potomac.

He proved to be a highly "political" officer, first acting as a yes-man for General G. T. Beauregard and then serving the same role for General Joseph E. Johnston, even rewriting, at Johnston's insistence, his

S

account of the Battle of Seven Pines to shift blame from General James Longstreet to General Benjamin Huger.

During the Peninsula Campaign, General Smith's performance was mediocre, and he tended to fall sick at critical times. Some questioned his courage, others thought he feared responsibility, and still others believed he suffered from a neurological condition, with stress bringing on bouts of temporary paralysis (something he had suffered even as a civilian). He nevertheless assumed command of the army after Joseph E. Johnston was wounded on May 31, 1862.

G. W. Smith commanded the army for one day. President Jefferson Davis showed up at headquarters and asked for a situation report. Smith's answer was incoherent babble. The president was shocked. On the way back to Richmond, he appointed Robert E. Lee commander of the army. General Lee promptly got rid of Gustavus Woodson Smith. He never again held an important combat command.

Smith was placed in charge of the Richmond defenses after Lee's victories in the Seven Days Battles, when the capital was no longer threatened. From November 17 to 21, 1862, he was interim secretary of war, following the resignation of George W. Randolph and before the arrival of James A. Seddon. Smith, meanwhile, became increasingly angry, because junior officers were being promoted over him. He resigned his commission on February 17, 1863. Neither Lee nor Davis made any attempt to talk him out of it.

On June 1, 1864, Governor Joseph Brown of Georgia appointed Smith major general of the Georgia Militia, a post which he held until the end of the war. He operated on the fringe of Union General William T. Sherman's March to the Sea, including the evacuation of Savannah, where he performed brilliantly in securing the Confederates' route of retreat. Along with part of his militia, he surrendered at Macon, Georgia, on April 20, 1865.

After the war, G. W. Smith worked as a manager for an iron firm in Tennessee before becoming insurance commissioner for Kentucky, a position he held from 1870 to 1876, after which he moved to New York, where he pursued business interests and wrote articles and books covering life insurance (on which he was an acknowledged authority) and the late war.

General Smith died in New York City on June 24, 1896, at the age of seventy-four. He is buried in Cedar Grove Cemetery, New London, Connecticut.

JAMES ARGYLE SMITH was born on July 1, 1831, in Maury County, south-central Tennessee. He attended West Point and graduated in 1853 as a second lieutenant of infantry. Smith served on the Western frontier from 1853 to 1861 and fought against Mormons in Utah and Lakota Sioux in Nebraska.

On May 9, 1861, three days after Tennessee passed its ordinance of secession, James A. Smith resigned his commission. He was immediately commissioned as a captain in the Confederate Army and appointed assistant adjutant general to General Leonidas Polk. He was promoted to major on March 21, 1862, and to lieutenant colonel of the 2nd Tennessee Infantry Regiment after the Battle of Shiloh in April 1862. In September, James Smith was promoted to colonel and given command of the 5th Confederate Infantry Regiment.

He distinguished himself in the Battle of Perryville. His division commander reported, "The fire of the Fifth Confederate regiment was particularly destructive, plainly thinning the enemy's ranks at every volley. Three times the flag of the enemy was cut down, and finally they were beaten back utterly whipped."

During the Second Battle of Murfreesboro, Smith again distinguished himself. He took part in the Tullahoma Campaign and the Battle of Chickamauga. After Brigadier General James Deshler was killed in action on September 20, Smith took command of his Texas brigade, which was part of Patrick Cleburne's division. He was promoted to brigadier general on September 30, 1863.

·S

During the Battle of Missionary Ridge, General Smith launched a counterattack against Sherman's flank, which prevented him from cutting off General Braxton Bragg's retreat. Smith was shot through both thighs in this battle. He was sent to Atlanta to recuperate and could not return to field duty until mid-July 1864. During the Battle of Atlanta (July 22), he overran three lines of Union trenches and captured fifteen artillery pieces. He was, however, wounded again. After he recovered, he was placed in command of a Georgia brigade.

Smith rejoined the Army of Tennessee at Tuscumbia, Alabama, in November 1864. He took part in the Franklin-Nashville Campaign. When General Cleburne was killed in action during the Battle of Franklin, Smith assumed command of the division, which he led at Nashville. He and his men were part of John Bell Hood's retreat to Tupelo, Mississippi. He then marched to North Carolina with the remnants of the Army of Tennessee in early 1865. He led half of General Benjamin Cheatham's corps at Bentonville (March 19–21, 1865), where he performed brilliantly.

Smith surrendered with the Army of Tennessee at Bennett's Place, North Carolina, on April 26, 1865. He was paroled in Greensboro on May 1.

After the war, James Smith settled in Mississippi, where he started a farm. He was elected state superintendent of education and served from 1878 to 1886. Later, he became an agent of the Bureau of Indian Affairs (1893–97). He also served as marshal of the Mississippi Supreme Court. General Smith died on December 6, 1901, in Jackson, Mississippi, at age seventy. He is buried in Greenwood Cemetery, Jackson.

He was among the best brigade and division commanders of the Civil War.

MARTIN LUTHER SMITH was born in Danby, New York, on September 9, 1819. He entered West Point in 1838 and graduated in 1842. He started his career as a topographical engineer, assigned to Florida and Georgia, where he improved coastal defenses and navigation.

During the Mexican War, he joined General Winfield Scott's engineer staff, where he worked with Robert E. Lee, G. T. Beauregard, and George B. McClellan. His most noteworthy accomplishment was reconnoitering and mapping the approaches and defenses of Mexico City. For this contribution, he was brevetted first lieutenant.

Smith's subsequent engineering assignments took him to Texas, Georgia, and Florida. By 1861, Martin Luther Smith was unquestionably one of the finest military engineers in the country. He resigned his commission in the U.S. Army on April 1 and was appointed a major of engineers in the Confederate Army. He was posted to New Orleans, where he was chief engineer of Fort Jackson and Fort St. Philip on the Mississippi River and later commander of the 21st Louisiana Infantry Regiment, which carried with it a promotion to colonel.

Smith was promoted to brigadier general on April 11, 1862. Despite his lack of command experience, Smith was named commander of Vicksburg after the fall of New Orleans in late April. He was commander of the fortress city for more than a year, which included the First Siege of Vicksburg, (May 18 to July 27, 1862).

In December 1862, Union General William T. Sherman tried to take Vicksburg via a surprise amphibious assault. The key position was Chickasaw Bluffs, eight miles north of the city. But when Sherman finally launched his major attack on December 29, Smith was waiting for him. The Yankees lost 1,900 men in this battle; Smith lost 200.

When the second siege began on May 18, 1863, General John C. Pemberton was in overall command, and Smith's division held his northern flank. It repulsed two major attacks from Sherman and the Union XV Corps and held its positions until the city surrendered.

After Vicksburg, Smith was taken prisoner and not exchanged until March 1864. On April 5, he was named chief engineer for Robert E. Lee's Army of Northern Virginia and proved invaluable as both a scout and engineer. It was his reconnaissance that allowed Confederate General James Longstreet to roll up Union General Winfield Scott Hancock's left flank during the Battle of the Wilderness. Smith developed much of the Confederate defensive line at Spotsylvania Court House and proposed using the bluffs on the south bank of the North Anna River as a major defensive position. This fortification was so strong that even a commander as aggressive as Union General Ulysses Grant refused to attack it.

On July 20, 1864, General Smith was named chief engineer of the Army of Tennessee, a post that he held until Atlanta fell. He was then ordered to erect defenses for Macon, Columbus, Augusta, and finally the forts around Mobile. He was again named chief engineer of the Army of Tennessee on December 4, 1864. He surrendered with the army on April 26, 1865. General Smith was paroled at Macon on May 8.

After the war, Martin Luther Smith worked as a civil engineer until July 29, 1866 (the day after his twentieth wedding anniversary), when he suddenly died in Savannah, Georgia, at age forty-six. He was buried in Oconee Hill Cemetery, Athens, Georgia.

PRESTON SMITH was born on December 25, 1823, in Giles County, Tennessee. He was educated in local schools and at Jackson College in Columbia, Tennessee. He studied law in Columbia, was admitted to the bar, and practiced for a time in Waynesboro, Tennessee. He eventually settled in Memphis, where he was highly successful, but he shut down his office after Tennessee seceded.

In May 1861, Smith was elected colonel of the 154th Tennessee Militia. He remained in command after the regiment was incorporated into the Confederate Army later that month; however, the Richmond government required that the designation "senior" be added to it, so it became the 154th Senior Tennessee Infantry Regiment.

Colonel Smith led his regiment in the Battle of Shiloh on April 6 and 7, 1862, until he caught a minié ball in his right shoulder. He was

S

out of action until May 14, when he returned to duty as a brigade commander in Patrick Cleburne's division of the Army of Mississippi.

Smith participated in Braxton Bragg's Kentucky Campaign of 1862 and distinguished himself in the Battle of Richmond. Although only a colonel, he assumed temporary command of the division after General Cleburne was wounded. He was promoted to brigadier general on October 27, 1862.

General Preston Smith led a brigade in the Second Battle of Murfreesboro, the Tullahoma Campaign, and Bragg's Chickamauga offensive, where he led a night attack in support of General James Deshler's brigade. Night attacks were rare in the Civil War, because darkness greatly inhibited a commander's ability to control his forces, and in the confusion, General Smith blundered into the Union lines. He was shot in the chest and fell from his horse. The general was alive when his men found him, but he died less than an hour later.

General Benjamin Cheatham, his division commander, praised Smith as "[a]ctive, energetic and brave, with a rare fitness to command, full of honorable ambition in perfect harmony with the most elevated patriotism," and added, "[T]he whole country will mourn his fall."

Brigadier General Preston Smith was thirty-nine years old. His body was taken from the field and buried in Atlanta. In 1868, it was exhumed and reinterred in Elmwood Cemetery, Memphis, Tennessee.

THOMAS "TOM" BENTON SMITH was born on February 24, 1838, probably in Rutherford County, Tennessee, near the community of Triune. His father was a carpenter who made cotton gins. The family owned 105 acres and lived in a two-room log house. At age fifteen, Smith invented and patented a cowcatcher for locomotives.

Smith was educated in local schools, the Nashville Military Academy, and, for a year, at West Point. He returned to Tennessee and worked for the Nashville and Decatur Railroad.

In the spring of 1861, after Tennessee's secession, Smith helped raise a militia company at Triune. It became Company B of the 20th Tennessee Infantry Regiment, and Smith was elected second lieutenant but was soon promoted to first lieutenant. He was described as "the beau ideal of a soldier."

Smith first saw action in the Battle of Fishing Creek (January 1862), where General Felix Zollicoffer was killed. His regiment fought one of its hardest battles at Shiloh, where it lost 187 of its 400 men. When the regiment reformed at Corinth on May 8, Tom Smith was elected colonel.

The 20th Tennessee fought in the First Siege of Vicksburg (1862), the Battle of Baton Rouge, and the Second Battle of Murfreesboro, where he was seriously wounded on January 2, 1863, when a bullet cut across his chest and penetrated his left arm.

After participating in the Tullahoma Campaign, Smith fought at Chickamauga, where he was again wounded in the arm on September 19. He remained in command during the subsequent Siege of Chattanooga. During the Battle of Missionary Ridge, Colonel Robert C. Tyler, his brigade commander, was seriously wounded. Thomas Smith replaced him and led the brigade for the next thirteen months. He was promoted to brigadier general (temporary rank) on July 29, 1864.

The brigade participated in the Atlanta Campaign and in General John Bell Hood's ensuing march into Tennessee. It fought at Franklin, in the Third Battle of Murfreesboro (where it greatly impressed General Nathan Bedford Forrest), and at Nashville, where it was overwhelmed by vastly superior forces and Smith was captured.

A drunken Union colonel cursed and abused Smith, now an unarmed prisoner of war, and struck him in the head with his sword—three times before he was stopped. Smith suffered permanent brain damage. Smith remained a prisoner and was transferred to Fort Warren in Boston Harbor. He was paroled and released on July 24, 1865.

When he returned home, he was employed as a brakeman, freight conductor, and passenger conductor and even made an unsuccessful run for Congress. After his mother's death, however, he fell into deep depression, his mind deteriorated further (to the point of declaring himself an Indian chief, riding naked on a horse, and threatening people with bows and arrows), and in 1876 he was committed to the Central Hospital for the Insane, where he spent the rest of his life.

Tom Smith died in the asylum on May 21, 1923, at the age of eighty-five. He was survived by only two other Confederate generals. He was buried in Mount Olivet Cemetery, Nashville.

WILLIAM "EXTRA BILLY" SMITH was born on September 6, 1797, in Marengo, Virginia. He was educated in private schools in Virginia and at Plainfield Academy in Connecticut. He read law, was admitted to the bar, and began practicing in Culpeper in 1818.

In 1827, Smith established a stage line through Virginia, later expanded into the Carolinas and Georgia, to carry passengers and mail. During a congressional investigation, it was found that Smith had utilized several additional routes to generate more billing with the postal department. As a result, a senator dubbed him "Extra Billy" Smith, and the sobriquet stuck.

Smith became a successful politician, serving in the state senate from 1836 to 1841, in Congress from 1841 to 1843, and as Virginia's governor from January 1, 1846 to January 1, 1849. His efforts, however, to gain a U.S. Senate seat failed, so he moved to California during the Gold Rush and headed up the first Democratic statewide convention.

He then returned to the Old Dominion and was reelected to Congress, serving from 1853 to 1861. He was an advocate for states' rights and slavery.

After secession, Smith at first declined the offer of a commission as a brigadier general, but on June 1, 1861, he was involved in the Battle of Fairfax Court House as a civilian. Smith found the experience of combat exhilarating and arranged to become colonel and commander of the

·S

49th Virginia Infantry Regiment on June 17. He fought in the Battle of First Manassas and performed well.

Billy Smith was an eccentric commander to say the least. He disliked uniforms and, in the field, carried a blue cotton umbrella and wore a high beaver hat. He disdained West Pointers and urged his officers to use common sense rather than standard military tactics—as if the two were always mutually exclusive. He was, however, fearless in battle.

Smith fought in the Peninsula Campaign, the Battle of Seven Pines (where he was wounded), the Seven Days Battles, and the Maryland Campaign. He temporarily commanded Jubal Early's brigade at Sharpsburg, where he was wounded three times. He apparently had not recovered by the time of the Battle of Fredericksburg, where his regiment was commanded by his lieutenant colonel.

He was elected to the Confederate Congress while simultaneously serving in the army. He resigned from Congress in April 1863, preferring to remain in the field, despite his advanced age of sixty-five.

On January 31, 1863, Smith was promoted to brigadier general and assumed command of a brigade. He was a good regimental commander, but leading a brigade seems to have been too much for him. His performance at Chancellorsville was lackluster at best, and at Gettysburg it was worse, prompting General Early, now Smith's divisional commander, to order another brigadier general to supervise Smith's brigade.

Early praised all his generals at Gettysburg, except for Smith, who submitted his resignation on July 10. It was not accepted. Instead, Smith was promoted to major general on August 12. Smith was running for governor of Virginia, and it is likely President Jefferson Davis wanted his future cooperation.

William Smith was elected governor and inaugurated on January 1, 1864. Although he was a Jeffersonian Democrat, he sided with the centralizing tendency of the Davis administration when it came to the war effort. He was an excellent governor.

Smith surrendered to the Union provost of Richmond on June 8, 1865. He was paroled and returned to Monterosa, (Monte Rosa), his home in Warrenton.

The former governor became a farmer. He continued to dabble in politics, but it was no longer his profession. He was elected to the Virginia House of Delegates at age eighty and served from 1877 to 1879. General Smith died in Warrenton, Virginia, on May 18, 1887, at the age of eighty-nine. He is buried in Hollywood Cemetery in Richmond, Virginia.

WILLIAM DUNCAN SMITH was born on July 28, 1825, in Augusta, Georgia, the son of a Scottish immigrant. He entered the U.S. Military Academy at West Point in 1842 and graduated in the famous class of 1846. He was sent to Mexico with the 2nd Dragoons and fought in the Siege of Veracruz and the battles of Cerro Gordo, Contreras, and Churubusco. He was severely wounded at Molino del Rey on September 8, 1847.

After he recovered, Smith served on the Western frontier. He was on garrison or frontier duty from 1848 to 1858 and was on a leave of absence to Europe from 1859 to 1861. He was promoted to captain in 1858.

Smith resigned his commission on January 16, 1861, three days before Georgia seceded. He entered the Confederate Army as a captain but was soon promoted to major in the 1st Regular Georgia Infantry Regiment. He was named assistant adjutant general of Savannah's defenses on June 25, and colonel of the 20th Georgia Infantry Regiment on July 14. In September, Smith and his men took positions on Mason's Hill, not far from Washington, D.C.

He was promoted to brigadier general on March 7, 1862. On April 30, Smith was named commander of the 1st Brigade, District of South Carolina, and was given responsibility for defending James Island, located south of Charleston.

In early June, elements of two Union divisions (6,600 men) landed on the southern end of James Island and marched north. Confederate General John C. Pemberton reinforced the island. On June 16, the Rebels threw back the Yankee invaders at the Battle of Secessionville, and

·S

the Northerners abandoned James Island altogether on July 7. It was a small but brilliant Confederate victory, defeating the main Union attempt to capture Charleston by land. William Smith acquitted himself well at Secessionville; it was also his only battle of the war.

Smith died of yellow fever in Charleston on October 4, 1862, at the age of thirty-seven. The South lost a promising young officer. He was buried in Magnolia Cemetery, Augusta, Georgia.

GILBERT MOXLEY SORREL, who went by the name "Moxley" and sometimes "Gill," was born in Savannah, Georgia, on February 23, 1838, the son of a successful businessman. Moxley was a twenty-two-year-old clerk in the banking division of a railroad when the war began.

Sorrel had no military education, but he went to Virginia and met James "Old Pete" Longstreet, beginning an association that lasted throughout the war. He served as a volunteer aide until September 11, 1861, when he was appointed captain and acting assistant adjutant general to Longstreet. Before long he was Longstreet's de facto chief of staff. Although quiet and taciturn, he adapted to military life surprisingly well and came to be regarded as one of the best staff officers in Confederate service. He served in the Peninsula Campaign and was promoted to major on May 5, 1862.

One reason many people considered Longstreet a great commander during the war was that his command always featured excellent staff work. Longstreet deserves primary credit for this, of course, but some of the praise must go to his chief of staff, Sorrel. He continued with Old Pete in the Seven Days Battles, the Battle of Second Manassas, and the Battle of Sharpsburg. Here, on September 17, 1862, he helped members of Longstreet's staff man a cannon while Longstreet held their horses' reins. Later, while delivering a dispatch, his horse was shot from under him. Still later, a shell fragment struck him and knocked him senseless. He was taken to the rear and was disabled for a time.

S.

Sorrel was present at the Battle of Fredericksburg and in the Suffolk Campaign. He was promoted to lieutenant colonel on June 18, 1863. At Gettysburg on July 2, a shell burst directly over him. One of the large pieces of shrapnel struck him on the right arm near the shoulder. It did not break the bone, but it was a painful wound and paralyzed the arm for at least ten days and turned the limb black from the shoulder to the wrist. Despite his wound, he took part in Pickett's Charge on July 3, where his horse was shot from under him.

Sorrel did much of the staff work for the transfer of Longstreet's I Corps from Virginia to Chickamauga, where the South won an impressive victory. He also took part in the Siege of Knoxville and the subsequent return to Virginia.

On the morning of May 6, 1864, during the Battle of the Wilderness, Longstreet ordered Sorrel to take charge of the somewhat disorganized units on the Confederate right and then to attack the left flank of Union General Winfield Scott Hancock's II Corps. Sorrel took charge of three brigades and attacked an hour later. After the war, Hancock told Longstreet: "You rolled me up like a wet blanket and it was some hours before I could reorganize for battle." Sorrel was promoted to brigadier general on October 27, 1864, bypassing the rank of colonel altogether.

Sorrel's brigade performed well in the Siege of Petersburg, and he was popular with his men. His tendency to get wounded, however, continued. In January 1865, during the Siege of Petersburg, a bullet knocked him out of the saddle. On February 7, 1865, during the Battle of Hatcher's Run, a bullet smashed through his chest and almost killed him. He was sent to Roanoke County to recover. In April 1865, he tried to return to the Army of Northern Virginia, but he only reached Lynchburg when he learned General Robert E. Lee had surrendered. He was paroled at Lynchburg on June 20, 1865.

Moxley Sorrel was only twenty-six years old when the war ended. He became a merchant and then the manager of a steamship company. After he retired, General Sorrel wrote *Recollections of a Confederate Staff Officer*, which was published posthumously in 1905. Dr. Douglas Southall Freeman called it one of the best accounts of the war by a major participant.

General Gilbert Moxley Sorrel died at the Barrens, the estate of his brother near Roanoke, Virginia, on August 10, 1901 at age sixty-three. His body was taken back to Georgia and buried in Laurel Grove Cemetery, Savannah.

LEROY AUGUSTUS STAFFORD was born on April 13, 1822, at Greenwood Plantation near Cheneyville, Louisiana, into a distinguished family. He was educated at a private school in Bardstown, Kentucky, and went to college in Nashville, Tennessee. He returned to Louisiana in 1843, ran plantations in Rapides Parish for a couple of years, and was elected parish sheriff. He served in the Mexican War as a private in the Rapides Rifles, which fought in the Battle of Monterrey. He resumed plantation management after the war.

With sectional tensions rising, Stafford raised a volunteer company, the Stafford Guards, and became its captain. It was mustered into Confederate service as part of the 9th Louisiana Infantry. The regiment was sent to Virginia and on April 24, 1862, enlisted for the duration of the war, with Stafford elected colonel.

Stafford served in Stonewall Jackson's Valley Campaign of 1862—in which General Richard Taylor praised his fine leadership—and in the Seven Days Battles, during which Stafford took command of a brigade after the acting brigade commander was killed. As part of the Stonewall Division, Stafford and the 9th Louisiana fought at Cedar Mountain, Second Manassas (where it was heavily engaged), and Chantilly, gaining a distinguished reputation.

Colonel Stafford continued to perform well in the Maryland Campaign, including the Battle of Sharpsburg, where he became an acting brigade commander after Brigadier General William E. Starke was killed, and Stafford was wounded.

The 9th Louisiana Infantry Regiment was in reserve at Fredericksburg but still lost twelve men killed or wounded to artillery fire. Colonel

Stafford fought in the Battle of Chancellorsville until May 4, 1863, when he was captured at Salem Church. He was exchanged in June 1863, took part in the Battle of Gettysburg, and fought at Cemetery Hill. He was officially commended for his conspicuous gallantry.

On October 8, 1863, following the retreat to Virginia, Leroy Stafford was promoted to brigadier general and named commander of the 2nd Louisiana Brigade of the Stonewall Division. The Brigade was involved in the Mine Run and Bristoe campaigns, as well as the Overland Campaign. High casualties forced its consolidated with the 1st Louisiana Brigade. One of those casualties was Stafford himself. On May 5, 1864, during the Battle of the Wilderness, a minié ball pierced General Stafford's spinal cord. He was taken to the Spotswood Hotel in Richmond, where he died on May 8. He was forty-two years old. The loss of generals of Stafford's quality was a cost the Army of Northern Virginia could not afford.

Brigadier General Leroy A. Stafford was buried in Hollywood Cemetery, Richmond, with full military honors. After the war, his body was reinterred in the family cemetery on Greenwood Plantation, Rapides Parish, Louisiana.

PETER BURWELL STARKE was born in Brunswick County, Virginia, in 1815, the younger brother of William Edwin Starke, another future Confederate general. The Starke brothers operated a stage line in the 1830s. In the 1840s, Peter moved to Bolivar County, Mississippi. He ran unsuccessfully for Congress in 1846 but was elected to the state legislature, serving in the Mississippi House of Representatives from 1850 to 1854 and in the Mississippi Senate from 1856 to 1862.

In early 1862, he organized the 28th Mississippi Cavalry Regiment. It numbered nearly seven hundred men and operated in northern Mississippi, where it skirmished against Northern cavalry.

Starke and his men joined W. H. "Red" Jackson's Cavalry Brigade and fought in the victory at Thompson's Station (March 1863). Jackson was promoted to division commander, and Starke assumed command of the brigade on December 23, 1863. On February 24, 1864, he launched a stinging attack on the Federals at Sharon, Mississippi, and won the praise of General Stephen Dill Lee, who commended Starke's "skill and gallantry."

Colonel Starke took part in the Atlanta Campaign and was promoted to brigadier general on November 4, 1864. He saw action in the disastrous Franklin-Nashville Campaign and was then assigned to guard northeastern Mississippi against a Union invasion that never came. He surrendered with General Richard Taylor in May 1865 and was paroled at Gainesville, Alabama, on May 12, 1865.

Starke returned to Mississippi after the war and served on the Mississippi Levee Commission. He also served a term as sheriff of Bolivar County. He returned to Brunswick County, Virginia, in 1873, near Lawrenceville, where his second wife owned property and a farm. He died in Lawrenceville on July 13, 1888. He is buried in the Percival family cemetery, Lawrenceville, Virginia.

WILLIAM EDWIN STARKE, the brother of Confederate Brigadier General Peter E. Starke, was born in Brunswick County, Virginia, in 1814. He operated a small stagecoach line in Virginia with his brothers in the 1830s. William Starke moved to Alabama in 1840 and became a cotton broker in New Orleans and Mobile, where he grew wealthy. He returned to Virginia when the war began and was named lieutenant colonel of the 53rd Virginia Infantry Regiment in June 1861. In July, he was serving as a volunteer aide to Brigadier General Robert S. Garnett, who was killed in action at Corrick's Ford on July 13 during the disastrous retreat from the defeat at Rich Mountain. Starke's "coolness and judgment in the midst of the confusion that followed the death of

General Garnett were highly commended by Colonel William B. Taliaferro, who succeeded in command," Major Jed Hotchkiss wrote later.

After serving as an aide-de-camp to Robert E. Lee (June to August), Starke was promoted to colonel and given command of the 60th Virginia Infantry on October 12, 1861. He was sent to Lewisburg, Virginia, to support General John B. Floyd and then to Bowling Green, Kentucky. Finally, the 60th returned to Virginia, where it fought in the Seven Days Battles, and Starke was again commended for his gallantry. He was promoted to brigadier general on August 6, 1862, and given command of the 2nd Louisiana Brigade.

At the Battle of Second Manassas, Starke took command of the Stonewall Division, after its commander, General William B. Taliaferro, was wounded.

During the Maryland Campaign, he led a brigade in the siege of Harpers Ferry, and at Sharpsburg on September 17, 1862, his brigade came under heavy attack. When his men wavered, he rallied them by grabbing and waving a battle flag. The enemy shot him three times, and he died within an hour.

General Bradley Johnson, reflecting on Starke's performance at Second Manassas, said, "The buoyant dash with which he [Starke] led his brigade into the most withering fire on Friday, though then in command of the division; the force he showed in the handling of this command; the coolness and judgment which distinguished him in action, made him to me a marked man, and I regretted his early death as a great loss to the army and the cause."

Brigadier General William E. Starke was undoubtedly a fine brigade and division commander. His body was transported to Richmond, where it was buried in Hollywood Cemetery, next to his youngest son, who was killed at Seven Pines.

WILLIAM STEELE was born on May 1, 1819, in Albany, New York. He attended West Point, graduated in 1840, and fought in the Second Seminole War (1841–42). Afterward, he was stationed at Fort Jesup, Louisiana.

Steele's cavalry regiment served with General Zachary Taylor in Mexico, including at the battles of Palo Alto and Monterrey, before being transferred to General Winfield Scott's Army of Mexico. Steele took part in the Siege of Veracruz and the battles of Cerro Gordo, Contreras, Churubusco, and Molino del Rey. He was brevetted captain for gallantry and meritorious service at Contreras and Churubusco.

After the Mexican War, Steele was stationed in Mississippi, Texas (which he considered home after marrying a Texas woman), the New Mexico Territory, Kansas, the Dakota Territory, Missouri, and Nebraska. He was promoted to captain in 1852 and was a well-experienced Indian fighter, having battled Apache, Sioux, Kiowa, and Comanche.

On May 30, 1861, after more than twenty years of U.S. Army service, Steele resigned his commission and "went south," choosing to serve his adopted state of Texas. Initially, he was appointed lieutenant colonel in the 4th Texas Mounted Volunteers (later designated the 4th Texas Cavalry). He was named colonel of the 7th Texas Cavalry on October 29, 1861.

Assigned to Henry Sibley's Army of New Mexico, Steele did not take part in the fighting at Valverde and Glorieta Pass but instead guarded the El Paso and Mesilla areas. He led an expedition to Tucson, Arizona, in early 1862, and was named governor and military commander of the Arizona Territory. He was promoted to brigadier general on September 12, 1862, by which time the Confederacy had lost both New Mexico and Arizona.

On January 1, 1863, General Steele was named commander of the Indian Territory. Confederate President Jefferson Davis was impressed by his energy and administrative ability. "His service was efficient and of inestimable value," the president noted.

In December, he turned the Indian Territory over to Brigadier General Samuel B. Maxey and took command of the defenses of Galveston, Texas. He then became a brigade commander in Tom Green's cavalry division and saw action in the Red River Campaign and the battles of Mansfield and Pleasant Hill, where he earned praise from General Richard Taylor, the commander of the Army of Western Louisiana. Steele was commanding a cavalry division in Texas when the Confederacy surrendered. He was paroled in San Antonio on August 4.

After the war, William Steele worked in the commission cotton and mercantile businesses in San Antonio from 1866 to 1873. When the corrupt Republican administration collapsed at the end of the Reconstruction era, Steele was named adjutant general of Texas. He served from January 1874 to January 1879 and directed the reorganization of the Texas Rangers.

General William Steele died on January 12, 1885, in San Antonio. He was sixty-five years old. He is buried in Oakwood Cemetery in Austin, Texas.

GEORGE HUME "MARYLAND" STEUART was born in Baltimore, Maryland, on August 24, 1828, the descendant of Scottish immigrants. His father, a planter, owned 2,000 acres and 150 slaves.

Steuart attended West Point and graduated with the class of 1848. He was assigned to the 2nd Dragoons and served mainly in the West, fighting against the Cheyenne, Mormons, and Comanches.

He resigned his commission on April 22, 1861, and was named a captain in the Regular Army of the Confederacy. On June 17, 1861, he became lieutenant colonel of the 1st Maryland Infantry Regiment, which distinguished itself at the Battle of First Manassas. When Arnold Elzey, the regiment's commander, was promoted to brigadier general, Steuart became the colonel of the 1st Maryland.

Like Elzey, Steuart was a strict disciplinarian and was at first regarded as a bit of a martinet. He drilled his men to the point of exhaustion and was unpopular, although the soldiers eventually came to appreciate him. He was most rigorous in enforcing the sanitary regulations, and the 1st Maryland may have had the cleanest camp in the Confederate Army. Its rate of loss due to disease was correspondingly low.

Steuart acquired the nickname "Maryland" to distinguish him from J. E. B. Stuart, who operated in the same area. George Steuart was promoted to brigadier general on March 6, 1862, and commanded a brigade in Richard Ewell's division during Stonewall Jackson's Valley Campaign of 1862. On May 24, Jackson gave Steuart command of a two-regiment cavalry brigade. He performed poorly during the First Battle of Winchester and was slow to pursue the routed Federals. A few days later, both of his regimental commanders requested that their units be transferred. Ewell and Jackson agreed, and Steuart's cavalry brigade was dissolved.

George Steuart resumed command of the 1st Maryland, helped defeat the Federals at the Battle of Cross Keys on June 8, but was badly wounded by a Union canister shot that smashed his shoulder and broke his collar bone. He could not return to duty until May 1863, when he was given command of an infantry brigade. He never got another cavalry command.

General Steuart's brigade command did well in the Second Battle of Winchester (June 13–15), where it captured more than one thousand Yankees at a cost of nine killed and thirty-four wounded. On July 3, at Gettysburg, he was ordered to launch a bayonet charge against the Federals on Culp's Hill. In fierce fighting, Steuart lost seven hundred of his two thousand men.

On November 27, 1863, in the Battle of Mine Run (Payne's Farm), Steuart moved boldly and blocked the main Union attack, preventing a Northern breakthrough. Steuart was severely wounded in the arm. He had recovered by the Battle of the Wilderness, where he again distinguished himself.

During the Battle of Spotsylvania Court House, Steuart was captured when his line was overwhelmed on May 12. He was exchanged on August 3, 1864.

Steuart was then given command of a brigade in George Pickett's division during the Siege of Petersburg. He was present at the Battle of Five Forks on April 1, 1865. Because Pickett had left his troops to attend a shad bake, Steuart was the acting division commander. Attacked by overwhelming forces, Steuart lost three thousand of his ten thousand men but continued to lead the remnants of his brigade until the Confederate surrender at Appomattox Court House on April 9. He was paroled on April 12.

The irony of Steuart's Civil War career is that he was an above-average infantry commander and a below-average cavalry officer, despite having spent thirteen years in the U.S. Cavalry. After the war, George Steuart became a farmer at Mount Steuart, near the South River in Anne Arundel County, Maryland. He served as the commander-in-chief of the Maryland Division of the United Confederate Veterans for many years.

General George H. Steuart passed away on November 22, 1903, on his South River estate. He was seventy-five years old. He was buried in Green Mount Cemetery, Baltimore.

CLEMENT HOFFMAN "ROCK" STEVENS was born in Norwich, Connecticut, on August 14, 1821, the son of a U.S. naval officer. He grew up in Florida, where his father owned a sugar plantation, and South Carolina, where the family moved because of Indian troubles and because it was his mother's home state.

Stevens was apprenticed to the Navy, serving as secretary to two sea-going relatives, one a rear admiral, the other a commodore. He returned to shore in 1842, worked in banking and for a railroad construction company, and was an inventor (one of his inventions was a portable bread oven). He also joined the South Carolina Militia, became an ordnance expert, and was a colonel when the state seceded.

His talents were put to use immediately. Clement Stevens designed and constructed the first iron-plated artillery battery and (arguably) the first armored fortification in military history. It was located on Morris Island and was used to bombard Fort Sumter on April 12 and 13, 1861.

Stevens was commissioned as a colonel in the Confederate Army and appointed as an aide to Brigadier General Barnard Bee, his brother-in-law. At the Battle of First Manassas, Bee was mortally wounded and Stevens was severely injured. After Stevens recovered, he assumed command of a South Carolina militia regiment in Charleston. During the winter of 1861–62, he served as an aide to General Roswell Ripley. On April 1, 1862, he assumed command of the 24th South Carolina Infantry Regiment. He led the regiment into battle at Secessionville on James Island on June 16, 1862.

His regiment was sent to defend Jackson, Mississippi, and after the fall of Vicksburg in July 1863, it was sent to the Army of Tennessee and fought at the Battle of Chickamauga, where Colonel Stevens had two horses shot out from under him and was wounded. General States Rights Gist called him "iron-nerved," and General W. H. T. Walker recommended him for promotion. On January 20, 1864, Stevens became a brigadier general.

In February 1864, he assumed command of a brigade in Walker's division and led it in the Atlanta Campaign. On July 20, 1864, he was shot in the head while leading an attack at the Battle of Peach Tree Creek. He died in Atlanta on July 25, at age forty-two. "Rock" Stevens, a nickname he earned during the war, was initially buried in Magnolia Cemetery in Charleston, but he was later reinterred, and his remains now lie in St. Paul's Episcopal Church Cemetery, Pendleton, South Carolina.

WALTER HUSTED STEVENS was born in Penn Yan, New York, on August 24, 1827. Admitted to West Point, he graduated in 1848. Commissioned as a brevet second lieutenant of engineers, Stevens spent most of his U.S. Army career in Texas and Louisiana, where he married the sister of future Confederate General Louis Hébert. By 1861, Stevens was thoroughly converted to the Southern cause and considered himself a Texan. When Texas left the Union, he submitted his resignation.

He was commissioned as a captain of engineers in the Confederate Army, was quickly promoted to major, and was stationed at Pensacola, Florida.

Stevens became chief engineer of the Army of Pensacola in April 1861 but was sent to Virginia as chief engineer of the Army of the Potomac (later called the Army of Northern Virginia) in June. He was with General G. T. Beauregard during the Battle of First Manassas. Later, he served with General Joseph E. Johnston in the Peninsula Campaign. He was promoted to lieutenant colonel on January 31, 1862.

After Johnston was wounded at the Battle of Seven Pines on May 31, Robert E. Lee took command of the army and placed Stevens in charge of the Richmond fortifications as chief engineer. During the next two years, he was engaged in strengthening and expanding Richmond's defenses. He was promoted to colonel on March 3, 1863.

On July 20, 1864, during the Siege of Petersburg, Colonel Stevens was reappointed chief engineer of the Army of Northern Virginia. He was promoted to brigadier general on August 28, 1864. During the evacuation of Richmond, he was reportedly the last uniformed soldier to cross the Mayo Bridge on the night of April 2–3, 1865.

After the war, General Stevens went to Mexico, where he was superintendent and chief engineer for the Mexican Imperial Railroad, which was completed in July 1867. It ran from Veracruz to Mexico City.

General Walter H. Stevens died of yellow fever in Veracruz on November 12, 1867. He was forty years old. He is buried at Hollywood Cemetery, Richmond.

CARTER LITTLEPAGE STEVENSON, JR., was born on September 21, 1817, at Fredericksburg, Virginia, the son of a prominent attorney. He attended West Point, graduated in 1838, and was sent to Wisconsin. In 1840, he was transferred to Florida, where he fought in the Second Seminole War.

Stevenson took part in the military occupation of Texas in 1845. He fought in the Mexican War, seeing action in the battles of Palo Alto and Resaca de la Palma in northern Mexico. He was promoted to captain in 1847.

After the Mexican War, he fought Apaches in the West, Seminoles in Florida (again), and Mormons in the Utah War (1857–58). He was on frontier duty from 1858 to 1861.

Stevenson joined the Confederate Army as a major of infantry and was soon promoted to colonel of the 53rd Virginia. He was advanced to the rank of brigadier general on February 27, 1862, and eventually assumed command of a division in General Edmund Kirby Smith's Army of East Tennessee. He helped drive U.S. General George W. Morgan from the Cumberland Gap, took part in the invasion of Kentucky, and retreated with the army to Murfreesboro. He was promoted to major general on October 10, 1862.

In December 1862, Stevenson's division (ten thousand men) was hurriedly transferred from the Army of Tennessee to the Army of Mississippi to help defend Vicksburg. His men were heavily engaged in the Confederate defeat at Champion Hill (May 16), and he commanded the retreating Confederate columns into Vicksburg after the Battle of Big Black River Bridge (May 17).

Besieged at Vicksburg, Stevenson turned back major Union assaults on May 19 and 22. He successfully defended his line until July 4, when the fortress surrendered. He was exchanged on October 16 and was made a divisional commander in the Army of Tennessee.

General Stevenson fought in the Siege of Chattanooga, the Atlanta Campaign, and the Tennessee Campaign of 1864, where his division was smashed in the Battle of Nashville. Stephen Dill Lee, his corps commander, was wounded on December 17, 1864, and Stevenson became acting corps commander. He commanded his division again in the Carolinas Campaign, during which, reduced to a strength of 2,600 men, it fought at the Battle of Bentonville.

Stevenson was with General Joseph E. Johnston when he surrendered on April 26. He was paroled at Greensboro, North Carolina, on May 1, 1865.

Carter Stevenson was a competent but colorless commander—solid, but certainly not dynamic or brilliant.

After the war, he was employed as a mining and civil engineer. He died on August 15, 1888, in Caroline County, Virginia. He is buried in the Confederate Cemetery in Fredericksburg.

ALEXANDER PETER "OLD STRAIGHT" STEWART was born in Rogersville, East Tennessee, on October 2, 1821, and was educated in local schools. His parents were devoutly religious and strongly antislavery. He was admitted to West Point in 1838 and graduated in 1842 as an artillery officer. He resigned from the army in 1845 to become a professor of mathematics and experimental philosophy at Cumberland University in Lebanon, Tennessee. Except for a year at the University of Nashville, he was at Cumberland until 1861. By the time the war began, he was chair of the mathematics and natural and experimental philosophy department.

Stewart gained his nickname "Old Straight" because of his straightforward moral uprightness. A Whig by political conviction, Stewart strongly opposed secession, but like many others throughout the South, his loyalty was with his state, not the Washington government.

On May 17, 1861, he was commissioned as a major in the Tennessee Militia and on August 15, 1861, he became a major of artillery in the Confederate States Army. He was promoted to brigadier general on November 8, 1861, and was given command of a brigade in the Columbus (Kentucky) District under Leonidas Polk.

A. P. Stewart was a quiet, unassuming, and very effective officer. He was also a model Christian gentleman and an elder in his church. During the war, he occasionally preached to his men and conducted baptisms. He was a staunch Presbyterian most of his life but became a Jehovah's Witness in his later years.

Stewart's brigade fought during the early stages of the Island Number 10 Campaign. During the Battle of Belmont, he commanded the heavy artillery from the Kentucky side and blasted U.S. General Ulysses Grant's raiding party. The brigade's first major action was at Shiloh, where Stewart led his men in attacks on the Hornet's Nest. He took part in the retreat to Corinth and then Tupelo. Stewart fought in the battles of Perryville and Second Murfreesboro, where he helped rout the enemy's right wing. He became a division commander in April 1863 and was promoted to major general on June 2.

Stewart's division served in the Tullahoma Campaign and at Chickamauga, where he was slightly wounded on September 19. Stewart later took part in the Siege of Chattanooga and the Battle of Missionary Ridge.

During the Atlanta Campaign, Stewart fought in all the major battles, including Resaca, where he had three horses shot out from under him. When General Leonidas Polk was killed in action at Pine Mountain, Stewart was named his replacement and promoted to lieutenant general (temporary rank) on June 23, 1864. His first battle as a corps commander was Kennesaw Mountain, where he helped General Joseph E. Johnston give Sherman a stinging tactical defeat.

A. P. Stewart directed his corps throughout the rest of the Atlanta Campaign until the Battle of Ezra Church (July 28), where he was wounded in the forehead by a minié ball. He was temporarily blinded and had to be led from the battlefield. He returned to his command on August 15.

Stewart led his III Corps in the battles around Atlanta until the city fell on September 2. He then took part in General John Bell Hood's Tennessee Campaign, including the Battle of Franklin, where the morale of his corps was shattered. In the Battle of Nashville, the greatly depleted III Corps's performance did not measure up to its previous standards, and it broke on the second day of the battle (December 16). It retreated into Alabama and Mississippi with the remnants of the Army of Tennessee and later marched east to take part in the Carolinas Campaign. By this time, Stewart's corps had fewer than five thousand men.

"As a commander he was quiet and modest, but he always inspired his soldiers with confidence and daring," General Clement A. Evans

S

wrote later. Stewart was not a charismatic corps commander, but he was a good and solid one.

The Army of Tennessee surrendered on April 26, 1865. Stewart was paroled at Greensboro on May 1. He returned to Cumberland University in Lebanon, Tennessee, and resumed his professorship. He remained there until 1869, when he took a position as an insurance executive in St. Louis, Missouri. In 1874, he became chancellor of the University of Mississippi. He held this post for a dozen years.

In 1886, Alexander P. Stewart became a commissioner of the Chickamauga and Chattanooga National Military Park. In 1903, he had a stroke. He was no longer able to speak, and the right side of his face and the left side of his body were paralyzed. Remarkably, he made a complete recovery. Lieutenant General Alexander P. Stewart retired in 1905 and died in Biloxi, Mississippi, on August 30, 1908. He was eighty-six years old. Before his passing, Stewart was the highest-ranking living Confederate officer. He was buried in Bellefontaine Cemetery, St. Louis, Missouri.

MARCELLUS AUGUSTUS STOVALL was born in Sparta, Georgia, on September 18, 1818. His father was a wealthy merchant who sent his son to Wesleyan Christian Academy in Wilbraham, Massachusetts, where he received an excellent education. He returned to Georgia and in 1835 enlisted in the Richmond Blues of the Georgia State Volunteers, a mounted infantry unit, and served in the Second Seminole War. The following year, he entered West Point but resigned in 1837 due to a severe and prolonged attack of rheumatism.

After recovering his health, Stovall became a captain in the militia. In August 1861, Governor Joseph E. Brown appointed him colonel of the 2nd Georgia Militia Artillery Regiment. On October 8, 1861, he accepted a demotion to lieutenant colonel to become commander of the 3rd Georgia Infantry Battalion, which was accepted into

Confederate service in December. After doing garrison duty at Richmond and Lynchburg, Virginia, and Goldsboro, North Carolina, it first saw action in a skirmish at Walden's Ridge, East Tennessee, on July 5, 1862. It accompanied Edmund Kirby Smith into Kentucky in 1862 and fought at Richmond.

Stovall's battalion was thoroughly well drilled and was noted for its discipline and high morale. Stovall was a natural leader at the battalion level. In October 1862, he joined Braxton Bragg's Army of Tennessee and fought at the Second Battle of Murfreesboro, where he distinguished himself by leading an aggressive counterattack. When his brigade commander, General James Edwards Rains, was shot through the heart, Marcellus Stovall was selected to replace him. He was promoted to brigadier general on January 20, 1863.

Stovall's brigade was sent west during the Vicksburg Campaign and took part in the First Battle of Jackson, Mississippi (May 14). The brigade returned to the Army of Tennessee and fought in the Battle of Chickamauga, after which General John C. Breckinridge commended Stovall for his courage and skill. The brigade also took part in the unsuccessful Siege of Chattanooga and the Atlanta Campaign.

After Atlanta fell, Stovall participated in John Bell Hood's Tennessee Campaign, including the Battle of Nashville, where his brigade was one of the few to retain its cohesion. The brigade marched to Mississippi with Hood and then traveled east to join General Joseph E. Johnston in the Carolinas Campaign, where it fought in the Battle of Bentonville. It surrendered on April 26, and Stovall was paroled on May 9, 1865.

General Stovall returned to Augusta after the war, where he organized and operated the Georgia Chemical Works for many years. He served as city alderman and became the first police commissioner of Augusta. He was also quite active in the Confederate Survivors Association.

General Marcellus Augustus Stovall died of heart disease on August 4, 1895. He was seventy-six years old. He is buried in Magnolia Cemetery, Augusta, Georgia.

OTHO FRENCH STRAHL, was born on June 3, 1831, in Malta Township, near McConnelsville, Ohio. He came from an antislavery Quaker background and was educated at Ohio Wesleyan University, although he did not graduate. In 1855, he and fellow student Daniel H. Reynolds—another future Confederate general— decided to study law under Judge John Harris in Somerville, Tennessee. Strahl supported himself by teaching at a school in the village of New Castle, twelve miles away. "Otho Strahl had a way of inspiring admiration," Charles M. Cummings wrote later. Strahl was remembered as "the most perfect gentleman and best teacher that ever was in that section." Sumner Cunningham later remarked, "General Strahl was a model character, and it was said of him that in all the war he was never known to use language unsuited to the presence of ladies."

Strahl was admitted to the bar, moved to Dyersburg, Tennessee, opened a law office in 1858, and was elected mayor in 1860. A strong believer in states' rights, he raised a company of volunteers immediately after the Rebels fired on Fort Sumter. In May 1861, it was incorporated into the 4th Tennessee Infantry Regiment as Company K, and Strahl was elected captain. The regiment was mustered into Confederate service in Germantown, near Memphis, on May 15, and Strahl was elected lieutenant colonel.

At the Battle of Shiloh (April 6–7, 1862), Strahl led a bayonet charge against a Union battery. General A. P. Stewart commended him for his "gallant bearing and conduct." The regiment's commander, however, was court-martialed for drunkenness, so when the 4th Tennessee was reorganized on April 24, 1862, Strahl was elected colonel.

Strahl fought in the Battle of Perryville, where he had three horses shot out from under him. Shortly before the Second Battle of Murfreesboro, his regiment was consolidated with the 5th Tennessee to form the 4th/5th Tennessee Infantry. Strahl retained command and again performed well at Murfreesboro. He replaced A. P. Stewart as brigade

·S

commander on June 6, 1863, and was promoted to brigadier general on July 28.

Strahl's brigade took part in the Tullahoma Campaign, the Battle of Chickamauga, the Siege of Chattanooga, and the retreat into Georgia.

Meanwhile, a religious revival swept the camps of the Army of Tennessee. On April 20, 1864, Strahl was baptized by Dr. Charles Todd Quintard, an Episcopalian priest and later a bishop. Also baptized at that meeting were Generals William J. Hardee, Francis Shoup, and Daniel C. Govan.

On Saturday, May 7, the Atlanta Campaign began. Members of Strahl's brigade later claimed that they were under fire for sixty consecutive days. General Strahl was severely wounded during the Battle of Atlanta on July 22. He could not return to active duty until September, after Atlanta fell.

Strahl took part in General John Bell Hood's Tennessee Campaign of 1864. At the Battle of Franklin, on the morning of November 30, perhaps sensing his own demise, Strahl gave away his favorite horse to Chaplain Quintard. He led an attack that pushed to the base of the Union Army's earthworks. Here, he loaded rifles for his sharpshooters until a Union bullet struck him in the neck. Officers of Strahl's staff tried to lift the general and carry him to the rear when another bullet struck him. Finally, a Union volley mortally wounded General Strahl. His last words were an order to his men: "Keep on firing." He was thirty-three years old.

Strahl's body was taken to Carnton, the home of Colonel John McGavock, about a mile and a half southeast of Franklin, where it was placed on the long back gallery beside the remains of Generals Patrick Cleburne, John Adams, and Hiram Granbury. Buried at St. John's Episcopal Church south of Columbia, Tennessee, he was reinterred in Dyersburg City Cemetery in 1901 and now lies at the base of a ten-inch Columbiad siege gun.

JAMES EWELL BROWN "JEB" STUART was born on February 6, 1833, at his family's Laurel Hill Plantation in Patrick County, southwestern Virginia. His father was not particularly prosperous but was a noted charmer and bon vivant. Jeb's mother, however, raised him with a strong religious background and an aversion to alcoholic beverages. He promised her he would never drink, and he never did.

Stuart enrolled at Emory and Henry College when he was fifteen and entered West Point in 1850. Stuart's nickname at the Point was "Beauty" for his plain features and his short chin. Later, he grew a magnificent beard to hide them.

He graduated from West Point in 1854 and served primarily with the cavalry in Texas and Kansas. On July 29, 1857, he fought in an action against three hundred Cheyenne warriors and shot an Indian who was about to kill Lunsford Lomax, who later became one of his brigadiers. A few moments later, an Indian shot Stuart in the chest from a distance of about two feet. The bullet glanced off a bone without striking any major organs. The lieutenant was fortunate that he was not killed. He healed quickly.

In 1859, Stuart played a leading role in the capture of the abolitionist-terrorist John Brown. He was promoted to captain in 1861 but resigned his commission effective May 14. He was already appointed captain in the Provisional Army of the Confederacy and was promoted to lieutenant colonel on May 10. He was sent to Harpers Ferry, where General Stonewall Jackson placed him in charge of half his cavalry.

On July 16, Stuart was appointed colonel of the 1st Virginia Cavalry, and on July 21 he was given command of a cavalry brigade. That afternoon, during the Battle of First Manassas, he attacked the enemy's far right flank and helped rout the Federals. He was promoted to brigadier general on September 24, 1861.

During the winter of 1861–62, Stuart commanded the cavalry of General Joseph E. Johnston's Army of the Potomac (later the Army of Northern Virginia), screening its front, standing outpost duty, conducting reconnaissance, launching an occasional raid, and enjoying parties thrown by pretty local belles. General Stuart assembled a staff that was both efficient and jovial. They often danced, frolicked, sang, and made merry until all hours, led by their dashing young general, who soon assembled his own band. He was adored by the ladies, enjoyed flirting, and had charisma and romantic charm, but he was steadfastly loyal to his wife. The esteem in which the civilian population held him bordered on hero worship.

Stuart's cavalry fought in the Peninsula Campaign, and then, from June 12 to 16, he electrified the entire world when he rode completely around McClellan's Army of the Potomac. He also confirmed to General Robert E. Lee that the Union Army's right flank was exposed. This led to the Seven Days Battles, during which Lee saved Richmond.

The horse regiments of the Army of Northern Virginia were organized as a division that summer, with Stuart as its commander. He was promoted to major general on July 26, 1862. He fought in the Battle of Second Manassas and the Maryland and Fredericksburg campaigns. From October 10 to 12, he made another audacious move for which he became famous: he again rode around McClellan's army, 130 miles in 60 hours.

At Chancellorsville, on the night of May 2, 1863, Stonewall Jackson was mortally wounded, and A. P. Hill assumed command of II Corps. Shortly after, Hill was also wounded and ordered Stuart to take command. He led the II Corps for the rest of the battle—until May 6, when Hill returned to duty—and did an excellent job.

Stonewall Jackson died on May 10, and Stuart was devastated. He tried to raise everyone's morale when on June 8 he and his cavalrymen were bivouacked near Brandy Station. His cavalry conducted a grand review for General Robert E. Lee. The next day, Union General Alfred Pleasonton launched a surprise attack with 11,500 men on Stuart and his 9,500 men in an attempt to disperse the Confederate cavalry. It was the largest predominately cavalry action of the war. The result was a somewhat inconclusive Confederate victory, but Stuart was surprised and embarrassed at Brandy Station (Fleetwood Hill). More important, the Union cavalry made a contest out of it and performed better than ever before, auguring ill for the future of the Confederacy.

Stuart tried to recoup his somewhat damaged reputation during the Gettysburg Campaign. Taking advantage of discretionary orders, he made a third ride around the Army of the Potomac (June 28 to July 3). In doing so, he left General Robert E. Lee blind in enemy territory. The result was that the Rebels blundered into the Battle of Gettysburg, and the Army of Northern Virginia suffered a decisive defeat. Stuart rejoined the army on the afternoon of July 2. General Lee was quite angry with his former cadet. Later, on September 9, Lee reorganized his army and created the cavalry corps. It is significant that Stuart was not promoted to lieutenant general. Some historians have averred that there was no implied rebuke here, but I believe there was.

During the winter of 1863–64, Stuart again performed brilliantly. He ambushed Judson Kilpatrick's cavalry near Chestnut Hill (October 19), routed it, and chased it for miles. The battle subsequently went down in history as the "Buckland Races."

During the Overland Campaign of 1864, Stuart again performed brilliantly. He skillfully delayed the Union advance on Spotsylvania Court House for five vital hours, allowing Robert E. Lee to arrive in strength before Grant's legions.

Shortly after, Union General Phil Sheridan attempted to capture Richmond by a surprise raid. Stuart blocked it at Yellow Tavern on May 11. During the battle, a dismounted Union soldier shot Stuart in the left side with a .44-caliber revolver. The bullet sliced through his stomach and out his back. He was in great pain as he was carried to the home of Dr. Charles Brewer in Richmond.

Major John Esten Cooke recalled, "[H]is last hours were tranquil, his confidence in the mercy of heaven unfailing." His last words were "I am going fast now; I am resigned. God's will be done."

General Jeb Stuart died at 7:38 p.m. on May 12, 1864, in Richmond, Virginia. He was thirty-one years old. General Lee remarked that he could hardly keep from weeping when Stuart's name was mentioned. Stuart was buried in Hollywood Cemetery, Richmond.

T

TALIAFERRO – TYLER

WILLIAM BOOTH TALIAFERRO (pronounced TOL-i-var) was born on December 28, 1822, in Belleville, Gloucester County, Virginia, into a prominent family. He attended the College of William and Mary and after graduation studied law at Harvard.

In early 1847, Taliaferro joined the U.S. Army and served in the Mexican War. He arrived in Mexico too late to see combat but was part of the occupation force in Mexico City (1847–48). He was discharged as a major.

Taliaferro served in the Virginia state legislature from 1850 to 1853 and was a presidential elector in 1856. From 1858 to 1861, he was a major general in the Virginia Militia, and on May 1, 1861, he became commander of the 23rd Virginia Infantry and a colonel in the Confederate Army. He was sent to western Virginia and fought in the Battle of Corrick's Ford. His troops were also lightly engaged in the retreat from Laurel Hill. He was given command of a brigade on September 8 and performed well.

General Taliaferro was a rigid disciplinarian who was disliked by his subordinates. A drunken private even assaulted him on one occasion. He feuded with his army commander, Thomas J. "Stonewall" Jackson, and petitioned the War Department to have Jackson removed after the Romney Campaign. Jackson, in turn, opposed Taliaferro's advancement. He was nevertheless promoted to brigadier general on March 4, 1862.

Despite their personal antipathy, as battlefield commanders Taliaferro and Jackson worked well together. During the Valley Campaign, Taliaferro played a major role in the Confederate victory at McDowell and led his brigade in the Confederate victories at Cross Keys and Port Republic. He missed the Seven Days Battles because of illness but returned to fight at the Battle of Cedar Mountain. He assumed command of the Stonewall Division after General Charles Winder was killed on August 9, 1862. During the Battle of Groveton in the Second Manassas Campaign, Taliaferro was shot three times. The last wound, in his arm, forced him to leave the field.

T.

Taliaferro returned to command in December 1862. His division was in reserve at Fredericksburg, but Taliaferro was slightly wounded by Union artillery fire. He thought he deserved advancement to major general, but Jackson blocked his promotion. Taliaferro asked to be transferred, and Jackson happily obliged. Each man was pleased to be rid of the other.

Taliaferro was transferred first to Savannah, Georgia, and then in July to Charleston, where he commanded the defenses of Morris Island and played a credible role in the defense of Battery Wagner. He subsequently took command of a division on James Island.

In February 1864, Taliaferro was given command of the District of East Florida. A month later, he returned to James Island. That spring he commanded a South Carolina district. In December he took charge of all army forces in the state and kept open Confederate General William J. Hardee's escape route as Sherman closed in on Savannah.

Taliaferro was with the Army of Tennessee when the war ended. There is no written record of his promotion to major general, but the Federals paroled him at that rank in Greensboro on May 2.

After the war, General Taliaferro returned to Virginia and practiced law. He served in the legislature from 1874 to 1879 and was chairman of the state Democratic Party in 1876. From 1880, he devoted himself mostly to his successful law practice.

He was a judge in Gloucester County from 1891 to 1897, when he resigned because of failing eyesight. General Taliaferro died on February 28, 1898, at Dunham Massie, his home in Gloucester County. He was seventy-five years old. He was buried in Ware Episcopal Church Cemetery, Gloucester.

JAMES CAMP TAPPAN was born in Franklin, Tennessee, on September 9, 1825. He was educated at Exeter Academy in New Hampshire and at Yale University, from which he graduated in 1845. He then studied law in

Vicksburg, Mississippi, and was admitted to the bar the following year. He moved to Helena, Arkansas, in 1848.

Tappan served in the state legislature (1850–51) and was elected circuit court judge. When the war began, he was commissioned as a captain, and on July 23, 1861, he was named colonel of the 13th Arkansas. The regiment was sent to Missouri and saw action in the Battle of Belmont, where the Confederate forces handed U.S. General Ulysses Grant a marginal defeat.

Tappan and his men fought in the Battle of Shiloh, where the regiment suffered more than a hundred casualties (mainly at the Hornet's Nest). Tappan took part in the retreat to Corinth and in the Kentucky Campaign, where he fought in the battles of Richmond and Perryville.

James Tappan was promoted to brigadier general on November 5, 1862, and given command of an Arkansas brigade that, with other Confederate forces, tried and failed to hold Little Rock in the fall of 1863. He was sent to northwest Louisiana in March 1864 and fought at Pleasant Hill on April 9, where he was acting commander of General Thomas J. Churchill's division. He then returned to Arkansas and helped halt the U.S. VII Corps' drive on Shreveport. He also fought at Camden and Jenkins' Ferry.

General Tappan remained in southern Arkansas for the rest of the war and was a good brigade commander. He was paroled in Shreveport on June 8, 1865. After the surrender, he resumed his law practice. He returned to legislature in 1897, served until 1900, and was speaker of the house in 1897 and 1898. Highly thought of in Democratic circles throughout the state, he twice declined the Democratic nomination for governor.

General James Camp Tappan died in Helena, Arkansas, on March 19, 1906, at age eighty. He was buried in Maple Hill Cemetery, Helena.

RICHARD "DICK" TAYLOR was the only son of General and President Zachary Taylor and his wife

Margaret (the daughter of a Maryland planter) and was the brother-in-law of Confederate President Jefferson Davis. (Taylor's sister was Davis's first wife; she died only three months after her marriage, but Richard Taylor and Jefferson Davis remained close, lifelong friends.)

Taylor was born on his family's plantation, Springfield, near Louisville, Kentucky, on January 27, 1826. He spent much of his childhood on military bases before attending preparatory schools in Kentucky and Massachusetts. He enrolled at Harvard, didn't like it, and transferred to Yale, from which he graduated in 1845.

Dick Taylor stood five feet, eight and a half inches tall and had dark, hazel eyes, a deep, tan complexion, and a thick, black beard. He smoked, drank, chewed tobacco, and enjoyed fine food and wine. He grew "as fat as a Dutchman" (to use a nineteenth-century expression) but lost his excess weight during the war via active campaigning. He was highly cultured, possessed a magnetic personality, and had an aristocratic air. He was very well read, had a fine memory, could quote long passages from literature or the Bible, and was both an original thinker and a man prepared to take risks.

Dick Taylor had chronic rheumatoid arthritis and suffered from poor health throughout his life. He eventually bought his own plantation thirty miles north of New Orleans. Named Fashion, it covered more than 1,200 acres and initially employed 64 slaves. Ultimately, Taylor would own 147 slaves. He believed that slavery was a necessary evil, unfortunately interwoven into Southern society and the South's economy, but that it would eventually fade away, presumably into a form of paid farm labor. He regarded abolitionists as meddlesome extremists. By the standards of the day, he treated his slaves well and, true to his ideals, even paid them occasionally.

Taylor was elected to the Louisiana Senate in 1855, even though he refused to campaign. In the legislature, he never made a speech but still had a reputation for honesty, integrity, and forthrightness—three virtues rare in the Louisiana legislature, even then. He was easily reelected. He was reluctant to embrace secession, but when Louisiana opted to leave the Union, he voted with the majority.

Taylor initially joined General Braxton Bragg's staff at Pensacola as a civilian advisor. On July 7, 1861, Governor Thomas Overton Moore appointed him colonel of the 9th Louisiana Infantry. He and his regiment departed for Virginia immediately, but it was too late to fight at the Battle of First Manassas. On October 21, 1861, he was promoted to brigadier general.

As a military commander, Taylor was just as tough and as brilliant as General George S. Patton would be in World War II. But Taylor was more ornery, more pigheaded, more independent-minded, less diplomatic, and likely even more profane. Patton could at least pretend to be contrite, but Taylor never pretended anything. He was brilliant, and he knew it—to the point of arrogance. Patton got into trouble for slapping a soldier; Taylor hanged two Confederate soldiers before he ever saw his first armed Yankee.

Taylor's brigade served under Stonewall Jackson in the Valley Campaign of 1862, and Taylor distinguished himself in combat. Stonewall Jackson recommended him for promotion.

Dick Taylor was ill and missed part of the Seven Days Battles. Much of the time he directed his brigade from the back of an ambulance. On July 28, he was promoted to major general and sent to Louisiana, where New Orleans and Baton Rouge had fallen to the Federals and the military situation for the Confederates was deteriorating rapidly.

Taylor directed several small but brilliant campaigns in Louisiana. His masterpiece was the Red River Campaign of 1864. With 8,800 men, Taylor attacked Union General Nathaniel Banks at Mansfield on April 8. Banks had 32,000 men, but they were strung out along twenty miles of bad roads and piney Louisiana woods. Taylor knocked them down like so many dominoes. The Union Army of the Gulf was routed. The Confederate Army of Western Louisiana took 2,500 prisoners and captured 20 guns. The next day, it fought an inconclusive battle at Pleasant Hill, after which the Yankees retreated. Taylor pursued them for two hundred miles and even surrounded them twice, but they escaped, and Taylor placed the blame squarely on General Edmund Kirby Smith, who had stripped Taylor of three of his four infantry divisions. Taylor's dispatches became so insulting that Kirby Smith felt he had little choice but to place him under arrest. Taylor was relieved of his command on June 10, but was promoted to lieutenant general on July 18, 1864, to date from April 8.

It was clear that the South needed commanders of Taylor's caliber, and on August 15, President Davis named him commander of the Department of Alabama and East Mississippi, headquartered at Meridian.

Taylor's department was a shambles when he arrived, but he promptly restored law and order through most of the area. He served as acting commander of the Army of Tennessee from January 23 to February 22, 1865, when he was replaced by Joseph E. Johnston, and Taylor resumed command at Meridian. He commanded the last Confederate forces east of the Mississippi and surrendered on May 8, 1865, at Citronelle, Mississippi. He was paroled at Meridian on May 11.

Taylor's fortune was swept away by the war. His plantation was gone, and he was forced to file for bankruptcy in 1866. He ended up going to Europe, where he represented the business interests of Samuel Barlow, a prominent lawyer. Even so, he continued to work tirelessly in the interests of the South and was instrumental in securing President Davis's release from prison.

After Taylor's wife died in 1875, the former general moved to Winchester, Virginia, where he lived with his daughter. Here, he wrote *Destruction and Reconstruction: Personal Experiences of the Late War*, which was published posthumously in 1879. Dr. Douglas Southall Freeman later remarked that it was the only memoir by a major participant in the Civil War that should be classified as literature.

On April 12, 1879, during a business trip to New York City, Taylor died of congestive heart failure at the home of his friend Barlow. Richard Taylor was fifty-three years old. He is buried in Metairie Cemetery, Orleans Parish, Louisiana.

THOMAS HART TAYLOR was born on July 31, 1825, in Frankfort, Kentucky. He attended Kenyon College in Ohio and Centre College in

Kentucky. In 1847, during the Mexican War, Taylor became a first lieutenant in the 3rd Kentucky Infantry, although he did not see action. After the war, he returned to Kentucky, where he farmed, practiced law, and participated in two cattle drives to California.

On April 8, 1861, Taylor was appointed a captain of cavalry in the Confederate Army. He later joined the 1st Kentucky Infantry Regiment. It was sent to Virginia, and Taylor was promoted rapidly—to lieutenant colonel on July 3 and to full colonel and regimental commander on October 14.

The 1st Kentucky had a skirmish or two, spent most of its time drilling, and fought at the Battle of Dranesville in December, where it supported J. E. B. Stuart's cavalry in an attack against a Union force that outnumbered it three to one. Taylor was cut off behind enemy lines, but he kept his composure and waited for nightfall. Then he escaped.

In March, his regiment was sent to the peninsula and took part in the Siege of Yorktown, but its enlistments expired—it was a twelve-month regiment—and its men were discharged at Camp Winder near Richmond in May 1862.

After the 1st Kentucky dissolved, Thomas Taylor reported to General Edmund Kirby Smith, the commander of the Army of East Tennessee, at Cumberland Gap. He commanded the 5th Brigade in General Carter L. Stevenson's division at the Gap and in the Kentucky Campaign, and on November 4, 1862, he was promoted to brigadier general. President Davis, however, did not forward his nomination to the Senate, and his appointment was unconfirmed.

Taylor accompanied General Stevenson to Vicksburg. He remained in brigade command until April 1863, when he became provost marshal on General John C. Pemberton's staff and reverted to the rank of colonel. After Vicksburg fell, he was paroled, exchanged, and became provost marshal for the District of South Mississippi and East Louisiana under the command of Stephen Dill Lee.

T

Thomas Taylor was sent to Mobile, Alabama, in November 1864. Here, he directed an ad hoc formation called "Taylor's Command." It consisted of the City Battalion (four special service companies under Major William Hartwell) and the Pelham Cadet Battalion under Captain P. Williams, Jr. It was more concerned with maintaining order in the city than fighting Yankees. He was in Mobile when the city fell to the Federals on April 12, 1865.

After the war, General Taylor pursued business interests in Mobile until 1870, when he returned to Kentucky and served five years as U.S. deputy marshal. From 1881 to 1892, he was chief of police of Louisville. Taylor spent three years as superintendent of the Louisville and Portland Canal (1886–89). Thomas Hart Taylor died in Louisville of typhoid fever on April 12, 1901, at age seventy-five. He is buried in Frankfort Cemetery in Frankfort, Kentucky.

JAMES BARBOUR TERRILL was born on February 20, 1838, in Bath County, Virginia. His older brother was Union Brigadier General William R. Terrill, who was killed at Perryville on October 8, 1862.

James Terrill enrolled at the Virginia Military Institute in 1854, where he was given the nickname "Bath." He graduated in 1858. He then studied law, was admitted to the bar, and became a lawyer in Warm Springs, Virginia.

Terrill enlisted in the Confederate Army and on May 23, 1861, was elected major of the 13th Virginia Infantry, when it was organized at Harpers Ferry. It was moved by rail to Manassas on July 21 but was posted on the Confederate right flank and was not engaged during the First Battle of Bull Run.

On February 24, 1862, the regiment's colonel, A. P. Hill, was promoted to brigadier general, Lieutenant Colonel James A. Walker became colonel, and Terrill was promoted to lieutenant colonel. He fought in the Valley Campaign of 1862 and was officially commended for his actions at Cross Keys and Port Republic.

The 13th Virginia saw action in the Seven Days Battles, at Cedar Mountain, in the Battle of Second Manassas, in the Battle of Chantilly, during the Maryland Campaign (though it was not at Sharpsburg), in the Battle of Fredericksburg, and in the Battle of Chancellorsville. Throughout all these campaigns it performed very well. Colonel Walker was promoted to brigadier general on May 15, 1863, and Terrill was advanced to colonel that same day.

The 13th Virginia remained at Winchester during the Pennsylvania Campaign but fought in the Bristoe and Mine Run campaigns. On May 5, 1864, Terrill assumed temporary command of John Pegram's brigade after the latter was wounded in the Battle of the Wilderness. He led the brigade with considerable success at Spotsylvania Court House and on the North Anna River.

On May 30, during the Cold Harbor fighting, Terrill's men took part in the Battle of Totopotomoy Creek (Bethesda Church), near Mechanicsville. Colonel Terrill deployed his regiment to attack but was shot through the body. He struggled to his feet and ordered his men to attack, and a Union bullet pierced his head. He was twenty-six years old.

Despite his death, Terrill was nominated for promotion on May 31 and was posthumously confirmed as a brigadier general by the Confederate Senate that same day. He was buried on the battlefield by Union soldiers. His remains now lie in an unknown grave on the Bethesda Church Civil War Battlefield.

WILLIAM TERRY, the last commander of the Stonewall Brigade, was born in Amherst County, Virginia, on August 14, 1824. He is sometimes confused with General William R. Terry, another Confederate general from Virginia.

Terry was educated locally and attended the University of Virginia, from which he graduated in 1848. He taught school, studied law, was admitted to the bar (1851), and began practicing in Wytheville. On April 26, 1861, he became a lieutenant in the 4th Virginia Infantry, which was forming at Winchester. It was assigned to the 1st Virginia Brigade, which became famous as the Stonewall Brigade, and fought at the Battle of First Manassas. Terry and his regiment took part in the brutal Romney Campaign and the Battle of Kernstown (March 23, 1862), where the 4th Virginia suffered 37 percent casualties.

The army was reorganized in April, and the men of 4th Virginia reenlisted for three years, or the duration of the war. Terry was elected major on April 22, 1862. The regiment fought in the Valley Campaign of 1862, the Seven Days Battles, and the Battle of Cedar Mountain. On August 28, during the Battle of Groveton, Terry was wounded in the left elbow. He returned to duty by October.

During the Battle of Fredericksburg, the Stonewall Brigade was heavily engaged. The regimental commander, Colonel Robert Gardner, was seriously wounded by a Federal artillery shell, and Major Terry took command of the regiment. He directed it in the Battle of Chancellorsville, in the Second Battle of Winchester, and at Culp's Hill during the Battle of Gettysburg, where it lost 137 men out of 257 engaged. Terry was promoted to colonel on September 11, 1863, and fought in the Mine Run Campaign.

Colonel Gardner, the regiment's permanent commander, returned to duty on April 9, 1864. He led it on May 12 at the Mule Shoe in the Battle of Spotsylvania Court House, where the Stonewall Brigade was at last overwhelmed and most of it was captured. Colonel Terry suffered two slight wounds but was the only senior officer in the brigade to escape. He spent the next two days organizing survivors. By May 15, he organized the remnants of ten Virginia regiments, including 249 survivors of the Stonewall Brigade, into an ad hoc brigade. During the Battle of North Anna, Terry's brigade was in reserve. He was promoted to brigadier general on May 19, 1864.

Terry become a general via attrition rather than brilliance, although he was unquestionably a brave and tenacious warrior. In the trenches during the Overland Campaign, the South definitely needed men like him. He directed Terry's Consolidated Brigade in the Cold Harbor Campaign and in the Shenandoah Campaign of 1864. On September 19, 1864, General Terry was seriously wounded during the Third Battle of Winchester. He did not return to active duty until February 1865, when he rejoined his brigade in the trenches at Petersburg. During the Battle of Fort Stedman, he was wounded at Hare's Hill by the same shell that killed his horse. He could not rejoin the army before Appomattox. When he learned General Robert E. Lee had surrendered, William Terry joined the Army of Tennessee. He surrendered with it on April 26.

Terry was partially disabled by the three serious wounds he suffered during the war. He returned to Wytheville and resumed his law practice. He was elected to Congress, serving from 1871 to 1873, and from 1875 to 1877. He was a delegate to the Democratic National Convention in 1880.

On September 5, 1888, General Terry was swept off his horse and drowned while trying to ford Reed Creek near Wytheville. He was buried in East End City Cemetery, Wytheville.

WILLIAM RICHARD "ROCK" TERRY was born on March 12, 1827, in Bedford County, Virginia. He spent four years at the Virginia Military Institute, from which he graduated in 1850. He then became a farmer and a merchant.

After Virginia seceded on April 17, 1861, William Terry raised a cavalry company in Bedford County, with himself as captain. On July 21, he took part in the cavalry charge that helped rout the Union right wing in the Battle of First Manassas. Colonel Jubal Early was quite impressed with Terry's performance. When Early was formally promoted to brigadier general in September, he appointed Terry commander of the 24th Virginia, his old regiment. Terry was promoted to colonel on September 21, 1861.

Colonel Terry fought in the Peninsula Campaign of 1862. On the afternoon of May 5, 1862, during the Battle of Williamsburg, "Rock" Terry launched a sharp attack and earned a reputation as "an inspiring and irresistible leader," according to Jed Hotchkiss. U.S. General Winfield Scott Hancock, who commanded Federal forces opposing them, declared that the two regiments (the 24th Virginia and 5th North Carolina) deserved to have the name "Immortal" inscribed on their banners.

Colonel Terry was seriously wounded in the face at Williamsburg. It was the first of seven wounds he suffered during the war. It took him weeks to recover, but he was back on duty by August 1862. Terry assumed command of James Kemper's brigade when Colonel Montgomery Corse, the acting commander, was wounded. Terry led it during the Battle of Second Manassas. Kemper returned to the command of his old brigade during the Maryland Campaign, and Terry returned to the leadership of the 24th Virginia, which he directed at South Mountain and Sharpsburg.

Terry and his men were part of General James Longstreet's Suffolk Expedition in the spring of 1863 and fought at Gettysburg as part of Pickett's Charge, where the 24th Virginia's casualties were 47 killed, 83 wounded, and 33 missing or captured. Among those who fell severely wounded was William R. Terry.

Terry returned to duty by the end of July. He assumed command of Kemper's old brigade in September 1863 and led it for the rest of the war (Kemper was too badly wounded to return). Again part of Pickett's division, Terry fought in the unsuccessful operations against New Bern in the spring of 1864.

In May 1864, Terry's brigade was hurried to Virginia, where it defended Drewry's Bluff in the battle of May 16 and played a major role in saving Richmond from the Union Army of the James. William R. Terry was rewarded on May 31 with a promotion to brigadier general.

Terry's brigade fought in the Battle of North Anna, the Battle of Cold Harbor, and the Siege of Petersburg. On March 31, 1865, near

Dinwiddie Court House, General Terry's horse was killed by a shell, and Terry's leg was broken.

The records do not show what happened to General Terry during the last days of the war, and no record of his capture or parole has been found. After the war, he returned to Bedford County and the practice of law. In 1868, he was elected to the Virginia Senate and served two terms, from 1869 to 1877. He was also active in the Masons and was Master of the Liberty Masonic Lodge. After leaving the state senate, he was superintendent of the state penitentiary and, from 1886 until 1893, directed the Robert E. Lee Camp Confederate Soldiers' Home in Richmond.

General Terry suffered a stroke in 1887 and never fully recovered. He retired due to ill health in 1893 and died of paralysis on March 28, 1897, at Chesterfield Court House, Virginia. He was seventy years old. William R. Terry is buried in Hollywood Cemetery, Richmond. He was a man of incredible courage and was a very effective regimental and brigade commander.

ALLEN THOMAS was born in Howard County, Maryland, on December 14, 1830. He was educated at the College of New Jersey (now Princeton), from which he graduated in 1850. He established a law practice in Maryland and remained there until 1857, when he married into a wealthy family from Ascension Parish, Louisiana. He was the brother-in-law of Richard Taylor and Confederate Congressman Duncan Kenner; all three men married Bringier sisters.

Thomas moved to south Louisiana and became a lawyer, a planter, and a colonel in the Louisiana Militia. When Louisiana seceded, he raised an infantry battalion of five companies. In July 1861, he became its major. On May 3, 1862, Thomas's battalion was expanded and upgraded to the 29th Louisiana Infantry Regiment (sometimes referred to as the 28th/29th Louisiana), and he was promoted to colonel.

Thomas served in the First Siege of Vicksburg, mainly at Warrenton, south of the city. In December 1862, when U.S. General William T. Sherman attempted to take Vicksburg from the north, Thomas was made commander of a provisional brigade that defended Chickasaw Bluffs as part of General Stephen Dill Lee's ad hoc division. General Lee reported, "Col. Allen Thomas exhibited great gallantry and . . . did splendid service."

After Sherman withdrew and the threat had passed, Thomas's brigade was dissolved, and he returned to command of the 28th/29th. It remained in Vicksburg until April 2, 1863, when it took part in operations around Greenville, Mississippi, in which it cleared out some Union raiders. It returned to the Chickasaw Bluffs area in mid-April.

On May 17 and 18, the 28th/29th moved into the trench line at Vicksburg. It formed part of General Francis Shoup's Louisiana Brigade of General Martin Luther Smith's division. It faced major Union assaults on May 19 and twenty-second and turned them back with heavy enemy losses. It remained in the trenches for forty-seven days until Grant finally starved the garrison into surrender on July 4.

After Thomas was exchanged, he was assigned to Richard Taylor's District of West Louisiana, where he was given the task of collecting and organizing exchanged prisoners. He was promoted to brigadier general on February 4, 1864. In September 1864, he was given command of a brigade, which was assigned to Prince Camille Armand de Polignac's division. Thomas held this post until March 17, 1865, when Polignac left for Europe on a diplomatic mission for Jefferson Davis, and Thomas succeeded him. He held the post until the surrender of the Trans-Mississippi Department. General Edmund Kirby Smith went on record as saying Thomas was an able divisional commander.

On June 8, 1865, General Thomas was paroled at Natchitoches. He resumed his life as a planter. He was a member of the board of supervisors of Louisiana State University in 1882 and a professor of agriculture from 1882 to 1884.

Thomas lived in Florida from 1889 to 1907. He worked as a coiner at the U.S. mint in New Orleans during President Grover Cleveland's first term and was U.S. minister to Venezuela during Cleveland's second term.

General Allen Thomas died of malaria in Waveland, Mississippi, on December 3, 1907. He was just short of seventy-seven years old. He was buried in the Bringier family tomb in Ascension Catholic Cemetery, Donaldsonville, Louisiana.

BRYAN MOREL THOMAS was born on May 8, 1836, in Baldwin County, Georgia, near Milledgeville. He was educated locally and at Oglethorpe University in Atlanta. He entered West Point in 1854, graduated in 1858, and was commissioned brevet second lieutenant of infantry. He was stationed in New York, in the Utah Territory, and at Fort Union, New Mexico Territory. After Georgia seceded, he resigned his commission effective April 6, 1861, and was appointed a major in the Confederate Army.

In July 1861, Thomas became a major in the 18th Alabama Infantry, which was forming in Auburn, Alabama. On December 20, he became an ordnance officer in the District of Alabama. On March 18, 1862, he was appointed artillery commander in Brigadier General John K. Jackson's brigade of Jones M. Withers's division. He was promoted to assistant adjutant general and de facto chief of staff of Jackson's brigade eight days later. He fought in the Battle of Shiloh, after which General Withers reported that he had "discharged his duties on both days of the battle with active zeal and gallantry." General Leonidas Polk was also impressed with Thomas.

In July 1862, Thomas became commander of the Reserve Corps Artillery and by the time of the Second Battle of Murfreesboro was an inspector general on the staff of General Withers. In the autumn of 1864, Bryan Thomas was given command of a brigade of Alabama reserves. On August 4, 1864, Thomas was promoted to brigadier general.

Thomas's brigade was assigned to the District of the Gulf, and his principal mission was the defense of Mobile. While there, in 1865, he married the daughter of General Withers, his former commanding officer.

Thomas was part of the garrison of Fort Blakeley when it was besieged on April 1, 1865. In this battle, about 20,000 Union troops faced 4,500 Rebels under the overall command of St. John R. Liddell. Most of those under Thomas's command were young boys, but they fought well. The final attack came late in the day on April 9, when the garrison was overwhelmed. Both Generals Liddell and Thomas were captured, along with General Francis Cockrell and 3,700 of their men. General Thomas was paroled at Fort Gaines, Alabama, in June.

After the war, Bryan Thomas was a planter in Dooly County and Whitfield County, both in Georgia. He also served as a deputy U.S. marshal and a schoolteacher. From 1891 to 1900, he was superintendent of public schools in Dalton, Georgia. He died on July 16, 1905, in Dalton at age sixty-nine. General Bryan Morel Thomas is buried in West Hill Cemetery, Dalton.

EDWARD LLOYD THOMAS was born in 1825 in Clarke County, Georgia. He grew up in a devoutly Christian family. "His private life was pure, that of a true Christian gentleman," Joseph T. Derry wrote later. "No profane expression ever soiled his lips."

Thomas graduated from Emory University and became a farmer in Whitfield County, northwest Georgia. He served in the Mexican War as a second lieutenant in a Georgia mounted rifle company and fought in all the major battles between Veracruz and Mexico City. He performed so well that the secretary of war offered him a Regular Army commission. Thomas, however, declined it.

Many prominent people in antebellum Georgia urged Thomas to seek public office, but he always refused. Although he had strong

Southern sympathies, he worked his plantation and did not enter public life until his state seceded. When it did, he promptly raised the 4th Georgia Infantry Battalion, with himself as lieutenant colonel.

President Jefferson Davis knew of Thomas's military experience and fitness for command. He authorized him to recruit a regiment. The result was the 35th Georgia, which was mustered into Confederate service on October 15, 1861, with Thomas as its colonel. In the spring of 1862, the 35th Georgia was sent to Richmond. Thomas's regiment fought in the Battle of Seven Pines and the Seven Days Battles, including Frayser's Farm (June 30), where General Joseph R. Anderson was seriously wounded. Colonel Thomas assumed command of the brigade and led it for the rest of the war. He fought in all of the major campaigns of the Army of Northern Virginia and was promoted to brigadier general on November 1, 1862. He surrendered at Appomattox on April 9, 1865.

In the devastated postwar South, General Thomas returned to Georgia to run his plantation in Newton County, but without his previous success. President Grover Cleveland appointed him as special agent with the Bureau of Land Management in Kansas in 1885. Later, he became an Indian Agent at the Sac and Fox Agency in the Indian Territory, which soon became Oklahoma. He remained in this position for the rest of his life. Edward Lloyd Thomas died on March 8, 1898, in South McAlester, Oklahoma Territory. He is buried in Kiowa City Cemetery, Kiowa, Oklahoma.

LLOYD TILGHMAN (pronounced TIL mon) was born at Rich Neck Manor, Claiborne, Maryland, on January 26, 1816. He was educated in Baltimore and entered the U.S. Military Academy at West Point, graduating with the class of 1836. He resigned his commission, however, on September 30, 1836, preferring to work as a civil engineer rather than a military one. Among his projects was spending four years in Panama building a railroad across the isthmus.

When it appeared obvious that a fight with Mexico was on the horizon, Lloyd Tilghman returned to the colors. He became captain of the Maryland and District of Columbia Artillery Battery and fought in the Battles of Palo Alto and Resaca de la Palma. He was discharged in 1848.

In 1852, Tilghman settled in Paducah, Kentucky. He joined the state guards militia and on July 5, 1861, was appointed colonel of the 3rd Kentucky Infantry. He was promoted to brigadier general in the Confederate States Army on October 18, 1861, and was given command of Fort Henry on the Tennessee.

Fort Henry was one of the worst-located forts in Civil War history. On February 6, 1862, it was attacked by a flotilla of U.S. gunboats backed by General Grant's ground forces. Knowing that his position was doomed, Tilghman evacuated 2,500 of his men to Fort Donelson and then tried to hold Fort Henry as long as possible. He surrendered the fort and his remaining 94 men after a two-hour engagement. He was transported to Fort Warren, Massachusetts, as a prisoner of war.

Tilghman was exchanged on August 15, 1862. On October 6, he was appointed to command a brigade in W. W. Loring's division. Tilghman performed well against Grant's army during the winter of 1862–63. On December 5, he set a brilliant ambush for the Yankees along the Water Valley–Coffeeville Road that inflicted 311 casualties on the Northerners while the Confederates suffered only 60.

That winter, Tilghman helped hold the Yalobusha River line near Grenada, Mississippi. He also checked the advance of General Grant's forces in the Yazoo Pass and Steele's Bayou Expeditions that spring.

Tilghman had been an old friend of General John C. Pemberton, commander of the Army of Mississippi, but a dispute over Tilghman's abandonment of a large number of tents in a retreat from northern Mississippi in the fall of 1862 had festered into a major feud that pitted Generals Tilghman and Loring against Pemberton. On the morning of May 16, 1863, during the last Vicksburg Campaign, Pemberton relieved Tilghman of his command. Later that morning, the fractious and foul-mouthed General Loring confronted Pemberton and threatened to resign if Tilghman was not restored to command. Pemberton capitulated, but Tilghman paid a horrible price: that afternoon, a three-inch piece of metal from an exploding Parrott shell almost cut him in half. He lived about three more hours but never regained consciousness. He was forty-seven years old.

His son, Lieutenant Lloyd Tilghman, Jr., carried his father's remains to Cedar Hill Cemetery, Vicksburg, where they were interred in the Searles family plot. In 1902, General Tilghman's body was removed from the Vicksburg Cemetery by his two surviving sons (who were successful New York stockbrokers) and reburied beside his wife in the Tilghman plot in Woodlawn Cemetery, Bronx, New York.

ROBERT AUGUSTUS "BOB" TOOMBS was born in Wilkes County near Washington, Georgia, on July 2, 1810. He was educated at Franklin College (now part of the University of Georgia), from which he was expelled for playing cards, unbecoming conduct, and drinking—at age fourteen. He transferred to Union College in Schenectady, New York, from which he graduated in 1828. He then studied law and was admitted to the bar in 1830.

Bob Toombs joined the Georgia Volunteers and fought in the Creek War (1836–37). He was discharged as a captain and was almost immediately elected to the Georgia House of Representatives, serving from 1837 to 1843. Toombs was a genial, charismatic man and a superb orator. He also had a drinking problem. "Stupid, he would have been dismissible," one colleague is reported to have said. "Sober, he would have been a statesman for the ages. Alas, he was neither."

Toombs was a Whig and had a distinguished career as a U.S. congressman (1845–53), a senator (1853–61), and the first Confederate secretary of state (February 25 to July 19, 1861). By the standards of the time, he was a moderate and only joined the Democratic Party reluctantly, after the Constitutional Union Party failed to gain national traction. He was almost elected president of the Confederacy, but when a delegation came to discuss the matter with him, he was drunk, and his shirt was stained with tobacco juice. Jefferson Davis was selected instead.

Toombs expected the war to be brief and wanted to take to the field before the war ended. He arranged to be appointed brigadier general on July 21, 1861. His brigade fought in the Siege of Yorktown, the retreat up the peninsula, and the Seven Days Battles. At Malvern Hill, he retired without orders and received a thorough dressing down from D. H. Hill. Toombs challenged the general to a duel and was fortunate that Hill did not court-martial him.

Dr. Ulrich B. Phillips, a fervent admirer of Toombs, wrote, "He was so firmly convinced of the superlative value of his own ideas of grand strategy that he could not refrain from making himself obnoxious by his censure . . . [of all] who rejected his proposals."

One night, while Toombs was having dinner with a friend, General James Longstreet ordered Toombs's men to guard a ford on the Rapidan. Toombs did not think the dreary outpost duty was necessary and ordered his men back to camp. Their absence allowed Yankee cavalry to cross the river unopposed and raid General J. E. B. Stuart's headquarters, where they captured documents that revealed Robert E. Lee's plans. Lee had intended to trap U.S. General John Pope's army between the Rapidan and the Rappahannock; now Pope was able to escape. When Longstreet learned what had happened, he had Toombs arrested and did not release him until the Battle of Second Manassas.

The high point of Toombs's war was the Battle of Sharpsburg on September 17, where he defended Burnside's Bridge. He held off vastly superior Union forces much of the day and was wounded when a ball passed through his left hand.

For some reason, Toombs thought he deserved promotion to major general. Lee, Longstreet, and D. H. Hill must have been astonished at this demand. When he saw that no promotion was forthcoming, Toombs resigned his commission on March 3, 1863.

Back in Georgia, Toombs was appointed colonel in the Georgia Militia. He was promoted to brigadier general of militia on February 6,

1864. He went on sick leave after the fall of Savannah (December 21) and never returned to duty.

Robert Toombs escaped to Cuba after the war. He returned to the United States via Canada in 1867 and resumed his lucrative law practice in Washington, Georgia. He spent his last years nearly blinded and ravaged by alcoholism. He died on December 15, 1885, in Washington, Georgia, at age seventy-five. He is buried in Rest Haven Cemetery, Washington, Georgia.

THOMAS FENTRESS TOON was born on June 10, 1840, in Columbus County, North Carolina. He attended Wake Forest College, graduated in June 1861, and joined his half brother's company, the Columbus Guard Number 2. On June 17, he was elected first lieutenant of the Guard, which was incorporated into the 20th North Carolina Infantry the next day. Thomas Toon was elected captain and company commander.

The 20th North Carolina was stationed at Smithville (now Southport) until May 1862. Sent to Virginia, it fought in the Battle of Seven Pines and the Seven Days Battles. Because of casualties, Thomas Toon's half brother, William, became acting commander. Thomas Toon was slightly wounded at Seven Pines on May 31 and wounded again at Gaines' Mill on June 27. He would be wounded seven times during the war.

Thomas Toon was promoted to major in June 1862. His regiment fought in the battles of Second Manassas, South Mountain, and Sharpsburg, where it was in the Sunken Lane.

The 20th North Carolina was in reserve at Fredericksburg on December 13, but it suffered a few casualties due to artillery fire. William Toon resigned in February 1863, and Thomas Toon was selected to replace him. He was promoted to colonel on February 26, 1863.

A winter of inactivity ended with the Battle of Chancellorsville, where Toon formed part of Stonewall Jackson's famous flanking attack

T

on May 2, 1863. He was forced to leave the field after being wounded no fewer than three times the following morning. He was not present at Gettysburg.

On October 11, near Morton's Ford, Toon played a major role in defeating Union General John Buford's cavalry brigade and driving it back across the Rappahannock. It also took part in the Mine Run Campaign, the Battle of the Wilderness, and the Battle of Spotsylvania Court House, where it distinguished itself launching a charge and restoring the Confederate line. Toon received a commendation from General Robert E. Lee. Two days later, on May 14, Toon was wounded yet again.

On May 31, 1864, Thomas Toon was promoted to brigadier general (temporary rank) and assigned to command Robert D. Johnston's North Carolina Brigade. He took part in the Cold Harbor operation and fought in the Shenandoah Valley Campaign of 1864. On August 7, 1864, Thomas Toon reverted to colonel when General Johnston returned to the brigade. Toon fought in the Third Battle of Winchester and at Cedar Creek before returning to Petersburg, which was now under siege.

On March 25, 1865, Toon and his men took part in the Fort Stedman operation, where he suffered his most severe wound of the conflict. For him, the war was over.

As a military commander, Toon does not rank in the genius category, but he was definitely a solid commander and demonstrated courage and genuine leadership throughout the war. He had no military training when the war began and was only twenty-four years old when Lee surrendered. One wonders what he might have accomplished and how high he might have risen had he been older. The fact that senior officers stepped aside for him to be promoted in 1863 says something very positive about him.

Toon spent the rest of his life in education. In 1900, he was elected superintendent of public instruction for the state of North Carolina.

On February 19, 1902, he died suddenly from heart failure. He was sixty-one years old. He was buried in Oakwood Cemetery, Raleigh, North Carolina.

EDWARD DORR TRACY, JR., was born on November 5, 1833, in Macon, Georgia, the son of a judge. He became a lawyer and moved to Huntsville, Alabama. He was a fervent supporter of John C. Breckinridge for president and stumped the northern counties of Alabama on his behalf. After Abraham Lincoln was elected, he organized a militia company in Huntsville and became its captain. On May 2, 1861, it became part of the 4th Alabama Infantry and was sent to Virginia, where it was attached to Barnard E. Bee's brigade. Tracy was appointed major of the 12th Alabama Infantry on July 17 but declined the promotion, probably because he did not want to miss the Battle of First Manassas. Tracy and his company were heavily engaged in the fighting on Matthews Hill on July 21. Every field-grade officer of the 4th Alabama was either wounded or killed.

On October 12, 1861, Edward Tracy accepted the post of lieutenant colonel of the 19th Alabama Infantry, then in Pensacola, Florida. His colonel was Joe Wheeler. The 19th Alabama fought in the Battle of Shiloh, where it lost 110 killed and 240 wounded out of 650 men engaged. Tracy was not wounded, although he did have a horse shot out from under him. He was then sent to East Tennessee, where he impressed General Edmund Kirby Smith, who recommended him for promotion. On June 29, 1862, all the Alabama regiments in the Army of East Tennessee were collected into a brigade with Tracy as its commander. He was appointed brigadier general on August 16, 1862.

Tracy's brigade was part of Carter L. Stevenson's division. In December, during the Battle of Chickasaw Bluffs, it was sent to Vicksburg. It remained in the area of the fortress until late April, when U.S. General Ulysses Grant landed at Bruinsburg, near Grand Gulf, south of Vicksburg. With 1,500 men, Tracy marched to Port Gibson and on May 1, 1863, engaged the enemy in fierce combat. Near mid-afternoon, a minié ball struck him in the back of the neck. He said, "Oh, Lord," and fell dead. General Tracy was twenty-nine years old.

Louisiana historian W. H. Tunnard recalled that Tracy "was one of the most efficient brigade commanders in the army, and his loss was irreparable." Brigadier General Edward D. Tracy is buried in Rose Hill Cemetery, Macon, Georgia.

JAMES HEYWARD TRAPIER was born on November 24, 1815, at Windsor, near Georgetown, South Carolina. He entered the U.S. Military Academy in 1834 and graduated in 1838. Trapier joined the Corps of Engineers and worked on U.S. coastal defenses, primarily at Charleston Harbor, Fort Pulaski (in Georgia), and various forts in New York. He also served in the war against Mexico.

Trapier resigned his commission on February 28, 1848, and returned to South Carolina to become a planter. He became a colonel in the South Carolina Militia. In April 1861, Trapier entered Confederate service as a captain of engineers and as aide-de-camp to Governor Francis Pickens. He was soon with General G. T. Beauregard, constructing batteries in Charleston Harbor, and was engineer in chief on Morris Island, south of Fort Sumter. On June 19, 1861, he was promoted to major and named assistant quartermaster.

On October 21, 1861, James Trapier was promoted to brigadier general. Two weeks later, on November 5, he was appointed commander of the District of Eastern and Middle Florida, where he was criticized by General Braxton Bragg, the Florida State Convention, and citizens of the district. He asked to be relieved in March 1862 and was ordered to report to General Albert Sidney Johnston in Alabama. He was given command of a brigade in the Army of Mississippi but was not present at the Battle of Shiloh. On April 14, he assumed command of a division in Leonidas Polk's I Corps. He remained in northern Mississippi while most of the army took part in the Heartland Campaign. General Trapier commanded his division at Farmington and in the Siege of Corinth.

Apparently, his performance again left something to be desired. He was relieved of his command and sent back to South Carolina.

After a period of unemployment and possible ill health, Trapier spent the rest of the war in minor subdistrict (territorial) assignments in South Carolina.

General James H. Trapier died at a friend's house on December 21, 1865, in Georgetown, South Carolina. He was fifty years of age. He was buried in Prince George Winyah Cemetery, Georgetown.

ISAAC RIDGEWAY TRIMBLE was born on May 15, 1802, in Frederick County, Virginia, but he was moved to Culpeper County as a child. His parents died of fever when he was young, and he was raised by a half brother in Kentucky. He attended West Point, graduated in 1822, and was commissioned in the artillery.

On May 31, 1832, Trimble (who was still a second lieutenant) resigned to work on railroad development as a civilian construction engineer. He worked for several railroads from 1832 to 1861.

In April 1861, Isaac Trimble commanded citizens' organizations for the defense of Baltimore. When Union troops overran the state, Trimble went to Virginia, where, on May 25, 1861, he became a colonel of Virginia State Troops. He built defenses for Norfolk and along the Potomac and was promoted to brigadier general in the Confederate Army on August 6, 1861.

On November 16, Trimble assumed command of a brigade in Richard Ewell's division. He first saw combat in Stonewall Jackson's Valley Campaign of 1862, where he performed well. He particularly distinguished himself in the Battle of Cross Keys, where he commanded two brigades. He was prominent in the Seven Days Battles, where he personally led a charge at Gaines' Mill. He fought at Cedar Mountain, and on August 27, Trimble and 500 men marched thirty-four miles without food or rest and captured Manassas Junction, taking 300 prisoners without losing a man. He also captured 8 guns and a huge volume of supplies. In his official report, Stonewall Jackson called it the most brilliant achievement of the war.

On August 29, during the Second Manassas Campaign, Trimble was wounded by a sharpshooter. The bullet was an explosive ball. It struck the leg three inches above his left ankle, burst in the tibia, left three exit wounds, and took a long time to heal.

Stonewall Jackson recommended Trimble be advanced to major general, although he noted that he did not consider him a good disciplinarian. Trimble was promoted on January 17, 1863.

Trimble returned to the army in June during the Pennsylvania Campaign. He no longer had a command, so he attached himself to Ewell's headquarters as a supernumerary (an excess senior officer).

Isaac Trimble lacked tact. He quarreled frequently with Ewell and was not on friendly terms with J. E. B. Stuart. At Gettysburg on July 1, he forcefully advocated taking Cemetery Hill, but Ewell would not attack it, nor occupy Culp's Hill. Ewell told Trimble that when he wanted advice from a junior officer, he usually asked for it. Upon hearing this, Trimble threw down his sword and declared that he would never again serve under that officer.

Meanwhile, General Pender was wounded, and General Robert E. Lee selected Trimble to replace him. On July 3, 1863, Trimble's new command was one of the three divisions to take part in Pickett's Charge. He was again shot in the left leg, and this time the lower third of it had to be amputated.

The sixty-one-year-old General Trimble was not deemed fit to travel, even in an ambulance. He was left behind when the Rebels finally retreated, and he was captured on July 5. He was hospitalized for months. Union orderlies supplied him with an artificial leg before he was transferred to Johnson's Island prison camp in September.

Gettysburg was Isaac Trimble's last battle. Former U.S. Secretary of War Simon Cameron believed that he was too valuable a prisoner to trade because of his extensive knowledge of Northern railroads. He was probably correct on this point. In any case, in March 1865, General Grant finally ordered that he be exchanged. He was sent to City Point, Virginia, but was unable to rejoin the army before Lee surrendered. Trimble was paroled at Lynchburg on April 16.

Postwar, Isaac Trimble returned to the railroad business as chief engineer of the Baltimore and Potomac. After a three-week illness, he died of bronchitis and pneumonia on January 2, 1888, in Baltimore. He was eighty-five years old. He was buried in Green Mount Cemetery, where Joseph E. Johnston and John Wilkes Booth are also interred.

WILLIAM FEIMSTER TUCKER was born on May 9, 1827, in Iredell County, North Carolina. He attended Emory and Henry College in Virginia and graduated in 1848. Without financial means, he moved to northern Mississippi, settled in Houston, Mississippi (which was then a frontier town), and became a schoolteacher, while simultaneously reading law. He passed the bar, set up a law office, and became a probate judge.

Tucker helped form the Chickasaw Guards, a militia unit, and became its captain in January 1861. The Guards were ordered to Corinth and became Company K of the 11th Mississippi Infantry on May 4, 1861.

The 11th Mississippi was sent to Virginia and assigned to Barnard E. Bee's brigade, and part of it fought at the Battle of First Manassas. Afterward, Tucker's company was sent back to Mississippi, where he was promoted to colonel on May 8, 1862, as commander of the 41st Mississippi Infantry Regiment, which formed at Pontotoc, Mississippi, that summer.

Colonel Tucker distinguished himself in the Battle of Perryville, where he was severely wounded in the right arm. It would be stiff and of little use for the rest of his life. He nevertheless returned to duty in time to lead the 41st in the Second Battle of Murfreesboro. After taking part in the Tullahoma Campaign, Tucker fought at Chickamauga, where his regiment suffered 39.4 percent casualties in two days of heavy fighting.

On October 31, 1863, William F. Tucker succeeded James Patton Anderson as brigade commander and led his brigade in the Battle of Missionary Ridge and the subsequent retreat into northern Georgia. On March 1, 1864, he was promoted to brigadier general.

On May 14, 1864, during the Battle of Resaca, General Tucker was struck in the left arm by a shell fragment. After he recovered, his left arm was three inches shorter than his right, but, as he said, it was "preferable to [having] no arm."

With two damaged arms, General Tucker was precluded from field duty. In April 1865, however, he was able to assume a territorial command: the District of Southwestern Mississippi and Eastern Louisiana. He surrendered the following month and was paroled on May 15, 1865, at Jackson, Mississippi.

Tucker returned home after the war, settled in Okolona, Mississippi, and resumed his law practice. He was elected to a two-year term in the Mississippi legislature (1876–78). He ran for Congress in 1880 but was defeated.

On September 14, 1881, he was lying on his bed, reading a letter from his son, when someone from outside his bedroom window shot him through the chest. Three defendants were tried for his murder, but all were acquitted.

General Tucker was fifty-four years old when he died. He was buried in the Odd Fellows Cemetery in Okolona.

DAVID EMANUEL "TIGER" TWIGGS was the oldest general to serve in the Civil War. He was born on Good Hope plantation in Richmond County, Georgia, near Augusta, on February 14, 1790. His father was John Twiggs, who had served in the American Revolution, won fame as "the savior of Georgia," and had been a major general in the Georgia militia.

Young Twiggs joined the army on March 8, 1812. He was commissioned captain in the infantry and fought in the War of 1812. He was officially discharged in June 1815, but he had showed such promise during the war that he was accepted into the post-war army as a captain and brevet major.

David Twiggs fought against the Seminoles in Florida (1817–18) and in the Black Hawk War (1832), where he distinguished himself. He was promoted to major (1825), lieutenant colonel (1831), and colonel (1836). He commanded the 2nd Dragoons, which under his leadership was generally regarded as the best cavalry unit in the army. The regiment fought the Second Seminole War and was stationed at Fort Jesup, on the Louisiana border with the Republic of Texas, and at Fort Towson, Indian Territory, among other postings.

During the Mexican War, Twiggs led a brigade in the battles of Palo Alto and Resaca de la Palma. He was promoted to brigadier general on June 30, 1846, and was brevetted major general after the Battle of Monterrey, during which he commanded the 2nd Regular Division. He fought in all the battles from Veracruz to the fall of Mexico City and was wounded at Chapultepec.

Twiggs was commander of the Department of the West, headquartered in St. Louis, from 1848 to 1857. He then became commander of the Department of Texas, with headquarters in San Antonio. In 1861, David Twiggs was outranked only by General Winfield Scott. Twiggs, however, was strongly pro-Southern, believing that secession was a constitutional right and that if secession came he would go with his home state of Georgia.

General Twiggs resigned his commission on January 13, 1861, but his resignation was not accepted until January 28, and he was still unaware of its acceptance on February 1, when Texas seceded. Three days later, the Texas Convention appointed commissioners to meet with Twiggs to demand the surrender of all government property—or have it taken by force. Negotiations continued until February 16, when Twiggs, who did not want to fire on the Texans, capitulated. He surrendered his entire department, which included the Federal Arsenal at the Alamo, 20 military installations, 44 cannons, about 1,000 horses, and tens of thousands of dollars' worth of supplies and equipment. Many people in

T

the North, including the Federal government, took his surrender to be an act of treachery.

Twiggs joined the Confederacy and was named commander of the District of Louisiana on April 17. On May 22, he was commissioned as the senior major general in the Confederate Army, with headquarters in New Orleans. He was, however, too old and infirm to exercise his command, and he retired on October 11.

Major General David Emanuel Twiggs died of pneumonia in Augusta, Georgia, on July 15, 1862, at the age of seventy-two. He was buried in Twiggs Cemetery in Augusta under a simple tombstone. His grandson, John Twiggs Myers, commanded the American Legation Guard at Peking, China, during the Boxer Rebellion and later became a lieutenant general in the U.S. Marine Corps.

ROBERT CHARLES TYLER was the last general on either side to be killed in action. He was one of the more obscure Civil War generals. It is not certain where or when he was born. He stated that his age was twenty-eight when he enlisted in the 15th Tennessee on April 18, 1861. It was reported that he was raised in Baltimore. Little is known about his life until 1852, when he lived in California. After this, he no longer called himself "Robert Tyler," but used the name "R. Charles Tyler," or "Reuben C. Tyler," apparently to escape his creditors. In any case, in 1856 he joined William Walker's first filibuster expedition to Nicaragua. After this expedition was defeated, Tyler lived in Baltimore briefly before settling in Memphis, Tennessee, where he helped organize the Knights of the Golden Circle (KGC), a secret organization whose goal was to form a "golden circle" of slave-holding territories that would include Central America, parts of Mexico, and the Southern United States.

When the Civil War began, Tyler enlisted in the 15th Tennessee as a private and was immediately promoted to quartermaster sergeant. In September 1861, he was promoted to major on the staff of General

Benjamin F. Cheatham but returned to the 15th Tennessee in December. He was regimental commander at Shiloh, where he was wounded. In June, he was elected colonel, but that same month General Braxton Bragg named him provost marshal of the Army of Mississippi (later the Army of Tennessee) for the Heartland (Kentucky) Campaign. After the Battle of Stones River, he returned to the command of his regiment, which consolidated with the 37th Tennessee and was now designated the 15th/37th Tennessee. He was seriously wounded at Chickamauga.

Braxton Bragg was impressed with Robert C. Tyler and again named him provost of the army on November 20, 1863. Five days later, he was so badly wounded during the Battle of Missionary Ridge that his left leg had to be amputated.

On February 23, 1864, Tyler was promoted to brigadier general. Two days later, he was given command of a brigade in William B. Bate's division. He was usually absent, however, because of his health, and his brigade was commanded by Thomas Benton Smith. In January 1865, Tyler was placed in command of the post of West Point, Georgia.

On April 16, U.S. General James H. Wilson attacked with overwhelming force, outnumbering the Confederates by as many as thirty to one. General Tyler defended the town at an earthwork called Fort Tyler. He only had a few militias, some local defense forces, and a smattering of detached soldiers. Tyler had refused to burn the houses in front of his works, and a Union sharpshooter used one of them to shoot Robert Tyler. He was taken to the base of the flagstaff, where he died about an hour later. He was about thirty-two years old. He is buried in Fort Tyler Cemetery at West Point, Georgia.

T·

V

VANCE – VILLEPIGUE

ROBERT BRANK VANCE was born at his family's home on Reems Creek, Buncombe County, North Carolina, on April 24, 1828. His father, Captain David Vance, died when Robert was a teenager. Vance was homeschooled by his mother, who had access to an extensive library left by an uncle. Robert was elected clerk of the court of common pleas for Buncombe County at age twenty and remained in office until 1858, when he decided not to seek reelection. He became a merchant in Asheville (the seat of Buncombe County).

Robert Vance and his younger brother Zebulon (who became the Confederate governor of North Carolina) were Whigs and supported the political philosophy of Henry Clay. They opposed secession and backed John Bell and his Constitutional Union Party in the presidential election of 1860. Their primary loyalty, however, was to their state. As the war approached, Robert Vance formed the Buncombe County Life Guards, a militia company, and was elected its captain in 1861. In September 1861, Vance was elected colonel of the 29th North Carolina, to which his militia unit had been assigned as Company H.

The 29th North Carolina was posted to East Tennessee in November, where it defended the Bristol-Chattanooga Railroad from guerrillas and raiders. In February 1862 it was sent to the Cumberland Gap. The Federals captured the gap on June 18 but were forced to abandon it in September during Confederate General Braxton Bragg's Heartland Campaign. The regiment also fought in the victory at Tazewell.

Vance's regiment fought in the Second Battle of Murfreesboro, where he had a horse shot out from under him and where he was slightly wounded. His brigade commander, General James E. Rains, was killed in action on December 31, and Vance replaced him. He was selected as permanent commander and promoted to brigadier general on March 4, 1863. Vance was not long with the brigade, however; after Bragg retreated to Shelbyville in January 1863, Vance came down with typhoid fever and almost died. He did not return to active duty until September

16, 1863, when he was named commander of the District of Western North Carolina.

General Vance was captured at Crosby Creek on January 14, 1864. In Union captivity, he was named special assistant for prisoner exchange and purchased clothing for Confederate prisoners of war.

Vance received his parole at Fort Delaware on March 10, 1865. He returned to the political arena in 1872, when he successfully ran for Congress, and served from 1873 to 1885. He did not seek reelection in 1884.

From 1885 to 1889, he was employed as an assistant commissioner of patents in Washington, D.C. He also wrote several volumes of poetry. After he left Washington, he became a lecturer and served in the North Carolina House of Representatives.

Robert B. Vance died of uremic poisoning (kidney failure) in Asheville, North Carolina, on November 28, 1899. He was seventy-one years old. He is buried in Riverside Cemetery, Asheville.

EARL "BUCK" VAN DORN, a grandnephew of President Andrew Jackson, was born on September 17, 1820, in Claiborne County, Mississippi, near the town of Port Gibson. His father was a lawyer, judge, and state legislator.

Buck Van Dorn was admitted to West Point in 1838, graduated in 1842, and was commissioned a brevet second lieutenant of infantry. He married an Alabama woman in 1843 but had four children by other women. Sent to Texas in 1845, he was involved in the defense of Fort Brown (near Brownsville, Texas) during the early days of the Mexican War. He also fought in the Battle of Monterrey before being transferred to General Winfield Scott's army. He fought in all the major battles from Veracruz to the storming of the Belén Gate at Mexico City (September 13, 1846). He was brevetted captain for his actions at Cerro Gordo and major for his performance at Contreras and Churubusco. He was wounded in the foot near Mexico City on September 3 and took a musket ball to the foot at the Belén Gate.

Van Dorn fought in the Second Seminole War and was promoted to captain in the 2nd U.S. Cavalry in Texas in 1855. In 1858, Van Dorn was transferred to the Indian Territory, where he fought Comanches. He was wounded four times during the Battle of Wichita Village on October 1. He was fully recovered by 1860, when he was promoted to major.

Earl Van Dorn resigned his commission on January 31, 1861, and became a major general in the Mississippi Militia and then a colonel in the Confederate Army. He was commander of the Department of Texas and, with a group of Texas volunteers, captured thirteen companies of U.S. infantry at Saluria on April 24.

Van Dorn was promoted too rapidly: to brigadier general on June 5, 1861, and to major general on September 19, 1861. He was one of those officers of great promise from whom much was expected. Unfortunately, he delivered little.

From September 24, 1861, General Van Dorn commanded a division in northern Virginia. He was named commander of the Trans-Mississippi Department and the Army of the West on January 10, 1862. He assembled an army of 16,000 men and moved to attack U.S. General Samuel Curtis's Army of the Southwest (10,500 men). Unfortunately for the South, Van Dorn did not understand the importance of logistics. His inadequately supplied men were defeated at Pea Ridge on March 7 and 8, 1862.

Ordered to join the main army east of the Mississippi River, Van Dorn served under General G. T. Beauregard in the Siege of Corinth and on July 2 became commander of the Army of West Tennessee, which became the Army of Mississippi. He was in overall command of the Rebel forces during most of the First Siege of Vicksburg (May 18 to July 27, 1862). After the Union flotillas withdrew, he ordered General John C. Breckinridge to recapture Baton Rouge, but this effort was unsuccessful.

As the Confederate commander of Mississippi, Van Dorn was a failure. His rule was arbitrary. He placed most of the state under martial law, tossed many civilians into stockades, hanged six, imposed price controls and restricted trade, shut down newspapers that covered him unfavorably, and outraged public opinion by his high-handed actions, as well as his drunkenness and womanizing. The Army of Mississippi's logistical infrastructure was also a mess. Van Dorn and his two corps commanders, Sterling Price and Mansfield Lovell, badly mishandled the Battle of Iuka and the Second Battle of Corinth and almost got the Army of Mississippi trapped and destroyed. At this point, President Jefferson Davis demoted Van Dorn to a corps commander and replaced him with John C. Pemberton. General John S. Bowen went further and preferred charges against Van Dorn for neglect of duty at Corinth. President Davis, however, did not want to dispense with Van Dorn entirely, so he stacked the court with men sympathetic to him, and Van Dorn was acquitted. He was not, however, acquitted in the court of public opinion.

It was obvious to all that, as an army and department commander, Earl Van Dorn had been promoted over his head. Pemberton, however, suspected that he might be an excellent cavalry leader. He gave Van Dorn command of his horsemen and sent him on a raid to Holly Springs to destroy the main supply depot of U.S. General Ulysses Grant's invading army. Van Dorn succeeded brilliantly. He captured 1,500 Yankees and dozens of horses, burned Grant's main supply depot, and then escaped.

After the Holly Springs Raid, General Joseph E. Johnston transferred Van Dorn's cavalry to General Braxton Bragg in Tennessee. On March 5, 1863, Van Dorn destroyed a Federal force at Thompson's Station, netting two thousand prisoners and suffering only three hundred casualties. On March 16, he was appointed commander of the cavalry corps of the Army of Tennessee. He proved to be a fine cavalry commander.

On May 7, 1863, at his headquarters in Spring Hill, Tennessee, General Van Dorn was shot in the back of the head and killed by Dr. George B. Peters. The general was forty-two years old. Peters later declared that he had shot Van Dorn for "violating the sanctity of [his] home." Van Dorn was indeed having an affair with Jessie Peters, the doctor's wife, but that was not the full story. Professor Bridget Smith uncovered the truth well over a century later: Van Dorn was hardly the first of Jessie's lovers. Peters shot Van Dorn because he was simultaneously having an illicit liaison with Peters's fourteen-year-old daughter, Clara. The affair produced a daughter after Van Dorn's death.

General Van Dorn is buried in Wintergreen Cemetery, Port Gibson, Mississippi.

ALFRED JEFFERSON VAUGHAN, JR., was born in Dinwiddie County, Virginia, on May 10, 1830. He enrolled at the Virginia Military Institute in 1848 and graduated in 1851. He settled in Marshall County, Mississippi, on the Tennessee border, and became a planter.

Vaughan strongly opposed secession but followed his adopted state out of the Union. He formed a company, the Dixie Rifles, and when Mississippi was not able to arm them, he led his men across the border to Moscow, Tennessee (near Memphis), and joined the 13th Tennessee Infantry Regiment. Vaughan became a captain in May 1861. When the regiment was reorganized, Vaughan was elected its lieutenant colonel on June 7.

The 13th Tennessee fought in the Battle of Belmont on November 7, 1861, where it took the brunt of the Federal attack. When the regiment was reorganized, Vaughan was elected colonel on December 4, 1861. The 13th Tennessee fought at the Battle of Shiloh, where on April 6, 1862, Vaughan was struck by a spent ball but not seriously injured. His solid reputation as a combat officer continued to develop in all the campaigns of the western army. Between Shiloh and Chickamauga, he had eight horses shot out from underneath him. He fought at Richmond, Kentucky, and when General Patrick Cleburne was wounded, Vaughan's brigade commander, Preston Smith, assumed temporary command of the division, and Vaughan took charge of the brigade.

Colonel Vaughan joined General Braxton Bragg in time for the Battle of Perryville. Still under Vaughan's command, the brigade retreated to Tennessee. It fought in the Second Battle of Murfreesboro and then retreated to Shelbyville, where General Smith returned to command of his brigade and Vaughan resumed the leadership of the much-reduced 13th Tennessee.

Vaughan took part in the Tullahoma Campaign and the Battle of Chickamauga, where General Smith was killed in action on September 19, 1863. Smith was replaced by Alfred J. Vaughan, who was promoted to brigadier general on November 18.

Vaughan's brigade took part in the Siege of Chattanooga, the Battle of Missionary Ridge on November 25, and the retreat to Dalton, Georgia. He fought in the Atlanta campaign, and on July 4, 1864, at the Battle of Vinings Station, he was about two hundred yards from the front line and was lighting his pipe when his left foot was struck by an exploding shell. His right leg was also severely injured. Surgeons amputated Vaughan's left leg, and he was transported via freight train to Macon. He was incapable of further field duty. After the Confederate surrender, Vaughan was paroled at Gainesville, Alabama, on May 10, 1865.

After the war, he returned to farming in Mississippi, but in the early 1870s, he gave that up in favor of a mercantile business in Memphis, as well as working to help farmers and communities in Tennessee, Mississippi, and Arkansas as part of the Grange movement. In 1878, he was elected clerk of the criminal court of Shelby County (Memphis). He was reelected in 1882. He was also the head of the United Confederate Veterans for the Division of Tennessee. In 1897, he published a book, *Personal Record of the Thirteenth Regiment, Tennessee Infantry*.

In his last years, General Vaughan suffered from cancer. The month before he died, he was sent to Indianapolis, Indiana, to consult with cancer specialists. He passed away on October 1, 1899, at the age of sixty-nine. He was buried in Elmwood Cemetery, Memphis.

JOHN CRAWFORD VAUGHN was born on February 24, 1824, in Monroe County, Tennessee, the son of a county sheriff. Vaughn volunteered for service in the

Mexican War and was elected captain in the 5th Tennessee Volunteers. He reached Mexico City, but only after the fighting was over. He returned home and became a merchant in the village of Sweetwater, East Tennessee.

In 1850, Vaughn sought his fortune in California. He returned home to Sweetwater a couple of years later and built a hotel to serve railroad travelers. He was elected sheriff of Monroe County in 1856.

On April 12, 1861, Vaughn was in Charleston, South Carolina, on a business trip and witnessed General G. T. Beauregard firing on Fort Sumter. With war in the offing, he rushed home to recruit a regiment for the South. The result was the 3rd Tennessee Infantry, also known as the 3rd Tennessee Mounted Infantry. Vaughn became its colonel on May 3, and it left for Virginia on June 2.

Vaughn's regiment fought in the Battle of First Manassas. It returned to East Tennessee in early 1862, where it chased outlaws and bushwhackers. The 3rd Tennessee took part in the recapture of the Cumberland Gap on September 17 and then rejoined General Braxton Bragg in Kentucky, but it was too late to fight in the Battle of Perryville. John C. Vaughn was promoted to brigadier general on September 22, 1862.

Vaughn's brigade consisted largely of recent draftees from East Tennessee, and they were not particularly loyal to the Confederacy. Many of them were Union sympathizers. The brigade was routed in the Battle of Big Black River Bridge on May 17, 1863. It was the first time in the war that a sizable Confederate force ran away. The remnants of Vaughn's brigade fought in the Siege of Vicksburg, which surrendered on July 4, 1863.

After Vaughn was exchanged in October, he formed a cavalry brigade. He worked with General James Longstreet in his failed effort to take Knoxville and successfully operated against marauders and Union guerrillas in East Tennessee and southwest Virginia until the spring of 1864, when he was sent to the Shenandoah Valley. He fought in the Battle of Piedmont on June 5, where the Rebel forces were routed and some of Vaughn's men refused to fight. After General William "Grumble" Jones was killed, Vaughn successfully extracted the remnants of the Rebel forces and joined General Jubal Early but was severely wounded at Martinsburg, (West) Virginia, on July 3.

After he recovered, General Vaughn returned to East Tennessee in September 1864, following the death of General John Hunt Morgan, and assumed command of the Confederate forces there. He was wounded again on September 18. He continued to operate in the rural Appalachian Mountains for most of the rest of the war and experienced some success. On April 19, 1865, he and his men joined President Jefferson Davis's escort. General Vaughn surrendered on May 10, the day Jefferson Davis was captured by Union cavalry.

John Vaughn was indicted for treason by the Republican government in Tennessee, so he and his family fled the state in October 1865. He moved to Thomas County, Georgia, but returned to Sweetwater by 1870. He was elected to the state senate and held office from 1871 to 1873, where he functioned as presiding officer. In 1874, he pled guilty to using false identities in order to defraud a certain widow's pension fund. He was fined $1,000. After that, he returned to southern Georgia and became a merchant.

General John C. Vaughn died of meningitis on September 10, 1875, in Thomasville, Georgia. He was fifty-one years old. He was buried in Laurel Hill Cemetery, Thomasville.

JOHN BORDENAVE VILLEPIGUE (pronounced VIL-uh-PIG) was born on July 2, 1830, in Camden, South Carolina. He entered West Point in 1850 and graduated in 1854. He was a cavalry officer and served mainly on the frontier in Kansas and Nebraska, where he fought the Sioux. Stationed at Fort Lookout, Dakota Territory, in 1856, he participated in the Utah Expedition of 1857–58.

Villepigue resigned his commission on March 31, 1861, and was immediately commissioned as a captain of artillery in the Confederate Regular Army. On April 16, he was promoted to major in the 1st Georgia Infantry

Battalion and in September became lieutenant colonel of the 36th Georgia Infantry Regiment. He was promoted to colonel on October 29. He was placed in charge of the defenses of Fort McRee in Pensacola Harbor.

On November 22, the fort was heavily bombarded by the USS *Niagara* and USS *Richmond* as well as the guns of Fort Pickens. McRee's gunners seriously damaged the *Richmond*. Colonel Villepigue was severely wounded in the arm during the bombardment. By late afternoon, the fort's guns were silenced, and half of them were dismounted, but the gunboats withdrew when darkness fell and the tide went down. The Yankees renewed their bombardment the next day, and the guns of Fort McRee remained silent, but the Federals did not launch an amphibious attack. The fort did not fall until the Confederates evacuated Pensacola in May 1862.

General Braxton Bragg praised Villepigue for remaining in command despite his wound and for his coolness and courage in the battle, setting an inspiring example for the defenders of Fort McRee, most of whom were raw recruits. He noted that the colonel had been specially selected for this dangerous post, that his performance had vindicated his selection, and that his worthy Christian humility had been much in evidence.

On January 27, 1862, John Villepigue was appointed as chief of engineers and artillery in the Department of Alabama and West Florida. He relocated to Mobile, where, on March 13, 1862, he was promoted to brigadier general.

General G. T. Beauregard held Villepigue in high esteem and named him commander of Fort Pillow, a major installation about fifty miles north of Memphis. Its guns blocked the Union Navy's only approach to the River City from the north. In May 1862, the Northern fleet attacked, and Villepigue conducted an able and skillful defense. The Union gunboats were checked and forced to withdraw. But U.S. ground forces southeast of the fort threatened to cut it off. Villepigue was ordered to evacuate the fort—which he did on June 4.

In early June, John Villepigue became a brigade commander. He was one of the few Confederate generals who distinguished himself in the Second Battle of Corinth, both in the opening attack and in covering General Earl Van Dorn's withdrawal. He was promised a promotion and was sent to Port Hudson, Louisiana, to command the defenses there, even though he was ill with river fever. Instead of improving as expected, his condition deteriorated rapidly and developed into pneumonia. General Villepigue died at Port Hudson on November 9, 1862. He was buried in the Quaker Cemetery, Camden, South Carolina, where Confederate Generals Joseph B. Kershaw and John D. Kennedy are also buried.

W

WALKER – WRIGHT

HENRY HARRISON "MUD" WALKER was born at Elmwood in Sussex County, Virginia, on October 15, 1832. He was appointed to the U.S. Military Academy at West Point and graduated in 1853. He was commissioned in the infantry and served in Kentucky, New Mexico, Kansas, and California. Walker was on frontier duty at Fort Churchill, Nevada, when Virginia seceded. He resigned his lieutenancy on May 3, 1861, and was named a captain in the Confederate Regular Army.

In November 1861, "Mud" Walker became lieutenant colonel of the 40th Virginia. He performed well during the Seven Days Battles and was highly praised by General A. P. Hill, his division commander.

On June 27, 1862, during the Battle of Gaines' Mill, he was wounded twice. The second wound was severe, and he spent two months convalescing. When he returned to duty in September 1862, it was as commanding officer of a convalescence camp.

Despite having never commanded a regiment, he was promoted to brigadier general on July 1, 1863, bypassing the rank of colonel altogether. Initially, he commanded Henry Heth's old brigade, which had suffered heavy losses in Pickett's Charge. On July 11, he was given command of James J. Archer's old brigade, which was also badly depleted. He would lead both brigades until October.

On October 14, 1863, Walker distinguished himself in the Battle of Bristoe Station. He later fought in the Mine Run Campaign, the Battle of the Wilderness, and the Battle of Spotsylvania, where on May 10, 1864, his left foot was shattered. Taken to a field hospital, surgeons amputated it that same day. General Walker was in hospitals until July, followed by a recuperative furlough in Savannah. He did not return to active duty until November 7, 1864, when he was assigned to court-martial duty with the Judge Advocates' Office in the Department of Richmond.

Walker was on limited active duty until February 1865, when he was given the mission of defending the Richmond and Danville Railroad during the Siege of Petersburg. This mission ended with the evacuation of Richmond on April 2. It was reportedly Walker who brought the news of Robert E. Lee's surrender to Jefferson Davis. Walker was paroled at Richmond on May 7, 1865.

After the war, Henry H. Walker moved to New Jersey, where he found a new career as an investment broker. He suffered from a form of dementia in his last days. General Walker died of "senile pneumonia" in Morristown, New Jersey, on March 22, 1912, at the age of seventy-nine. He was buried in Evergreen Cemetery, Morristown.

JAMES ALEXANDER "BULLDOG" WALKER was born on August 27, 1832, at Mount Meridian, Virginia. Nicknamed "Jim," "Bulldog," and later "Stonewall Jim," he was educated in private schools until 1848, when he entered the Virginia Military Institute. The hot-tempered Walker was a senior in the spring of 1852 when he took offense at a comment Professor Thomas J. Jackson made in the lecture room. One word led to another, and Jackson had him court-martialed and expelled for insubordination. Walker challenged the future Stonewall to a duel. Despite their different stations, Jackson seriously considered accepting the challenge but in the end did not do so.

After VMI, Walker worked for a railroad for eighteen months and then studied law at the University of Virginia (1854–55). He was admitted to the bar in 1856 and set up a law practice at Newbern in Pulaski County, Virginia.

Following the terrorist attack on Harpers Ferry in October 1859, Walker joined the Pulaski Guards, a local militia unit, and became its captain. When the war began, it became Company C of the 4th Virginia Infantry. On May 17, 1861, the 13th Virginia was organized at Harpers Ferry. A. P. Hill was elected its colonel. James Walker was elected lieutenant colonel. On February 26, 1862, A. P. Hill was promoted to brigade commander, and Walker became colonel.

Walker's regiment fought in Stonewall Jackson's Valley Campaign of 1862. On June 8 and 9, Walker was acting brigade commander during the battles of Cross Keys and Port Republic. Stonewall Jackson noticed that Walker was fearless and at the front of every attack. Past grievances were put aside, and they became friends.

Walker led his regiment in the Seven Days Battles until his brigade commander, Brigadier General Arnold Elzey, was wounded. Walker took charge of the brigade until he was superseded by General Jubal Early on July 1. He led his regiment at Cedar Mountain and in the Battle of Second Manassas. On September 1, James Walker became acting commander of Isaac Trimble's brigade, which was heavily engaged at Sharpsburg. Three of its four regimental commanders were killed or seriously wounded, and Colonel Walker was painfully wounded by a piece of shrapnel from the same shell that killed the horse he was riding.

In December 1862, Colonel Walker received his third brigade of the year when he became acting commander of Early's brigade, which he led at Fredericksburg. After General Elisha F. Paxton was killed during the Battle of Chancellorsville, Jackson named Walker commander of the famous Stonewall Brigade. Jackson recommended him for promotion to brigadier general on his deathbed. Walker was promoted May 15, 1863.

Walker continued to be at the front of all the major battles of the Army of Northern Virginia, including Gettysburg, Bristoe Station, Mine Run, and the Wilderness. On May 12, 1864, during the Battle of Spotsylvania Court House, a Union bullet fractured his left elbow. At Walker's urging, his surgeon avoided amputating the limb but was forced to remove six to eight inches of bone. Not ready to return to full combat duty, he was assigned to guard the Richmond and Danville Railroad, upon which General Robert E. Lee relied for his supplies.

General Walker successfully defended the rail lines from Union raiders and earned the praise of Lee and his senior generals. In February 1865, he asked to be returned to a combat command and was given John Pegram's division. (Pegram was killed on February 6.) He led it to Appomattox, where he surrendered on April 9.

General Walker returned home to Pulaski County, where he labored as a farmer and a lawyer. Walker was elected to the legislature as a Democrat, serving from 1871 to 1874.

In 1876, General Walker was elected lieutenant governor of Virginia. When he returned to the political arena in 1893, it was as a Republican. He was elected and reelected to Congress, serving from March 4, 1895, to March 3, 1899. He was defeated for reelection in 1898. He ran again in 1900 and lost again. James Walker contested both elections. One of the depositions in 1899 led to shots being fired, and Walker was wounded.

General Walker died October 20, 1901, in Wytheville, Virginia. He was sixty-nine years old. He is buried in East End Cemetery, Wytheville. James Alexander Walker was a violent and sometimes fractious man, but he was also a fearless one and an unquestionably excellent tactician.

JOHN GEORGE WALKER was born in Jefferson City, Missouri, on July 22, 1821 or 1822. He was educated at the Jesuit College in St. Louis (now St. Louis University) and on May 27, 1846, was commissioned directly into the Mounted Rifle Regiment of the U.S. Army as a first lieutenant. He was sent to Mexico, where he joined General Zachary Taylor's army in the capture of Monterrey and later served with General Winfield Scott in the drive on Mexico City. He was brevetted captain for bravery at San Juan de los Llanos (August 1, 1847) and was severely wounded at Molino del Rey on September 8. After the Mexican War, Walker served in Arizona, California, Oregon, and New Mexico and fought Indians on the West Texas frontier.

Walker resigned his U.S. Army commission in July 1861 and was commissioned as a major in the Confederate States Army. In August, he became lieutenant colonel of the 8th Texas Cavalry and colonel of the regiment the following month. On September 13, Walker became a brigade commander. He was promoted to brigadier general on January 9, 1862.

General Walker fought in the Seven Days Battles and was wounded at Malvern Hill. He was given command of a division in July and remained in the Richmond area watching Union General George B. McClellan during the Second Manassas Campaign. He rejoined the Army of Northern Virginia for the Maryland Campaign and seized Loudoun Heights overlooking Harpers Ferry. He fought at Sharpsburg and was credited as being one of the men who saved Robert E. Lee's army on September 17. President Jefferson Davis promoted Walker to major general on November 8, 1862, and ordered him to Arkansas to assume command of the Texas Division.

Davis had reports that the division was in a horrible condition, but Walker soon whipped it into shape. The unit was soon known as the Greyhounds, so rapidly did it march. After his long service in Texas, Walker understood the Texas mentality, and he was extremely popular with his men. When he appeared, the troops often placed their hats on their bayonets and cheered him loudly. "No commander could surpass him," one private wrote. "Devoid of ambition, incapable of envy, he was brave, gallant and just."

The Greyhounds first saw action on June 7, 1863, in the Battle of Milliken's Bend, where Ben McCulloch's brigade pushed the Federals to the edge of the river but was unable to destroy them because of fire from the Union gunboats. The Greyhounds lost 185 men, as opposed to 652 for the Yankees.

The Texans later marched west to join Richard Taylor's Army of Western Louisiana and performed brilliantly in the Battle of Mansfield, where 8,800 Rebels routed Nathaniel Banks's 32,000-man army. The next day, Walker was shot through the groin at the Battle of Pleasant Hill. He continued to command from a stretcher until General Taylor arrived and ordered him taken to the rear.

Walker could not return to field duty until after the Red River Campaign was over. On June 10, 1864, Walker succeeded Taylor as commander of the Army of Western Louisiana. On August 4, General Edmund Kirby Smith transferred Walker to command of the District of Texas. In September, he simultaneously became commander of the

III Corps of the Trans-Mississippi Army. He held both posts until March 31, 1865, when he became cavalry commander of the District of Texas, New Mexico, and Arizona.

John G. Walker was undoubtedly one of the best junior generals in the war. He fled to Mexico after the surrender and lived in England for a time. He eventually returned to the United States and served as U.S. consul general to Bogotá, Colombia. Later, he was special American commissioner to the South American republics. In July 1893, in Washington, D.C., he suffered a stroke. After lying in a coma for four days, he died on July 20, 1893. He was buried in Stonewall Jackson Cemetery, Winchester, Virginia.

LEROY POPE WALKER was born on February 7, 1817, near Huntsville, Alabama, the son of Alabama's first U.S. senator. The future Confederate general was educated by private tutors and attended the University of Alabama (1833–35), followed by the University of Virginia, where he studied law. He was admitted to the bar and represented Lawrence County in the legislature in 1843 and 1844. Walker moved to Lauderdale County in extreme northwest Alabama in 1845 and represented it in the legislature from 1847 to 1850, when he was elected a circuit judge. He returned to the legislature in 1853 and served a term as speaker of the house.

LeRoy Walker moved back to the Huntsville area in 1855. He became a brigadier general in the Alabama Militia, despite having no military training. Walker was an ardent secessionist and a delegate to both Democratic conventions in 1860. When the Confederacy was formed, President Jefferson Davis appointed him secretary of war on February 21, 1861. Walker was energetic and very confident, if seriously lacking in military experience and knowledge. After Fort Sumter surrendered, for example, he predicted that Washington, D.C., and Boston would fall to Confederate forces by May 1.

Walker faced huge obstacles in his new position, not the least of which was his boss, Jefferson Davis, who was a micromanager. Davis was, in effect, his own secretary of war, and Walker was often little more than a glorified clerk. In that capacity, he was a poor administrator and failed to forge cooperation among bickering governors. He faced growing criticism, because while he had mobilized two hundred thousand men, he was unable to equip or supply them properly. He worked hard, but his health began to deteriorate, and he was frequently absent with colds.

On September 21, 1861, Walker resigned and accepted a commission as a brigadier general the same day. He commanded troops at Montgomery and Mobile and in March 1862 commanded a brigade in Daniel Ruggles's division. He resigned on March 31, shortly before the Battle of Shiloh, because of bad health. Walker returned to duty as a military judge (with the rank of colonel) on April 6, 1864.

After the war, Walker resumed his law practice. He was, without question, a fine attorney, and he successfully represented several celebrities. In his most celebrated case, he won an acquittal for his client, outlaw and bank robber Frank James, in 1883.

General Walker was president of the Alabama Constitutional Convention in 1875. He passed away from peritonitis on August 23, 1884, in Huntsville. He was sixty-seven. He is buried in Maple Hill Cemetery, Huntsville.

LUCIUS MARSHALL "MARSH" WALKER was born on October 18, 1829, in Columbia, Tennessee. He was the brother-in-law of Confederate General Frank C. Armstrong.

As a nephew of President James K. Polk, Walker had no problem gaining admission to West Point in 1846. He graduated in 1850 and served in the cavalry on the Texas frontier. He resigned in 1852 and returned to Tennessee, where he established a successful mercantile business. He joined the Confederate Army as lieutenant colonel of the 40th Tennessee when it was formed in

Memphis in October 1861. On November 11, he became colonel of the regiment. He was commandant of Memphis for a time before he was posted to Madrid Bend. In February and March 1862, a combined Union Army-Navy task force advanced on the New Madrid–Island Number 10 sector. He successfully withdrew the 40th Tennessee from an untenable position. Walker was promoted to brigadier general on March 11, 1862.

Walker was not a man of robust health, and he missed Shiloh due to illness. He took part in the retreat to Corinth, where on May 9, 1862, he fought in the Battle of Farmington. Here, he launched an effective counterattack. He later took part in the retreat to Tupelo.

General Walker was frequently criticized for his poor performance and leadership. General Braxton Bragg was particularly dissatisfied with him. In the fall of 1862, Walker was sick with dysentery. He received a medical furlough in November. On March 23, 1863, he returned to duty and was ordered to the Trans-Mississippi Department, then headquartered in Little Rock. General Edmund Kirby Smith gave him command of a cavalry brigade.

Lucius Walker performed poorly as a cavalry brigade commander. He fought in the Battle of Helena, Arkansas, in early July 1863, where he failed to support Brigadier General John S. Marmaduke as planned. Marmaduke was furious, but Walker was his senior and thus nominal commander. On August 27, 1863, at the Battle of Reed's Bridge, Walker retreated without notice, leaving Marmaduke's entire command exposed. Marmaduke nevertheless checked the Union advance. Afterwards, Marmaduke demanded that he be removed from Walker's command, or he would resign. Walker took that as a reflection on his courage. One of Walker's staff officers challenged Marmaduke to a duel on Walker's behalf, but without his general's knowledge. Walker nevertheless decided to meet Marmaduke on the field of honor. Sterling Price, their mutual superior, ordered both officers to remain in their tents, but they did not.

The two generals met on the north bank of the Arkansas River on the morning of September 6, 1863, virtually within sight of the enemy, and faced each other with six-shot Colt Navy revolvers. They both missed on their first shots, but on the second try, Marmaduke's bullet struck Walker in the right side. General Lucius Walker died the following evening. He forgave Marmaduke before he passed. He was thirty-three years old. He is buried in Elmwood Cemetery, Memphis.

REUBEN LINDSAY "RUBE" WALKER was born in Logan, Albemarle County, Virginia, on May 29, 1827. His father, a former captain, was well-to-do and sent his son to the Virginia Military Institute, from which Reuben Walker graduated in 1845. "Rube" was reportedly a very popular cadet. After graduation, he worked as an engineer and a farmer.

After John Brown's terrorist attack on Harpers Ferry, Walker became the captain of the Purcell Artillery, a part of the Virginia Militia. In May 1861, he was commissioned a captain of artillery in the Confederate Army. His battery of six Parrott guns reached the battlefield at Manassas in time to shell the retreating Federals. After that, he was stationed at points near the Potomac River. He was promoted to major on March 20, 1862.

He missed the Seven Days Battles because of illness. He returned to duty on July 2, 1862, and was promoted to lieutenant colonel the next day. As chief of artillery for General A. P. Hill's Light Division, he fought in the Second Manassas Campaign, the reduction of Harpers Ferry, and the battles of Sharpsburg and Fredericksburg, in which General Hill reported that Walker "directed the fire from his guns with admirable coolness and precision." He was promoted to colonel on March 14, 1863.

When the Army of Northern Virginia was reorganized following the death of Stonewall Jackson, Walker was appointed chief of artillery of the III Corps on May 30, 1863. He commanded sixty-three guns during the Battle of Gettysburg. He directed the III Corps Artillery with distinction during the Overland Campaign and the Siege of Petersburg. He was promoted to brigadier general on February 18, 1865.

On April 8, 1865, Walker was struck by Union General George Armstrong Custer's cavalry between Appomattox Court House and Appomattox Station. He stopped several attacks. He surrendered the next day. General Walker had fought in sixty-three battles. Despite the fact that he was often found in the thick of the fighting (and was a large target at six feet four), he was never wounded.

Walker was paroled on May 8, 1865, in Richmond. He devoted the next seven years to farming. In 1872, he moved to Alabama, where he worked as a civil engineer and superintendent of the Marion and Selma Railroad. He returned to Virginia in 1876. Eight years later, he moved to Texas, where he was involved in the construction of railroads and in building the Texas state capitol.

Rube Walker returned to Virginia once again in 1888 and lived on his farm at the confluence of the James and Rivanna Rivers. He died on June 7, 1890, in Fluvanna County, Virginia. He was sixty-three years old. He is buried in Hollywood Cemetery, Richmond.

WILLIAM HENRY TALBOT WALKER (often called William H. T. Walker or W. H. T. Walker when in Confederate service), was born in Augusta, Georgia, on November 26, 1816. His father was a lawyer, a U.S. senator in the 1820s, and a mayor of Augusta.

Walker entered West Point in 1832 and graduated in 1837, after being set back a year for academic reasons. He was commissioned in the infantry and was soon on his way to Florida to fight the Seminoles.

On December 25, 1837, at Lake Okeechobee, he was wounded several times (in the neck, shoulder, chest, left arm, and left leg) and left for dead. He was brevetted first lieutenant for his courage, but when a special, accelerated promotion did not materialize, Walker resigned in disgust on October 31. This move was indicative of his main failings, both as a man and as a military leader: he was headstrong, stubborn, and unable to tolerate differing opinions.

Unhappy with civilian life, Walker managed to get himself reinstated in the army at his previous rank. He was promoted to captain in 1845.

In the Mexican War, Walker fought at Veracruz and was slightly wounded at Churubusco. He was brevetted major for his gallantry at Contreras and Churubusco. He was so seriously wounded at Molino del Rey that the doctors initially gave up on him. But he later recovered and was brevetted lieutenant colonel.

Walker was commandant of cadets at West Point (1854–56). He was promoted to major in 1855.

William H. T. Walker was not a healthy man. He suffered from asthma, such that he had to sleep with his back upright. He had been shot so many times he was called "Shot Pouch." He spent half of the next decade on sick leave. He was irritable, fractious, bad-tempered, and prideful but was recognized as a sound tactician.

Politically, Walker was an ardent secessionist. He resigned his commission the same day South Carolina left the Union. After Georgia seceded on January 19, 1861, Walker was given command of one of the state's first two volunteer regiments. He was promoted rapidly: to major general of Georgia Militia (March 13); colonel, Confederate Army (April 25); and brigadier general (May 25). He was stationed at Pensacola but chafed under General Braxton Bragg and asked for a transfer. On August 26, he was ordered to report to General Joseph E. Johnston's army at Manassas. (He and Johnston were old friends.) He was given command of a brigade of Louisianians.

In October 1861, the army was reorganized, and Walker was shifted to command a brigade of Georgians. He was, however, incensed that Richard Taylor, the brother-in-law of Jefferson Davis, had taken command of his former brigade of Louisianians and resigned his commission on October 29, 1861.

While the Confederacy won impressive victories, Walker remained in unhappy retirement in Augusta. The South, however, needed every good general it could get, and on February 9, 1863, Walker was recommissioned as a brigadier general. He was sent to a relatively unimportant sector—Savannah, Georgia, which was then under the command of General G. T. Beauregard.

When Joe Johnston was charged with relieving Vicksburg, he asked for Walker as a division commander, and the War Department approved.

Walker fought in the First Battle of Jackson (May 14), was promoted to major general on May 23, 1863, and was involved in Johnston's half-hearted Vicksburg relief campaign. In the summer of 1863, his troops were transferred to the Reserve Corps of the Army of Tennessee. Walker performed well commanding the corps at Chickamauga, but, inevitably, he disagreed with Braxton Bragg's strategy at Chattanooga. Walker went home on leave in mid-November and missed the Battle of Missionary Ridge.

After Missionary Ridge, Walker was effectively demoted. His corps was disbanded, and he was again a divisional commander in the Atlanta Campaign that began on May 7, 1864. On July 22, 1864, during the Battle of Atlanta, Walker was shot and killed by a Union rifleman. He was forty-seven years old. His body was transported back to Augusta and buried at the city arsenal. It is now buried in the Walker family cemetery, Augusta.

WILLIAM STEPHEN WALKER was born on April 13, 1822, in Pittsburgh, Pennsylvania. He was raised by his uncle, a secretary of the treasury and U.S. senator, and grew up in Georgetown in the District of Columbia and in Mississippi. During the Mexican War, he secured a commission as a first lieutenant in the 1st U.S. Voltigeurs Regiment, which fought from Veracruz to Mexico City. He was brevetted captain for his services at Chapultepec. He was discharged when the regiment disbanded in 1848.

In 1855, Walker rejoined the army as a captain of cavalry. He served in "Bleeding Kansas" and in operations against the Cheyenne on the Western frontier. He resigned on May 1, 1861, and was appointed as a captain in the Confederate Army. He joined Thomas C. Hindman's Arkansas regiment on June 11. That fall, he was named assistant inspector general for the Department of South Carolina, and, in November and December, served as aide-de-camp to the department commander, General Robert E. Lee. He was advanced to assistant adjutant general in December. On March 14, 1862, General John C. Pemberton assumed command of the department and named Walker his adjutant and inspector general. He was promoted to colonel on March 22.

On May 6, Pemberton appointed Walker commander of the 4th and 5th Subdistrict of South Carolina, which covered the area between the Ashepoo River and Oketie (Okatie) Creek. In July, his territory was expanded, and he alternately commanded the 4th and 3rd Military Subdistricts of South Carolina until 1864. On October 22, 1862, he was promoted to brigadier general.

On April 19, 1864, General G. T. Beauregard placed Walker in command of the Tramp Brigade. Walker and his men served in the defense of Petersburg.

On May 20, Beauregard (eighteen thousand men) charged the lines of U.S. General Benjamin Butler's Army of the James (thirty thousand men) near Ware Bottom Church during the Bermuda Hundred operation and forced the Yankees back. Walker's advance, however, lacked coordination. In the smoke and heavy underbrush, he blundered into the 67th Ohio, which delivered a full volley. Walker's horse was hit sixteen times and killed. The general was wounded in the left arm, hip, and leg and was captured.

William Stephen Walker was exchanged on October 29, 1864. On January 6, 1865, he assumed command of the army post at Weldon, North Carolina, and served there until the end of the war. He was paroled at Greensboro, North Carolina, on May 1, 1865.

After the war, Walker moved to Georgia. He died on June 7, 1899, in Atlanta, at age seventy-seven and was buried in Oakland Cemetery, Atlanta.

WILLIAM HENRY WALLACE was born on March 24, 1827, in Laurens County, South Carolina. He entered South Carolina College in 1846, graduated in 1849, and set up as a planter.

In 1857, he became the publisher of the *Union Times* newspaper. He also studied law, passed the bar in 1859, and established a law office. He was elected to the legislature in 1860.

Walker enlisted in Company A of the 18th Carolina Infantry in January 1861 and was soon appointed regimental adjutant. The regiment remained in Charleston until the summer of 1862. Meanwhile, in January 1862, Walker received promotions to first lieutenant and captain, and on May 5, 1862, was elected lieutenant colonel. The regiment was sent to Virginia in the summer of 1862 and was assigned to Nathan "Shanks" Evans's Tramp Brigade. The 18th South Carolina fought at the Battle of Second Manassas and suffered 50 percent casualties, including the death of its commanding colonel. Walker replaced him.

He led the regiment in the Maryland Campaign, including the battles of South Mountain and Sharpsburg (September 17, 1862), where it was part of John Bell Hood's division. After the retreat to Virginia, it was sent to the Kinston and Goldsboro areas of North Carolina. Later, in 1863, the regiment saw duty in South Carolina, Mississippi, and Georgia and by September was defending Charleston, South Carolina.

In February 1864, the 18th was on detached duty in Florida. In May, it was posted to Wilmington, North Carolina. Later that month, it fought in the Bermuda Hundred Campaign and joined the Army of Northern Virginia in the trenches around Petersburg.

On July 30, the 18th was heavily engaged in the Battle of the Crater, where four of its companies were devasted when the Union detonated explosives beneath their positions. With General Stephen Elliott badly wounded, Wallace took charge of what was left of the brigade and ejected the enemy from his trenches. He performed well and was promoted to brigadier general (temporary rank) on September 30, 1864.

Wallace's brigade remained in the trenches south of Petersburg until the lines finally broke on April 2, 1865. The brigade retreated to Appomattox, where Wallace and his men finally surrendered on April 9.

General Wallace returned home to Union, South Carolina, and resumed practicing law. In 1872, he was one of the few Democrats elected to the state legislature. He was reelected in 1874 and 1876. In 1877, he was elected a circuit judge. He was repeatedly reelected without opposition until 1893, when he retired from public life.

Despite being "retired," William Henry Wallace remained active, both as a planter and as a stockholder in at least three cotton mills. He was also deeply interested in promoting economic growth and industrial development in his town and state. He died suddenly on March 21, 1901, in Union, South Carolina, days away from being seventy-four years old. He is buried in Forest Lawn Cemetery, Union, South Carolina.

EDWARD CARY WALTHALL was born in Richmond, Virginia, on April 4, 1831. His father, a merchant, went bankrupt in 1841 and moved the family to Holly Springs, Mississippi. Despite his father's financial difficulties, Edward attended St. Thomas Hall, an Episcopalian academy, where he received an excellent classical education. He studied law while working as deputy clerk of the court in Holly Springs. He was admitted to the bar in 1852 and moved to Coffeeville, where he established his law practice.

In 1856, he was elected district attorney and was reelected in 1860. When the war broke out, he resigned his office and joined the Yalobusha Rifles, which later became part of the 15th Mississippi Infantry Regiment. On April 27, 1861, he was elected first lieutenant, and on July 21, he was elected lieutenant colonel.

Walthall fought at Fishing Creek (Mills Springs), eastern Kentucky. Though a Confederate defeat, Walthall handled his men with vigor and skill. His performance impressed his superiors.

On April 11, 1862, Walthall was elected colonel of the 29th Mississippi Infantry Regiment. He served in the Siege of Corinth and in the Kentucky Campaign, where he took part in the assault on Munfordville. In December, he was promoted to brigadier general and given command of a brigade of Mississippi troops.

Walthall missed the Second Battle of Murfreesboro due to illness. He was involved in the Tullahoma Campaign. the Battle of Chickamauga, and the Siege of Chattanooga. On November 24, 1863, Walthall's 1,500-man brigade was attacked by about 10,000 Federals, who advanced under cover of fog, at the Battle of Lookout Mountain. The fighting was fierce, and by the time Walthall retreated to Missionary Ridge, he had lost most of his brigade. The next day, the remnants of Walthall's brigade were overrun, and General Walthall was severely wounded and captured. He was exchanged in early 1864.

Walthall commanded a brigade at the Battle of Resaca on May 15 and was wounded. On June 6, 1864, he was promoted to major general (temporary rank) and became a division commander. He fought in all of the major battles around Atlanta. After the city fell, he served with General John Bell Hood in the Franklin-Nashville Campaign. On November 30, 1864, during the Battle of Franklin, he was wounded and had two horses shot out from under him.

Following the disastrous Rebel defeat at Nashville, Walthall commanded the infantry portion of the rear guard and operated so well that even General George H. Thomas, the Union commander, praised his performance. Walthall and his division served with the Army of Tennessee in North Carolina and fought in the Battle of Bentonville. They surrendered with the rest of the army on April 26, 1865. General Walthall was paroled on May 1.

Although largely unknown today, Edward C. Walthall was one of the greatest commanders of the Civil War. Joseph E. Johnston later said, "If the Confederate War had lasted two years longer, Gen. Walthall would have risen to the command of all the Confederate armies."

Walthall returned to Coffeeville after the war but moved to Grenada in 1871, where he worked as a corporate lawyer for a railroad. In 1885, the state legislature chose Walthall to an unexpired term in the U.S. Senate. He was elected to a full term in 1886 and served from March 9, 1885, to January 24, 1894. He resigned due to poor health but returned to the Senate on March 4, 1895. In early April 1898, General Walthall developed typhoid pneumonia and, after an illness of two weeks, died in Washington, D.C., on April 21. He was sixty-seven years old. Edward C. Walthall was buried in Hill Crest Cemetery, Holly Springs.

RICHARD WATERHOUSE was born in Rhea County, Tennessee, on January 12, 1832. He ran away from home as a teenager to fight in the Mexican War but rejoined his family when it moved to San Augustine, Texas, in 1849. He worked in the family's mercantile business from then until the outbreak of the Civil War. He helped raise the 19th Texas Infantry Regiment and on May 13, 1862, was elected its colonel. It had 886 men.

Waterhouse's entire career was spent in the Trans-Mississippi Department. In June 1862, he and his regiment marched to Arkansas and joined Henry McCulloch's (later John G. Walker's) division. His regiment was often on the march—in the early months of 1863 it marched from Vicksburg to northwest Arkansas and back again five times—but did not see combat until May 31, 1863, when its artillery exchanged fire with Union gunboats. Waterhouse's first real battle was at Milliken's Bend on June 7, 1863, where the colonel distinguished himself in the inconclusive fighting. After the battle, his regiment remained in Louisiana and was plagued by desertion, poor rations, and disease.

In 1864, however, the 19th Texas was heavily engaged in the Red River Campaign. It fought in the victory at Mansfield (April 8) and the indecisive battle at Pleasant Hill (April 9), as well as several smaller fights. It then marched to Arkansas and fought in the Battle of Jenkins' Ferry (April 30). General Edmund Kirby Smith was impressed by Waterhouse, gave him command of a brigade (which he lead to the end of the war), and promoted him to brigadier general. Confederate President Jefferson Davis, however, did not officially promote Waterhouse until March 17, 1865.

After the war, Richard Waterhouse returned to the mercantile business. He fell down the stairs of a Waco hotel on March 18, 1876. This was followed by a severe case of pneumonia. He died in Waco on March 20 at age forty-four. He was interred in Oakwood Cemetery, Jefferson, Texas.

STAND WATIE, a three-quarters Cherokee, was born on December 12, 1806, in Oothcaloga Cherokee Nation (now Calhoun, Georgia). He was born Degataga, which is translated "standing firm." At various times, Watie was known as "Standhope Uwatie," "Tawkertawker," and "Isaac Watie." He was the only Indian on either side to become a full general officer in the Civil War.

The Watie family was converted to Christianity by missionaries from the Moravian Church, known in German as the Herrnhuter Brüdergemeine, or the Unity of Brethren, one of the oldest Protestant denominations in the world, dating back to fifteenth-century Bohemia. They taught Stand Watie to read and write. As a young man, Watie wrote articles for the *Cherokee Phoenix*, said to be the first Indian newspaper. It published articles in both Cherokee and English. Stand's brother, Elias Boudinot, was the editor.

In 1836, Stand was one of the signatories of the Treaty of New Echota, agreeing to the removal of the Cherokee from Georgia in exchange for new lands in Oklahoma. He migrated to the Indian Territory by 1837 with little difficulty. (The Trail of Tears incident happened the next year.) He settled in the Honey Creek area in what is now extreme northeastern Oklahoma.

Under Cherokee Blood Law, any group of Cherokees who surrendered ancient Cherokee lands forfeited his life, and several Cherokee supporters of the Treaty of New Echota were assassinated, including Watie's brother and other relatives.

In Oklahoma, Watie became a plantation owner in the Spavinaw Creek area and held slaves. As a leader of the Cherokee Nation, he served on the Cherokee Council from 1845 to 1861. He was speaker of the council from 1857 to 1859. When the tribe divided into pro-Union and pro-Confederacy factions, Watie became the acknowledged chief of the Confederate Cherokees. In April 1861, he was commissioned as a captain in the Confederate Army.

Stand Watie was promoted to colonel on July 12, 1861, and was the commander of the 1st (later 2nd) Cherokee Mounted Rifles. He led his men against Yankees, pro-Union Cherokees, and Creeks and Seminoles who supported the North. He took part in the Battle of Pea Ridge.

For three years, Watie's regiment continually harassed Federals. It staged hit-and-run raids against both white and Indian targets and engaged in numerous small battles and skirmishes.

On May 6, 1864, Watie was promoted to brigadier general and commander of a brigade of two regiments: his own mounted rifles and three battalions of Cherokee, Seminole, and Osage infantry.

On September 19, 1864, Watie fought in the Second Battle of Cabin Creek, Indian Territory. He and Brigadier General Richard Gano routed the 2nd Kansas Cavalry and captured 130 wagons and 740 mules. For this victory, Waite received the official thanks of the Confederate Congress.

In February 1865, Watie was named commander of the Indian Division of Indian Territory, but the region was now dominated by Federal forces. On June 23, 1865, Stand Watie surrendered. He was the last Confederate general to do so. He served on the Cherokee Council that negotiated the tribe's peace agreement with the United States.

Watie was exiled in the Choctaw Nation until 1867. He then returned to Honey Creek to rebuild his home and fortune. As a former Confederate general, he prudently stayed out of politics.

As a general, it has been estimated that Watie's troops fought more battles west of the Mississippi than any other group, though his actions were not without controversy. During his famed raid at Cedar Creek, his men massacred a detachment of black hay cutters at Wagoner, Oklahoma.

After a lengthy period of ill health, General Stand Watie died on September 9, 1871. He was sixty-four years old. He was buried in Old Ridge Cemetery (now Polson Cemetery) in Delaware County, Oklahoma.

THOMAS NEVILLE "NIVELLE" WAUL was born on January 5, 1813, in Sumter County, near Stateburg, South Carolina. He attended South Carolina College for three years, which was all he could afford, and left without graduating. He moved to Florence, Alabama, where he taught school.

Apparently not happy as a schoolteacher, Waul moved to Vicksburg, where he studied law. Waul was admitted to the bar in 1835 and eventually became a circuit judge.

In 1850, Thomas Waul moved to Gonzales County, Texas, where he practiced law and established a cotton plantation on the Guadalupe River. In 1859, he ran for Congress but was unsuccessful. In 1861, however, the secession convention appointed him to the Confederate Congress. He took his seat on February 19, 1861. In November 1861, he ran for a seat in the Confederate Senate but was defeated.

Waul returned to Brenham, Texas, in the spring of 1862 and recruited Waul's Legion, a regimental-sized command. He was commissioned its colonel on May 17. The legion was assigned to General John

C. Pemberton's Army of Mississippi, fought in the Vicksburg campaigns, and was besieged in the city.

On May 22, 1863, the Yankees forced a serious breach in the Confederate line. Waul summoned forty men, charged the invaders, restored the line, and took one hundred prisoners. Generals Carter L. Stevenson and Stephen Dill Lee officially commended Waul for his actions. Vicksburg surrendered on July 4, 1863. Waul was still a prisoner of war when he was promoted to brigadier general on September 18, 1863. He was exchanged on October 16 and became a brigade commander in John George Walker's Greyhound Division.

Waul took part in the Red River Campaign, including the Battles of Mansfield and Pleasant Hill. He then marched to Arkansas and fought in the Battle of Jenkins' Ferry on April 30. Here he was severely wounded and returned to Texas to convalesce. He did not return to active duty until September 1864, when he assumed command of a brigade in the District of Texas. He held this post until the end of the war.

After the Trans-Mississippi Department surrendered on May 26, 1865, Waul returned to Gonzales County and reestablished his law practice. He was elected to the constitutional convention of 1866 but never again sought public office after. From 1866 to 1893, he practiced law in Galveston. He was thought highly of and was a faithful member of the Baptist church. He retired to his farm near Greenville, Hunt County, in 1893.

General Thomas Neville Waul died of tuberculosis in Hunt County, Texas, on July 28, 1903, at age 90. He had no blood relations alive at the time of his passing. He is buried in Oakwood Cemetery, Fort Worth, Texas.

HENRY CONSTANTINE WAYNE was born in Savannah, Georgia, on September 18, 1815. He was the son of James M. Wayne, a U.S. congressman and associate justice of the U.S. Supreme Court. In 1834, Henry dropped out of Harvard to attend the U.S. Military Academy, from which he graduated in 1838.

Wayne was commissioned a second lieutenant of artillery and was sent to Maine during the Aroostook War, a border dispute between the United States and Canada that was resolved without fighting. Lieutenant Wayne was sent back to West Point in 1841 as an instructor of artillery and cavalry. He was Master of the Sword at the academy from 1843 to 1846. He authored a book on the subject, *The Sword Exercise, Arranged for Military Instruction*, which was published in 1850.

In 1846, Wayne was promoted to captain and transferred to the quartermaster branch. He rejoined the artillery during the Mexican War and earned a brevet promotion to major for his courage in the battles of Contreras and Churubusco. While in Mexico, he met Captain George H. Crosman. Crosman convinced Wayne that the military should use camels instead of horses in the American Southwest.

When Jefferson Davis became secretary of war in 1853, he decided to put this idea into practice, and Wayne became head of the U.S. Camel Corps, with an eventual strength of seventy-four camels. The War Department proposed buying a thousand more, but the Civil War intervened, the project was scrapped, and the Army's camels were sold or released into the wild.

After Abraham Lincoln was elected president, Henry C. Wayne resigned his commission. On December 13, 1860, he was appointed adjutant and inspector general of the Georgia Militia with the rank of colonel. On December 16, 1861, he was appointed as a brigadier general in the Confederate Army, but he resigned this appointment on January 11, 1862, and returned to his former position as adjutant general of the Georgia Militia. He was promoted to major general of Georgia state troops on January 11, 1862, and commanded the Georgia Militia until June 1, 1864, when he was relieved of his command and assigned to administrative duties. He was succeeded by G. W. Smith.

During Sherman's March to the Sea, Wayne briefly commanded Confederate troops at the Battle of Ball's Ferry (November 23–26, 1864), but he could not stop the Federals from crossing the Oconee River.

General Wayne surrendered on May 7, 1865, and was paroled the next day. After the war, he worked as a timber merchant in Savannah.

Henry C. Wayne died in Savannah on March 15, 1883, at the age of sixty-seven. He was buried in Laurel Grove North Cemetery, Savannah.

DAVID ADDISON WEISIGER was born at the Grove in Chesterfield, Virginia, on December 23, 1818, the grandson of a German immigrant. During the Mexican War, Weisiger was a second lieutenant in the 1st Virginia Infantry, but his regiment never saw combat. While pursuing a successful business career in Petersburg, Virginia, he remained active in the Virginia Militia and was officer of the day when John Brown was hanged.

David Weisiger joined the Confederate Army in April 1861 as a major in the 4th Virginia Militia Battalion (five companies). It was expanded into the 12th Virginia Infantry Regiment, of which he was elected colonel on May 9. It was assigned to the Norfolk garrison and remained there until the city was evacuated on May 9, 1862. It marched to Richmond and joined the Army of Northern Virginia.

Weisiger led the regiment in the Battle of Seven Pines, the Seven Days Battles, and the Battle of Second Manassas, during which, on the afternoon of August 30, he briefly commanded a brigade after General William Mahone was wounded. Shortly after, Weisiger himself suffered a serious bullet wound. He was not able to return to command of the 12th Virginia until July 1863.

The regiment was part of Mahone's brigade when the Overland Campaign began on May 4, 1864. Weisiger again became acting brigade commander when Mahone was severely wounded on May 7. He led the brigade in the battles of the Wilderness, Spotsylvania Court House, and Cold Harbor. He was appointed brigadier general (temporary rank) on May 31, but his promotion was canceled that summer. Colonel Weisiger nevertheless remained in command of the brigade. (He and Mahone did not get along, but they nevertheless worked well together.)

On July 30, Weisiger's brigade (eight hundred men) was part of Mahone's division, which was in reserve at Petersburg when the Yankees blew a four-ton mine underneath Confederate lines. Along with Malone, he led the counterattack at the ensuing Battle of the Crater. He was wounded but succeeded in smashing the Union advance. He was again promoted to brigadier general on November 1, to date from July 30.

Weisiger led his depleted brigade until April 9, 1865, when he and the rest of the Army of Northern Virginia surrendered at Appomattox Court House. He returned to Petersburg and worked first as a bank cashier and then as a businessman in Richmond. General David Addison Weisiger died on February 23, 1899. He was eighty years old. He was buried in Blandford Cemetery, Petersburg, Virginia.

GABRIEL COLVIN "GABE" WHARTON was born on July 23, 1824, in Culpeper County, Virginia. He attended the Virginia Military Institute and graduated with the class of 1847. He went to work as a civil engineer and later moved to the Arizona Territory as a mining engineer.

On July 1, 1861, he was elected major of the 45th Virginia Infantry in southwestern Virginia. On July 17, he became colonel of the 51st Virginia Regiment, which was attached to the Army of the Kanawha. Wharton fought in the Western Virginia Campaign, including the Battle of Carnifex Ferry (September 10), where General John B. Floyd suffered a defeat.

Wharton accompanied Floyd to Kentucky in early 1862 and then to Fort Donelson. He performed well against Grant's campaign against the fort and was praised by General Gideon Pillow for his gallantry. On the night of February 15–16, Floyd escaped from Fort Donelson by steamboat along with Wharton's 51st Virginia and the 56th Virginia Infantry. Wharton and his men took part in the evacuation of Nashville. On May 17, 1862, they defeated a Union regiment at Princeton, southwest Virginia.

Wharton joined General William W. Loring's command and led one of his brigades in the Kanawha Valley Campaign in September 1862. He then commanded an ad hoc division in the mountains of western Virginia until February 1863, when he was posted at Abingdon.

Wharton remained a brigade commander in the Department of Western Virginia until July 1863, when General Robert E. Lee needed troops. Wharton was detached, and the department commander, General Sam Jones, recommended him as an "admirable officer." Wharton was promoted to brigadier general on July 8, and he temporarily commanded the Valley District, with headquarters in Winchester.

After Lee was defeated at Gettysburg and returned to Virginia with his army, Wharton returned to his former station, guarding the Virginia and Tennessee Railroad. He joined General John C. Breckinridge in the Shenandoah Valley in April 1864 and helped him defeat U.S. General Franz Sigel's army in the Battle of New Market. He was sent to Richmond, where he took part in the victory at Cold Harbor. General Wharton then defended Lynchburg and helped chase U.S. General David Hunter from the Shenandoah Valley. Wharton was with General Jubal Early when he invaded Maryland and pushed to the outskirts of Washington, D.C. Remaining in the Army of the Valley, Wharton was given command of his own division on September 20, 1864. He led it until the Battle of Waynesboro (March 2, 1865), when his troops were scattered and many were captured. He only had a handful of men at the end of the war.

General Wharton surrendered on May 2, 1865, and was paroled in Lynchburg on June 4. After the war, he served in the Virginia legislature, worked as a mining engineer, and assisted in building the railroad in New River Valley.

By all accounts, Gabe Wharton was a good brigade and division commander. He died in Radford, Virginia, on May 12, 1906. He was eighty-one years old. He is buried in the Radford family cemetery.

JOHN AUSTIN WHARTON was born near Nashville, Tennessee, on July 3, 1828. His family moved to

Brazoria County, Texas, when he was very young, and he grew up on his father's and uncle's plantations. He was educated by private tutors and in a private school at Galveston. From 1846 to 1850, he attended South Carolina College, where he became commander of the cadet corps.

After graduation, Wharton returned to Texas and studied law. He was admitted to the bar and set up a law office in Brazoria. He was also a highly successful planter and became wealthy. Wharton was a presidential elector for John C. Breckinridge in 1860 and a member of the Texas Secession Convention in 1861, voting for secession.

In February 1861, Wharton joined the Confederate Army and was promptly promoted to captain in the 8th Texas Cavalry (Terry's Texas Rangers). The 8th Texas first saw combat on December 17, 1861, at Woodsonville, Kentucky, where Colonel Benjamin Franklin Terry was killed, and the regiment's lieutenant colonel fell sick and died shortly after. The regiment then elected Wharton colonel.

John Wharton distinguished himself at Shiloh on April 6, 1862, where he dismounted his men and led a ground attack. He pushed back the Federals but was wounded.

John Wharton's regiment took part in General Nathan Bedford Forrest's raid into central Tennessee, and on July 13, he spearheaded the attack on Murfreesboro. He literally ran over the sleeping Yankees in their tents and personally shot their commander, Colonel William Duffield, who was badly wounded and captured. Wharton suffered a severe wound a few moments later.

Colonel Wharton was given command of a brigade in General Joe Wheeler's cavalry on September 27, 1862, after the Heartland Campaign, and was promoted to brigadier general on November 18. He was placed in charge of a division on January 22, 1863. He took part in Wheeler's ill-advised attack on Fort Donelson, Tennessee, on February 3, 1863, the Tullahoma Campaign in July, and the Battle of Chickamauga in September, where he distinguished himself. He was promoted to major general on November 10, 1863. He fought in the Chattanooga Campaign but was so at odds with General Wheeler that he conspired to replace him.

Instead, President Jefferson Davis transferred Wharton to the Trans-Mississippi Department. He joined General Richard Taylor's army just after the Battle of Mansfield, was given a cavalry division on April 12, 1864, and successfully harassed the Yankee rear guard. Wharton became cavalry corps commander after General Taylor sacked Hamilton Bee on April 21. John Wharton led the corps until September 1864.

Wharton's corps took part in Sterling Price's disastrous raid into Missouri and was downgraded to a 5,400-man division after he returned to Texas, where he remained for the rest of the war. On April 6, 1865, he had an altercation with Colonel George W. Baylor, who shot him. Wharton died almost instantly. He was thirty-six years old.

General Wharton was first buried in Hempstead, Texas, near his home. Later he was reinterred with full military honors in Texas State Cemetery, Austin. Wharton was a fine cavalry commander. He was bold without being rash and was loved by his men. He could communicate equally well with uneducated privates and Bourbon aristocrats, inspiring both.

JOSEPH "FIGHTIN' JOE" WHEELER was born on September 10, 1836, in Augusta, Georgia. He was educated at Episcopal Academy in Cheshire, Connecticut. He gained admission to West Point and graduated in 1859.

A cavalryman, Wheeler was stationed in New Mexico, where he fought Indians and earned the nickname "Fightin' Joe." He was a colorful character, small of stature (sometimes called "Little Joe"), and was a lax disciplinarian.

Lieutenant Wheeler resigned his U.S. Army commission on April 22, 1861, and became a first lieutenant in the Confederate Army. He was posted initially to the Pensacola garrison, serving under General Braxton Bragg. On September 4, 1861, Wheeler was named colonel of the 19th Alabama Infantry, which he led at Shiloh, fighting well. He and his men took part in the

Siege of Corinth and the subsequent withdrawal to Tupelo and then joined Braxton Bragg for the Kentucky Campaign.

Wheeler fought in all the major campaigns of the Army of Tennessee except for General John Bell Hood's Tennessee Campaign of 1864. On September 14, 1862, Bragg named Wheeler commander of a cavalry brigade. He was promoted to brigadier general on October 30, 1862, and became a major general on January 23, 1863, at age twenty-six.

"Little Joe" showed his greatest skill in screening the army's movements, smashing Union forays into the Confederate rear, and covering retreats. He was not so good as a raider. His attack on Fort Donelson (February 3, 1863) was a debacle. From October 1 to Ocotber 9, he launched a raid into the Union rear, which was another disaster.

On November 27, during the Battle of Ringgold Gap, he was wounded by an exploding shell near La Vergne, Tennessee. It was one of three wounds he suffered during the war. He also lost thirty-six staff officers (mostly aides) killed or wounded and had sixteen horses shot from under him during the conflict.

After Atlanta fell to the Yankees on September 2, 1864, John Bell Hood decided to invade Tennessee. He left behind Joe Wheeler and his 3,500 men to defend Georgia from U.S. General William T. Sherman and his more than 66,000 men. Wheeler's troops were notoriously ill-disciplined, and General D. H. Hill noted that "the whole of Georgia [was] full of bitter complaints of Wheeler's cavalry."

In January 1865, General G. T. Beauregard's chief of staff inspected Wheeler's cavalry and found it deficient in every category. In February, at Beauregard's request, Wade Hampton was promoted to lieutenant general, and Wheeler and his cavalry were put under Hampton's command, where they remained until the end of the war.

Fightin' Joe Wheeler joined Jefferson Davis's escort but was captured on May 9, 1865, at Conyers Station, Georgia. The Federals placed him in solitary confinement. He was paroled at Fort Delaware on June 8.

After the war, General Wheeler moved to Louisiana, tried his hand at the carriage and hardware business, failed at that, returned to Alabama, studied law, was admitted to the bar, opened a law practice in what is now known as Wheeler, Alabama, and set himself up as a planter. He ran for Congress in 1880 and was elected in a heated contest. He served as a U.S. congressman from March 4, 1881, to June 3, 1882 (except for six weeks in 1883), and from 1885 to 1900.

In 1898, at the outbreak of the Spanish-American War, President William McKinley appointed him a major general of U.S. Volunteers. He commanded the American cavalry division in Cuba, which included Theodore Roosevelt's Rough Riders. Later, as a brigadier general in the Regular Army, Wheeler served under General Arthur MacArthur in the Philippine War. He retired from the U.S. Army in 1900 and settled in New York.

He was the author of several books, including *A Revised System of Cavalry Tactics, for the Use of the Cavalry and Mounted Infantry* (1863), which was used by the Confederate Army during the war, *The Santiago Campaign* (1898), and *Confederate Military History: Alabama* (1899).

General Joseph Wheeler died in Brooklyn, New York, January 25, 1906, after a short illness. He was sixty-nine years old. He was buried in Arlington National Cemetery.

JOHN WILKINS WHITFIELD was born on March 11, 1818, near Franklin, Tennessee. During the Mexican War, he was a captain in the 1st Tennessee Infantry and later lieutenant colonel of the 2nd Tennessee; he fought in the American victories at Fort de la Tenería and Monterrey.

Whitfield served two terms in the Tennessee legislature (1848 to 1851). He moved to Missouri in 1853, where he was Indian Agent to the Pottawatomie Indians at Westport. Later he became an agent to the Arkansas Indians. He was selected as the delegate to Congress from the Territory of Kansas, serving from late 1854 to 1857. He was strongly pro-Southern and anti-abolitionist.

From 1857 to 1861, Whitfield was register of the land office at Doniphan, Kansas. In 1860, he purchased 1,500 acres on the Navidad River in Lavaca County, Texas. He moved there in 1861 and organized a company of cavalry in Lavaca County. It was later redesignated Company D, 27th Texas Cavalry Battalion. Whitfield became its captain in July 1861.

On September 29, 1861, he was promoted to major and commander of the battalion. It only had four companies. He led his command, which was sometimes called the Whitfield Legion or the 1st Texas Legion, in the Battle of Pea Ridge. On April 2, the 27th was increased from four companies to thirteen, and Whitfield became its colonel.

The expanded Whitfield Legion became an infantry unit and was assigned to Sterling Price's division of the Army of the West (later the Army of West Tennessee) on April 29. It was officially known as the 27th Texas Cavalry Regiment (Dismounted). On September 19, it fought in the Battle of Iuka, where Colonel Whitfield was wounded twice. General Price praised the "dashing boldness and steady courage" of Whitfield and his men, which placed them "side by side with the bravest and the best."

John W. Whitfield never really recovered from the wound he took in his right shoulder at Iuka. He nevertheless returned to his command when it was stationed at Yazoo City, Mississippi, and again became a cavalry unit. It was sent to Tennessee as part of William "Red" Jackson's brigade and fought in the Battle of Spring Hill (March 5, 1863). Colonel Whitfield performed well and was promoted to brigadier general on May 9, 1863. On July 4, 1863, he attacked and defeated five hundred U.S. cavalry at Messinger's Ferry, a victory that was overshadowed by the fall of Vicksburg to the Federals that same day.

The Federals recognized Whitfield's talents. On September 17, 1863, Union General William T. Sherman wrote to U.S. General Henry Halleck that the Confederate cavalry serving under Confederate General Stephen Dill Lee, including Whitfield's brigade, was "the best cavalry in the world." In October 1863, U.S. General James B. McPherson wrote to General Ulysses Grant confessing that the Confederate cavalry he faced, including Whitfield's brigade, was "far superior" to their own.

But on October 2, 1863, Stephen D. Lee reported that wounds and rheumatism had made Whitfield too ill for active field duty. Doctors recommended he be transferred to a healthier climate. In December 1863, he left for Texas, where he stayed for the rest of the war. Whitfield was paroled in Columbus, Texas, on June 29, 1865.

After the war, Whitfield labored as a farmer and stockman in Lavaca County. He served as a delegate to the constitutional conventions of 1866 and 1875. General Whitfield died on October 27, 1879, near Hallettsville, Lavaca County, Texas. He was sixty-one years old. He was buried in Hallettsville Cemetery.

WILLIAM HENRY CHASE "LITTLE BILLY" WHITING was born in Biloxi, Mississippi, on March 22, 1824. His father, a Massachusetts native, was a career army officer and a lieutenant colonel in the 1st Artillery when he died in 1852. Educated in Boston and at Georgetown College, D.C., young Whiting entered the U.S. Military Academy in 1841 and graduated at the head of his class in 1845. He was commissioned a second lieutenant in the Corps of Engineers.

Lieutenant Whiting worked on river and harbor improvements, lighthouses, and coastal fortifications in California, on the Gulf of Mexico, and the southeastern coast. He also did a tour of duty on the Texas frontier.

The Southern Confederacy was formed on February 8, 1861. Whiting resigned his commission twelve days later and became a major in the Confederate Army. He was present at the bombardment of Fort Sumter and became a brigadier general in the North Carolina Militia on April 21. On May 24, he joined Joseph E. Johnston's Army of the Shenandoah as chief engineer and de facto chief of staff. Johnston thought highly of Whiting, who was charged with demolishing the armory at Harpers Ferry and arranging the transportation of the Army of the Shenandoah from the Shenandoah Valley to Manassas. On July 21, 1861, on the battlefield at Manassas, President Jefferson Davis promoted Whiting to brigadier general and gave him command of General Bernard Bee's brigade, after Bee fell mortally wounded. Whiting fought at Yorktown and Seven Pines and in the Seven Days Battles (during which he commanded a division).

On July 17, 1862, he was transferred to the command of the District of Cape Fear in the Department of North Carolina. His area of responsibility included Wilmington and Fort Fisher.

Whiting did a marvelous job at Wilmington, which became the South's leading blockade-running port, and he strengthened and expanded the defenses of Fort Fisher. The result was a steady flow of supplies to the South until almost the end of the war. In recognition of his services, Little Billy was promoted to major general on February 28, 1863.

General Whiting constantly asked the War Department to transfer him to a more active theater of operations. These requests were generally ignored because of his superior performance in North Carolina and because Whiting did not get along well with his fellow officers, whom he looked down upon, almost uniformly, as his intellectual inferiors. But early in the Siege of Petersburg, Whiting was given command of an ad hoc brigade under General George Pickett and did a good job. As soon as the emergency passed, however, he was returned to Wilmington.

While Whiting was unpopular with officers, he was quite popular with his men. They were the ones who nicknamed him "Little Billy." Daniel Harvey Hill, Jr., wrote that his men "almost worshiped" him.

In late December 1864, Whiting defeated General Benjamin Butler and Admiral David Porter's attempt to seize Fort Fisher. Bracing for another assault, he requested reinforcements; his request was denied. Arriving at Fort Fisher, Whiting told Colonel William Lamb that he had come to share his fate. "You and your garrison are to be sacrificed."

After a two-day naval bombardment, the Union launched the largest amphibious landing in American history before World War II. On January 15, 1865, the Federals attacked with more than 11,000 soldiers, sailors, and marines, supported by 58 ships. Colonel Lamb met them with 1,900 men. As the Yankees overpowered the defenders, General Whiting fought them hand-to-hand. He was hit with two bullets. One struck his right leg and the other went through his hip. He was taken prisoner and transported to Union Military Hospital at Fort Columbus, on Governors Island, New York Harbor. He died of his wounds and illness on March 10, 1865. He was forty years old. General William H. C. Whiting was buried in the Green-Wood Cemetery in Brooklyn.

In 1900, his wife had his body exhumed and reburied in Oakdale Cemetery, Wilmington; she is buried next to him.

WILLIAMS CARTER WICKHAM was born in Richmond, Virginia, on September 21, 1820. He spent much of his youth on his father's 3,200-acre plantation, Hickory Hill, which was located about 20 miles north of Richmond. Educated at the University of Virginia, he was admitted to the bar in 1842.

Wickham was elected to the Virginia House of Delegates in 1849 as a Whig and to the Virginia Senate in 1859. He joined the local militia company, the Hanover Dragoons, and became its captain. He was elected to the Virginia Secession Convention and voted against secession. When the Old Dominion left the Union anyway, Wickman and his company joined the Confederacy and fought in the Battle of First Manassas.

In September 1861, Governor John Letcher appointed him lieutenant colonel of the 4th Virginia Cavalry. The regiment took part in the Peninsula Campaign, and during a cavalry charge at the Battle of Williamsburg (May 4, 1862), Wickman was badly wounded by a saber thrust. He went to his father's home in Ashland (five miles from Hickory Hill), where he was captured by a Yankee patrol on May 29. He was exchanged that summer and was promoted to colonel on July 28.

As part of Fitzhugh Lee's brigade, William Wickham led his regiment during the Battle of Second Manassas, the Maryland Campaign, and the retreat to Virginia. On November 3, during a skirmish against the Federals, he was wounded when a shell fragment struck him in the neck. He recovered in time to fight at the Battle of Fredericksburg and in the Chancellorsville Campaign. In May 1863, he was elected to the Confederate Congress for the Richmond district but opted to remain with the army and left his seat temporarily vacant.

Wickham fought at Brandy Station and in the Gettysburg Campaign. He was promoted to brigadier general on September 2, 1863, to rank from September 1. On September 9, J. E. B. Stuart's cavalry was reorganized into a corps, and Wickham took charge of Fitz Lee's old brigade.

General Wickham fought in the battles of Bristoe, Brandy Station, and Buckland Mills and helped smash Union General Judson Kilpatrick's raid on Richmond in February 1864. He took part in the battles of the Wilderness, Spotsylvania, Beaver Dam, and Yellow Tavern.

In August 1864, he and his men were sent to join Jubal Early's Army of the Valley in the Shenandoah. He covered the Confederate retreat after the Battle of Winchester (September 19), and the Battle of Fisher's Hill (September 22). He resigned his commission on October 5 to take his seat in Congress.

After the Confederate surrender, William C. Wickham aligned himself with the Republican Party. He went into the corporate world and became president of the Virginia Central Railroad and later president and then vice president of the Chesapeake and Ohio Railroad. He was a member of the Electoral College in 1872, voting for President Ulysses Grant. He was a member of the state senate as an independent from 1883 until his death.

General Wickham died of a heart attack in Richmond on July 23, 1888. He was sixty-seven years old. He was buried in Hickory Hill Cemetery, Ashland, Virginia. Many of the men of his old command, who split from him politically, insisted that the legislature erect a statue to his memory. It was unveiled in Richmond in 1891. It was toppled from its pedestal in 2020 as part of a widespread leftist campaign against American history.

LOUIS TREZEVANT WIGFALL was born on his father's plantation near Edgefield, Edgefield County, South Carolina, on April 21, 1816. He was privately educated before attending the University of Virginia and South Carolina College. He was an indifferent student: proud, quarrelsome, more interested in taverns than study halls, and keen on issuing challenges to duels. He believed that chivalry, slavery, and agrarianism were the foundations of civilization.

Wigfall dropped out of school in order to fight in the Second Seminole War, where he achieved the rank of lieutenant of volunteers. He then returned to school, graduated in 1837, and was admitted to the bar around 1839.

Wigfall was deeply involved in the gubernatorial election of 1840, during which, in a five-month period, he got involved in a fistfight, two duels, and three other challenges and was charged with killing a man, although he was not indicted. He met future Congressman Preston Brooks on the field of honor, and Brooks put a bullet through both of his thighs. Although this was Wigfall's last duel, he continued to espouse the code duello throughout his life, as an important "factor in the improvement of both the morals and manners of the community." He may have been right about that.

Wigfall squandered his inheritance on drinking and gambling and had to sell his property to help cover his debts. He moved to Marshall, Texas, hoping for a new start. He was a great stump speaker and was elected to the Texas House of Representatives in 1850 and to the Texas Senate in 1857. He capitalized on the fear engendered by John Brown's attack on Harpers Ferry and was elected to the U.S. Senate, serving from December 5, 1859, to March 23, 1861, when the Senate expelled him for supporting the "rebellion." (He had also been a delegate to the Provisional Congress of the Confederate States of America in February 1861.)

Wigfall was a volunteer aide to General G. T. Beauregard in Charleston, South Carolina, during the siege of Fort Sumter. In a bit of a stunt, he took a skiff to the fort and demanded its surrender. The mission was unauthorized, but it did result in the garrison commander's running up the white flag. The incident greatly increased Wigfall's celebrity. On April 12, he was formally appointed colonel of the 1st Texas Infantry Regiment.

At the start of the war, Wigfall was a close friend of President Jefferson Davis and served as one of his aides-de-camp from May to August 1861. Their friendship later disintegrated under Wigfall's frequent and harsh criticisms.

Despite his falling out with the president, Wigfall was promoted to brigadier general on October 21, 1861, and became commander of the Texas Brigade. He established his headquarters at a tavern in Dumfries, Virginia, and was frequently and obviously drunk, as well as very nervous. No one was upset when he resigned his commission on February 20, 1862, to take a seat in the Confederate Senate, though he remained active in military affairs. While still a senator, Wigfall served as a volunteer aide to General Joseph E. Johnston from February 1864 until April 1865.

After the war, he fled to England. He returned to the United States in 1870, living first in Colorado, then in Baltimore, and finally in Galveston, Texas. He died of a stroke on February 18, 1874. He was fifty-seven years old and was buried in Trinity Episcopal Cemetery, Galveston.

CADMUS MARCELLUS "CAD" WILCOX was born in Wayne or Greene County, North Carolina (depending on the source consulted) on May 20, 1824. His family moved to Tipton County, Tennessee, when he was two. He attended the University of Nashville and entered West Point in 1842. He graduated in 1846.

Wilcox had an exuberant nature. He was personable, had a dry sense of humor, was often charming, and was a nervously active man. He also had a touch of hypochondria.

Wilcox served in Winfield Scott's army in Mexico and fought from Veracruz to Mexico City. His subsequent military service took him from Missouri to fighting Seminoles in Florida, as well as from Texas to West Point, where he was an assistant instructor of infantry tactics. In November 1857, Wilcox was sent to Europe, where he visited the French Army's school at Vincennes. (He was fluent in French.) He returned to America in early 1859, and published *Rifles and Rifle Practice: An Elementary Treatise Upon the Theory of Rifle Firing, Explaining the Causes of Inaccuracy of Fire, and the Manner of Correcting It*. It became a standard text at West Point.

Wilcox fought against the Navajos in New Mexico and was promoted to captain in late 1860.

Wilcox opposed slavery but favored secession. As soon as he learned that North Carolina and Tennessee had seceded, he resigned his commission. He was appointed a captain of artillery in the Confederate Regular Army.

On July 9, 1861, he was assigned to command the 9th Alabama Infantry in northern Virginia. The colonel was not popular with many of his troops because he imposed discipline. On the recommendation of General G. T. Beauregard, he was promoted to brigadier general on October 21, 1861, and took charge of Edmund Kirby Smith's old brigade. It fought in the Peninsula Campaign and at Seven Pines, where Wilcox commanded three brigades. He proved to be a fine brigade commander. He was engaged in heavy combat at Gaines' Mill and Frayser's Farm, where his men captured two six-gun batteries. Still commanding three brigades, Cadmus M. Wilcox did well in the Battle of Second Manassas and the subsequent pursuit of the Federals. He missed the Battle of Sharpsburg due to a bout of dysentery. Back in brigade command, his troops were lightly engaged at Fredericksburg.

During the Chancellorsville Campaign, after the Federals broke General Jubal Early's line, Wilcox marched to Salem Church on his own initiative and checked a major Union attack. He also fought at Gettysburg, after which he replaced William Dorsey Pender as commander of the Light Division. He was promoted to major general on August 13, 1863, to rank from August 3.

As a leader, Cad Wilcox was blunt, tactless, often profane, overtly ambitious, and occasionally jealous. He was nevertheless a fine commander—at the brigade level. His performance at the divisional level was mixed.

On May 6, 1864, during the Battle of the Wilderness, Wilcox's and Henry Heth's divisions were surprised and scattered when the U.S. II Corps and VI Corps attacked at dawn. The Confederate generals had neither conducted an adequate reconnaissance nor ordered their men to dig in. Heth later recalled that General Robert E. Lee "never forgave Wilcox or me for this awful blunder."

Wilcox fought in the Battle of Spotsylvania and the subsequent retreat to Petersburg. He blundered in the battle on Jerusalem Plank Road and failed to support Billy Mahone, costing the South a potentially significant victory. On the other hand, he performed brilliantly at Ream's Station and bagged 2,100 prisoners and nine guns.

For nine months, Wilcox's division held a four- to five-mile trench line at Petersburg and slowly bled to death due to casualties, illness, disease, and desertion. On April 2, 1865, the Yankees broke Wilcox's line. He rushed what troops he could to plug the gaps and delayed the Federals long enough for General Lee to conduct a reasonably orderly withdrawal. He surrendered with the rest of the army at Appomattox on April 9, 1865.

General Wilcox went to Mexico after the war. He returned to the United States in 1866 and eventually became a messenger for the U.S. Senate. Like many Southerners of his era, he had fallen a long way. He was later promoted to assistant doorkeeper of the Senate.

From 1886 to 1890, Wilcox was chief of the Railroad Division in the U.S. Land Office. He also wrote articles for the Southern Historical Society and had begun writing a book, *History of the Mexican War*, which his niece edited and published after his death in 1892.

General Cadmus M. Wilcox suffered a bad fall and died of a cerebral hemorrhage in Washington, D.C., five days later on December 2, 1890. He was sixty-six years old. He was buried in Oak Hill Cemetery, Washington, D.C.

JOHN STUART "CERRO GORDO" WILLIAMS
was born on June 28, 1818, in Mount Sterling, Kentucky. He was educated at Miami University in Oxford, Ohio, from which he graduated in 1838. He then studied law, was admitted to the bar, and began practicing law in Paris, Kentucky.

Williams volunteered for service in the Mexican War and became captain of an independent company attached to the 6th U.S. Infantry. He played such a prominent role in the Battle of Cerro Gordo that he bore the sobriquet "Cerro Gordo" for the rest of his life. He later became colonel of the 4th Kentucky Infantry Regiment.

He was with Winfield Scott's army throughout the war, including the capture of Mexico City. He then returned to Kentucky and his law practice. He also acquired a farm and was very interested in stock raising.

Politically, Williams was a Whig. He served in the Kentucky legislature from 1851 to 1855. He opposed secession but supported states' rights and opposed President Abraham Lincoln's policy of keeping the Southern states in the Union by force. On November 16, 1861, he joined the Confederate Army as colonel of the 5th Kentucky Infantry.

Williams, who was promoted to brigadier general on April 16, 1862, spent most of the Civil War in the Appalachian Mountains, where he fought pro-Union bushwhackers, invaded eastern Kentucky with General Humphrey Marshall, battled the U.S. Army of the Ohio's advance into eastern Tennessee, and fought in numerous minor battles and skirmishes, including Blue Springs and Henderson's Mill.

In June 1864, Williams assumed command of a brigade in Joe Wheeler's cavalry corps and fought in the Atlanta Campaign. At one point, he was arrested by General Wheeler, but the charges were later dropped.

General Williams returned to the mountains after the fall of Atlanta and played a decisive role in the Confederate victory at Saltville on October 2, 1864. From April 9, 1865, until the surrender, Cerro Gordo

Williams commanded a brigade in Wade Hampton's cavalry. He was paroled at Washington, Georgia, on May 9, 1865.

After the war, Williams returned to his farm near Winchester, Kentucky. He eventually resumed his political career, served two terms in the Kentucky legislature, was an unsuccessful candidate for governor in 1875, and was a Democratic presidential elector in 1876. In 1878, he was elected a U.S. senator, serving from 1879 to 1885. Defeated for reelection in 1884, he retired from politics and returned to farming and raising livestock.

In the late 1880s, he promoted Florida land development and was copublisher of the Louisville *Courier-Journal*. He also established Naples, a resort town on the Florida Gulf coast.

General John Stuart Williams died on July 17, 1898, in Mount Sterling, Kentucky. He was eighty years old. He is buried in Winchester Cemetery, Winchester, Kentucky.

CLAUDIUS CHARLES WILSON was born in Effingham County, Georgia, on October 1, 1831. He graduated from Emory College in 1851, went on to study law, was admitted to the bar in 1852, and was solicitor general for eastern Georgia in 1859 and 1860. In April 1861, he enlisted in the Bryan Guards, which later became Company D of the 25th Georgia Infantry Regiment. He was mustered into Confederate service on August 9, 1861, as a captain.

Despite a lack of military experience, Claudius Wilson was elected colonel of his regiment on September 2, 1861, and occasionally served as brigade commander. The 25th Georgia's primary role was defending the coastlines of Georgia and South Carolina, until May 1863, when it fought at the Battle of Jackson in Mississippi. In June, Wilson became a brigade commander in General William H. T. Walker's division.

He took part in the Tullahoma Campaign, distinguished himself in the Battle of Chickamauga (launching a counterattack that captured several guns), and saw action in the Siege of Chattanooga.

On November 16, 1863, he became a brigadier general, though his appointment was confirmed posthumously. Claudius Wilson came down with "camp fever" (possibly yellow fever) and was sent back to Georgia. He died at Ringgold on November 27, 1863. He was thirty-two years old. General Wilson was buried in Bonaventure Cemetery, Savannah.

CHARLES SIDNEY WINDER (pronounced WINE-der) was born in Talbot County, on the Eastern Shore of Maryland, on October 18, 1829, the son of a captain in the 2nd Dragoons. His family owned Wye, an enormous estate, and was quite wealthy.

Winder attended St. John's College in Annapolis, Maryland, and graduated from West Point in 1850. He was commissioned a brevet second lieutenant in the artillery. After serving in New York and Rhode Island, he was ordered to the Pacific coast. His transport ship was sunk by a hurricane, and for several weeks Winder was presumed lost. Finally, rescued by a Britain-bound ship, he made it to California—via Liverpool, England.

Promoted to captain, he fought Indians in Oregon and the Washington Territory. He was home on leave during the secession crisis. On April 1, 1861, he resigned his commission in the U.S. Army and was appointed a major of artillery in the Confederate Army. He was present during the bombardment of Fort Sumter. After temporarily commanding the Charleston Arsenal, he became colonel of the 6th South Carolina Infantry Regiment on July 8, 1861. His regiment was sent to Virginia and served in the Centreville-Manassas sector throughout the winter of 1861–62.

After briefly commanding a brigade in A. P. Hill's Light Division, Winder was transferred to the Shenandoah Valley, where General

Thomas J. Jackson named him commander of the Stonewall Brigade. Winder was promoted to brigadier general on March 5, 1862, to rank from March 1.

The Stonewall Brigade had loved its previous commander, Richard Garnett, and gave Winder a cool reception. Winder was a brutal disciplinarian who hanged stragglers by their thumbs. Winder's officers and men despised him, but he was a very good battlefield tactician. On May 25, 1862, during the First Battle of Winchester, he both checked a flanking maneuver by the Union infantry and advised Jackson on turning the Union right, leading to a rout of the Federals. At Port Republic, he spearheaded a victorious Confederate assault. Winder, in fact, played a significant role in virtually every battle during Jackson's Valley Campaign. He also distinguished himself during the Battle of Gaines' Mill.

After the Seven Days Battles, Charles Winder was given command of Jackson's old division for the Battle of Cedar Mountain. There, on August 9, 1862, he was directing an artillery battery in his shirtsleeves when a shell fragment ripped through his left arm and side. Placed on a stretcher, he was taken to a nearby home, where he died a few hours later. He was thirty-two years old.

Charles Sidney Winder's remains were buried in Wye House Cemetery, Easton, Talbot County, Maryland.

JOHN HENRY WINDER was born on February 21, 1800, at Rewston in Somerset County, Maryland. He entered the U.S. Military Academy at West Point in 1814 and graduated in 1820. He was commissioned as a second lieutenant in the artillery. In 1823, family financial difficulties compelled him to resign his commission and help manage his father-in-law's plantation. He returned to the colors in 1827 as a second lieutenant and fought in the Second Seminole War. He was promoted to captain in 1842 and given command of Fort Sullivan in Eastport, Maine, where he commanded Company G, 1st

Artillery. During the War with Mexico, he was brevetted major for his gallantry at Contreras and Churubusco and brevetted lieutenant colonel shortly after the capture of Mexico City.

John H. Winder sold his plantation in 1849 and made some shrewd real estate investments, including a building in Washington, D.C., that later housed the War Department. He was a wealthy man by 1854.

He was promoted to major in late 1860 but resigned his commission on April 20, 1861. He was then commissioned as a colonel of infantry in the Confederate Army on May 21, 1861, and was promoted to brigadier general on June 21. He was simultaneously named inspector general of the Camps of Instruction, with headquarters in Richmond. (He was too old for a field command.) He held this appointment until October 21, when the War Department abolished his job. General Winder was unemployed for several months.

On March 1, 1862, President Jefferson Davis declared martial law in Richmond and appointed Winder provost marshal general. He immediately prohibited the sale of alcohol and ordered all citizens to turn in their guns. He hired the members of a Baltimore street gang, the Plug Uglies, as policemen. Winder was quickly dubbed "the dictator of Richmond" and was accused of instituting a "reign of terror."

Winder stirred further controversy with his management of prisoner-of-war camps. He appointed Henry Wirz as commandant of Camp Sumter at Andersonville, Georgia, and briefly commanded the camp himself. The peak population of the prison was thirty-three thusand men, and it became notorious for overcrowding, poor provisions, disease, and death. Winder made efforts to enlarge the camp and to better feed, clothe, and house the prisoners, but without notable success. From July 26 to November 21, 1864, Winder was commanding general of prisons in Alabama and Georgia. He then became commissary general of all prisoners east of the Mississippi.

General Winder was vilified by the Northern press both during and after the war, even though it was Ulysses S. Grant who stopped the practice of exchanging prisoners. That left tens of thousands of Union soldiers trapped in prison camps that had inadequate supplies. The Union's blockade and destruction of Southern farms and transportation networks only made the situation worse. Confederate prisoner-of-war camps held 194,743 Union solders. Of these, 30,218 died—a mortality rate of 15 percent. Of the 214,865 Rebel prisoners held in Northern camps, 25,976 died—a mortality rate of 12 percent. And yet, the North had good transportation facilities and plenty of food, whereas the South could barely feed its own soldiers.

Shortly before his death, Winder recommended that all Union prisoners be paroled and sent home because the Confederacy could not meet its obligations to them. He died in Florence, South Carolina, on February 7, 1865, of a massive heart attack. He was buried in Green Mount Cemetery, Baltimore, Maryland.

HENRY ALEXANDER WISE was born on December 3, 1806, at Drummondtown in Accomack County, Virginia. His father was a wealthy landowner. He was well educated by private tutors at Margaret Academy and at Washington College (now Washington and Jefferson College) in southwestern Pennsylvania. After graduation, he attended Henry St. George Tucker's law school in Winchester. He was admitted to the bar in 1828. In 1830, he returned to the Eastern Shore of Virginia, purchased a modest farm, and became a farmer and politician.

In 1832, he was elected to the U.S. House of Representatives as a Jacksonian Democrat but broke with the party in the mid-1830s, became a Whig, and then was a Democrat again. He remained a loyal ally of John Tyler of Virginia and supported his election as vice president. Unlike many Whigs, Wise supported Tyler throughout his presidency.

Henry Wise was considered very intelligent, both a fine orator and a fierce opponent. He served in Congress from 1833 to 1843 and was then appointed U.S. minister to Brazil (1844–47). His tenure was controversial because he criticized Brazil's continued participation in the international slave trade. He ran for governor in 1855 and was elected as a Democrat. He served as governor from January 1, 1856, to January 1, 1860.

Wise defended slavery but initially opposed secession. It was only after the election of Abraham Lincoln as president that he believed that compromise between the North and South was impossible. On June 5, 1861, Henry Wise was appointed a brigadier general in the Confederate Army, though Wise had no military training whatsoever. He was placed in charge of the Army of the Kanawha and led it in the Western Virginia Campaign of 1861, with disastrous results. He could not or would not cooperate with General John Floyd, another former governor of Virginia. President Jefferson Davis replaced both of them. In February 1862, Wise was given command of the District of Roanoke. Wise was ill when the Yankees attacked Roanoke Island, and the South suffered a disastrous defeat. He was given command of a brigade in Theophilus H. Holmes's division during the Seven Days Battles. When General Robert E. Lee moved north against General John Pope, Wise remained behind guarding Richmond. He was then given command of a subdistrict in South Carolina, where he remained until 1864.

When Henry A. Wise returned to Virginia in the spring of 1864, his military leadership had improved markedly. He fought in the Siege of Petersburg, where his performance was good to excellent. His brigade's defense against the first Union assaults in June 1864 was a major contributing factor in saving the city.

On April 6, 1865, during the retreat to Appomattox, General Bushrod Johnson abandoned his men at Sayler's Creek. The next day, General Lee relieved Johnson of his command and replaced him with Wise. Two days later, the army surrendered.

After the war, with his plantations confiscated, Wise resumed his law practice in Richmond, where he lived for the rest of his life. He never sought a pardon for his Confederate service. He wrote a book, *Seven Decades of the Union*, based on the life of John Tyler. In it, he sought to minimize his own role in Virginia's secession. It was published in 1872. Governor Wise's grandson, Barton H. Wise, wrote a biography of him.

General Henry A. Wise died in Richmond on September 12, 1876. He was sixty-nine years old. He was buried in Hollywood Cemetery, Richmond. Wise County, Virginia, and Wise County, Texas, are named after him.

JONES MITCHELL WITHERS was born in Huntsville, Madison County, Alabama, on January 12, 1814, the son of a planter. He attended Greene Academy in Huntsville, was admitted to West Point in 1831, and graduated in 1835. He was commissioned in the cavalry and stationed at Fort Leavenworth, Kansas. Lieutenant Withers resigned his commission on December 5, 1835, to study law.

In 1836, he served as a staff officer in the Alabama Militia during the Creek War. Withers passed the state bar examination in 1838 and subsequently practiced law in Tuscaloosa but eventually settled in Mobile, where he became a cotton broker. He returned to the colors in 1846 when the Mexican War began and became lieutenant colonel of the 13th U.S. Infantry and then colonel of the 9th U.S. Infantry and led it in the Battle of Mexico City. In May 1848, Colonel Withers again resigned his commission and returned to Alabama.

A highly respected member of his community, he was elected to the state legislature in 1855. He served as mayor of Mobile from 1856 until the start of the Civil War. On April 28, 1861, he was elected colonel of the 3rd Alabama Infantry. It was the first Alabama regiment to be mustered into Confederate service and was assigned to the Department of Norfolk.

On July 10, 1861, Withers was sent home to organize the state's Gulf coast defenses against a potential invasion. On March 29, 1862, he assumed leadership of a division in Braxton Bragg's II Corps of the Army of Mississippi and distinguished himself in the Battle of Shiloh. He also fought in the Siege of Corinth and in the subsequent retreat to Tupelo.

Withers was appointed commander of the Reserve Corps, Army of Mississippi, on June 30, and took part in the Kentucky Campaign. On August 16, 1862, he was promoted to major general, with a date of rank of April 6—the first day of the Battle of Shiloh.

Withers commanded a division in Leonidas Polk's corps during the Second Battle of Murfreesboro. He was heavily engaged on the first day, losing 2,500 of his 7,700 men. Polk and Bragg praised his courage and leadership.

Throughout the war, Withers suffered from poor health. On July 13, 1863, he resigned his commission. Implored to reconsider, he asked for a role that did not involve active campaigning. He was restored to rank on July 21 but was relieved on August 13 because of ill health.

Nevertheless, on February 6, 1864, General Withers returned to duty as commander of the District of North Alabama. On July 27, Secretary of War James Seddon named him commander of the Reserve Forces of Alabama. He was responsible for organizing boys and old men for possible combat. He held this post until May 4, 1865, and was paroled at Meridian on December 28, 1865.

Withers returned to Mobile and again worked as a cotton broker. For a time, he was also editor of the *Mobile Tribune*. He served another term as mayor of Mobile (1866–67). In 1878, he was elected city treasurer.

General Jones M. Withers was a highly capable leader at every level in which he exercised command; his only weakness was his health. He died of heart disease in Mobile on March 13, 1890. He was seventy-six years old. He was buried in Magnolia Cemetery, Mobile.

WILLIAM TATUM WOFFORD was born on June 28, 1824, near Toccoa in Habersham County, Georgia. The family moved to Bartow County in northwestern

Georgia in 1827. In 1844, he graduated from Franklin College, which is now part of the University of Georgia system.

In 1847, Wofford joined the army and served in the Mexican War as a captain in the Georgia Mounted Rifles. He was discharged in 1848 and became a planter and an attorney. He was twice elected to the legislature and was later elected clerk of the Georgia House of Representatives. In 1852, he became editor of the *Cassville Standard*.

He was elected to the Georgia Secession Convention as a Unionist and spoke against secession. When Georgia seceded anyway, he became a captain in the Confederate Army. He was elected colonel of the 18th Georgia on April 22, and in August his regiment was in Richmond, guarding prisoners captured at the Battle of First Manassas.

In November 1861, the 18th was assigned to John Bell Hood's Texas Brigade and fought in the Peninsula Campaign, the Battle of Seven Pines, and the Seven Days Battles, during which it distinguished itself in the Battle of Gaines' Mill. It also fought in the battles of Second Manassas, South Mountain, and Sharpsburg, where Wofford commanded the Texas Brigade. At Sharpsburg, the brigade lost 560 men killed or wounded out of 854 engaged.

Back in regimental command, Colonel Wofford led his men into the Battle of Fredericksburg in December 1862. He took command of the brigade when T. R. R. Cobb was mortally wounded and defended the stone wall at the base of Marye's Heights. William Wofford was promoted to brigadier general on January 17, 1863.

General Wofford fought in the battles of Chancellorsville and Gettysburg. In the fall of 1863, under James Longstreet's command, he participated in the unsuccessful Knoxville Campaign. After a hard winter in East Tennessee, General Wofford rejoined the Army of Northern Virginia and fought in the Battle of the Wilderness, where he was wounded. He was wounded again at Spotsylvania and was with Joseph B. Kershaw in the fighting around Richmond and Petersburg. Wofford's brigade accompanied Kershaw's division to the Shenandoah Valley and participated in the Battle of Cedar Creek.

At the request of Governor Joseph E. Brown, Wofford was named commander of the Subdistrict of North Georgia, which he directed from January 20, 1865, until the end of the war. In this position, he raised more than seven thousand troops (many of them former deserters) to combat outlaws. He obtained corn and distributed it among the starving people of North Georgia. He even received permission from the Union commander in North Georgia to feed hungry people behind Federal lines.

General Wofford surrendered at Resaca, Georgia, on May 2, 1865, and was paroled the same day. He returned to his plantation near Cass Station. Highly respected throughout northern Georgia, he was elected to Congress in 1865, but like other Southern senators and congressmen, he was denied his seat by the Radical Republicans.

General Wofford went into the railroad business and grew quite prosperous. He was also a trustee of Cherokee Baptist College and Cassville Female College and served as a presidential elector for Horace Greeley in 1872 and an elector for Samuel Tilden in 1876. In 1877, he was elected to the state constitutional convention.

William Tatum Wofford died May 22, 1884, in Cassville, Georgia. He was fifty-nine years old. He is buried in Cassville Cemetery.

STERLING ALEXANDER MARTIN "SAM" WOOD was born on March 17, 1823, in Florence, Alabama. His father was the first mayor of Florence. Sam attended St. Joseph's College in Kentucky in 1841 and studied law in Columbia, Tennessee. He was admitted to the bar in 1845 and joined his brother to form a law partnership in Florence.

He was elected to the Alabama legislature and served from 1857 to 1861. He was simultaneously a district solicitor and the editor of the Florence *Gazette* newspaper.

Sam Wood became a captain and company commander of the Florence Guard, an Alabama infantry unit, on April 3, 1861. On May 18, he was elected colonel of the 7th Alabama when it was organized in Pensacola, Florida. He remained in Pensacola until the beginning of 1862, when he was ordered to join Albert Sidney Johnston's Army of Central Kentucky in Bowling Green, Kentucky. On January 7, 1862, he was promoted to brigadier general. At Shiloh, his first attack went well, and he captured six enemy guns.

During the first day's battle, his horse was wounded and threw him off, but his foot was caught in the stirrup and dragged him through the Union tents. He suffered a concussion but was not captured and was taken to the Confederate infirmary, where he remained for three hours. His division commander, General Thomas C. Hindman, practically accused Wood of malingering. He and Hindman never did like each other.

General Wood fought bravely in the Battle of Perryville but was badly wounded when a shell fragment hit him in the head. He was out of action until November 20, 1862. Transferred to Patrick Cleburne's division, he won Cleburne's praise for his performance at the Second Battle of Murfreesboro. At Chickamauga, however, his brigade advanced through an open field that exposed it to enemy fire. The other two brigades in the division wisely advanced through the woods. When Cleburne did not mention him in his official report on Chickamauga but praised all his other brigade commanders, Wood, who was both ill and aggrieved, resigned his commission on October 17, 1863.

After he quit, Wood returned home and resumed his law practice. He served another term as an Alabama legislator and from 1889 to 1890 was a professor of law at the University of Alabama.

General Sterling A. M. Wood died on July 26, 1891, in Tuscaloosa. He was sixty-eight years old. He was buried in Evergreen Cemetery, Tuscaloosa.

AMBROSE RANSOM "RANS" WRIGHT was born on April 26, 1826, in Louisville, Georgia. He read law, was admitted to the bar, and became interested in politics but was defeated in races for the Georgia legislature and the U.S. House of Representatives. In 1856, he was a presidential elector for Millard Fillmore. He took Abraham Lincoln's election as grounds for secession.

When the Civil War began, Rans Wright enlisted in the Georgia Militia as a private. He helped organize the 3rd Georgia Infantry Regiment in Augusta and was commissioned its colonel on May 18, 1861. His regiment was sent to Portsmouth, Virginia, and camped outside the naval yard. It was sent to Roanoke Island in September. In early October, Wright commanded Confederate forces in the minor Battle of Chicamacomico, which was a Rebel victory. The regiment returned to Portsmouth in December.

On April 12, 1862, the 3rd Georgia was involved in the Battle of South Mills, where Union forces under General Jesse L. Reno were repulsed. In May, it took part in the evacuation of Norfolk. It joined the main army for the end of the Peninsula Campaign and fought in the Battle of Seven Pines.

General Albert G. Blanchard's performance in the Battle of Seven Pines was deemed unsatisfactory. He was relieved of his command and replaced by Ambrose Wright, who was promoted to brigadier general on June 3. In the Seven Days Battles, Wright's brigade launched a fierce but ultimately unsuccessful attack on Malvern Hill. General D. H. Hill witnessed it and declared, "I never saw anything more grandly heroic." The brigade fought in the Battle of Second Manassas and at Sharpsburg, where General Wright was wounded twice and carried from the field. He recovered in time to fight at Fredericksburg. He was again wounded during the Battle of Chancellorsville, but not seriously.

On July 2, 1863, during the Battle of Gettysburg, Wright's brigade broke the Union line on Cemetery Ridge and captured twenty guns but was forced to retreat. Wright continued to distinguish himself throughout the Overland Campaign and in the early stages of the Siege of Petersburg. On August 9, 1864, however, his health gave way, and he was forced to give up command of his illustrious brigade. He was on sick furlough until November 24, 1864, when he was given command of the

Confederate forces in the area of Augusta, Georgia. He organized them into a division and was promoted to major general (temporary rank) on November 26. He remained there until the end of the war.

Following the capitulation, Ambrose Wright remained in Augusta and became editor of the Augusta *Chronicle & Sentinel*. He was elected to Congress in 1872 but died of brain inflammation on December 21, 1872, in Augusta, before he could take his seat. He was forty-six years old. General Wright was buried in City (now Magnolia) Cemetery, Augusta.

MARCUS JOSEPH WRIGHT has born on June 5, 1831, in Purdy, Tennessee, and received a classical education at a local private academy. He then studied law, passed the bar, set up a law practice in Memphis, and was a clerk for the common law and chancery court. On April 4, 1861, Wright became lieutenant colonel of the 154th Tennessee Militia Regiment, which was redesignated the 154th Senior Tennessee Infantry Regiment in the Confederate States Army on August 17, 1861. The commander of the regiment was Preston Smith.

Stationed at Columbus, Kentucky, the 154th was involved in the Battle of Belmont on November 7, where Wright commanded the regiment, as Colonel Smith was commanding a brigade. On April 6, 1862, he fought in the Battle of Shiloh and assumed command of the regiment after Smith was wounded. Wright was struck in right knee by a minié ball but continued to command although in great pain.

From June 10 to September 1, he was assistant adjutant general (and de facto chief of staff) for General Benjamin Cheatham. He fought in the Kentucky Campaign, including the battles of Munfordville and Perryville. On December 20, 1862, he was promoted to brigadier general, to rank from December 13.

Wright's first battle as a brigade commander was the Second Battle of Murfreesboro. His brigade fought well but suffered heavy losses. He was transferred to another brigade and in February 1863 commanded what was formerly Daniel Donelson's Tennessee Brigade.

Wright fought in the Tullahoma Campaign, Chickamauga, and Missionary Ridge. After the retreat from Chattanooga, bad health forced him to surrender command of his brigade and go on a medical furlough.

General Wright returned to duty in March 1864 and was named commandant of Atlanta, a post he held until August 6. Wright's health remained uncertain, and he was sent to Macon, where he was commandant of the city from August 23 until December 14, when he was named commander of the reserves, Military Division of the West.

Marcus Wright's last assignment during the war was as commander of the District of Northern Mississippi and West Tennessee, which he held from February 3 to May 4, 1865, when he surrendered in Grenada, Mississippi.

After the war, Wright worked as editor of the Columbia (Tennessee) *Journal* before he moved to Washington to practice law. From 1878, he was the principal agent of the War Department for the collection of Confederate military records. He was a major organizer and editor of the *Official Records of the War of the Rebellion*, which is an essential source for any Civil War historian.

Marcus Wright was a prolific author, covering everything from the Civil War (which he wrote about at great length in multiple volumes) to a biography of General Winfield Scott, from the *Official History of the Spanish-American War* to *The Social Evolution of Woman*.

General Wright passed away in Washington, D.C., on December 27, 1922. He was ninety-one years old. He was buried near the Confederate Monument in Arlington National Cemetery.

Y

YORK – YOUNG

ZEBULON YORK was born on October 10, 1819, in Avon, Maine, and educated in a local one-room schoolhouse. He later attended Maine Wesleyan Seminary and then enrolled at Transylvania University in Kentucky at age sixteen, graduating with honors. He liked the South and moved to Vidalia, Louisiana, where he began reading law. He eventually studied law at the University of Louisiana in New Orleans, graduated with honors, was admitted to the bar, and returned to Vidalia to establish a practice.

York entered in a business partnership with Elias J. Hoover and purchased a plantation. They were incredibly successful and bought another plantation, then another, and then another—until they owned six. By the outbreak of the war, they owned more than 1,500 slaves, produced 4,500 bales of cotton a year, and paid more in realty taxes than anyone in the state. York was a respected member of the community and was well-liked, with a reputation, according to his obituary, of being a "gentle and tender-hearted" master to his slaves, one of whom recalled that York "was sure good to us . . . [he] never 'loud [allowed] no one to beat us."

Following Abraham Lincoln's election as president in 1860, York was unanimously chosen to represent Concordia Parish in the secession convention. On January 26, 1861, the convention voted to leave the Union by a vote of 113 to 17. Zebulon York voted with the majority.

As soon as he returned home, Zebulon York and Elias Hoover organized the 1st Regiment, Polish Brigade, entirely at their own expense. (York was of Polish descent.) In April 1861, York became a captain and company commander. When the 14th Louisiana Infantry Regiment was organized in New Orleans in August, it became Company F.

York was promoted to major (September 2) and to lieutenant colonel (on February 19, 1862). The 14th Louisiana first saw action in the Siege of Yorktown and at the Battle of Williamsburg, where York was among the wounded. General James Longstreet officially commended him for his "skill and fearlessness."

After he recovered, York fought in the Seven Days Battles (in which he was slightly wounded at Gaines' Mill) and in the Battle of Second Manassas. As part of Stonewall Jackson's corps, York seized a vital railroad embankment, but in the process a Yankee bullet went through his neck and under his spine, and for a time there was fear that he might be paralyzed. When he was out of danger, he was sent back home to recuperate.

Zebulon York was promoted to colonel on October 3, 1862. After working as a training officer for General Richard Taylor in Louisiana, he returned to the Army of Northern Virginia in time to take part in the Overland Campaign of 1864, where he fought at the Wilderness and Spotsylvania. On June 2, he was promoted to brigadier general. York joined Jubal Early's Army of the Valley and took part in his raid on Washington and subsequent withdrawal to the Shenandoah Valley.

During the Third Battle of Winchester, General York's left arm was shattered by grapeshot during the fighting. He was taken to a field hospital where his arm was amputated. A friend offered his home as a place to recuperate, but York replied that the enemy would never capture him—although they could have the arm. He then mounted a horse and rode more than twenty miles to Fisher's Hill, where he received further medical attention.

No longer fit for frontline duty, Zebulon York became a recruiter in North Carolina in 1865. After Richmond fell, York—commanding about 1,200 hastily assembled men and a few pieces of artillery—successfully defended the Yadkin River Bridge against Union General George Stoneman's raiders, shielding Jefferson Davis's flight from the Yankees. After General Joseph E. Johnston capitulated in North Carolina, General York surrendered and was paroled in the Old North State on May 6.

York's Louisiana plantation properties were either destroyed or confiscated by the Federals. So, he settled in Natchez, Mississippi, became the proprietor of a boarding house called the York House, and ran five small steamboats that delivered goods and transported passengers.

Brigadier General Zebulon York died in Natchez on August 5, 1900. He was eighty years old. He is buried in Natchez City Cemetery.

PIERCE MANNING BUTLER YOUNG was born on November 15, 1836, in Spartanburg, South Carolina, the son of a physician, who moved the family to Bartow County in northwest Georgia. Young was educated at home by private tutors and at the Georgia Military Institute in Marietta, from which he graduated in 1856. He was appointed to the U.S. Military Academy in 1857 but withdrew two months before his gradation in 1861 because of Georgia's secession. He returned home and offered his services to the Confederacy, which appointed him a second lieutenant of artillery on May 7, 1861. He was promoted to first lieutenant of artillery in June and on July 24, 1861, became a first lieutenant in Cobb's Legion, which was also known as the 9th Georgia Cavalry Regiment. He was promoted to major on September 3, when he became commander of the legion's cavalry, and to lieutenant colonel on November 15, 1861. Meanwhile, he was sent to the Eastern Front and fought in the Peninsula Campaign, the Seven Days Battles, and Lee's first invasion of the North.

On September 13, 1862, near Crampton's Gap during the Maryland Campaign, he was wounded in the calf. It was the first of four wounds he received during the war.

After the retreat from Sharpsburg, Pierce Young became commanding officer of the 9th Georgia Cavalry and was promoted to colonel on November 1, 1862.

Colonel Young fought in all the major campaigns of the Army of Northern Virginia in 1862 and 1863 and was wounded near Brandy Station on August 1, 1863, by a pistol shot to the chest. He spent ten days in the hospital and went home on medical furlough. While there, he was promoted to brigadier general on September 28, 1863. He became a brigade commander on October 15, 1863.

He served in the Overland Campaign of 1864 and on May 31, near Cold Harbor, was again seriously wounded in the chest, but he gradually recovered. He was promoted to major general (temporary rank) at the end of December 1864 and assumed command of Wade Hampton's old division, which he led for the rest of the war, opposing Sherman's advance to Augusta and through the Carolinas.

After the war, Young returned home and attempted to make a living as a planter. He was elected to Congress, serving from July 25, 1868, to March 3, 1875. He later served as the U.S. commissioner to the Paris Exposition (1878) and was U.S. consul general to Russia (1885–87). In 1892, he commanded the Georgia Division of the United Confederate Veterans.

In 1893, President Grover Cleveland appointed him U.S. envoy extraordinary and minister plenipotentiary to Guatemala and Honduras. He returned to the United States on leave in 1896, suffering from gout and cirrhosis of the liver. He was hospitalized at Presbyterian Hospital in New York City and died there on July 6, 1896. His age was fifty-nine. He is buried in Oak Hill Cemetery, Cartersville, Georgia.

WILLIAM HUGH YOUNG was born on New Year's Day, 1838, in Boonville, Missouri, and educated at Washington College, Tennessee; McKenzie College, Texas; and the University of Virginia, where he was student at the outset of the Civil War. The university's cadet corps broke into two companies. Young commanded one, and Robert E. Lee, Jr., the other. They engaged in intensive training for six months; then Young received a commission from Governor Edward Clark of Texas (where Young's father commanded militia troops) to raise a regiment in sparsely populated North Texas. He rode all over the district and brought in recruits, who assembled in Dallas in September 1861 as the 9th Texas Infantry Regiment. Because of his age (he was only twenty-three), Young was not elected colonel but served as a captain.

At Shiloh, Captain Young distinguished himself leading the regiment's first charge against a Union battery. He and his men overran it and captured it. He captured several more Federal guns before the action was over. Afterward, the 9th Texas's commander, Sam Maxey, was promoted to brigadier general, and William H. Young was elected colonel.

Young took part in the Kentucky Campaign, including the Battle of Perryville, where the regiment suffered nearly 40 percent casualties. On December 31, 1862, Colonel Young was wounded in the right shoulder during the Second Battle of Murfreesboro and had two horses shot out from under him. He fought in the Vicksburg Campaign and was wounded in the leg on July 13, 1863. He returned to fight at Chickamauga, where he was shot in the chest on September 20, 1863. He took part in the Atlanta Campaign and suffered wounds to his neck and jaw at Kennesaw Mountain on June 27, 1864. He was promoted to brigadier general on August 15, 1864 (and had been an acting brigade commander since July 27). At age twenty-six, Young was one of the youngest generals in the Confederate Army.

General Young saw extensive action in the battles around Atlanta, and on October 5, 1864, his left foot was shattered by a shell splinter at the Battle of Allatoona Pass. He was placed in an ambulance, which unfortunately took the wrong road, and he was captured by Union cavalry. He received no medical attention for days, and the wound was gangrenous by the time a doctor saw it. Without using anaesthetic, a capable young surgeon strapped him to a stretcher and burned off the rotten flesh with nitric acid "until the smoke reached the ceiling." The procedure saved the leg. He was eventually incarcrated at Johnson's Island, Ohio, in the middle of Lake Erie. He was paroled there on July 24, 1865.

Despite his many wounds, William H. Young was still a young man when the war ended—enterprising and full of vigor. He became a lawyer and real estate agent in San Antonio, organized the Nueces River Irrigation Company, and owned a considerable amount of property, but he lost most of his money in an unsuccessful newspaper venture.

Y

Near the end of his life, General William Hugh Young suffered from heart disease. He died in San Antonio on November 27, 1901, at age sixty-three. He is buried there in the Confederate Cemetery.

·Y

Z

ZOLLICOFFER

FELIX KIRK ZOLLICOFFER was born on May 19, 1812, in Bigbyville, near Columbia, Middle Tennessee, the descendant of Swiss immigrants. The future Rebel general left school at age sixteen to became a printer's apprentice. He entered the newspaper business and worked his way up to editor and part owner of the *Columbia Observer*. In 1836, he was named as state printer for Tennessee.

In 1836, as a second lieutenant in the Tennessee Militia, he served in Florida in the Second Seminole War. After he returned, he edited the *Southern Agriculturalist*, and in 1843 he became editor of the *Republican Banner*, the press operation of the Tennessee branch of the Whig Party.

Zollicoffer served as comptroller of the state treasury (1845–49). He became a member of the state senate in 1849 and was elected to Congress as a Whig in 1852 and reelected twice as a member of the American (Know-Nothing) Party. In the presidential election of 1860, he campaigned for John C. Bell of the moderate Constitutional Union Party.

Felix Zollicoffer was a strong believer in states' rights but opposed Tennessee's secession until Abraham Lincoln was elected, after which he thought secession was justified and war inevitable. Governor Isham Harris commissioned Zollicoffer a brigadier general in the Provisional Army of Tennessee on May 9, 1861. After Tennessee joined the Confederacy, he was appointed a brigadier general in the Confederate States Army. He was placed in charge of the District of East Tennessee on July 26.

The people of East Tennessee were largely pro-Union. Politically, Zollicoffer tried to conciliate them. Militarily, he seized the Cumberland Gap on September 14 to prevent the Union Army from invading his sector. But there were four other potential routes of advance from Kentucky to East or Middle Tennessee, and he did not have the troops to adequately cover them all.

Zollicoffer initially performed quite well. He and his men launched several raids into Kentucky in the autumn and winter of 1861 and won a few minor victories. On December 6, he crossed to the northern bank of the Cumberland River, where he thought it would be easier to supply his troops. This was a disastrous decision. On January 2, 1862, Major General George Crittenden superceded Zollicoffer in command of the District of East Tennessee, and Zollicoffer beame a brigade commander in Crittenden's army for an invasion of Kentucky.

By January 18, U.S. General George Thomas approached the Rebel concentration. General Crittenden held a council of war and, against Zollicoffer's advice, ordered him to attack. On January 19, 1862, Zollicoffer marched his men through a pouring rain and met Thomas with about 3,500 men in the Battle of Mill Springs (Logan's Cross Roads). Thomas had 10,000 men in his columns, but only 5,000 could take to the field that day. The terrain featured thick forests, and the inexperienced Confederate regiments lost their cohesion. Even so, the battle seemed to be going the South's way until General Zollicoffer rode up to a Union regiment, which he mistook for a Confederate formation. The Yankees unleashed a volley, and multiple bullets hit Felix Zollicoffer, killing him instantly.

James D. Porter, a Confederate officer who later became governor of Tennessee, wrote that Zollicoffer "was a man of unblemished moral character, amiable and modest in deportment, but quick to resent an insult." He was the first Confederate general to fall in the Western Theater, and a doctor in the Union Army went to the trouble of embalming Zollicoffer's body before returning it to the Confederates.

General Zollicoffer was laid to rest in Nashville City Cemetery. He was forty-nine years old.

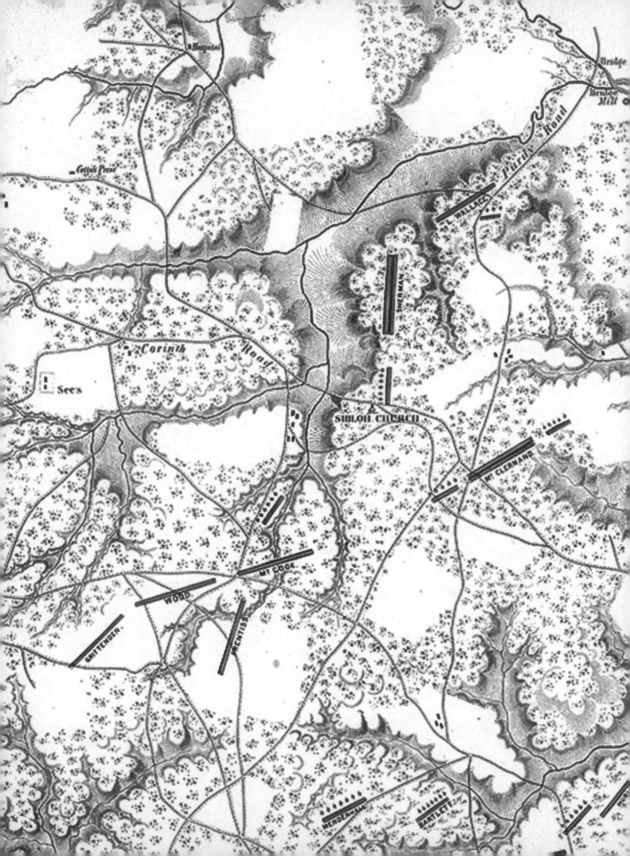

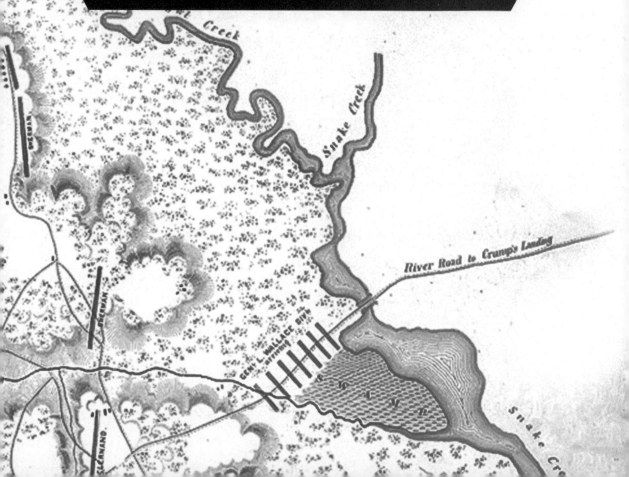

Appendix I

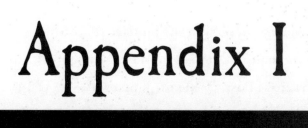

Alphabetical listing by place of the major campaigns, battles, and events of the war

A

Alabama, Secession of, January 11, 1861

Appomattox Campaign, March 29–April 9, 1865

Arkansas Post, Battle of, January 10–11, 1863

Arkansas, Secession of, May 6, 1861

Atlanta Campaign, May 7–September 2, 1864

Atlanta, Battle of, July 22, 1864

B

Ball's Bluff, Battle of October 21–22, 1861

Baton Rouge, Battle of August 5, 1862

Bean's Station, Battle of, December 14, 1863

Belmont, Battle of, November 7, 1861

Bentonville, Battle of, March 19–21, 1865

Bethesda Church, Battle of, May 30–June 3, 1864

Big Bethel, Battle of, June 10, 1861

Blair's Landing, Battle of, April 12, 1864

Brandy Station, Battle of, June 9, 1863

Brice's Cross Roads, Battle of, June 10, 1864

Buckland Mills, Battle of, October 19, 1863

Buffington Island, Battle of, July 19, 1863

C

Camden Expedition, March 23–May 3, 1864

Carolinas Campaign, January 1–April 26, 1865

Carthage, Battle of, July 5, 1861

Cedar Creek, Battle of, October 19, 1864

Cedar Mountain (Slaughter's Mountain), Battle of, August 9, 1862

Chambersburg, Burning of, July 30, 1864

Champion Hill, Mississippi, Battle of, May 16, 1863

Chancellorsville, Battle of, May 1–6, 1864

Chantilly, Battle of, September 1, 1862

Charleston, South Carolina, Fall of, February 18, 1865

Chattanooga, Siege of, September 22–November 25

Chickasaw Bluffs, Battle of, December 29, 1862

Cloyd's Mountain, Battle of, May 9, 1864

Cold Harbor, Battle of, May 31–June 3, 1864

Confederate States of America, Formation of, February 8, 1861

Corinth, Second Battle of, October 3–4, 1862

Corrick's Ford, Battle of, July 13, 1861

Crater, Battle of the, July 30, 1864

Cross Keys, Battle of, June 8, 1862

Cumberland Gap, U.S. Evacuation of, September 17, 1862

D

Dalton, Battle of, May 9–12, 1864

Dinwiddie Court House, Battle of, March 31, 1865

Dranesville, Battle of, December 20, 1861

Drewry's Bluff, Battle of, May 16, 1862

E

Ezra Church, Battle of, July 28, 1864

F

Falling Waters, Battle of, July 14, 1863

Farmington, Battle of, May 9, 1862

Farmville, Battle of, April 7, 1865

Fisher's Hill, Battle of, September 22, 1864

Fishing Creek, Battle of, January 19, 1862

Five Forks, Battle of, April 1, 1865

Florida, Secession of, January 10, 1861

Fort Blakely, Battle of, April 2–9, 1865

Fort Donelson, Battle of, February 12–16, 1862

Fort Fisher, Battle of, December 24–25, 1864, and January 13–15, 1865

Fort Gregg, Battle of, April 2, 1865

Fort Harrison, Battle of, September 29–30, 1864

Fort Henry, Battle of, February 6, 1862

Fort Jackson, Battle of, April 18–28, 1862. *See also* Fort St. Philip, Battle of.

Fort McRee, Battle of, November 22, 1861

Fort Morgan, Siege of, August 9–23, 1864

Fort Pillow, Battles of, April 14–June 5, 1862, and April 12, 1864

Fort Sanders, Battle of, November 29, 1863

Fort St. Philip, Battle of, April 18–28, 1862. *See also* Fort Jackson, Battle of.

Fort Stedman, Battle of, March 25, 1865

Fort Sumter, Battle of, April 12–13, 1861

Fort Tyler, Battle of, April 16, 1865

Franklin, Battle of, November 30, 1864

Frayser's Farm, Battle of, June 30, 1862

Fredericksburg, Battle of, December 13, 1862. *See also* Chancellorsville, Battle of.

Front Royal, Battle of, May 23 and May 30–31, 1862

G

Gaines' Mill, Battle of, June 27, 1862

Galveston, Battle of, January 1, 1863

Georgia, Secession of, January 19, 1861

Gettysburg, Battle of, July 1–3, 1863

Glorieta Pass, Battle of, March 26–28, 1862

Groveton, Battle of, August 28, 1862

H

Harpers Ferry, Battle of, September 12–15, 1862

Hatcher's Run, Battle of, February 5–7, 1865

Helena, Battle of, July 4, 1863

Holly Springs, Battle of, December 20, 1862

I

Island Number 10, Battle of, April 7–8, 1862

Iuka, Battle of, September 19, 1862

J

Jackson, First Battle of, May 14, 1863

Jackson, Second Battle of (Siege of), July 9–16, 1863

Jenkins' Ferry, Battle of, April 30, 1864

Jonesboro, Battle of, August 31–September 1, 1864

K

Kelly's Ford, Battle of, March 17, 1863

Kennesaw Mountain, Battle of, June 27, 1864

Kentucky Campaign, August 14–October 10, 1862

Kernstown, Battle of, March 23, 1862

Knoxville Campaign, November 17–December 4, 1863

L

Laurel Hill, Battle of, July 11, 1861

Lexington, Siege of, September 12–20, 1861

Little Rock, Fall of, September 10, 1863

Lookout Mountain, Battle of, November 24, 1863

Louisiana, Secession of, January 26, 1861

Lynchburg, Battle of, June 17–18, 1864

M

Malvern Hill, Battle of, July 1, 1862

Manassas (Bull Run), First Battle of, July 21, 1862

Manassas (Bull Run), Second Battle of, August 29–30, 1862

Mansfield, Battle of, April 8, 1864

Marks' Mills, Battle of, April 25, 1864

Maryland Campaign, September 10–19, 1862

McDowell, Battle of, May 8, 1862

Mechanicsville, Battle of, June 26, 1862

Meridian Expedition, February 3–March 5, 1864

Mill Springs, Battle of, January 19, 1862

Milliken's Bend, Battle of, June 7, 1863

Mine Creek, Battle of, October 25, 1864

Mine Run Campaign, November 26–December 2, 1863

Mississippi, Secession of, January 9, 1861

Mobile, Operations against, February 16, 1864–April 12, 1865

Monocacy, Battle of, July 9, 1864

Murfreesboro, First Battle of, July 13, 1862

Murfreesboro, Second Battle of, December 31, 1862–January 2, 1863

Murfreesboro, Third Battle of, December 6, 1864

N

Nashville, Battle of, December 15–16, 1864

New Bern, Battle of, March 14, 1862

New Hope Church, Battle of, May 25–June 5, 1864

New Madrid, Battle of, March 3–14, 1862

New Orleans, Fall of, April 25, 1862

Newburgh, Indiana, Raid on, July 18, 1862

Norfolk, Evacuation of, April 20, 1861

O

Olustee (Ocean Pond), Battle of, February 20, 1864

Overland Campaign, May 4–June 24, 1864

P

Payne's Farm, Battle of, November 27, 1863. *See also* Mine Run Campaign.

Pea Ridge, Battle of, March 7–8, 1862

Peachtree Creek, Battle of, July 20, 1864

Peninsula Campaign, April–June 1864

Pensacola, Battle of, May 9–12, 1862

Perryville, Battle of, October 8, 1862

Petersburg, Siege of, June 9, 1864–April 3, 1865

Piedmont, Battle of, June 5, 1864

Pine Mountain, Battle of, June 14, 1864

Pleasant Hill, Battle of, April 9, 1864

Plymouth, Battle of, April 17–20, 1864

Port Gibson, Battle of, May 1, 1863

Port Hudson, Siege of, May 21–July 9, 1863

Port Republic, Battle of, June 8–9, 1862

Port Royal, Battle of, November 3–7, 1861

Prairie Grove, Arkansas, Battle of, December 7, 1862

Princeton Court House, West Virginia, Battle of, May 15–17, 1862

R

Rappahannock Bridgehead, Battle of, November 7, 1863

Ream's Station, First Battle of, June 29, 1864

Ream's Station, Second Battle of, August 25, 1864

Richmond, Kentucky, Battle of, August 30, 1862

Richmond, Virginia, Fall of, April 2–3, 1865

Romney, Battle of, January 10, 1862

Romney Campaign, December 1861–January 24, 1862

S

Salem Church, Battle of, May 3–4, 1863

Savage Station, Battle of, June 29, 1862

Savannah Campaign (Sherman's March to the Sea), November 15–December 21, 1864

Sayler's Creek, Battle of, April 6, 1865

Secessionville, Battle of, June 16, 1862

Selma, Battle of, April 2, 1865

Seven Days Battles, June 26–July 1, 1862. *See also* Frayser's Farm, Battle of; Gaines' Mill, Battle of; Malvern Hill, Battle

Vicksburg, Siege of, May 18–July 4, 1863

Virginia, Secession of, April 17, 1861

W

Waynesboro, Battle of, March 2, 1865

Weldon Railroad, Battle of, August 18–21, 1864

Westport, Battle of, October 21–23, 1864

Wilderness, Battle of the, May 5–7, 1864

Williamsburg, Battle of, May 5, 1862

Wilmington, Fall of, February 22, 1865

Wilson's Creek, Battle of, August 10, 1861

Winchester, First Battle of, May 25, 1862

Winchester, Second Battle of, June 13–15, 1863

Winchester (Opequon), Third Battle of, September 19, 1864

Y

Yellow Tavern, Battle of, May 11, 1864

Yorktown, Siege of, April 5–May 4, 1862

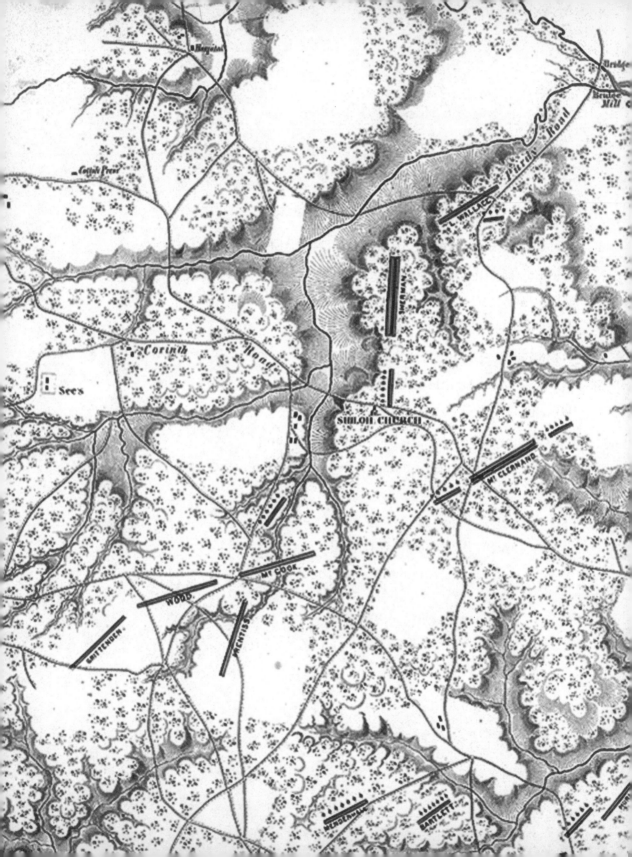

Appendix II

Major battles/events of the
Mexican War

1846

May 3–10: Battle of Fort Texas (Fort Brown)

May 8: Palo Alto

May 9: Resaca de la Palma

May 13: U.S. declares war

August 13: U.S. forces occupy Los Angeles

August 15: U.S. forces capture Santa Fe, New Mexico

September 20–24: Battle of Monterrey

1847

January: Taos Revolt, New Mexico

January 12: Mexican forces in California surrender

January 13: Mexican resistance in California ended

February 22: Battle of Buena Vista; end of resistance in northern Mexico

March 9–29: Siege of Veracruz

April 18: Cerro Gordo

May 1–August 7: Scott's Army of Mexico paused at Puebla

August 19–20: Contreras

August 20: Churubusco

September 8: Molino del Rey

September 13: Chapultepec

September 8–15: Storming of the Gates of Mexico City

1848

February 2: Treaty of Guadalupe Hidalgo

EPILOGUE

How good were the Civil War generals?

A superficial look at the figures does not do much to enhance the reputation of either side. The War for Southern Independence produced more casualties than all the rest of our wars combined, and high casualties are never indicators of great generalship. There were a number of reasons for these losses: the natural ferocity of the American combat soldier; the firm belief, on both sides, in the justness of the cause (preserving the Union or securing Southern independence); and, of course, courage. I agree with Aristotle, who declared that courage is the first virtue, because it makes all the other virtues possible. There is a flip side to this particular virtue, however: courage can get you killed. And it certainly did during the period of 1861 to 1865 in our history.

All but ignored by Civil War historians is the fact that both the Union and Confederate armies expanded too rapidly. Throughout their existences, both armies exhibited symptoms of hastily formed and inadequately trained forces. In 1860, the U. S. Regular Army had a strength of 16,367 men, of whom 14,657 were present for duty. This included 1,108 officers. When the war began, 286 active-duty officers "went south" and joined the Confederacy. Another 114 former officers returned to the colors and joined the North, while 99 former officers donned the gray. The number of generals in the United States Army increased from 5 to 586. During the course of the war, 426 men became general officers in the Rebel army—up from zero in February 1861, when the Confederacy was formed.

From very little, the United States Army formed 2,125 volunteer regiments during the course of the war. The Confederacy formed 804 regiments from nothing except a few militias.* In addition, both sides organized numerous independent battalions, squadrons, companies, and batteries. There were simply not enough qualified officers to go around. Graduates from The Citadel, the Virginia Military Institute, and other military schools narrowed this gap somewhat, but only to a small degree.

---

* The South had nine "legions": regiment-sized units with infantry, cavalry, and artillery components. They are included in the 804 regiments mentioned above.

It must also be pointed out that the top military school in the nation at that time was the United States Military Academy at West Point. Then, as now, it produced second lieutenants. In 1861, there were a handful of schools, such as the Cavalry School for Practice at Carlisle Barracks, Pennsylvania, but the United States Army had no advanced courses such as the Infantry Officers' Advanced Course or the Engineer Officers' Advanced Course. It had no Ranger School, Command and General Staff College, or Industrial War College, among others. Certainly it had nothing to even approach the Prussian War Academy.

Today, an American officer who spends twenty years in the service can expect to spend eight of them in various schools. No such infrastructure existed in 1861. To be blunt, both the Union and Confederate armies were filled with unqualified officers and non-commissioned officers from top to bottom.

The battlefield is no place for on-the-job training. But the Union and Confederate armies had no other choice. This is one big reason for the enormous number of casualties in the Civil War. Both sides improved markedly as the war progressed, but it was a costly process.

French Marshal Ferdinand Foch, the Supreme Allied Commander on the Western Front in World War I, once declared that it took ten thousand casualties to produce a good division commander. Although the number was lower in the Civil War, thousands of men died "training" their officers—or weeding out the incompetents.

The Northern supply of military brains was further sapped by the fact that it had thirty Regular Army regiments. Typically, each had more than thirty officers. Many of these officers were well-trained professionals who might have done well commanding volunteer regiments or brigades but instead remained in their Regular Army regiments the entire war. It is no accident that the North's top two generals (Ulysses S. Grant and William T. Sherman) had both left the Regular Army before the war began. Had they remained in a Regular Army regiment, they might have ended the war as majors.

Theoretically, the Confederacy also had a Regular Army, but it existed mainly on paper. One will occasionally see a reference to thus-and-so Confederate regiment, but that usually means the unit had companies from two or more states. Other than that, the most prominent regular Confederate units were floating bridge (engineer) companies.

The South was more fortunate than the North in the selection of its commander in chief. I know some people consider it almost sacrilegious to say anything even remotely negative about Abraham Lincoln, but he was—frankly—a military illiterate in 1861. His healthy common sense partially compensated for this fact, but not entirely. He was in the militia once, during the Black Hawk War (1832), and he served fewer than ninety days. All Lincoln managed to do was get busted from captain to private because of an absolute absence of military ability. Meanwhile, in that same war, Second Lieutenant Jefferson Davis—who had just graduated from West Point—rushed to the scene of action. He led only one patrol and personally captured Chief Black Hawk, ending the war. Neither man heard a shot fired in anger.

Davis, however, stayed in the Army for some time. He resigned his commission in 1835 and eloped with his commanding officer's daughter. He returned to the colors in 1846 when the Mexican War began, formed the elite 1st Mississippi Rifles, and saved the American Army in the Battle of Buena Vista, where he was seriously wounded. Later, he served as U.S. Secretary of War under President Franklin Pierce and did a marvelous job.

As commander in chief of the Confederacy, Davis's sometimes prickly personality, his micromanagement of the military, and his favoritism to West Pointers and political allies did not always serve the South well. Still, at the war's outset, he was Lincoln's superior as a commander in chief and acted essentially as his own secretary of war. Honest Abe's first secretary of war was Simon Cameron, a corrupt Pennsylvania politician whose most famous quote was that "An honest politician is one who, when he is bought, stays bought." Lincoln's wry defense of Cameron was thus: "I do not believe he would steal a red-hot stove."

Cameron's tour of duty as secretary of war (March 1861 to January 1862) was characterized by incompetence and terrible corruption. It took the North some time to overcome this bad start.

Both presidents appointed "political generals" to high military rank, but Lincoln appointed them more frequently and retained them longer. He selected Nathanial P. Banks and Benjamin Butler, both former Massachusetts congressmen, to command armies. They remained in command until May 1864 and early 1865, respectively, and they were responsible for a litany of disasters. Davis's worst appointment was (arguably) John Floyd, a former secretary of war and governor of Virginia. He was responsible for the Fort Donelson debacle. Davis fired him in March 1862. After that, he pretty much stuck with West Pointers at the higher levels. He did name former U.S. Vice President John C. Breckinridge his last secretary of war in early 1865, but by this time Breckinridge had spent four years in the army, mostly as a major general, and knew his profession. He did as good a job as anyone could have done during the last months of the war.

So which side had the best generals? In my humble opinion, the Confederacy did. I agree with Dr. Ludwell Johnson, who, in his classic *North against South*, wrote, "When all things are taken into account . . . [including] the oppressive disparity in resources—the Confederate high command performed well. Sometimes coordination was poor, but it was freer of politics and functioned more efficiently than its Union counterpart. Above all, it secured a better quality of leadership." Even Union Colonel Thomas L. Livermore, a prominent historian of the war, wrote, "The long and resolute contest maintained by the South, and their many successes against superior numbers, must always command admiration." They could not have accomplished this without some pretty solid commanders at every level. The North had a population base of roughly 22,000,000, while the South's white population base was 5,500,000. According to John H. Eicher and David J. Eicher, authors of the tome *Civil War High Commands*, the North had a "military population" (white males age 18 through 45) of 3,954,776, as opposed to 1,064,193 for the South. The North also employed 489,920 mercenaries from 15 foreign countries, as well as 191,000 African American soldiers and sailors. The South also had black soldiers, but estimates vary widely—from 3,000 to 96,000. In all, 2,898,304 men served in the Union Army. The estimated number of Rebel soldiers range from 600,000 to 1,500,000, with 800,000 to 850,000 being common estimates. The North's industrial base outweighed the South's by ten to one, and the North initially had 94 warships, as opposed to the South's 14 seaworthy warships, but this disparity grew as the war progressed. By the end of the war, the North had 671 combat vessels, and they imposed a very effective naval blockade on the Rebels and captured several major cities. Even so, the South fought on for four long years. The South's generals were better, in my opinion, but better in terms of degrees—not orders of magnitude. The soldiers of the Southern Confederacy demonstrated military skill at every level. In the end, of course, that was not enough to secure the independence for which they fought.

Confederate infantry on the attack, Seven Days Battles, Virginia, June 1862 (American Battlefield Trust).

BIBLIOGRAPHY

Abbeville Institute (website). Various posts and publications. https://www.abbevilleinstitute.org.

Adams, Henry. *The Education of Henry Adams: An Autobiography.* Boston and New York: Massachusetts Historical Society, 1918.

Aderhold, Mrs. Joseph. "Sketch of the Life of General John Forney." Ca. 1921. On file at the Old City Courthouse Library, Vicksburg, Mississippi.

Alexander, Edward Porter. *Fighting For the Confederacy: The Personal Recollections of General Edward Porter Alexander.* Edited by Gary W. Gallagher. Chapel Hill: University of North Carolina Press, 1989.

———. *Military Memoirs of a Confederate: A Critical Narrative.* New York: Charles Scribner's Sons, 1907.

Allardice, Bruce S. *Confederate Colonels: A Biographical Register.* Columbia: University of Missouri Press, 2008.

———. *More Generals in Gray.* Baton Rouge: Louisiana State University Press, 1995.

Anderson, Charles G. *Confederate General William Read "Dirty Neck Bill" Scurry (1821–1864).* Snyder, Texas: Snyder Publishing Company, 1999.

Anderson, Ephraim McDowell. *Memoirs: Historical and Personal; Including the Campaigns of the First Missouri Confederate Brigade.* St. Louis, 1868.

Anderson, Paul Christopher. "Dunovant, John." *South Carolina Encyclopedia.* University of South Carolina, Institute for Southern Studies. Originally published May 17, 2016. Updated September 15, 2016. https://www.scencyclopedia.org/sce/entries/dunovant-john/.

———. "Turner Ashby (1828–1862)." *Encyclopedia Virginia.* February 12, 2021. https://encyclopediavirginia.org/entries/ashby-turner-1828-1862/.

Arceneaux, William. *Acadian General: Alfred Mouton and the Civil War.* Lafayette: University of Southwestern Louisiana, 1972.

Arey, Frank. "Thomas Pleasant Dockery (1833–1898)." *Encyclopedia of Arkansas.* Updated October 21, 2020. https://encyclopediaofarkansas.net/entries/thomas-pleasant-dockery-1191/.

Ashby, Thomas A. *The Valley Campaigns: Being the Reminiscences of a Non-Combatant While between the Lines in the Shenandoah Valley during the War of the States.* New York: Neale, 1914.

Atkinson, Frank. "Winder, John H. (1800–1865)." *Encyclopedia Virginia.* https://www.encyclopediavirginia.org/Winder_John _H_1800-1865#start_entry.

Avery, A. C. *Memorial Address on Life and Character of Lieutenant General D. H. Hill.* Raleigh, North Carolina, 1893.

Baker, William D. *The Camden Expedition of 1864.* Little Rock: Arkansas Historical Preservation Program, 1993. https://www .arkansasheritage.com/docs/default-source/ahpp-documents /national-historic-landmarks/red_river_campaign_camden_new _nhl_new20378820-59ce-42a5-a3a9-4596f2713c78.pdf?sfvrsn =7a873762_5.

Ballard, Michael B. *Pemberton: A Biography.* Jackson: University Press of Mississippi, 1991.

Bankston, Marie Louise Benton. *Camp-Fire Stories of the Mississippi Valley Campaign.* New Orleans: The L. Graham Company, 1914.

Barefoot, Daniel W. *General Robert F. Hoke: Lee's Modest Warrior.* Winston-Salem, North Carolina: John F. Blair, 1996.

——. *Let Us Die Like Brave Men: Behind the Dying Words of Confederate Warriors.* Winston-Salem, North Carolina: John F. Blair, 2005.

Barrett, John G. "Hoke, Robert Frederick." In vol. 1 of *Dictionary of North Carolina Biography*, edited by William S. Powell. Chapel Hill: University of North Carolina Press, 1988. Reprinted in NCpedia. https://www.ncpedia.org/biography/hoke-robert -frederick.

——. "Ramseur, Stephen Dodson." In vol. 5 of *Dictionary of North Carolina Biography*, edited by William S. Powell. Chapel Hill: University of North Carolina Press, 1994. Reprinted in NCpedia. https://www.ncpedia.org/biography/ramseur-stephen -dodson.

Barringer, Sheridan R. *Fighting for General Lee: Confederate General Rufus Barringer and the North Carolina Cavalry Brigade.* El Dorado Hills, California: Savas Beatie, 2015.

Beck, Brandon H. *Winchester's Three Battles: A Civil War Driving Tour through Virginia's Most War-Torn Town*. Winchester, Virginia: Angle Valley Press, 2016.

Begley, Paul R. "Hagood, Johnson." *South Carolina Encyclopedia*. University of South Carolina, Institute for Southern Studies. Originally published April 15, 2016. Updated July 2, 2019. https://www.scencyclopedia.org/sce/entries/hagood-johnson/.

Bell, John L., Jr. "Johnston, Joseph E. (1807–1891)." *Encyclopedia Virginia*. https://encyclopediavirginia.org/entries/johnston-joseph-e-1807-1891/.

Bender, Robert Patrick. "Lucius Marshall (Marsh) Walker (1829–1863)." *Encyclopedia of Arkansas*. Updated November 24, 2020. https://encyclopediaofarkansas.net/entries/lucius-marshall-8521/.

Benner, Judith Ann. *Sul Ross, Soldier, Statesman, Educator*. College Station: Texas A&M University Press, 1983.

Bennett, Chet. *Resolute Rebel: General Roswell S. Ripley, Charleston's Gallant Defender*. Columbia: University of South Carolina Press, 2017.

Bevier, R. S. *History of the First and Second Missouri Confederate Brigades. 1861–1865. And From Wakarusa to Appomattox: A Military Anagraph*. St. Louis, 1879.

Blackburn, J. K. P. *Reminiscences of the Terry Rangers*. Austin: Littlefield Fund for Southern History, University of Texas, 1919.

Blackford, W. W. *War Years with Jeb Stuart*. New York: Charles Scribner's Sons, 1946.

Blair, Dan. "Kinston, Battle of." In *Encyclopedia of North Carolina*, edited by William S. Powell. Chapel Hill: University of North Carolina Press, 2006. Reprinted in NCpedia. https://www.ncpedia.org/kinston-battle.

Blessington, Joseph P. *The Campaigns of Walker's Texas Division*. New York, 1875.

Boggs, William R. *Military Reminiscences of Gen. Wm. R. Boggs, C.S.A.* Durham, North Carolina: The Seeman Printery, 1913.

Borcke, Heros von. *Memoirs of the Confederate War for Independence*. Philadelphia, 1867. Reprinted by Thebe Books, 2017.

Boykin, Samuel, ed. *A Memorial Volume of the Hon. Howell Cobb, of Georgia.*
Philadelphia, 1870.

Bradford, Gamaliel. *Confederate Portraits.* Boston and New York:
Houghton Mifflin, 1914.

Bradley, Michael R. *Nathan Bedford Forrest's Escort and Staff.* Gretna,
Louisiana: Pelican Publishing Company, 2006.

Branch, Paul. "Dockery, Thomas Pleasant." In vol. 2 of *Dictionary of
North Carolina Biography*, edited by William S. Powell. Chapel Hill:
University of North Carolina Press, 1986. Reprinted in NCpedia. https://www.ncpedia.org/biography/dockery-thomas
-pleasant.

————. "Leventhorpe, Collett." In vol. 4 of *Dictionary of North Carolina
Biography*, edited by William S. Powell. Chapel Hill: University
of North Carolina Press, 1991. Reprinted in NCpedia. https://
www.ncpedia.org/biography/leventhorpe-collett.

————. "Martin, James Green." In vol. 4 of *Dictionary of North Carolina
Biography*, edited by William S. Powell. Chapel Hill: University
of North Carolina Press, 1991. Reprinted in NCpedia. https://
www.ncpedia.org/biography/martin-james-green.

————. "Rains, Gabriel James." In vol. 5 of *Dictionary of North Carolina
Biography*, edited by William S. Powell. Chapel Hill: University
of North Carolina Press, 1994. Reprinted in NCpedia. https://
www.ncpedia.org/biography/rains-gabriel-james.

Brennan, Patrick. *Secessionville: Assault on Charleston.* Campbell, California: Savas Publishing, 1996.

Bridges, Hal. "A Confederate Hero: General William Y. Slack."
Arkansas Historical Quarterly 10, no. 3 (Autumn 1951): 233–37.
https://www.jstor.org/stable/40024252.

————. *Lee's Maverick General: Daniel Harvey Hill.* New York: McGraw-Hill,
1961. Reprinted in Lincoln: University of Nebraska Press,
1991.

Bromberg, Alan B. "Anderson, Joseph R. (1813–1892)." *Encyclopedia
Virginia.* https://www.encyclopediavirginia.org/anderson_joseph
_reid_1813-1892.

Brown, Russell K. *To the Manner Born: The Life of General William H. T. Walker*. Athens: University of Georgia Press, 1994. Reprinted in Macon, Georgia: Mercer University Press, 2005.

Bunn, Mike. "Jacob Hunter Sharp." *Mississippi Encyclopedia*. Center for Study of Southern Culture. Originally published July 11, 2017. Updated April 15, 2018. https://mississippiencyclopedia .org/entries/Jacob-hunter-sharp/.

Burton, E. Milby. *The Siege of Charleston, 1861–1865*. Columbia: University of South Carolina Press, 1970.

Bush, Bryan S. *Lloyd Tilghman: Confederate General in the Western Theatre*. Morley, Missouri: Acclaim Press, 2006.

Calhoun, W. L. *History of the 42d Regiment, Georgia Volunteers, Confederate States Army, Infantry*. Atlanta, Georgia: Sisson Printing, 1900.

Carmichael, Peters S. "William Nelson Pendleton (1809–1883)." *Encyclopedia Virginia*. https://encyclopediavirginia.org/entries /pendleton-william-nelson-1809-1883.

Carter, Arthur B. *The Tarnished Cavalier: Major General Earl Van Dorn, C.S.A.* Knoxville: University of Tennessee Press, 1999.

Cassidy, Vincent H., and Amos E. Simpson. *Henry Watkins Allen of Louisiana*. Baton Rouge: Louisiana State University Press, 1964.

Castel, Albert E. *General Sterling Price and the Civil War in the West*. Baton Rouge: Louisiana State University Press, 1968.

Causey, Donna R. "Biography: Edmund Winston Pettus Born July 6, 1821—Photograph," *Alabama Pioneers*. https://www .alabamapioneers.com/biography-edmund-winston-pettus -born-1821-with-photograph/.

Chesnut, Mary B. *Mary Chesnut's Civil War*. Edited by C. Vann Woodward. New Haven, Connecticut: Yale University Press, 1981.

Cisco, Walter Brian. *Wade Hampton: Confederate Warrior, Conservative Statesman*. Washington, D.C.: Brassey's, 2004. Reprinted in Washington, D.C.: Potomac Books, 2006.

Clark, Walter, ed. *Histories of the Several Regiments and Battalions from North Carolina in the Great War, 1861–'65*. 5 vols. Raleigh: State of North Carolina, 1901. Vol. 1: https://archive.org/details /cu31924092908536; Vol. 2: https://archive.org/details /cu31924092908544; Vol. 3: https://archive.org/details /historiesofsever03clar; Vol. 4: https://archive.org/details /cu31924092908569; Vol. 5: https://archive.org/details /historiesofsever05clar.

Combined Service Records. Various Generals. Unpublished documents. U.S. National Archives, Washington, D.C.

Connelly, Thomas L. *Army of the Heartland: The Army of Tennessee, 1861–1862*. Baton Rouge: Louisiana State University Press, 1967.

——. *Autumn of Glory: The Army of Tennessee, 1862–1865*. Baton Rouge: Louisiana State University Press, 1971.

Constitution (Atlanta, Georgia). Various Dates.

Coulter, E. Merton. *William Montague Browne: Versatile Anglo-Irish American, 1823–1883*. Athens: University of Georgia Press, 1967. Reprinted 2010.

Coyle, Steven. "Henry Watkins Allen." Lecture delivered to Camp 1714 of the Sons of Confederate Veterans, October 12, 2021.

Cubbison, Douglas. *The Entering Wedge: The Battle of Port Gibson, 1 May 1863: A Scholarly Monograph*. Saline, Michigan: McNaughton and Gunn for the Blue and Gray Education Society, 2002.

Cullum, George W. *Biographical Register of the Officers and Graduates of the United States Military Academy at West Point, N. Y. from Its Establishment, in 1802, to 1890: With the Early History of the United States Military Academy*. 3 vols. New York, 1868–91. https://penelope.uchicago.edu/Thayer/E/Gazetteer/Places/America/United_States/Army/USMA/Cullums_Register/home.html.

Cumming, Kate. *A Journal of Hospital Life in the Confederate Army of Tennessee from the Battle of Shiloh to the End of the War: With Sketches of Life and Character, and Brief Notices of Current Events during That Period*. Louisville, Kentucky, 1866.

Cummings, Charles M. "Forgotten Man at Fort Donelson: Bushrod Rust Johnson." *Tennessee Historical Quarterly* 27, no. 4 (Winter 1968): 380–97.

——. "Otho French Strahl: 'Choicest Spirit to Embrace the South.'" *Tennessee Historical Quarterly* 24, no. 4 (Winter 1965): 341–55.

——. *Yankee Quaker, Confederate General: The Curious Career of Bushrod Rust Johnson*. Rutherford, New Jersey: Fairleigh Dickinson University Press, 1971. Reprinted in Columbus, Ohio: General's Press, 1995.

Cunningham, S. A. *Confederate Veteran* 1–31. Various issues. 1893–1923.

Cutrer, Thomas W. "Crittenden, George Bibb." Handbook of Texas Online. Texas State Historical Association. December 1, 1994. https://tshaonline.org/handbook/online/articles/fcrmc.

———. "Harrison, Thomas." Handbook of Texas Online. Texas State Historical Association. Originally published 1952. Updated January 1, 1995. https://tshaonline.org/handbook/online/articles/fhaaf.

———. "Hawes, James Morison." Handbook of Texas Online. Texas State Historical Association. Originally published January 1, 1995. Updated August 1, 2020. https://tshaonline.org/handbook/online/articles/fhafd.

———. "Magruder, John Bankhead." Handbook of Texas Online. Texas State Historical Association. Originally published 1952. Updated August 3, 2020. https://www.tshaonline.org/handbook/entries/magruder-john-bankhead.

———. "Major, James Patrick." Handbook of Texas Online. Texas State Historical Association. Originally published 1976. Updated February 24, 2011. https://www.tshaonline.org/handbook/entries/major-james-patrick.

———. "McCulloch, Benjamin." Handbook of Texas Online. Texas State Historical Association. Originally published 1952. Updated July 31, 2020. https://www.tshaonline.org/handbook/entries/mcculloch-benjamin.

D., J. C. "Thomas F. Drayton." *Report of the Twenty-Second Annual Reunion of the Association of the Graduates of the United States Military Academy*. Obituary, June 12, 1891. Reprinted in http://penelope.uchicago.edu/Thayer/E/Gazetteer/Places/America/United_States/Army/USMA/AOG_Reunions/22/Thomas_F_Drayton*.html.

Dabney, Robert L. *Life and Campaigns of Lieut.-Gen. Thomas J. Jackson (Stonewall Jackson)*. Richmond, Virginia, and Philadelphia, 1866.

Daily News (Galveston, Texas). Various issues.

Daughtry, Mary Bandy. *Gray Cavalier: The Life and Wars of General W. H. F. "Rooney" Lee*. Cambridge, Massachusetts: De Capo Press, 2002.

Davis, Burke. *Gray Fox: Robert E. Lee in the Civil War*. New York: Fairfax Press, 1956. Reprinted in 1981.

——. *Jeb Stuart: The Last Cavalier*. New York: Fairfax Press, 1957. Reprinted in New York: Wings Books, 2000.

Davis, Jefferson. *The Rise and Fall of the Confederate Government*. 2 vols. New York, 1881.

Davis, Stephen. "A Georgia Firebrand: Major General W. H. T. Walker, C.S.A." *Georgia Historical Quarterly* 63, no. 4 (Winter 1979): 447–60.

Davis, William C. *Breckinridge: Statesman, Soldier, Symbol*. Baton Rouge: Louisiana State University Press, 1974. Reprinted in Lexington: University Press of Kentucky, 2010.

——. *The Orphan Brigade: The Kentucky Confederates Who Couldn't Go Home*. Garden City, New York: Doubleday Books, 1980.

Davis, William C., and Julie Hoffman. *The Confederate General*. 6 vols. Harrisburg, Pennsylvania: National Historical Society, 1991.

Delaney, Norman C. "Raphael Semmes." *Encyclopedia of Alabama*. Originally published September 20, 2007. Updated May 26, 2013. http://encyclopediaofalabama.org/article/h-1359.

Dickert, D. Augustus. *History of Kershaw's Brigade, with Complete Roll of Companies, Biographical Sketches, Incidents, Anecdotes, Etc.* Newberry, South Carolina, 1899. Reprinted in Dayton, Ohio: Morningside Bookshop, 1973.

Dillon, James. "Benjamin Jefferson Hill (1825–1880)." WikiTree. https://www.wikitree.com/wiki/Hill-7618.

Donovan, Timothy P., Willard B. Gatewood, Jr., and Jeannie M. Whayne, eds. *The Governors of Arkansas: Essays in Political Biography*. 2nd ed. Fayetteville: University of Arkansas Press, 1995.

Dorsey, Sarah A. *Recollections of Henry Watkins Allen, Brigadier-General, Confederate States Army, Ex-Governor of Louisiana*. New York, 1866.

Douglas, Henry Kyd. *I Rode with Stonewall*. Chapel Hill: University of North Carolina Press, 1940. Reprinted 1968.

Dowdey, Clifford. *Lee*. With photographs and maps by Samuel H. Bryant. Boston: Little, Brown, and Company, 1965.

Drennan, William. *Lieutenant Drennan's Letter: A Confederate Officer's Account of the Battle of Champion Hill and the Siege of Vicksburg*. Edited by Matt Atkinson. Gettysburg, Pennsylvania: Thomas Publications, 2009.

DuBose, John Witherspoon. *General Joseph Wheeler and the Army of Tennessee*. New York: Neale Publishing Company, 1912.

Dufour, Charles L. *The Night the War Was Lost*. Garden City, New York: Doubleday Books, 1960. Reprinted in Lincoln: University of Nebraska Press, 1990.

Duke, Basil W. *Reminiscences of General Basil W. Duke, C.S.A.* Garden City, New York: Doubleday, Page, and Company, 1911.

——. *History of Morgan's Cavalry*. Cincinnati, 1867.

Duncan, John A. "Brigadier General J. K. Duncan CSA." Clan Duncan Society. Updated April 6, 2009. https://www.clan-duncan.co.uk/duncanjk.html.

Dyer, John P. *From Shiloh to San Juan: The Life of "Fightin' Joe" Wheeler*. Baton Rouge: Louisiana State University Press, 1941. Revised 1961, reprinted 1992.

Early, Jubal A. *The Campaigns of Gen. Robert E. Lee: An Address before Washington and Lee University, January 19th, 1872*. Baltimore, 1872.

Early, Jubal A., and Ruth Hairston Early. *Lieutenant General Jubal Anderson Early, C.S.A.: Autobiographical Sketch and Narrative of the War between the States*. Philadelphia: Lippincott, 1912.

Eckert, Ralph Lowell. *John Brown Gordon: Soldier, Southerner, American*. Baton Rouge: Louisiana State University, 1989.

Edwards, John N. *Shelby and His Men: or, The War in the West*. Cincinnati, 1867.

Eicher, David J. *The Longest Night: A Military History of the Civil War*. New York: Touchstone, 2002.

Eicher, John H., and David J. Eicher, *Civil War High Commands*. Stanford, California: Stanford University Press, 2001.

Evans, Clement A., ed. *Confederate Military History: A Library of Confederate States History*. 12 vols. Atlanta, 1899.

——. *Intrepid Warrior: Clement Anselm Evans, Confederate General from Georgia: Life, Letters, and Diaries of the War Years*. Edited by Robert G. Stephens, Jr. Dayton, Ohio: Morningside, 1992.

Fahrner, Alvin A. "William 'Extra Billy' Smith, Governor of Virginia, 1864–1865: A Pillar of the Confederacy." *Virginia Magazine of History and Biography* 74, no. 1 (January 1966): 68–87.

Farnum, George R. "Edward Cary Walthall: Lawyer, Soldier and Statesman of the South." *American Bar Association Journal* 30, no. 6 (June 1944): 367–68, 376–77.

Farris, Charles Sherwood. *The American Soul: An Appreciation of the Four Greatest Americans and Their Lesson for Present Americans*. Boston: Stratford Company, 1920.

Faust, Patricia L., ed. *Historical Times Illustrated Encyclopedia of the Civil War*. New York: Harper and Row, 1986.

Find a Grave. Memorials of various generals and their relatives. https://www.findagrave.com.

Flood, Charles B. *Lee: The Last Years*. Boston: Houghton Mifflin Company, 1942. Reprinted 1981.

Foote, Shelby. *The Civil War: A Narrative*. 3 vols. New York: Random House, 1958. Reprinted 1974.

Freeman, Douglas Southall. *Lee's Lieutenants: A Study in Command*. 3 vols. New York: Charles Scribner's Sons, 1942–44.

———. *R. E. Lee: A Biography*. 4 vols. New York: Charles Scribner's Sons, 1933–35.

Fremantle, Sir Arthur J. L. *Three Months in the Southern States: April–June 1863*. Edinburgh, 1863. Reprinted in New York, 1864.

French, Samuel G. *Two Wars: An Autobiography of General Samuel G. French [. . .] Mexican War; War between the States, A Diary; Reconstruction Period, His Experience; Incidents, Reminiscences, Etc*. Nashville, Tennessee: Confederate Veteran, 1901.

Friedman, Morgan. "The Inflation Calculator." https://westegg .com/inflation/.

Fuller, A. James. "Joseph Wheeler." *Encyclopedia of Alabama*. Originally published May 12, 2009. Updated May 18, 2021. http://www .encyclopediaofalabama.org/article/h-2140.

Gallagher, Gary W. *Stephen Dodson Ramseur: Lee's Gallant General*. Chapel Hill: University of North Carolina Press, 1985.

———. "The Civil War: General Edward Porter Alexander." Address to the Virginia Historical Society, April 7, 2017. C-Span video, 55:08. https://www.c-span.org/video/?426654-1/confederate -general-edward-porter-alexander.

Gallagher, Gary W., and Joseph T. Glatthaar. *Leaders of the Lost Cause: New Perspectives on the Confederate High Command*. Mechanicsburg, Pennsylvania: Stackpole Books, 2004.

Generals of the American Civil War. "Confederate Generals." http://www.generalsandbrevets.com/sa/sa.htm.

Geni. "Brig. Gen. Rufus Barringer (CSA)." Updated May 24, 2018. https://www.geni.com/people/Brig-Gen-Rufus-C-Barringer-CSA/6000000017842185203.

———. "Brig. General Basil W. Duke (CSA)." Updated January 31, 2015. https://www.geni.com/people/Brig-General-Basil-W-Duke-CSA/6000000009946340206.

Gigantino, Jim. "Clement Evans." *New Georgia Encyclopedia*. Originally published December 20, 2005. Updated August 30, 2013. https://www.georgiaencyclopedia.org/articles/history-archaeology/clement-evans-1833-1911/.

Gordon, John B. *Reminiscences of the Civil War*. New York: Charles Scribner's Sons, 1903.

Gordon, Lesley J. *General George E. Pickett in Life and Legend*. Chapel Hill: University of North Carolina Press, 1998.

———. "George E. Pickett (1825–1875)." *Encyclopedia Virginia*. https://www.encyclopediavirginia.org/pickett_george_e_1825-1875#start_entry.

Gow, June I. "Military Administration in the Confederate Army of Tennessee." *Journal of Southern History* 40, no. 2 (May 1974): 183–98.

Grant, U. S. *Personal Memoirs of U.S. Grant*. 2 vols. New York, 1885.

Greene, A. Wilson. *The Final Battles of the Petersburg Campaign: Breaking the Backbone of the Rebellion*. Mason City, Iowa: Savas, 2000.

Grisamore, Silas T. *Reminiscences of Uncle Silas: A History of the Eighteenth Louisiana Infantry Regiment*. Edited by Arthur W. Bergeron, Jr. Baton Rouge: Le Comité des Archives de la Louisiane, 1981.

Groom, Winston. *Vicksburg, 1863*. New York: Alfred A. Knopf, 2009.

Gwynne, S. C. *Rebel Yell: The Violence, Passion, and Redemption of Stonewall Jackson*. New York: Scribner, 2014.

Hagood, Johnson. *Memoirs of the War of Secession, from the Original Manuscripts of Johnson Hagood, Brigadier-General, C.S.A.* Edited by Ulysses R. Brooks. Columbia, South Carolina: State Company, 1910.

Hallock, Judith Lee. *Braxton Bragg and Confederate Defeat.* Vol. 2. Tuscaloosa, Alabama: University of Alabama Press, 1991.

Hardeman, Nicholas P. "Hardeman, William Polk." Handbook of Texas. Texas State Historical Association. Originally published 1952. Updated August 1, 2020. https://www.tshaonline.org/handbook/entries/hardeman-william-polk.

Harden, William. "Gen. Alexander Robert Lawton." USGenWeb Archives. Uploaded October 13, 2004. http://files.usgwarchives.net/ga/chatham/bios/gbs143lawton.txt.

———. *A History of Savannah and South Georgia.* 2 vols. Chicago: Lewis Publishing Company, 1913.

Harris, William Charles. *Leroy Pope Walker: Confederate Secretary of War.* Tuscaloosa, Alabama: Confederate Publishing Company, 1952. Reprinted 1962.

Hattaway, Herman Morrell. "Stephen Dill Lee: A Biography." Unpublished PhD diss., Louisiana State University, 1969. https://digitalcommons.lsu.edu/cgi/viewcontent.cgi?article=2596&context=gradschool_disstheses.

Hatton, Roy O. "Prince Camille de Polignac and the American Civil War, 1863–1865." *Louisiana Studies* 3, no. 3 (Summer 1964).

Hawks, Steve A. "Confederate Regiments & Batteries." Civil War in the East. https://civilwarintheeast.com/confederate-regiments/.

Head, Thomas A. *Campaigns and Battles of the Sixteenth Regiment, Tennessee Volunteers, in the War Between the States, with Incidental Sketches of the Part Performed by Other Tennessee Troops in the Same War, 1861–1865.* Nashville, Tennessee: Cumberland Presbyterian, 1885.

Heitman, Francis B. *Historical Register and Dictionary of the United States Army: From Its Organization, September 29, 1789, to March 2, 1903.* Washington, D.C.: U.S. Government Printing Office, 1903. Reprinted in Urbana: University of Illinois Press, 1965.

Henry, Robert S. *"First With the Most" Forrest.* Indianapolis: Bobbs-Merrill, 1944.

Hess, Earl J. "Confederate General Braxton Bragg." Address at the Gettysburg College Civil War Institute Conference, June 10, 2017. C-Span video, 1:03:24. https://www.c-span.org/video/?429295-3/confederate-general-braxton-bragg.

———. *Lee's Tar Heels: The Pettigrew-Kirkland-McRae Brigade.* Chapel Hill: University of North Carolina Press, 2002.

Hesseltine, William B., and Hazel C. Wolf. *The Blue and Gray on the Nile.* Chicago: University of Chicago Press, 1961.

Hewitt, Lawrence L. *Port Hudson: Confederate Bastion on the Mississippi.* Baton Rouge: Louisiana State University, 1987.

Hill, Daniel Harvey. *Elements of Algebra.* Philadelphia, 1857.

Hood, John Bell. *Advance and Retreat: Personal Experiences in the United States and Confederate States Armies.* New Orleans, 1880.

Hood, Stephen M. *John Bell Hood: The Rise, Fall, and Resurrection of a Confederate General.* El Dorado Hills, California: Savas Beatie, 2013.

Hospodor, Gregory S. "Mexican-American War." *Mississippi Encyclopedia.* Center for the Study of Southern Culture. Originally published July 11, 2017. Updated July 5, 2018. https://mississippiencyclopedia.org/entries/mexican-american-war/.

Houghtalen, Robert. *I Am a Good Ol' Rebel: A Biography and Civil War Account of Confederate Brigadier General William H. F. Payne.* Bloomington, Indiana: AuthorHouse, 2016.

Howe, James Lewis. "George Washington Custis Lee." *Virginia Magazine of History and Biography* 48, no. 4 (October 1940): 315–27.

Huff, Leo E. "The Last Duel in Arkansas: The Marmaduke-Walker Duel." *Arkansas Historical Quarterly* 23, no. 1 (Spring 1964): 36–49.

Hughes, Nathaniel Cheairs, Jr. *General William J. Hardee: Old Reliable.* Baton Rouge: Louisiana State University Press, 1965. Reprinted 1992.

———. "McNair, Evander." In vol 4 of *Dictionary of North Carolina Biography*, edited by William S. Powell. Chapel Hill: University of North Carolina Press, 1991. Reprinted in NCpedia. https://www.ncpedia.org/biography/mcnair-evander.

Hyman, Carolyn. "Greer, Elkanah Bracken." Handbook of Texas. Texas State Historical Association. Originally published 1952. Updated January 1, 1995. https://tshaonline.org/handbook/online/articles/fgr42.

Jefferds, Joseph C., Jr. "Alexander Welch Reynolds." *e-WV: West Virginia Encyclopedia*. Updated December 8, 2015. https://www.wvencyclopedia.org/articles/73.

Johnson, Adam Rankin. *The Partisan Rangers of the Confederate States Army: Memoirs of General Adam R. Johnson*. Edited by William J. Davis. Louisville, Kentucky: George G. Fetter Company, 1904.

Johnson, Flora Smith. "The Civil War Record of Albert Gallatin Jenkins, C.S.A." *West Virginia History* 8, no. 4 (July 1947): 392–404. https://archive.wvculture.org/history/journal_wvh/wvh8-1.html.

Johnson, Ludwell H. *North against South: The American Iliad, 1848–1877*. 3rd ed. Columbia, South Carolina: Foundation for American Education, 1993. Originally published as *Division and Reunion: America, 1848–1877*. New York: John Wiley and Sons, 1978.

———. *The Red River Campaign: Politics and Cotton in the Civil War*. Baltimore: Johns Hopkins Press, 1958.

Johnston, Joseph E. *Narrative of Military Operations, Directed, During the Late War between the States*. New York, 1874.

Johnson, Robert Underwood, and Clarence Clough Buel, eds. *Battles and Leaders of the Civil War: Being for the Most Part Contributions by Union and Confederate Officers*. 4 vols. New York, 1884–88.

Johnston, William Preston. *The Life of Gen. Albert Sidney Johnston: Embracing His Services in the Armies of the United States, the Republic of Texas, and the Confederate States*. New York, 1878.

Joiner, Gary D. *Through the Howling Wilderness: The 1864 Red River Campaign and Union Failure in the West*. Knoxville: University of Tennessee, 2006.

Jones, J. William. *Personal Reminiscences, Anecdotes, and Letters of Gen. Robert E. Lee*. New York, 1874.

Jones, John B. *A Rebel War Clerk's Diary at the Confederate States Capital*. 2 vols. Philadelphia, 1866.

Jones, Samuel. *The Siege of Charleston and the Operations on the South Atlantic Coast in the War among the States*. New York: Neale Publishing Company, 1911.

Jones, Terry L. *Lee's Tigers: The Louisiana Infantry in the Army of Northern Virginia*. Baton Rouge: Louisiana State University Press, 1987.

Jordan, Thomas, and J. P. Pryor. *The Campaigns of Lieut.-Gen. N. B. Forrest, and of Forrest's Cavalry, with Portraits, Maps, and Illustrations.* New Orleans, 1868.

Jordan, Weymouth T., Jr., and John D. Chapla. "'O what A turbill affair': Alexander W. Reynolds and His North Carolina–Virginia Brigade at Missionary Ridge, Tennessee, November 25, 1863." *North Carolina Historical Review* 77, no. 3 (July 2000): 312–36.

Joslyn, Mauriel. "Patrick Ronayne Cleburne (1828–1864)." *Encyclopedia of Arkansas.* Updated April 18, 2017. https://encyclopediaofarkansas.net/entries/patrick-ronayne-cleburne-339/.

——, ed. *A Meteor Shining Brightly: Essays on Major General Patrick R. Cleburne.* Milledgeville, Georgia: Terrell House Publishing, 1997. Reprinted in Macon, Georgia: Mercer University Press, 2000.

Kearney, H. Thomas, Jr. "Clingman, Thomas Lanier." In vol. 3 of *Dictionary of North Carolina Biography*, edited by William S. Powell. Chapel Hill: University of North Carolina Press, 1979. Reprinted in NCpedia. https://www.ncpedia.org/biography/clingman-thomas-lanier.

Kennedy, James Ronald, and Walter Donald Kennedy. *The South Was Right!* Gretna, Louisiana: Pelican Publishing, 1991. Reprinted as 3rd edition in Columbia, South Carolina: Shotwell Publishing, 2020.

Kent, Tim. Tim Kent's Civil War Tales. http://trrcobb.blogspot.com.

——. "William Booth Taliaferro: The Man Who Couldn't Destroy a Stonewall." Tim Kent's Civil War Tales, July 31, 2011. http://trrcobb.blogspot.com/2011/07/william-booth-taliaferro-virginian-in.html.

Kinard, Jeff. *Lafayette of the South: Prince Camille de Polignac and the American Civil War.* College Station: Texas A&M University Press, 2001.

Koch, Peter. "General William Whedbee Kirkland: A North Carolinian at War." North State Rifles. http://www.northstaterifles.com/kirkland.htm.

Krieger, Marvin. "Barringer, Rufus Clay." In vol. 1 of *Dictionary of North Carolina Biography*, edited by William S. Powell. Chapel Hill: University of North Carolina Press, 1979. Reprinted in NCpedia. https://ncpedia.org/biography/barringer-rufus-clay.

Laidig, Scott. "Brigadier General John Pegram, Lee's Paradoxical Cavalier." Department of History. Ohio State University, February 1998. https://ehistory.osu.edu/articles/brigadier-general -john-pegram-lee%E2%80%99s-paradoxical-cavalier.

Lamb, John. "1st Maryland Infantry, CSA." Second Maryland Infantry, U.S.A. & Maryland in the Civil War. 1997–2008. http://2ndmdinfantryus.org/csinf1.html.

Lane, Walter P. *The Adventures and Recollections of General Walter P. Lane, a San Jacinto Veteran*. Marshall, Texas, 1887. Reprinted in Austin, Texas: Pemberton Press, 1970.

Lash, Jeffrey N. "A Yankee in Gray: Danville Leadbetter and the Defense of Mobile Bay, 1861–1863." *Civil War History* 37, no. 3 (September 1991): 197–218.

Laver, Tara. "William Thompson Martin." *Mississippi Encyclopedia*. Center for the Study of Southern Culture. Originally published July 11, 2017. Updated April 14, 2018. https://mississippiencyclopedia.org/entries/william-thompson -martin/.

Lee, Susan Pendleton. *Memoirs of William Nelson Pendleton, D.D., Rector of Latimer Parish, Lexington, Virginia; Brigadier-General, C.S.A.; Chief of Artillery, Army of Northern Virginia*. Philadelphia, 1893.

Liddell, St. John Richardson. *Liddell's Record*. Edited by Nathaniel Cheairs Hughes, Jr. Dayton, Ohio: Morningside, 1985. Reprinted in Baton Rouge: Louisiana State University Press, 1997.

Lipscomb, David. *Gospel Advocate*. May 29, 1913.

Long, A. L., and Marcus J. Wright. *Memoirs of Robert E. Lee: His Military and Personal History, Embracing a Large Amount of Information Hitherto Unpublished*. New York, 1886.

Long, E. B. with Barbara Long. *The Civil War Day by Day: An Almanac, 1861–65*. Garden City, New York: Doubleday Books, 1971.

Longacre, Edward G. "Fitzhugh Lee (1835–1905)." *Encyclopedia Virginia*. https://encyclopediavirginia.org/entries/lee-fitzhugh-1835-1905/.

Longstreet, James. *From Manassas to Appomattox: Memoirs of the Civil War in America*. Philadelphia, 1895. Reprinted as 2nd ed. in Philadelphia: Lippincott, 1903.

Losson, Christopher T. "Samuel Wragg Ferguson." *Mississippi Encyclopedia*. Center for the Study of Southern Culture. Originally published July 11, 2017. Updated April 23, 2018. https://mississippiencyclopedia.org/entries/samuel-wragg-ferguson.

Lowery, Mark P. "General M. P. Lowery: An Autobiography." *Southern Historical Society Papers* 16 (1888): 365–76. http://www.perseus.tufts.edu/hopper/text?doc=Perseus%3Atext%3A2001.05.0273%3Achapter%3D1.40.

Luebke, Peter C. "Floyd, John B. (1806–1863)." *Encyclopedia Virginia*. https://www.encyclopediavirginia.org/Floyd_John_B_1806-1863.

Maberry, Robert, Jr. "Wharton, John Austin." Handbook of Texas. Texas State Historical Association. Originally published 1952. Updated August 26, 2020. https://tshaonline.org/handbook/online/articles/fwh04.

Manigault, Arthur M. *A Carolinian Goes to War: The Civil War Narrative of Arthur Middleton Manigault, Brigadier General, C.S.A.* Edited by R. Lockwood Tower. Columbia: University of South Carolina Press, 1983. Reprinted 1992.

Marrin, William J. "Thomas Jordan. No. 1057. Class of 1840." *Report of the Twenty-Seventh Annual Reunion of the Association of the Graduates of the United States Military Academy*. Obituary, June 11, 1896. Reprinted in Bill Thayer's Web Site. http://penelope.uchicago.edu/Thayer/E/Gazetteer/Places/America/United_States/Army/USMA/AOG_Reunions/27/Thomas_Jordan*.htm.

Maury, Dabney H. *Recollections of a Virginian in the Mexican, Indian, and Civil Wars*. New York, 1894.

Mayes, Edward. *Lucius Q. C. Lamar: His Life, Times, and Speeches, 1825–1893*. Nashville, Tennessee, 1896.

McCabe, William Gordon. *Major-General George Washington Custis Lee*. Richmond, 1914.

McCawley, Patrick. "Chesnut, James Jr." *South Carolina Encyclopedia*. University of South Carolina, Institute for Southern Studies. Originally published April 15, 2016. Updated January 22, 2019. http://www.scencyclopedia.org/sce/entries/chesnut-james -jr/.

McCormick, Arley H. "Phillip Dale Roddey, 'The Defender of North Alabama.'" In *North Alabama Civil War Generals: 13 Wore Gray, the Rest Blue; A Selection of Essays from the Authors of the Tennessee Valley Civil War Round Table*, edited by Arley H. McCormick and Jacquelyn Reeves, 79–87. Madison, Alabama: Tennessee Valley Civil War Round Table, 2014. http://huntsvillehistorycollection.org/hh /hhpics/pdf/book2/North_Alabama_Generals.pdf.

McCutchan, Joseph D. *Mier Expedition Diary: A Texas Prisoner's Account*. Edited by Joseph Milton Nance. Austin: University of Texas Press, 1978.

McKim, Randolph H. *A Soldier's Recollections: Leaves from the Diary of a Young Confederate with an Oration on the Motives and Aims of the Soldiers of the South*. New York: Longmans, Green, and Company, 1910.

McKnight, Brian D. "Hope and Humiliation: Humphrey Marshall and the Confederacy's Last Change in Eastern Kentucky." Ohio Valley History 5, no. 3 (Fall 2005): 3–20.

McMurray, W. J. *History of the Twentieth Tennessee Volunteer Infantry, C.S.A.* Nashville, Tennessee: The Publication Committee, Consisting of W. J. Murray, Deering J. Roberts, and Ralph J. Neal, 1904.

McPherson, James M. *Battle Cry of Freedom: The Civil War Era*. New York: Oxford University Press, 1988.

McWhiney, Grady. *Braxton Bragg and Confederate Defeat*. Vol. 1. Tuscaloosa, Alabama: University of Alabama Press, 1969.

Miller, Francis T., and Robert S. Lanier, eds. *The Photographic History of the Civil War*. 10 vols. New York: The Review of Reviews Company, 1911.

Mitcham, Samuel W., Jr. *Bust Hell Wide Open: The Life of Nathan Bedford Forrest*. Washington, D.C.: Regnery History, 2016.

——. "Louisiana's Warrior Governor." Abbeville Institute, August 26, 2019. https://www.abbevilleinstitute.org/louisianas -warrior-governor/.

——. *Richard Taylor and the Red River Campaign of 1864*. Gretna, Louisiana: Pelican Publishing Company, 2012.

——. *Vicksburg: The Bloody Siege that Turned the Tide of the Civil War*. Washington, D.C.: Regnery History, 2018.

Montgomery, Don. "Thomas James Churchill (1824–1905)." *Encyclopedia of Arkansas*. Updated November 19, 2020. https://encyclopediaofarkansas.net/entries/thomas-james-churchill -92/.

Montgomery, Walter A. *Life and Character of Major-General W. D. Pender: Memorial Address, May 10, 1894*. Raleigh, North Carolina, 1894.

Moore, Edward A. *The Story of a Cannoneer under Stonewall Jackson, in Which is Told the Part Taken by the Rockbridge Artillery in the Army of Northern Virginia*. New York: Neale Publishing Company, 1907.

Murray, R. Smith, and Chris Young. "The Enigma of the Confederate Gen. S. A. M. Wood." *Chattanooga Time Free Press* (Chattanooga, Tennessee). October 12, 2014.

Nash, Charles E. *Biographical Sketches of Gen. Pat Cleburne and Gen. T. C. Hindman, Together with Humorous Anecdotes and Reminiscences of the Late Civil War*. Little Rock, Arkansas, 1898.

National Park Service. "The Civil War: Search for Battle Units." https://www.nps.gov/civilwar/search-battle-units-detail.htm.

Nichols, C. Howard. "Some Notes on the Military Career of Francis T. Nicholls." *Louisiana History: The Journal of the Louisiana Historical Association* 3, no. 4 (Autumn 1962): 297–315.

Nichols, James L. *Confederate Engineers*. Tuscaloosa, Alabama: Confederate Publishing Company, 1957.

Noel, Theophilus. *Autobiography and Reminiscences of Theophilus Noel*. Chicago: Theophilus Noel Company Printing, 1904.

Noll, Arthur Howard. *General Kirby-Smith*. Sewanee, Tennessee: The University Press at the University of the South, 1907.

Norris, David A. "William H. C. Whiting." *Mississippi Encyclopedia*. Center for the Study of Southern Culture. Originally published July 11, 2017. Updated April 15, 2018. https://mississippiencyclopedia.org/entries/william-hc-whiting/.

O'Reilly, Francis A. *The Fredericksburg Campaign: Winter War on the Rappa-hannock*. Baton Rouge: Louisiana State University Press, 2003.

Osborne, Charles C. *Jubal: The Life and Times of General Jubal A. Early, CSA, Defender of the Lost Cause*. Chapel Hill, North Carolina: Algonquin Books of Chapel Hill, 1992.

Owen, Richard and James Owen. *Generals at Rest: The Graves Sites of the 425 Official Confederate Generals*. Shippensburg, Pennsylvania: Beidel Printing House, 1997.

Owen, Thomas McAdory. *History of Alabama and Dictionary of Alabama Biography*. 4 vols. Chicago: The S. J. Clarke Publishing Company, 1921.

Owen, William Miller. *In Camp and Battle with the Washington Artillery of New Orleans*. Boston, 1885.

Parker, William L. "Brigadier General James Dearing, C.S.A." Unpublished master's thesis, Virginia Polytechnic Institute and State University, Blacksburg, 1969.

Parks, Joseph Howard. *General Edmund Kirby Smith, C.S.A.* Baton Rouge: Louisiana State University Press, 1954.

———. *General Leonidas Polk, C.S.A.: The Fighting Bishop*. Baton Rouge: Louisiana State University Press, 1962. Reprinted 1992.

Parrish, T. Michael. *Richard Taylor: Soldier Prince of Dixie*. Chapel Hill: University of North Carolina Press, 1992.

Patterson, Gerard A. *From Blue to Gray: The Life of Confederate General Cadmus M. Wilcox*. Mechanicsburg, Pennsylvania: Stackpole Books, 2001.

Paxton, Elisha Franklin. *Memoir and Memorials: Elisha Franklin Paxton, Brigadier-General, C.S.A.; Composed of His Letters from Camp and Field While an Officer in the Confederate Army, with an Introductory and Connecting Narrative Collected and Arranged by His Son, John Gallatin Paxton*. Edited by John Gallatin Paxton. New York: Neale Publishing Company, 1907. https://docsouth.unc.edu/fpn/paxton/paxton.html.

Pemberton, John C. *Pemberton, Defender of Vicksburg*. Chapel Hill: University of North Carolina Press, 1942.

Penner, Kristl Knudsen. "Whitfield, John Wilkins." Handbook of Texas. Texas State Historical Association. Originally published 1952. Updated November 11, 2011. https://tshaonline.org /handbook/online/articles/fwh38.

Pfanz, Donald C. *Richard S. Ewell: A Soldier's Life*. Chapel Hill: University of North Carolina Press, 1998.

Phillips, Ulrich B. *The Life of Robert Toombs*. New York: Macmillan, 1913.

Poché, Felix Pierre. *A Louisiana Confederate: Diary of Felix Pierre Poché*. Edited by Edwin C. Bearss. Translated by Eugenie Watson Somdal. Natchitoches: Louisiana Studies Institute, Northwestern State University of Louisiana, 1972.

Pollard, Edward A. *The Lost Cause: A New Southern History of the War of the Confederates*. New York, 1867.

Powell, William S., ed. *Dictionary of North Carolina Biography*. 6 vols. Chapel Hill: University of North Carolina Press, 1979–96.

Prince, Sigsbee C., Jr. "Edward A. Perry, Yankee General of the Florida Brigade." *Florida Historical Quarterly* 29, no. 3 (January 1951): 197–205.

Pryor, Sara Agnes Rice. *My Day: Reminiscences of a Long Life*. New York: Macmillan, 1909.

Raab, James W. *A Dual Biography: Lloyd Tilghman and Francis Asbury Shoup; Two Forgotten Confederate Generals*. Edited by John McGlone. Murfreesboro, Tennessee: Southern Heritage Press, 2001.

———. *Loring: Florida's Forgotten General*. Manhattan, Kansas: Sunflower University Press (an Open Library), 1996.

Reidinger, Martin. "Vance, Robert Brank." In vol. 6 of *Dictionary of North Carolina Biography*, edited by William S. Powell. Chapel Hill: University of North Carolina Press, 1996. Reprinted in NCpedia. https://www.ncpedia.org/biography/vance-robert-brank-0.

Robarts, William Hugh. *Mexican War Veterans: A Complete Roster of the Regular and Volunteer Troops in the War between the United States and Mexico, from 1846 to 1848*. Washington, D.C., 1887.

Robertson, James I., Jr. "Braxton Bragg: The Lonely Patriot." In *Leaders of the Lost Cause: New Perspectives on the Confederate High Command*, edited by Gary W. Gallagher and Joseph T. Glatthaar. Mechanicsburg, Pennsylvania: Stackpole Books, 2004.

———. "Confederate Failure." Radio IQ/WVTF. Radio broadcast. Originally aired December 6, 1996. https://www.wvtf.org/post /confederate-failure#stream/0.

———. *General A. P. Hill: The Story of a Confederate Warrior*. New York: Random House, 1987.

———. *Stonewall Jackson: The Man, the Soldier, the Legend*. New York: Macmillan, 1997.

Robson, John S. *How a One-Legged Rebel Lives: Reminiscences of the Civil War: The Story of the Campaigns of Stonewall Jackson, as Told by a High Private in the "Foot Cavalry": From Alleghany Mountain to Chancellorsville: With the Complete Regimental Rosters of Both the Great Armies at Gettysburg*. Durham, N.C., 1898. https://web.archive.org/web/20050923091734/http:// docsouth.unc.edu/robson/robson.html.

Roland, Charles P. "P. G. T. Beauregard." In *Leaders of the Lost Cause: New Perspectives on the Confederate High Command*, edited by Gary W. Gallagher and Joseph T. Glatthaar. Mechanicsburg, Pennsylvania: Stackpole Books, 2004.

Rose, Victor M. *The Life and Services of Gen. Ben McCulloch*. Philadelphia, 1888.

Rowland, Dunbar. *Military History of Mississippi, 1803–1898*. Spartanburg, South Carolina: Reprint Company, 1978. Excerpt reprinted from Rowland, Dunbar. *The Official and Statistical Register of the State of Mississippi*. Nashville, Tennessee: Press of the Brandon Printing Company, 1908.

Saturday Herald (Decatur, Illinois), May 3–9, 1885. https:// newspaperarchive.com/decatur-saturday-herald-may-09-1885 -p-1/.

Scott, Robert N., ed. *The War of the Rebellion: A Compilation of the Official Records of the Union and Confederate Armies*. 128 vols. Washington, D.C.: U.S. Government Printing Office, 1880–1901.

Scott, Winfield. *Memoirs of Lieut.-General Scott, LL. D.* 2 vols. New York, 1864.

Semmes, Raphael. *Memoirs of Service Afloat during the War between the States*. Baltimore, 1869.

Shalhope, Robert E. *Sterling Price: Portrait of a Southerner*. Columbia: University of Missouri Press, 1971.

Shea, William L., and Earl J. Hess. *Pea Ridge: Civil War Campaign in the West*. Chapel Hill: University of North Carolina Press, 1992.

Shenandoah Civil War History. "The Confederate Yankee: Zebulon York." Shenandoah Valley's Civil War. November 15, 2018. https://shenandoahcivilwarhistory.blog/2018/11/15/the-confederate-yankee-zebulon-York/.

Sherman, William T. *Memoirs of Gen. William T. Sherman*. 2 vols. Edited by Willis Fletcher Johnson and O. O. Howard. New York: 1891.

Shiver, Joshua. "Philip Dale Roddey." *Encyclopedia of Alabama*. Originally published April 16, 2020. Updated May 25, 2021. http://www.encyclopediaofalabama.org/article/h-4196.

Sifakis, Stewart. *Who Was Who in the Confederacy: A Comprehensive, Illustrated Biographical Reference to More Than 1,000 of the Principal Confederacy Participants in the Civil War*. New York: Facts on File, 1988.

A Sketch of the Life and Service of General William Ruffin Cox: Including the Address of Hon. Frank S. Spruill at the Presentation of Portrait of General William Ruffin Cox to the State of North Carolina. Richmond, Virginia: Whittet and Shepperson, 1921.

Slagsvol, Whitt. "Evander McIver Law: Teacher and Confederate General." Unpublished paper, College of Charleston, March 2011. https://cpb-us-w2.wpmucdn.com/blogs.cofc.edu/dist/f/392/files/2011/03/Evander-McIver-Law.pdf.

Smith, Bridget. *Where Elephants Fought: The Murder of Confederate General Earl Van Dorn*. Mechanicsburg, Pennsylvania: Sunbury Press, 2015.

Smith, Timothy B. *Champion Hill: Decisive Battle for Vicksburg*. New York: Savas Beatie, 2004.

———. "Claudius Wistar Sears." *Mississippi Encyclopedia*. Center for the Study of Southern Culture. Originally published July 11, 2017. Updated April 15, 2018. https://mississippiencyclopedia.org/entries/claudius-wistar-sears/.

Sorrel, G. Moxley. *Recollections of a Confederate Staff Officer*. 2nd ed. New York: Neale Publishing Company, 1917.

Southern Historical Society Papers. Vols. 1–42 of 52. 1876–1917.

Southern Publishing Company. *Biographical Encyclopedia of Texas*. New York, 1880.

Stanchak, John E. "Jackson, Alfred Eugene." In *Historical Times Illus-trated History of the Civil War*, edited by Patricia L. Faust. New York: Harper and Row, 1986.

Strother, Faye O. "Dandridge McRae—An Arkansas General." *Arkansas Democrat*, December 30, 1862.

Stroud, David V. "Ector, Mathew Duncan." Handbook of Texas. Texas State Historical Association. Originally published 1952. Updated January 1, 1995. https://tshaonline.org/handbook /online/articles/fec02.

Sutherland, Daniel E. "Mansfield Lovell's Quest for Justice: Another Look at the Fall of New Orleans." *Louisiana History: The Journal of the Louisiana Historical Association* 24, no. 3 (Summer 1983): 233–59.

———. "No Better Officer in the Confederacy: The Wartime Career of Daniel C. Govan." *Arkansas Historical Quarterly* 54, no. 3 (Autumn 1995): 269–303.

Symonds, Craig L. *Joseph E. Johnston: A Civil War Biography*. New York: W. W. Norton and Company, 1992. Reprinted 1994.

———. *Stonewall of the West: Patrick Cleburne and the Civil War*. Lawrence: University Press of Kansas, 1997.

Taylor, Richard L. *Destruction and Reconstruction: Personal Experiences of the Late War in the United States*. New York, 1879.

Thomas, John P. *Career and Character of Gen. Micah Jenkins, C.S.A.* Colum-bia, South Carolina: The State Printing Company, 1903.

Thompson, Edwin Porter. *History of the Orphan Brigade*. Louisville, Kentucky, 1898.

Toon, Thomas F. "Twentieth Regiment." In *Histories of the Several Regiments and Battalions from North Carolina in the Great War, 1861–'65*, edited by Walter Clark, 111–127. Raleigh, North Carolina: E. M. Uzzell, 1901. https://archive.org/details/cu31924092908544 /page/n157/mode/2up.

Trescot, William Henry. *Memorial of the Life of J. Johnston Pettigrew, Brig. Gen. of the Confederate States Army*. Charleston, South Carolina, 1870.

Tucker, Phillip T. *The Forgotten "Stonewall of the West": Major General John Stevens Bowen*. Macon, Georgia: Mercer University Press, 1997.

Tunnard, W. H. *A Southern Record: The History of the Third Regiment, Louisiana Infantry*. Baton Rouge, 1866.

U.S. Bureau of Labor Statistics. "CPI Inflation Calculator." https://www.bls.gov/data/inflation_calculator.htm.

Vandiver, Frank E. *Ploughshares into Swords: Josiah Gorgas and Confederate Ordnance*. Austin: University of Texas Press, 1952.

Wakelyn, Jon L. and Frank E. Vandiver, ed. *Biographical Dictionary of the Confederacy*. Westport, Connecticut: Greenwood Press, 1977.

Walker, C. Irvine. *The Life of Lieutenant General Richard Heron Anderson of the Confederate States Army*. Charleston, South Carolina: Art Publishing Company, 1917.

Walsh, George. *"Damage Them All You Can": Robert E. Lee's Army of Northern Virginia*. New York: Forge, 2002. Reprinted 2004.

Walters, Ryan S. "Joseph Robert Davis." *Mississippi Encyclopedia*. Center for Study of Southern Culture. Originally published July 10, 2017. Updated April 13, 2018. https://mississippiencyclopedia.org/entries/joseph-robert-davis/.

Warner, Ezra J. *Generals in Blue: Lives of the Union Commanders*. Baton Rouge: Louisiana State University Press, 1964.

——. *Generals in Gray: Lives of the Confederate Commanders*. Baton Rouge: Louisiana State University Press, 1959.

Weiss, Harold J., Jr. "McCulloch, Henry Eustace." Handbook of Texas Online. Texas State Historical Association. Originally published 1976. Updated November 20, 2014. https://tshaonline.org/handbook/online/articles/fmc35.

Welker, David A. "Cowards in the Cornfield? (Part Two): The Complicated Story of Virginia's General John R. Jones." Antietam's Cornfield. August 21, 2016. https://antietamscornfield.com/2016/08/21/cowards-in-the-cornfield-part-two-the-complicated-story-of-virginias-general-john-r-jones/.

Welsh, Jack D. *Medical Histories of Confederate Generals*. Kent, Ohio: Kent State University Press, 1995.

Wert, Jeffry D. *General James Longstreet: The Confederacy's Most Controversial Soldier: A Biography*. New York: Simon and Schuster, 1993.

White, Henry A. *The Making of South Carolina*. New York: Silver, Burdett and Company, 1906.

White, J. T. *National Cyclopaedia of American Biography*. New York, J. T. White Company, 1900.

Wikipedia. https://www.wikipedia.org.

Williams, Max R. "Cox, William Ruffin." In vol. 1 of *Dictionary of North Carolina Biography*, edited by William S. Powell. Chapel Hill: University of North Carolina Press, 1979. Reprinted in NCpedia. https://www.ncpedia.org/biography/cox-william-ruffin.

Williams, Nancy A., and Jeannie M. Whayne. *Arkansas Biography: A Collection of Notable Lives*. Fayetteville: University of Arkansas Press, 2000.

Williams, T. Harry. *P. G. T. Beauregard: Napoleon in Gray*. Baton Rouge: Louisiana State University Press, 1954.

Willis, Brian Steel. *A Battle from the Start: The Life of Nathan Bedford Forrest*. New York: HarperCollins, 1992.

Wilson, Clyde N. *Carolina Cavalier: The Life and Mind of James Johnston Pettigrew*. Athens: University of Georgia Press, 1990.

Winters, John D. *The Civil War in Louisiana*. Baton Rouge: Louisiana State University Press, 1963.

Wise, Barton H. *The Life of Henry A. Wise, 1806–1876*. New York, 1899.

Wise, Henry A. *Seven Decades of the Union: The Humanities and Materialism; Illustrated by a Memoir of John Tyler, with Reminiscences of Some of His Great Contemporaries; The Transition State of This Nation—Its Dangers and Their Remedy*. Philadelphia, 1872.

Wise, Jennings C. *The Long Arm of Lee; or, The History of the Artillery of the Army of Northern Virginia, with a Brief Account of the Confederate Bureau of Ordnance*. 2 vols. Lynchburg, Virginia: J. P. Bell and Company, 1915.

Wolverton, Jeff. "Thomas Benton Smith, The Boy General." Abbeville Institute. December 14, 2017. https://www.abbevilleinstitute.org/thomas-benton-smith-the-boy-general/.

Womack, Marlene. "Out of the Past: Southern Hero Seen as Crotchety Old Man, Gracious Gentleman." *News Herald* (Panama City, Florida), May 27, 2001. https://archive.is/20070528100016/http://www.newsherald.com/archives/article.display.php?id=49306.

Woodward, Colin. "Rebel General from Abolitionist Enclave Massachusetts." HistoryNet. Originally published in *Civil War Times*, April 2020. https://www.historynet.com/rebel-general -from-abolitionist-enclave-massachusetts.htm.

Woodworth, Steven E. *Jefferson Davis and His Generals: The Failure of Confederate Command in the West*. Lawrence: University Press of Kansas, 1990.

Wright, John D. *The Routledge Encyclopedia of Civil War Biographies*. New York: Routledge, Taylor, and Francis Group, 2013.

Wright, Louise Wigfall. *A Southern Girl in 1861: The War-Time Memories of a Confederate Senator's Daughter*. Garden City, New York: Doubleday Books, 1905.

Wright, Marcus J. "Diary of Brigadier-General Marcus J. Wright, C.S.A. April 23, 1861–February 26, 1863: Electronic Edition." 1861–63. Documenting the American South. University of North Carolina Chapel Hill. Uploaded 1998. https://docsouth .unc.edu/fpn/wrightmarcus/wright.html#note2.

Yeary, Mamie. *Reminiscences of the Boys in Gray, 1861–1865*. 2 vols. Dallas, Texas: Smith and Lamar, 1912

YesterYear Once More. "The Double Death Which Disgraced Mississippi." October 5, 2010. https://yesteryearsnews.wordpress .com/2010/10/05/the-double-death-which-disgraced -mississippi/.

Young, Bennett H. *Confederate Wizards of the Saddle: Being Reminiscences and Observations of One Who Rode with Morgan*. Boston: Chapple Publishing Company, 1914.

Young, Hugh H. "Two Texas Patiots [Generals Hugh Franklin and William Hugh Young]." *Southwestern Historical Quarterly* 44, no. 1 (July 1940): 16–32.